ESSAYS IN LAW AND HISTORY FOR DAVID IBBETSON

Over the last 40 years, David Ibbetson has paved the way in a remarkably broad range of fields.

In ancient law, his scholarship has spanned both the detailed doctrine of the Roman law of obligations and the cross-pollination of legal influences around the ancient Mediterranean. His work on English legal history has ranged from the earliest days of the common law through to the turn of the 20th century, combining forensic archival research with a sensitivity to how lawyers thought about their subject. In European legal history, he has shown the porousness of the civil law and the extent to which it has been shaped by other areas of intellectual life, from theology to rationalist philosophy.

The contributions to this volume in his honour mirror both the breadth and the depth of Ibbetson's scholarship. The book combines chapters from leading legal historians, close colleagues and over a dozen of Ibbetson's students. Some chapters build upon or respond to Ibbetson's ideas, others his areas of interest. The contributions are introduced by Ibbetson's valedictory lecture on the importance of legal history to modern practice and scholarship, and the work yet to be done.

Essays in Law and History for David Ibbetson

Querella

Edited by
Joe Sampson
and
Stelios Tofaris

•HART•
OXFORD • LONDON • NEW YORK • NEW DELHI • SYDNEY

HART PUBLISHING

Bloomsbury Publishing Plc

Kemp House, Chawley Park, Cumnor Hill, Oxford, OX2 9PH, UK

1385 Broadway, New York, NY 10018, USA

29 Earlsfort Terrace, Dublin 2, Ireland

First published in Great Britain 2024

A catalogue record for this book is available from the British Library.

A catalogue record for this book is available from the Library of Congress.

Library of Congress Control Number: 2024944175

ISBN: HB: 978-1-50997-065-0
ePDF: 978-1-50997-067-4
ePub: 978-1-50997-066-7

Typeset by Compuscript Ltd, Shannon

ACKNOWLEDGEMENTS

As ever in a collaboration of this type, the editors have accumulated several debts of gratitude that they wish to acknowledge. The Maitland Fund at the University of Cambridge kindly provided funding towards the symposium marking David Ibbetson's retirement. Trinity College Cambridge provided funding towards the cost of copy-editing several chapters, this work being very ably carried out by David's most recent doctoral student, Ros Acland. For the title of the volume, we owe thanks to Ben Spagnolo. Particular thanks are due to the team at Hart, especially Verity Stuart and Kate Whetter, for their patience with the editors.

TABLE OF CONTENTS

PART III
COMPARATIVE LEGAL HISTORY

PART IV
HISTORY AND MODERNITY

LIST OF CONTRIBUTORS

Paul Babie is Bonython Chair in Law and Professor of Law at Adelaide Law School, University of Adelaide. David co-supervised his DPhil at Oxford on 'Crown Land in Australia'.

John Baker is Emeritus Downing Professor of the Laws of England at the University of Cambridge and Honorary Fellow of St Catharine's College, Cambridge. He supervised David's PhD at Cambridge on 'The Development of the Action of Assumpsit 1540–1620'.

John Bell is Emeritus Professor of Law (1973) at the University of Cambridge and Emeritus Fellow of Pembroke College, Cambridge.

Paul Brand is Emeritus Professor of Legal History at the University of Oxford and Emeritus Fellow at All Souls College, Oxford.

Matthew Dyson is Professor of Civil and Criminal Law at the University of Oxford, Fellow of Corpus Christi College, Oxford and Global Professor, Notre Dame London Law Programme. David supervised his PhD at Cambridge on 'Interfacing Crime and Tort: Legal Development in England and Spain Since 1850' as part of David's AHRC-funded project on the development of tort law in Europe, together with John Bell.

Wolfgang Ernst is Regius Professor of Civil Law at the University of Oxford and Fellow of All Souls College, Oxford.

David Feldman is Emeritus Rouse Ball Professor of English Law at the University of Cambridge, Emeritus Fellow of Downing College, Cambridge and Honorary Fellow of Exeter College, Oxford.

David Foxton is a Justice of the King's Bench Division and a Judge of the Commercial Court, England and Wales.

Joshua Getzler is Professor of Law and Legal History at the University of Oxford and Fellow of St Hugh's College, Oxford. David supervised his DPhil at Oxford on 'Rules Writ in Water: A History of Riparian Rights and Property Use Doctrine in England to 1870'.

Emily Gordon is College Associate Lecturer in Private Law at St John's College, Cambridge. David supervised her PhD at Cambridge on 'The Doctrine of Privity in Negligence, 1842–1932'.

David Ibbetson is Emeritus Regius Professor of Civil Law at the University of Cambridge, formerly President of Clare Hall, Cambridge, and Emeritus Fellow of Magdalen College, Oxford.

Neil Jones is Professor of English Legal History at the University of Cambridge and Fellow of Magdalene College, Cambridge.

Michael Lobban is Professor of Legal History at the University of Oxford and Senior Research Fellow of All Souls College, Oxford.

Catharine MacMillan is Professor of Private Law at the Dickson Poon School of Law, King's College London.

Mike Macnair is Fellow by Resolution of St Hugh's College, Oxford. Until retirement, he was Ann Smart Fellow & Tutor in Law at St Hugh's College and Associate Professor of Law at the University of Oxford. David supervised his DPhil at Oxford on 'The Law of Proof in Early Modern Equity'.

Colm Peter McGrath is Senior Lecturer in Tort Law at the Dickson Poon School of Law, King's College London and Global Associate Professor, Notre Dame London Law Programme. His PhD at Cambridge on 'The Development of Medical Liability in Germany 1800–1945' was part of David's AHRC-funded project on the development of tort law in Europe, together with John Bell.

Paul Mitchell is Professor of Laws at University College London.

Jonathan Morgan is Professor of English Law at the University of Cambridge and Fellow of Corpus Christi College, Cambridge.

Joe Sampson is Assistant Professor of Legal History at the University of Cambridge and Fellow of Trinity College, Cambridge. David supervised his PhD at Cambridge on 'The Historical Foundations of Grotius's Analysis of Delict'.

Helen Scott is Regius Professor of Civil Law at the University of Cambridge, Fellow of Downing College, Cambridge, Honorary Research Fellow at Lady Margaret Hall, Oxford, and Honorary Professor at the Department of Private Law, University of Cape Town.

Warren Swain is Professor of Law at the University of Auckland. David supervised his DPhil at Oxford on 'Aspects of the Action of Assumpsit Circa 1750–1855'.

Stelios Tofaris is Associate Professor of Law at the University of Cambridge and Fellow of Girton College, Cambridge. David supervised his PhD at Cambridge on 'A Historical Study of the Indian Contract Act 1872'.

Alain Wijffels is Emeritus Professor of Legal History at the University of Leiden, Emeritus Professor of Legal History at KU Leuven and Professeur Extraordinaire Émérite at UC Louvain.

Ian Williams is Associate Professor of Law at the University of Oxford and Fellow of St John's College, Oxford. David supervised his PhD at Cambridge on 'English Legal Reasoning and Legal Culture, c.1528–c.1642'.

1

Introduction

JOE SAMPSON AND STELIOS TOFARIS

It would normally fall to an introductory chapter in a festschrift to introduce the honouree, their work, and their significance. The editors of this volume have been spared much of that task – the honouree decided to do it for himself. For a full introduction from the horse's mouth, please turn to chapter two.

We will instead fill in the gaps that David has left for us, which largely pertain to his own history and the magnitude of his influence on legal history today. David joined Corpus Christi College, Cambridge in the mid-1970s, and quickly marked himself out as a superlative student. Among his accolades were distinction ('Starred First') results in both the second and third years of his undergraduate degree. The Faculty of Law of the 1970s was marked out by many larger-than-life academic personalities, and long after David would speak of the influence of the likes of Peter Stein on his own approach to academia. David stayed on at Corpus for doctoral research into the history of assumpsit with John Baker, the first of many fruitful collaborations between the pair.

In 1980, David was appointed to his first teaching post: a Tutorial Fellowship at Magdalen College, Oxford. Like many of his future research students, David had built up a broad range of teaching experience during his doctoral studies, but took matters to a new level once in post, with claims to have taught up to ten papers at a time. Alongside the expected papers in Legal History and Roman Law, he would routinely offer tutorials in modern subjects such as Tort Law, Criminal Law and Family Law. David also took on major college officerships at Magdalen, including a spell as Senior Tutor and a legendary stint as Senior Dean of Arts – three decades later, alumni still reminisce about college parties being 'Ibboed'. Much of David's research at Oxford focused on English legal history, work that culminated in his best-known publication, *A Historical Introduction to the Law of Obligations*. This remains a reference point for legal historians, private lawyers and judges. The book is replete with insights, the profoundness of which is masked by the succinctness with which they are encapsulated. Over 20 years after its publication, the book deserves to be read and reread and reread again.

After 20 years in Oxford, David returned to Cambridge and Corpus to take up the Regius Professorship in Civil Law. As in Oxford, David's contributions to academia through his research, his teaching and his service to the broader community were prodigious. During his second Cambridge life, David's research took on an increasingly comparative dimension, reflected in a long-term project recently published,

The Cambridge Comparative History of Ancient Law (co-edited with Caroline Humfress and Patrick Olivelle). He served as Chair of the Faculty of Law, on innumerable College, Faculty and University Committees, and spent seven happy years as the President of Clare Hall. And throughout his commitment to teaching was unwavering.

David's willingness to supervise and mentor research students is unparalleled. It has fostered the next generations of legal historians and many more besides. No better evidence exists than the sheer number of scholars who started their career by doing a PhD thesis under David. His teaching of undergraduate students was no less inspiring. Generations of lawyers were set on a journey to discovering answers, guided along the way by questions, prompts and the odd sardonic comment. The discovery could be satisfying but it was the journey which had a lasting impact, demonstrating how to engage with law and how engaging law could be. At the heart of everything was a common trait: selfless devotion to his students. It is no surprise that so many of them have become his friends.

This volume is a testament to the breadth and depth of David's influence on legal historical scholarship. When David retired from the Regius Professorship of Civil Law at the University of Cambridge in September 2022, almost 40 of his past doctoral students gathered in Cambridge for three days of papers and festivities. However, it soon became apparent that there were many more scholars who wished to pay a tribute to David. In putting together this festschrift, we are conscious there are many others who would have been equally well placed to contribute. Such is the central role David has played in fostering legal history as a discipline throughout his career. Our hope is that the volume balances the different areas of David's academic life: as a researcher, a teacher, and a colleague.

2

Acta et Agenda*

DAVID IBBETSON

Inaugural lectures can be intimidating. My distant predecessor, the first Regius Professor, Thomas Smith, had every reason to be concerned when he gave his pair of inaugural lectures in 1542.[1] His only qualification as a scholar of Roman law was that he was the second best scholar of Greek in Cambridge and, he said, he had bought a copy of Justinian's *Digest* and dipped into it in his leisure hours. History does not record whether that was enough to convince the scholars in his audience that he was the right person to hold what was then a well-endowed office.

But an inaugural lecture does have something approaching a template. A few deprecative words of praise for one's predecessors, whether genuinely meant or not, are followed by the new professor laying out his or her stall, saying how they see their subject and what is important within it. For Thomas Smith, this meant stressing the newly fashionable humanist learning that he had picked up in France and Italy, departing from the earlier exegetical *mos italicus*. History does not record whether this was what he actually did. The marginal notes he made on his copy of Justinian's *Digest* perhaps suggest that he stuck to the old exegesis.

A valedictory lecture has no such template. It is by nature backward looking. If an inaugural is a *credo*, a valedictory risks being an *apologia pro vita sua*. Answering the normally unspoken question, 'What has he been doing all these years and has he learnt anything from it?'. But I remember as a student being inspired by the valedictory lecture of our late friend and colleague, Kurt Lipstein. In its published form,[2] its title was *Acta et Agenda*, the title I have borrowed today, loosely translatable as 'What I have done and what remains to be done'. It was not the content of Kurt's lecture that had had an effect on me so much as the title. Even on retirement at what then seemed to be an old age, a scholar could still look forward. Thirty years later Kurt was still doing so. So this lecture is what I have done, what I have learnt, and what remains to be done.

* This is a very lightly edited version of the valedictory lecture given on 22 November 2022. I claim the privilege of a valedictorian to restrict citations to my own works, except where references to quotations are needed.

[1] I rely on the text as transcribed by my predecessor-but-two, Patrick Duff, now in the Squire Law Library.

[2] K Lipstein, 'Acta et Agenda' (1977) 36 *CLJ* 47.

I should begin with some personal reflections. Stepping down from the chair I look back at those to whom I owe debts of gratitude. To my friends and family, who kept me more or less sane and made sure I didn't forget that there was life outside the academy; to those from whom I learnt so much;[3] to my colleagues, who have forever stimulated me into thinking about law, even when I have disagreed with them profoundly; and to my students, undergraduates who raised questions I could not answer at first sight and graduate students who answered questions I had never thought to ask.

I never gave an inaugural lecture, but if I had done I would have said that I would carry on working on the history of English private law though with an eye to its relationship with Roman law, and more generally working on comparative legal history. I have spent the last 20 or so years doing just this, though the Roman law I have been looking at has broadened into the whole Romanised tradition on the European continent and elsewhere. Sometimes this has involved metaphorically looking under stones to see if there is anything there; though, probably more commonly it has been the result of metaphorically picking up a shiny stone and discovering by pure chance something interesting under it.

An important figure in my work has been the eighteenth-century polymath and lawyer, Sir William Jones.[4] He is probably better known today as the philologist who identified the genetic relationship between Sanskrit, Greek and Latin and hence triggered the study of Indo-European linguistics, but many lawyers will have heard of his little *Essay on the Law of Bailments*, first published in 1781, even if few have actually read it. The title promises more than the book delivers. It does not deal with all the legal problems that the bailment relationship gives rise to, and they are many, but only one: the standard of care owed by the bailee, the borrower, to the bailor, the lender; how much care he ought to take of the property while it is in his possession. But this was in truth a big enough topic in itself. The English case law on the subject before 1700 was extraordinarily confused, and the situation had only been made worse by attempts to impose order on the topic by treatise writers from Bracton and his colleagues in the mid-thirteenth century to Christopher St German in the early sixteenth. But the subject had been reduced to something like order in 1703, in the great case of *Coggs v Barnard*.[5] Chief Justice Holt had there reinterpreted the earlier case law and aligned it with what he repeatedly called 'the law', that is, Roman law. Holt's reasoning was utterly opaque and on analysis totally incoherent, but it did produce a few general principles, a great deal easier to apply than the confused mish-mash of the previous law. It was neither the first nor the last case where a welcome result was reached by transparently bad reasoning and never subsequently questioned.

[3] It is right that I acknowledge specifically the debt I owe to the two Cambridge colossi of legal history of the last century, Toby Milsom and John Baker: see 'Milsom's Legal History' (2017) 76 *CLJ* 360; 'The Renaissance of English Legal History' (2021) 80 *CLJ* 91. But *inclusio duorum* should not be taken as *exclusio aliorum*.

[4] 'Sir William Jones as a Comparative Lawyer', in A Murray (ed), *Sir William Jones, 1746–94* (Oxford, Oxford University Press, 1998) 19; 'Sir William Jones' (2001) 7 *Transactions of the Honourable Society Cymmrodorion* 66; 'Sir William Jones and the Nature of Law' in AS Burrows and Lord Rodger (eds), *Mapping the Law* (Oxford, Oxford University Press, 2006) 619; *Sir William Jones, Essay on the Law of Bailments* (Welsh Legal History Society, 2007).

[5] 'Coggs v Barnard (1703)' in C Mitchell and P Mitchell (eds), *Landmark Cases in the Law of Contract* (Oxford, Hart Publishing, 2008) 1.

When Jones came to write his little book, the rules defined in *Coggs v Barnard* had been in place for three quarters of a century and he was able to say that his work was 'merely a commentary' on the earlier decision. Maybe, but Jones went a good deal further than Holt had done. He did not merely reproduce the law of Justinian's *Institutes*, 'the law' as Holt had described it, but ventured into a critique of the more detailed texts in the *Digest*, analysing them and even from time to time arguing for an emendation of a received text. Unlike Holt, he also cited more modern scholars' writings on the Roman texts, and even if some of his references were blind citations picked up from other writers, he had clearly looked at some of the books he had referred to. Perhaps most significantly with hindsight, he made use of the works of Robert-Joseph Pothier, which he had introduced into England and which were to be the main source of the principles of modern English contract law. Sometimes, I am afraid, he plagiarised them shamelessly. It was more difficult to shoehorn the English case law into the framework which he had derived from Roman law, and it has to be said that he was as cavalier in his use of the earlier cases as Holt had been, sometimes reading facts into decisions to make them say what he wanted them to say, sometimes blatantly reinterpreting them. Did he need to do this? Could he not simply have started with *Coggs v Barnard* and ignored the pre-1700 decisions by saying that they had already been explained?

The answer, I think, lies in an important assumption about the nature of the common law. Like many English lawyers of the eighteenth century, he was in thrall to a theory of natural law,[6] making this explicit in his essay:

> [I]f law be a science, and really deserve so sublime a name, it must be founded on principle, and claim an exalted rank in the empire of reason; but, if it be merely an unconnected series of decrees and ordinances, its use may remain, though its dignity be lessened, and He will become the greatest lawyer, who has the strongest habitual, or artificial, memory.[7]

The whole of his essay is structured around the methodological assumption that law is indeed a science. Following the German Johann Gottlieb Heineccius, whose works he would undoubtedly have become familiar with while studying at Oxford, he begins with an analytical part, delineating the subject from first principles of natural reason. Then comes the empirical part, showing how the rules of developed systems conformed to this model. Finally the brief synthetic part, detailing the fundamental rules. Roman law was undoubtedly a developed system; the common law too was a developed system, and in Jones' view it had been a developed system from at least the thirteenth century. It followed that their rules, even the law of the fourteenth-century Year Books, must surely be congruent with his starting point of natural law. And why limit it to English and Roman law? He also refers from time to time to Gothic, Greek, Hebrew, Turkish, Visigothic, Bavarian, Frankish, Welsh and Hindu law, though only of course where they were consistent with his natural law starting points.

Although the natural law writers of the seventeenth and eighteenth centuries claimed to be building up their ideal systems from unquestionably true starting points, their reasoning from these starting points was frequently rather more questionable. For all of them, I think, the ideal system they had in their minds was that of sixth-century Rome,

[6] 'Natural Law and Common Law' (2001) 5 *Edinburgh Law Review* 4.
[7] *Essay on the Law of Bailments* (n 4) 195 (1781 edn, 123).

the law of Justinian's *Corpus Iuris* and especially the law of the classical Roman jurists. It was unsurprising therefore that Roman law turned out to be more or less consistent with the principles of natural law. English law was not such an obvious fit; even a shoehorn might not have been enough and a straitjacket was needed.

But let me return to Jones himself. The law of bailments might have been the very worst topic to have chosen as the first of a series of projected monographs ('no more published', as a bookseller's catalogue might describe it). From a Roman perspective, bailments were contracts, the so-called real contracts, and the standards of care appropriate to each contract were default rules in the absence of any agreement to the contrary. But by the eighteenth century it was not so easy for the natural lawyers. It was coming to be treated as axiomatic that contractual liability stemmed from the meeting of the minds of the parties, and it was not enough to say that in a gratuitous deposit for safe keeping, for example, the bailee was only liable for gross negligence or deliberate wrongdoing, it was necessary to say why this was so if there had been no express agreement between the parties. Like a good common lawyer of today Jones said we could infer or imply that this was their tacit agreement, but every good common lawyer of today knows in his or her heart, whenever we say that something is inferred or implied we may well be sheltering behind a weasel word to allow us to get to a desired conclusion. Jones' inference or implication was always just that, with little reason to suppose that it was anything more. Worse, cases of bailment in English law were situated rather uncomfortably between contract and tort. In form they were tortious, from the 1360s actions of trespass on the case; but from 1500 the action for breach of contract was also trespass on the case, and it was in practice impossible to say whether the action was tortious or contractual in cases on the boundary. Either view raised potential difficulties in practice because of technical rules of procedure. Jones, like Chief Justice Holt before him, categorised them as contractual, though unlike Holt he simply assumed it. Twenty or thirty years later, they were clearly being seen as tortious. Jones was able to carry across the Roman contractual rules into England without too much extra trouble, but there was the potential for friction.

Why does this matter? Well, it was already coming to be said, and again derived from natural law, that you were under a duty to take reasonable care not to injure your neighbour.[8] But the core Roman contract rule, central to Jones, was slightly different: the duty to take the care that would be taken by a *bonus paterfamilias*, or, as we would say in the nineteenth or twentieth century, by a reasonable man. From the 1830s, not only were bailment cases tortious, but this reasonable man standard had come to apply generally in the law of tort. Reasonable care, and the care of a reasonable man, were almost equivalent; but only almost. If the duty was to take the reasonable care, it was for the jury to use its own standards of reasonableness; if the duty was to take the care of a reasonable man then the standard was one external to them. Juries might not think it was reasonable that railways killed so many people, but if they were asked what a

[8] I have traced the history of the tort of negligence from this point in 'The Law of Business Rome: Foundations of the Anglo-American Tort of Negligence' [1999] *Current Legal Problems* 74; 'The Tort of Negligence in the Early Common Law', in EJH Schrage (ed), *Negligence* (Berlin, Duncker & Humblot, 2001) 229; '*George v Skivington* (1869)' in C Mitchell and P Mitchell (eds), *Landmark Cases in the Law of Tort* (Oxford, Hart Publishing, 2010) 69; 'The Tort of Negligence in England' in N Jansen (ed), *The Development and Making of Legal Doctrine* (Cambridge, Cambridge University Press, 2010) 46.

reasonable railway company would do they might feel constrained to accept the normal practice – unless, of course, they simply ignored the judge's direction. We are stuck with this terminology today, though the law has been able to adjust its reasonable person standard to achieve desired results: a 15-year-old has to act as a reasonable 15-year-old, by contrast a learner driver has to act as a reasonable qualified driver. We are back in the pre-Jones world of asking what constituted reasonable care in the circumstances.

It is not difficult to see the attraction of natural law, and behind it Roman law, to Jones. It was a well-structured system, scientific in the sense that Jones had used the word, and it was self-consciously underpinned by attractive ethical principles. Had he lived to 1808 he would have had some sympathy with the deputy in the Louisiana Assembly who successfully argued that Louisiana should have a code based on the model of the French *Code Civil* rather than wading into what he described as 'the horrible chaos of the common law', '*el horrible caos del common law*'.[9] But there were negative sides to natural law too. Fundamentally, as I think Jones recognised and could not resolve, there was a tension between the well-structured system founded upon abstract propositions (but throwing up many points of potential disagreement) and the need for authority to resolve those disagreements at the risk of destroying the self-consistency of the system. My own belief is that it was this tension that brought the classical period of Roman law to an end early in the third century – too many points on which very able jurists could disagree – and allowed the system of imperial authority to replace it. One authoritative answer to a legal question was far better than two or three intellectually convincing but inconsistent answers. A second problem was that it was too easy to believe that the propositions of natural law were fundamentally true, that all legal systems were at heart the same. Hence, having become a judge in India in 1783 and taken up the study of Sanskrit, he translated the important Hindu work of perhaps the second or third century CE, the *Mānavadharmaśāstra*, publishing it as *The Institutes of Indian Law, or the Ordinances of Menu* in 1794. The title makes it clear that for Jones this was the equivalent of the Institutes of Justinian, the basic manual of Hindu law. But it was nothing of the sort, and although it did contain norms we would certainly describe as law, it is better to think of it as a guide to proper conduct. He also set in train the creation of an ambitious *Digest* of Hindu law, consisting of extracts from texts sewn together in the manner of Justinian's *Digest* and reflecting very closely some of the detail. It should contain, he said, 'a more ample repertory of Hindu laws, especially on the twelve different Contracts, to which *Ulpian* has given specifick names, and on all the others, which, though not specifically named, are reducible to four general heads'.[10] Hindu law, surely, must be structured in the same way as Roman law, just as the English law of bailments mimicked the Roman law of real contracts. The same assumption was made explicitly by judges in India in the generations after Jones' death; it was a commonplace observation in the Anglo-Indian courts and in the British parliament that so far as contract was concerned, Hindu law was the same as English law. It was a classic example of what has been described as a process of 'converting Indian forms of knowledge into European objects'.[11]

[9] Quoted by A Guzmán Brito, 'La Influencia del Código Civil Francés en las Codificaciones Americanas' (2005) *Cuadernos de Análisis Juridico* 25 at fn 81.

[10] G Cannon, *The Letters of Sir William Jones* (Cambridge, Cambridge University Press, 1970) 797.

[11] BS Cohn, 'The Command of Language and the Language of Command' in R Guha (ed), *Subaltern Studies IV: Writings on South Asian History and Society* (Delhi, Oxford University Press, 1985) 282.

I suspect that this was inevitable, given the eighteenth-century belief in the objective, universal validity of natural law principles, an assumption explicit in Blackstone's Commentaries:

> This law of nature, being co-eval with mankind and dictated by God himself, is of course superior in obligation to any other. It is binding over all the globe, in all countries, and at all times: no human laws are of any validity, if contrary to this …

Such a view of natural law as the basis of common law fell out of fashion in the nineteenth century as the positivism of John Austin took over. But we may be moving along the same lines today, with private law theorists identifying 'true' principles, and more generally as we impose a liberal western set of values onto different cultures through the fetishisation of human rights. Should we see in Jones a reflection of a tension within ourselves? He was a thoroughgoing anti-colonialist, a strong supporter of American independence and a strong believer in allowing Indians to be governed by their own customary laws; but at the same time he was blinkered into granting a universal validity to the natural law which was in truth a projection of Roman law.

Thus far on the *acta* side of the line with Jones; but there is something on the *agenda* side too, a fascinating loose end I have not tied up. That is Jones' share in the making of the Second Amendment of the US Constitution, the right to bear arms. He had been caught up in the Gordon Riots in 1780. The civil authorities had lost control of the city and Jones played his part in the Inns of Court militia, in time regaining control of the streets. Reflecting on this, he published a pamphlet on the proper mode of the suppression of riots, arguing that all citizens should arm themselves in some way and train regularly, ready to be called on to support the civil power. A duty to bear arms. Slightly later, the result of a conversation with Benjamin Franklin among others, he penned his *Dialogue between a Scholar and a Peasant* in which he reduced his libertarian political philosophy to principles so simple that they could be understood by anyone. One of those principles was the right of individuals to arm themselves to protect themselves against the abuse of governmental power, the dialogue leading to the peasant saying that he will certainly keep a flintlock in his farmhouse for the purpose. A right to bear arms. Franklin, we know, approved of the pamphlet, which incidentally gave rise to what must be one of the more absurd episodes in English legal history as Jones was very hurriedly shipped off to take up a judgeship in India at the same time as his brother-in-law was being prosecuted for sedition for disseminating Jones's pamphlet in Welsh. We can see his developed views on the bearing of arms in an address to the Grand Jury of Calcutta in which he described the rights most fundamental to the protection of the individual: the right to play a part in the election of the legislature, the right to trial by jury, and the right – and duty – to arm oneself. I shall leave it to others to burrow deeper into this rabbit hole.

Let me return to private law. One topic I have several times returned to, as a dog returns to its vomit you might privately think by the time I have finished, is the area of law which we probably know as unjust enrichment or restitution, though in continental Europe it is generally known as unjustified enrichment.[12] It has proved useful over the

[12] 'Unjust Enrichment in England before 1600' in EJH Schrage (ed), *Unjust Enrichment* (Berlin, Duncker & Humblot, 1995) 121; 'Unjust Enrichment in English Law' in EJH Schrage (ed), *Unjust Enrichment and the*

last eight or nine centuries as a way of providing remedies in a variety of situations. Its anchor point in Roman law was a Stoic philosophical principle that it was fair that no-one should be enriched to the detriment of another, though a second version of the text says that no-one should be enriched to the detriment and wrong of another. But this was a very general statement with no more bite than that one should give every man his due. The legal core was the remedy known as the *condictio*, applicable principally either when there was a contract to pay a fixed sum of money or where there had been a transfer which ought to be reversed, typically where money had been paid in the mistaken belief that it was owed or where it had been transferred without a legally recognised cause. Finally there were the quasi-contractual obligations, where a person was liable as if there had been a contract when there had not been. I shall spare you all the ins and outs of the last nine centuries or so. They are legion. Medieval scholars of Roman law stuck largely with the Roman texts, though from the late thirteenth century there was something of a dalliance with the idea that a *condictio* should lie whenever it was equitable that it should. This idea found its home in Holland, Frisia and Germany in the seventeenth and early-eighteenth centuries, for the first time I think linking the availability of the remedy to the general principle that none should be enriched at the expense of another. The English common law was having none of this. Legal practice just squeezed difficult situations into existing remedies without any attempt to theorise. The treatise known as *Bracton* from the mid-thirteenth century reproduces the Roman texts on the so-called quasi-contracts without comment; it bears no relation whatsoever to what was happening in courts. Only in the seventeenth and early-eighteenth centuries do we find recognisably non-contractual remedies, for example in the form of indebitatus assumpsit for money had and received or non-contractual actions of quantum meruit. Text writers kept their heads in the sand and tended to speak of them as based on implied contracts. After all, the form of action was assumpsit and assumpsit was normally contractual. It was only with Lord Mansfield that there was any serious attempt to generalise. Borrowing either from the Frisian Huber or the German Heineccius – the same Heineccius as Sir William Jones borrowed from – he articulated a general principle that money or other property could be claimed whenever it was just that it should be.[13] But this was far too broad and within a few years he backtracked, leaving equity with its overtones of the Court of Chancery behind. England drifted back into its implied contract analysis. With apologies to non-lawyers present, and possibly to lawyers too, I cannot resist quoting Frederick Pollock's explanation of the law in the latter part of the nineteenth century:

> It does not follow that because there is no true contract, there may not be cases falling within this general description in which it is just and expedient that an obligation analogous to contract should be imposed upon the person receiving the benefit. In fact there are such

Law of Contract (The Hague, Kluwer Law International, 2001) 33; 'Unjust Enrichment and Lord Mansfield' in M Schermaier, H Dondorp and B Sirks (eds), *De Rebus Divinis et Humanis* (Göttingen, V&R Unipress, 2019) 193; 'Development in Common Law' in E Bant, K Barker and S Degeling (eds), *Research Handbook on Unjust Enrichment* (Cheltenham, Edward Elgar Publishing, 2020) 28; 'What's in a Name: Historical Foundations of Unjust(ified) Enrichment' in S Turenne (ed), *Reasons and Contexts in Comparative Law* (Cambridge, Cambridge University Press, 2023) 63.

[13] It is worth noting in passing that the whole problem in the leading case of *Moses v Macferlan* had stemmed from legislation preventing the review of a lower court's decision by the common law judges.

> cases: and as the forms of our law do not recognise quasi-contracts in any distinct manner, these cases are dealt with by the fiction of an implied previous request, which often has to be supplemented (as in the action for money had and received) by an equally fictitious promise. The promise, actual or fictitious, then relates back to the fictitious request, so that the transaction which is the real foundation of the matter is treated as forming the consideration in a fictitious contract of the regular type.[14]

So much for English law being a science. Meanwhile, in Germany, the great Friedrich von Savigny had explained the law in terms of the reversal of transfers made without a legally recognised cause, *grundlose Bereicherung*, unjustified enrichment. But when this was translated into French it came out as *enrichissement injuste*, unjust enrichment. This was picked up by the American legal historian James Barr Ames in 1888 as the explanation of a set of seventeenth-century English cases, and the terminology of unjust enrichment stuck, conveniently sucking in some ideas of the Chancery with their rooting in equity. Now we find German lawyers questioning the whole idea of unjustified enrichment and English lawyers questioning the whole idea of unjust enrichment.

There is no better antidote to a belief in the timeless and fundamental rationality of the law than a good dose of legal history.

Let me turn from the sheer confusion of the enrichment remedy to the perhaps calmer waters of contract law. This was the starting point of my research career. My PhD thesis dug deep into manuscript law reports of the sixteenth century in an attempt to elucidate what appear to be the foundations of the modern law of contract in the action of assumpsit. The starting point was in the middle of the fourteenth century, in what we would think of as the law of torts. A person who had been injured by faulty medical treatment, for example, had come to be excluded from the core action of trespass, which required an allegation that there had been a forcible breach of the king's peace. Breach of the king's peace could not properly be alleged when the defendant had been acting with the consent of the victim. The same applied when property was damaged by a bailee. The solution was to allow the action to proceed without an allegation of a breach of the king's peace but with a brief statement of the circumstances in which the alleged wrong had been committed. Since the problem in many of these cases was that the defendant had been acting with the consent of the victim, it became common to allege that he had undertaken to do something but had done it badly. There was a problem when the form of pleading was used in cases of non-performance. After a century of uncertainty, it was settled that it might be used in such circumstances, the contractual dimension being stressed by the addition of an allegation that the defendant had not merely assumed to act but had also promised to do so. The action became popular since it avoided some procedural difficulties of the orthodox contractual action of debt and by 1600 it had substantially eclipsed the older remedy. History is perhaps repeating itself today in the way in which some fringe cases of negligence, especially cases where there has been an omission rather than a positive act or where the rules of the law of contract have come to be seen as excessively rigid, are being brought in by alleging that there has been an assumption of responsibility.

One of the doctrines that crystallised in the sixteenth century was consideration, the rule that in the absence of a sealed document an undertaking was legally enforceable

[14] F Pollock, *Principles of Contract at Law and Equity* (London, Stevens and Sons, 1876) 29.

only if something had been given or done in exchange. This perhaps made sense in the sixteenth century, when social relations were underpinned by the giving of gifts in the expectation of receiving a gift in return. The only difference between a gift and a contract was that in a contract the counter-performance had been agreed in advance whereas in a gift it was for the receiver to choose how and when to reciprocate. This medieval approach was perhaps on the way out at the time – Lord Chancellor Francis Bacon found to his cost that a gift might easily be characterised as a bribe – and by the eighteenth century it was being argued that the doctrine of consideration had passed its sell-by date; the new model of contract had come to the fore, based on the meeting of minds of the parties. But consideration survived, the fossilised detritus of the earlier model of contract. We are stuck with it today, though it is easily avoided by putting the agreement in writing and including a few magic words. Fail to do that and there is no enforceable contract, though the merciful courts have at their disposal a whole toolbox of devices to avoid that. Assumption of responsibility, promissory estoppel, proprietary estoppel, the invention of a nominal consideration, commercial exceptions and so on.

If we get one lesson from legal history it is that the common law is not terribly good at discarding rules and doctrines once they have got their place in the textbooks. Perhaps my favourite example of this inertia is the rule of privity of contract, the rule that only a party to a contract can enforce it. It looks to have come from Roman law, where it made sense. In England it was an inconvenience and from about 1240 any competent lawyer drafting a contract to be put in writing could avoid it, unless an unborn child was involved. It remained as a snare to trap the unwary until 1999.

There are, of course, bits of the jigsaw of the history of contract waiting to be filled in. One is the relationship between the emergent doctrine of consideration of the sixteenth century and the Roman, or continental European, idea of *causa*. There are hints that some English lawyers were aware of the romanised rule but I have seen no evidence that the development of the English doctrine was influenced by it. A more important agendum is the crystallisation of the legal boundary between contracts which were made in a sealed document and those which were not. I have spent, but I think not wasted, many hours, days and months beginning to make some sense of this by looking at the formalisation of the action of covenant around 1300, one of the most important factors shaping the whole history of the English law of obligations right up to the present day.[15] But covenant was the tip of the iceberg, and there is a great deal still to be done. I suspect that on a thorough investigation it will be revealed as a prime example of the spawning of a naturalised common-law distinction out of a rather different Roman-law distinction in the course of the thirteenth and fourteenth centuries. But I will leave that investigation to others.

As the holder of a chair in Roman law I have of course spent some time on the law of the ancient world. Whether I have said anything worthwhile about the law of Rome it will be for others to say. What I have written on the subject has been rather aimed at clearing away the brushwood and debris of several centuries of commentary in an attempt to elucidate what was actually happening to the law in the millennium between the Twelve Tables and Justinian. I have been more concerned with the comparative

[15] 'Words and Deeds: the Action of Covenant in the Reign of Edward I' (1986) 4 *Law and History Review* 71; 'The Requirement of a Deed in the Action of Covenant' (2021) 42 *Journal of Legal History* 233.

legal history of the ancient world. I believe a straight line can be drawn from the Mesopotamian world at the end of the third millennium BCE through the Hittites of second millennium Anatolia and the Greeks to Rome.[16] The great significance of Roman law lay not so much in its rules as in its methods developed from the end of the Republic, in particular the reliance on reasoning by analogy. I have suggested, perhaps eccentrically, that the relatively recent discovery and translation of the Hittite texts has caused us to underestimate the importance of this still rather obscure system. It looks to me to have been possibly the first legal culture to have generalised legal rules from decisions in actual cases, a very important step in the development of the idea of law as we think of it today. Some of these early texts have an eerily modern ring to them. A Sumerian text of the first decades of the second millennium BCE deals with the problem of a landowner who neglects his land with the result that thieves are able to break into his neighbour's property. I wonder if they discussed what was the right result at as great a length as the House of Lords did in 1987?

More recently, I have been heavily involved in a project which is nearing its end, a comparative investigation of ancient legal systems. Mesopotamia, Anatolia, Egypt, Greece and Rome have enough features in common for us to think of them as a legal-cultural unity, but the same cannot be said for India and China. Neither had a word which we can safely translate as 'law', but there are occasionally equivalent practices in very different systems. In early China there seem to have been special formalities for the sale of slaves and cattle, just as there were in early Rome. Across Eurasia we see the parties to a formal contract mixing their blood or smearing it onto a document of some form, generally transmuting the mixing of blood into the ritual sharing of wine. Independent developments? Evidence of age old contacts through central Asia along what would come to be known as the Silk Road? Or practices which could be traced back for many, many millennia? Our project may be nearing completion, but we have only scratched the surface of questions of this type. Something else for the agenda.

My time is coming to an end, at least in the sense that this lecture is reaching its close. But I should say something about legal education. I shall keep it brief since with this audience I suspect I may be preaching to the converted. Why should we teach Roman law, comparative law and legal history? Let me begin with Roman law. It is a fact that most of the world's legal systems deal with private law in a very Roman way. My own belief is that this is true also of Common-law systems because of the work of Sir William Jones and his ilk in the eighteenth century. This prevalence of thought traceable back to Roman law is not simply a consequence of colonial domination. Such an explanation would not account for the Japanese code of 1898 or the first Chinese civil code, drafted in 1911. Nor does it really explain the experience of the newly independent states in South America in the nineteenth century, rejecting the Spanish and Portuguese-based laws of the colonial powers and choosing to replace them with a code based on a French or German model. We can say that a knowledge of Roman law helps us to understand the conceptual vocabulary of those systems, but it is more than that. If we ask why those responsible for the drafting of civil codes have repeatedly turned to a Romanised model,

[16] 'Wrongs and Responsibility in Pre-Roman Law' (2004) 29 *Journal of Legal History* 99; 'Revolutions in Private Law?' in S Worthington, G Virgo and A Robinson (eds), *Revolution and Evolution in Private Law* (Oxford, Hart Publishing, 2018) 11.

the answer has to be that it was a rather good model. It would not be going too far to say that Roman law was one of the crucial forces shaping modern civilisation, and was the single most important force in the shaping of modern legal culture.

What about comparative law? I have no pretensions to be a comparative lawyer myself, but I have learnt a lot from working with comparative lawyers. The value of studying the subject is emphatically not that pointed to by Jones in 1778, it reveals to the patriot the superiority of his own system. If legal systems reach different results in some particular cases we can learn from asking why that might be; and if they reach the same result by different routes we might well seek to ask which route is the more efficient.

Finally legal history. We can, no doubt, conceive of law as a static system. When consulted by a client, the lawyer is expected to say what the relevant law is. But it is also a dynamic system, and the good lawyer advising a client must be concerned with what the law is becoming. You cannot see what the law is becoming without knowing where it has come from, and in English law, which has developed without any radical break for nearly a millennium, the dynamic dimension may involve looking back for centuries. Perhaps more importantly in a common law system, there is value in being able to identify rules and doctrines which made sense when they were introduced but have been left behind as detritus from a past age. Jeremy Bentham said that in order to reform the law you had to know what it was; he might have added that you had to understand where it had come from.

In the opening pages of his *De Legibus* Cicero tells of being asked by his friend Atticus to turn himself to writing a history. Cicero replies that you can only really write a history when free of work and worry, ie when you retire. His is a good model for a Professor of Roman law to follow. So I turn now to writing the legal history which I should have been writing for the last three decades. I'm sure I will carry on looking under metaphorical stones, but when I find something interesting there I will pass it on to someone else and turn back to my book. At least one person in the room today will be pleased to hear it.[17]

[17] I should record that at this point Professor Baker nodded vigorously.

PART I

Ancient Law

3

Chasing, Lying and Persuading: D 47.2.52.19–24 in Context

HELEN SCOTT*

I. Preface: The Ibbetsonian School

I first encountered David Ibbetson in 2000 when I studied Roman Law Delict on the BCL. Peter Birks delivered the seminars while David taught the tutorials, so I didn't actually meet him until late in the academic year, when the seminars were finished and exams were looming. Each week during Trinity Term I made my way from Holywell Manor to Magdalen. Sometimes I would have to wait for a long time outside his door while he, as Dean, attended to some undergraduate emergency. Once inside, he would lie full length on what I remember to have been a chaise longue and would drape a handkerchief across his face while I read out my essay on *furtum*, *iniuria*, the quasi-delicts, or some aspect of the *lex Aquilia*. Occasionally he would groan terribly in response to something I had said; I would pause, expecting correction on a fundamental point, but he would just wave his hand (without removing the handkerchief) and murmur encouragingly 'go on, go on.' I later realised that the groans disclosed deep thought rather than suffering. Sometimes long periods would elapse during which no sign of life issued from under the handkerchief and I would begin to wonder whether he had fallen sleep. But after one particularly prolonged silence, when I happened to suggest that a text in Digest 9.2 had been interpolated, his entire body seemed to rise horizontally into the air and the handkerchief was abruptly cast off as he demanded, furious ('where? where does it say that? show me where!'), that I justify this (to my mind quite uncontroversial) assertion. In this way I discovered that the lesson I had absorbed from my previous encounters with Roman law – that one could deconstruct the classical texts more-or-less at will – was not universally accepted practice.

* I am indebted to the Edinburgh Roman Law Group, and to Professor Paul du Plessis in particular, for giving an audience to an early draft of this paper in March 2021; to Professor Ernie Metzger, who pointed me to the work of Platschek cited in n 13 below; to Dr Guy Westwood, for help with Sophocles; and to Dr Benjamin Spagnolo, for help with both the substance of the piece and the translation of D 47.2.27, D 47.2.50, D 47.2.52.14, and D 47.2.52.19–24 itself. All remaining errors are mine. As ever, I owe an enormous debt of gratitude to the students at both Oxford and Cambridge who have helped me to refine my thinking regarding this passage.

As the term went on, I realised that David's tutorials were utterly transforming my understanding of classical Roman law: rather than the monolith of principle and abstraction I had understood it to be, in fact juristic writing was casuistic, heterodox, even playful. It turned out that the Roman jurists were as distinctive and contentious as the people who taught on the BCL. The thing was to pay close attention to the fact patterns they were discussing, as you would in reading a case; to try to get into their heads and really understand what they were saying. A few years later, when I was labouring through the foothills of a DPhil, I discovered *An Historical Introduction to the Law of Obligations* and found the common law represented there with same humour, sensitivity to nuance, and lightness of touch that had characterised David's Roman law tutorials: details were lightly sketched in, and the evolution of a key doctrine over centuries summed up in a single elegant paragraph. I tried to imitate this style in my accounts of nineteenth-century South African law, with limited success. I had, in fact, become a card-carrying member of the Ibbetsonian school.

Of the many ideas that impressed me during the course of that Trinity Term, one of the most compelling was David's account of the delict of *furtum*, offered in 'The danger of definition: *contrectatio* and appropriation'[1] and elaborated in tutorials. Through careful contextualisation of certain key passages in D 47.2, and in particular by means of a sensitive reading of D 47.2.21 pr–8, David not only defended the text against the charge of being 'irredeemably corrupt'[2] but relied on it to build an argument that while classical *furtum* was defined in terms of *contrectatio*, interference, the popular conception of theft as carrying off (*asportatio*) or taking away (*amotio*) continued to inform the scope of the delict. As the physical element of the delict became increasingly attenuated, the jurists relied heavily on the mental element – the intention to steal (*animus furandi*), acting in order to make a gain (*lucri faciendi gratia*) – to hold the boundaries of *furtum* in place. But sometimes it was necessary to grasp the nettle: to deny liability for theft even where both *contrectatio* and *animus furandi* were clearly present. It was this tension between definition and concept that Ulpian[3] was exploring in D 47.2.21 pr-8: '[i]f I follow Ulpian's reasoning, his argument takes the form of an extended critique in four sections … of the notion (of Sabinus?) that the simple handling of the thing with the appropriate mental state is sufficient in itself to constitute *furtum*.'[4] Only if his subject in this passage is correctly identified is it possible to make sense of the argument that Ulpian is making. In the piece that follows I have tried to put into practice the lessons that David taught me 24 years ago, emulating his method in affording the portion of Ulpian's edictal commentary preserved in D 47.2.50 and 52 and in particular the sequence at 52.19–24 what I hope is a sympathetic and imaginative (but not too imaginative) reading. Approached as a coherent argument, rather than as a series of disconnected fragments, and situated in the wider context of Ulpian's commentary on

[1] DJ Ibbetson, 'The Danger of Definition: *Contrectatio* and Appropriation' in ADE Lewis and DJ Ibbetson (eds), *The Roman Law Tradition* (Cambridge, Cambridge University Press, 1994) 54.

[2] '[T]he fact that it is extremely difficult to make sense of the highly condensed argument is not in itself a reason for so concluding; what follows is based on the assumption that the text is substantially genuine, and that it makes substantial sense.' See Ibbetson, '*Contrectatio* and Appropriation' (n 1) 63.

[3] Not Paul: see Ibbetson, '*Contrectatio* and Appropriation' (n 1) fn 61, as well as the discussion of this text by Tony Honoré in *Justinian's Digest: Character and Compilation* (Oxford, Oxford University Press, 2010) 138–39.

[4] Ibbetson, '*Contrectatio* and Appropriation' (n 1) 63.

the words of the formula of the *actio furti nec manifesti*, the meaning of this difficult passage is unlocked. That my substantive conclusions align with the view of *furtum* articulated by David in 1994 surprises me not at all.

II. The Edictal Element in D 47.2

Digest 47.2 begins with a passage excerpted from Book 39 of Paul's Edictal Commentary, a passage that concludes with Paul's famous definition of *furtum*:

> Theft is a fraudulent interference [*contrectatio*] with a thing with a view to gain [*lucri faciendi gratia*], whether by the thing itself or by the use or possession of it. This natural law proscribes.[5]

The last fragment in the title, D 47.2.93, is excerpted from Book 38 of Ulpian's Edictal Commentary:

> It must be remembered that now criminal proceedings for theft are common and the complainant lays an allegation. It is not a kind of public prosecution in the normal sense, but it seemed proper that the temerity of those who do such wrongs should be punishable on extraordinary scrutiny. Still if that be the party's wish, he can bring civil proceedings for theft.[6]

Thus the first and last words in this long title are taken from the edictal commentaries of Paul and Ulpian. But the impression that their prominence creates – that the raw material of D 47.2 is predominantly edictal – turns out to be misleading. The first half of the title consists of extracts from their commentaries on the works of Sabinus, along with significant contributions from Gaius (Commentary on the Provincial Edict) and Pomponius (Commentary on Sabinus): in the case of Ulpian, mainly Book 41; in the case of Paul, mainly Book 9. Extracts from these two books alternate, giving the expression of a conversation between the jurists: this is particularly evident in the section from D 47.2.22 to 45. They appear to have been read together.[7] But almost immediately after the final fragment taken from Ulpian's commentary on Sabinus at D 47.2.48 we encounter a cluster of texts which are, like D 47.2.1 and D 47.2.93, taken from Ulpian and Paul's commentaries on the Edict: first, a long passage from Book 37 of Ulpian (this appears at 47.2.50 and 47.2.52); then a short passage from Book 38 of his Edictal Commentary (at D 47.2.53) – this is the same book from which 47.2.93 is taken; and finally a longer passage from Book 39 of Paul's Edictal Commentary (at D 47.2.54) – again, the same book from which D 47.2.1 is taken. These works appear to have been read by members of the same committee that read the Sabinian works, although not necessarily by the same people.[8] As in the case of Paul and Ulpian's commentaries on Sabinus, these books (37 and 38 of Ulpian, 39 of Paul) appear to have been read together.[9]

[5] D 47.2.1.3 (Paul Book 39 On the Edict). The translation is that given in A Watson (ed), *The Digest of Justinian* (Philadelphia, University of Pennsylvania Press, 1985).

[6] Translation in the Watson edition.

[7] See the revised version of the Bluhme-Krüger *Ordo Librorum Iuris Veteris in Compilandis Digestis Observatus* offered by Honoré in *Justinian's Digest* at 151–61 and especially 151 (the *ad Sabinum* group), as well as ch 3.

[8] See Honoré's revised *Ordo* in *Justinian's Digest* at 152 (the middle edictal commentaries group), which – like the *ad Sabinum* group – forms part of the Sabinian mass, as well as ch 3.

[9] ibid.

Why did the Compilers choose to include these portions of Ulpian and Paul's commentaries on the Edict in addition to the extensive extracts from their commentaries on Sabinus that dominate the first half of the title? In particular, why was the long extract from Ulpian's Book 37 chosen? There is, in fact, considerable overlap between the subject matter of the Sabinian passages and the material included here. But the extract preserved at 50 and 52 is distinctive insofar as it addresses in detail a topic only briefly dealt with by Ulpian elsewhere, namely complicity:[10] it contains a sustained analysis of the mental state and conduct necessary to sustain accomplice liability.

III. D 47.2.50.1–52.24 (Ulpian Book 37 On the Edict)

A. 50.1–4

D 47.2.50 begins with an unambiguous statement of general principle: 'In the *actio furti*, it is not the interest [*quod interest*] that is quadrupled or doubled but the true value [*verum pretium*] of the thing.' And indeed the entirely of 50 pr deals with the calculation of damages under the *actio furti manifesti* and *nec manifesti*, and in particular with the effect on those damages of either the destruction or deterioration of the thing or of an increase in its value between the commission of the theft and the commencement of action.[11] This issue reoccurs later in the fragment.[12] But Lenel took 50.1 to be the start of Ulpian's commentary on the words 'si paret Aulo Agerio a Numerio Negidio opeve consilio Numerii Negidii' in the formula of the *actio furti nec manifesti*:[13]

> 1. Celsus says that a theft has been committed with one's help and advice [*ope consilio furtum factum*] not only if what one did was in order to enable one's associates to steal [*si idcirco fuerit factum ut socii furarentur*] but also if one did it not in order to enable one's associates to steal but rather for the sake of ill-will [*inimicitiarum causa*]. 2. Pedius rightly says that just as no one commits theft [*furtum facit*] without wrongful intent [*dolo malo*], equally no one can offer either help or advice [*ope consilio*] without wrongful intent. 3. A person is deemed to give advice [*consilio*], who persuades and directs and provides advice in order to get a theft committed [*qui persuadet et impellit atque instruit consilio ad furtum faciendum*]; he gives help [*ope*] who provides aid or assistance for taking things [*qui ministerium atque adiutorium ad subripiendas res praebet*]. 4. An *actio furti* lies against he who waved a red flag and put cattle to flight so that they fell into the hands of thieves [*ut in fures incideret*], if indeed he did it with wrongful intent [*dolo malo*]. But even if he did not do this for the purpose of committing theft

[10] The only treatment of complicity in the fragments of Ulpian's Commentary on Sabinus excerpted in Digest 47.2 appears at D 47.2.36 (Ulpian Book 4 On Sabinus).

[11] For Lenel, 50.pr refers to a passage from the Twelve Tables, specifically 'si adorat furto, quod nec manifestum erit …'. See O Lenel, *Palingenesia Iuris Civilis*, Vol II (Leipzig, B Tauchnitz, 1889) 675, §1040.

[12] In 52.14 and 52.25 ff. *cf* section II(B) below.

[13] Lenel (n 11) 675, §1041. The reconstruction of the *actio furti nec manifesti* given here is taken from D Mantovani, *Le formule del processo privato romano*, 2nd edn (Milan, Wolters Kluwer, 1999) 62–63 but is essentially the same as the version Lenel assumes in his *Palingenesia*. See also O Lenel, *Das Edictum Perpetuum*, 3rd edn (Leipzig, B Tauchnitz, 1927) 324–30. But *cf* now J Platschek, 'Die Klageformel gegen den peregrinen Dieb in Gai. 4,37 Zugleich zum Aufbau der actio furti' (2014) 131 *Zeitschrift für Rechtsgeschichte: Romanistische Abteilung* 395.

> [*furti faciendi causa*], such a destructive game [*lusus perniciosus*] should not go unpunished; for this reason Labeo writes that an *actio in factum* should be given.[14]

It seems that Ulpian is concerned here with the mental state necessary to render someone who in fact enables another to steal an accomplice to theft. Whereas Celsus apparently thought that an act that enabled another to steal amounted to complicity, even where that was not the actor's intention (ie where he was motivated merely by ill-will towards the owner of the thing), Pedius thought that *dolus malus* – translated here as 'wrongful intent' – was necessary to constitute someone an accomplice to theft, just as it was necessary to constitute someone a thief. It was this latter view that Ulpian preferred.[15] Thus in the case set out in 50.4, where someone set cattle running with the result that they fell into the hands of thieves, he is liable to the *actio furti* only insofar as he acted for the purpose of committing theft.[16] A lesser mental state – the playing of a 'destructive game' – attracts only liability under an *actio in factum*.[17] It was not enough to make him an accomplice that the chaser's conduct in fact enabled another's theft.[18]

B. 52 pr–18

Following an extract from Gaius Book 13 on the Provincial Edict, Ulpian's analysis continues at 52 pr. 52 pr–52.2 is concerned with theft from husbands by wives – whereas a husband cannot bring the *actio furti* against his wife, he can sue her accomplice in theft – while 3 deals with a wife's liability for theft from her husband by her slave. 52.4, 5 and 6 then deal with liability for theft as between fathers and sons in power, the case of theft from his father by a slave forming part of the son's *peculium castrense* discussed in 4 forming a bridge, with 3, between the two groups of cases. At 7 Ulpian appears to change direction, considering the case in which a creditor retains a pledged object after the debt has been paid and approving Mela's view that he is liable for theft [*teneri furti*] if acting *celandi animo*, in order to conceal the object. Lenel thought that 52.7 marked the transition from Ulpian's commentary on the words 'si paret Aulo Agerio a Numerio Negidio opeve consilio Numerii Negidii' to his commentary on the words 'furtum factum esse', 'theft has been committed'.[19] If this were so, we would expect to find in this text and those following it analysis of what amounts to theft for the purposes of the *actio furti*, and indeed that is what we appear to find in 7: its interest lies in the fact that in omitting to return the pledged item, the defendant committed no new act but simply adopted a different mental state.[20] But in 8, 9, 10 and 11 Ulpian turns to the

[14] My translation (I have tried to render the Latin as literally as possible).

[15] *cf* also D 47.2.91.1 (Javolenus Book 9 From the Posthumous Works of Labeo).

[16] I have translated 'ut in fures incideret' in 50.4 as a result clause; by contrast, 'furti faciendi causa' later in the same fragment expresses purpose. Similarly 'ut socii furarentur' in 50.1 expresses purpose.

[17] *cf* Gaius III.202: in the same case the chaser's mental state is described as *lascivia* and his actions are said to give rise to an *actio utilis* modelled on the *lex Aquilia* (also D 47.2.51. Gaius Book 13 On the Provincial Edict).

[18] D 47.2.36 pr (Ulpian Book 41 On Sabinus) and D 47.2.37 (Pomponius Book 19 On Sabinus) suggest that Pomponius at least thought differently: ie he took the view that one whose actions enabled another's theft should be treated as an accomplice whatever his mental state.

[19] Lenel (n 11) 676, §1042; Mantovani (n 13) 63.

[20] *cf* D 41.1.44 (Ulpian Book 19 On the Edict).

question of standing: whether it is the owner of land or the *colonus* who can bring the *actio furti* of the theft of sulphur from pits on the land; whether a *paterfamilias* has the *actio furti* in respect of the theft of clothes stolen from a slave or son who has received them for cleaning; whether the unwitting purchaser of stolen goods has the *actio furti* in respect of the theft of those goods from him; where someone impersonates another in order to obtain flour from a corn merchant, whether it is the merchant or the person impersonated who has the *actio furti*:

> 11. It is said by Labeo that if a person tells a corn merchant to give flour to anyone who may come and ask for it in his name [*nomine eius*] and a passer-by who has heard this does so ask, and acquires [*accepit*] the flour, it is the corn merchant, not I, who has the *actio furti* against him; for the merchant conducted his own transaction [*negotium*], not mine.[21]

Similarly, 12 considers a case where an act of giving – in this case, the handing over of a slave to his putative master by a duumvir – is prompted by a mistake as to the identity of the recipient: while the true owner of the slave has an action against the official to make available his action on any verbal guarantees given, in the absence of such guarantees the owner can bring the *actio furti* against the person who secured the slave's release.

In 13 Ulpian considers the case in which someone knocks gold or silver coins [*nummos*] (or something else) out of someone's hand: if he did it in order for another to pick the coins up, and if they did indeed do so, he is liable for theft.[22] As in 50.1–4, we are concerned here with the conditions under which someone can be held liable to the *actio furti* as an accomplice, although the phrase '*ope consilio*' is not used. Not only must he intend to enable a theft; theft must in fact be committed. The reference to precious metals in 13 leads, in 14, to a case that appears to raise a new issue in this context, the characterisation of the thing stolen: 'if someone stole [*subripuerit*] my unwrought silver and made it into cups, I can have the *actio furti* or the *condictio* in respect of the cups or the metal. The same applies in the case of grapes, unfermented wine, and grapeskins; for it is possible to bring an *actio furti* in respect of the grapes and the must and the skins, but it is also possible to bring the *condictio*.' The point seems to be that the *actio furti* (and *condictio*) lies both in respect of the goods as they were when they were stolen and in respect of their final form. This text thus evokes 50 pr, in which it was argued that damages under the *actio furti* could be calculated either with reference to the value of the goods when stolen or with respect to their value at the time of trial, whichever was higher. But 15 picks up once again the question explored in 11, namely the effect of mistake on an act of giving: where a slave asserts that he is free, or a son in power asserts that he is a *paterfamilias*, in order to obtain a loan [*ut sibi pecunia crederetur*], he does not commit theft [*furtum non facit*] because he does no more than assert that he is a suitable borrower.[23] A contrast with the facts in 11 (which involved an error as to the identity of the recipient) is implied. 16 then considers the case where someone acquires money [*pecuniam acceperit*] from another to pay to that other's creditor and,

[21] Note that I have adjusted the translation in the Watson edition, which reads '... it is against him, not against me, that the corn merchant will have the action for theft.'

[22] *cf* G III.202 and D 9.2.27.21 (Ulpian Book 18 On the Edict) where this case is also discussed.

[23] *cf* D 47.2.43.3 (Ulpian Book 41 On Sabinus): 'If a man does not lie with respect to his identity but does use words misleadingly, he is a fraud [*fallax*] not a thief; for example, he says that he is wealthy or that he intends to put the money he receives into trade ...' (translation in the Watson edition).

by chance owing the same amount to the same creditor, pays it over in his own name [*suo nomine solverit*]: for Julian, he commits theft [*furtum facere*]. Again, there is an echo of the case discussed in 11, where flour is asked for (and received) in another's name [*nomine eius*]. But (Ulpian continues in 17) where Titius sells another's thing and receives coins [*accepit nummos*] from the purchaser, he does not seem to commit theft of the coins. Finally, 18 considers a case involving multiple potential plaintiffs: 'if there be two partners in a partnership of all assets and one receive a pledge which is then stolen, Mela says that only the recipient, not the other partner, has the action for theft.'[24] We are thus brought round once again to the topic addressed in 8, 9, 10, 11 and 12: that of standing to sue.

It is not always easy to follow Ulpian's train of thought in the passage running from 52.pr to 52.18, perhaps because the text has been shortened by the Compilers. Nevertheless, its central themes are clear: throughout the passage, Ulpian is interested in questions of standing and liability under the *actio furti*; often the cases discussed involve multiple potential plaintiffs (as in 8, 11, 12, 18) or more than one wrongdoer (pr, 1, 2, 3, 4, 13), the latter category comprising cases of complicity, a topic already addressed in 50.1–4. Prominent throughout are cases in which the defendant purports to be someone else, or purports to have a different status than he really has, or acts for himself when bound to act for another: this is the subject matter of 11, 12, 15, 16 and 17. Some of these cases involve only two parties, but the defendant's simulation or dissimulation seems to bring them into line with those involving multiple plaintiffs or wrongdoers. At the same time, these dis/simulation cases form a bridge between the three-party cases and the two-party case in 7: what the complicity cases, 7, 11, 12, 15, 16 and 17 all have in common is that they involve a defendant who has not stolen according to the popular conception of theft – someone who had not taken away or carried off a thing belonging to the plaintiff – but who is nevertheless liable to the *actio furti*.

These cross-cutting themes suggest that, contrary to Lenel's view, 50.1–52.6 and 52.7–52.18 do not speak (in the first case) to complicity and (in the second case) to the question of what amounts to theft for the purposes of the *actio furti* but rather form part of a single integrated analysis.[25] In fact, it may be that Lenel's reconstruction of the formula of the *actio furti nec manifesti* in his *Palingenesia* – and thus his understanding of our text – relied on a flawed reading of Gaius's *Institutes* 4.37.[26] Johannes Platschek argues that in truth the formula of the *actio furti nec manifesti* read, 'quod furtum factum est paterae aureae a Numerio Negidio, qua de re agitur, quam ob rem eum, si civis romanus esset, pro fure damnum decidere oporteret …'.[27] If this reconstruction of the formula is correct, is seems likely that both D 47.2.50.1–4 and D 47.2.52 pr–24 originally pertained to the words, 'quod furtum factum est', 'that theft has been committed'.

[24] Translation in the Watson edition.

[25] Indeed, on the evidence of 52.14, we might break from Lenel also in excluding 50 pr from this integrated analysis. See further section III below.

[26] See the sources referred to in n 13 above.

[27] Platschek (n 13) 399.

Nor does Ulpian abandon this analysis at 52.18.[28] Ulpian is often thought by commentators to be exploring in D 47.2.52.19–24 the meaning of *contrectatio*.[29] This belief coheres with Lenel's view that Ulpian's discussion of *ope consilio* concluded at 52.6, and indeed it is unsurprising given the way the passage begins: 'One commits theft [*furtum facit*] neither by word nor by writing; for our rule is that theft cannot occur without *contrectatio*.' The remainder of our text (52.20–24) is then understood as a series of examples designed to illustrate this rule.[30] But in fact Ulpian is here exploring further the themes identified in 50 and in 52 pr–18: in particular – as in 50.1–4 and 52.13 – the conditions under which someone could be held liable to the *actio furti* as an accomplice, alongside the wider question of when a person who had not stolen in the lay sense of the word could nevertheless be held liable for theft.

C. 52.19–24

A literal translation of 52.19–24 reads as follows:

> 19. One commits theft [*furtum facit*] neither by word nor by writing [*neque verbo neque scriptura*]; for our rule is that theft cannot occur without *contrectatio*. For this reason providing help [*opem ferre*] or giving advice [*consilium dare*] likewise imports liability [*nocet*] only when *contrectatio* has followed. 20. If someone will have driven off my male ass and set him loose among his own mares merely in order to impregnate them [τῆς γονῆς dumtaxat χάριν], he is not liable for theft unless he also had theftuous intent [*furandi animum*]; I gave the same reply to my pupil, Herennius Modestinus, who consulted me from Dalmatia concerning horses to which a man was alleged to have submitted his mares for the same purpose, that he would be liable for theft insofar as he had done it with theftuous intent [*furandi animo*]; if not, it would be necessary to bring an *actio in factum*. 21. When I wished to lend money to Titius, an honourable man, and you presented to me a different, penniless Titius as if he were rich, and shared the coins received [*nummos acceptos*] with him, you are liable for theft on the basis that theft has been committed [*furtum factum sit*] through your help and advice [*ope tua consilioque*]; but Titius will also be liable for theft. 22. Someone lent you heavier weights when you were buying by weight; Mela writes that he is liable to the seller for theft; as also are you if you knew; for you do not acquire [*accipis*] in accordance with the will of the seller [*ex voluntate venditoris*] since he is in error as to the weight. 23. If someone persuaded my slave to remove [*tolleret*] his debt [*nomen*] from, say, a document of purchase [*instrumento emptionis*], Mela wrote, and I think [*ego puto*], that a theft action lies [*furtum agendum*]. 24. But if the slave were persuaded to transcribe my tablets [*tabulas meas describeret*], I think that if indeed the slave were persuaded to do it, the *actio servi corrupti* must be brought, but if he himself did it, the *actio de dolo* must be given.[31]

[28] Continuity between 52.7–18 and 52.19–24 is accepted by Lenel: as we have seen (text to n 19 above), he understands everything from 52.7 to 52.24 to be a comment on the words 'furtum factum esse' in the formula of the *actio furti nec manifesti*.

[29] According to Lenel, at D 47.2.52.25 Ulpian turns his attention to the words 'paterae aureae'. See Lenel (n 11) 677, §1043 as well as Mantovani (n 13) 63 and Platschek (n 13).

[30] As in eg P Birks, 'The Case of the Filched Pedigree: D 47.2.52.20' in *Sodalitas: Scritti I Onore di Antonio Guarino*, Vol II (Napoli, Jovene, 1984) 731, 736 especially fn 11; P Ferretti, *Complicità e furto nel diritto romano* (Milan, Giuffrè, 2005) 199–200.

[31] This translation is based on Watson's but has been adjusted in order to render the Latin as literally as possible.

Setting aside for the moment the abstract propositions in 19, the text considers four cases (with variants), one of which appears to have derived from Ulpian's own experience (or at least from that of Modestinus, his pupil), while the others appear to have had a long history in the juristic tradition. 52.20 involves the theft of semen, or the theft of stud services (*furtum usus*), or perhaps even the theft of the genetic material of a male animal:[32] one man drives another's donkey to his own mares, or (more difficult) submits his stallions to another's mares, for the purpose of insemination. It is said, in respect of both variants, that the owner of the female animals will be liable for theft only insofar as he acts with theftuous intent (*animo furandi*). These references to intention are widely suspected of having been interpolated,[33] and some commentators go further, arguing that Ulpian originally denied liability unless *contrectatio* (in the sense of touching) could be demonstrated.[34] In 52.21, someone ('you') persuades another ('I') to lend money to a third person by presenting him as 'honourable Titius' whereas in fact he is 'penniless Titius'. 'You' and Titius share out the money between them. 'You' is liable on the basis that theft has been committed with his help and advice, *ope consilio*. Titius is also liable for theft. This text, like 20, is suspected of interpolation. Several commentators have doubted whether 'you' could indeed be said to be an accomplice (as Ulpian claims) if indeed he shared the money with Titius and therefore contrected it: either the reference to *ope consilio* must be interpolated or the reference to sharing the coins with Titius must be.[35] In 52.22 someone lends weights that are too heavy (ie heavier than indicated) to another ('you') who then goes shopping in the market. It is said – at least by Mela – that the lender of the weights is liable for theft. If 'you' knows, he is also liable, for the seller's error as to the weight of the goods handed over means that 'you' does not acquire them with his consent. Commentators have doubted the implication of the first sentence, that the lender of the weights could be liable for theft even where the purchaser was innocent, ie in the absence of any relationship of complicity or indeed any principal thief.[36] Without *animus furandi* on the part of 'you', the lender's conduct must itself amount to *contrectatio*, which is thought to be implausible. It is therefore suggested that the qualification regarding the knowledge of the purchaser ('as also are you if you knew') must be interpolated, or perhaps a late gloss, and that Mela in fact meant such knowledge on the part of the purchaser to be assumed.[37] Finally, in 52.23 someone persuades 'my' slave to remove his (the wrongdoer's) debt (literally, 'name') from a document evidencing a sale, with the result that my contractual claim against him is effectively extinguished because

[32] But note that we are not told how the story ended, ie whether the defendant's female animals in fact became pregnant.

[33] It is suspected that the original Ulpianic text either affirmed or denied liability on these facts without reference to *animus furandi*: see the sources cited in G Broggini (ed), *Index Interpolationum: Quae In Iustiniani Codice Inesse Dicuntur* (Weimar, Böhlau, 1969) 493 as well as A Watson, 'D 47.2.52.20: The Jackass, the Mares and "Furtum"' in *Studi in Onore di Edoardo Volterra*, Vol II (Milan, Giuffrè, 1971) 445, 445–46 and the sources referred to there. But *cf* JAC Thomas, '*Animus Furandi*' (1968) 19 *IURA* 14.

[34] Birks (n 30).

[35] See again the sources cited in Broggini (n 33) 493 as well as G MacCormack, 'Ope Consilio Furtum Factum' (1983) 51 *Tijdschrift voor Rechtsgeschiedenis* 271, 290.

[36] See the sources cited in Broggini (n 33) 493. But *cf* M Rizzi, '"Maiora quis pondera tibi commodavit cum emeres ad pondus" Note a D. 47.2.52.22 (Ulp. 37 ad ed.)' (2016) 44 *Index* 307, 318–21.

[37] See eg WAJ Watson, '"Contrectatio" Again' (1962) 28 *SDHI* 338, rescinding his own previously expressed view in WAJ Watson, '*Contrectatio* as an Essential of *Furtum*' (1961) 77 *Law Quarterly Review* 520, 532.

it can no longer be enforced.[38] Both Mela and Ulpian thought that these facts would give rise to a theft action. But (in 24) if the slave were merely persuaded to transcribe my documents, the *actio servi corrupti* must lie; if he himself did it, the *actio de dolo*. Of 23 it is said that Mela (and presumably also Ulpian?) is indifferent to *contrectatio* insofar as he does not explicitly say that the defendant acts as accomplice to the slave, who is the principal thief,[39] and even Lenel believed that much of the second half of 24 had been interpolated.[40] Overall, if the cases set out in 20 through 24 are construed as a series of illustrations of a general requirement of *contrectatio* set out in 52.19, they seem to have been badly distorted by the Compilers, who – it is said – had a wider view of *contrectatio* than Ulpian, and accorded much greater prominence to intent.

If, however, we admit the possibility that 52.19–24 contains a coherent analysis, one original to Ulpian, and if we place it in the wider context of D 47.2.50 and 52, we begin to see a clear argument emerging. Whereas it is the mental state necessary to render someone liable as an accomplice that is Ulpian's focus in 50.1–4 – again, in 50.2, 'Pedius rightly says that just as no one commits theft [*furtum facit*] without wrongful intent [*dolo malo*], equally no one can offer either help or advice [*ope consilio*] without wrongful intent' – this passage deals with the conduct necessary to sustain liability in cases involving accomplices (or accomplice-like figures): according to the second sentence of 52.19, *ops* or *consilium* gives rise to liability under the *actio furti* only where *contrectatio* 'has followed', because (as set out in the first sentence), theft cannot occur without *contrectatio*. It is not an accident that the conduct at issue here is the same as that at issue in 50.4, namely, chasing.

In a standard complicity scenario, the necessary *contrectatio* is provided by another person, one to whom one might refer, somewhat anachronistically, as the principal thief.[41] That is certainly the only plausible reading of cases where the person in the accomplice role deploys trickery or persuasion on the plaintiff,[42] or on another wrongdoer,[43] or indeed on the object of the theft[44] in order to get the theft committed: after all, '[o]ne commits theft [*furtum facit*] neither by word nor by writing [*neque verbo neque scriptura*].' But this assumption is less secure where the intervention of the accomplice figure goes beyond mere words or writing: in cases of this kind, acts of complicity can themselves amount to *contrectatio* as negatively defined by Ulpian in the first sentence of 52.19. It is this issue – locating the necessary *contrectatio* in a complicity scenario – that is Ulpian's concern in 19–24. In pursuing it, he considers not only cases of actual

[38] This interpretation of the text is strongly suggested by D 47.2.27 (Ulpian Book 41 On Sabinus), especially 27.3.

[39] See eg HF Jolowicz, *Digest XLVII.2* De Furtis (Cambridge, Cambridge University Press, 1940) 78.

[40] See again the sources cited in Broggini (n 33) 493. For Buckland, '[i]n all probability the original pointed out that this case had none of the characteristics of theft': see WW Buckland, 'Digest XLVII. 2 (De Furtis) and the Methods of the Compliers' (1930) 10 *Tijdschrift voor Rechtsgeschiedenis* 117, 128.

[41] While Ulpian refers to liability as an accomplice, *ope consilio*, in 50.1, 2 and 3 and in 52.19 and 21, there is no terminology equivalent to 'principal thief' in his surviving analysis. Rather, he emphasises that a defendant commits theft, '*furtum facit*', as in eg 50.2 and 52.19.

[42] As in D 47.2.52.21, discussed below.

[43] As in D 47.2.52.23, discussed below.

[44] As in D 47.2.36 pr, which gives the case of one who persuades a slave to run away so that another might steal him as an example of liability *ope consilio*, and presumably of liability *consilio* in particular (*cf* the reference to *malum consilium* earlier in the same text).

complicity but also cases that involve only one wrongdoer, albeit cases where the theft is accomplished by more than one actor, human or otherwise.

The case considered in 52.20 is of this second kind. Here there is only one wrongdoer, the owner of the female animals. To the extent that he is liable for theft, it must therefore be he who provides the necessary *contrectatio*, either by chasing another's donkey to his mares or by driving his mares to another's stallions. As we saw in Section III(A) above, the chaser in the first case discussed in D 47.2.50.4 was liable only insofar as he set the plaintiff's animal running *so that it might fall into the hands of thieves*.[45] That is why Ulpian emphasises the chaser's *animus furandi* here: the fact that he intended to steal – to make a gain for himself – is important because it explains why this is still a case of theft, even without the involvement of a third party. The *contrectatio* in the second alternative is even more remote from the gain that the chaser hopes to make, and it is therefore unsurprising that Ulpian again emphasises his mental state, repeating in respect of that variant also that liability depends upon the presence of *animus furandi*. But despite his mental state, as a mere chaser (whether of another's animals or his own) the defendant seems to be cast in the role of accomplice. It is a quirk of these particular facts – arising from the capacity of the animals to move themselves – that both things can be true at once. In introducing them, Ulpian appears to be making the point that the *contrectatio* necessary to give rise to liability under the *actio furti* can be provided by one in an apparently accessorial role.[46]

In the next case, discussed in 52.21, there are two wrongdoers and two potential defendants to the *actio furti*. And there is little ambiguity in the conduct of 'You' in deceiving 'I' into lending money to Titius: by Ulpian's own definition in 19, mere speaking cannot constitute *contrectatio*, and indeed You's conduct falls neatly within *consilium* as defined in 50.3. Thus You is said to be liable on the basis that theft has been committed with his help and advice, while Titius is also liable.[47] It seems that Titius, regarding whose identity I is mistaken, commits theft despite I's act of giving – he has merely accepted the coins – the way already having been prepared by Ulpian in 52.11 and in the sequence running from 52.15 to 52.17. But on closer examination the text turns out to be less straightforward than it first appears. First, it seems that both Titius and You contrect (ie commit *contrectatio* in respect of) the money: Titius – we assume – hands some (most?) of the coins received to You. The case might therefore be understood to suggest that providing *contrectatio* did not necessarily preclude one's being liable as an

[45] The facts envisaged in the second alternative in 50.4 seem to be those discussed by Gaius towards the end of G III.202, or in a fragment of his Commentary on the Provincial Edict preserved at D 47.2.51: there, the cattle run over a cliff, giving rise to an *actio utilis* modelled on the *actio legis Aquiliae*. In 52.20, however, it does not seem that the plaintiff's animals are lost, and therefore it is not clear whether the *actio in factum* that Ulpian mentions is indeed modelled on the *actio legis Aquiliae*.

[46] Cases involving a standard accomplice/principal configuration were no good for making this point, as *contrectatio* would invariably be provided by the principal, making it impossible to test whether the accomplice's actions were themselves sufficient to substantiate liability.

[47] *cf* also D 47.2.67.4 (Paul Book 7 On Plautius): 'If you commend Titius to me as a suitable person to whom to advance money and I make inquiries about Titius and then you bring forward someone else as being Titius, you commit theft because I believe him to be Titius, that is, if the person who is presented also knows; if he does not know, however, you do not commit theft, nor can the person who presented him be said to be an accomplice, because no theft has been committed; but an *actio in factum* will be given against the person who presented him.' (translation in the Watson edition).

accomplice only,[48] although to this it might be responded that the handling of the coins by 'you' is superfluous, the theft being complete when Titius receives them. But this difficulty points to a further one: like the wrongdoer in 20, the mental state of You is not really that of accomplice but rather that of thief: he is the author of the scheme, committing theft on his own account: he 'shares the coins with Titius', whereas Titius, presented to I by You, seems to be playing the role of accomplice. Again, the relationship between *contrectatio*, *animus furandi* and complicity seems less than straightforward.

The third case – the case of the weights – is like that discussed in 20 insofar as the lender of the weights, while apparently in an accessorial role, is the only possible defendant in the picture: at least in the first version of the story, the purchaser ('You') is apparently ignorant of the deception and therefore proof against the *actio furti*.[49] On the other hand, like 21, this case involves lying: through the false markings on the weights, the seller is tricked into handing over more goods than he intended. But the facts are stronger: whereas You in 21 merely spoke, the lender in 22 has acted: as in 20, his conduct goes beyond mere speaking or writing and is therefore capable of amounting to *contrectatio*.[50] It was perhaps for this reason that Mela at least thought that the lender was liable to the seller for theft, just as the chaser was liable in 20. Admittedly, Ulpian does not seem to agree with Mela's view of this first variant – there is a clear contrast with 23, where he agrees explicitly. This is unsurprising: unlike the chaser in 20, or indeed You in 21, the lender here intends to facilitate a gain on the part of the purchaser, rather than making a gain on his own account.[51] In fact, it is arguable that he lacks any theftuous intent at all: he is like the chaser in the second alternative discussed in 50.4, one who engages in a destructive game, or like the person discussed by Celsus in 50.1 who acts through ill-will [*inimicitiarum causa*]. But neither does Ulpian disclaim Mela's view, and he must have thought it at least consistent with his analysis.[52] In fact, it seems that 22, like 20, is employed by Ulpian to make a counter-intuitive point, namely, that the *contrectatio* necessary to constitute theft can be provided by one in an apparently accessorial role.[53]

What of the second alternative? Here, following the logic of 11, 15–17 and 21, the seller's mistake as to the amount of grain (for example) he is handing over entails theft on the part of the purchaser, You, despite this being a case of giving rather than taking. As in 11 and 21, we assume that You's conduct amounts to *contrectatio*: the vitiation

[48] *cf* MacCormack, who assumes that one who contrects is necessarily a principal thief, and that liability *ope consilio* is characterised by the absence of *contrectatio*: see MacCormack (n 35) 289–90.

[49] *cf* the similar facts discussed by Paul in D 4.3.18.3 (Paul Book 11 On the Edict): 'In the case of one who knowingly lent incorrect weights for the seller to weigh out goods to the buyer, Trebatius gave an action for fraud [*de dolo dabat actionem*]. But if he lent weights which were too heavy, the excess amount of goods can be recovered by a *condictio*; if they were too light, the goods still due can be recovered by the action on sale, unless the goods were sold on condition that they be determined by means of these particular weights and the lender, intending to deceive, asserted that he had correct weights.' (translation in the Watson edition).

[50] *cf* D 47.2.67.4 (Paul Book 7 On Plautius): where the person who was presented did not know of the deception, no theft was committed, because mere speaking by 'I' was not sufficient to sustain the theft.

[51] *cf* again D 47.2.67.4 set out in n 47 above: Paul explored this problem (the guilty accomplice and innocent principal) in the context of the case discussed by Ulpian in 21, reaching a firm 'no' because (we assume) of the absence of any plausible *contrectatio* on the part of the presenter.

[52] It appears that Ulpian is pursuing two distinct goals here: to preserve past decisions, and to create a coherent analysis.

[53] *cf* n 46 above.

of the victim's intention means that ownership in the flour, money, or grain (*vel sim*) does not pass to the recipient.[54] On the other hand, whereas the victim's error as to the identity of the recipient in 11 and 21 meant that he committed theft of everything handed over, here it is not clear whether the purchaser steals all the grain or only that part attributable to the seller's error. But unlike in those cases, here the reason why this is treated as theft is spelled out: 'for you do not acquire [*accipis*] in accordance with the will of the seller [*ex voluntate venditoris*] since he is in error as to the weight.' As in 21, then, we seem to have two *contrectationes*. But unlike in 21, both actors are liable in their own right, rather than the lender's being liable merely as an accomplice. Indeed, it is not clear that there is any co-operation between the parties, even in the second alternative.

In the fourth case, as in 21 and the second alternative in 22, there are two wrongdoers, but this time there is only one defendant: the slave, being property of the victim, cannot be sued by him, just as the wrongdoer's animals in 22 could not be sued. Unlike the chaser in 20 and the lender in 22 but like You in 21, the defendant's conduct – mere persuading – cannot constitute *contrectatio*. Only the slave who removes the defendant's debt (or name) from the document of purchase can plausibly be said to have committed *contrectatio*: again, deleting text goes beyond mere speaking or writing, and in fact this case is dealt with in D 47.2.27, excerpted from Book 41 of Ulpian's Commentary on Sabinus:

> pr One who takes away tablets [*tabulas*] or *cautiones* is liable in theft not only for the value [*pretii*] of the tablets themselves but for the (plaintiff's) interest [*eius quod interfuit*], which is assessed with reference to the sum contained in these tablets, provided that his interest was that great; thus, if the tablets were acknowledgements of debt [*chirographa*][55] for ten gold pieces, we say that this is doubled. But what if they were already worthless, because payment was tendered, surely it seems that there should be assessment of the value [*pretii*] of the tablets themselves only? For what was the interest? Yet it can be said that because debtors not infrequently seek to have tablets restored to them, and not infrequently falsely allege that the amount paid was not due, it is in the creditor's interest [*interesse creditoris*] to keep these tablets from them, lest perhaps he meet with controversy regarding this matter. And generally, it is to be said that the interest is doubled … 3 But if a person does not remove documents of this kind [*amovit huiusmodi instrumenta*] but strikes out text [*interlevit*], not only the *actio furti* will lie but also the *actio legis Aquiliae*; for he who spoilt them seems to have committed *rumpere*.[56]

Where text is deleted from a document that provides evidence of a debt, damages are calculated according to the amount of the debt, at least in some circumstances.[57] This is to be contrasted with the variant set out in the next text, 24, where no such *contrectatio* is committed: here the slave transcribes the document's contents rather than effacing text – again, mere writing – and only the *actio servi corrupti* lies[58] (or *actio de dolo* if

[54] *cf* again D 47.2.67.4 set out in n 47 above ('you commit theft because I believe him to be Titius') as well as the contrary view of Trebatius reported by Paul in D 4.3.18.3, set out in n 49 above.

[55] *cf* G III.134.

[56] My translation. I have resisted translating 'tabulae' as 'account books' because that seems to be at odds with Ulpian's meaning in this passage. On the other hand, 'documents' seems insufficiently precise to distinguish *tabulae* from *instrumenta*. cf D 47.2.52.24 above.

[57] further D 47.2.27.1–2, as well as D 47.2.32 (Paul Book 9 On Sabinus).

[58] *cf* D 11.3.1.5 (Ulpian Book 23 On the Edict): 'One also makes a slave worse if … one persuades a slave-agent to tamper with or falsify his master's accounts [*rationes*], or to confuse accounts entrusted to him …'.

the defendant did it himself). 23 therefore appears to resemble 21: the slave commits the theft, in which the defendant is a mere accomplice. But in fact the case is not so straightforward.

First, unlike You in 21, it is not clear that the defendant in 23 commits any act of complicity: it does not seem that what he did – persuading the slave to delete his name from the document – amounted to complicity as Ulpian himself understood it. In D 47.2.36 pr (Book 41 Commentary on Sabinus) Ulpian appears specifically to exclude from the scope of complicity one who persuades a slave to run away:

> A man who persuades a slave to run away is not a thief. For a man who gives another bad advice [*malum consilium*] no more commits theft than one who advises another to throw himself from a height or to kill himself: these acts do not give rise to the action for theft. …[59]

Justinian seems to have regarded the exclusion of this case – persuading a slave to steal – from the scope of *furtum* as the expression of a broader principle:

> [I]t is certain that a person who has not assisted in the commission of a theft, but has only given advice [*consilium dedit*] and urged [*hortatus est*] the commission of theft, is not liable for theft.'[60]

But this reading of D 47.2.36 pr is difficult to reconcile with what Ulpian says in D 47.2.50.3. Again,

> A person is deemed to give advice [*consilio*], who persuades and directs and provides advice in order to get a theft committed [*qui persuadet et impellit atque instruit consilio ad furtum faciendum*]

Thus Ulpian might be thought to be making the different point in 36 pr, namely, that a slave who runs away does not steal himself, just as a slave who kills himself does not do so, and that persuading him to run away cannot therefore amount to complicity in theft. On the other hand, Ulpian's precise formulation in 50.3 should be carefully noted: it is persuading (etc) *in order to get a theft committed* that constitutes *consilium*. What Ulpian appears to have primarily in mind here is a case like that described in 52.21, where it is the persuading of I by You (ie to lend the money) that enables Titius to carry out the theft, or a case like that described later in 36 pr, where one person persuades a slave to run away so that another might steal him. It seems that for Ulpian, simply persuading a slave to steal was *servi corruptio* rather than complicity in theft.[61] And a passage in Gaius's *Institutes* makes it clear that where someone persuaded a slave to bring his master's goods to him, he became liable only once he himself committed *contrectatio* of the goods, not when the slave took them.[62]

On which side of the line do the facts in 52.23 lie? It could be said that the defendant has simply urged the victim's slave to act. But in fact his intervention goes beyond mere persuasion to commit theft: it is through persuading the slave to remove the defendant's name from the document that theft has been accomplished, at least if the theft is

[59] My translation.
[60] J IV.1.11.
[61] D 11.3.1.5 (Ulpian Book 23 On the Edict): 'One also makes a slave worse if one persuades him to commit *iniuria* or *furtum* [or] to run away …' (Watson translation).
[62] G III.198. The relevant portion of the passage is repeated in J IV.1.8.

understood to have occurred in respect of the sum evidenced in the document. Yet this interpretation of the case discloses a still greater difficulty. Unlike the actions of Titius in 21, the slave's actions here do not in themselves clearly amount to stealing. He handles the document, but his intention in deleting the defendant's name from it is to enable the defendant to gain, not to gain on his own account. The slave himself has no interest in the document in the sense identified by Ulpian in 27 pr: it has value only to the victim of the theft, who is the creditor, and of course to the defendant, of whose debt it is evidence.[63]

What, then, are we to make of this text? Perhaps we are dealing here with a case involving two accomplices, one of whom provides *consilium* accompanied by *animus furandi*, the other of whom provides *ops* accompanied by the intention to enable another to steal. Or – and I incline to this view – Ulpian means to suggest that while the slave is an accomplice, it is the defendant who commits theft, having stolen the sum evidenced in the document. After all, unlike in 21, Ulpian does not say that he is liable *ope consilio*. In fact, in some respects this case resembles the first alternative in 22: there, the person who gained committed no *contrectatio*, while the person who provided the *contrectatio* made no gain, nor did he intend to do so – he intended only to enable the defendant to gain. Again, Ulpian merely reported Mela's view that the lender of the weights was liable for theft. But here, like the chaser in 20 and the persuader in 21, the person who gained clearly has *animus furandi* in the sense of intention to gain. It must be this – the *animus furandi* of the defendant in 23 – that is making the difference. That is why Ulpian explicitly agreed with Mela that a theft action was available.

This second view may seem deeply improbable. After all, as we have seen, no *contrectatio* can be detected on the part of the defendant. And we should note carefully the '*ego puto*' with which Ulpian introduces his conclusion in 23: this might be translated as 'I at least think'. Clearly, this was not a universal view. Nevertheless, it seems that Ulpian was advancing, albeit tentatively, a revolutionary proposition. Building on the point made in 20 and 22 – that *contrectatio* could be provided by one in an accessorial role – but subverting the expectations engendered by 21 – that the defendant was accomplice and the slave principal – he demonstrates that *contrectatio* was neither necessary nor sufficient to make one a thief: it was enough to give rise to the *actio furti* that there was *contrectatio* somewhere else in the picture, even if was supplied by an accomplice. Indeed, that is what Ulpian says in 52.19: again, 'our rule is that theft cannot occur without *contrectatio*. For this reason providing help or giving advice likewise imports liability only when *contrectatio* has followed.'

IV. Ulpian

The passage that forms the focus of this piece – 52.19–24 – contains an analysis of an important question: what conduct was necessary to sustain liability for theft in cases

[63] *cf* again D 47.2.50 pr: 'In the *actio furti*, it is not the interest [*quod interest*] that is quadrupled or doubled but the true value [*verum pretium*] of the thing.' If we read this text alongside D 47.2.27, it seems that 'true value' must encompass also value to the plaintiff (and the defendant) ie market value to only a few individuals. Value [*pretium*] cannot, however, be depressed beyond market value with reference to *quod interest*: *cf* D 9.2.21.2 and 23 pr–6.

involving accomplices? Ulpian considered three kinds of conduct in particular: chasing (physically interfering with the plaintiff's property); lying (to the plaintiff); and persuading (either the plaintiff himself or another agent).[64] His analysis necessarily entailed an examination of the borderline between the *actio furti nec manifesti* on the one hand and the *actio doli* and *actio servi corrupti* on the other. The linked question of the mental state necessary to make someone liable as an accomplice had already received close attention in 50.1–4. Here, the relevant borderline was with the *actio in factum* modelled on the *lex Aquilia*. 52 pr–18 contains further analysis of who could bring the *actio furti nec manifesti*, against whom, and in respect of what. As such, 52.19–24 forms part of an integrated account of that action.

The analysis of Ulpian's analysis set out in section III(C) above vindicates many of the conclusions reached by Tony Honoré in his *Ulpian*.[65] We observe, for example, the relatively simple sentence structure and abundant conjunctions and introductory phrases said to characterise Ulpian's 'oral style',[66] as well as the use of Greek that showed him looking towards the expanded citizenry of the post-212 legal order.[67] Most strikingly, 52.19–24 offers abundant evidence of the 'empirical method' identified by Honoré.[68] Ulpian treats the views of his predecessors as authoritative and reasons almost exclusively by analogy, employing a technique Benjamin Spagnolo has called 'an antiphonal structure of paired texts.'[69] It is difficult to imagine any common lawyer navigating more carefully around precedent, sticking more closely to the facts of the cases, or drawing more fine-grained distinctions between them. At the same time, the sophistication of the analysis contained in 52.19–24 is equal to anything produced by contemporary Anglophone legal scholarship.[70] On the other hand, the degree of integration discernible in Ulpian's analysis casts some doubt on Lenel's view that D 47.2.50.1–52.24 consists of self-contained commentaries on successive portions of the text of the *actio furti*. In particular, it is difficult to see D 47.2.50.1–4 and 52.19.24 as discrete from one another. From this the inference may be drawn that the entirety of this passage pertained to a single phrase, probably 'furtum factum esse'.[71] Or – more boldly – we may infer that Ulpian's commentary on the *actio furti* was not after all

[64] cf the triad of force, trickery and persuasion found in e.g. Sophocles' *Philoctetes* and indeed throughout ancient Greek tragedy and history. For Ulpian too, these seem to represent the three essential modes by which human beings act on one another.

[65] T Honoré, *Ulpian: Pioneer of Human Rights*, 2nd edn (Oxford, Oxford University Press, 2002).

[66] See ch 2.

[67] As in ch 3, 'The Cosmopolis and Human Rights' at p 90: '... a more typical use of the language is for him to insert a Greek word or two in a Latin sentence as being more expressive or conveying nuances that the Latin equivalent would not convey.' cf the use of τῆς γονῆς dumtaxat χάριν in D 47.2.52.19.

[68] See ch 4.

[69] As here, in D 9.2.27.17–25 and perhaps also in 13–16 and 25–28, Ulpian appears to be working with blocks of four texts. See B Spagnolo, '*Quasi* and (*Cor*)*ruptio*' in B Spagnolo and J Sampson (eds), *Principle and Pragmatism in Roman Law* (Oxford, Hart Publishing, 2020) 171, 192–94.

[70] It is said by Analise Acorn of John Gardner that, 'he could hold steady multiple, interlocking logical structures in at least three dimensions.' See www.law.ox.ac.uk/content/john-gardner-1965-2019. The same is most assuredly true of Ulpian. In 52.20, 21 22 and 23, he keeps at least three balls in the air. First, the conduct of the accomplice figure, namely chasing/lying/lying/persuading: ABBC. Second, whether the conduct of the accomplice figure amounts to *contrectatio* (as in 20 and 22) or merely *consilium* (as in 21 and 23(?)): ABAB(?). Finally, the intention of the accomplice figure: *animus furandi* (in 20 and 23) vs the intention to enable another to gain (in 21(?) and 22): AB(?)BA.

[71] As per Platschek (n 13) 399.

lemmatic in the way that, for example, his commentary on the words of the *lex Aquilia* was, but rather pertained to the formula as a whole.[72]

Despite its procedural focus, it is possible to draw certain conclusions from D 47.2.52.19–24 regarding Ulpian's conception of theft. As we have seen, *contrectatio* was for Ulpian a condition of liability, not the gist of the wrong of *furtum*. What, then, was Ulpianic *furtum*? Neither the chaser in 20 nor Titius in 21 nor the purchaser in 22 nor the persuader in 23 had physically removed (*amotio*) or carried off (*asportatio*) anything belonging to the plaintiff. Yet each had obtained something – the stud, the money, the extra goods, the debt – from the plaintiff. As spelt out in 22, this was theft because 'you do not acquire [*accipis*] in accordance with the will of the seller [*ex voluntate venditoris*] since he is in error as to the weight.' Of course Ulpian could simply be taken to be making the point that the seller's error prevents ownership in the extra goods from passing to the purchaser by virtue of a valid *traditio*, which means, in turn, that the purchaser commits *contrectatio* of the goods. That was the assumption underlying the analysis in previous section. But it may be that what mattered, rather, was what Ulpian actually says: it was the fact that the purchaser knowingly acquired something from the seller without the seller's consent that made him a thief.[73]

Thus it seems that Ulpianic *furtum* was not the wrong of interfering with another's corporeal property, as the *contrectatio* requirement seemed to suggest, but rather the wrong of acquiring something from the plaintiff without his consent. The absence of volition on the part of the plaintiff specified by Ulpian in D 47.2.52.22 was not simply the inverse of a potential defence of consent but was significant in its own right, as an essential element of the wrong. Thus conceptualised, theft could comprise the taking of incorporeal property as well as corporeal objects. That was why it was possible to steal genetic material or a debt. It is easy to miss the significance of this development. After all, the theft of an incorporeal thing is entirely uncontroversial in the context of modern criminal law. But insofar as Ulpian was describing an *actio in personam*, albeit a penal one, his analysis entails that acquiring something from another without his consent – even acquiring a thing that cannot be handled or interfered with – gives rise to a corresponding right and duty on the part of the plaintiff and defendant respectively. As such, his concept of theft seems to have radical implications for the modern law of tort[74] and unjust enrichment.[75]

[72] If that view is taken, the exclusion of 52.25–29 from the scope of my account becomes difficult to justify.

[73] *cf* also D 47.2.46.7–8 (Ulpian Book 42 On Sabinus).

[74] *cf* eg *OBG Ltd v Allan* [2007] UKHL 21, [2008] 1 AC 1.

[75] See H Scott, 'Interference without Ownership: The Theft of Incorporeal Money in the South African Law of Unjustified Enrichment' in T Naude and D Visser (eds), *The Future of Contract: Essays in Honour of Dale Hutchison* (Cape Town, Juta, 2021) 343; 'Property | Unjust Enrichment' in W Day and J Grower (eds), *Borderlines in Private Law* (Oxford, Oxford University Press, 2024) forthcoming.

4

D 9.2.27.14 (Ulp 18 *ad Ed*): Weed in the *Digest*

WOLFGANG ERNST

I. The Text Read as Justinianic Law

A. The Outer Limits of (*cor*)*rumpere*

This chapter revisits the well-known text D 9.2.27.14 (Ulp 18 *ad Ed*), with a greater emphasis on the role of the interdict as an instrument to liquidate damages.

> Et ideo Celsus quaerit, si lolium aut avenam in segetem alienam inieceris, quo eam tu inquinares, non solum quod vi aut clam dominum posse agere vel, si locatus fundus sit, colonum, sed et in factum agendum, et si colonus eam exercuit, cavere eum debere amplius non agi, scilicet ne dominus amplius inquietet: nam alia quaedam species damni est ipsum quid corrumpere et mutare, ut lex Aquilia locum habeat, alia nulla ipsius mutatione applicare aliud, cuius molesta separatio sit.

As Bruce Frier has noticed, the English translation edited by Watson is flawed for this text.[1] In his tracks, the following is suggested:

> And so Celsus asks, if you sow tares or wild oats in another man's crops and spoil them, not only can the owner (or, if the farm is leased, the tenant) bring the *interdictum quod vi aut clam*, but he can also proceed *in factum*. And if a tenant farmer proceeds thus, he must warrant that there will be no further proceedings, obviously lest the landlord should stir up matters further. For it is one sort of damage to spoil or alter something so that the *lex Aquilia* applies and quite another to add something that is a nuisance to separate, but without any other change being made.

The text originates from the part of Ulpian's commentary on the Edict where he elucidates the three operative verbs in Chapter III of the *lex Aquilia*. For the verb *rumpere*, already understood as *corrumpere*, he turns to a case presented to Celsus with

[1] A Watson (ed), *The Digest of Justinian*, rev English-language edn, vol 1 (Philadelphia, University of Pennsylvania Press, 1998) 285.

the lead question of whether the act qualifies as *corrumpere*.[2] In Ulpian's commentary, the text brings the very first illustration of the outer limits of the verb. Further legal issues are intertwined in this text, concerning a problem of concurrence of actions and interdicts and matters of standing. The reader does not find the first issue addressed in *lectio continua*, but one can link the three pertinent bits of the text together easily:

> si lolium aut avenam in segetem alienam inieceris, quo eam tu inquinares … in factum agendum <est> … nam alia quaedam species damni est ipsum quid corrumpere et mutare, ut lex Aquilia locum habeat, alia nulla ipsius mutatione applicare aliud, cuius molesta separatio sit.

The last sentence explains why the act does not qualify as (*cor*)*rumpere*, and no direct action can lie, whereas an *actio in factum* should be granted. The context suggests that this *actio in factum* will be modelled after the action on Chapter III of the *lex Aquilia*. The unavailability of the direct action is not based on the fact that a *colonus* is in play: there is *damnum*, as required by the wording of the *lex*, but the *damnum* is not brought about by an adverse change of the targeted object. It emerges as the necessity to make an effort on the victim's side to get rid of the weed from tares or wild oats. The statement of law is an important elucidation of the outer limits of liability based on (*cor*)*rumpere*.

B. *Interdictum quod vi aut clam*, the *colonus*, and the *cautio de amplius non petendo*

i. The interdictum quod vi aut clam *as a Damages Remedy*

The *interdictum quod vi aut clam* was an *interdictum restitorium*, which ordered the adversary to stop interfering violently or clandestinely with landed property that is in the applicant's possession and/or to undo changes that resulted from such a violent or clandestine act of interference.[3] The *restituere* in the interdict's formula was seen as comprising a variety of orders, inter alia ceasing and desisting (*patientiam praestare*), but also the compensation for damage which is factored into the *aestimatio litis*; D 43.24.15.7 (Ulp 69 *ad Ed*):[4]

> Hoc interdicto tanti lis aestimatur, quanti actoris interest id opus factum esse. Officio autem iudicis ita oportere fieri restitutionem iudicandum est, ut in omni causa eadem

[2] On this aspect, see B Spagnolo, '*Quasi* and (*Cor*)*ruptio*' in B Spagnolo and J Sampson (eds), *Principle and Pragmatism in Roman Law* (Oxford, Hart Publishing, 2020) 171, 176–77; F Musumeci, 'Molesta separano, difficilis separano ed esperibilità dell'actio legis aquiliae' in *Studi in onore de Remo Martini*, vol 2 (Milan, Giuffrè, 2009) 821. I have not been able to read A Samir, 'Ulpijan, Celz i zagađenje zemljišta korovom (D. 9.2.27.14)' (2011) 45 *Zbornik radova Pravnog fakulteta, Novi Sad* 615.

[3] On this interdict, see L Isola, 'Interdikte' in U Babusiaux et al (eds), *Handbuch des Römischen Privatrechts* (*HRP*) (Tübingen, MohrSiebeck, 2022) vol 2, 1808, 1832 ff; P van Warmelo, 'Interdictum Quod Vi Aut Clam' (1964) 15 *Acta Juridica 1962* 15.

[4] On this text, see I Fargnoli, *Studi sulla legittimazione attiva all'interdetto 'quod vi aut clam'* (Milano, Giuffrè, 1998) 122 ff.

> condicio sit actoris, quae futura esset, si id opus, de quo actum est, neque vi neque clam factum esset.

Similar statements can be found concerning the *interdictum de vi et de vi armata*; these statements are relevant here as well, as they pertain to the same concept of *restituere*. The first is D 43.16.1.41 (Ulp 69 *ad Ed*):

> Non solum autem fructuum ratio in hoc interdicto habetur, verum ceterarum etiam utilitatium habenda est: nam Vivianus refert in hoc interdicto omnia, quaecumque habiturus vel adsecuturus erat is qui deiectus est, si vi deiectus non esset, restitui aut eorum litem a iudice aestimari debere eumque tantum consecuturum, quanti sua interesset se vi deiectum non esse.

The second one is D 43.16.1.31 (Ulp 69 *ad Ed*):

> Qui vi deiectus est, quidquid damni senserit ob hoc quod deiectus est, reciperare debet: pristina enim causa restitui debet, quam habiturus erat, si non fuisset deiectus.

With the function of indemnifying the applicant, the interdict comes into play in our text. Unlike the direct action under Chapter III of the *lex Aquilia*, the interdict did not require the adverse physical change of the object at stake. It was sufficient that the perpetrator had violently or clandestinely interfered with someone else's landed property with a negative effect on the current possessor. Therefore, the availability of the interdict here is a direct one; no tweaking of its formula is needed. The two remedies, the *lex Aquilia*-based *actio* (*in factum*) and the interdict can be employed to essentially the same effect, namely securing compensation for damages.[5]

ii. The colonus's *Standing for the* interdictum quod vi aut clam

The text starts with the bilateral case of the owner and the mischievous perpetrator. For this case, the owner's ability to use the interdict is a triviality, presupposing that he also possesses the field. The text gets interesting as it informs us that when the land is worked by a *colonus*, the *interdictum quod vi aut clam* can be brought by the *colonus*, too. In Justinian's law, there was a detailed regime for the *colonus*'s standing to bring the *interdictum quod vi aut clam*. Following the broad principle that this interdict can be granted to those who, as possessors or detentors, have an interest that the intervention, the critical *factum*, should not have happened, the *colonus* is acknowledged as having standing, too; D. 43.24.12 (Ven 2 *Int*):

> Quamquam autem colonus et fructuarius fructuum nomine in hoc interdictum admittantur, tamen et domino id competet, si quid praeterea eius intersit.

The *colonus* can bring the interdict in view of the field, insofar as the plants he cultivates are affected. The *interdictum quod vi aut clam* can only be brought for the protection of landed property. Once the fruits have been harvested, they become

[5] The action based on the *lex Aquilia* has the litiscrescence mechanism, but it is doubtful whether the *actio in factum* replicated this feature.

moveable property, losing the protection of this interdict, as we learn from D. 43.24.7.5 (Ulp 71 *ad Ed*):

> Notavimus supra, quod, quamvis verba interdicti late pateant, tamen ad ea sola opera pertinere interdictum placere, quaecumque fiant in solo. Eum enim, qui fructum tangit, non teneri interdicto quod vi aut clam: nullum enim opus in solo facit. At qui arbores succidit, utique tenebitur, et qui harundinem et qui salictum: terrae enim et quodammodo solo ipsi corrumpendo manus infert. Idem et in vineis succisis. Ceterum qui fructum aufert, furti debet conveniri. Itaque si quid operis in solo fiat, interdictum locum habet. In solo fieri accipimus et si quid circa arbores fiat, non si quid circa fructum arborum.

We can conclude that the *fructus* here mentioned D 9.2.27.14 (Ulp 18 *ad Ed*) is corn still on the grass. The *colonus* gets the same standing as the *usufructuarius* who holds a *ius in rem*. Both sue *suo nomine*, as it is their interest that is protected. These two potential claimants do not displace the owner who still can sue with this interdict, in view of the damage sustained.

iii. The cautio de amplius non petendo

The *cautio* can be identified as the *cautio de amplius non petendo*. This *cautio* usually, but not necessarily comes combined with the *cautio ratam rem haberi*.[6] Both *cautiones* are given for a different effect.[7] The *cautio ratam rem haberi* is required from a claimant launching a suit on someone else's behalf, without prior authorisation. He has to guarantee that the person on whose behalf he comes to court will ratify his application and hence be barred from using the same remedy *suo nomine*. On the strength of the *ratihabitio*, the action is consumed as it would be had the principal launched it himself. It is the effect of the *ratihabitio*, which the *alieno nomine*-claimant promises will be given, that the same *actio* cannot be brought by the principal himself.

The *cautio de amplius non petendo* had a different, albeit related function. It made sure, it is suggested here, that the person on whose behalf the lawsuit was launched cannot sue on another basis, ignoring the fact that the defendant had already been made to satisfy what seems to be the same interest. The *cautio ratam rem haberi* eliminates the risk of being sued with the very same action, in case an agent had brought that action first. But what if the principal has two remedies to choose from? While the *actio* employed by the agent cannot be brought again, because it has been neutralised by way of the guaranteed *ratihabitio*, any other remedy remains available. The *consumptio*-effect of the *ratihabitio* did not pertain to any other actions but the one brought by the agent. With the *cautio de amplius non petendo* the defendant can be assured that the principal will not use another remedy against him after he has been

[6] On these *cautiones*, see J Platschek, 'Formularprozess: Verhandlung *in iure*' in *HRP* (n 3) vol 1, 405; T Rüfner, '*Vadimonium* und andere Prozessstipulationen' in *HRP* (n 3) vol 2, 1985; S Dieckmann, *Die ratihabitio im klassischen römischen Recht* (Berlin, Duncker & Humblot, 2023) 303–26; O Lenel, *Edictum Perpetuum*, 3rd edn (Leipzig, Tauchnitz, 1927) 541; L Debray, 'La cautio amplius non peti' (1912) 36 *Nouvelle revue historique de droit français et étranger* (*NHRD*) 5.

[7] Platschek (n 6) points out that further research into the evolution of these two *cautiones* is necessary.

successfully sued once. The *cautio de amplius non petendo* is an instrument to handle the concurrence of actions if one action is being used by an agent. To regulate the concurrence of actions when both actions play out between the same plaintiff and defendant, there were other, more standard instruments in play. The *exceptio doli* was one of those instruments, but it may not have worked against the principal who has had no prior dealing with the defendant. The *cautio rem ratam haberi* is an instrument to protect the defendant against being sued twice with the same remedy, filed first *alieno* and then *suo nomine* – the *cautio de amplius non petendo* protects the defendant against being sued a second time, the principal now using another, concurring remedy that has not been consumed by his *ratihabitio*. The *cautio de amplius non petendo* (scilicet: *alia actione de eadem re*) thus supplemented the *cautio ratam rem haberi* and possibly both were integrated into the same standard template that had to be used by any agent suing *alieno nomine*.

The *cautio de amplius non petendo* could also come into play as a stand-alone *cautio*, not linked to the *cautio rem ratam haberi*, in cases where no agent was in play. A good example is D 23.3.29 (Ulp 36 *Sab*): a father promises a dowry to the bridegroom and sets up an identical legacy for his daughter, the bride. After the father's death, the former can sue the heir on the strength of the promise, the latter on the strength of the legacy. The text addresses, inter alia, the variant that the father did not intend to see the gratuity doubled: if the daughter sues, she must give a warranty that her husband will not sue as well. Here, both potential claimants would sue *suo nomine*.

In D 9.2.27.14 (Ulp 18 *ad Ed*), the *cautio de amplius non petendo* makes sure that the owner does not come onto the scene after the *colonus* has successfully sued the perpetrator using the *interdictum*. The action that the *dominus* could use to sue for a top-up would be his Aquilian action. In our case, the option to sue for 'more of the same' is a result of interdict and *actio* (*in factum*) being geared here at the same effect, namely damages in pecuniary terms.[8] The owner can sue, of course, using his Aquilian action, but that would trigger the warranty given by the *colonus*. Since the *colonus* is using the interdict *suo nomine*, he is not required to give the *cautio ratam rem haberi*, hence the *cautio de amplius non petendo* here is a stand-alone *cautio*.

D 9.2.27.14 (Ulp 18 *ad Ed*) states the necessity to provide a *cautio* only for the *colonus*. Should the owner proceed with the interdict, he does not have to provide the *cautio de amplius non petendo*. Indeed, there is no need for a symmetrical *cautio* to be given by the *dominus* because the *colonus*, as we shall see, has no Aquilian action that he could use to extract additional damages from the perpetrator who has already been made to pay to the *dominus*. It is quite a different matter whether the *dominus*, who has been compensated for the damage to his field, must share or absorb an eventual loss of the *colonus* one way or another. This issue is not our authors' concern here.[9]

[8] Should the *actio in factum* have come with the litiscrescence mechanism, the perpetrator who denied the owner's Aquilian claim, pointing to his payment to the *colonus*, would have run the risk of paying damages three times over.

[9] On issues of *remissio mercedis*, see P du Plessis, *A History of Remissio Mercedis and Related Legal Institutions* (Rotterdam, Kluwer, 2003); W Ernst, 'Das Nutzungsrisiko bei der Pacht' (1988) 105 *Zeitschrift der Savigny-Stiftung für Rechtsgeschichte Romanistische Abteilung* 541.

C. An *Aquilian actio in factum* for the *colonus*?

i. The actio utilis ex interdicti causa

Does the *colonus* have two remedies he can choose from, the *actio in factum* (Aquilian style) as well as the *interdictum*? A bulk of Justinianic texts confirm that Aquilian protection is given primarily to the owner and in exceptional cases to holders of a *ius in rem*, but not to mere detentors holding a thing on the strength of a contractual position. Should one have to read our text as granting an Aquilian action to a tenant, its alignment with conventional wisdom would pose a considerable challenge.

Eam should stand for *actionem*, although that noun does not feature in the foregoing text. The presumed reference to an *actio* must be the main reason why the necessity to provide a *cautio* has been linked to the *actio in factum*, Aquilian style, and thus to the assumption that the *colonus* can bring this *actio*, too.[10] However, since the time Diocletian abolished the special type of process for the interdict (C. 8.1.3 [Diocletian and Maximian to Pompeianus, 28 December 293]) the traditional juxtaposition of *actio* and *interdictum* was gradually blurred. In the context of the prevailing *cognitio*-procedure, the remedy was referred to as *actio utilis ex interdicti causa*.[11] Exploring the classical jurists' language, Fritz Schulz found:

> to apply for an interdict is accordingly never called *agere* ... Nor have the classical lawyers ever used *interdicere* with reference to the plaintiff ... The classical jurists know only the terms *interdicto uti* and *experiri*. Finally, the parties to whom the interdict is addressed are never called *actor* and *reus* ... This transformation inevitably led to numerous alterations of classical texts. Thus we meet in pseudo-classical texts interdicts called *actiones*. The plaintiff called *actor*, *interdicere* used for *agere interdicto*.[12]

In Justinian's law, the new terminology is declared to be the norm, I. 4.15.8:

> De ordine et veteri exitu interdictorum supervacuum est hodie dicere: nam quotiens extra ordinem ius dicitur, qualia sunt hodie omnia iudicia, non est necesse reddi interdictum, sed perinde iudicatur sine interdictis, atque si utilis actio ex causa interdicti reddita fuisset.

van Warmelo concluded that where *Digest* texts refer to the *interdictum quod vi aut clam* as *ea actio*, the text cannot be classical.[13] As we shall see, in D. 9.2.27.14 (Ulp 18 *ad Ed*) the passage about the *colonus*'s interdict is likely to have been marred by a Justinianic

[10] As assumed by, inter alia, JAC Thomas, *Textbook of Roman Law* (Cambridge, Philip McDonald, 2015) 384, fn 49; Spagnolo (n 2) 176; GD MacCormack, '*Celsus quaerit*: D. 9.2.27.14' (1973) 20 *Revue Internationale des Droits de l'Antiquité (RIDA)* 341.

[11] R Fercia, '"Actiones" ed "actio utilis ex causa interdicti": vicende storiche, anomalie, opacità' (2009) 8 *Diritto e Storia, Rivista Internazionale di Scienze Giuridiche e Tradizione Romana*, www.dirittoestoria.it/8/Tradizione-Romana/Fercia-Actio-utilis-ex-causa-interdicti.htm.

[12] F Schulz, *Classical Roman Law* (Oxford, Clarendon Press, 1951) 61–62. As the shift into procedures *per cognitionem* accelerated in late classical times, Schulz allowed for the possibility that the new terminology can perhaps be found occasionally with late and post-classical authors already. Indeed, to give but one example, C Theod 4.22.1 (Constantine to Severus, 23 October 326) (= C. 8.5.1.1) already uses the term *actio recuperandae possessionis* for the *interdictum unde vi*. On this constitution, see L Solidoro Maruotti, *La tutela del possesso in età costantiniana* (Naples, Jovene, 1998) 107–12.

[13] van Warmelo (n 3) 18 fn 10, 27 ff.

intervention, one way or another. The use of *actio* for the *interdictum quod vi aut clam* is in line with contemporary, ie, sixth-century terminology. In this view, *eam* can and should be read as *actionem utilem ex interdicti causa.*[14] The necessity to provide a *cautio* as stated for the *colonus* then refers to his interdict-based damage claim. Read this way, nothing is left in the text that would point to an Aquilian action made available to the *colonus.*

We could rest our case here but need to briefly address two strands of arguments that have tried to 'explain' the *colonus*'s standing for an Aquilian-style action that one assumed must be acknowledged in the text. The following review will *a limine* dismiss the idea that the *colonus* can sue on an Aquilian basis and hence also the two following explanations that have been advanced.

ii. Aquilian Remedy for the Effect on the colonus*'s Harvest?*

A harmonisation was found in the idea that the object that the perpetrator interfered with was not the land but the grain already harvested.[15] According to this theory, the legal content, for which one must read between the lines, is the following: after *separatio,* the *colonus* is the owner of the harvested grain. That grain is spoiled as an effect of the mischievous perpetrator's attack, but, as the owner's land in the principal case, this object is not adversely altered, although the labour of separating the useful grain from the weed constitutes a *damnum.* So, one goes on reasoning, the *colonus* gets the *actio in factum.* In line with this understanding, the *cautio de amplius non esse petiturum* would have to be given by the *colonus* who brings his Aquilia-based action.

This theory is just a sorry example of the fine-spun '*solutiones contrariorum*', which Fritz Schulz found 'lack any juristic values, since they are not the product of juristic reflection on juristic problems, but of sham and empty cleverness and pseudo-philology'.[16] It is not doubtful, as a matter of law in both classical and Justinian's times, that in this situation the *colonus* enjoys the protection of the Chapter III action under the *lex Aquilia.* The issue here is only whether that statement of law is expressed in D 9.2.27.14 (Ulp 18 *ad Ed*).

It is not possible to take the harvested grain as the target since this would make the *interdictum quod vi aut clam* inapplicable, which the text states can be brought by the *colonus,* too. And what function could a *cautio* have had, which the *colonus* had to give to pursue an Aquilian claim for the spoiling of his harvest: if the *colonus* were granted an action for the damage he has suffered in relation to the corn he has made his own, it seems impossible to preclude the *dominus* with a *cautio de non amplius petendi* from suing for damages that he, and not the *colonus,* has suffered with regard to his agricultural land.[17] Or should one assume that the *cautio* is meant to bar the owner

[14] If this passage had a basis in Ulpian's (or another classical jurist's) writing, *eam* could have been put in for *interdictum,* as *interdictum exercere* seems to be a good technical phrase.

[15] A Di Porto, *La tutela della 'salubritas' fra editto e giurisprudenza,* vol 1 (Milan, Giuffrè, 1990) 36–39.

[16] F Schulz, *History of Roman Legal Science* (Oxford, Clarendon Press, 1946) 331.

[17] OE Tellegen-Couperus, 'The Tenant, the Borrower and the lex Aquilia' (1995) 42 *RIDA* 415, at 418, with others, identifies the *lolium* as a poisonous grass and *avena* as a weed that plagues the farmer for many years: even if the weed that has been cut down together with the corn plagues the farming *colonus,* who now has to separate 'the wheat from the chaff', there is a lasting problem for the field itself, too.

(as possessor) from relying on the interdict? The idea meets the same difficulties as the assumption that the *dominus* should be barred from seeking Aquilian compensation for his own loss.

iii. The colonus *as Claimant with Standing for the Aquilian Position of the* dominus*?*

We must also dismiss the idea that the *colonus* is, by mandate or constructively, authorised to bring the Aquilian-style action *alieno nomine*, on behalf of the *dominus*. This idea has been pondered by Geoffrey MacCormack.[18] MacCormack assumed that the *cautio* points to a lawsuit launched on someone else's behalf, and as many others have done, linked the *cautio* to an Aquilian action which he sees granted to the *colonus*. However, the *cautio* here mentioned is the *cautio de non amplius petendi* and not the *cautio rem ratam haberi*, which is linked to the concept of procedural agency. While a *mandatum praesumptum* that allows the *colonus* to sue on behalf of the absent owner can be found in C. 8.5.1 (Constantine to Severus, 23 October 326), it is limited to the *interdictum unde vi* which needs to be applied for with some urgency, in order to get back onto the land.[19] No similar mechanism existed for Aquilian actions. The text does not hint at, but rather rules out the idea that the *dominus* has expressly authorised the *colonus* to act as his *procurator*.

D. Paraphrasing D 9.2.27.14 (Ulp 18 *ad Ed*)

A paraphrasis of the core legal content of *lex* 27.14, read as part of Justinian's law, could run as follows:

> If someone throws tares or wild oats into a cornfield, the owner does not have the direct action under Chapter III for *(cor)rumpere*, but can rely on an *actio in factum*. To recover his damage, he can also use the *interdictum quod vi aut clam*. Should a *colonus* work the field, the *interdictum quod vi aut clam* can be brought by him (*suo nomine*), but he has to give the *cautio de amplius non petendo*.

There is nothing out of the ordinary or mysterious to be found here. Quite certainly, the text has not and cannot be read as stating that any *conductor* could sue under the *lex Aquilia* for damage done to the leased object of his *locator*, or for damage caused without adverse change of such a leased object itself, using an *in factum* variant of the Chapter III action. In Justinian's time, the *colonus* had become a special case, subject to wide-ranging regulations, going way beyond the traditional law of *locatio conductio*.[20] Even when narrowed down to *coloni*, it is hardly conceivable that Justinian's law would allow the *colonus* to bring an Aquilian-based action for a damaging interference with the cornfield that is not his.[21] In the modern history of civil law, however,

[18] MacCormack (n 10).
[19] AJB Sirks, *The Colonate in the Roman Empire* (Cambridge, University Press, 2024) 111.
[20] On the colonate in Justinian's law, see Sirks (n 19) 30–146.
[21] For the opposite view, see the authors named in n 10 above.

D 9.2.27.14 (Ulp 18 *ad Ed*) was occasionally used, from the sixteenth century onwards, as an argument that Roman law allowed tenants to use the *lex Aquilia*.[22] Most civilians took a sceptical view[23] and the issue remained controversial, but this is a story for another day.

E. Concurrence of Actions

The case harbours problems of concurrence of actions and interdicts, in that two potential claimants and two potential remedies are in play. Ernst Levy and Detlef Liebs have analysed the fragment in this regard.[24] The text gives us one piece of direct information only: should the *colonus* bring the interdict, he has to give a *cautio* protecting the perpetrator against being sued for a second time, now by the *dominus* on an Aquilian basis. For all other aspects of the concurrence issue, the user of Justinian's codification must turn to evidence found elsewhere or general principles.

One may assume that the victim (*dominus*) can choose between bringing the *actio in factum*, modelled after the Chapter III Aquilian action, or the *interdictum quod vi aut clam*. If the owner brings an Aquilian action, he will be restricted in bringing the interdict, too, as we learn from D 47.7.11 (Paul 22 *ad Ed*):

> Sed si de arboribus caesis ex lege Aquilia actum sit, interdicto quod vi aut clam reddito absolvetur, si satis prima condemnatione gravaverit reum, manente nihilo minus actione ex lege duodecim tabularum.

When someone who has cut off trees on another man's property has been sued with the *actio legis Aquiliae* and is then sued again, this time with the *interdictum quod vi aut clam*, the judge will absolve him, provided that the first *condemnatio* seems sufficient. This is a case of so-called judicial consumption. Paulus tells us that the action for felled trees, as granted by the XII Tables, remains available. This is not surprising as it is a penal action for the *duplum*.

A similar statement, in more general terms, can be found in D 43.24.15 (Ulp 71 *ad Ed*):

> Quia autem hoc interdictum id quod interest continet, si quis alia actione fuerit consecutus id quod interfuit opus non esse factum, consequens erit dicere ex interdicto nihil eum consequi oportere.

Finally, in case the owner proceeds with the interdict first, it is doubtful whether an *actio in factum* would still be granted to him, as no gap-filler is called for anymore. If the Aquilian action would have been available, it should have been possible to rebut the owner suing again with the *exceptio doli*.

[22] N Vigelius, *Methodus universi iuris civilis absolutissima* (Basel, Oporinus, 1586) pars 6 lib 22 cap 10 qu 1 reg 2, col 1796 ff; CF Glück, *Ausführliche Erläuterungen der Pandecten*, vol X/1 (Erlangen, Palm, 1808) 375.

[23] WA Lauterbach, *Collegii theoretico-practici* (Tübingen, Cotta, 1714) lib 9 tit 2, IV, XXI, 668, 677.

[24] E Levy, *Die Konkurrenz der Aktionen – Band 2* (Berlin, Franz Vahlen, 1922; reprint Aalen, Scientia, 1964) 216–21 (mostly doubtful); D Liebs, *Die Klagenkonkurrenz im römischen Recht* (Göttingen, Vandenhoeck & Ruprecht, 1972) 215–16.

II. Text and Law in Classical Times

There is a *communis opinio* that D 9.2.27.14 (Ulp 18 *ad Ed*) does not give us the authentic passage from Ulpian's commentary.[25] Apart from difficulties of grammar, the avoidance of the term *interdictum* and – perhaps – the fact that the *conductor* is addressed as *colonus* point to interventions of the sixth-century compilers. With regard to the preceding passages, explaining *urere*, a *confronto* with Coll 12.7.1–3, 10 shows how surgically yet intensively the compilers have reworked the Ulpianic original.[26] It would not come as a surprise should the same *modus operandi* be found in the ensuing passage.[27] The following deliberations come with a degree of uncertainty and the best we can hope for is singling out the hypothesis of greatest likelihood.

This is the narrative that seems to suggest itself in light of the interpolation criticism: reviewing Ulpian's commentary, the compilers found that the case could come in a variant, namely the cultivation of the land by a *colonus*. It may be recalled that the regulation of the colonate was a specific concern for Justinian's legislation, as evidenced by several Codex titles that address legal aspects of the colonate, C. 11.48 to C. 11.53.[28] Wondering whether something needed to be said about the protection of the *colonus* in this case, the compilers remembered that the *colonus* had supplementary standing for the *interdictum quod vi aut clam*, so they added that both *dominus* and *colonus* could bring the *interdictum*: *quod vi aut clam dominum posse agere vel, si locatus fundus sit, colonum*. This raised the issue of a potentially doubled liability caused by both *dominus* and *colonus* proceeding against the perpetrator on different grounds. Hence the *cautio* merited a mention. The uncouth implantation of the *colonus*'s protection by way of interdict has, however, damaged the structure of the text and has led readers astray.

Before we comment on this scenario, it must be stressed that whatever manipulation the text has gone through in the sixth century, its statements of law do not distort what Ulpian, or jurists in Ulpian's time, could have said. There is no legal content that we could identify as postclassical, Justinianic innovation. If the text was meddled with, it was not to implement a law reform, but merely to insert additional information about the law as it was in force then and had been in force in Ulpian's time already. It may or may not be the case that the text in the 18th book of Ulpian's commentary dealt with no more than the outer limits of *corrumpere*, to be later expanded by the compilers.[29]

[25] A last attempt to defend the authenticity of the text was made by L Debray, 'Le fermier et la loi Aquilia: Autour du fr. 27, § 14, D. IX, 2' (1909) 33 *NHRD* 643.

[26] *cf* W Ernst, '*Insulam exurere*: Reading Collatio 12.7.1–3 closely' in Spagnolo and Sampson (n 2) 159.

[27] On the working of Justinian's compilers, see the balanced resume by JHA Lokin, 'The End of an Epoch: Epilegomena to a Century of Interpolation Criticism' in R Feenstra et al (eds), *Collatio Iuris Romani*, vol 1 (Amsterdam, Gieben, 1995) 261; see also the contributions to M Avenarius et al (eds), *Gradenwitz, Riccobono und die Entwicklung der Interpolationenkritik: Methodentransfer unter europäischen Juristen im späten 19. Jahrhundert = Gradenwitz, Riccobono e gli sviluppi della critica interpolazionistica: Circolazione di modelli e metodi fra giuristi europei nel tardo Ottocento* (Tübingen, MohrSiebeck, 2018); FJ Andrés Santos, 'Brevissima storia della critica interpolazionistica nelle fonti giuridiche romane' (2011) 23 *Revista de estudios histórico-jurídicos* 65.

[28] Sirks, (n 19) 32–61.

[29] It is also possible that Ulpian mentioned the *interdictum quod vi aut clam* with regard to the *dominus* only, and the compilers added the variant dealing with the *colonus*.

As the element that could be suspected as engrafted is not at odds with our knowledge of the law of classical times, the compilers could have taken it from another text, written by Ulpian himself or another classical author.[30]

An intervention by the compilers may well have had another cause. Commenting on the operative verbs of the *lex Aquilia*, Ulpian used a pertinent disquisition by Celsus, from the 37th book of Celsus's *Digesta*.[31] The original case (*dominus*/ perpetrator) was put to Celsus.[32] It has been suggested that Celsus was asked for his legal view on the Parable of Wheat and Tares (Matthew 13.24–30).[33] It is a nice thought, no more. We know from Coll 12.7.10 that Celsus's views regarding the leeway in interpreting the operative verbs of the *lex* were controversial, and find these controversies suppressed in Justinian's *Digest*. It may well be that there had been a controversy regarding our case, too, but it seems impossible to make out the conflicting positions.[34] We cannot even be sure that the solution Ulpian sets out, granting the *actio in factum*, was already Celsus's, but as Celsus in other instances willingly supplemented Aquilian liability with an analogous action it is quite a plausible assumption. Ulpian's original may have entailed more information about both Celsus's view and that of other jurists, and the unsatisfactory text may be the result of these bits being cut out.

With apologies to my students

for whom I set this text

as a Finals question.

[30] In this case, the compilers could have simply exchanged *eam* for *interdictum*, as they may well have done in a systematic manner, to get classical texts in line with I. 4.15.8.

[31] O Lenel, *Palingenesia Iuris Civilis* (Tauchnitz, Leipzig, 1889) vol 1, cols 166–67, correcting the *Collatio* which attributes the passage to the 27th book.

[32] Tellegen-Couperus (n 17) 422–23 assumes that the case put to Celsus already concerned the involvement of a tenant.

[33] G von Beseler, 'Fruges et Paleae II' in H Niedermeyer and W Flume (eds), *Festschrift Fritz Schulz*, vol 1 (Weimar, Hermann Böhlaus Nachfolger, 1951) 3, 20–22.

[34] Earlier jurists who could have been reluctant to go from the statutory *rumpere* to the wider *corrumpere* may have found the owner sufficiently protected by the long-established *interdictum quod vi aut clam*.

5

Felling Trees in Mesopotamia and Rome

JOE SAMPSON

Many reading this volume will know of David Ibbetson through his research, and many of the chapters pick up on themes from across his published works. While my own contribution also seeks to build upon an article of David's, it was with the goal of recognising David the Teacher that I decided on my topic for this chapter. I had the pleasure of being taught by David across six years, three degrees and two Faculties. In these six years he broadened my intellectual horizons in a way that no one else has. But his single greatest influence on me came through the teaching we did together. For four years the two of us would supervise *Civil Law II* together in the President's Lodgings at Clare Hall in Cambridge. We would spend Friday afternoons sat in his living room talking through the details of the Roman law of property and delict with a rotating cast of students. We must have spent as much time scrutinising the views of one another as we did those of the students, and looking to our occasionally bewildered onlookers to tell us whose interpretation of a text was the more convincing. It was an entirely egalitarian intellectual experience, with every idea deserving careful consideration and – more often than not – precise demolition.

These afternoons shaped my understanding of what it is to be an academic. Research is preparation for teaching. It gives you fresh material through which you can understand your subject and seek to make it understandable to your charges. The ultimate goal it serves is the communication of essential messages about what law is and what law does. Perhaps the most striking aspect of David's teaching style is his use of comparison, a method that also characterises his research.[1] When a particular development looks opaque, he finds a comparable analogue[2] from elsewhere to cast light on the inner workings of the law, its concepts or its practitioners. In his teaching David would draw on an even wider range of comparators, from far beyond the typical realms of legal scholarship, to help his lessons land.

[1] His case for comparison as a foundational method in legal historical scholarship is made in DJ Ibbetson, 'Comparative Legal History: A Methodology' in A Musson and C Stebbings (eds), *Making Legal History* (Cambridge, Cambridge University Press, 2012) 131–45.

[2] Or, more commonly, analogues. A recent example is DJ Ibbetson, 'What's in a Name? Historical Foundations of Unjust(ified) Enrichment' in S Turenne (ed), *Reasons and Context in Comparative Law: Essays in Honour of John Bell* (Cambridge, Cambridge University Press, 2023) which includes examples from over two dozen jurisdictions from around the world.

This chapter is an attempt at recreating the style of comparison David's students encountered in his teaching. It ties into a broader debate, one of David's favourites, about the potential influence of earlier legal systems on the first stages in Rome's legal development. This is something that David has written on only rarely and with an abundance of caution, but which has cropped up with regularity in our discussions over the years.[3] This reflects the difference between David the Researcher and David the Teacher. Any account of the intellectual origins of the Twelve Tables is necessarily speculative by virtue of the incomplete survival of those laws. From what survives it seems apparent that the Twelve Tables are the confluence of several prior streams of thinking about law, and the extent to which any one of those sources represents a dominant influence cannot be known. Nevertheless, I hope this attempt at recreating David's style of teaching results in a new data point in favour of seeing Mesopotamian influence in the melting pot.

I. Setting the Scene: Mesopotamian Influence on Early Roman Law

The focus of this chapter is a little-discussed provision in the Twelve Tables that imposed a fixed financial penalty for the felling of productive trees.[4] The text is unusually unambiguous for an early law, and the provision has no obvious connection to the mainstream of delict in the developed Roman law.[5] As the pillars of later delict emerged in the mid-to-late Republic, this wrong faded into the background. Indeed, the main question that leaps to mind is why, given the ambit of wrongdoing in what survives of the Twelve Tables, the felling of trees attracted legal consequences at all. An answer to this might tentatively be provided by juxtaposing the early Roman wrong with remarkably similar provisions in several ancient near eastern bodies of law, a world in which the reasons for such a norm are far more readily discernible.

In the anglophone literature today the argument for a connection between the Twelve Tables and earlier near eastern codes is principally associated with Raymond Westbrook.[6] His controversial[7] hypothesis saw traces of near-eastern influence across

[3] DJ Ibbetson, 'Wrongs and Responsibility in pre-Roman Law' (2004) 25 *Journal of Legal History* 99–127. By the time this chapter is published, we ought to hear much more of his views on the theme: C Humfress, DJ Ibbetson and P Olivelle (eds), *The Cambridge Comparative History of Ancient Law* (Cambridge, Cambridge University Press, 2024).

[4] Unless specified otherwise, references to the Twelve Tables will be to Crawford's reconstruction: MH Crawford, *Roman Statutes*, vol 2 (London, Institute of Classical Studies, 1996) 555–721. Crawford gives the text as: 'Si arborem felicem succiderit, XXV poenae sunto' (1.16).

[5] It is on the possible connections between the XII Tables wrong and the developed law that one of the longest sustained treatment of the provision in the modern literature focuses: MF Cursi, 'Gli illeciti privati' in MF Cursi, *XII Tabulae: Testo e commento* (Naples, Edizioni Scientifiche Itaiane, 2018) 561–646, 631–34.

[6] Though there are certainly earlier incarnations of the hypothesis: one example is D Müller, *Die Gesetze Hammurabis und ihr Verhältnis zur mosaischen Gesetzgebung sowie zu den 12 Tafeln* (Vienna, Alfred Hölder, 1903).

[7] One review of Westbrook's collected papers described his positions as 'provocative, controversial, and to certain quarters of academia [they] are considered as revisionist; however, they reveal the open texture of the available evidence as well as the need and pitfalls of an interdisciplinary approach' (IN Arnaoutoglou, 'And the Law Came from the East' (2016) 66 *The Classical Review* 470–72, 470).

early Greek and Roman culture, with arguments about the content of early legal sources carrying over into philosophy and poetry.[8] The argument can be adopted with lesser degrees of intensity, and today it is widely recognised that there was some degree of borrowing and recycling in societies around the ancient Mediterranean, albeit not on the scale or with the sense of purpose that Westbrook proposed.[9]

Westbrook argued there was discernible direct influence from the near east on the Twelve Tables, visible in both the form and content of the early Roman laws.[10] What are now described as legal codes were a genre of literature that circulated through ancient near eastern societies as paradigmatic texts.[11] Less stringently, other have seen the potential for the ancient near east to have influenced Greece then Rome through the assimilation (rather than transplantation) of material, with Raaflaub arguing in relation to Greece that 'where [they] did incorporate foreign impulses, they transformed and adapted them thoroughly to fit their own conditions and needs'.[12] Westbrook's account of the Twelve Tables focuses on two core curiosities in the surviving fragments. Firstly, the provisions we have are ill-suited to the needs of practice, with little on fundamentals such as the forms of action.[13] Secondly, the near-total absence of core Roman social institutions and structures, not least the separation of the patricians and plebians, which feature centrally in the traditional origin story of the legislation.[14] Taken together, these give the impression of a body of rules only loosely tethered to Roman society: 'the bulk of the rules deal with very ordinary aspects of private law … They could apply to almost any period or society'.[15] In particular, Westbrook argues that the absence of any political scars gives the lie to traditional story of a political compromise leading to legislation, in turn introducing the possibility of explanations that differ from the Roman's own history.

In substantiating his argument, Westbrook relies heavily on material concerning wrongdoing.[16] And it is in his writing on wrongdoing that Ibbetson offers tentative

[8] See eg the essays collected in R Westbrook (D Lyons and S Démare-Lafont (eds), *Ex Oriente Lex: Near Eastern Influences on Ancient Greek and Roman Law* (Baltimore, John Hopkins University Press, 2015)) stray into classical literature with a piece on the Iliad, and anthropology in a theoretical essay on the nature of legal development in early societies.

[9] See, for instance, the overview of existing literature in J Clackson, 'Roman Law in its Italic Context' in S Bell & P du Plessis (eds), *Roman Law Before the Twelve Tables: An Interdisciplinary Approach* (Edinburgh, Edinburgh University Press, 2020) 9–23, 9–10. There are also compelling accounts of the origins of the Twelve Tables that conform broadly to the Roman's own origin myth: C Cascione, 'Il contesto storico della legislazione decemvirale' in MF Cursi, *XII Tabulae: Testo e commento* (Naples. Edizioni Scientifiche Itaiane, 2018) 1–30. Other leading historians of the Twelve Tables look for closer influences, eg MH Crawford, 'From Ionia to the Twelve Tables' in K Muscheler (ed), *Römische Jurisprudenz-Dogmatik, Überlieferung, Rezeption: Festschrift für Detlef Liebs zum 75. Geburtstag* (Berlin, Duncker & Humblot, 2011) 153–60.

[10] Indeed, he argued the influence was still visible in legislation as late as the *lex Aquilia*: R Westbrook, 'The Coherence of the *lex Aquilia*' (1995) 42 *RIDA* 437.

[11] R Westbrook, 'Codification and Canonization' in R Westbrook (B Wells and R Magdalene eds), *Law from the Tigris to the Tiber, Volume 1: The Shared Tradition* (Winona Lake, Indiana, Eisenbrauns, 2009).

[12] K Raaflaub, 'Early Greek Political Thought in its Mediterranean Context' in RK Balot (ed), *A Companion to Greek and Roman Political Thought* (Oxford, Wiley-Blackwell) 51–52.

[13] R Westbrook, 'The Nature and Origins of the Twelve Tables' in *Ex Oriente Lex* (n 8) 72.

[14] Noting that the sole provision that mentions the two social classes (11.1) deals not with a point of political reconciliation but enduring separation: it prohibits intermarriage.

[15] Westbrook (n 13) 72.

[16] Wrongdoing also forms the basis of arguments for the extra-Mesopotamian influence of Hammurabi in P Barmash, *The Laws of Hammurabi: At the Confluence of Royal and Scribal Traditions* (Oxford, Oxford

support for the Westbrook thesis.[17] Ibbetson is cautious in navigating Westbrook and his controversial hypothesis. It is made clear that the argument is not one of doctrinal transplantation but intellectual influence: '[our] concern is with legal values rather than legal rules; all that is important is that we my suppose that the values found in the texts reflect a particular legal tradition'.[18] This facilitates a different pattern of analysis to Westbrook. Westbrook focused on similarities at a textual level – comparable constructions, terminological curiosities. Ibbetson's analysis cuts across a greater range of individual laws from a variety of systems to construct an overarching concept of liability for wrongs that informed the earliest laws of Rome. In doing so, he avoids being committed to the sort of direct influence, bordering on transplantation, that Westbrook saw behind the Twelve Tables. It does, nevertheless, presuppose intellectual crosspollination around the ancient Mediterranean.

II. The Roman Wrong

The Twelve Tables wrong in question simply imposed a penalty of 25 on anyone who felled a productive tree.[19] Reconstructions of the laws invariably assume the penalty was in asses, and though this is based on Pliny the Elder's account of the law authored some four centuries later there is no reason to doubt this.[20] Pliny notes the extraordinarily low value attached to fruit trees by the Romans of the early Republic, to be contrasted with enormous value of Crassus's mythical lotus trees. A classic story of the excesses of the second century BCE, the six lotus trees are valued at ten million sesterces by Crassus' co-censor. The paltry penalty of the ancient law has nevertheless been an important factor in categorising the wrong in modern reconstructions. Crawford places the wrong immediately after the supposed trifecta of *os fractum*, *membrum ruptum* and *iniuria*, linking the third of these to felling trees by the identical penalty imposed.[21]

Several reconstructions of the Twelve Tables add an additional requirement: that the wrong be done *iniuria*.[22] This is justified by the classical discussion of the liability that attached to felling trees, which frequently includes references to the need for stealth

University Press, 2020) ch 7. The possibility of a biblical bridge is explored in DP Wright, 'The Compositional Logic of the Goring Ox and Negligence Laws in the Covenant Collection (Ex 21:28-36)' (2004) 10 *Zeitschrift für altorientalische und biblische Rechtsgeschichte* 93–142. Other areas of law, or law-adjacent activity, offer further support. For example Yaron notes that in a treaty between the Romans Latins in 493BCE language forbidding subsequent variation is used which is extremely common in treaties from the ancient Near East: R Yaron, 'Semitic Elements in Early Rome' in A Watson (ed), *Daube Noster* (Edinburgh, Scottish Academic Press, 1974) 348–51.

[17] Ibbetson (n 3) 99–127.

[18] Ibbetson (n 3) 99, fn 5.

[19] Crawford, 1.16: 'Si arborem felicem succiderit, XXV poenae sunto'.

[20] Pliny the Elder, *Natural History*, 17.1.7.

[21] Crawford, *Roman Statutes*, 1.16 (*iniuria* in 1.15: 'si iniuriam ?alteri? faxsit, uigintiquinque poenae sunt'.

[22] See eg PF Girard and H Senn, *Les lois des Romains* (Naples, Jovene, 1977) 8.11; S Riccobono, *Fontes iuris romani antejustiniani* (Florence, Barbèra, 1941) I, 8.11; C Bruns, *Fontes iuris Romani antique* (Tubingen, 1909) I, 8.11. Elements of the modern literature continue the association of the *actio de arboribus succissis* with *iniuria*, eg N Jansen, *The Structure of Tort Law* (Oxford, Oxford University Press, 2021) 2.2.2.

(albeit not *iniuria*),[23] defined as acting without the knowledge of the tree's owner, and with the intent to conceal the actions from the owner.[24] This reflects the conflation of the Twelve Tables wrong with a later action, the *actio arborum furtim caesarum*, which is the subject matter of the Digest title from which the references to stealth are taken. Lenel begins his commentary on the later action with a warning: 'the *actio arborum furtim caesarum* must not be confused with the *actio de arboribus succissis* of the Twelve Tables'.[25] Instead, Lenel emphasises that the Twelve Tables wrong consisted simply in the act of felling trees.[26]

The provision sits awkwardly within what might loosely be described as the treatment of wrongs in the Twelve Tables. There is an inevitable danger in identifying any particular provision as concerning wrongdoing. The very label suggests an artificial boundary between the provisions so categorised and the residue of the Twelve Tables, giving rise to an anachronistic taxonomy. This is problematic given the typical conditional form in the Twelve Tables, where a conditional construction imposes a consequence for conduct already performed results in a sanction-based model of rules. The following list is necessarily tentative, and based on provisions that adopt this conditional form with a clear course of conduct prohibited, with the patently undesirable consequence imposed. This risks under-inclusion, insofar as it omits provisions where the consequence is not provided, or else where the nature of either the conduct or consequence is ambiguous. But it provides the minimum content of what might be termed the wrongs of the Twelve Tables.

It is an eclectic list: *membrum ruptum*, or bodily maiming (talion unless a compromise reached);[27] breaking the bone of a free person (300 asses);[28] breaking the bone of a slave (150 asses);[29] manifest theft (where the defendant was free, flogging and enslavement; where the defendant was a slave, flogging and death by being thrown from the Tarpeian Rock; where the defendant was below the age of puberty, flogging and a duty to compensate);[30] non-manifest theft (double damages);[31] loss caused by a quadruped (surrender the animal);[32] cutting a crop by night (hanged in dedication

[23] See eg D 47.7.1 (Paul), D 47.7.1 (Paul), D 47.7.6.pr (Pomponius), D 47.7.7.pr (Ulpian), D 47.7.7.1 (Ulpian citing Pedius), D 47.7.8.1 (Paul).47.7.6.pr (Pomponius), D 47.7.7.pr (Ulpian), D 47.7.7.1 (Ulpian citing Pedius), D 47.7.8.1 (Paul).

[24] D 47.7.7.pr (Ulpian).

[25] O Lenel, *Das edictum perpetuum*, 3rd edn (Leipzig, Tauchnitz, 1927) 326: 'Die actio arborum furtim caesarum darf nicht verwechselt warden mit der aus den zwölf Tafeln stammenden actio de arboribus succisis'. There is a sole text that refers to the Twelve Tables wrong having a stealth element: D 19.2.25.5 (Gaius), though this can be explained through Lenel's argument that the compilers sought to present the two actions as one.

[26] Though the wrong is little discussed in the modern literature on the Twelve Tables, there is still a tendency to insert the classical *furtim* element into the original wrong despite Lenel's warning. See eg O Dilberto, 'Una palingenesis "aperta"' in M Humbert, *Le Dodici Tavole: dai decemviri agli Umanisti* (Pavia, IUSS Press, 2005) 217–38, 225.

[27] Crawford, 1.13: si membrum rupit, ni cum eo pacit, talio esto.

[28] ibid.

[29] Crawford, 1.14: si os fregit libero, CCC, <si> seruo, CL poena<e> su<n>to.

[30] Crawford, 1.19: <<<si furtum manifestum est, ni pacit, uerberato>>> transque dato. <<<si seruus, uerberato deque saxo deicito. si impubes, uerberato noxiamque sarcito.>>>.

[31] Crawford, 1.21: si adorat furt <i>quod nec manifestum erit, <<<duplum poenae esto.>>>.

[32] Crawford, 8.2: si quadrupes pauperiem <faxit>, <<<ni sarcit, noxae dato.>>>.

to Ceres; if below puberty, flogging and double damages);[33] burning a building or pile of corn near a building (beaten then killed by fire; if it happened accidentally, there is instead a duty to repair);[34] guardians acting deceitfully (double damages);[35] patrons defrauding their clients (renders the defendant *sacer*);[36] bearing false witness (death by being hurled from the Tarpeian Rock);[37] and bringing a false claim (three arbiters appointed to determine damages, which are then doubled).[38] To this we can add a wrong of uncertain content: *inuiria*, typically (though not confidently) thought to be violence or humiliation that merited a penalty of 25 asses.[39] There are then further measures which might have been wrongs, but which do not provide penalties: curses;[40] singing in enmity or composing songs;[41] bewitching fruits or the harvest of another;[42] sending animals to pasture on another's fruit;[43] and a range of provisions concerning burial rites.[44]

Within this list, four patterns of outcome can be seen.[45] Firstly, there are forms of punishment that appear to be culturally significant to the early Romans: the specificity of hurling a condemned person from the Tarpeian Rock, of offering them to Ceres or rendering the defendant *sacer* make the connected provisions unlikely candidates for importation. Secondly, there is at least one example of talion. *Membrum ruptum* makes use of the term *talio* in the surviving formulation, and is direct in the retribution imposed. A sense of like-for-like punishment looks to lie behind the penalty imposed for arson, but there is a clear mismatch between setting a building on fire and setting the defendant on fire. Thirdly, there is limited recourse to assessed damages, including the creation of processes by which reliable assessments might be made. Fourthly, limited use is made of fixed financial penalties.

The felling of trees belongs to the fourth category, sharing the title of puniest penalty with *iniuria*. Each of the other Twelve Tables wrongs that imposes a fixed penalty has been argued to represent influence from the ancient near east.[46] There is also a clear

[33] Crawford, 8.5: <<<si nox segetem pauerit secueritue, Cereri suspensus esto. si impubes, uerberato duplioneque damnum decidito.>>>.

[34] Crawford, 8.6: <<<si aedes aceruumue frumenti iuxta ?domum? positum combusserit, uinctus uerberatus igni … si casu …, noxiam sarcito … >>>.

[35] Crawford, 8.9: <<<si tutor dolo malo … duplione damnum decidito.>>>.

[36] Crawford, 8.10: si patronus clienti fraudem fecerit, sacer esto. On the meaning of *sacer esto*, see Bennett, 'Sacer esto', (1930) *Transactions of the American Philology Society* 5.

[37] Crawford, 8.12: <<<si falsum testimonium dixerit, de saxo deicito.>>>.

[38] Crawford, 12.3: si uindiciam falsam tulit, s<t>litis arbitros tris dato; eorum arbitrio duplione damnum decidito.

[39] Crawford, 1.15: si iniuriam ?alteri? faxsit, uigintiquinque poenae sunto.

[40] Crawford, 8.1: qui malum carmen incantassit … <quiue> occentassit carmen<ue> cond<issit> ….

[41] ibid.

[42] Crawford, 8.4: qui fruges excantassit … ?quiue? alienam segetem pellexeri<t> ….

[43] Crawford, 8.3: <<<glande in alieno pastum ne inmittito.>>>.

[44] Crawford, 10.1-10.

[45] A different categorisation of the four, influenced by developed Roman law, is provided by M Humbert, 'La codificazione decemvirales: tentative d'interpretazione' in M Humbert, *Le Dodici Tavole: dai decemviri agli Umanisti* (Pavia, IUSS Press, 2005) 3–50, 26. He suggests (1) *poena*; (2) *damnum*; (3) *noxia*; (4) *addictio*, corporal punishment or loss of civic status. The manner in which he navigates the boundary between the first and second cases, which turns on the later distinction founded on the purpose for which damages are paid, is difficult to reconcile with the limited information the texts provide.

[46] Ibbetson (n 3) 108–13.

mismatch in severity between felling trees and what appear to be cognate wrongs. While cutting an individual fruit-bearing tree merits the lowest penalty known, taking an entire crop from a field merits capital punishment. It is also striking that there are few other examples of property damage. The severity of the penalties attached to theft show that the protection of property was taken seriously. Yet the range of property damage provisions is narrow, and the outcomes highly variable. A total of three wrongs (cutting a crop, damage by fire, felling a tree) result in five possible outcomes: execution, corporal punishment, double damages based on assessment, a duty to compensate, and fixed penalties. It is difficult to believe this mismatch of approaches represent a single moment in time or a single set of influences.

III. The Mesopotamian Wrongs

If the Roman wrong is anomalous *in situ*, can ancient near eastern analogues provide insight into its possible origins? Provisions attaching consequences to the felling of trees are found in several of the surviving texts.[47] The earliest example of a rule about felling trees comes from the Code of Lipit-Ishtar, which predates the much better-known Code of Hammurabi by approximately a century. The wrong is straightforwardly stated: 'If a man cut down a tree in the garden of (another) man, he shall pay one half mina of silver'.[48] By contrast, the Code of Hammurabi provided: 'If a man has cut a tree[49] in a man's grove[50] without (the knowledge of) the owner of the plantation, he shall pay half a maneh of silver'.[51] Although the correspondence between the two is not perfect (though how the term translated out of Sumerian as 'garden' and translated out of Akkadian as 'grove' differ is difficult to know), in his comparison of the two codes, Steele thought the provisions concerning trees were among just one of seven instances of 'almost exact correspondence'.[52] Even in the earliest records of ancient near eastern law there is the suggestion of recycling between codes in relation to this wrong.

Hammurabi's incarnation of the wrong appears in a sequence on the cultivation of trees, leading Driver and Miles to assert that this provision specifically concerned the felling of palm trees, the most agriculturally significant type of tree cultivated.[53] They rely upon a tablet from the time of Cyrus (ie the late sixth century BCE) to suggest the market value of a palm tree was a full maneh of silver. That the penalty for

[47] Any account of the 'codes' of the ancient near east immediately encounters a terminological difficulty. It is evident that the texts were not codes in the modern sense, and it is unclear to what extent they operated as law at all.

[48] Law 10; FR Steele, *The Code of Lipit-Ishtar* (Philadelphia, University Museum of the University Pennsylvania, 1948) 15.

[49] Literally 'wood' – I am very grateful to Nicholas Postgate for his help with understanding the significance of the terminology chosen in this clause.

[50] GR Driver and JC Miles, *The Babylonian Laws* (Oxford, Clarendon, 1960) use 'planation', likely due to their association of this law with date palms which were systematically farmed. The term used certainly suggests cultivation, hence 'grove' here.

[51] Law 59.

[52] Steele (n 48) 28. There are several further instances where there are degrees of parallelism, but where there are also key respects in which Hammurabi departed from the earlier laws.

[53] Driver and Miles (n 50) vol 2, 160.

felling a tree would only meet half the price of replacement is initially curious, though their suggestion that the intervening twelve centuries entailed a change in the value of silver is certainly plausible. The importance of the date palm to agricultural activity in the ancient near east is difficult to overstate, with the shade provided by palm's fronds allowing for the cultivation of other less hardy crops that would otherwise not survive.[54] Tengberg describes a common three-storey method of cultivation, beginning with the palm as the central tallest pillar providing shade, with fruit trees (such as figs and pomegranates), and then finally cereals, pulses and vegetables closest to the ground. Such an approach to agriculture is found in Mesopotamia well before the Code of Hammurabi, with remains found from the middle of the fifth millennium BCE.[55] The agricultural significance of date palms, coupled with the decades-long growth period before they can fulfil this purpose, provide some insight into why this wrong merited a serious penalty.

This wrong is not the only provision concerning agriculture. Elsewhere in Hammurabi we find provisions underscoring the importance of maximising the exploitation of agricultural resources. However, these laws do not impose financial penalties even in cases of waste. One sequence of provisions concerns those who agreed to work another's fields. Where a defendant made such an agreement but failed to grow any corn, they were expected to pay over to the owner of the field the amount of corn raised in neighbouring fields.[56] If the field was not just neglected but left to waste, not only did this amount of corn need to be delivered, but the neglectful labourer was expected to plough the field and prepare it for the following year – in other words, to undo any deleterious effects of the waste.[57] Driver and Miles note that the enforcement of law against felling trees is evidenced in a range of tablets, indicating that the offence was sufficiently weighty to merit recording.[58] The social gravitas of the wrong can also be seen in religious texts, including a curse equivalent to that placed upon those found to be using false weights applicable to anyone who felled tamarisks and palms, or tore up briars.[59] This, they conclude, was a serious wrong.

The same level of financial penalty is found in various instances of violence. It was the sum owed where a freeperson was killed in an affray, so long as the wrongdoer was willing to swear that the blow was not struck intentionally.[60] It was also imposed where a villein pregnant woman was killed by physical violence.[61] It ranks below most instances of personal injury, where the penalty was typically talion where the victim was free or else a financial penalty, though there are some wrongs that impose a penalty

[54] M Tengberg, 'Beginnings and Early History of Date Palm Garden Cultivation in the Middle East' (2012) 86 *Journal of Arid Environments* 139–47, 139. The same article notes the non-agricultural uses of the palm tree.

[55] ibid 143.

[56] Law 42.

[57] Law 43. See also law 44 on the effect of three years of waste.

[58] Driver and Miles (n 50) 160.

[59] ibid 160.

[60] Law 206. If the deceased was a villein, the penalty was 1/3 a maneh of silver instead. The language of villein is that used by Driver and Miles.

[61] Law 212. If the deceased was free, the wrongdoer's daughter was put to death in an instance of talion (Law 210). If the deceased was a slave, the penalty was 1/3 a maneh of silver (Law 214).

below ½ a maneh of silver.[62] It is also noteworthy how this wrong appears to fit into Hammurabi's taxonomy of wrongs. Though theft is a crime typically punished by death, damage to property is largely absent. Indeed, this is the only freestanding wrong that affects property other than slaves. Other instances of property damage are redressed only within a contractual context, as with the above examples of tenant farming, and result in directly compensatory outcomes. Unlike the Twelve Tables, Hammurabi is a complete body of rules, and so felling trees has the appearance of an archetypical form of property damage. This further underscores the importance of felling trees as a social problem.

Provisions concerning the felling of trees are not a universal feature of the surviving records of the ancient near eastern legal landscape. Lipit-Ishtar is the earliest found; earlier Sumerian codes such as Ur-Namma do not have a surviving analogous provision, though these sources are also extremely fragmentary.[63] Prominent later legal texts similarly lack an analogous provision.[64] Liability for felling trees next appear in the Hittite texts, written between roughly 1650 and 1500 BCE. The closest provision to that found in Hammurabi is law 104:

> If anyone cuts down a pear (?) tree or plum (?) tree, he shall pay [... shekels] of silver. He shall look to his house for it.[65]

Drawing parallels between this and the earlier codes is made difficult by the corruption of the text. What would otherwise be clear indicators of similarity, such as the penalty, cannot be relied upon. There are two evident points of departure: the specificity of the trees mentioned, and the addition of a final provision instructing the condemned defendant to 'look to his house' in meeting the penalty. The former is a matter of differences between nouns relating to trees in the different languages, and the latter is an extremely common provision in the Hittite texts.[66]

Unlike Hammurabi, the Hittite texts contain other provisions imposing liability for harming plants independently of a pre-existing relationship. Law 104 sits in the middle of a run of such wrongs. These begin with three species of theft: of vines,

[62] See eg law 201, 204. A table setting out systematically the various wrongs, their penalties and variants for different types of victim can be found in Driver and Miles (n 50) vol 2, 409.

[63] Similarly, the so-called 'Laws of X' (so named because the initial ascription to a ruler is missing) has just eighteen surviving provisions, many of which are so corrupt as to be unintelligible: see MT Roth, *Law Collections from Mesopotamia and Asia Minor* (Atlanta, Scholars Press, 1997) 36–39.

[64] See eg the Middle Assyrian Laws, though these depart dramatically from Hammurabi in many respects. MAL B (Roth (n 63) 176–82) deals with a cluster of wrongs to do with land, and is a largely complete tract. It makes no mention of felling trees but does deal with, to take one example, growing crops on another's land. It is difficult to know the extent to which the Middle Assyrian Laws were organised thematically; it might be significant that MAL B begins with the inheritance of land, moves on to transfers of land, and then considers non-consensual cultivation of another's land. It is not obvious that straightforward property damage such as felling another's tree absent some other legal relationship between the parties would belong in this sequence *if* it is thematically organised. The far more fragmentary MAL E (Roth (n 63) 186) looks to have dealt with wrongdoing independently of a relationship, but only four provisions survive, three so corrupt as to be indecipherable (my claim that they concern wrongdoing independent of a relationship is based on the use of the word 'strike' connected with 'head' in MAL E 2, and the range of consequences in MAL E 1).

[65] Roth (n 63) 230.

[66] The clause appears in Laws 1–5,7–8, 11–15, 17, 19b–20, 25a, 57–63, 67, 69–70, 72, 77a, 81–83, 87–88, 91, 94, 96–97, 104–105, 119, 121–24, 127, 129–33, 143, and 149.

garlic or onions;[67] of wood from some manner of pond;[68] and plants (perhaps in a residual sense, capturing any not dealt with under other wrongs), with a penalty according to the size of the plot affected.[69] Law 104 marks the bridge from theft to damage, and is followed a pair of wrongs addressing damage by fire.[70] There is then an instance of waste, and a final pair concerning theft then damage to fruit still on a tree.[71] The sequence is not comprehensive, and wrongs of a similar nature appear dotted throughout the laws.[72] It is nevertheless telling that Law 104 sits at the head of those provisions dealing with damage to plants.

IV. A Question of Influence

At this point in the supervision, David would put the two sets of sources side-by-side and ask what we make of the similarities. We have a wrong of peculiar narrowness resulting in a fixed financial penalty. It is also one of the few fixed financial penalties to be found in the surviving text. The level of the penalty corresponds closely to other fixed penalties for personal injury. And the wrong is the prime form of property damage that does not concern slaves. Given these points of correspondence, and the otherwise curious inclusion of a wrong about felling trees in the Twelve Tables, might we be looking at an example of influence?

The potential for Mesopotamian law to have influenced the Twelve Tables, whether directly or indirectly, is clear; the extent and nature of any such influence is unknowable. Few now believe that the early Roman republic was a hermetically sealed society, and arguments turn not on whether there was external influence, but which external influence had the greatest effect on the early Roman mindset. Crawford, in a recent chapter on Greek influences on the Twelve Tables, concluded:

> So we are in my view in the fifth century BC in a world of borrowing of approaches to inscribing legislative texts; but we are also in a world of borrowing and creation of alphabets, of the Etruscan and – probably independently, the Sabine alphabets; of the Umbrian, Faliscan and Latin alphabets, on the basis of the Etruscan alphabet … Given these very precise and identifiable borrowings, we should look with new eyes at 'some quite precise parallels between specific provisions of the Twelve Tables and some Athenian legislation', of the mythical mother city of the Ionian Dodekapolis.[73]

Reaching back to Mesopotamia can be justified through the same sort of logic, with the borrowing and creation of alphabets facilitated by the legal texts they formed. We know, for example, that as late as the seventh century BCE the Code of Hammurabi was being translated into new scripts in Anatolia.[74]

[67] 101 (Roth (n 63) 229).
[68] 102 (Roth (n 63) 229).
[69] 103 (Roth (n 63) 229).
[70] 105 and 106 (Roth (n 63) 230).
[71] Waste: 107; fruit: 108 and 109 (Roth (n 63) 230).
[72] See eg Law 124.
[73] Crawford (n 9) 158.
[74] For surviving examples see the entries marked 'neuassyrisch' in R Borger, *Babylonisch-assyrische Lesestücke* (Rome, Pontificium Institutum Biblicum,1994) 2–4.

Whether students were (or readers are) convinced by the parallels drawn is another matter. But with David's teaching, it was often the case that the answer reached was secondary to the path taken. In engaging with the argument, students were made to read texts closely and agonise over the possible implications of the author's choice of language. They were encouraged to immerse themselves in legal cultures they had not encountered before, and to think about the ideas that sat beneath the language used. It was not unusual for consecutive supervision groups to reach very different conclusions based on the points of detail to which they attached significance. But it was often the case that small points of detail unlocked new ways of participating in much larger arguments. In this respect, I hope this contribution has given a taste of what it was like to be taught by David.

PART II

English Legal History

6

Taking Thirteenth-Century Statutes Seriously: The Strange History of Remedies Based on Chapter 7 of the Statute of Gloucester (1278)

PAUL BRAND

In Easter term 1310 pleading took place in the Common Bench at Westminster in a suit brought by Walter of Strickland against Roger of Burnside. Walter was claiming three messuages, 36 acres of arable and two acres of meadow at Strickland Ketel in Westmorland in the far north-west of England. William of Strickland (Walter's father) had held the land in curtesy after the death of his wife and Walter's mother, Elizabeth.[1] He had then granted the land in fee to Thomas of Kymbe and his wife Agnes who had in turn granted the land to the current tenant, Roger of Burnside. Walter asserted that since William's grant had been in breach of an (unspecified) statute he was now entitled to sue for immediate possession of this land. Roger of Burnside, the current tenant, had previously vouched Agnes, by now the widow of Thomas of Kymbe, to warranty for this land. She appeared and warranted the land to Roger. She then challenged Walter's writ. It claimed to be based on a statutory provision but it was not. Walter could not deny this and so his claim was dismissed.

This is at any rate all that the plea roll tells us.[2] There are, however, fortunately also at least four different printed reports of this same case: one in the Vulgate edition of 1678, the other three edited by Maitland in 1905. These add materially to our knowledge of the arguments and tell us of an otherwise unrecorded sequel to the case.[3] They show, firstly, that counsel for the warrantor made the more precise objection to the writ that although it purported to be based on the Statute of Gloucester the statute did not in fact cover this case. The reference is to chapter 7 of the Statute of Gloucester (1278), which had stated that:

[1] She was already dead by Michaelmas term 1276: KB 27/28, m 1 [Anglo-American Legal Tradition (AALT) image 7961] but in 1276 her heir was Walter's elder brother William. He had evidently died without issue before 1301 when her heir was Walter: see JUST 1/989, m 2 [AALT image 1262].

[2] CP 40/181, m 136d [AALT image 0288].

[3] *Les Reportes des Cases Argue et Adjudge in le Temps del Roy Edward le Second* … (London, 1678) 75; FW Maitland (ed), *YB 3 Edward II* (Selden Society 20, 1905) 106–109. Curiously of the three reports edited by Maitland the first says that the basis of the claim was an alienation by a tenant for life (not a curtesy tenant) and that the writ specifically spoke of a breach of the Statute of Gloucester (which the enrolment suggests that it did not); the third turns it into a curious hybrid of a writ of entry *cui in vita* and a writ based on the statute.

> It is likewise provided that if a woman sell or give in fee or for a life term a tenement that she holds in dower the heir or other to whom the land ought to revert after the death of the woman is to have immediate recovery to claim the land by writ of entry [to be] provided for this purpose in the chancery.[4]

The statute had indeed said nothing about grants made by curtesy tenants. The different reports then give two counter-arguments against this objection. One was that the Statute of Westminster II (1285) (the reference is to chapter 24 of the statute) had authorised Chancery to provide similar remedies to existing ones where the situations were similar but no writ (and thus no remedy) was currently available,[5] and the cases of the curtesy tenant (and also of the tenant who held for life by special grant) were similar to that of the doweress. The writ was therefore jointly authorised by the two statutes and had properly been issued by the clerks of Chancery. The second was that similar writs had always been granted in the past and had been upheld by the justices and had allowed claimants to recover on such grants. The reports also differ as to the identity of the justice who gave final judgment in the case: some make it the Chief Justice, William of Bereford; others the puisne Justice Hervey of Staunton. But they agree on the reason given for the judgment. The writ purported to be based on the Statute of Gloucester but the statute did not mention this specific situation. One report cites Bereford as saying that, if there had not been such a direct citation of the statute, the writ might have been upheld.

Only one report tells us of the sequel. Four days afterwards Bereford went to Chancery and met with the senior Chancery clerks, Barlby (Bardelby) and Osgodby, and other (unnamed) examiners of writs. They agreed that in future writs issued for such cases were to mention only reversion for breach of 'the statute provided in a like case' (*in consimili casu provisi*), not breach of 'the statute'. The reporter then gives what looks like a specimen writ. It is not, however, for this particular case, nor even for an alienation by a tenant in curtesy, but for an alienation by a tenant who was a grantee for life.[6] Evidence from a register of writs dating from less than a decade later indicates that by then writs of entry were indeed available to give immediate recovery to reversioners on purported alienations in fee made both by curtesy tenants and by tenants for life by grant, and that they all cited as grounds for the recovery the terms of the 'statute provided in a like case' (*per formam statuti in casu consimili inde provisi*).[7]

This case and its sequel have been well known to legal historians since Plucknett discussed it in his *Statutes and Their Interpretation in the First Half of the Fourteenth Century* in 1922.[8] Despite what the reporter (and counsel) had said about the prior

[4] 'Ensement si femme vent ou donne en fee ou a terme de vie tenement que el tient en dowaire establi est qe le heir ou autre a qi la terre devereit revertir apres le deces la femme eit meintenaunt recoverir a demaunder [la tere] par bref de entre fet de ceo en la chauncelerie': *The Statutes of the Realm* (*Stat Realm*), vol 1 (London, 1810) 48.

[5] 'set decetero cum in uno casu conceditur breve et in consimili casu simili remedio indigenti sicuti prius fit breve': *Stat Realm*, i, 48.

[6] It is probably significant that the original alienee named in this specimen writ was the recently deceased senior Chancery clerk, William of Hambleton (Hamilton).

[7] For writs against the alienees of tenants for life by grant see E de Haas and GDG Hall (eds), *Early Registers of Writs* (Selden Society 87, 1970) R 839, R 840, R 845, R 852, R 854; for writs against curtesy tenants see ibid R 836–38. For the date of Register R see ibid lvi.

[8] TFT Plucknett, *Statutes and their Interpretation in the First Half of the Fourteenth Century* (Cambridge, Cambridge University Press, 1922) 53, 83.

availability of a remedy for alienations made by tenants in curtesy and tenants for life by grant, Plucknett thought that no remedy had been available in such cases prior to 1310 and that *Strickland v Burnside* (*alias Stirkelande v Brunolfshead*) and some earlier cases (discussed below) showed the justices being unwilling to extend the statutory remedy beyond the case mentioned in the statute (that of the doweress), and Bereford solving the problem by the invention of the writ *in consimili casu*. In 1963 Milsom suggested a drastic revision of this picture. What had happened in 1310 was much less revolutionary. It was 'no more than the provision of a new writ' and not a new remedy since a 'remedy had long been obtained by writs professedly based upon the statute of Gloucester'.[9] His evidence was not just what was said by counsel and justices in the course of the case (and by the reporter) but also two cases reported in the printed Year Books of Edward I (of 1294 and 1304). In both a reversioner had sought to recover land granted away by a tenant for life by grant through a writ citing the terms of the statute, and in neither of them was 'any objection made on the ground that the wrongdoer was grantee for life rather than doweress'.[10] There were also, Milsom noted, specimen counts in the pleading manual *Novae Narrationes* which showed actions for reversioners on grants both by curtesy tenants and by tenants for life by grant being explicitly based on the Statute of Gloucester.

An examination of the plea rolls of the Common Bench and the General Eyre and of the surviving (but as yet unpublished) law reports for the period between 1278 and 1307 confirms Professor Milsom's suggestion about the prior availability of such remedies and provides much fuller evidence to support his general conclusion. It also shows (as will be seen) just how soon after 1278 Chancery began issuing writs purportedly based on the statute but for the use of reversioners claiming immediate possession of land after grants by life tenants other than doweresses, and the courts accepting such writs even though they were not in fact warranted by the statute.

I. Tenants for Life by Grant

The earliest action brought by a reversioner claiming the possession of land granted away in fee by a tenant for life by grant was heard in the Common Bench in Trinity term 1282.[11] In it John Buffard claimed the Warwickshire manor of Cubbington against the Master of the Templars. This is only two terms later than the earliest action brought by a writ that really was authorised by the Statute of Gloucester (on an alienation by a doweress), which was heard in Hilary term 1282.[12] It also came three years before the enactment of the Statute of Westminster II and thus shows that Chancery was willing to

[9] E Shanks and SFC Milsom (eds), *Novae Narrationes* (Selden Society 80, 1963) cxxxix.

[10] ibid cxxxviii. In fact, the first of these cases belongs to Michaelmas 1291 rather than to the Middlesex eyre of 1294: (1291) YB 21 & 22 Edw I, 563.

[11] CP 40/46, m 30d [AALT image 0246].

[12] The case is *Thomas Weyland v Robert son of Philip [of Little Whelnetham]*: CP 40/44, m 1d [AALT image 5676]. The claimant was the court's Chief Justice and the writ issued for the case was enrolled (evidently as a specimen writ since the marginal heading is *novum breve factum secundum statutum Glouc*') as the first entry on the dorse of the Close Roll in November 1281: C 54/99, m 8d (calendared in *Calendar of Close Rolls, Edward I: Volume 2, 1279–1288* (London, 1902) 175).

extend the provisions of the Statute of Gloucester even before it was given any specific statutory authority for doing so. The grant in fee that had been made by the tenants for life (Henry de Seymour and his wife Ermengard) was specifically said in the writ to have been 'contrary to the terms of the king's statute of Gloucester' (*contra formam statuti regis Glouc'*) and the reversion claimed (by the brother and heir of the original grantor, Walter de Ottesford) was said to be under the terms of the same statute (*per formam ejusdem statuti*). The tenant (or his counsel) is recorded on the roll as objecting to the writ on the grounds that the 'said statute of Gloucester makes no mention of such a demise made by any kind of tenant for a life term' (*predictum statutum Glouc' nullam facit mencionem de hujusmodi dimissione facta per qualemcumque tenentem ad terminum vite*). Judgment on this objection was adjourned and none is recorded.[13] A second such action was heard in Easter term 1284, again prior to the 1285 statute. This was *Walter of Amersham v Humphrey de Bohun earl of Hereford* and in it Walter claimed extensive lands at Stocks in Aldbury in Hertfordshire which William of Cotton had held of him for his life. William had, he alleged, granted these lands to the Earl to Walter's disinheritance and 'contrary to the terms of the king's statute provided by the common council of the king's kingdom on such grants' (*contra formam statuti regis de communi consilio regni regis super hujusmodi dimissionibus provisi*).[14] Although no longer specified, the 'statute' can only be the Statute of Gloucester. This was certainly the belief of the tenant, for he again objected to the writ on the grounds that 'the statute does not mention anything other than grants by women who hold lands in dower' (*statutum non facit mencionem nisi de dimissionibus factis per mulieres que tenent terras in dotem*). Judgment was adjourned, and the parties subsequently made a final concord under which Walter quitclaimed all right in the land to the Earl.[15] It is not clear, though, that this implies any acknowledgment of the weakness of his claim. The Earl was likely to be a strong and tenacious opponent and may have been willing to pay to buy out the claim (though the final concord mentions only a nominal sore sparrowhawk).

Between 1284–1307 a further 45 such actions were brought by reversioners after alienations made by tenants for life. Only in one (*Simon of Newnham v Henry son of Walter of 'Bechull'*) is there any further evidence of a tenant attempting to object that the writ was not warranted by the statute. The case was heard in Michaelmas term 1296 and the enrolment of the case says nothing of any such challenge.[16] Two out of the three identified reports of the case, however, do so. In one Henry Spigurnel, counsel for the tenant's warrantor, excepted to the writ on the grounds that 'the statute on which you base your writ supports no writ except in the case where a woman alienates in fee

[13] The original grant of the manor for the lives of the couple by John's brother, Walter de Ottesford, was by final concord made in Michaelmas term 1273: E Stokes, FC Wellstood and FTS Houghton (eds), *Warwickshire Feet of Fines, vol. I (1195–1284)* (Dugdale Society, 1932) 195 (no 908). The final concord under which Henry and Ermengard quitclaimed all right to the manor to the Templars for themselves and her heirs was made in Michaelmas term 1281: ibid 207 (no 961). John had registered his claim when that fine was made. For the complicated history of the litigation about this manor see the notes to 79 Assize 1 in PA Brand (ed), *The Earliest English Law Reports* (EELR), vol 4 (Selden Society, 2007) 479–81.

[14] CP 40/53, m 43 [AALT image 7979].

[15] *VCH Herts*, ii, 145; the final concord is CP 25/1/86/40, no 153 [AALT image 0246]. Walter of Amersham had only acquired his title to the reversion of lands then held for life by William of Cotton and his wife Maud in 1281: CP 25/1/86/39, no 136 [AALT image 0226].

[16] CP 40/115, m 171 [AALT image 0371].

tenements which she holds in dower' (*le statut sur qay vous fundez vostre bref maynteynge nul bref fors en cas ou feme aliene en fee tenemenz qe el tent en dower*). Counsel for the claimant told him he had left it too late to say this as he had already given a higher response, and Bereford J told him 'This writ will not abate' (*Ceti bref ne abaterra mie*).[17] In the second report, it is again Spigurnel who excepts to the writ on the grounds that 'the statute does not aid them for the statute only applies to those who hold in dower, not for a life term, who make alienation in fee' (*le statut ne se lye fors qe a genz qe tenent en douwere, ne pas a terme de vie, qe funt alienacion en fee*). Again counsel for the claimant told the tenant he had left it too late to make this response but this report does not mention any remarks by Bereford suggesting unwillingness to quash the writ.[18] Although this case may suggest that similar objections might have been made and waived or overruled in other cases of which there are no surviving reports, we can reasonably exclude that possibility in the six other cases of this type for which we do have reports but no evidence of this exception being made.[19] Even where we do not have reports, we can at least be certain from the enrolments that no such exceptions were ever successful. Counsel was also certainly right in the 1310 report about claimants having recovered possession of land on the basis of such writs. Judgments were given for claimants after pleading prior to 1307 in at least six such cases.[20]

II. Tenants by Curtesy

The earliest action brought by a reversioner on the basis of a grant made by a curtesy tenant (a widower holding his late wife's land) is only to be found later. The first such case seems to be that of *John of Shrewsbury and his wife Alice v William son of Deodatus of Tyringham*, heard in Hilary term 1288. In it, John and Alice claimed a messuage (less a shop) at Newport Pagnel in Buckinghamshire on the grounds that it had been

[17] British Library (BL) Egerton MS 2811, fos 107r–v.

[18] BL Hargrave MS 375, fos 80r–v.

[19] These are the Easter 1289 case reported in PA Brand (ed), *EELR*, vol 2 (Selden Society, 1996) 317 (1289.5); the unidentified case of Michaelmas 1291 reported in (1291) YB 21 & 22 Edw I, RS p 563; the Easter 1302 case of *Thomas de Hastings v Miles son of Philip de Hastings* reported in Bodleian Library Hatton MS 28, fo 84r (enrolled on CP 40/142, m 1 [AALT image 0003]); what may be the Easter 1303 case of *Robert son of John d'Eyville of Deighton and his wife Maud v William son of Robert Bret of Eryholm* reported in BL Add MS 31826, fo 144v (enrolled on CP 40/147, m 131d [AALT image 0594]); the Michaelmas 1304 case of *Thomas Kyde v Robert of Berden* reported in (1304) YB 32 & 33 Edw I, RS pp 277–79 and in BL Add MS 31826, fo 344v, Lincoln's Inn Miscellaneous MS 738, fo 27r, BL Harley MS 25, fo 65r (enrolled on CP 40/149, m 249d [AALT image 1444]); the Hilary 1306 case of *Henry of Grainsby v William Tuchet* reported in (1306) YB 33–35 Edw I, RS p 157 and BL Hargrave MS 375, fo 140v (enrolled on CP 40/158, m 118 [AALT image 0251]).

[20] After a favourable jury verdict in the Michaelmas 1290 case of *Richard of South Aller v John de Tracy* (CP 40/86, m 218 [AALT image 0474]); the Hilary 1291 case of *Simon de Bruly and wife Joan, Adam of Whilborough and wife Maud and Margaret daughter of Agnes of Luddington v Amabilla daughter of Walter of Luddington* (CP 40/87, m 105d [AALT image 0557]); the Easter 1293 case of *Nicholas del Gardin v Walter of Tey* (CP 40/100, m 111 [AALT image 0230]); the Michaelmas 1306 case of *Robert of Aldridge and wife Alice v Simon le Grece of Weston and wife Juliana* (CP 40/161, m 261d [AALT image 1719]). On a surrender by the tenant in the Trinity 1302 case of *Simon of Brobury v Richard son of Walter of Brobury and his wife Margaret* (CP 40/143, m 70 [AALT image 0160]). On a finding that land was not ancient demesne as claimed by the tenant in the Trinity 1304 case of *William of Greenmere v William fizSeneschal of Hemsby and his son Richard* (CP 40/152, m 161 [AALT image 0337]).

granted to William by Hugh Maltmaker and that Hugh had only held it in curtesy of Alice's inheritance (Alice being her mother's heiress). As this grant was 'contrary to the terms of the king's statute' (*contra formam statuti regis*) the messuage ought to revert to John and Alice 'under the terms of the said statute' (*per formam statuti predicti*).[21] William's response was to assert that this had been Hugh's own property and that he had held it in fee simple, not curtesy. When a jury found that not to be the case the claimants recovered. Between 1288–1307 there were a further 15 such cases, mainly in the Common Bench. In only one of them, the case of *Henry of Clitheroe v Robert son of Adam of Preston and Richard del Hurst* heard in the 1292 Lancashire eyre, did a litigant (here a warrantor) object that although the writ claimed to be founded on the Statute of Gloucester the statute had mentioned only grants by tenants in dower. It may have been a court unsympathetic to this particular plea that suggested to him that it was wise to waive this exception and plead instead that the land had been the said husband's own right and not his wife's (which a jury then confirmed).[22] Again it is normally only in the reported cases (which are characteristically more generous in recording ultimately unsuccessful arguments than are enrolments) that we have a good chance of knowing whether tenants or their warrantors had tried similar arguments on other occasions as well. Only three cases are the subject of such reports. None mentions any such arguments being made.[23] Here, too, we have the positive evidence that the courts gave judgments in favour of claimants after pleading in at least three such cases.[24]

III. Tenants in Tail, Reversioners and Remaindermen

The doweress who alienated in fee (whose case was the only one covered in express terms by chapter 7 of the Statute of Gloucester) was, of course, and had to be, the sole tenant for life, and the curtesy tenant to whom the statute came to be extended was also inevitably a sole tenant for life. As has been seen, however, the very first action brought on an alienation by a tenant for life by grant (in 1282) was in fact brought against the alienee of two joint tenants (a husband and wife) for life (or rather their lives),[25] and in later cases too we encounter alienations allegedly made by two brothers who held jointly for their lives (in a case of Easter 1295)[26] and by another man and his wife (in a case of

[21] CP 40/70, m 65d [AALT image 7332].

[22] JUST 1/408, m 28d [AALT image 0903].

[23] The reported cases are the Michaelmas 1300 case of *Robert Davilliers of South Frodingham v prior of Bridlington*, reported in BL Add MS 37657, fos 49r–v and BL Add MS 31826, fo 87r (enrolled on CP40/131, m 177d [AALT image 1191]); the Easter 1302 case of *Alexander of Harlow v Pelagia daughter of Nicholas of Harlow*, reported in BL Add MS 31826, fos 136r–v, BL Add MS 37657, fo 182r, and Cambridge University Library MS Ee.6.18, fo 56r (enrolled on CP 40/142, m 72 [AALT image 0155]); the Hilary 1303 case of *Avicia widow of William Malet of Irby v Gilbert Rayner of Great Grimsby*, reported in LI Miscellaneous MS 87, fo 2v (enrolled on CP 40/146, m 115 [AALT images 0241–42]).

[24] In the Hilary 1288 case of *John of Shrewsbury and wife Alice v William son of Deodatus of Tyringham* (CP 40/70, m 65d [AALT image 7332]); the 1292 Lancashire eyre case of *Henry of Clitheroe v Robert son of Adam of Preston and Richard del Hurst* (JUST 1/408, m 28d [AALT image 0903]); in the Easter 1302 case of *Alexander of Harlow v Pelagia daughter of Nicholas of Harlow* (CP 40/142, m 72 [AALT image 0155] (but this judgment seems later to have been superseded).

[25] See text to n 13 above.

[26] *Geoffrey of Roding v Joan widow of William of Hadstock*: CP 40/108, m 53 [AALT image 0111].

Michaelmas 1295).[27] There is also one example of an action brought on an alienation made by the survivor of two joint tenants for life, a husband and wife who had been granted land for their lives, in a case of Michaelmas 1306.[28] We may suspect, but cannot know for sure, that at least some of these joint life tenants were in reality tenants in tail, perhaps tenants in tail without issue, whose tenancy was being treated as though it had been a life tenancy, particularly when it emerges from the pleading that the tenants for lives were now themselves dead and have died without issue. In the Michaelmas 1295 case, for example, we know from the pleading that the husband at least (the joint tenant for life with his wife) was now dead, and that he had died without issue. It may also be significant that the enrolment records that the warrantor making the defence subsequently had it placed on record that he did not in fact admit that the initial grant had been only a grant for life.[29]

Some of those who are described in claimants' writs as being sole tenants for life may also in fact have been tenants in tail. In a 1287 action Nicholas of Redesdale sued Robert son of William Reeve of Peatling for a messuage and virgate at Peatling Parva in Leicestershire, claiming that Robert had gained title to it through William of Blaby and that William had been granted the land for life by Roger, the grandfather of the claimant. Robert vouched William of Blaby to warranty. William then pleaded that his original estate was not a tenancy for life, but a grant in frankmarriage made on his marriage to Roger's daughter, Agnes. As Nicholas could not deny this the court dismissed his claim.[30] A subsequent action of formedon in the reverter between the same parties heard in Trinity 1292 (apparently after William's death, since this time he was not vouched to warranty) indicates that William and Agnes had produced children, but suggests that both had died in their father's lifetime, for the issue taken in this case was whether or not the issue had been living when the alienation had been made.[31] If the alienation was made after their deaths and after the death of Agnes, the alienation had indeed been made after the possibility of issue was extinct, and such an alienation might reasonably be seen as an alienation made effectively, or constructively, by a tenant for life.[32] The court was perhaps still resisting this conclusion in 1287.

The statute had explicitly authorised an action not only for the heir to whom the land held in dower was supposed in the normal course of events to revert after the death of the doweress, but also for any third party to whom the heir had granted the reversion of a holding. The earliest case to be brought against the alienee of a doweress was

[27] *William de Ros and his wife Eustachia v Joan daughter of John de la Warre*: CP 40/110, m 17 [AALT image 0635].

[28] *Richard son of David of Coleham and his brother Richard v Richard Stury*: CP 40/161, m 289 [AALT image 0596].

[29] *Postea quia justiciarii recordantur quod predictus Philippus non cognovit quod predictus Johannes senior etc. dimisit predictum tenementum predictis Johanni de la Haye et Johanne tenendum ad terminum vite ipsorum Johannes et Johanne etc. ideo cognicio illa nullius sit momenti etc.* An additional complication in this case is that the husband seems to have been the son and heir of the original grantor and to have made the grant after his father's death and in order to resettle the manor on himself and his wife, who was probably the current tenant.

[30] CP 40/68, m 64d [AALT image 4414].

[31] CP 40/95, m 65 [AALT image 0137]. Reported in BL Add MS 31826, fo 67r; BL Add MS 5925, fos 84r–v.

[32] For evidence that such a tenant was being treated by the 1320s for some purposes (such as restraint on his alienation) as a tenant for life, see DW Sutherland, *The Assize of Novel Disseisin* (Oxford, Clarendon Press, 1973) 115, fn 1.

indeed one brought by the grantee of a reversion, albeit a very special grantee, no less than Thomas Weyland, the Chief Justice of the court where the action was brought,[33] and of the 15 other pre-1307 pleaded cases brought against the alienees of doweresses, five more were brought by the grantees of reversions,[34] and one by the heir of such a grantee.[35] A much smaller proportion of the actions brought against the alienees of tenants for life by grant were brought by grantees of the reversions, only two of the 47 claimants,[36] but as many as 23 of the 47 claimants made it clear through their writs that they were the heirs of the original grantors of the life estate. None of the cases brought against the alienees of curtesy tenants were brought by claimants who did not claim to be the heir of the wife whose inheritance the land had been. There is, however, at least one case (*Robert Davilliers of South Frodingham v prior of Bridlington*) initially heard in 1300 and repleaded on a new (and apparently amended) writ in 1302 where the claimant explicitly stated in his writ and his claim that he was the heir of his mother under an entail, a grant made by his grandmother to his mother and her issue.[37]

All this could be seen as falling within the spirit, if not exactly the letter, of the statute. The first sign that Chancery might be willing to go further than this came in Easter term 1299. In the case of *Robert of Stokes v Ralph de Glynlee and his wife Joan and others* the claimant asserted his claim to 36 acres of arable and two acres of meadow at Rickmansworth in Hertfordshire which had been granted by John Kenelm to Henry of Stokes and Nicholas of Stokes jointly for their lives, with remainder over to the right heirs of Henry. Nicholas had allegedly granted the land to the current tenants in breach of the provisions of the king's (unspecified) statute.[38] This action was brought not by the grantor or his heir (who no longer had any interest in the land), but by Henry's brother and heir, Robert, who claimed that the land ought now to 'revert' to him immediately (rather than after the death of Nicholas) under the terms of the (unspecified) statute. No challenge seems to have been made to the form of the writ. Certainly, none is recorded on the roll. Issue was taken instead on whether or not the quitclaim produced by the tenants in Robert's name and purporting to have been made by him at Fleet Street in London was genuine. Perhaps Chancery avoided using the term 'remain' in the writ so as to avoid drawing attention to the fact that it was a remainderman, not a reversioner,

[33] See text to n 12 above.

[34] *William of Saham v John Ode of Lynn*: CP 40/75, m 104 (Michaelmas term 1288) [AALT image 8925]; *Adam Bacun v Edmund de Munpinzun*: CP 40/142, m 67 (Easter term 1302) [AALT image 0145]; *Richard of Thorpland v John son of William of Shottisham and his wife Maud*: CP 40/149, m 252d (Michaelmas term 1304) [AALT image 1449]; *William son of Reginald of Scotton and his wife Emma v Peter Jonel of Lincoln*: CP 40/161, m 147d (Michaelmas term 1306) [AALT image 1487]; *Master John of Maldon v William de Boneville*: CP 40/163, m 186d (Easter term 1307) [AALT image 1041].

[35] *Warin son of Gerard de Lisle v Roger Page of Marlborough*: CP 40/109, m 110 (Trinity term 1295) [AALT image 0230].

[36] *John Othetoun v Adam of Hepworth and his wife Alice and Walter of Lockwood and his wife Parnel and Adam their son*: CP 40/149, m 151d (Michaelmas term 1304) [AALT image 1242]; *Roger Bendiste v Geoffrey son of Thomas of Brumstead*: CP 40/158, m 99d (Hilary term 1306) [AALT image 0875]. Another case may be *Walter of Amersham v Humphrey de Bohun earl of Hereford*: CP 40/53, m 43 (Easter term 1284) [AALT image 7980], where the writ as enrolled says the grantor held of the claimant for life but not that the claimant had granted him his life estate.

[37] CP 40/131, m 177d [AALT image 1191] (reported in BL Add MS 37657, fos 49r–v; BL Add MS 31826, fo 87r); CP 40/141, m 16 [AALT image 0040].

[38] CP 40/127, m 61 [AALT image 0133].

who was now being given a remedy. But the case was a reasonably strong one, since it was only the remainderman who had any interest in the land after the current tenant for life, not the original grantor. The only reason for hesitation might have been that, if the two tenants for life were brothers (as seems possible), Robert would also have been his uncle's heir after his death as well as his own father's. Allowing him to bring an action during his uncle's lifetime would in effect have allowed him to avoid being barred by his uncle's warranty.

A similar form of settlement and a similar claimant, another remainderman, brought a second such case in Hilary term 1307 for a messuage in High Wycombe in Buckinghamshire (*Roger de la Grene of Wycombe v Bernard East of Rickmansworth*).[39] Roger claimed the messuage as having been granted by Geoffrey of Desborough to Emma the wife of John de la Grene and her husband John jointly for their lives with a remainder over in fee simple to the right heirs of John, and as having been alienated in fee by Emma to the tenant Bernard (evidently after John's death) 'contrary to the terms of our statute of Gloucester'. He claimed not as heir to the grantor, but as the brother and heir of John de la Grene. Again, his writ talked of the property as 'reverting' to Roger under the terms of the statute. The tenant, Bernard, defaulted. Emma herself then appeared and asked to be allowed to defend her title to the land and was admitted to do so. Only the reports of the case explain why. She had recently recovered the land from Bernard through a successful action brought by a writ of entry *causa matrimonii prelocuti* because her alienation to Bernard had been part of the arrangements preceding a second marriage which had not then taken place. Emma's defence to the claim was that at the time of the alienation she was not just a life tenant but had possessed fee and free tenement in the land. The claimant denied this and issue was joined. Only the reporter adds an explanation. The messuage lay in a borough where tenants had a right of devise. Her late husband had left her a fee simple interest in the messuage.

In a third such case heard in Trinity term the same year (*Robert of Bootton v Ralph of Skeyton*) the claimant sought seven messuages, 28 acres of arable, six acres of meadow, six acres of pasture and the moiety of a mill at Bootton, Witchingham and Reepham in Norfolk as having been granted by Eborard of Thorton to John of Baldeswell and his wife Agnes for their lives, with a remainder over in fee simple to John's heirs. This holding had, he alleged, been alienated in fee by Agnes after the death of John to Richard of Skeyton, probably the father of the current tenant.[40] He asserted that it ought now to 'revert' to Robert, as John's brother and heir, by virtue of the alienation contrary to the terms of the statute. Robert was, of course, a remainderman rather than a reversioner. Ralph, the tenant, claimed to be under age and the case stood over until his age.

In each of these three cases, Chancery had moved significantly beyond the protection of the reversioner after a life estate to the protection of the interests of a remainderman under a settlement. It could, however, be argued these three claimants all belonged to the class of particularly deserving remainderman, for their remainder was in fee simple, and they were claiming as the heirs of named individuals who were themselves already dead by the time the litigation was brought. But a further step was taken by Chancery

[39] CP 40/162, m 48 [AALT image 0098]. Reported in (1307) YB 33–35 Edw I, RS pp 399–401; BL Hargrave MS 375, fo 175v.

[40] CP 40/164, m 125 [AALT image 0254].

in issuing the writ used in a case pleaded in Hilary term 1307, *Lawrence de St Michael junior v Alice widow of Walter de Beauchamp*.[41] The property at stake in this case was an extensive holding of two carucates of arable, 28 acres of woodland and a rent of 65 shillings and two hens plus three-quarters of a messuage at [East] Wickham, Bexley, Lessness and Woolwich in north-west Kent. The claimant asserted that this land had been settled by William of Stapleton on Lawrence de St Michael senior and his (late) wife Eve for their lives with a remainder over to the heirs of their bodies under a final concord made in the Common Bench while Thomas Weyland was its Chief Justice. The final concord shows that it was indeed in these terms but also with a final remainder over in fee simple to Lawrence's own right heirs and that it had been made at the quindene of Easter 1280.[42] Lawrence junior asserted that this property ought now to 'remain' to him (as the son and heir of his father Lawrence senior, by Eve) because his father (Lawrence senior) had granted the property to Robert Burnel (the late Bishop of Bath and Wells and king's Chancellor) 'contrary to the terms of the statute made by the common counsel of the realm on such grants', a reference to the Statute of Gloucester. As recorded on the plea roll, the tenant excepted to the writ on the grounds that there was no warrant in the statute for it. The claimant called in aid the Statute of Westminster II as extending the remit of the Statute of Gloucester to similar cases and claimed that Chancery had given him the writ on the basis of that clause 'because his case was sufficiently in agreement with the case expressed in the statute of Gloucester' (*eo quod casus suus sufficienter concordans est casui in predicto statuto Glouc' expresso*). The Court looked at the writ and the statutes and decided for several reasons not further explained *(videtur curie pluribus racionibus*) that the writ was not warranted by the statute and therefore dismissed the case. The reports are again helpful in explaining more clearly what went on, both in the pleading of the case and in the final judgment.[43] They show that the claimant tried to cut off argument on the writ on the grounds that the tenant had previously requested a view of the land and had thereby affirmed the form of the writ. This argument was, however, rejected by Bereford J on the grounds that the exception was in effect an exception to the action, not just to the form of the writ, and so could still be made after a request for the view. They also show that serjeant Harle, arguing for the claimant, made the claim that Lawrence senior was in effect a tenant for life, with the fee and right resting in the claimant. This would indeed have made this case close to those where the statutory action had already been accepted as applying. This conceptualisation was, however, explicitly rejected by Bereford. He saw the claimant as being no more than a remainderman under the entail, without any current vested interest in the fee and right. The printed report suggests that it was because the statute did not extend to the protection of rights under entails that the writ was rejected. A second, unprinted report, however, suggests that the Court ultimately adopted two other related reasons for quashing the writ. The claimant's own writ showed him claiming as a remainderman and the statute (even as extended by Westminster II) only gave an action to reversioners, not to remaindermen. As we have seen, the Court itself had not been quite consistent about this and in another case in

[41] CP 40/162, m 77d [AALT image 0926].
[42] CP 25/1/98/62, no 153 [AALT image 0394].
[43] BL Add MS 5925, fos 119v–120r [printed in (1307) YB 33–35 Edw I, RS pp 427–29]; (ii) BL Hargrave MS 375, fo 176r.

the same term and in the case heard in Trinity term 1307 had in fact accepted actions brought by remaindermen. The second was that the writ described Lawrence junior as the son and heir of Lawrence senior (and Eve), though Lawrence senior was still alive and no man could be the heir of another in their own lifetime. Chancery had gone too far for the Common Bench. The Court was happy enough to accept actions based on the statutory provisions covering not just alienations in fee by doweresses but also by other kinds of life tenant. It would even at a pinch accept actions brought by remaindermen who possessed a vested fee simple interest in the remainder on alienations made by sole surviving tenants for life. But it drew the line at accepting an action brought by a remainderman where the claimant's interest was only a possibility, not a vested remainder (as it was bound to remain until his father died), and where the remainder was in fee tail, not fee simple. No one seems to have mentioned the fact that the alienation to Burnel in 1283 had taken the form of a second final concord or argued that this barred all claims not then registered within a year and a day.[44]

In Hilary term 1310 the Court (now presided over by William Bereford as Chief Justice) was again faced with an action purportedly based on statute (implicitly, but not explicitly, the Statute of Gloucester) brought by a remainderman.[45] Stephen son of John Devereux (through his guardian) was claiming the Herefordshire manor of Lyonshall (with some fairly substantial exceptions) against William Touchet as that which had been given by Robert Burnel to William Devereux and his wife Lucy for their lives, and which ought to 'remain' to the same Stephen after the alienation in fee made by William and Lucy to Walter [de Langton], Bishop of Coventry and Lichfield. As enrolled, the tenant immediately objected to the claim to a remainder on the grounds that there was no statutory authority for such a writ. The Court agreed and dismissed the case. Again, the reports are more helpful (if in part also clearly inaccurate). They show that the form of the settlement gave the manor to William and Lucy for their lives, with a remainder over to John Devereux (Stephen's father and perhaps their son) and his heirs. They seem also to show that the writ was quashed because it was brought by a remainderman. This remainderman, however, unlike the remainderman in the 1307 case, had an interest that had already vested, since his father was already dead. The Court had now apparently moved on from rejecting a particular kind of remainderman to rejecting actions brought by remaindermen in general. We also learn of a sequel, which is also a prequel to the scene in the reports of the case of the following term with which this paper started. One of the two reports of this case tells us that the claimant subsequently made a complaint to Chancery about having had his writ quashed. The clerks of Chancery asked Bereford to come to Chancery to explain his action in quashing the writ. When he appeared, he told them that the writ was not maintainable by statute. Barlby responded that the statute had given a remedy for the alienation of the doweress and Westminster II had authorised the provision of a like remedy in a like case. Bereford apparently said that he would uphold the remedy if they made a suitable writ.

It is against this context, then, that we must place the Easter 1310 case with which this paper began. The Common Bench had been alerted by the 1307 case of

[44] For the fine see CP 25/1/98/63, no 197 [AALT image 0446].
[45] *Devereux v Tuchet* in Maitland (n 3) 16–19.

St Michael v Beauchamp to the fact that Chancery was willing to offer litigants writs purporting to be based on the Statute of Gloucester but in fact going far beyond not just the wording, but also perhaps even the spirit, of that statute. In general principle it was clearly right that remedies purporting to be based on the terms of a statute should in fact be supported by the actual wording of the statute, and those based on an extension by analogy should mention that fact (however indirectly) in their formulas. But in insisting that Chancery make clear through the wording of the writ that the remedy being offered was one based on an extension of the statute by analogy the Court was perhaps trying to draw some sort of line. There can have been little chance that the courts would now repudiate the remedies for reversioners on alienations by curtesy tenants and tenants for life by grant that had been allowed for so long. But insistence on the new form of words may perhaps have been intended to ensure that there would now be more scrutiny of the more questionable attempts to extend the remedy beyond these more obviously acceptable cases.

IV. Conclusions

The history of remedies based on chapter 7 of the Statute of Gloucester (1278) is a curious one. The makers of the 1278 statute were evidently much concerned with controlling the use and abuse of their rights by life tenants. Chapter 5 of the statute dealt with the commission of waste and introduced the new penalty of a loss of the property wasted and triple damages for waste committed by tenants for life. It made it clear that the new rules were to apply to curtesy tenants (who came first on the list), other tenants for life (evidently in this context tenants for life by grant) and doweresses (as well as tenants for a term of years), and not just to one of those categories of life tenant. Chapter 3 of the statute dealt with alienations made by members of one of the two groups to whom the statutory remedy came to be extended, tenants in curtesy, but only apparently in the context of remedies brought after their deaths by the heirs of their late wives, making it clear that even if the wife's heir was the husband's heir as well he or she was not to be barred from bringing his assize of mort d'ancestor (or his *sur cui in vita)* for his mother's land except to the extent he had inherited assets from the husband. So the fact that chapter 7 dealt only with alienations made by the doweress looks to be not so much a drafting oversight by draftsmen unable to think beyond the single case of a single set of circumstances which had given rise to the demand for legislation as a quite deliberate choice on the part of the drafters to confine themselves to this one particular case and this particular type of life tenant, and not to extend the new remedy to cover other types of life tenant as well. Despite this, as has been seen, Chancery showed itself willing within four years of the enactment of the statute to extend the availability of the statutory remedy beyond the specific case covered by the statute, first to the tenant for life by grant, and then to the tenant in curtesy. As has been seen, that extension was challenged initially and occasionally thereafter by those against whom the extended remedies were brought precisely on the grounds that the statute did not authorise them, but the courts did not uphold such challenges. After 1285 claimants could (and did) add an argument from the provisions of Westminster II, chapter 24, allowing 'similar remedies' in similar cases, to their repertoire of arguments, even if the statute did not specifically mention the possibility of doing anything other than extending existing common law remedies, not those created by statute. The end result was an ironic one. During the years between 1278–1307 significantly more actions were purportedly brought under the Statute of Gloucester (or implicitly brought under its provisions) that were in fact outside the scope of the statute than those which it had authorised: a total of 47 actions brought by reversioners against the alienees of tenants for life (or possibly in some cases tenants in tail) and 16 actions against the alienees of curtesy tenants, as against only 16 actions against the alienees of doweresses, the actions warranted by the statute. By the end of the thirteenth century Chancery was even beginning to issue writs extending the statutory remedy to protect the interests of fee simple remaindermen after life tenants and to give them an immediate remedy on any purported alienation in fee. It was only when Chancery went still further and allowed a fee tail remainderman whose estate had not yet vested to bring such an action on an alienation by the life tenant in possession in 1307 that the courts finally called a halt to the extension of the statutory remedy, and having done this once did it again in 1310 even where the remainder was (apparently) in fee simple and vested. The greater scrutiny these cases induced of actions purportedly based on the statute then seems to have led to the decision that even those actions long allowed but not strictly speaking warranted by the statute should in future be correctly described as based on the statute provided 'in like case' not the 'statute provided in this case'. Only a single word differed in the Latin, but honour was satisfied and a bright line drawn that perhaps made it more difficult for Chancery to smudge it thereafter.

7

John Selden's Commonplace-Book (1608)

JOHN BAKER

Professor Ibbetson, while being the foremost representative of the surviving English Civilians, has at the same time achieved well-deserved renown as a historian of the common law. The only English legal historian who stands comparison with him in this double respect is John Selden (1584–1654). So much has been written about Selden – there have been nine books about him in the last 35 years – that it might seem superfluous to add to the literature. But there is one piece of evidence about Selden which has been overlooked, thanks to the unhelpful catalogue of the Harleian manuscripts – which also managed to draw a curtain around Coke's autograph notebooks for two centuries. Harleian MS 1674 has the eighteenth-century binder's title 'Law Common Places' and was described by Humphrey Wanley (1672–1726) as: 'A Paper-book in small fol. wherein are written, by some Person of Learning, a Collection of Law Common-Place, in Order Alphabetical; perhaps worthy the Perusal of those who are Students of our Law'. No doubt Wanley was ahead of his time in giving even as much information as that; but his description, printed in the 1759 catalogue[1] and from thence copied verbatim into the 1808 catalogue,[2] has never been altered. Wanley and his successors as custodians of the collection never showed much interest in legal materials, and it has to be admitted that the 'Students of our Law' – with the notable exception of Professor Ibbetson – have been almost equally remiss in not delving more frequently into the manuscripts to find out which ones are in fact worthy of their perusal.

The manuscript may be dated with reasonable confidence from the contents, which are so extensive as to suggest that nothing available to the compiler was omitted. The latest printed sources cited are Cowell's *Institutiones Juris Anglicani* (Cambridge, 1605) (passim) and his *Interpreter* (Cambridge, 1607) (fos 113, 144, 148, 149v); the sixth volume of Coke's *Reports* (London, 1607), which is cited 13 times (fos 35, 54, 63, 75, 81, 85, 89v, 121, 124, 143v, 144v, 146, 174v), and the seventh volume (1608), which is cited only twice (fos 46, 61). The latest statutes cited are from 1605 (fos 77, 149), and the latest cases cited from life are a Common Pleas case of Easter term 1605,[3] cited three times

[1] H Wanley and others, *Catalogue of the Harleian Collection of Manuscripts*, vol 1 (London, 1759) no 1674.

[2] *A Catalogue of the Harleian Manuscripts in the British Museum*, vol 2 (London, 1808) 170. This is the catalogue still in use.

[3] The modern reports without citations, perhaps attributable to Selden himself, seem to begin in 1603 (fo 59). For manuscript reports which he is known to have owned, see n 36 below.

(fos 92v, 93v, 101) and *Calvin's Case* (1608) (fo 94v).[4] The book would therefore seem to date from around 1608. Its history in the half-century after 1654 is unknown; but it came into the extensive collection of Colonel Henry Worsley (1672–1740), who gave it to Harley some time before 1713.[5] There is no indication of authorship in the manuscript, or in the catalogues; but Wanley was guilty of severe understatement in acknowledging it as the work of 'some Person of Learning'. The range of sources, outlined below, points to a person of most uncommon learning. Indeed, it points inexorably to John Selden, who in 1608 was aged 24 and still a student below the bar. Probably no other common lawyer of the time could have compiled such a book.[6] Only Selden would have mixed Roman law, modern European law and common law, cited histories both English and foreign, referred to manuscripts in the Inner Temple, and written here and there in Hebrew, Greek and Anglo-Saxon characters. In any case the hand does, indeed, seem to be Selden's. The Greek and Latin are accomplished enough, but the Hebrew – used only occasionally, once for biblical references,[7] and several times to encode the surnames of manuscript owners[8] – is imperfectly written. It seems that the future 'chief rabbi of England' had not yet begun to acquire much proficiency as a Hebraist.[9] But the marvel is that any Hebrew letters at all should be seen in a common lawyer's notebook.[10]

The catalogue description of the manuscript as a 'commonplace' is followed here, but only for want of a better word. It does not adequately reflect its uniqueness. Legal commonplace-books are, on the whole, a rather dull genre. The dullest are arranged by traditional titles, say from 'Account' to 'Withernam', and assemble under each title a varying quantity of relevant references to the yearbooks, Dyer and Plowden, and sometimes the student treatises by Littleton and Perkins and Fitzherbert's *Novel Natura Brevium*; in the seventeenth century they may include later reports as well, especially Coke's. In their lowliest manifestations they contain nothing of value to the legal historian, other than to show the extent of the compilers' studies; and most compilers are anonymous. The more interesting (and much less common) examples of the genre include references to unpublished reports, lectures in the inns of court, and personal communications. Some will even consist entirely or mostly of unpublished material, and may be considered as abridged original reports arranged alphabetically. To a casual observer, such as the eighteenth-century cataloguer, MS Harley 1674 might well have appeared to be a perfectly ordinary 'Law Common-Place'. It is arranged more or less alphabetically, with recognisable titles from 'Admesurement de Pasture' to 'Wast'.[11] Wanley did not know

[4] Coke's report was printed in 1608: *Calvin's Case* (1608) 7 Co Rep 1.

[5] CE Wright, *Fontes Harleiani* (London, British Museum, 1972) 399, 561. Wright gave Worlsey's dates as 1675–1747.

[6] The only other common-law work comparable for its range, albeit written a few decades later, was Edward Littleton's *The Newe Littleton* (Harvard Law School MS 2106), as to which see JH Baker, *Collected Papers on English Legal History*, vol 2 (Cambridge, Cambridge University Press, 2013) 768–81. Littleton was admitted to the Inner Temple in 1608 and became well known to Selden.

[7] Under 'Dismes' (fo 110v), with a note on Hebrew dating.

[8] The names appear to be Broughton (fos 87, 151; identified at n 27 below), Cotton (fo 91) and probably Prideaux (fos 89v, 164; see n 18 below). The last was a member of Clifford's Inn and owned a 'M.S. Statutorum et Hengham'. Why Selden used Hebrew to encrypt these names is a mystery, especially since Broughton is written in full on fo 90v. Professor Anna Sapir-Abulafia provided invaluable assistance with the decipherment.

[9] J Rosenblatt, *Renaissance England's Chief Rabbi: John Selden* (Oxford, Oxford University Press, 2006).

[10] There are printed Hebrew characters in Selden's *Jani Anglorum Facies Altera* (London, 1610).

[11] The order is not exact: eg, 'Accompt' follows 'Auncien demesne'. There is a short note on 'Leges' on fo 1.

enough to decide for sure whether it was even worth perusal by those acquainted with the law. Closer attention would have revealed a few unusual headings such as 'Chose in Action', 'Property' and 'Possession', suggestive of juristic thinking, while a nascent interest in public law might be discerned in headings such as 'Praemunire' and 'Praerogative' (both disappointingly brief) and the somewhat fuller 'Quinzin, Subsidy & Custom' (with divisions on 'Marchaunts' and 'Admiralty'). Even 'Testaments' is not a title found in most commonplace-books, since the learning was mostly Civilian. But these are only slight enlargements of the usual range of headings and fall largely within the common law tradition. Upon still further perusal, however, MS Harley 1674 proves to be remarkably different from any other legal commonplace.

In the first place, it includes numerous cases and materials from an earlier period than those usually found in student commonplace-books. Cases from the time of Edward I and Edward II, even when taken from Fitzherbert's *Abridgment*, were not ordinary student fare. Selden not only cited such cases from the abridgments but also (as will be shown below) from manuscripts. His interest in legal history is further shown by the many citations to *Glanvill* and *Bracton*, occasional recourse to *Britton and Novae Narrationes*, and acquaintance with the four unpublished medieval treatises *Hengham Magna* and *Parva*,[12] *Fleta* (presumably the manuscript in Sir Robert Cotton's library[13]) and the *Mirror of Justices* (fos 107, 150v),[14] not to mention occasional pieces of Anglo-Saxon law – written in Anglo-Saxon characters – taken from William Lambarde's *Archaionomia* (London, 1568).[15] Record sources appear also, particularly the rolls of parliament,[16] the patent and close rolls, and the plea rolls – all, of course, unprinted in 1608. The historical material was approached critically: for example, Selden was already aware of differences between the Magna Carta granted by King John (as reported by Matthew Paris), 'nostre Magna Charta' (that is, the charter of 1225), and the law as stated in *Bracton*, concerning debts owing to Jews (fo 22v), and he also noted a passage from the 1215 charter,[17] omitted in 1225, found in a manuscript belonging to a student of Clifford's Inn (fo 89v).[18] In discussing

[12] Selden published it in 1616 from a manuscript owned by Francis Tate (d 1616) of the Middle Temple. But Selden may have been acquainted first with the manuscript belonging to Robert Broughton of the Inner Temple: n 29 below.

[13] Selden produced the first printed edition of this also, but not until 1647.

[14] The only medieval text is thought to be that given to Corpus Christi College, Cambridge, by Matthew Parker. But Sir Edward Coke had a transcript before 1613, and Francis Tate (see n 12 above) had another: WJ Whitaker (ed), *The Mirror of Justices* (London, Selden Society, 1895) ix–xi. Doubtless other copies were made: eg, MS Harley 314 was transcribed by Simonds D'Ewes in 1624.

[15] Selden drew particular attention to this in *Janus Anglorum*, 50, adding the hope that it would produce the harvest it deserved ('Sua digni suo sit messis').

[16] Most of the citations are simply by year, but cp fo 91: 'in les rolls del parliamentes que fuerunt in le tower del an. 30 Ed. 1 [Parl. Westm. octab. Sancti Joh. Baptist. ann. Ed. 1. 30. rotul. 2. extract. è lib. rubeo Rob. {Cotton *in Hebrew characters*} militis]' (concerning Margaret Painell's claim to dower). The words in square brackets are in the margin.

[17] The text is c 27 of the 1215 charter, as now numbered. Selden linked it with Magna Carta 1225, c 18, which he had transcribed first, continuing 'mes in un manuscript jeo ay view ceux parolx …', without here explicitly identifying the manuscript text as part of John's charter.

[18] 'M.S. magistri [Prideaux] Cliff. hosp. et Ed. H. Int. Temp.' The first name is represented by two imperfectly written Hebrew characters which cannot be deciphered with complete certainty. The most likely reading (Prideaux) is corroborated if 'Ed. H.' is Edmund Hampden (d 1627), admitted to the Inner Temple in 1600 at the instance of Master [Edmund] Prideaux (d 1628). Edmund Prideaux's eldest son Peter was admitted to the

an apparent divergence between *Glanvill* and the decretals on the subject of divorce, Selden pointed out that *Glanvill* was written in the time of Henry II, whereas (according to Wesenbeck) Gratian was earlier, having been first written in 1109 and then revised by Irnerius in 1150 (fo 91v). The date of *Glanvill* also showed that Polydore Vergil was wrong in tracing the commencement of wardship to the time of Henry III; indeed, according to Buchanan, there was an example in Scotland in the year 1000, during the reign of Malcolm II (fo 119).

Such old sources were all made relevant to the legal topic in hand. The headings were not specially chosen for historical purposes, though many of the entries explored origins and revealed parallels. As with Coke and Hale, legal history was not for Selden a separate branch of learning but a necessary and integral part of legal scholarship. It is true that much of the old common law had become obsolete, but very little of it had been extirpated by statute, and so a profoundly learned lawyer still had to know about topics such as darrein presentment (fo 147v)[19] and frankmarriage (fo 160). If Selden omitted subjects of greater current importance, such as *indebitatus assumpsit*, uses,[20] and perpetuities, this was perfectly normal among his contemporaries. Such matters were to be found in modern law reports, which circulated widely in manuscript, but not as a rule in commonplace-books with traditional titles.

Another departure from the general run of commonplace-books is in the degree of analysis within each heading.[21] It is not, for the most part, a random gathering of jottings made at different times, but a series of brief essays written coherently. The title 'Action sur le case' (fos 10–15) provides a good example. There are 14 divisions: (1) the writ; (2) misconduct by an office-holder; [2a] things prejudicial to the commonwealth (no action); (3) hindrances to doing something (franchises); (4) things touching freehold (nuisance); (5) nonfeasance; (6) malfeasance and misfeasance; [6a] sales without title; (7) corrupt victuals and warranties (deceit); (8) beasts (*scienter*); (9) innkeepers; (10) vexatious litigation; (11) false protections; (12) misconduct by a bailee; (13) fire; and (14) process in the action. The analysis here is more by factual subject-matter than legal formulae; for instance, *assumpsit* is not treated as a single entity, or even mentioned by name. The treatment is not particularly profound, but it shows a mastery of the older case-law, attempting to explain seeming discrepancies, and is more complete than anything in print in 1608.[22]

Inner Temple in 1608. It seems probable that Peter is the Mr Prideaux of the citation, and that he migrated from Clifford's Inn soon after the time of writing; he was to succeed to his father's baronetcy in 1628. The citation is unusual in indicating dual ownership, but on fo 164 (citing the same passage) the 'Lib. M.S. statutorum et Hengh[am]' is assigned to Prideaux alone (again in Hebrew characters).

[19] Tellingly, perhaps, there is no section on novel disseisin, though there is a page on 'Seisin pur assise' (fo 153v).

[20] There is a heading 'Uses' (fo 179), but it consists only of four lines on usufruct in Roman law.

[21] The first comparable example in print is H Rolle, *Abridgement des Plusieurs Cases* (London, 1668), compiled in the 1620s or 1630s. Henry Rolle, like Edward Littleton, was only five years junior to Selden in the Inner Temple.

[22] There is a brief mention of *Slade's Case*, but the reference is to an obiter dictum rather than the decision. The most probable explanation for the omission of *assumpsit* for money is that in substantive terms it belonged with debt. Oddly, however, there is no heading for either debt or contract.

I. Authorities and Sources Outside the Common Law

Selden's unusually deep interest in the longer term is obvious on almost every page. But even this is not the most remarkable feature of the Harleian manuscript. Besides the massive quantity of references to the yearbooks, abridgments and other English sources mentioned above, there is an extraordinary range of citations reaching way beyond the ambit of the common law. The *Digest* and *Institutes* of Justinian are regularly referred to throughout, with occasional mention of the glosses by Accursius (fo 163) and Bartolus (fos 111, 163, 171). The *Corpus Iuris Canonici* is also cited, though less frequently, with a mention of the gloss by Panormitanus (Nicolò de' Tudeschi) (fo 46v), and there are references to William Lyndwood's *Provinciale* (fos 46v, 90, 116, 146v) and the older general councils. Of modern Civilian authors, there was little from England to be cited. Regular use is made of John Cowell's *Institutes*, which were an attempt at comparative law, by reducing English law to a Roman method, but they are not used uncritically: for instance, on fo 13v Selden criticises Cowell for quoting a passage in *Bracton* without indicating that it was no longer law. There are at least six references to Alberico Gentili's *De Nuptiis* (Hanover, 1601) (fos 46v, 47, 97, 120v, 135v, 161v), but it would be a stretch to count him as English. Henry Swinburne's book on *Testaments* (London, 1590–91) earns at least two references (fos 90, 163). But the most cited jurists are German (Gaill, Mynsinger, Oldendorp and Wesenbeck),[23] followed by the French (Cujas, Duaren, Godefroy, Grégoire, Hotman and Rebuffi).[24] Italy may claim Scipione Gentili (fo 163v) if not also his brother Alberico (above), besides the more ancient Oberto Dall'Orto (fo 1) and the humanists Andrea Alciato (fo 91), Carlo Sigonio (fo 91v) and Lorenzo Valla (fo 163). The customs of Normandy make several appearances,[25] and there are allusions to Scots law[26] and Byzantine law, in the person of Constantine Harmenopoulos (fo 90). As with the English books, these authorities are not merely quoted but engaged with. Vocabulary was crucial: the different meanings of *dos* were a familiar source of difficulty (fo 89), but Selden also noticed that what Wesenbeck called *fidelitas* should be understood in English as homage rather than mere fealty (fo 38). Moreover, the Continental books were cited not merely as an exercise in two-dimensional comparative law, spotting coincidences. This was comparative legal history, driven by a sense that similarities and differences can only be understood by tracing them back to their origins.

Selden's citations are by no means restricted to legal authorities. There are plentiful references to the English medieval chronicles of Matthew Paris (fos 22v, 48, 49, 50, 95v,

[23] Andreas Gaill (d 1587) (fo 163); Joachim Mynsinger (d 1588), *Scholia* (fos 3, 8, 10, 18, 46, 62, 90, 163, 163v, 165v); Johann Oldendorp (d 1567), *Lexicon Juris* (fo 163); Matthaeus Wesenbeck (d 1586), *Oeconomia Iuris* (fos 38, 91v), *Paratitla in Pandectis* (fos 49, 76, 90, 135).

[24] Jacques Cujas (d 1590) (fo 135); François Duaren (d 1559), *De Beneficiis* (fo 116); Gothofredus (Denis Godefroy, d 1622) (fos 54, 135); Petrus Gregorius (Pierre Grégoire, d 1597), *De Beneficiis* (fo 144); François Hotman (d 1590) (fos 37v, 90, 163v); Rebuffus (Pierre Rebuffi, d 1557) (fos 5v, 110).

[25] 'Custom. Norman.' (fo 37v); 'Coust. Norm.' (fos 90, 94); 'Cust. Norm.' (cited on fo 107 to show that tenancy by the curtesy of England was not peculiar to England); 'Graund custom. de Norm.' (fo 113). *cf* 'Cust. gen. d'Artois' (fos 90, 94, 172); 'Cust. gen. de Bretagne' (fo 172).

[26] 'Skene de verb. signif.' [J Skene, *De Verborum Significatione* (Edinburgh, 1597)] (fos 113, 163); *cf* 'Buchan. Scoticarum' (fo 119), which is historical rather than legal. The absence of *Regiam Majestatem* (Edinburgh, 1609) is further confirmation of the date of the manuscript.

149, 164) and Thomas Walsingham (fos 48, 49v, 50, 60, 110, 119, 148), and occasional references to Ranulf Higden (fo 90), Roger de Hoveden (fos 49v, 149) and Florence of Worcester (fo 163v). Modern histories of England are represented by William Camden's *Britannia* [1st edn (London, 1587)] (fos 48, 119) and Polydore Vergil's *Anglica Historia* (Basle, 1555) (fos 50, 89, 95v, 116, 119, 149). Histories from further afield include George Buchanan's *Rerum Scoticarum Historia* [1st edn (Edinburgh, 1582)] (fo 119), Daniel Chytraeus's *Chronologia* [1st edn (Strasbourg, 1563)] (fo 90), Georgius Codinus Curopalata's *De Officiis* [1st edn (Heidelberg, 1588)] (fo 54) and Albert Krantz's *Daniae Historia* (Frankfurt, 1583) (fo 163v). The search for origins did not stop at medieval times. There are scattered quotations from the ancients: Aristotle (fo 171), Caesar (fo 89), Cicero (with Mario Nizolio's observations) (fo 54), Diodorus Siculus (fo 120v), Hesiod (fo 111), Horace (fos 89, 135v), Livy (fo 163v), Pliny (fo 46), Plutarch (fo 89), Seneca (fo 163v), Aelius Spartianus (*Vita Adriani*) (fo 163v), Strabo (fo 89), Suetonius (fo 90), Tacitus (fo 163v), Varro (fo 76) and Virgil (fo 136). Even science has its place in a law notebook written by the young Selden: on questions of conception and gestation, reference is made to Hippocrates (fo 46) and Johannes Schenck's *Observationes Medicae* (Basle, 1584) (fo 46v), and on insanity to Andreas Laurentius [Lars Andersson, *Opera Anatomica* (Hanover, 1595)] (fo 135v).

II. The Broughton Manuscript

In addition to the printed sources mentioned above, Selden made use of a few manuscripts in private possession. The volume containing the *Statuta Vetera* and *Hengham* which belonged to a member of Clifford's Inn, probably Peter Prideaux, has already been mentioned. More frequently cited was a manuscript yearbook of Edward I and the first two years of Edward II belonging to Robert Broughton (d 1617) of the Inner Temple.[27] The same manuscript is cited in Selden's 'Collectanea G', now in the W A Clark Library, Los Angeles (MS 1 H 9 D) as 'e lib. MSS. Rob. Br. et soc. Int. Temp.'[28] Either the same or another manuscript of Broughton's contained cases from the second and third years of Edward III.[29] Robert Broughton was admitted to the Inner Temple a year after Selden, on 30 January 1605, as of Broughton, Shropshire, and called in 1616, but he died the following year without issue.[30] A close association with Selden appears from the verses prefaced to Arthur Hopton's *Concordancy of Yeares* (London, 1616).

[27] 'Mich. 31 Ed. 1. in MSS. Rob. Br.' (fo 151); 'M. 32 Ed. 1. R. B. 27. et Hill. 33 Ed. 1. fol. 43a' (fo 135v); 'H. 33 Ed. 1. c. Prior de Walsingham. R. B.' (fo 87); 'P. 34 Ed. 1. in MSS. R. B.' (fo 145); 'P. 34 E. 1. fol. 11b. R. B.' (fo 147v); 'M. 34 Ed. 1. fo. [...] 4. R. B.' (fo 90); 'P. 35 Ed. 1. R. B.' (fo 91); 'T. 1 Ed. 2. cas. 35. in MSS. R. Broughton de Int. Temp. cas. John Hidan et Will. Hatton. il est enter T. 34 Ed. 1. rot. 203. assisa' (fo 90v); '1 Ed. 2 in MSS. R. [Broughton *in Hebrew characters*]' (fo 87); '2 Ed. 2. R. B.' (fo 51).

[28] JH Baker, *English Legal Manuscripts in the United States of America*, vol 2 (London, Selden Society, 1990) 29, no 241, where it was wrongly conjectured that 'Rob. Br.' might be Robert Brerewood of the Middle Temple.

[29] 'T. 2 Edw. 3. in MSS. lib. Rob. [Broughton *in Hebrew characters*] ex Int. Temp.' (fo 151); '[3 Ed. 3, fo. 21b] in le MSS. R. Br.' (fo 128v); 'In MSS des cases etc. miscell. Rob. Br. Int. Temp.', which seems also to have included a Hengham (fo 35v).

[30] G Grazebrook and JP Rylands (eds), *The Visitation of Shropshire Taken in the Year 1623*, pt 1 (London, Harleian Society, 1889) 87.

He is not otherwise known as a manuscript collector, but he may have inherited the books from his father Richard Broughton (1542–1604), justice of Chester, also of the Inner Temple. Richard is thought to be the 'Mr Broughton' who belonged to the Elizabethan Society of Antiquaries in 1599.

III. Selden's Own Manuscripts

There are several references to manuscript yearbooks without the name of their owner, and since Selden was usually precise with his citations it seems likely that these were his own.[31] If that is so, they show that he was collecting old manuscripts in his 20s. The principal item was a yearbook of 21–32 Edward I, in at least 304 folios,[32] but there seems to have been another with eyres of Edward III.[33] There are also references to a manuscript of Harper's reports, from the time of Queen Elizabeth, which circulated widely but were never published; as was often the case with reports attributed to Harper, the contents here extended beyond Harper's lifetime.[34] Again, the citations are without indication of the manuscript's location.[35]

On the subject of cases, a few further observations may be made. On fo 169 there is a reference to a case of 1594, without citation,[36] and on fo 173v another case of that year cited only from the roll.[37] But other cases cited by year, without mention of manuscripts, are from the printed yearbooks and abridgments. Fitzherbert's abridgment is, as usual, cited simply by the alphabetical title and case-number, without the compiler's name; and where the title is the same as the title in the commonplace, Selden used the abbreviation 'h. t.' (*hoc titulo*) or an 'I' with a tittle (perhaps for *ibi, ibidem*). Several references to 'Cas. incerti temp.' are not to a manuscript but to the central portion of 'Keilwey', edited by John Croke (London, 1602), now identified as readers' cases in the Inner Temple rather than law reports in the usual sense. A reference on fo 171v to

[31] *cf Titles of Honor* (London, 1631) 782 ('21 Ed. 1, fol. 66. in codice meo', the case of Robert of Bentham's ransom). On the end-leaves of *The Historie of Tithes* (London, 1618) is a list of Selden's own manuscripts used in the work, including the eyre of Derby, *Britton* and *Bracton*.

[32] Arranged in sequence, the citations are: '21 Ed. 1. fo. 3b' (fo 46v); '21 E. 1. fol. 11. MSS.' (fo 161v); '21 Ed. 1. fo. 15b. MSS.' (fo 153); '21 E. 1. 15b' (fo 101v); '22 Ed. 1. fol. 27a' (fo 85v); '27 Ed. 1. fo. 155a' (fo 46v); '27 E. 1. fo. 173a' (fo 46v); '27 Ed. 1. fol. 243a' (fo 144); '28 E. 1. 205a' (fo 146v); '30 Ed. 1. fol. 226' (fo 96); '30 Ed. 1. fol. 287b' (fo 150v); '30 Ed. 1. fol. 304' (fo 144); '32 Ed. 1. fol. 283' (fo 33). The text dated 32 Edward I seems to have come between two dated 30 Edward I.

[33] A solitary reference: 'Itin. Ed. 3. fol. 138 … Itin. Pick[ering] fol. 180' (fo 150). See also the reference in 1618 to his own manuscript of the eyre of Derby: n 31 above.

[34] Richard Harper (or Harpur), justice of the Common Pleas, died in 1577. The reports proper seem to end in 1573.

[35] Arranged in sequence, the citations are: 'M. 2 Eliz. Harper. fol. 7a' (fo 97v); '2 Eliz. Harper. fol. [*blank*]' (fo 128v); 'Grayes case Tr. 3 Eliz. in les rep. de J[ustice] Harper [fol. 19a]' (fo 94v); 'T. 3 Eliz. Harp. fo. 19a' (fo 101); 'P. 6 Eliz. in rep. Harp.' (fo 126v); 'P. 6 Eliz. Harper. fol. 25' (fo 158v); '[7 Eliz.] Rep. Harp. fol. 31 et 34' (fo 18); '7 Eliz. Harp. fol. 34' (fo 173v); '15 Eliz. Harp. pag. 64' (fo 171); '23 Eliz. Harp. fol. 89a' (fo 161).

[36] 'Les preignotaryes del commen bank certyfy in bank le roy 36 Eliz. … 36 Eliz. Ba. ro. c. Sr Ralph Heyworth'. Selden owned MS reports of 33–36 and 42 Elizabeth I, 4 and 7 James I, and undated 'Reports of King James and Queene Eliz.' (nos 151, 156, 171, 264, 372–73 and 375 in Selden's library catalogue, Bodleian Library, MS Selden supra 11, fos 1–12; in DM Barratt (ed), (1951) 3 *The Bodleian Library Record* 256–74).

[37] 'M. 36 & 37 Eliz. rot. 25 in B. R. … inter Gray et Paulet', *recte Parlet v Gray* (1594) KB 27/1331, m 25. This was reported privately by Coke but not printed: 138 SS 609.

'21 H. 7. Cr.' is also to Croke's edition of 'Keilwey'. Some cases are cited from the plea rolls, but these are mostly taken from William Rastell's *Colleccion of Entrees* (London, 1566) ('Lib. Intr.'), not always with acknowledgment.[38] Elizabethan cases are otherwise from Plowden, Dyer and 'Cocus'.

IV. The Inner Temple 'Winchedon' Manuscript

Of particular interest to the legal historian, for reasons which will appear presently, are 18 or 19 references to a yearbook in the library of the Inner Temple.[39] It appears from the citations to have been a volume running from 1–12 Edward II, in at least 164 folios, and it was described in 1618 as 'The yeeres of Edward the second at large'.[40] It is also cited in *Titles of Honor* (1614).[41] There was no such volume in the Inner Temple in the early twentieth century, having been lost much earlier,[42] probably in one of the seventeenth-century conflagrations which ravaged the Temple.[43] But it may be identified with the puzzling Winchedon manuscript which Selden discussed in his dissertation on *Fleta*.[44] Maitland was intrigued by Winchedon as possibly the only named yearbook reporter,

[38] An exception, besides that in the previous note, is 'Tr. 13 Eliz. rot. 858' (fo 13v), identifiable as *Bromwich v Newman* (1571) CP 40/1293, m 858d (a *scienter* action).

[39] Arranged in sequence, the citations are: 'Pas. 3 Ed. 2. Int. Temp.' (fo 36v); '4 Ed. 2. in M.S. Int. Temp. fol. 35. pl. 1' (fo 104); '5 Ed. 2. term. Hill. in MSS. Int. Temp.' (fo 27); '5 Ed. 2. Int. Temp. MSS. fol. 60 et 61. c. Thomas de Botoner' (fo 160); '[5 Ed. 2] M.S. Int. Temp. fol. 62. 63' (fo 92); 'Int. Temp. MS. 5 E. 2. fol. 67a' (fo 27); 'H. 7 E. 2. MS. Int. Temp. fol. 107a' (fo 95v); 'Pasch 7 Ed. 2. MSS. Int. Temp. fol. 113b' (fo 110v); '7 Ed. 2. in le Inner Temple Library [fol. 114a] in Labbot de Tewkesburyes case ... Issint auxi in 10 Ed. 2 [fol. 134b] in mesme liver ... et in Trin. 12 Edw. 2. ibid. [fo. 168a]' (fo 38v); '7 Ed. 2. Int. Temp. fol. 114a. c. Abb. de Tewkesb.' (fo 70v); '9 Ed. 2. MS. in biblioth. Inter. Templ. fol. 122b' (fo 14v); 'Tr. 9 Ed. 2. M.S. Int. Temp. fol. 123a' (fo 104v); '9 Ed. 2. MSS. Int. Templi' (fo 120); 'Pasch. 10 Ed. 2. in MS. Int. Temp. fol. 133b. et 12 Ed. 2. ibid. fol. 151' (fo 16v); '10 Ed. 2. fol. 134b' (fo 38v, above); 'Tr. 10 Ed. 2. M.S. In. Temp. fol. 135a' (fo 94v); '10 Ed. 2. M.S. Int. Temp. fol. 137b' (fo 93v); 'Trin. 12 Edw. 2. fol. 168a (fo 38v, above); '12 Ed. 2. Dower 159. M.S. Int. Templ. fol. 163b' (fo 95v); 'P. 12 Ed. 2. MSS. Int. Temp. fol. 164a' (fo 173v). See also '2 Ed. 2. Age 78. in M.S. fol. 25' (fo 21v): the first reference here is to Fitz Abr, *Age*, pl 78, but the second (to 'fol. 25') is almost certainly to the Inner Temple MS.

[40] *The Historie of Tithes* (London, 1618), in the list of authorities on the end-leaves.

[41] *Titles of Honor* (London, 1614) 278 ('Mich. 5. Ed. 2. fol. 66. Ms. Int. Temp. Biblioth.'); and in the 1631 edn, at 689 ('Mich. 5 Ed. 2. Ms. in Biblioth. Int. Temp. fol. 66.').

[42] E Worrall, *Bibliotheca Legum* (London, 1756) 157 says that 'Year Books, by Richard de Winchendon, prior to those above, may be seen in the Inner Temple Library'; this statement remained in the 1777 edition, but was dropped in 1788, presumably because it had been challenged. *cf* M Davies, *Icon Libellorum* (London, 1715) 332: 'Those Law-Annals were first collected together in the present Form, as 'tis thought, by one Richard de Winchedon, a Gentleman of the Long Robe, in Edward the Sixth's [*sic*] time; which very Original *autographon* of that Collector coming to the Possession of Sir John Barker [*sic*] Chancellor of the Exchequer under Phillip and Mary, he gave it to the Library of the Inner-Temple: That Manuscript is so fairly writ that it is easier to be read than the first Editions in Print.' GJ Turner took this as indicating survival in 1715: 26 SS lx, fn 1 (referring to p '322'). However, given the inaccuracies in the passage, it is more likely that the last sentence was an embroidery upon Selden's 'annalibus juridicis ... perpulchre descriptis' rather than eye-witness testimony; there was only one printed edition of Edward II, that of 1678, but Davies seems to have been referring to all the yearbooks.

[43] Plucknett's conjecture: 70 SS lxxii. Maitland, relying on Inderwick, elected for optimism: 20 SS xvi ('there is room for hope that the missing volume will once more come to the surface: *latitat et discurrit*').

[44] J Selden, *Ad Fletam Dissertatio*, appended to *Fleta* (London, 1647) 528–29 (Latin); translated by FW Maitland, 20 SS xvii–xix; and by D Ogg, *Ioannis Selden ad Fletam Dissertatio* (Cambridge, Cambridge University Press, 1925) 149–53.

though it seems possible (*pace* Selden[45]) that he was just the scribe rather than the author. Selden's principal interest, on the other hand, was in the relationship between common lawyers and Roman law in the time of Edward II. The Inner Temple manuscript showed that 'the very words and maxims of the Civil law' were mentioned in lawsuits before the king's justices, occasionally even with references, though Selden admitted that instances of this were 'rarissimae'. Although the deployment of Latin maxims by serjeants in this period was actually more common than he supposed,[46] the explicit citation of texts was almost unknown.

Selden's evidence began with a pair of cases concerning civil (as opposed to natural) death, cited as 'Mich. 12 Ed. 2, fol. 151a', and 'Pasch. 10 Ed. 2, fol. 133b'. These citations in 1647 are in exactly the same format as in the commonplace and refer to the two cases noted together on fo 16v of the latter. The case of 12 Edward II is the Prior of Wallingford's case, which occurs in numerous other manuscripts. The Selden Society edition reads:[47]

> Et fut agard bon quia duplex est mors, scilicet civilis et naturalis, et in hoc casu jure civili mortuus est Prior [*sic*] quia dignitate privatur.[48] Et en ceo plee Berr' alegga coment en un derrein presentment le defendaunt dit qe la persone ne fust pas mort, quasi diceret quod non sit mortuus morte naturali; sic ex parte ista.

Selden's account seems to have convolved this case with that of Easter term, 10 Edward II, which he copied in his commonplace (fo 16v):

> Prior de Lantony port trespas … Uncore tenus nul plea car le deposition est mors civilis et come ils la diont sicome deportatio in insulam quae iure civili est capitis quedam diminutio. Pasch. 10 Ed. 2. [fol. 133b] in cas. praedicti et 12 Ed. 2 [fol. 151] in casu Prioris de Walingford.

The Prior of Llanthony's case is not in the Selden Society edition of this term (vol 54). Indeed, Plucknett could not find any case concerning the prior in nearby terms either and suggested that it was actually the Prior of Lenton's case in 4 Edward II.[49] That is possible, since the subject-matter was similar, but there is no textual affinity between the two reports. The reference to *deportatio in insulam* is certainly Roman, but there is no explicit citation of the text (*Institutes* 1.16.2).

None of the other 16 citations to the Inner Temple manuscript in the commonplace give any hint of its having been suffused with Roman law. It seems that in 1647 Selden made rather too much of it for his purpose, even to the extent of

[45] Selden thought Winchedon was the 'clericus qui librum istum scripsit', and that the reference to Roman law was interpolated by the copyist 'qui codicem descripsit'. But he did not indicate precisely how Winchedon's name appeared in the manuscript. (The ambiguity is discussed by Maitland in 20 SS xix–xxi.) The editors of *Les Reports des Cases Argue & Adjudge in le Temple del' Roy Edward le Second* (London, 1678) read too much into Selden's account and (in the preface) attributed all the yearbooks of Edward II to Winchedon.

[46] See JH Baker, 'Roman Law at the Third University of England' (2002), reprinted in *Collected Papers*, vol 1, 367, 374–75, 391–93; D Seipp, 'Roman Style in the Year Books' in 'Bracton, the Year Books, and the Transformation of Elementary Legal Ideas in the Early Common Law' (1989) 7 *Law and History Review* 195–98.

[47] *Prior of Wallingford v Raundes* (1318) 65 SS 9; CP 40/225, m 18; discussed by Plucknett, 70 SS lxxv–lxxix.

[48] Collas misunderstood this passage, thinking that 'prior' was a description of the plaintiff. Selden himself had read it correctly.

[49] Printed in 9 SS 134–36.

Romanising the names of the parties as Seius and Titius.[50] Selden based his claim on two passages. Since he compared the Inner Temple manuscript with a Lincoln's Inn manuscript,[51] we may trust his observation that the former contained an additional note by the copyist (unusually written in the first person) on *media capitis diminutio*, 'prout memoriae meae occurrit in Jure Civili'. This refers to an exile 'qui deportatur in insulam', suggesting it may have been prompted by the widely circulated earlier report of 10 Edward II. The allusion to Roman law, though vague, is certainly explicit.

Selden's second illustration, 'Pasch. 5 Ed. 2, fol. 73b',[52] seemed to him to show the copyist inserting an explicit citation to the *Regulae Juris* into an argument at the bar, though it was actually a remark by a clerical judge with some knowledge of Roman law.[53] Only one other report of this case is at present known, and it contains no reference to Roman law;[54] but it seems probable that the maxim did occur in the Inner Temple report and that the copyist (again, most unusually) supplied chapter and verse. That was no doubt a unique feature of the Inner Temple manuscript, but almost certainly not of the underlying yearbook text itself, and it was probably an isolated example. If there had been more instances of such citation in the manuscript, Selden would surely have mentioned them. Nevertheless, Plucknett – following Maitland's lead – came to the conclusion that[55]

> the Winchedon manuscript was not in the common law tradition, that it did not circulate among common lawyers (for nobody copied it), and that it was the peculiar product of some learned cloister where it had no bearing upon professional common law studies.

That now seems to be completely mistaken. On the contrary, it seems that in all probability the Inner Temple manuscript was just an ordinary yearbook, in the common law tradition, into which a copyist had interpolated a single citation in the Roman manner, much as a modern editor might insert a footnote, and added an inexact note on Roman law ('as my memory serves me') in another place.[56] There is indeed some evidence – previously unnoticed – that Winchedon was a professional copyist. There survives in the British Library a text of some statutes of Edward II signed with his name, bound up with yearbooks of 13–21 Edward III.[57]

[50] Maitland was surely right in supposing that the Roman names did not occur in the manuscript. They do not occur in any other yearbooks, including the surviving reports of the case in question.

[51] 'Eadem decisio memoratur in annalium ejusdem regis juridicorum MSS. In bibliotheca Hospitii Lincolniensis'.

[52] This is not cited in the commonplace. Nor is Selden's final example, 'Hil. 12 Edw. 2, fol. 156a'. But both citations fit the folio sequence.

[53] Selden attributed the citation to 'Hervaeus actricis advocatus' (counsel for the plaintiff), but Hervey de Staunton, a cleric, was in fact a judge without having been a serjeant. For his knowledge of Roman law, see AJ Horwood (ed), *Year Books 33–35 Edward I* (London, Rolls Series, 1879), 470–71.

[54] Printed from a single manuscript (Cambridge University Library MS Gg.5.20) in 31 SS 217. Bolland's editorial comment on the case (ibid xxxvii–xxxviii) does not mention Selden's version.

[55] 70 SS lxxix.

[56] Maitland said of this, 'his acquaintance with the text of the Institutes was by no means as close as it might have been': 20 SS xxi.

[57] Harley MS 741, fo 8v: 'Explicit totum […] peramat bene potum etc. etc. R. de Wynchedon etc.'

Selden noted that the Winchedon manuscript had been given to the Inner Temple by Sir John Baker (d 1558), a bencher in the time of Henry VIII and under-treasurer of England under Queen Mary.[58] The gift was presumably recorded in an inscription, and it would have had a special interest for Selden, who claimed kinship with the 'knightly Baker family of Kent' and used the same arms as Sir John Baker with a crescent for difference.[59] But what interested him most was the way in which references to Roman law could be woven into the common law, in cases where the two concurred.[60]

V. Conclusion

Harley MS 1674, though written in Selden's own hand, is a fair copy with very few alterations and additions. Earlier notes and drafts must have lain behind it. Perhaps, therefore, it was intended for publication. He had already composed *Analecton Britannicon Libri Duo* (Frankfurt, 1615), which has a preface dated 1607, and would soon publish *Jani Anglorum Facies Altera* (London, 1610), in which he informed the reader that (despite his tender years) he had for a long time had the desire to see the origins of 'our civil law' made clearer (*liquidius*).[61] But the alphabetical manuscript, seemingly completed between those two works, was not to see the light of day for another 415 years. It is unique among legal manuscripts, but that is because Selden – like Ibbetson – was exceptional among his contemporaries. It does not revolutionise our understanding of Selden, since his early immersion in universal historical learning was already apparent from *Janus Anglorum*.[62] That, however, was a search for origins, whereas the manuscript is more concerned with basic legal principles. It shows that, while Selden was becoming a significant historian, he had simultaneously managed to master the whole of the common law and to gain some familiarity with most other legal systems about which information could be had. All this he had achieved within four years of entering the Inner

[58] There is no mention of books in Baker's will (Public Record Office, PCC 11/42A/229). A manuscript yearbook of Henry VI which he owned passed to John Scott, probably Sir John Scott (d 1616), grandson of his daughter Elizabeth, and is now Harley MS 452, fos 146–236 (if not the whole volume).

[59] Baker, *Collected Papers*, vol 2, 755, fn 1. The suggestion there about Selden's grandfather is erroneous. The inscription in Temple Church said Selden was 'ex equestri Bakeriorum in Cantio familia filius e cunis superstitum unicus'. But his maternal grandfather was Thomas Baker (d 1561) of Rustington, Sussex, and any connection with the *equestris familia* must be traced back before him. The crescent indicates a second son.

[60] *cf Historie of Tithes* (1618) 481: 'And heretofore some texts of [the Civil law] have been in our Courts cited; not only as at this day sometimes is done (when the words only of some of the *regulae iuris* is brought into an argument) but the Title and Law, after the Civilians' fashion, hath been remember'd at the Barre, and so afterward exprest in the Report, as I have seen in an example or two in the Mss. yeers of Edward the second. [In Biblioth. Int. Templi]'.

[61] *Janus Anglorum* (1610) sig A4: 'Diu pro mea est aetatula, quod summis primulum habui in votis, uti Prisca Juris nostri Civilis Origo, et processus liquidius constaret'.

[62] He pointed this out himself in the preface, sig A4v: 'Subsecivae aliquot pellegendis Historicis, Chronographus, Palaeologis, absumtae mihi sunt horae exoticis, conterraneis, vetustis, et novitiorum politioribus'.

Temple and well before his call to the bar in 1612. As an Inner Templar with a strong historical curiosity, it was perhaps inevitable that he should have discovered and studied the Winchedon manuscript 40 years before he wrote his perplexing account of it in *Ad Fletam Dissertatio* (1647). What is more notable is that a student manuscript of 1608, which appears on its outside to be merely a 'Collection of Law Common-Place … perhaps worthy the Perusal', is found already to be suffused by Selden's fascination with the interrelationship between the laws of all nations and their histories. It fills a major gap in the recorded history of Selden's life and scholarly formation.

8

Early Seventeenth-Century Common Injunctions

NEIL JONES

In *Hutchins v Martin* (1613) the Court of Chancery was informed that some eight years earlier the plaintiff had gone as the defendant's factor aboard the *Blessings of Plymouth* to the island of St Michael's, entering a bond to make a true account for the venture. The plaintiff arrived at St Michael's with the defendant's merchandise shortly after a proclamation that all Flemish goods being landed should be forfeit. The *Blessings*' cargo – unknown to the plaintiff comprising Flemish goods – was seized and the plaintiff imprisoned, whence 'with great trouble and hazard of his life', he escaped. The defendant nonetheless threatened to put the bond in suit at law, whereupon the plaintiff sought relief in Chancery. The matter being ready for hearing, it appeared that the defendant had arrested the plaintiff in Plymouth upon the bond. It was thereupon ordered that unless cause were shown to the contrary, 'an injunction is awarded against the defendant his counsellors attorneys and solicitors for stay of [his] proceedings at the common law upon the … bond until the matter shall be heard and determined or otherwise ordered by this court'.[1]

While the facts of *Hutchins v Martin* may catch the eye, it is merely one instance of the injunctions against proceedings in another court – known as common injunctions[2] – which appear with great frequency in the early seventeenth-century Chancery register's books. It is very well known that the issuing of common injunctions after judgment at law

[1] C 33/125, fo 18v [IMG_0020a]. All manuscripts are in The National Archives (TNA). Where available, references to TNA manuscripts are accompanied by the relevant image number in the digital archive assembled by Robert C Palmer, Elspeth K Palmer, and Susanne Brand, 'The Anglo-American Legal Tradition', available at aalt.law.uh.edu/, which has much assisted with the research for this chapter. Quotations from manuscript have been rendered into modern spelling and orthography. The year is taken to begin on 1 January. For reasons of space, references are not given for statistical statements, but are available from the author. Unless otherwise indicated, references to parties to litigation as 'plaintiff' and 'defendant' refer to their respective roles in Chancery (as opposed to their roles in a related action at law).

[2] The record refers both to injunctions against actions in another court, and to stays of such actions, between which there seems to have been a procedural distinction. Thus in *Hitch v Parsons* (1617), C 33/133, fo 31 [IMG_0033], it was ordered that one of the defendants be examined upon interrogatories, the defendants' proceedings at law being 'stayed' until further order, provided that 'the plaintiff may take an injunction for that purpose if he please'. See likewise, *Wright v Trapps* (1605), C 33/109, fo 15 [IMG_6782] and *Roe v Check* (1618), C 33/135, fo 37 [IMG_1202]. It seems probable that a stay and an injunction had similar effects, the latter, involving a writ (see eg *Leeds v West* (1605) C 33/109, fo 14 [IMG_6781]), being the more formal.

was at the heart of the controversy between Sir Edward Coke CJKB, and Lord Ellesmere C which flared up in the 1610s.[3] But little is otherwise known about common injunctions in the early seventeenth century. Drawing upon a sample of just over 300 entries concerning common injunctions[4] gathered from the first 50 folios of register's books for 1605–06, 1613–14, 1614–15, 1615–16, 1616–17, 1617–18 and 1626–27,[5] together with a small number of instances gathered from earlier years, this chapter begins to fill the gap.

I. Actions Upon Bonds

In involving proceedings upon a bond, *Hutchins v Martin* was not unusual. Thus of the 31 entries involving common injunctions in the first 50 folios of the register's book for 1613–14 where the nature of the claim at law is stated, 23 (approximately three-quarters) involve a bond or similar obligation (or, occasionally, an action upon an informal debt). A very similar pattern appears in the first 50 folios of most of the other books sampled:[6] early seventeenth-century common injunctions were to a substantial extent an aspect of Chancery relief upon bonds.

An injunction itself might be stayed, as in *Golding v Frith*, C 33/127, fo 29 [IMG_0030], where the injunction, remaining 'in the plaintiff's attorney's hand', was 'stayed', not to be delivered until counsel had been heard. And, as in *Cavendish v Hicks* (1615), C 33/129, fo 43 [IMG_0046], a petition that proceedings at law be 'stayed' might be answered by the award of an injunction. In this chapter the terms 'injunction' and 'stay' are not used interchangeably.

[3] See eg JH Baker, *The Reinvention of Magna Carta 1216–1616* (Cambridge, Cambridge University Press, 2017) ch 10.

[4] Of these a handful concern injunctions against proceedings in non-common law jurisdictions, including the Court of Requests (*Mitchell v Wood* (1615), C 33/129, fo 32 [IMG_0034]) and (probably) the London Mayor's Court (*Saltenstall v Saltenstall* (1614), C 33/127, fo 14 [IMG_0016]), but the vast majority are against actions at law.

[5] Respectively C 33/109, 125, 127, 129, 131, 133 and 151. These years have been chosen as encompassing the Coke–Ellesmere dispute, with outlying samples respectively some years before and after that period. The following figures relate to the number of entries in the first fifty folios of the register's books commencing in the years stated in which it is clear that a common injunction was considered (though not necessarily granted): 1605, 34; 1613, 34; 1614, 44; 1615, 27; 1616, 45; 1617, 41; 1618, 49; 1626, 28. Caution has been exercised in compiling these figures, which may in consequence be an understatement. These figures exclude a small number of injunctions against the enforcement of recognizances or statutes merchant or staple. Such writings obligatory 'were designed to cut out litigation' (AWB Simpson, *A History of the Common Law of Contract: The Rise of the Action of Assumpsit* (Oxford, Oxford University Press, 1975) 130), and injunctions against their enforcement are not directly comparable to the standard form of common injunctions. In each book the first 50 folios also contain entries in which a 'stay' of an action at law was considered (though not necessarily granted), the numbers of which (excluding entries where a stay was awarded as a preliminary to a possible injunction) are: 1605, 10; 1613, 3; 1614, 3; 1615, 3; 1616, 5; 1617, 5; 1618, 3; 1626, 2. In all cases figures are based only upon the information available from the record entries in the sample. Of the entries in the sample, just under 200 show the grant of a common injunction (1605, 18; 1613, 26; 1614, 29; 1615, 21; 1616, 26; 1617, 22; 1618, 28; 1626, 24). In the other entries an injunction was considered but not granted; or, in a handful of cases dissolved as having been improperly obtained. In a substantial proportion of the entries where an injunction was considered but not granted, grant was subject to a condition, for example a master's report that there were grounds for an injunction, or action by one of the parties, such as bringing a sum of money into court. In some of these cases an injunction will probably in due course have been awarded.

[6] On the same basis, the approximate proportion of actions on bonds or similar obligations, or, in a few instances for an informal debt, in the sample for 1605 is 59%; 1614, 70%; 1615, 70%; 1616, 74%; 1617, 77%; 1618, 79%; and 1626, 72%. Given that it is not invariably possible to determine the nature of the claim at law from the entry in the sample, it is in principle possible that the claims at law in entries where the nature of

The grounds for common injunctions against actions upon bonds and other writings obligatory were various. In a number of cases it was a matter of the defendant's misbehaviour.[7] Defendants, for example, not infrequently sought to gain time to proceed at law by seeking a commission to take their answers in the country.[8] Other varieties of misbehaviour also appear. In *Barnard v Hall* (1613),[9] so as to 'prevent the [Chancery's] judgment', the defendant gave warning to the plaintiff to go to trial at law upon the bond in question against the plaintiff's surety, which action was enjoined until the matter was heard and determined or otherwise ordered in Chancery, and in *Lyard v Leigh* (1616)[10] an injunction was granted – if cause were not shown to the contrary – to enjoin proceedings at law against the plaintiff, newly come of age, who had been drawn into bonds and the granting of a lease without receiving what had been promised by the defendants.[11]

Turning to more substantive matters, in a number of cases it was claimed that all money due upon a bond put in suit at law had already been paid.[12] Thus in *Searchfield v Lady Anne Harte* (1618)[13] it was held that since it was 'vehemently to be suspected' that the money due upon the bond in question had been paid by the deceased testator,

the dispute is not clear were disproportionately not upon bonds or similar obligations, though given that significant numbers of claims which clearly did not turn upon bonds or similar obligations are apparent in the sample, such disproportion seems unlikely.

[7] It was possible conversely that misbehaviour by the plaintiff might lead to dissolution of an injunction, as in *Jones v Edwards* (1605), C 33/109, fo 34 [IMG_6803], where, despite making no payment upon a bond, the plaintiff had obtained an injunction against the defendant's proceeding at law while delaying hearing in Chancery, and to prevent special bail upon the bond had had himself sworn an attorney of the Common Pleas, 'which this court misliketh'. The plaintiff was ordered to put in security to abide by the Chancery's order or the defendant was to have liberty to proceed at law.

[8] For other examples see *Southworth v Foxcroft* (1605), C 33/109, fo 50v [IMG_6821a]; *Verchill v Williams* (1613), C 33/125, fo 13 [IMG_0015]; *Suckley v Evett* (1614), C 33/127, fo 49 [IMG_0051] (where the defendant was alleged to intend in the meantime to obtain judgment upon a verdict already obtained); *Wood v Ollver* (1617), C 33/133, fo 11v [IMG_0013a] (where the defendant had obtained a commission to take his answer in the country on condition that he did not in the meantime proceed further at law, but had nevertheless 'stolen down a trial and obtained a verdict'); and *Stebbing v Nunne* (1618), C 33/135, fo 42v [IMG_1208a]. The award of injunctions in such cases was sufficiently frequent to be addressed by the commissioners of the great seal in an order of 26 November 1649, to the effect that to avoid in future the need for a motion to seek an injunction to stay proceedings at law pending taking of the answer in the country, the plaintiff's six clerk was to prepare, without motion, a 'docquett and writ of injunction', 'in the usual form', to be signed by 'the six clerks which are attornies in the cause or their respective deputies', GW Sanders, *Orders of the High Court of Chancery*, vol 1, pt 1 (London, Maxwell & Son, 1845) 220–21.

[9] C 33/125, fo 7 [IMG_0009].

[10] C 33/131, fo 29v [IMG_0031a].

[11] For other instances of common injunctions in the context of misbehaviour by the defendant see, for example, *Whitinge v Morden* (1613), C 33/125, fo 49 [IMG_0051] (verdicts obtained at law by the plaintiffs' attorney in combination with the defendants, without the plaintiffs' knowledge); and *Broade v Eaton* (1618), C 33/134, fo 43v [IMG_1209a] (proceeding at law upon a bond and books of account while evading Chancery process to answer).

[12] In other cases it was alleged that some part of the principal money had been paid, for example, *Speede v Barringer* (1605), C 33/109, fo 9v [IMG_6778a] (petition for an injunction against proceedings at law for a debt 'the most part' of which was already paid referred to a master); and *Chapple v Sherland* (1617), C 33/133, fo 5 [IMG_0007] (alleged that £10 of the principal sum had been paid, and the remaining £7 10s had been tendered; injunction awarded, on condition of the plaintiff bringing £7 10s into court). In *Willson v Blake* (1618) concerning a trader's book debts, Master Hussey reported in favour of an injunction, finding it not reasonable that the defendant should both keep the book and sue at law for 'so small a sum as fifteen pounds', C 38/33, report dated 19 October 1618 (the volume is not foliated or paginated).

[13] C 33/135, fo 21 [IMG_1186].

there was 'no cause in equity' for the defendant's action at law, which was enjoined, subject to the plaintiff bringing a specified sum into court.[14]

Questions arose also of late tender of the principal sum on conditioned bonds. In *Martin v Marke* (1626)[15] the plaintiff sought relief upon such a bond. The defendant, having obtained verdict, sat out a Chancery attachment for not answering while pressing to enter judgment and take execution, 'whereas', the plaintiff argued, 'it appeared upon the … trial that the principal money upon the bond was paid … though after the day of payment limited by the condition of the … bond'. The defendant's proceeding at law was enjoined until the making of a perfect answer and other order taken to the contrary.[16] A similar question arose in *Dodman v Miller* (1613),[17] where the coming of the cause into Chancery had been facilitated by the trial judge. The defendant had obtained a verdict at law upon a bond of £20 'for not payment of £10 at the day'. The *postea*, however, had been

> stayed by Mr Justice Dodderidge before whom the trial passed until he … should be further moved for the same for that though the … money was not paid at the day yet it was paid within a year after and the bond was promised to be delivered up.

Upon this the defendant's further proceeding at law was enjoined until the matter had been heard and determined or otherwise ordered in Chancery.

Such action by a common law judge was not new in 1613. In *Harringe v Styles* (1605)[18] it appeared in Chancery that the plaintiff had made a lease to the defendant upon trust to try title, yet the defendant had brought an action of covenant against the plaintiff on the lease, recovering £225 in damages, which the Chancery was 'clear of opinion is very unjust and unconscionable', and 'for that the court of King's Bench by an order of this term have made stay of judgment to the intent the plaintiff might seek relief in this court', it was ordered that all actions at law by the defendant on the matter should cease, the plaintiff in Chancery paying the defendant £20 for his charges about the trial of title.

Walker v Lumley (1613)[19] provides another example of this approach. The defendant had obtained a verdict upon a bond made 14 years since, but 'the justice of assize

[14] The bringing into court of the principal sum was not invariably required in such cases. In *Wythers v Sheldon* (1614), C 33/127, fo 30v [IMG_00331a], for example, an injunction was awarded without bringing in of the principal, the court being informed that the money due on the bond had been 'paid and satisfied twelve years since'. A common injunction might also be awarded to support an agreement that the sum owed on a bond be paid over a period of time from income from an annuity, as in *Worthington v Worthington* (1605), C 33/109, fo 23v [IMG_6792a], an additional factor in this case being that the parties were brothers.

[15] C 33/151, fo 21v [IMG_0025].

[16] For another example see *Larder v Court* (1614), C 33/127, fo 29v [IMG_0030a], where again it was said that the principal sum had been paid after the date specified, and that the defendant had obtained a verdict. Here, too, an injunction was to be awarded, subject to a master reporting the substantial truth of the allegation. And in *Wilks v Iston* (1616), C 33/131, fo 33v [IMG_0035a] it was alleged that through illness the plaintiff had missed by two weeks one quarterly payment of £5 upon an annuity of £20, upon which the defendant sought to forfeit the bond conditioned for payment of the annuity. An injunction was awarded upon a master's report that the defendant's answer did not allege that payment was more than £2 behind, C 38/26, report dated 22 October 1616 (the volume is not foliated or paginated).

[17] C 33/125, fo 20 [IMG_0022].

[18] C 33/109, fo 29 [IMG_6798].

[19] C 33/125, fo 30v [IMG_0032a].

hath stayed the *postea* … to the end the plaintiff might move [the Chancery] in the mean time for a further stay thereof'. The defendant's proceeding at law was enjoined until he should appear and answer in Chancery and other order should be taken to the contrary. Similarly, in *Haidon v Garrett* (1613),[20] the plaintiff had bought land from Godfrey Garrett, one of the defendants, entering into a bond for the price. A question of title arising at about the time at which it was due, the plaintiff had delayed payment of the price. Payment was subsequently made through Thomas Thetford, another of the defendants, the bond being delivered by Garrett to Thetford who, as the plaintiff thought, had destroyed it. But Thetford, by confederacy with Garrett, had put the bond in suit at law. The matter came for trial before Sir Thomas Fleming CJKB – who in the same year wrote to King James complaining that the Chancery was hearing suits determinable at law[21] – 'before whom the debt was proved to have been paid though not at the just day', upon which 'by order of the Court of King's Bench judgment was stayed to the end the plaintiff might seek relief in' Chancery. It was ordered that a master consider the proceedings at law and Thetford's confession that the money had been paid, and if the information on these points was true, an injunction would be awarded against the Chancery defendants to forbear to call for judgment or take out execution upon the verdict until the matter had been heard and determined or otherwise ordered in Chancery.[22]

In some instances the defendant had obtained a verdict for the penalty on a conditioned bond, and upon the plaintiff bringing the principal sum into court, the defendant's proceeding at law was enjoined until the matter had been heard in Chancery or further order had been taken. Thus in *Smith v Kidd* (1626),[23] an injunction was granted until hearing or further order to prevent entry of judgment following a verdict upon a conditioned bond, provided that the Chancery plaintiff bring into court the principal money due and £5 more for costs. This injunction, as with many others, was granted until further hearing or other order to the contrary, though it was possible for a common injunction against proceedings upon a bond to be final.[24] Thus in *Lincolne v Emes* (1613)[25] the defendants had obtained verdict at law upon a bond, the plaintiff having brought into court the £30 principal debt. An injunction was awarded to stay judgment upon the verdict, the plaintiff to pay the defendants 20 nobles for costs of suit, and the £30 principal debt together with a sum for the forbearing of it. That being done, 'the matter shall take end and all bonds touching and concerning the said money be delivered up unto the … plaintiff'.

[20] C 33/125, fo 19v [IMG_0021a].

[21] JH Baker, *Collected Papers on English Legal History*, vol 1 (Cambridge, Cambridge University Press 2013) 487–88.

[22] A somewhat similar approach was taken by a common law judge in *Garret v Garret* (1605), C 33/109, fo 14v [IMG_6782a] concerning a question of title to land. The matter having come to trial twice already, Anderson CJCP, with the assent of counsel and 'for avoiding of all further controversies', stayed a third trial, directing that a bill be exhibited in Chancery.

[23] C 33/151, fo 19v [IMG_0023a].

[24] It seems to have been thought that common injunctions should not have perpetual effect without a decree or final order in Chancery: in *Good v Merton College, Oxford* (1626), C 33/151, fo 6 [IMG_0009] the college's counsel objected that the injunction in the cause was 'perpetual' and 'without precedent there being no decree or final order made'. The injunction was ordered to stand until hearing next term and other order taken. No entry in the case has been found in the three succeeding terms.

[25] C 33/125, fo 15 [IMG_0017].

In the case of actions at law upon bonds and other writings obligatory, numbers in the sample are sufficient to permit generalisation. Other types of claim at law are significantly less numerous. They include: ejectment;[26] an action to recover possession of mortgaged land;[27] an action of false imprisonment;[28] an action for rent on a lease;[29] trespass to land;[30] actions concerning title to copyhold and freehold land;[31] trespass to recover money;[32] trover;[33] *assumpsit*;[34] covenant;[35] *devastavit*;[36] a writ of dower;[37] and an assize of fresh force.[38] None of these types of claim appears in the sample in substantial numbers.

II. Injunctions after Verdict, and after Judgment

Turning from the basis for the grant of common injunctions, a question arises as to the stage which had been reached in the actions at law which were enjoined. In a significant number of entries in the sample reference is made in broad terms to the defendant prosecuting suit at law. In many, if not most, such cases the common law action probably had yet to reach trial.[39]

In 64[40] instances in the sample the common law action was said to have reached verdict, the injunction being sought to stay the *postea*, or entry of judgment.[41] A straightforward ground for such injunctions arose, as in *Mone v Pleage* (1614),[42] where a defendant had obtained a verdict at law while failing to answer, or delaying answer, in Chancery.[43] More substantively, where the defendant had obtained a verdict for the

[26] *Browne v Earl of Lincoln* (1605), C 33/109, fo 7 [IMG_6776]; *Pearson v Pearson* (1615), C 33/129, fo 27v [IMG_0029a]; *Nicholls v Thomas* (1626), C 33/151, fo 5 [IMG_0008].

[27] *Mynne v Slany* (1626), C 33/151, fo 13 [IMG_0016].

[28] *Jeffs v Jeffs* (1626), C 33/151, fo 16 [IMG_0020].

[29] *Dillingham v Willington* (1626), C 33/151, fo 24v [IMG_0028a].

[30] *Mone v Pleage* (1614), C 33/127 fo 6 [IMG_0007].

[31] See eg *Browne v George* (1605), C 33/109, fo 32 [IMG_6801]; *Leedes v West* (1605), C 33/109, fo 46v [IMG_6817a]; *Shuter v Shuter* (1613), C 33/125, fo 4 [IMG_0006]; *Hodge v Congden* (1615), C 33/129, fo 34 [IMG_0037].

[32] *Bradley v White* (1613), C 33/125, fo 5 [IMG_0007].

[33] See eg *Colston v Foxe* (1614), C 33/127, fo 6v [IMG_0007a].

[34] See eg *Wright v Trapps* (1605), C 33/109, fo 6 [IMG_6782].

[35] See eg *Firme v Barnes* (1614), C 33/127, fo 23 [IMG_0024].

[36] *Goslinge v Goslinge* (1613), C 33/125, fo 9v [IMG_0011a].

[37] *Farwell v Strange* (1613), C 33/125, fo 33v [IMG_0035a].

[38] *Wilkinson v Tusser* (1605), C 33/109, fo 33 [IMG_6802].

[39] It is possible that in some of these cases the action at law had reached verdict or even judgment, though at least in the case of judgment, and perhaps also in that of verdict, it seems probable that this would be reflected in the entry.

[40] 1605, 3; 1613, 12; 1614, 13 (including one special verdict); 1615, 2; 1616, 8; 1617, 10; 1618, 8; 1626, 8. Beyond these instances, in *Arundel v Butler* (1617), C 33/133, fo 45 [IMG_0047], an injunction was granted to stay proceedings at law, including staying entry of judgment upon a verdict, should the defendant proceed to trial, and in *Powle v Cordall* (1618), C 33/135, fo 41v [IMG_1207a], the entry indicates that the defendant had proceeded to trial at law, but does not make clear whether a verdict had been obtained.

[41] In addition, stays were sought after verdict in five entries in the sample.

[42] C 33/127 fo 6 [IMG_0007].

[43] See likewise, *Nashe v Dormer* (1614), C 33/127, fo 17 [IMG_0019], and *Raymond v Triggs* (1614), C 33/127, fo 45v [IMG_0047a] (defendant, being an attorney, alleged to have obtained a verdict by default while failing to answer). Injunctions were also awarded in such circumstances where proceedings at law appear

penalty upon a conditioned bond, an injunction against proceeding upon the verdict may readily have been granted: in such a case it was ordered, for example, in *Saunders v Nashe* (1618)[44] that should a master find the facts to be as alleged, an injunction to stay the *postea* would be awarded without further motion, the *postea* being stayed in the meantime.[45] In contrast, it was arguable that an injunction after verdict should be denied where the remedy at law would be in damages only, as in a covenant action in *Barron v Langham* (1617),[46] such matters being 'not fit to be dealt withall in this court'.[47]

The award or continuation of injunctions against proceeding upon a verdict might be affected by the timing of the Chancery suit in relation to the verdict.[48] Questions of common injunctions arose also where verdicts had been obtained by default, as in *Denington v Eustace* (1616),[49] where the defendant having deliberately failed to proceed at the assizes when the plaintiff was ready, had had the case called again and had obtained verdict by default. A master was ordered to consider the sufficiency of the defendant's answer, an injunction to be awarded should it prove insufficient.[50]

In contrast to the relative frequency with which actions at law were enjoined after verdict but before judgment, the number of instances in the sample in which common injunctions were sought after judgment is small.[51] It is well known that issuing of common injunctions after judgment by Wolsey C had caused tension with the judges.[52] Such injunctions recurred in the time of Elizabeth. Thus in *Sadler v Sowthcote* (1585),[53] the plaintiff sought an injunction to stay the defendant's proceeding in the King's Bench upon a judgment on an obligation given by default long since. The matter was 'long debated', with the eventual order that the plaintiff proceed to a new trial, the original judgment to 'stand and remain in force for doubt of some fraudulent conveyance made since the … judgment by the plaintiff', until the new trial was had. Were the new trial to turn out for the plaintiff, 'then the … plaintiff shall be acquitted as well against the …

not yet to have reached verdict, see, for example, *Whalley v Backhouse* (1617), C 33/133, fo 24v [IMG_0026a]; *Pallmer v Pallmer* (1618), C 33/135, fo 7 [IMG_1172]; *Quirk v Collard* (1626), C 33/151, fo 27 [IMG_0031].

[44] C 33/135, fo 6v [IMG_1171a].

[45] The question of an injunction after verdict might arise also where the plaintiff claimed to have paid the principal sum due on a conditioned bond, as in *Seymor v Apprice* (1618), C 33/135, fo 36v [IMG_1201a], where an action on a bond had been 'let fall', it becoming apparent that the principal sum had been paid. The question of an injunction arose through creditors of the defendant now suing upon the bond in the defendant's name, the defendant having 'fallen into decay and departed the kingdom'.

[46] C 33/133, fo 3 [IMG_0005].

[47] It is possible that in considering the award of an injunction the Chancery would attach some weight to a verdict obtained on a point of title to land. In *Leedes v West* (1605), C 33/109, fo 46v [IMG_6817a], the defendant denying certain allegations in the bill, and because 'the defendant hath had a verdict at the common law in affirmance of his title' to certain copyhold land, the injunction sought by the plaintiff was stayed.

[48] See eg *Vallentyne v Bower* (1614), C 33/127, fo 45 [IMG_0047] (bill in Chancery not exhibited until after verdict at law, injunction against proceeding upon the verdict dissolved).

[49] C 33/131, fo 24v [IMG_0026a].

[50] For further examples of consideration of an injunction in the case of a verdict by default see *Raymond v Triggs* (1614), C 33/127, fo 45v [IMG_0047a], and *Suckley v Evett* (1614), C 33/127, fo 49 [IMG_0051]. For Elizabethan examples concerning judgment by default see text at nn 53–54, below.

[51] In some cases an injunction was awarded against proceedings at law before judgment, while providing that if judgment were obtained no execution should be taken out upon it, for example, *Stransham v Ower* (1615), C 33/129, fo 7v [IMG_0009a], C 38/23, report dated 6 November 1615 (the volume is not foliated or paginated); and *Roe v Check* (1618), C 33/135, fo 37 [IMG_1202].

[52] JA Guy, *The Public Career of Sir Thomas More* (Brighton, Harvester Press, 1980) 86–87.

[53] C 33/71, fo 11v [IMG_0013a], fo 50v [IMG_0052a].

first judgment as from the last trial and judgment thereupon to be had', but should it go the other way, the original judgment 'shall stand in force'. Rather than enjoining execution upon the original judgment, Chancery's order sought to cure any defect in it by having the matter reconsidered at law.[54]

In contrast, in *Harvie v Smith* (1605),[55] an injunction had been granted for stay of the defendants' proceeding upon any action at law concerning the lands in question, whereupon the court was informed that the defendants had already recovered some part of the land, and had had judgment and execution, by virtue of which they were possessed. It was ordered that the injunction should not affect any possession so obtained, but should stand in force in respect of all other the land in question.

Harvie v Smith aside, the entries in the sample in 1605 show two injunctions after judgment at law, both of which were subsequently dissolved. In *Parker v Grantham*[56] an injunction had been awarded for stay of execution of a judgment[57] until a master had reported. The plaintiff, failing to attend the master, brought a writ of error upon the judgment, and ceased to prosecute his suit in Chancery. The injunction was dissolved. In *Countess of Rutland v Dean and Chapter of the Church of Christ, Oxford*,[58] following a master's report, it was ordered that the injunction against execution of a judgment be dissolved and the matter dismissed. The defendants had previously been licensed to proceed to trial at law, but not to judgment 'without the special licence and order of this court'. Such licence had been granted, in part at least on the basis that the dean of Christ Church was shortly to be preferred as bishop of 'Colchester',[59] and should such preferment occur before judgment, the 'trial would be lost'.[60]

The entries in the sample in 1613 show no injunction issued after judgment at law. Those in the sample in 1614 show two such injunctions, one granted by assent of the parties and the other dissolved.[61] In *Page v Foxwell*[62] the defendant had obtained judgment upon a bond with a *cessat executio* until the first day of the present term, and as he 'did now assent that no execution should be taken forth till the cause should receive a

[54] The plaintiff was successively represented in Chancery by Serjeant Fenner and Mr Yelverton, both future justices of the King's Bench. The meaning of the plaintiff being 'acquitted' against the original judgment is unclear. It might perhaps be read to extend to a claim to act against the judgment itself, though it may refer only to an injunction against execution of the original judgment as had first been requested. For another instance in the same year of consideration of an injunction after judgment by default see *Pyke v Mychell* (1585), C 33/71, fo 13 [IMG_0015].

[55] C 33/109, fo 18 [IMG_6787].

[56] C 33/109, fo 31v [IMG_6800a].

[57] The entry in the sample refers simply to 'execution'. That this was execution upon a judgment at law is confirmed by an earlier entry in the case, C 33/107, fo 144v [IMG_5168a].

[58] C 33/109, fo 40v [IMG_6810a].

[59] This appears to be an error for Gloucester. Thomas Ravis, dean of Christ Church, was consecrated bishop of Gloucester in March 1605, resigning the deanery in August of that year. CS Knighton, 'Ravis, Thomas', *Oxford Dictionary of National Biography*, doi.org/10.1093/ref:odnb/23175.

[60] C 33/107, fo 260v [IMG_5290a]. In addition to the cases considered in the text, *Mitchell v Vosper* (1605) concerned an action which had gone to judgment at law, though here the injunction had been against proceedings upon the verdict, judgment having been obtained following dissolution of the injunction upon 'very slender' suggestions, C 33/107, fo 13v [IMG_5038], C 33/108, fo 259v [IMG_7046a].

[61] Additionally, in *Oram v Merchaunt* (1614), C 33/127, fo 46 [IMG_0048], the defendant had obtained a verdict, but not yet judgment. It was ordered that the defendant should enter judgment, but forbear execution, provided that the plaintiff brought £100 into court and had the matter set down to be heard in the next term.

[62] C 33/127, fo 43 [IMG_0045].

hearing in this court', an injunction was issued to stay proceedings upon the judgment until the matter had been heard and determined or otherwise ordered. In *Hallse v Orchard*,[63] in contrast, an injunction against the defendants' proceeding at law in an action concerning land was 'clearly dissolved', it appearing that the bill had not been exhibited until after one of the defendants 'had verdict and judgment at law … and was in … possession of the lands at such time as the … injunction was served on them'.

The cases in the sample for 1615 reveal two injunctions after judgment at law, one of which was dissolved, the other being by assent of the parties. As in *Halles v Orchard* (1614), in *Colston v Vaiver*[64] it was found that verdict, judgment and execution had passed upon a single bill before the injunction was granted. This being so, and the plaintiff failing to reply to the defendant's answer and confessing that the bill in question had not in fact been promised to be delivered up to him, the injunction was dissolved 'and the matter of the … bill clearly dismissed'. And in *Sparrye v Acton*[65] the defendant was 'contented to stay execution' upon a judgment at law upon a bond. The plaintiff putting in security to stand to the order of the court, it was ordered that the defendant 'shall forbear to take out execution upon the … judgment or otherwise to proceed at … law', until the matter had been heard and determined or otherwise ordered in Chancery, for which 'the plaintiff may take an injunction if he will'.

The 1616 sample reveals six cases in some way involving the question of an injunction after judgment at law, but, as in previous years, few of them will readily support the judges' fear, as reported by Coke in *Throckmorton v Finch* (1597), that Chancery intervention after judgment at law would risk the Chancery becoming a court of general resort.[66] In *Johnson v Hardres*,[67] it was found that the plaintiff had pleaded so as to delay trial upon a bond, and having exhibited his bill in Chancery had delayed replication until the day after judgment was given against him at law. Not explaining this, the plaintiff had obtained an injunction against the defendant's proceeding upon the judgment. The true situation becoming apparent, the injunction was absolutely dissolved, 'notwithstanding anything now said by [the plaintiff's counsel] to the contrary'. In *Hazard v Peacock*[68] the defendant claimed to be owed money by the intestate to whom the plaintiff was administrator, and had obtained judgment at law. It appeared, however, that the defendant had already received £142 more than he had been owed, and – disobeying a decree to pay that sum to the plaintiff – had sold his house and goods, intended to sell his land, and 'for further vexation' had sought a *scire facias* upon the judgment. The court finding that the judgment had been satisfied and should be discharged, an injunction was issued to stay process upon it, and the defendant – already incarcerated for contempt – was ordered to be shut up a close prisoner. Neither of these cases will easily support a narrative of expansive Chancery intervention after judgment at law.

Other instances in 1616 concerning injunctions after judgment turned upon the order of events at law and in Chancery. Thus in *Fines v Wheatley*[69] the plaintiff had not

[63] C 33/128, fo 7 [IMG_0011] (the B book; part of the entry is missing in the A book).
[64] C 33/129, fo 11 [IMG_0013].
[65] C 33/129, fo 26v [IMG_0028a].
[66] Baker (n 3) 287–88.
[67] C 33/131, fo 21v [IMG_0023a].
[68] C 33/131, fo 28 [IMG_0038].
[69] C 33/131, fo 7v [IMG_0010a].

exhibited his bill in Chancery until after judgment at law with a release of errors. The defendant's demurrer to the bill for lack of equity was referred to consideration by a master. No further action in the case has been found in the record up to 1618, and it may be that no injunction was granted. In *Farmer v Brocas*,[70] in contrast, the defendant had taken judgment at law despite an injunction which had already been granted for stay of his proceedings. Execution of the judgment was stayed, the defendant being required to answer for his contempt.

An injunction after judgment at law was granted in *Wharton v Musgrave*,[71] but so as to allow the master of the rolls to 'take the opinion of some of the judges'. Only in *Michelson v Fletcher*[72] is there an indication in the 1616 sample of the Chancery acting in effect to review a common law judgment. It being alleged that the defendant had sought execution of a judgment 'indirectly and unconscionably gotten', consideration of the pleadings was referred to a master to report whether he found sufficient confessed to move the court to grant an injunction for the plaintiff, the defendant in the meantime being enjoined not to call for or take out execution. No further action in the case has been found in the record up to 1618.

The 1617 sample shows three cases concerning an injunction after judgment at law, in at least one of which the injunction was dissolved. In *Biddle v Commander*[73] the plaintiff's suit in Chancery had not been commenced until after the defendant had obtained judgment, 'upon a fair trial', against the plaintiff in an action of debt. The plaintiff had obtained an injunction against execution of the judgment, while also proceeding upon a writ of error, commencing suit on the matter in Star Chamber, and having one of the defendants committed for contempt for non-payment of costs, despite agreement that costs be remitted. It was ordered that the injunction be dissolved and the Chancery suit be dismissed. In *Drebell v Vanlore*[74] the plaintiff had obtained an order that arbitrators consider their award and certify their doings so that order might be taken, and had sought an injunction in the meantime against the defendant's proceeding at law upon the bond in question, 'which his lordship did forbear to order', but 'by way of motion did advise and wish the … defendant thereunto'. It appearing that the defendant had already obtained judgment 'upon full hearing' in the King's Bench, in respect of which judgment the plaintiff was proceeding in error, it was ordered that the defendant might proceed upon the judgment unless cause were shown to the contrary.[75] In *Eckington v Parshewe*[76] the defendant, failing to answer, had obtained judgment at law against the plaintiff upon a counterbond to save the defendant harmless upon a bond 'long since satisfied'. An injunction was awarded against the proceeding at law until the defendant had directly answered and other order had been taken to the contrary.

[70] C 33/131, fo 34 [IMG_0036].
[71] C 33/131, fo 44 [IMG_0046].
[72] C 33/131, fo 25v [IMG_0027a].
[73] C 33/133, fo 26 [IMG_0028].
[74] C 33/133, fo 32 [IMG_0034].
[75] In a fourth case, *Lacon* v *Pesse* (1617), C 33/133, fo 10 [IMG_0012], an injunction was awarded against the defendant's proceeding at law upon a bond – in relation to which the plaintiff was a surety, and alleged that satisfaction had been made for the principal sum – subject to the plaintiff bringing the principal sum into court. The injunction was to stay the defendant's proceedings upon the verdict, or, if judgment were obtained, to stay execution of the judgment.
[76] C 33/133, fo 26v [IMG_0028a].

The sample for 1618 shows five cases concerning an injunction after judgment at law. In two cases the injunction reflected misbehaviour by the defendant. In *Owen v Alden*,[77] the defendant, avoiding subpoenas to answer, had 'stolen' a trial at law and had obtained verdict and judgment upon a bond of £120, 'there being but £7 due at first and lent twenty years past'. The defendant's proceeding at law was enjoined until she had directly answered and the court had given other order to the contrary. In *Reake v Arnold*,[78] a master reported that the plaintiff had been bound as surety in a conditioned bond for the debt of John Arnold, one of the defendants, to William Arnold, another defendant, John and William being cousins. Intending to lay the whole debt upon the plaintiff as surety, William caused an action to be brought at law upon the bond, confederating with an attorney to appear on behalf of both John and the plaintiff, and to confess the action, judgment being thereby obtained without the plaintiff's knowledge, the attorney having had no contact with him.[79] An injunction was awarded to stay proceedings upon the judgment until the matter had been heard and determined or otherwise ordered.

In two cases in 1618 provision was made in Chancery for payment of sums owed upon the bonds in question. In *Dowthwaite v Crase*[80] the defendant had obtained judgment at law upon a conditioned bond, and had had the plaintiff in execution, which was released upon his giving security for payment of the principal sum, and an injunction was granted against the defendant's proceeding at law. The plaintiff having brought in the principal sum with costs, the injunction was continued, the defendant being ordered to bring in the bonds to be cancelled and to acknowledge satisfaction. In *Brooke v Dowse*[81] the defendant had obtained judgment on a bond, and an order had been drawn up in Chancery whereby the bond and judgment were to be delivered up and discharged, the plaintiff paying a specified sum to the defendant. The defendant claiming that he had not been fully heard, a rehearing had been ordered, despite which the defendant had proceeded upon the judgment and gone about to obtain execution. An injunction was awarded against the defendant's proceeding at law until the matter had been heard and determined or otherwise ordered. And in the fifth 1618 case, *Laxton v Harman*,[82] the defendant's action at law lacked foundation. The defendant owed money to the plaintiff upon a sale of land, of which the defendant had taken possession without paying the full price. Contrary to the court's order, the defendant had obtained judgment upon a bond for repayment of the price should the sale not take effect. An injunction was awarded against execution of the judgment, albeit difficulties arose through execution having been obtained before service of the injunction.

Of the cases in the sample for 1626, only one shows an injunction after judgment at law, in the context of misconduct by the plaintiff. In *Sheeres v Leonard*,[83] an injunction had been granted to stay the defendant's proceeding at law until he had directly answered, but he had nevertheless obtained judgment upon the bond in question.

[77] C 33/135, fo 33v [IMG_1198a].
[78] C 33/135, fo 39 [IMG_1204].
[79] C 38/32, report dated 26 June 1618 (the volume is not foliated or paginated).
[80] C 33/135, fo 27v [IMG_1192a]. For an earlier entry see C 33/131, fo 10v [IMG_0012a].
[81] C 33/135, fo 38 [IMG_1203].
[82] C 33/135, fo 44v [IMG_1210a].
[83] C 33/151, fo 29 [IMG_0033].

It appeared that judgment and service upon the defendant of process to answer had occurred at about the same time. The plaintiff had persuaded the defendant not to answer, promising to make speedy payment of the money due with damages and not to take advantage of want of an answer, but had paid nothing and had obtained the injunction for want of answer. It was ordered that unless cause were shown, the injunction was to be dissolved.

III. Conclusion

This chapter represents no more than an initial foray into early seventeenth-century common injunctions: conclusions from some 300 entries must necessarily be tentative. The vast majority of common injunctions in the sample concerned actions at law. Of these actions, a clear majority concerned bonds and other writings obligatory. It may be that had the outcome of the controversy between Coke and Ellesmere gone the other way, things 'could have turned out very differently indeed'[84] for the development of the proprietary consequences of equitable rights, but contemporary common injunction practice seems to have been predominantly concerned not with equities of redemption or beneficial interests under trusts, but with the classic Chancery jurisdiction to relieve upon formal obligations, in which context the common injunction cases in the sample may contribute to understanding of informal relief upon writings obligatory at common law in the seventeenth century, showing the possibility, early in the century at least, of staying the *postea* or judgment at law to allow relief to be obtained in Chancery.[85]

While discussion of early seventeenth-century common injunctions has focused on their use after judgment at law, the sample reveals very small numbers of such injunctions, few of them suggesting any strong assertion of Chancery jurisdiction in this respect, with some indication of a tendency for positions established by judgments at law to be respected in Chancery. It may be possible to take from the heat of the controversy which led up to the *Earl of Oxford's Case* (1615)[86] an exaggerated impression of jurisdictional tension in the early seventeenth century. No doubt the Chancery very frequently enjoined litigants at law, but had the court been unable, for example, to prevent a judgment at law being obtained while the same matter was pending in Chancery, it is difficult to see how the jurisdiction could have functioned at all. Common injunctions were normally temporary, albeit they might in some cases have decisory effect. And while capable of being seen as an indicator of tension, common injunction practice may equally suggest co-operation between the jurisdictions.

Thus it seems to have been accepted in Chancery that actions at law 'where either party may recover his just damages' were 'more fit to be decided by the course of the

[84] DJ Ibbetson, '*The Earl of Oxford's Case* (1615)' in C Mitchell and P Mitchell (eds), *Landmark Cases in Equity* (Oxford, Hart Publishing, 2012) 1, at 26.

[85] See text at nn 17–22, above. For informal relief against penalties in the early-modern period more generally, see PG Turner, '*Lex Sequitur Equitatem*: Fusion and the Penalty Doctrine' in JCP Goldberg et al (eds), *Equity and Law: Fusion and Fission* (Cambridge, Cambridge University Press, 2019) 254, at 256 ff.

[86] 1 Chan Rep 1.

common law' and would therefore not normally be enjoined,[87] and in *Dirickson v Bland* (1618) 'the scope of the plaintiff's bill after a writ of error by him brought at the common law [being] to falsify a verdict obtained by the defendant at the common law', 'which precedent of so dangerous a consequence this court doth not think meet to admit or relieve any suit of that nature', it was ordered that unless the plaintiff showed cause 'the matter of the plaintiff's bill is clearly and absolutely dismissed out of this court'.[88] In some instances, indeed, Chancery and the judges worked directly together. Thus in *Rowe v Martin* (1605),[89] witnesses having been examined in Chancery and an injunction having been granted, the matter came to trial in the King's Bench, which referred the ending of it to the lord chief justice, and by Chancery order the same matter was likewise referred to the chief justice. In the same year in *Bedle v Beard*[90] the matter concerning a parsonage having been fully heard and debated in Chancery, the court thought not fit, 'for that the matter is of great consequence', to give any judgment or decree, but ordered that a case be made to the lord chancellor, 'who will be pleased to confer with the judges therein and then give order', the defendant's proceeding at law in the meantime to be stayed.

As WJ Jones observed, the Chancery had to 'work in close alignment with the system of law from which it had sprung'.[91] Such alignment – even at the height of the controversy over common injunctions after judgment – is suggested by *Paule v Watts* (1616)[92] in which an action at law by Watts, for the sum of £1,300 promised for his wife's jointure, had come before Coke CJKB at Northampton summer assizes in 1615, the year in which the King's Bench gave judgment for Magdalene College, Cambridge, in the *Earl of Oxford's Case*.[93] By a previous Chancery decree Watts had been awarded £200, it being found that 'a great part of the … portion [had been] paid before'. Dissatisfied, Watts had had his own suit dismissed, and the matter had been referred to arbitrators who awarded £300, certain land, and everything appointed to Watts by the Chancery decree. But Watts refused to perform the award, instead bringing the action at law. Coke CJ made an order before verdict for the assent of the parties that Watts be paid £400 and that assurance be made according to the Chancery decree. Verdict then following for Watts for the whole £1,300 claimed, the chief justice stayed the *postea*. The £400 was brought into the King's Bench but Watts refused it, obtained return of the *postea*, and called for judgment, whereupon it was ordered in Chancery that Watts forbear to call for judgment and show cause why he should not accept and perform the chief justice's order. It is difficult not to see this as an example, not of tension between the chief justice of the King's Bench and the Chancery, but of co-operation between the jurisdictions with a view to reaching a settlement in face of Watts's intransigent insistence upon what he regarded as his entitlement.

[87] *Bretton v Sheres* (1617), C 33/133, fo 43v [IMG_0045]. See also *Ferme v Barnes* (1614), C 33/127, fo 23 [IMG_0024], and *Barron v Langham* (1617), C 33/133, fo 3 [IMG_0005].

[88] C 33/135, fo 120v [IMG_1286a]. This was said to be according to a master's report. The report, by Master Wolveridge, has not been found; while listed in the contemporary index to the relevant volume of Chancery reports and certificates (C 38/30), it does not appear in the volume.

[89] C 33/109, fo 24 [IMG_6793].

[90] C 33/109, fo 181v [IMG_6872a] (not involving a common injunction).

[91] WJ Jones, *The Elizabethan Court of Chancery* (Oxford, Oxford University Press, 1967) 497.

[92] C 33/131, fo 41v [IMG_0043a].

[93] 1 Chan Rep 1.

In *Martin v Marshall*,[94] likewise in 1615, the question arose in the Common Pleas whether a municipal corporation could have a court of equity by grant or by prescription. Serjeant Hitcham had argued that a court of equity could not be by prescription, nonetheless emphasising that 'the High Court of Chancery at Westminster is a court known at common law'. But on another day the judges would not hear Hitcham argue this point, 'because it trenched upon the High Court of Chancery here [,a]nd said that the four great courts at Westminster are by prescription'. In Hobart CJCP's words 'the High Court of Chancery at Westminster is part of the government of the kingdom, and so as ancient as the common law. Every prescription is against common right; the Chancery is not but is common right', a view which the evidence of contemporary Chancery practice over common injunctions does little to contradict.

[94] WH Bryson (ed), *Cases Concerning Equity and the Courts of Equity*, vol 2 (Selden Soc vol 118) (London, Selden Society, 2001) 444, no 231, at 447.

9

The Burden of Proof in English Criminal Proceedings after the Revolution

MIKE MACNAIR

I owe David a lot. He taught me undergraduate legal history in 1980–81, in 1981 certified for the Law Society that my out-of-date Criminal Law from the Law Moderations exam in March 1973 had been updated, participated with Jeffrey Hackney in teaching the BCL course 'Legislation of Edward I' when I took it in 1981–82, and supervised my D.Phil., which ended up as *The Law of Proof in Early Modern Equity*.[1] That project was originally intended to be one on common law evidence but mutated, as these things do – in this case because of the abundance of sources.

The Law of Proof in Early Modern Equity did have things to say about the history of evidence at common law, but these have been effectively marginalised by the dominance of the school of thought initiated by John H Langbein's work since his 1978 article 'The Criminal Trial before the lawyers'.[2] My thesis and book were inconvenient for the chronological claims of this school, but could be set on one side as being equity. My subsequent work has been more on the 'equity' and 'common law and civil law' side. In the last couple of years, however, I have been dragged back into the 'common law evidence' side of the issue by work on the *substantive* criminal law of 1689–1760 for *Oxford History of the Laws of England* volume IX. This makes a return to common law evidence, I hope, an appropriate offering to David as the supervisor of the original project, and hence contribution to this collection.

The reason I have been pulled back to the issue is that two distinct lines of argument in the recent literature suggest fundamental change in the conceptual shape of criminal *law* taking place during or after the post-revolutionary period. George P Fletcher's *Rethinking Criminal Law* (2000) argues for a shift, in or after our period, from a pattern of 'manifest criminality' which focussed on the *actus reus* of a crime, to the modern

[1] M Macnair, *The Law of Proof in Early Modern Equity* (DPhil dissertation, University of Oxford, 1991); revised version published by Duncker & Humblot, 1999.

[2] JH Langbein, 'The Criminal Trial before the lawyers' (1978) 45 *U Chic LR* 263; further developed especially in JH Langbein, 'Shaping the Eighteenth Century Criminal Trial' (1983) *50 U Chic LR* 1; JH Langbein, 'Historical Foundations of the Law of Evidence: a View from the Ryder Sources' (1996) 96 *Col LR* 1167; and JH Langbein, *The Origins of Adversary Criminal Trial* (Oxford, Oxford University Press, 2003).

form of criminal law focussed on the *mens rea*, the mental state of the offender.[3] Nicola Lacey's 2008 *Women, Crime and Character* and her more generalised 2016 *In Search of Criminal Responsibility* both argue for a shift, taking place after our period, from a focus on the general character of the person charged with crime in our period, to a narrower focus on the specific offence, which also, like Fletcher's argument, entails an increased focus on the *mens rea* of the specific offence charged.[4] Both these arguments, in spite of their different character, at the end of the day *rest on* the picture of criminal trial in 'Criminal Trial before the Lawyers', Langbein's own subsequent work, and that of other authors – especially JM Beattie's 1986 *Crime and the Courts in England, 1660–1800*.[5] Langbein's argument is that the jury trial before 'lawyerisation' can be seen to be an 'accused speaks' trial in which a defendant is forced to account for him or herself; it is this picture of the *trial* which seems to call for a different conceptualisation of the substantive criminal law, whether as focussing on the *actus reus*, or on the accused's general character.

Fletcher and Lacey on *mens rea* have been sharply criticised by Elizabeth Papp Kamali and Thomas A. Green, pointing to the presence of *mens rea* conceptions already in thirteenth century England – and also to the circumstance that both Fletcher and Lacey focus on the trial by petty jury (and subsequent proceedings) to the exclusion of the *prior* proceedings which filtered out a good many allegations.[6]

It could be, of course, that *mens rea* conceptions had disappeared or a 'presumption of guilt' emerged between the late middle ages and the early eighteenth century (Bruce P Smith, in contrast, argues for the development of *statutory* presumptions of guilt in certain *summary* forms of theft-related liability).[7] But, just to take a single example, in one of the relatively few felony cases to be found in the law reports, *Meeres* (1689), the Old Bailey jury found a special verdict that the defendant, tenant of a furnished room, ran away with the furniture. The issue was argued before several judges at Serjeants' Inn whether this amounted to larceny, Sir Bartholomew Shower and Edward Northey being briefed for the prisoner (on the instruction of Holt CJ). Shower argued inter alia that:

> Felony is according to the original intent, but then it must be found there was such an intent, and, *in favorem vitæ*, nothing is to be intended, or presumed against the party: there is nothing found of an intention, to take away the goods when they took the lodgings …[8]

Shower *also* argued the need for the taking of the goods to be trespassory (ruled out by the landlord's delivery of them), as did Northey – which is closer to Fletcher's

[3] GP Fletcher, *Rethinking Criminal Law* (Oxford, Oxford University Press, 2000) Part I.

[4] N Lacey, *Women, Crime and Character: from Moll Flanders to Tess of the D'Urbervilles* (Oxford, Oxford University Press, 2008); N Lacey, *In Search of Criminal Responsibility: Ideas, Interests, and Institutions* (Oxford, Oxford University Press, 2016).

[5] JM Beattie, *Crime and the Courts in England, 1660–1800* (Oxford, Clarendon Press, 1986); the discussion of the trial in ch 7.

[6] The point is directly argued against Fletcher and Lacey in TA Green and E Papp Kamali, 'A Crossroads in Criminal Procedure: The Assumptions Underlying England's Adoption of Trial by Jury for Crime' in TR Baker (ed), *Law and Society in Later Medieval England and Ireland: Essays in Honour of Paul Brand* (Abingdon, Routledge, 2018), the point about their missing out the pre-trial processes at 65; Papp Kamali's case for the importance of *mens rea* in medieval felony ideas in depth is developed in E Papp Kamali, *Felony and the Guilty Mind* (Cambridge, Cambridge University Press 2019).

[7] BP Smith, 'The Presumption of Guilt and the English Law of Theft, 1750–1850' (2005) 23 *LHR* 133–71.

[8] 1 Show KB 50, 89 ER 441, 53/443.

'manifest criminality'. Holt CJKB, Atkyns CB, Nevil, Turton, and Ventris JJ took the view that this was not larceny, without giving much explanation; Rokeby J 'thought it no felony, because no intent found to steal, either in the taking the lodgings or in carrying away the goods'; Pollexfen CJCP dissented.[9] *Mens rea was* thus commonly understood to be an essential element in felony as of 1689; and, moreover, one that could not be 'presumed'.

The substantive law *mens rea* problem thus unavoidably involves confrontation with the account of early eighteenth century evidence law in the narrative of the 'accused speaks' trial.

There are two issues which mar the clarity of the image of the 'accused speaks trial'. The first is features of the 'late pre-modern' or 'early modern' felony *procedure* which Green and Papp Kamali adverted to, and which become apparent from the literature on the practical functioning of the criminal justice system. The second is issues about the *sources* of 'crown law' and about the historical sources from which evidence of legal argument can be drawn.

I. Procedure

The procedural points relate in the first place to *which cases went to trial*. There were two levels of selection before the arrival at trial before a petty jury: the examining magistrates (Justices of the Peace), and the Grand Jury. We don't have clear numbers for the number of potentially indictable felony charges which were disposed of by JPs by dismissal for insufficiency of evidence, by down-charging, or by arbitration or mediation by the JPs themselves or other local figures, for want of enough clear surviving records. But we do have a good deal of evidence of individual JPs pursuing one or another of these avenues of disposal.[10] The second stage was the grand jury finding of true bill or *ignoramus*. Here we do have some quantitative evidence of the level of dismissal, and it was fairly high, though tending to some extent to fall over the period.[11]

Taking these two matters together, it seems that cases which went to trial must have been selected for the strength of the evidence against the accused, as well as for the determination of the prosecutor, the seriousness of the individual charge, and the antecedent character (so far as known) of the accused. This is a significantly narrower class of cases than cases which would have gone to trial between the nineteenth century 'modernisation' of criminal procedure, and the very late twentieth century explosions of forms of 'diversion', of CPS refusal to charge, and of plea-bargaining.[12]

[9] ibid 54–55/444; the result was reversed by statute in 1692, 3 Will. & Mary, c 9 s 5 (royal assent 24 Feb 1691/92), still requiring an intent to steal, but *at the time of taking away* the furniture.

[10] See eg N Landau, *The Justices of the Peace 1679–1760* (Oakland, U Calif Press, 1984) chs 6–7; RB Shoemaker, *Prosecution and Punishment* (Cambridge, Cambridge University Press, 1991) ch 4; R Paley (ed), *Justice in Eighteenth-Century Hackney: the Justicing Notebook of Henry Norris and the Hackney Petty Sessions Book* (London Record Society, 1991) xvii-xix; N Landau, 'Indictment for Fun and Profit' (1999) 17 *LHR* 507; P King, *Crime, Justice and Discretion in England 1740–1820* (Oxford, Oxford University Press, 2000) 82–110.

[11] See eg Beattie (n 5) 400–406; King (n 10) 231–33.

[12] 'Modernisation' of criminal procedure: K Smith in W Cornish et al, *Oxford History of the Laws of England vol XIII* (Oxford, Oxford University Press, 2010) Part I, esp. 58–67, 112–15. Regarding the rise of 'diversion', it

On the other hand, as Tim Hitchcock and William J Turkel have pointed out, there is a substantial class of cases which went to trial which would in modern times go to a plea of guilty and matter led in mitigation.[13] Judges, in fact, pressed defendants who wanted to plead guilty to plead not guilty. The reason is that in the first place the jury had a recognised role in sentencing – both by 'down-charging' to turn murder into manslaughter, burglary or robbery into larceny, grand larceny into petty larceny, and so on; and by recommendations towards mercy. They could not play this role if the accused pleaded guilty: a point made by Langbein himself.[14] There was, indeed, no mechanism for matter to be led in mitigation after a guilty plea or verdict in felony,[15] other than extrajudicially petitioning the Crown for a pardon. In this latter procedure the trial judge was expected to report on the strength of the case against the convict and any other matters for or against them. They could not do so if there had been no trial. So even if the case was completely open and shut, there would usually be a not guilty plea and a (very brief indeed) trial. The high frequency of such cases creates the *appearance* of a trial procedure which either presumes guilt, or focusses on the defendant's general character rather than on specific guilt of the offence charged.

II. Sources

The issue of sources starts with the point already made that rather few felony cases appear in the regular law reports in the period. There are around 21,000 printed reports in the period in the *English Reports*; making a generous allowance of one third for duplicates, and so on, this would be around 14,000 reported cases. Among these there are 21 cases on the substantive law of homicide; 15 cases on larceny; nine on burglary; three on robbery; two on piracy; one on arson; one on buggery, and none on rape.[16] These are small numbers; though it should, of course, be noted that law reports on the civil side, too, are heavily dominated by issues of procedure.

As to *why* this is the case, the *apparent* answer is that felony defendants were not usually legally represented, so that points of law would not be taken; but the existence of Sir John Kelyng's reports, judicial reports of criminal cases c. 1660–68, show that the result does not necessarily follow. It is probably more explanatorily significant that the procedural forms in felony did not commonly lead to public rulings by the court *en banc*, which is where most reports were made; judicial consultations at Serjeants' Inn

is not easy to find longitudinal studies, but there is some discussion, see eg www.crestadvisory.com/post/the-use-of-out-of-court-disposals-and-diversion-at-the-front-end. CPS: there is some longitudinal discussion in K Sosa, *In the Public Interest: reforming the Crown Prosecution Service* (Policy Exchange, 2012); also recent discussion in *2020 charging inspection* (HMCPSI Publication No. CP001:1274, 2020). Plea bargaining: see eg discussion in *Young Minds, Big Decisions* (Fair Trials 2022).

[13] T Hitchcock and WJ Turkel, 'The Old Bailey Proceedings, 1674–1913: Text Mining for Evidence of Court Behavior' (2016) 34 *LHR* 929, esp. 940–55.

[14] Langbein, *Origins* (n 2) 57–61 summarises the position, and his characterisation of the petty jury trial as a sentencing proceeding is for many cases clearly appropriate.

[15] This *was* possible in misdemeanour: *Templeman* (1702) 7 Mod 40, 87 ER 1081, 1 Salk 55, 91 ER 54; *Woolston* (1729) 1 Barn KB 266, 94 ER 181.

[16] There are more on procedural issues, but not enough to radically increase 'felony reporting'.

or in Chambers would only be reported by a judge, or by one of the counsel briefed to argue, unless the judges decided on a public statement.[17] In contrast, reported *misdemeanour* cases in King's Bench and in trial reports were not uncommon.

Langbein's solution to the 'sources problem' the lack of reports creates, also used by Beattie and hence by subsequent authors who have relied on this work, was to make use of the *Old Bailey Sessions Papers* published from 1674 on, and similar trial reports; Langbein also used the judicial trial notebooks of Sir Dudley Ryder.[18] These sources are illuminating for certain aspects of criminal justice practice, but bias any account of substantive criminal law or the law of criminal procedure in two ways. The first is the point already made, that cases which went to petty jury trial are a selective sample of strong cases, including many which would go to a guilty plea in modern practice. The second point, made by Robert Shoemaker, is that the editorial purposes of *OBSP* were to show that crime did not pay, and, on the other hand, that the authorities were effectively protecting the public from crime. There was also an aspect of titillation from sensational stories. These editorial purposes led to the active editorial exclusion of points of law that were actually argued.[19]

To give a single example: *Anne Hawkins* (1704) was charged with burglary of the 'mansion house' of one Samuel Story, in fact an apartment in the offices of the Royal Africa Company. Holt CJ, Tracy J and Bury B sitting at the Old Bailey ruled that 'the apartment of Story could not be called his mansion-house; because he and the others inhabit in the house merely as officers and servants of the company.' The indictment was therefore discharged and a new one written to charge her with burgling *the Company's* house.[20] The *OBSP* report of the case says on the point of law merely that 'there being a fault in the Indictment, she was acquitted'.[21] Silence of *OBSP* reports therefore cannot be treated as evidence of the absence of rules of law. This is a very important general point.

Judicial trial notebooks are of limited value for a different reason. This is that the function of these was as notes of the evidence to refresh the trial judge's memory in case they had to report – on the civil side or in misdemeanour cases – on an application for a new trial on the ground of the verdict being against evidence; in treason or felony cases, on an application for reprieve or pardon.[22] *Legal* arguments would only really be pertinent to the judicial note-taking exercise if they substantially affected the weight of

[17] For example, *Meeres* quoted above is reported by Shower, who was briefed to argue; *Wiseman* (1718) Fort 92, 92 ER 774, is known only from Fortescue Aland J's note and draft letter to the Lord Chancellor about the case included in his reports. Judges decided on a public statement: eg *Huggins* (1730) 2 Stra 882, 93 ER 915, 1 Barn KB 396, 94 ER 267, Fitz-Gib 177, 94 ER 708, 186/712 (2 Ld Raym 1574, 92 ER 518 is a judicial report).

[18] *OBSP* is now accessible at www.oldbaileyonline.org. Non-London sets of trial proceedings have to be pursued individually. See Langbein's use of Ryder in 'Shaping the Eighteenth Century Criminal Trial' (n 2) and also in 'Albion's Fatal Flaws' (1983) 98 *Past & Present* 96.

[19] R Shoemaker, 'The Old Bailey Proceedings and the Representation of Crime and Criminal Justice in Eighteenth-Century London' (2008) 47 *JBS* 559–80.

[20] Foster 38, 168 ER 20, (from Tracy J's manuscript).

[21] *Old Bailey Online* (*OBO*) reference number (#) t17040426-1. From the report of the trial on the second indictment, *OBO* # t17040426-13, it appears that on the evidence the jury acquitted her of burglary and convicted her of larceny, for which she was able to take clergy.

[22] Langbein makes this point in 'Shaping the Eighteenth Century Criminal Trial' (n 2) at 5–7, though he downplays its significance. On the civil side, J Oldham, *The Mansfield Manuscripts and the Growth of English Law in the Eighteenth Century* (Chapel Hill, UNC Press, 1992, 2vv) i, 164–65.

the evidence led, eg if there was a failed application to exclude evidence; since if there was a serious point of substantive law at issue, it would be possible to obtain a special verdict for later full argument. This 'aide-mémoire' character is very visible in Lord Hardwicke's trial notes from the period while he was CJKB.[23]

The converse question is, what could be cited as authority, in the limited number of felony cases where we *do* have evidence of legal argument? The answer includes statutes (obviously) and reported cases (less obviously, given the dearth of felony reports);[24] Kelyng's reports were printed by Holt CJ, with three of his own judgments, in 1708, perhaps to add to the supply of available reports of felony cases.[25] Proportionately much more frequently than on the civil side, given the small number of felony reports, books of authority were cited: Staunford's *Plees del Coron*, Pulton's *De Pace*, Dalton's *Countrey Justice*, Coke's *Third Institute*, Hale's *Summary* and (after 1736) *History, of the Pleas of the Crown*.[26] Hawkins' *Treatise* became citable rather rapidly (within the life of the author).[27]

Through the treatises the cases they cited were used; and this class included, on the one hand, cases of considerable age; and, on the other hand, fairly recent cases printed as trial pamphlets (mostly now usually accessed through the *State Trials* collections beginning with that of Thomas Salmon).[28] This usage is visible in the text *Tryals per Pais in Capital Matters* attached to the trial lawyers' handbook *Tryals per Pais* from the fourth edition of 1702, and in Hawkins.[29] Direct citation of the printed trials as authority can also be found in reported cases.[30]

This point has to be made because Langbein and other authors who have relied on *OBSP* as a source for criminal procedural and substantive law have discounted the

[23] Samples of Hardwicke's notebooks, from BL Add MS 36028: London Sittings, November 1733–July 1734; Add MS 36036: Circuit Crown side, 1734–36; Add MS 36038 – King's Bench, November 1733–February 1734; and Add MS 36039 – King's Bench, February–July 1734, have been transcribed by Dr George Artley as part of research assistant work for the *OHLE IX* project; they are, as Langbein already pointed out in 'Shaping the Eighteenth Century Criminal Trial' (n 2), uninformative. Oldham, *Mansfield Manuscripts* (n 22) does not use Mansfield's notes of felony trials. From a slightly earlier date, Rokeby J's diary includes judicial notes of this sort – again mainly aide-mémoire in character and not very informative: *The Diary of Mr Justice Rokeby* (privately printed, 1887; reprint, Gale MOML, n.d.).

[24] See eg the several cases cited in *Keat/ Keate* (1696) 5 Mod 287, 87 ER 661, Skin 666, 90 ER 298, Comb 406, 90 ER 557, (*Keite*) 1 Ld Raym 138, 91 ER 989, 1 Comy 13, 92 ER 934.

[25] Holt CJ, *A Report of Divers Cases in Pleas of the Crown, … Collected by Sir John Kelyng Knt …* (London, 1708).

[26] For bibliographical data on these books see HW Maxwell and LF Maxwell, *A Legal Bibliography of the British Commonwealth of Nations vol 1*, 2nd edn (London, Sweet & Maxwell, 1955). Evidence of citations from results of searches in the *English Reports* CDROM is available from the author on request.

[27] See eg *Ward* (1727) 2 Stra 747, 93 ER 824; *Westbeer* (1739) 1 Leach 12, 168 ER 108.

[28] *Tryals for high-treason, and other crimes. With proceedings on bills of attainder, and impeachments. For three hundred years past. …* (4 vv, London, 1719), several later enlarged editions, now usually cited from the Cobbett/ Howell edition of 34vv, 1809–28.

[29] *TPP*: in the separately paginated *Tryals per Pais in Capital Matters*, 'To the reader', sig. A2v-A3r: 'I have herein cited several publick Tryals which though not of equal authority with Reports, yet being printed with the allowance of the Chief Justices, ought in my opinion to be esteemed something more than bare historical narratives'. Hawkins: in Volume I (London, 1716), which was written before the appearance of Salmon's collection, eg *James Nayler* (1656) at 7; the reversal of the attainder of *Algernon Sidney* at 38; in vol II (London, 1721) citations are concentrated in chs 39 (counsel for prisoner), 43 (challenges to the jury), 44 (trial by peers) and 46 (evidence).

[30] See eg in *Crosby* (1695) 5 Mod 15, 87 ER 491; *Layer* (1722) Fort 396, 92 ER 907; *Burridge* (1735) 3 P Wms 439, 24 ER 1133, Peere Williams for the prosecutor at 456–457/1140; *Townley* (1746) Foster 7 168 ER 4, 8/5.

State Trials as a source, largely on the basis of critiques of the *older* (pre-Restoration) narratives in the collection, and of the special case of the 'Whig Martyrology' of 1685 trials, produced in the 1690s.[31] Many of the 'State Trials' of the Restoration and later, however, were contemporaneous stenographic transcripts authorised by the presiding judges; hence the willingness of eighteenth century lawyers to use them in constructing accounts of criminal law and procedure.[32] The second aspect of Langbein's critique – that cases reported in the *State Trials* are few and unrepresentative, being *causes célèbres* – is valid for their use to describe *routine practice*; but not valid for them as a *source of law* analogous to reported cases. They report, however, even fewer cases than those in the law reports; and sometimes points of law discussed by the judges in law reports do not appear in the *State Trials* report.[33]

What about misdemeanour cases, however? There are, in fact, quite a lot of reported misdemeanour cases. It is practically infeasible to pin down numbers because of the sheer range of offences involved. While the expression 'misdemeanour' was in this period used as a term for 'offence less than felony',[34] it continued to be used in the wider sense of 'misconduct' generally, including breaches of bylaws; and the reports of misdemeanour cases usually refer merely to the individual offence. Hawkins has 26 chapters on misdemeanours, giving a list which is certainly incomplete. For a very arbitrary and certainly incomplete sample of misdemeanours *not* in Hawkins, I have found a further 21 indictable misdemeanours in reported cases, 1689–1760, in which there is some reference to 'prove' or 'proof'.[35]

Langbein has argued that misdemeanours are not really 'criminal' but closer to civil proceedings.[36] There is a little direct support for this idea: thus in *Earbery/ Erbury* (1723) the defendant in seditious libel was outlawed for non-appearance and sought a writ of error to reverse the outlawry. Raymond AG argued that this required the consent of the Crown. Fortescue Aland J's report comments that 'indeed this is in the nature of a civil action, being only for a misdemeanor.'[37]

The argument was pressed more extensively in relation to information in the nature of *quo warranto*, since statute had applied some features of civil proceedings to these.

[31] Langbein, 'Criminal Trial' (n 2) 264–67, relying on G Kitson Clark, *The Critical Historian* (Abingdon, Routledge 1967) and JG Muddiman, *State Trials: the need for a new and critical edition* (privately printed, 1930). The basic reliability of the printed trials is asserted by M Mendle, 'The "prints" of the trials: the Nexus of Politics, Religion, Law and Information in Late Seventeenth-Century England' in J McElligott (ed), *Fear, Exclusion and Revolution: Roger Morrice and Britain in the 1680s* (Aldershot, Ashgate, 2006) ch 7; *Contra*, P Monod, 'Politics and sentiment in the Jacobite State Trials' in B Cowan and S Sowerby (ed), *The State Trials and the Politics of Justice* (Woodbridge, Boydell, 2021) ch 10, reasserting the Muddiman/ Kitson Clark view.

[32] *cf* my review of *The State Trials and the Politics of Justice* (2022) 37 *The Seventeenth Century* 862.

[33] See eg *Gregg* (1707) WH Bryson ed, *Samuel Dodd's Reports 1678–1713 and Miscellaneous Exchequer Cases 1671–1713* (Durham, NC, Carolina Academic Press, 2001) 211 (cited from manuscripts in *Hensey* (1758) 2 Keny 366, 96 ER 1212, 368/1213, 1 Burr 642, 97 ER 489, 646/), (1708) 14 ST 1371. Since Gregg pleaded guilty, the legal issues discussed by the judges were not publicly discussed, hence were absent from the *State Trials* report.

[34] WS Holdsworth, *History of English Law* iv (N Yorkshire, Methuen 1924) 512–21, relying mainly on statutory usages.

[35] Found by search on the *English Reports* CDROM. Results available from the author on request.

[36] Langbein, 'Historical Foundations' (n 2) 1177; Langbein, *Origins* (n 2) 36–37 (less categorically than in 1996).

[37] (1723) Fort 37, 92 ER 751, 40/752; apparently his notes. The point is not in the report at 8 Mod 177, 88 ER 130.

But the result of these arguments was merely a split among the judiciary on the issue, which is inconsistent with misdemeanour proceedings *in general* being seen as civil.[38] And in *Hooper* (1734) an information for false imprisonment in Newfoundland was denied on the ground that all criminal proceedings are local, and in *Wych/ Whych* in the following term of the same year misdemeanour proceedings were ruled to be sufficiently criminal to exclude the use of a Quaker's affirmation.[39]

Some of the misdemeanours in which 'proof' was mentioned *could* be conceived as civil proceedings, but this is hardly true of the political offences (eg seditious libel; failure of a public official to take the required oaths timeously), or of the offences against the revenue (eg excise offences by distillers and others; being 'concerned in' unshipping smuggled goods). Nor do the purity offences fit this paradigm (eg building a playhouse to act lewd plays; attempted sodomy; constable permitting escape of an arrested street-walker).

III. Burden of Proof in Reported Cases

The Latin tag *onus probandi* is already present in Coke's reports.[40] It was applied to criminal matters in argument in *Cobbold* (1713) (game laws), and *Foley* (1717) (extortion), and judicially used in *Harvey* (1747) (a statutory felony connected with smuggling), the latter two cases explicitly asserting that the *onus probandi* was on the Crown.[41] The English translation, 'burden of proof' seems to appear first in the printed reports in 1786.[42]

This is a limited number of references. But there are a larger number of cases in the reports in which it is clear that a prosecution fails for want of sufficient proof of essential matters, which makes it clear that the burden of proof is *in general* on the prosecution; and a few cases in which we are explicitly told of reasons which do cast the burden of proof on the defendant – some of which may help to explain some of the *OBSP* cases where the burden of proof appears in some sense to be placed on the defendant.

To start with the necessity of proof: in *Haines* (1695) the defendant was charged with acting as an alderman without having timeously taken the required oaths. At the end of the argument, the court said that 'the offence alledged is for acting after the time limited in the Act for taking the oaths, having neglected to take them; of which acting after the 22d. of Jan no pretence of proof was offered, and therefore the Court directed the jury to find the defendant not guilty.'[43]

[38] *R v Bennett* (1718) 1 Stra 101, 93 ER 412, *R v Jones* (1723) 8 Mod 201, 88 ER 146 (in both these cases the court was split 2-2, and a general meeting of the judges was also split, on the availability of a new trial after acquittal); *R v Ellams* (1734) Ridgeway t Hardw 82, 27 ER 765, 7 Mod 220, 87 ER 1202.

[39] *Wych* (1730) 2 Stra 872, 93 ER 907, (*Whych*) 1 Barn KB 346, 94 ER 233. *cf Hooper* (1734) W Kely 190, 25 ER 562.

[40] *Hynde's Case* (1591) 4 Co Rep 70b, 76 ER 1040, 71b/ 1042-43 'he who strives to avoid the bargain, ought to make manifest proof thereof, for *actori incumbit onus probandi*'. The tag is Glossatorial – already in Azo: *Brocardica Aurea Azonis Bononiensis* (Venice 1566) col. 41: 'actori incumbit necessitas probandi'.

[41] *Cobbold* (1713) Gilb Cas 11, 93 ER 276; *Foley* (1717) 1 Stra 52, 93 ER 379; *Harvey* (1747) Foster 51, 168 ER 26.

[42] *Spieres v Parker* (1786) 1 TR 141, 99 ER 1019, Lord Mansfield CJ, 144/1020.

[43] Skin 583, 90 ER 262, 586/263. *cf* also *Knell* (1728) 1 Barn KB 305, 94 ER 207.

In *Tracy* (1703) (extortion) counsel for the defendant refers to:

> an indictment against the players of Drury Lane … where the indictment was for building a scandalous house for the acting of profane and lewd plays, and that they acted such plays; and though they could prove the acting of immoral plays, yet, because they could not prove the building, the defendants were acquitted.[44]

In *Muscot* (1713) Parker CJ, summing up to a jury in a perjury trial, said that:

> there is this difference between a prosecution for perjury and a bare contest about property, that in the latter case the matter stands indifferent; and therefore a credible and probable witness shall turn the scale in favour of either party; but in the former, presumption is ever to be made in favour of innocence, and the oath of the party will have a regard paid to it, until disproved.[45]

In *Kinnersley and Moore* (1719) the defendants were charged with conspiring to accuse the Earl of Sunderland of attempted sodomy, and on a motion in arrest of judgment it was argued inter alia that the expression 'conatus fuit rem veneream habere' for the allegation was uncertain. Reeve for the prosecution responded that 'This goes to their own charge; from which we could not vary, but were obliged to lay it as we could prove it.'[46]

At the Old Bailey in 1724 the defendant was charged with stealing goods, the property of a person unknown. Gilbert B ruled that:

> though an indictment might be good for stealing the goods *cujusdam ignoti*, yet a property must be proved in somebody at the trial, otherwise it shall be presumed that the property was in the prisoner, by his pleading 'not guilty' to the indictment; for a man shall not be found guilty of felony, and hanged upon presumption.[47]

OBO has one case which might be this ruling, *John Mills*, 26 February 1724, before a panel including Gilbert B, charged with stealing a silver tankard, the property of a person unknown, on the evidence of the person to whom he attempted to sell it; 'It appear'd the Prisoner was a Gentleman of a good Family, but reputed Crazy, there not being Proof he stole it, he was acquitted'.[48] If this is the same case, it illustrates the limits both of OBSP on the one hand, in excluding points of law argued, and of the law reporters, on the other hand, in hearsay transmission producing date and other errors. But both versions have the lack of *proof of stealing* fatal to the prosecution.

A particular aspect of the issue is the difference between general and special verdicts. In general verdicts in misdemeanour cases, the court on after-verdict motions in arrest of judgment was willing to 'intend' – that is, presume – that the jury could not have found a verdict of guilty unless the essentials of the offence were proved.[49]

[44] 6 Modern 30, 87 ER 795, 31/795. The case cited is probably the 'old playhouse' case of Easter 1702, reported in the press to have failed due to 'a flaw being in the indictment' or 'the indictment being wrong laid': J Milling, '"Abominable, impious, prophane, lewd, immoral": prosecuting the actors in early eighteenth-century London' (2007) 61 *Theatre Notebook* 132–43 at 137–38.

[45] 10 Mod 192, 88 ER 689, 194/690.

[46] 1 Stra 193, 93 ER 467, 194/468.

[47] 8 Mod 248, 88 ER 177.

[48] *OBO* # t17240226-29.

[49] Argument for the Crown in *Roberts* (1692) 4 Mod 100, 87 ER 286 (extortion); *Lammas* (1694) Skin 562, 90 ER 252 (excise offence); Holt CJ in *Greep/ Griepe* (1697) 12 Mod 139, 88 ER 1220, 143/223, Comb 459, 90 ER 591, 461/592, 1 Ld Raym 256, 91 ER 1067, 261/1070; *Wind* (1729) Sess Cas 129, 93 ER 130 (riot),

Where a special verdict was given, in contrast, the court would not 'intend' anything not in the verdict. Thus in *Plummer* (1702) an 'owler' was killed by friendly fire in an exchange of fire with customs officials. Holt CJ said that:

> it does not appear anywhere in the verdict that the person who did shoot off the fusee did shoot it against any of the King's officers; for if that had been found, it had been murder in them all; but that being not found, we cannot intend it; though upon the circumstances of the evidence, as it did appear, there was enough for the jury to have found such a verdict.[50]

The point is applied in several other cases.[51]

The same principle was applied in relation to summary convictions before JPs. Since there was no jury, the conviction had to recite the evidence, so that the King's Bench could decide on certiorari whether it was sufficient; and essential elements of the offence could not be 'intended'.[52]

Turning to cases where 'the proof', effectively meaning the burden of proof, was said to be on the defendant: in *Parsons* (1691) the prosecution argued (unsuccessfully) that the prerogative of pardon was restricted by statutory provisions in relation to murder, by virtue of Article 1 of the Bill of Rights 1689 on the dispensing power. The court is reported as giving as an argument for the retention of the prerogative:

> For suppose a bastard-child should be born dead, and the mother conceals it, and it is afterwards discovered that she had such a child; if she cannot prove by one witness that it was born dead, it is murder in her by the statute 21 Jac. 1, c. 27; but it would be a very hard case, if, upon such circumstances, the King should not have a power of pardoning.[53]

The argument assumes that the statutory reverse burden of proof is abnormal: otherwise this would not be 'a very hard case'.

In *Beare /Beere* (1698) (seditious libel) the jury found a special verdict that the defendant had only copied and collected the libels, but was not otherwise guilty. Holt CJ is reported in 12 Modern as saying that 'The defendant has had great favour in this verdict; for when a libel is produced, written with the proper hand of a man, and the author of it is not known, this puts the proof on him; and if he cannot produce the composer, the verdict shall be against him, and shall be as bad as taking one in possession of a horse that is stolen. …' Lord Raymond has the passage as 'The defendant Beare has had great favour in the verdict; for when a libel is produced written by a man's own hand, and the author of it is not known; he is taken in the manner ["taken with the mainour"], and that throws the proof upon him; and if he cannot produce the composer, the verdict will be against him. …'[54]

Lord Raymond CJ, 130/131; *Lady Lawley* (1730) Fitz-Gib 122, 94 ER 682, (1731) 2 Stra 904, 93 ER 930, 1 Barn KB 459, 94 ER 309, 460/309 (conspiracy to pervert justice).

[50] 12 Mod 627, 88 ER 1565, 627/2565, 1 Ld Raym 256, 91 ER 1067.

[51] See eg *Hayes* (1728) 2 Ld Raym 1518, 92 ER 485, 2 Stra 843, 93 ER 888 (forgery); *Frances/Francis* (1735) 2 Comy 478, 92 ER 1167, Cunn 165, 94 ER 1129.

[52] *Green* (1714) Gilb Cas 132, 93 ER 283, 133; *Marriott* (1717) 1 Stra 66, 93 ER 388; *Theed* (1731) 2 Stra 919, 93 ER 941, 2 Barn KB 16, 73, 94 ER 327, 365, (1732) Sess Cas 120, 93 ER 122; *Lloyd/ Floyd* (1733) W Kely 285, 25 ER 617, Sess Cas 67, 93 ER 68, (1734) Cunn 84, 1343, 94 ER 1078, 1109, 2 Stra 996, 93 ER 992; *Bryan* (1738) Andrews 81, 95 ER 307. Procedural correctness, as in that the defendant had been summoned, *could* be 'intended': *Venables* (1725) 8 Mod 377, 88 ER 268.

[53] *Rex v Anonymous [Parsons]* (1691) 4 Mod 61, 87 ER 263, 63/264.

[54] *Beere* (1698) 12 Mod 218, 88 ER 1274, 220-221/ 1275–76; *Beare* (1698) 1 Ld Raym 414, 91 ER 1175, 417/ 1177. *cf* also *George* (1703) 6 Mod 57, 87 ER 818.

Simpson (1714–17) was a game laws case in which the defendant had been convicted *in absentia*, not having appeared on summons. The objection that he had been convicted without a hearing was rejected, Parker CJ saying that 'in some of the cases put before, the law proceeds to condemn the party not only in his absence, but for his absence, or, which is all one, esteems his absence so strong an argument of guilt, that further proof is esteemed superfluous; whereas here the justices only proceed to examine, whether the charge be true; and do not condemn the offender, but on proof by oath'.[55]

Marriott (also 1717) is an early instance of the debates about reversed burden of proof in statutory exemptions and provisos, which have continued in modern times[56] – game laws again, here the defendant was convicted of keeping a greyhound while not having any of the statutory qualifications. Parker CJ began by arguing that it was for the defendant to show that he *was* qualified, but was persuaded that the form of the conviction was bad, because it relied on the witness merely swearing that the defendant was not qualified: 'he ought not to swear generally a man is not qualified, and such a general proof will not be good.'[57]

In *Empson* (1731–32) the defendant had been foreman of the Howdenshire jury under a commission of sewers, and was fined £60 for refusing to answer the commissioners' questions in relation to alleged alterations in a 'book of pains' delivered to him in this capacity. On certiorari, the conviction was objected to inter alia on the basis that the order was bad on self-incrimination grounds, and Crowle for the Crown argued that the question was not incriminatory, because 'though he should have answered it in the strongest manner against himself, viz. that the book was not in the same condition, when it was delivered to him, yet this would be far from convicting him for altering it; for the book was intrusted to the care of every one of the jurymen, as well as the foreman; and therefore it might have been any one of them, that altered it; and there was as much proof of that, as there was of the defendant's doing it'. Lord Raymond CJ and all the court agreed that the self-incrimination objection was fatal, since 'for if the defendant had answered, that the book was not in the same condition, when it was delivered to him, it would have been a very strong evidence against him, as he was foreman of the jury; and would have turned the proof upon him, that some other of the jurymen altered it.'[58]

In *Hassel* (1730) (larceny of a banknote by postal worker) the point takes a formal form. At the close of prosecution's evidence, defendant's counsel submitted that there was no case to answer, on the basis either that this was embezzlement, not larceny, or that the 1728 statute making it grand larceny only applied to 'banknotes', etc, in the plural:

> The Court, after consulting upon the subject, declared that it was their clear and unanimous opinion, that there was nothing in either of the objections; but that the offence, if the Jury believed the witnesses for the King, was clearly felony without the benefit of clergy.

[55] (1714) 10 Mod 248, 88 ER 713, (1717) 10 Mod 378, 88 ER 771, 380/772.

[56] *Turner* (1816) 5 M&S 206, 105 ER 1026; on the history see A Zuckerman, 'The Third Exception to the Woolmington Rule' (1976) 92 *LQR* 402; for continued relevance of the issue see P Roberts and A Zuckerman, *Criminal Evidence*, 3rd edn (Oxford, Oxford University Press, 2022) 290–305.

[57] 1 Stra 66, 93 ER 388, 66–67, 67/388. *cf* also *Gage* (1723) 8 Mod 63, 88 ER 51, 65/52, conviction on a defendant's confession is good, since 'the conviction should be on good proof, and a better cannot be had than the confession of the party against himself'; same point in *Thorogood* (1723) 8 Mod 179, 88 ER 131.

[58] 2 Barn KB 2, 25, 66, 171, 94 ER 317, 333, 360, 428, 171–72, 172/429.

> The prisoner was accordingly put on his defence, and he called several witnesses, who established a probable alibi; upon which he was acquitted.[59]

The Crown has *discharged* the burden of proof: therefore the defendant is 'put on his defence'.

IV. Burden of Proof in Printed Trials

I have already mentioned that the silence of *OBSP* reports cannot, given the editorial policy of the series, be treated as evidence of the absence of rules. There are, however, a number of cases in which more than mere silence has been used by supporters of the idea that the burden of proof was absent, or on the defendant to clear him or herself, in felony trials.

A few examples, from cases which have been cited in the literature as evidence of a presumption of guilt, obligation on the accused to speak, or reliance on accused's bad character to prove guilt: Langbein cites *James Watts and others* tried at Old Bailey Dec 10 1684 as an example of burden of proof on the defence, due to 'not being able to bring any proof, where they were at the time the Robbery was Committed, [Watts and Barnwell] were found Guilty'. Before the passage quoted by Langbein comes the information that the complainant

> finding his Saddle at a private house upon the Road where [the robbers] had left it, with a direction to send it to the Bell Inn in the Strand, he … carryed the Saddle accordingly as it was directed to the Tapster, desiring him to stop any Person that should come for it, when soon after, Brian O Cane came to demand it, for his Master James Watts, who being accordingly stayed, gave directions how to find his Master, who in fine, was taken together with Peter Barnwell, after some resistance at Chelsey, and the gelding found at the Bell-Inn in Westminster, Watts owning the Saddle and the Horse, and Barnwell having about him a Handkerchief and Necklace, taken from Winlows Wife, and in Watts Chamber a broken Ring found, being part of the goods of Winlow

In short, Watts and Barnwell were 'taken with the mainour' later on the day of the robbery.[60]

Anthony Gery, tried at the Old Bailey April 7 1714 for robbery, is cited by Langbein as an example of reliance on the accused's bad character to convict. Before the bad character was used, a witness 'depos'd, That having been to fetch some Oysters in a Porringer, as she was coming home, she met the Prisoner and another; and while the other catch'd hold of her pretending to kiss her, the Prisoner snatch'd the Porringer, and being pursu'd and taken, threw it under a Stall, where it was found.' This is not *quite* 'taken with the mainour' but even so is a pretty open and shut case and would in modern criminal practice be most likely to result in arguments in mitigation on a guilty plea.[61]

[59] 1 Leach 1, 168 ER 103, 5/105.
[60] Langbein, *Origins* (n 2) 57, fn 231; *OBO* # no. t16841210-43.
[61] Langbein, *Origins* (n 2) 194 (n 77); *OBO* # t17140407-4.

Langbein gives *Joseph Still*, tried at the Old Bailey for murder on 27 February 1717, as an example of the use of accused's bad character to convict. Again we should look at what came before the use of the bad character: the witnesses for the Crown stated that they arrested Still struggling with his dying victim, who he had just hit on the head with a bill-hook. Not 'taken with the mainor', but literally caught red-handed.[62]

Beattie cites *John Durham*, tried at Kingston-on-Thames Lent Assizes 1739 for housebreaking, as an example of burden of proof on the accused. The householder's wife, finding the house broken into, raised the hue and cry, and Durham was rapidly arrested in possession of the goods stolen: 'taken with the mainour'. His defence was that an unknown third party had asked him to hold a bundle containing the goods. While this implausible story *might* be true, for the Court to say to Durham 'you must prove that' is not evidence of a presumption of guilt, nor of any stronger obligation on the accused to offer evidence than the pressure which would apply to a late twentieth or twenty-first century accused who offered in an English Crown Court only his own *ipse dixit* to support such a story after such damning evidence had been led for the prosecution.[63]

What these cases – and others like them – show is what was in much of the twentieth century called the shifting of the burden of proof – an idea to which recent evidence lawyers are rather allergic, talking instead of a shifting 'tactical' burden.[64] The prosecution has led enough evidence that, in the absence of evidence from the defence side to call it into question, the jury could perfectly properly convict. If the jury believes the prosecution's evidence, the *practical* risk of non-persuasion of the trier of fact now falls on the defendant.

More generally, it is perfectly *possible* that practice may contradict legal-doctrinal sources, or supply indirect evidence of law in their absence. But the question of the burden of proof in criminal cases between 1689 and 1760 is not such a case. There is a good deal of material in the legal-doctrinal sources, and the material in the *OBSP* and similar sources – so far as they are not merely silent – is *consistent with* the doctrinal sources on these issues. It is then unnecessary to produce a theorisation of the nature of criminal *law* on the basis of the supposed characteristics of the 'accused speaks' trial.

[62] Langbein, *Origins* (n 2) 193 (fn 68) ('Sill' there is a typo); *OBO* # t17170227-13.

[63] Beattie (n 5) 349; *The Genuine Proceedings at the Assizes on the Home Circuit, March 1739* (London, 1739) 20. I reiterate that these cases from Langbein and Beattie are *examples*.

[64] Varying approaches in eg C Tapper, *Cross & Tapper on Evidence*, 12th edn (Oxford, Oxford University Press, 2010) 120–28; JD Heydon (ed), *Cross on Evidence*, 11th Australian ed (London, LexisNexis Butterworths, 2017) 330–32, 358–64; Roberts and Zuckerman (n 56) 249–50.

10

Motive and Malice Prepensed

JOSHUA GETZLER

David Ibbetson left a deep mark on 1990s Oxford. I remember clearly his intricate and well-attended lectures on the history of obligations, exploring ideas that were to inform the classic monograph just around the corner.[1] I prized those tightly organised, smudgily printed pages of comment on my draft chapters sent ahead of supervisions. I would open the notes arriving from Magdalen with great anticipation, looking forward to discussing the contents with David, and knowing that his lines would set me off into fresh discoveries in libraries and archives for a good few weeks or months. David emphasised to his legal history students the wider horizon of civilian and philosophical influence within the common law, whilst helping us enter the details of pleading, forensics and court exchanges from which the practical justice system was built. His friendly engagement and unfailing courtesy showed us all by example how to learn and debate together in the search for durable truths. 'How to enter into the Roman law as a newcomer from Australia?' I asked him early on, not a little daunted. 'Start with Buckland,' David told me. 'He sometimes writes like the engineer he once was. But it's really good scholarship.'

I am sure that the Pauline precept recorded in D 50.17.168.pr was written with David in mind.[2]

I. Purpose, Motive, and Legality

My springboard for this chapter in David's honour is the general problem of detecting and harnessing *motive* as a factor in determining liability in law. David deepened my interest in this topic with his work on the Elizabethan Court of Wards.[3] There he showed that the hunt for collusive arrangements denying the Crown the full value of its feudal incidents after the Reformation was nonetheless governed by a deep commitment to

[1] DJ Ibbetson, *A Historical Introduction to the Law of Obligations* (Oxford, Oxford University Press, 1999).

[2] *Rapienda occasio est, quae praebet benignius responsum*, 'The occasion of offering a mild reply must be seized.'

[3] DJ Ibbetson, 'Elizabethan Revenue Law: The Practice of the Court of Wards' in J Tiley (ed), *Studies in the History of Tax Law, Vol 4* (Oxford, Hart Publishing, 2010) 107–20.

legal proof and due process. Similar issues of rule-of-law propriety were raised whenever a court embarked on purposive interpretation of conduct, from the medieval mortmain tribunals holding feudal lords to account,[4] to the whole gamut of conciliar, prerogative, and church courts headed by Star Chamber[5] that regulated and maintained public order and morals, including defamation and treason. Adding to the police functions wielded by these courts, the historical Chancery jurisdiction up and running by the fifteenth century can be seen a system of control of contractual and proprietary powers looking for valid motives (*bona fides*, good conscience) in the acquisition and wielding of those powers.[6] By the eighteenth century, lawyers such as Lord Hardwicke C and Lord Mansfield CJ were extending the equitable tests for measuring purposeful powers to the arena of public administration via eleemosynary corporations.[7] The modern dogma that motive is irrelevant in the wielding of rights and the binding of duties does not match earlier legal consciousness, and may even be a poor fit for the law of our own times.[8]

There is another area of motive-driven litigation hiding in plain sight, in our criminal law. The historical law of murder revolved around tests for inferring malice aforethought or 'malice prepensed' from the surrounding facts of a killing; and here malice went beyond mere intention to harm or kill, and addressed the purposes in the mind of the perpetrator when contributing to the death of a victim. Conventional presumptions allowed culpable motive to be extrapolated from a more limited forensic observation of conduct. Judges and counsel debated in court how correct inferences could be drawn from acts, speech and context, revealing motivations relevant to liability and defences; and legislators periodically intervened to vary the presumptions and proofs establishing guilt. This chapter examines the legal search for motivation in felonious killing in the modern (post-1700) period, building on extant scholarly analyses of earlier law.[9]

II. Defining Malice Prepensed: Objective v Subjective Measures

Sir Edward East in his influential 1803 *Treatise of Pleas of the Crown*, defined 'malice aforethought express' in murder as 'where the deliberate purpose of the perpetrator was

[4] PA Brand, *Kings, Barons and Justices: The Making and Enforcement of Legislation in Thirteenth-Century England* (Cambridge, Cambridge University Press, 2009).

[5] I Williams, 'Learning the "New Law of the Star Chamber": Legal Education and Legal Literature in Early-Stuart England' (2022) 43 *JLH* 243.

[6] JH Baker, *The Oxford History of the Laws of England Volume VI: 1483–1558* (Oxford, Oxford University Press, 2003) 171–90, 653–86.

[7] *Charitable Corporation v Sutton* (1742) 2 Atk 400; 26 ER 642 (LC); *R v Windham* (1776) 1 Cowp 377, 98 ER 1139 (KB).

[8] OW Holmes Jr, 'Privilege, Malice and Intent' (1894) 8 *Harvard LR* 1; M Taggart, *Private Property and Abuse of Rights in Victorian England: The Story of Edward Pickles and the Bradford Water Supply* (Oxford, Oxford University Press, 2002).

[9] The classic analyses of early law of intent and motive in homicide are JF Stephen, *A History of the Criminal Law of England*, 3 vols (London, Macmillan, 1883) III, 1–108; and FW Maitland, 'The Early History of Malice Aforethought' in HAL Fisher (ed), *Collected Papers* (Cambridge, Cambridge University Press, 1911) I, 304–29. Leading recent contributions are TA Green, *Verdict According to Conscience: Perspectives on t e*

to deprive another of life, or do him some great bodily harm'. He adds to this overtly purposive definition of *mens rea* a significant extension:

> But he who wilfully and deliberately does any act which apparently endangers another's life, and thereby occasions his death, shall, unless he clearly proves the contrary, be adjudged to kill him of malice prepense.[10]

This problem was isolated two centuries earlier in Lambard's *Eirenarcha*, noting that the malice implied by law from voluntary conduct was actually a form of legal liability independent of the subjective motivations of the actor. He stated:

> Many times the law doth by the sequel judge of that malice which lurked before within the party, and doth accordingly make imputation of it … the law judgeth it [an act of unprovoked killing] to have proceeded of former malice, meditated within his own mind, however it be kept secret from the sight of other men.[11]

The phrases 'malice prepensed', 'former malice', a 'malice that lurked before within the party', later as in Blackstone 'malice aforethought' and 'implied malice',[12] connoted a widely accepted method of inferring evil intent and purpose from evidence of evil conduct, and then moving the onus of proof to the defendant to adduce justifications or excuses such as necessity or self-defence. But this inferential method, deriving initial guilt from observed conduct and then measuring defences, is also an irritant, colliding with the dogma that took hold in later centuries, namely that criminal intention as an element of liability must be proven by the prosecution as being subjectively held by the defendant in order to establish guilt and justify punishment.

Courts seem condemned to live with this destabilising irritation, a legal version of the Other Mind problem, where one person strives to grasp or reconstruct the thought and intentions of another, using inter-subjectivity as a tool to imagine thought outside one's own consciousness.[13] Historically the problem is solved (or evaded) by delegating adjudication of mind states to the lay jury; but this delegation does not completely allay the irritation, for jurors must be instructed by the judge as to what evidence is admissible and how to measure it. Despite the ideological emphasis on subjective proof of wicked intent, the courts are cognisant that objective tests in the form of evidentiary inferences are used to get at that intent.[14] The House of Lords decision in *DPP v Smith*[15]

English Criminal Trial Jury, 1200–1800 (University of Chicago Press, 1985); and EP Kamali, *Felony and the Guilty Mind in Medieval England* (Cambridge, Cambridge University Press, 2019); EP Kamali, 'The Audacity of Judging Mind in Medieval England' (2023) 53 *Journal of Medieval and Early Modern Studies* 493. *cf* SFC Milsom, *Historical Foundations of the Common Law*, 1st edn (London, Butterworths, 1969) ch 14, esp 353.

[10] EH East, *A Treatise on the Pleas of the Crown* (London, Strahan 1803) I, 222, 225. MN Dyson, *Explaining Tort and Crime: Legal Development Across Laws and Legal Systems, 1850–2020* (Cambridge, Cambridge University Press, 2022) deals with later periods when the framework of motivic analysis had faded almost completely.

[11] W Lambard, *Eirenarcha: or Of the Office of the Iustices of Peace, in foure Bookes: Reuised, corrected, and enlarged*, 2nd edn (Companie of Stationers, London, 1610) 239. This passage does not appear in the original 1581 edition and was introduced by later editors as a statement of the law at the time of James I.

[12] W Blackstone, *Commentaries on the Laws of England* (Oxford, Clarendon Press, 1765–69) bk 4, c 14.

[13] A Avramides, 'Other Minds', in EN Zalta and U Nodelman (eds), *Stanford Encyclopedia of Philosophy*, see plato.stanford.edu/archives/win2023/entries/other-minds/.

[14] See eg *R v Woollin* [1998] 1 AC 82 (HL).

[15] [1961] AC 290.

went too far in tilting the emphasis to objectivism, creating a legal presumption that one intends the natural and probable consequences of one's actions. This blunt objectivism was vehemently rejected by jurists and judges, notably by Dixon CJ and the High Court of Australia in *Parker v The Queen*,[16] and under this withering assault the *Smith* doctrine was abruptly overturned by Parliament.[17] But objectivist inferences are inevitable whenever one person seeks to judge the mind state of another; and it is more than likely that assessment of motive or purpose plays some part in that inferential process, whether as a matter of establishing initial liability or setting up a full or partial defence or rebuttal. The law, despite attempts at camouflage, will open windows into people's hearts and search for motives. And sometimes the desire to attribute purpose, will, agency and responsibility to the individual may result in working backwards, constructing motives and intentions in order to acknowledge the dignity of the criminal as a morally competent actor deserving of censure.[18]

The fact that modern courts[19] and commentators[20] have criticised and put to one side the old formulations of 'malice prepensed' or malice aforethought does not mean that the problem of assessing motive as a factor in criminal intent has vanished. Tracing the path of the malice theory through the historical cases and statutes can reveal much of what is at stake.

III. The History of Murder: Holt CJ's Account

An important, now rarely noted examination of the history of murder and malice prepensed is found in Holt CJ's speech in the case of *R v Mawgridge*, from the Court of Queen's Bench in 1706,[21] building on Holt's judgments in the cases of *Keat*[22] and *Plummer*[23] decided in 1701–2. The *Mawgridge* speech burst the bounds of a normal reserved judgment of the time; it may be compared to a reading or a moot assaying the origins and testing the direction of the law through an overt display of historical scholarship and policy speculation.[24] Sir John Holt (1642–1710) was appointed chief justice

[16] (1963) 111 CLR 610. The post-*Smith* debate is summed up in JE Stannard, 'Murder, Intention and the Inference of Intention' (1999) 34 *Irish Jurist NS* 202.

[17] Criminal Justice Act 1967, s 8.

[18] A von Hirsch, *Censure and Sanctions* (Oxford, Oxford University Press, 1993).

[19] See eg House of Lords in *Hyam v DPP* [1975] AC 55.

[20] See eg JJ Child, AP Simester, JR Spencer, FG Stark and GJ Virgo, *Simester and Sullivan's Criminal Law: Theory and Doctrine*, 8th edn (Oxford, Hart Publishing, 2022) 122–96, 637–40, 879 ff.

[21] (1706) Kelyng 119, 84 ER 1107 (QB). The report of *Mawgridge* was appended to the earlier Kelyng MS reports by Holt himself, as made plain in full title of the first 1708 edition: *A Report of Divers Cases in Pleas of the Crown, Adjudged and Determined, in the Reign of the late King Charles II, Collected by Sir John Kelyng, K*nt.*, Late Lord Chief Justice of His Majesty's Court of King's Bench. From the Original Manuscript, under his own Hand. To which is added, The Reports of Three Modern Cases*, Viz. *Armstrong* and *Lisle*, The KING and *Plumer*; The QUEEN and *Mawgridge*. (Cleave, Chancery Lane, 1708). Moreover, a prefatory note by 'J. Holt, John Powell, Littleton Powys, H. Gould' approves the publication of Kelyng's reports, 'and Three other Modern Cases added thereunto'. It was clearly important to Holt that the case should be widely known and noted. Of other reports, 17 State Trials 30, 57 more or less reproduces the Kelyng report; and (1706) Holt KB 484, 90 ER 1167 is a compressed summary only.

[22] *R v Keat* (1701) 5 Modern 287, 87 ER 661 (KB).

[23] *R v Plummer* (1706) Kelyng 109, 84 ER 1103 (QB).

[24] For another example of Holt CJ applying this method, see the bailment case of *Coggs v Barnard* delivered three years earlier, similarly replete with historical scholarship: (1703) 2 Lord Raym 909, 92 ER 107; 3 Lord

of King's Bench in 1689, and is counted the greatest jurist of the post-revolutionary period. Holt's analysis provides a helpful framing device to enter into a complex doctrinal history; it is well worth bringing this elaborate and influential judgment back into view.[25]

The facts of the case were these: the defendant Mawgridge was invited to a convivial gathering by one Lieutenant Cope of the Queen's Guards in Cope's rooms in the Tower of London; Mawgridge there insulted a female friend of Cope, and Cope reproached him for it; Mawgridge took umbrage and challenged Cope to a duel, who replied that this was neither the time nor place for it, and asked Mawgridge to be more civil or leave. Mawgridge departed, but on the way out threw a bottle at Cope hitting his head, and also drew his sword. Cope threw another bottle back, in turn hitting his assailant in the head. Mawgridge enraged then stabbed Cope with his drawn sword and killed him. The jury having established the facts on a special verdict asked the court to advise if they should be trying Mawgridge for murder or manslaughter. Mawgridge had meanwhile escaped custody, and the result of the case was that the court found on the stated facts he was guilty of murder in absentia, though Trevor CJ dissented. Kelyng reports the speech of Holt CJ with great care. Holt CJ himself notes the weighty burden of judgment requiring empanelment of an enlarged court, summing up the result of the case with added emphasis:

> This record being removed into this Court, the case hath been argued before all the Judges; and all of us, except my Lord Chief Justice Trevor, are of opinion that Mawgridge is guilty of murder.

Holt added for good measure, 'This hath been a case of great expectation.'[26]

Holt CJ began his discussion of the substantive law by describing murder as homicide 'committed in the worst manner'.[27] He notes that this modern concept of murder as distinguished from manslaughter was evolved 'by the statute of 23 H. 8 and other statutes that took away the benefit of clergy from murder committed by malice prepensed.' To understand what this idea of killing by malice prepensed might mean, Holt delved back into the history of clergyable and non-clergyable homicides, to see what the Tudor reforms sought to achieve.

Holt claimed that the word '*MURDER*' was originally known only in the British Isles, and began with laws of Edward the Confessor and before him Canute, describing murder as a secretive homicide of a Dane by an Englishman without witnesses or capture of suspect within a week and a month, in which case the vill or hundred would be levied a heavy fine as a collective punishment and inducement to produce the perpetrator.[28]

Raym 163, 92 ER 622; 1 Salk 26, 91 ER 25; 2 Salk 735, 91 ER 613; 3 Salk 11, 91 ER 660; 3 Salk 268, 91 ER 817; 1 Com 133, 92 ER 999; Holt 13, 90 ER 905; Holt 131, 90 ER 971; Holt 528, 90 ER 1190 (QB); anatomised in DJ Ibbetson, '*Coggs v Barnard* (1703)' in C Mitchell and P Mitchell (eds), *Landmark Cases in Contract* (Oxford, Hart Publishing, 2008) 1–22.

[25] The case attracted some brief discussion as an authority on provocation in *Parker v R* [1964] AC 1369 (PC), and again in *R v Smith (Morgan)* [2000] 1 AC 146 (HL), but otherwise has slipped from view.

[26] (1706) Kelyng 119, 121, 84 ER 1107, 1108 (QB). On one account the judges met to discuss the issues in a convenient London coffee house, to help Holt CJ decide the reserved point.

[27] SC 121, 1108.

[28] SC 121–22, 1108–09; Maitland (n 9) 306–307 by contrast finds earlier Germanic roots for the prosecution of *morth* or concealed homicide, with pre-Conquest England using the generic idea to denote particularly wicked slayings, eg by witchcraft or poisoning, as a subset of secretive killings.

William I revived this procedure after 1066 to apply to the insidious killing of a Norman by an Englishman. Henry I on his accession in 1100 adapted the rule as follows:

> *That if a man be found slain, he should be taken to be a Frenchman if it was not proved that he was an Englishman, and the country was bound to enquire whether the person slain was an Englishman or a French-man.* These inquisitions were taken before the coroner, and returned to the justices in eyre, and if the jury found him an Englishman, then the country was to be discharged, which law was called Englishrie, and the justices in eyre were also bound to enquire thereof …[29]

Holt observed that the 'presentment of Englishry', founding communal investigation and sanction for homicide chiefly on the ethnicity of victim and perpetrator, derived from a long past pre-Conquest world, when 'the Englishmen hated the Danes upon the account of their nation that had subdued them, and would upon all occasions seek their destruction', and later, where 'the Conqueror had the same reason to suspect the safety of his Normans.' By Angevin times these ethnically-based rules were seen to be divisive and unjust, requiring

> any one apprehended to be the murderer … to be tried by fire and water, though he killed him by misfortune; which was extended beyond reason and justice in favour of the Normans: but if an Englishman was killed by misfortune, he that killed him was not in danger of death, because it was not felony.[30]

The 1267 Statute of Marlborough[31] attempted to do away with the worst mischiefs of this unsatisfactory justice. The relevant section stated:

> Murther from henceforth shall not be judged before our Justices, where it is found Misfortune only: But it shall take place in such as are slain by Felony, and not otherwise.[32]

Holt CJ interpreted this gnomic provision to mean that 'if it was known that the person slain was a Frenchman, and was killed by misfortune, then the country should not be amerced if the manslayer was not taken, or if he were taken, he should not be put to his ordeal trial'. Holt read this alongside the 1225 reissue of Magna Carta (9 Hen 3 c 26), requiring reasonable modes of arrest and trial, to argue that by the later thirteenth century any man who killed in self defence or by accident, and was not arraigned by the sheriff's writ *de odio et atia* ('of ill-will and hatred') was presumptively not a felon and could be bailed; here he adopted Coke's a creative interpretation of the relevant statute law.[33] At any rate the whole collective prosecution of murder as concealed homicide of a Frenchman or foreigner was abolished by the fourteenth century by abolition of presentments of Englishry and concomitant development of the coronial inquest.[34]

[29] SC 122, 1109, emphasis in the original. For the full procedure see LJ Downer (ed), *Leges Regis Henrici Primi* (Oxford, Clarendon Press 1972) c 90–92 (279–93).

[30] SC 122, 1109.

[31] 'Statute of Marlebridge' in Holt's usage.

[32] 52 Hen 3, c 25; Holt's text erroneously denotes this as c 26.

[33] *Mawgridge*, 120–24, 1109–10, citing Coke, *Second Part of the Institutes of the Lawes of England* (London, Fletcher and Young, 1642) part 1, 42. The difficult history of the procedural changes to prosecutions in the wake of Magna Carta 1215 c 32–40 is exposed by S Jenks, 'The Writ and the Exception *de odio et atia*' (2002) 23 *JLH* 1.

[34] 14 Edw 3 st 1, c 4–9 (1340), precursed by Statutes of the Exchequer, 14 Edw 1 /51 Hen 3, c 4 & 5.

It is against this procedural background that Holt read the Bractonian substantive jurisprudence of homicide. The great thirteenth-century treatise *On the Laws and Customs of England*, compiled by a succession of jurists and ascribed to the royal judge Henry de Bracton (c 1210–c 1268), distinguished three classes of homicide: (i) intentional killing done with 'premeditated hatred'; (ii) avoidable killing through careless or reckless conduct but without premeditation, both these first two categories being culpable homicides; and (iii) unavoidable and necessary killing, including killing in self-defence and by judicial act, done with 'sorrow of heart', and not culpable; to which could be added (iv) death by misadventure, without fault and without liability.[35] The first, most atrocious category of homicide was analysed as follows:

> By intention, as where one in anger or hatred or for the sake of gain, deliberately and in premeditated assault, has killed another wickedly and feloniously and in breach of the king's peace.[36]

Holt CJ noted that in this context intentional homicide, definitely a felony to be punished with death by the king, was described by Bracton as 'murder' only if done in secret; this capital crime did not inevitably involve premeditated malice. One might deliberately and hatefully kill in the open (likely felony, but not murder); and one might kill unobserved, whether by misadventure or by purpose, and then act to conceal the death (possibly murder, with a distinct malice ascribed from the fact of concealment, and then requiring ordeal to escape the automatic full penalty). Hence avowal of a killing and surrender to the authorities by the perpetrator came to be seen as an essential prelude to seeking pardon for a homicide, as the confession took the killer out of the murder category and allowed him (or her) to argue that this was a death by misadventure, for example through justified self-defence in the midst of a sudden affray, suitable for the king of his royal grace to afford mercy.

Bracton's language further suggested that, by the time the work was completed, the procedural reform attempted by the 1267 Statute of Marlborough had succeeded in shifting the law, in that the crime of murder now applied regardless of status, ie whether an Englishman had insidiously killed a Frenchman, an Englishman, or any other.[37] This shift away from a particular justice favouring and protecting the Norman ruling class may be a result of the universalism implied in Henry II's centralisation of justice within a common-law system of courts, including a claimed royal monopoly over trial of felonies. These more serious crimes were now given added meaning as pertaining of treason or disturbance of the king's peace, overlaying with public law jurisdiction the private procedures of appeal by the victim or his family and presentment before a local jury. Allied to this centralisation of felony prosecution was a strengthening of the pardon system as a regular tool of government and administration rather than personal discretion or whim of the monarch. At the same time pardons were used adventitiously as a reward or incentive to shape subjects' behaviour; for example the Angevins were prone

[35] Bracton f 120–21, SE Thorne (ed and tr), *On the Laws and Customs of England* (Cambridge MA, Harvard University Press, 1968–77) II, 340–41.
[36] ibid, II, 341.
[37] *Mawgridge*, 123–24, 1109–10.

to use the pardoning power to recruit excused perpetrators to the army.[38] The flexibility of pardon in the time of Henry III is demonstrated in chapter 26 of the Statute of Marlborough 1267, which extended the reach of the prerogative of mercy and allowed a royal pardon for the slayer by misadventure even of a Norman, further removing the special protection of the old ruling class left over from the earlier period, and creating a more universal law sanctioning culpable homicide.[39]

It was the ready granting of royal pardon for non-murderous killing (equals non-concealed, admitted or confessed killings, and therefore not presumptively malicious / premeditated), together with the wide availability of benefit of clergy insulating literate Englishmen from the power of secular courts, that ultimately led to a shift in the concepts of felonious homicide to yield the modern distinction between manslaughter and murder. Holt CJ in *Mawgridge* puts it thus:

> It appears, that since that of Bracton the notion of *murder* is much altered, and comprehends all *homicides*, whether privately or publickly committed, if done by malice prepensed.[40]

The shift towards explicit punishing of 'malice prepensed' independent of concealment was accelerated in the reign of Richard II, who as a weak and partial king found his power of pardon resented by the elites. In 1389 the Commons petitioned the king to stop giving pardons for culpable homicides, which in their view served to undermine deterrence; the king assented to the petition in terms stating that any charter of petition for pardon of homicide should be abated where the victim 'was murdered or slain by await, assault or malice prepensed'.[41] Holt CJ comments that 'This is a plain description of murder, as it was taken to be according to the common understanding of men'. That is, 'murder', now connoting a culpable killing too serious to allow pardon, was assimilated to killing with malice prepensed, and so discarded the older elements of secretive and/or culpably careless killing.[42]

The late-fourteenth-century language denoting murder simply as killing with malice was enlarged by Tudor legislation curbing benefit of clergy. One might argue that the old protections of Danes and Normans which caused such discomfort had given way by the late fifteenth century to a class-based divide based on wealth and education, whereby literate actors who killed or maimed were given the benefit of the doubt as to their culpability by virtue of their higher social position evidenced by their relative sophistication compared to the illiterate populace. But this privileging of higher-born or wealthy perpetrators caused as much juridical and social unease as the older law of the Danes and Normans, which had singled out low-born English perpetrators for special sanction. Much of the history of felonious killing from the late fifteenth century can be portrayed as a renewed attempt to introduce equality of treatment for all, whether perpetrators or victims.

[38] Thorough examination in ND Hurnard, *The King's Pardon for Homicide before A.D. 1307* (Oxford, Clarendon Press, 1969). See further F Pollock and FW Maitland, *The History of English Law Before the Time of Edward I*, 2 vols (Cambridge, Cambridge University Press, 1895) II, 448–557; OW Holmes Jr, *The Common Law* (London, Macmillan, 1882) 39–76; Green (n 9); Kamali, *Felony* (n 9).

[39] *Mawgridge*, 122–23, 1109.

[40] SC 124, 1109.

[41] 10 Edw 3 stat 1 c 2 (1336).

[42] *Mawgridge*, 124–25, 1109–10.

Holt CJ continued his account of the development of murder with Henry VII's legislation passed in 1488[43] making benefit of clergy for homicide a one-off privilege; offenders were to be branded on the hand with an 'M' for a first manslaughter, and could not then claim church protection for a second. In 1496 petty treasons were excluded from benefit of clergy entirely. These initial statutes opened the gate to more thorough reform of the law of homicide, with benefit of clergy excluded by statute for any culpable killing (including now all petty treasons) involving 'wilful prepensed Murders' or 'prepensedly murder' in 1497.[44] Statutes followed further reducing benefit of clergy for 'murder upon malice prepensed' (1512),[45] 'wilful murder of malice prepensed' (1531),[46] and finally, 'murder of malice prepensed' (1547),[47] which became the stock phrase and was now to include poisoning or indirect killing, described as furnishing the means of death with malice prepensed.[48]

In the reign of Elizabeth, Sir William Stanford,[49] a judge of the Common Pleas, in his groundbreaking *Pleas of the Crown*, summed up the movement in the law as follows:

> At this day a man may define murder in another manner than it is defined by Bracton, Britton and Fleta: if any one of malice prepensed doth kill another, be he Englishman or foreigner, if secretly or publickly, that is murder. This was the definition long before the making of the statutes of 4 & 23 H. 8, and the other statutes that took away clergy. To define murder, there must be *malitia praecogitata* [malice prepensed] …[50]

Finally in 1603 the Statute of Stabbing[51] was passed holding that a person who killed by stab or thrust and was the first to draw blade shall be punished as if he had murdered, 'although it cannot be proved that the same was done of malice aforethought'. This ill-drawn statute caused no end of trouble in court, and the judges had to fit the statutory definition of presumptive malice within the new voluntarist definition of felony murder. Holt CJ concluded his analysis with the following explication of the consequences of the stabbing statute:

> One thing more is fit to be observed, that in all indictments for murder a man is not charged positively, that he did murder the person slain, but that he *ex malitia præcogitata, in ipsum insultum fecit, ac cum quodam gladio* [out of premeditated malice, he made an attack on him, and with a kind of sword], he gave him a wound whereof he died: *et sic ex malitia præcogitata ipsum murdravit* [and thus out of premeditated malice he murdered him], so the murder is charged upon him by way of conclusion, and as a consequence from the antecedent matter that is positively alledged.[52]

[43] 3 Hen 7, c 1 s 3.

[44] 12 Hen 7, c 7.

[45] 4 Hen 8, c 1.

[46] 23 Hen 8, c 1, also 25 Hen 8, c 3.

[47] 1 Edw 6, c 12, also 5 & 6 Edw 6, c 10.

[48] The expansion of homicides with malice prepensed counting as felonies outside the clergyable offences is charted in detail by King's Bench in *Powlter's Case* (1610) 11 Co Rep 29a, 77 ER 1181 (KB), and later in *The Case of William Nicholas* (1748) Foster 64; 168 ER 32 (Crown Cases Reserved). The judges in *Nicholas* noted that poisoning attracted a special horror comparable to the offence of treason, perhaps because death was administered in the guise of providing hospitality.

[49] Also spelled Staun(d)ford(e), Stamford.

[50] W Stanford, *Les Plees del Coron, diuisees in plusiours titles & common lieux, etc* (London, R Tottell, 1557) 18b, translation from the law French by Holt CJ, *Mawgridge*, 124, 1110.

[51] 1 Jac 1, c 8.

[52] *Mawgridge*, 125, 1110.

This way of thinking was taken from an influential passage in Coke's *Third Institutes*:

> Malice prepense is when one compasseth to kill, wound, or beat another, and doth it sedato animo [with settled will]. That is said in law to be malice forethought prepensed – malitia praecogitata. It is implied in three cases, (1) If one kills another without any provocation on the part of him that is slain. (2) If a magistrate or known officer … in doing or offering to do his office … is slain, that is murder by malice implied by law. (3) In respect of the person killing. If A assault B to rob him, and in resisting A killeth B, this is murder by malice implied, albeit he (A) never saw or knew him (B) before.[53]

The theory finally derived by Holt CJ from the historical sources may be summed as follows: wounding another to death will generally have malice prepensed assumed from the unprovoked violence, and will be taken to be murder, unless special circumstances are pleaded affording an excuse or justification. A fortiori if one kills a law officer, or kills while involved in a felony. One could not claim that mere verbal provocation, or a desire to chastise a servant or student or child, could take away the presumption of malice prepensed. The common law delineated the law of murder by stipulating those cases of presumptive malice where it was not possible to seek benefit of clergy, and where surrender and confession of homicide should not provide an avenue to royal pardon save in extraordinary circumstances.[54] Certain voluntaristic forms of killing, such as administering poison or stabbing with a weapon, were identified by statute as making a stronger presumption of malice prepensed, and made it more difficult for a perpetrator to rebut the inference that he acted with a guilty mind.

Holt CJ then turned to explore the reaches of malice prepensed in the context of Mawgridge's the killing of Lieutenant Cope. The precise question reserved for the court was whether Mawgridge's enraged attack following the mutual exchange of curses and bottles could involve a provocation defence that would exclude malice prepensed and reduce the crime to manslaughter. The answer was no: because the assailant had initiated the physical exchanges.

Holt CJ explained:

> Here is express malice, that appears by the nature of the action. Some have been led into mistake by not well considering what the passion of malice is; they have construed it to be a rancour of mind lodged in the person killing, for some considerable time before the commission of the fact, which is a mistake arising from the not well distinguishing between hatred and malice. Envy, hatred, and malice, are three distinct passions of the mind.
>
> 1. Envy properly is a repining or being grieved at the happiness and prosperity of another, *invidus alterius rebus macrescit opimis*.
>
> 2dly, Hatred, which is *odium*, is as Tully saith, *ira inveterata* [unyielding rage], a rancour fixed and settled in the mind of one towards another, which admits of several degrees. It may arrive

[53] E Coke, *The Third Part of the Institutes of the Laws of England, Concerning High Treason, and other Pleas of the Crown, and Criminall causes* (London, Flesher, 1644) 54. Probably written in Coke's last years and published a decade after his death in 1634, this volume emphasised treason, heresy and associated state crimes, with less material on interpersonal crimes, and clearly drew from Coke's 12 years' experience as Attorney-General from 1594 to 1606.

[54] See the discussion by the judges of a string of felonies at the Newgate Sessions on 14 October 1661, reported in *Raven's Case* (1661) Kelyng 24, 84 ER 1065, esp *Grey's Case* at 65, 1085: 'where one man killeth another without any provocation, the law judgeth it malice prepensed'.

> to so high a degree, and may carry a man so far as to wish the hurt of him, though not to perpetrate it himself.
>
> 3dly, Malice is a design formed of doing mischief to another; *cum quis data opera male agit*, he that designs and useth the means to do ill is malicious, 2 Inst. 42 [Coke]. *Odium* signifies hatred, *atia* malice, because it is eager, sharp and cruel. He that doth a cruel act voluntarily, doth it of malice prepensed, 3 Inst. 62 [Coke]. … If one doth such a mischief on a sudden, that is malice prepensed; for saith my Lord Coke, *If it be voluntarily, the law will imply malice*. Therefore when a man shall without any provocation stab another with a dagger, or knock out his brains with a bottle, this is express malice, for he designedly and purposely did him the mischief. This is such an act that is malicious in the nature of the act itself, if found by a jury, though it be sudden, and the words *ex malitia præcogitata* are not in the verdict.

Holt CJ observed that Mawgridge had insulted and initiated violence against Cope, who had responded lawfully to that attack, only to have Mawgridge rush to stab him, as if exploiting the response to his original violence to finish off his adversary. This could not fall within a provoked attack, but was rather a continuous stream of malicious attack. In other words, Mawgridge's behaviour to Cope had demonstrated a formed malicious desire to cause grave or deadly harm. Here the claimed provocation of Cope's bottle throw was really only a pretext to kill with malice prepensed. Holt concluded by giving further examples of reciprocal conduct that exceeded the bounds of provocation – killing in response to verbal insults; killing a trespasser or thief (not in the home) who gave no resistance; killing a householder in his own home who resisted a demand of entry; killing an 'obstinate or perverse' servant or dependant by chastisement with an inappropriate instrument or excessive force. Conversely one could be provoked by a physical slighting, by seeing one's family or friends under attack or wrongly imprisoned, or by witnessing one's spouse in an act of adultery.[55]

IV. Holt's Malice Presumption in Wider Context

Holt's *Mawgridge* speech can be seen to achieve two goals. He wished to establish ample authority for the idea that a voluntary unprovoked act causing death in itself showed malice prepensed and hence was presumptively a murder, thus assimilating the motive of murder to the intent to kill or harm. Direct violence was express malice; lesser causing of death implied malice. This criminal version of *res ipsa loquitur* had large moral and political implications, for in effect the presumptions grounded liability for a capital crime out of what might appear as an unexplained or accidental action ending badly. Holt dealt with this moral tension by setting out the types of defences that a judge could properly identify and put to the jury in order to soften and reverse the presumption of an evil mind whenever a death was caused.

This two-step process of presumptive liability softened by defences was justified by Holt CJ as the correct reading of the history of homicide cases and statutes as described above. Support was also drawn from authoritative treatise source such as Bracton and Coke. Holt CJ briefly cites Matthew Hale's then-unpublished discussion of homicide

[55] *Mawgridge*, 126–38, 1110–15.

in his *Pleas of the Crown*,[56] dating from the 1660s and by 1700 circulating widely in manuscript.[57] Hale's work was a rational restatement of past juridical work, typically adding case-law detail and precision to a core of ideas laid down in Coke's *Second* and *Third Institutes*, and a careful reading of Holt's *Mawgridge* speech shows that it was from Coke that many of the main ideas were derived. But if Holt and Hale were each quite Cokean in approach, we may also note that they were also drawing form a dense tradition of judicial debate over the forensics of motive and intention stretching back to Elizabethan times, and we will conclude by surveying this jurisprudence, breaking the law into separate themes.

V. Timing of Fatal Action

An important discussion of assessment of mind-states was afforded by the important 1561 King's Bench case of *Hales v Petit*,[58] ostensibly a trespass action for cattle damage but in effect a boundary dispute between freeholders. The criminal twist to this civil case was that the plaintiff traced title immediately from her deceased husband, a judge named Sir James Hales, who had drowned himself by casting himself in a river. The defendant brought a successful defence in bar that the widow lacked title to sue as her husband's estate was forfeit to the Crown as Sir James was presumptively a *felo de se*, a felon against himself. Plowden's report provided a lengthy record of debate between counsel and the judges as to how to understand the timing of homicide by seeking harm to self, with the plaintiff's side arguing that the self-destructive act of jumping into water was not the cause of death but rather the river itself. One could see the distinction by noting how a person who had cast himself into a river and then tried to save himself but yet drowned could not be said to have purposed his self-destruction at the time of death. The court rejected such subtleties, with Dyer J summing up the law in these terms:

> And as to the quality of the offence which Sir James has here committed, he said, it is in a degree of murder, and not of homicide or manslaughter, for homicide is the killing a man feloniously without malice prepense, but murder is the killing a man with malice prepense. And here the killing of himself was prepensed and resolved in his mind before the act was done. And also it agrees in another point with the ancient definition of murder, viz.[59] that *murdrum est occulta hominum occisio, nullo præsente, nullo sciente* [murder is the secret killing of men, with no one present and no one knowing]; so that always he who determines to kill himself, determines by the instigation of the devil to do it secretly, *nullo præsente, nullo sciente*, lest he should else be prevented from doing it. Wherefore the quality of the offence is murder.[60]

[56] M Hale in S Emelyn (ed), *The History of the Pleas of the Crown* (London, E& R Nutt et al, 1736) 451 ff; Stephen (n 9) 100 ff, 210 ff.

[57] A sole reference to 'Hale 42' appears at Kelyng 129, 84 ER 1111; as discussed at n 21, this report was edited and published by Holt himself, and his citation of the Holt MS is authentic.

[58] *Lady Margaret Hales, late Wife of Sir James Hales, late one of the Justices of the Common Bench v Cyriack Petit* (1561) 1 Plowden 253, 75 ER 387 (QB).

[59] Bracton f 134b, Britton c 6, S[tanford] P[rerogative] C[ases] [*Les Plees del Coron* (1560)] 12e, 17e.

[60] (1561) 1 Plowden 253, 261, 75 ER 387, 399–400.

By assimilating the crime of suicide to a secretive murder as in the early law of the Danes and Normans, Dyer J rooted the inference of a guiding felonious intent derived from the natural consequences of an act with the older legal policies of sanctioning unobserved conduct.

Dyer J went on to analyse the timing of any forfeiture for feloniously causing death. It was further proposed by counsel for the plaintiff that if the husband had only completed his felony at the point of death, then the succession of estate to his wife could have occurred at that same instant. This imaginative argument also failed, with Dyer J carefully analysing the nature of the self-victim's motivation and intent by setting in train his own demise:

> [T]he forfeiture here shall have relation to the time of the original offence committed which was the cause of the death, and that was the throwing himself into the water, which was done in his life-time, and this act was felony. And the indictment says, and may say, that he feloniously threw himself into the water; for that which caused the death may be said to be feloniously done. And therefore if one strikes another, so that afterwards he dies of it, the indictment ought to say that he struck him feloniously. So that the felony is attributed to the act, which act is always done by a living man, and in his life-time ... Sir James Hales was dead, and how came he to his death? It may be answered by drowning; and who drowned him? Sir James Hales; and when did he drown him? In his life-time. So that Sir James Hales being alive caused Sir James Hales to die; and the act of the living man was the death of the dead man. And then for this offence it is reasonable to punish the living man who committed the offence, and not the dead man. But how can he be said to be punished alive when the punishment comes after his death? Sir, this can be done no other way but by devesting out of him, from the time of the act done in his life which was the cause of his death, the title and property of those things which he had in his life-time.[61]

The problem of timing an ascription of felonious malice within a series of connected acts caused puzzlement again in the 1606 case of *George Leak*.[62] Leak was a fraudulent Chancery clerk who had written out a valid writ ready to receive the Great Seal on a thin slice of parchment that he had affixed to a thicker page, with the upper piece acceding to the lower so it could not be detected. Once the seal had been affixed Leak removed the upper layer and wrote out a fraudulent grant of lands to himself, so that the second writing appeared as validly authorised by the authentic seal on the parchment. The 1351 treason statute (25 Edw 3) had made counterfeiting the Great Seal a high treason, and the legislative rule had later been interpreted to include the removal of a seal from one document to another. The question before the court was whether Leak's action of *subtracting* part of the parchment amounted to an action falling within the statutory offence. The court split on this question, with some judges believing there was no treasonous act unless Leak had *expressly* intended to procure the Great Seal fraudulently at the time of affixing, which criminal motive had to be specially proven. Hence the act of ex post forgery could only be rated as a high misprision warranting imprisonment rather than execution. But in the end the Chief Justice of King's Bench prevailed and the

[61] SC 262, 401. A similar analysis was offered in the modern case of *R v Elizabeth Burgess* (1862) Leigh and Cave 258, 169 ER 1387 (Crown Cases Reserved).

[62] (1606) 12 Co Rep 15, 77 ER 1297 (KB).

statutory treason was extended to encompass Leak's conduct, with this metaphoric and political justification taken from the history of murder:

> … as if a man in an affray kills a constable that comes to keep the King's peace without any express malice prepensed, this is murder in law; and the delinquent may be generally indicted of murder by malice prepensed.[63]

No special proof of intent is required when the action generally encompasses a felonious motivation.

VI. Excessive Chastisement and Resisting Arrest

The problem of fatal violence when resisting arrest mentioned in *Leak* recurs often in the contemporary case-law. In *Halloway's Case*[64] a parker caught a boy trespassing in his park; the boy surrendered, but the parker nonetheless beat him badly and tied and dragged him behind a horse, breaking his shoulder. The boy died of his wound and the parker was adjudged a murderer to be hanged, and the question was referred to all the judges and barons as to whether excessive chastisement showed a deliberate cruelty indicating malice prepensed to kill. All the judges save Hutton J agreed that in circumstances of unnecessary and cruel punishment 'the law implies malice; and it shall be said in law to be prepensed malice, he doing it to one who made no resistance.'[65] The principle that excessive force would demonstrate malice prepensed was developed by Holt CJ himself in the 1701 case of *R v Keat*, where a man beat his servant on the head with the flat of his sword to chastise him for not surrendering a key to his garden; the servant retaliated by brandishing a scythe that was to hand, and the master then ran him through. Holt CJ, in a lengthy and scholarly judgment rehearsing the long history of murder, applied the *Halloway* precedent to find malice prepensed, and excluded the mitigating factor of provocation through the servant's return of violence, which might have been expected due to the unprovoked initial act of the master.[66]

The judges did not always sanction violent resistance during arrest, as shown in the difficult 1655 case of *The Protector v Buckner* in Court of King's Bench.[67] There a man named Horwood went to collect a debt from the defendant Buckner, taking an armed bailiff with him, and together they attempted to arrest the debtor in his house. Buckner of a sudden drew a dagger and stabbed Horwood to death, and then claimed that having been imprisoned by force, the circumstances of the felonious slaying took him out of the 1603 statute and permitted him to claim benefit of clergy. Ask J argued that the exact words of the statute must deny benefit of clergy, which he decried as a popish privilege taking from the common law not only the power to punish accidental or provoked manslaughter but even a deliberate murder. The clergy rule was doubly obnoxious as excluding all women from its protection. '[T]he statute shall be taken beneficially for

[63] SC 17, 1299.
[64] (1628) Croke, Car 131, 79 ER 715 (KB).
[65] SC 131, 716.
[66] (1701) 5 Modern 287, 87 ER 661 (KB).
[67] (1655) Style 467, 82 ER 867 (KB).

the commonwealth', Ask J declared, the better to avoid 'diminution of the common law, and of regal power, yea, and of the law of God also'. Buckner's act, drawing a dagger from his pocket and stabbing suddenly, fell exactly within the statute, and there should be no wide reading that he was provoked by his arrest:

> for all the acts done by Horwood amounted but to a trespass, and cannot be such a provocation as should cause Buckner to fear his death, for no violence was used to his person by striking, or drawing of a weapon, or other ways, and the sending for bailifs to arrest him cannot be such a provocation as the statute intends, which is to put the party in fear of his life, and the party knew that Horwood came with an intent only to arrest him, and not to kill him, nor did the party slain do any thing against Buckner to provoke him; and there is by presumption of law a prepensed malice in Buckner to kill Horwood, which is seen by his sudden manner of stabbing him.[68]

Ask J argued against expanding cases of clergy, noting that not even a strong verbal provocation placed a murder outside the statute, though he conceded that killing a thief by stabbing was within clergy, as was proportionate defence from attack, or mere accident. He concluded by stating that the lawyers of Serjeants' Inn including three ex-judges had been consulted and supported his interpretation. However, Glyn CJ thought otherwise, and adopted the arguments of Heneage Finch, counsel for the defendant, namely that benefit of clergy should apply where a person killed under duress of arrest, as this was not a hot-blooded stabbing within the mischief of the statute but rather a reaction to personal violence, akin to slaying a thief in one's home. Glyn CJ claimed the support of a majority of the judges, and in a later hearing had Warburton J join him *en banc* to find for the defendant. Buckner was admitted to clergy, had his hand burnt and escaped further punishment.

VII. Joint Enterprise

In a number of cases in the late sixteenth and seventeenth centuries a doctrine of *res ipsa loquitur* was applied to accessories where joint enterprise with an acknowledged felon was held to imply a felonious premeditated intent. Interestingly servant violence could implicate a master, and vice versa.

In *Egerton v Morgan*[69] a man was killed in an affray with three assailants; the brother of the deceased brought an appeal of murder against Morgan, the only one of the three who could be found, the others having fled. King's Bench on 1 January 1610 abated the appeal after lengthy analysis of whether a solidary felony liability could rightly be imposed under such an appeal without the prosecutory participation of the sheriff by return summons. The court then went on to try Morgan singly under a plea of the Crown. The jury found that the victim had challenged Morgan to a duel the day before, which challenge had been accepted. The hostiles then met by chance the next day and on a sudden fight Morgan had stabbed the victim twice or thrice, with one of

[68] SC 469–70, 869–70.
[69] (1610) 1 Bulstrode 69, 80 ER 770 (KB).

the thrusts killing him. The judges put aside the defence that this was a voluntary duel as the combat and killing stood outside the zone of the earlier challenge; yet the fact of the challenge showed animosity between the parties and helped to establish an express malice prepensed.

Yelverton J summarised the law as follows:

> As this case is, the law is clear, that this is murder, and it is no excuse for him to say, that he bore no malice to him before: for if one stab another, this shall be murder, for the law in such cases, doth presume malice to be in him, otherwise this would not have so hapned, and this the law calls malice apparent, and though the same cannot be proved, it is not material; a man cannot kill another in his own defence, which is manslaughter, but he shall for this forfeit all his goods, and to have the benefit of his clergy allowed to him, and if he cannot read, then to be hanged: but in case of murder, he is not to have his book allowed to him: but in this case, he is to appeal to mercy.[70]

Fleming CJ explained the inference of malice from conduct in terms of public policy evolved through an interaction of statutory prohibitions and common law interpretation:

> As to the matter now in question, there can be no murder without malice, and malice may be proved divers ways, as touching the matters precedent, these are either publick, or secret, upon these the law passeth no judgment, but in some cases the law will adjudge this to be maliciously done, though that no proof can be made of the malice, as where a publicke officer is killed by another in execution of his office, this is murder, for the law doth here adjudge this to be maliciously done, and in this fact, there is malice implyed; and so it is, if that two have a purpose, and intention for to fight, and they accordingly fight, and the one kills the other, this is murder, for here the law intends malice. In this case now in question, clearly here appears to be sufficient malice, to make this fact here, to be murder, this abuse by reason of challenges, is now grown to be too frequent, and nothing can be more perilous and destructive, than to suffer this in civil government, without being severely punished, and this is so frequently and advisedly undertaken, and that animo deliberato, that the greater care ought to be had of this, by way of prevention; stabbing, which is made murder by stat[ute]. this was murder at the common law, before the statute of 1 Jac cap 8 by the statute of 1 E 6 cap 12. poysoning made murder, and all wilful killing shall be taken as wilful murder, and so of malice prepensed: stabbing was wilful murder at the common law, for that in this is included, by apparent inference, malice prepensed, to precede the fact, and that this was the cause of the stabbing.[71]

In the end Morgan won a royal pardon and was freed, perhaps because the excuse of duelling yet appealed to the mores if not the law of the time.[72]

The judges struggled to develop the joint enterprise rule coherently where a number of persons were involved in joint wrongdoing and one only of the party used fatal violence in an action independent in time and place from his accomplices. An extreme case involved a gamekeeper killed when lawfully resisting a trespass by a marauding party hunting on private land, led by Thomas Dacre, Lord Fiennes. Dacre was convicted and hanged for his servant's homicide – even though Dacre was some way off when the killing took place.[73] This strong inference of malice including transferred malice

[70] SC 86, 785–86.

[71] SC 88, 786.

[72] The problem of duelling or voluntary public combat is thoroughly aired in KJ Kesselring, *Making Murder Public: Homicide in Early Modern England, 1480–1680* (New York, Oxford University Press, 2019).

[73] *Lord Dacre's Case* (1541/43) Moore 86; Brooke 237.

developed independently of the benefit of clergy and stabbing statutes, and may have involved a political element; there was some surprise that the king issued no pardon for Dacre but was content for an aristocrat to die by the noose for another's actions.[74]

Later the judges set some limits to this dangerous doctrine of transference of malice: for example if persons consented with obvious malice prepensed to duel with one another where each had a mutual intent to kill, then a helper unaware of the duel but acting precipitately to aid a friend in the conflict might be guilty only of manslaughter without malice, as he would have thought in the moment that he acted lawfully to defend the one from the violence of another.[75] And even where a group were pursuing an unlawful purpose in concert and one of them let off a gun killing a law officer, the others might not be guilty even of manslaughter, unless it could be proved that the person causing the death had acted purposefully, in order to resist arrest, as part of the joint unlawful enterprise, and had not killed in the moment through some private spite or hapless accident disconnected from the joint enterprise.[76]

As the law of accessory felony developed in the eighteenth century it became clear that the decisions could be as much driven by policy instinct and instant moral judgment as by the wording of statutes and the fitting of precedents. The courts were noticeably harsher in cases of petty treason, for example where a lover aided and abetted one spouse in killing another; the fact that such malign conduct was harshly sanctioned by hallowed and ancient statutes as well as a stream of cases helped the judges to convict even tangentially connected accomplices.[77] In other cases, where the offence seemed more *malum prohibita* than *malum in* se, for example where a modern statute created new felonies, or liberally added the death penalty to hitherto lesser offences, or removed clergy or other historical defences, the courts might interpret the operation of the criminalising statutes to exclude accomplices from their reach. In other words the equity of the statute applied more lightly where a natural offence was not in play. In the important *Case of John Midwinter and Richard Sims* in 1760 three co-conspirators determined to intimidate and punish a local prosecutor who was bringing an action against them for illegal rabbit hunting.[78] The three broke into his close and two of them (Sims and Taylor) captured and held steady a valuable breeding mare, so that the third (Midwinter) could slash its belly with a sharp hook. The mare died, and this brought Midwinter within the terms of a penal statute making a capital crime of maliciously wounding and killing cattle, without benefit of clergy. Taylor turned evidence against his partners, so escaping prosecution; Midwinter was convicted as principal and sentenced to death. Foster J at trial found the third man Sims guilty of aiding and abetting but doubted that the statute in its precise terms excluded clergy for an accomplice. The problem was perplexing and important enough for all the common-law judges to convene on three separate occasions to discuss the correct approach between the initial trial and the review hearing; but

[74] S Payling, 'The hanging of Thomas Fiennes, Lord Dacre: Henry VIII and the abuse of law', thehistoryofparliament.wordpress.com/2021/11/23/the-hanging-of-thomas-fiennes-lord-dacre-henry-viii-and-the-abuse-of-law/ (13 November 2021).

[75] *Sir Charles Stanley's Case* (1662) Kelyng 86, 84 ER 1094 (KB); *Thody's Case* (1673) 1 Freeman 514, 89 ER 386 (KB).

[76] *R v Plummer* (1706) Kelyng 109, 84 ER 1103 (QB).

[77] *The Case of John Swan and Elizabeth Jefferys* (1748) Foster 104, 168 ER 52 (Crown Cases Reserved).

[78] (1760) Foster 413, 168 ER 90 (Crown Cases Reserved).

for all that effort no consensus emerged. In a further hearing at Crown Cases Reserved the judge, presumably Foster J again, gave a lengthy judgment on accomplice liability for malicious participation in statutory offences, and he decided that whilst the cattle-maiming statute did apply to Sims as aider and abettor, he would not apply the exclusion of clergy to him as the statute had not spelled out such an application to accomplices. Foster J reasoned that other statutes such as the 1603 law against murder by stabbing had spelled out disabilities binding accomplices; this statute was silent. The crimes of high treason tended to involve principals involved in joint enterprise, so that sanctioning statutes applied to all who were involved equally. Especially horrendous felonies such as murder, rape and buggery, robbery, and burglary might sanction all 'persons offending in such an offence', encompassing not only principals or direct perpetrators, but also agents, patients, aiders, abettors, or indeed anyone involved in the detestable act, thus serving to exclude clergy entirely. Here the judges came to extend the primary criminal sanction to all persons present at the offending as deemed principals. However, in lighter cases where a supreme duty to stop a heinous act in one's purview did not apply, then those not directly perpetrating the proscribed act should not lose clergy unless the criminalising statute in strict terms made this clear. Foster J found that the eminent authorities Hale, Coke and Stanford, had

> laid down as a general rule, That indictments grounded on penal statutes, especially the most penal, must pursue the statute, so as to bring the party precisely within it: and this rule holds as well with regard to statutes which take away clergy from felonies at common-law, as to statutes creating new felonies.[79]

On this basis Sims could claim benefit of clergy outside the statutory bar, even though malice prepensed was ascribed to him under the main provision of the statute as a principal in the lower degree committing the felony.

VIII. Modernising Malice Prepensed

In the King's Bench case of *R v Oneby* in 1726,[80] Raymond CJ speaking for all 12 judges of the common law directly affirmed the Holt doctrine expressed 20 years earlier in *Mawgridge*, joining Holt's jurisprudence to that of Hale:

> The notion of murder is agreed on all hands to be, the killing another of malice prepense, that is in other words, a killing with a wicked design. The malice necessary to make the act murder, may be either express or implied; and my Lord Hale in his Pleas of the Crown, when he is describing what is malice implied, lays a great stress upon the manner of doing the act; and therefore puts the case of a man exercising an unruly horse amongst a multitude, where from the circumstances of the act it is highly probable a mischief may ensue.
>
> If a man kills another without any provocation, this is malice implied; for the law supposes there must be some latent malice in the party, or otherwise he would not be so barbarous as to take away the life of another. It may be murder, though words, or even blows pass between

[79] SC 422, 94.
[80] (1726) 2 Str 766, 93 ER 835 (KB).

> them .... I take this opportunity to declare, that we are all of opinion that *Mawgridge's case* is law.

The idea of malice aforethought as an inference from conduct reached its summation in the 1762 *Discourses* of Sir Michael Foster, who stated that a violent action could circumstantially indicate 'the symptoms of a wicked, depraved, malignant spirit ... the plain indications of a heart regardless of social duty and fatally bent upon mischief'.[81] Perhaps what is being sanctioned here is really evil character, a predisposition to misconduct revealed by the resort to deadly violence – a theme that Nicola Lacey has developed for the eighteenth and nineteenth centuries.[82]

At any rate, the presumptions of malice prepensed, whether partaking of evil motives or evil dispositions, did not survive into the twentieth century. In the great case of *Vickers* in 1957,[83] the intricate early modern law of malice aforethought was put to one side and a new test was propounded whereby the evidence was to be tested for a simple intention to kill or cause grievous bodily harm, with such intention to be extrapolated by the jury from the evidence of the case. *Vickers* was described by Lord Hailsham in 1975 in the leading case of *Hyam v DPP*[84] as a 'fresh start' that cut off the legal past; and he further recommended that the phrase 'malice aforethought, and its variants 'malice prepense' or 'prepensed', be abandoned as misleading archaisms:

> The precise value of this phrase is open to doubt. As long ago as 1883 Stephen described it as 'a phrase which is never used except to mislead or to be explained away' [History of the Criminal Law of England, vol. III, p. 83] and advised its abolition as a term of art and the substitution for it of a 'definite enumeration of the states of mind intended to be taken as constituent elements of murder.'
>
> ...
>
> the sooner the phrase is consigned to the limbo of legal history the better for precision and lucidity in the interpretation of our criminal law.[85]

In argument in *Hyam* the judges noted that malice aforethought was historically associated with evil motive or purpose and was used to ground a finding of initial liability for murder arising from the brute fact of homicide. The judges tried to quarantine the concepts of 'immediate' and 'ultimate purpose' as seeking a particular result from an operative intention to act with foresight of the likely consequences, even if those consequences were not purposed or desired.[86] Proof of subjective motive or purpose was therefore excluded as extraneous to any defence involving denial of intention. It was in this great case that the long history of malice prepensed as a formal category in the English courts came to an end; the courts no longer read back from harmful intention an evil motive as part and parcel of the nature of murder. But the haunting presence of

[81] Sir Michael Foster, *Discourses Upon a Few Branches of the Crown Law* (Oxford, Clarendon Press, 1762) 256–57.

[82] N Lacey, *Women, Crime, and Character: From Moll Flanders to Tess of the D'Urbervilles* (Oxford, Oxford University Press, 2008); N Lacey, *In Search of Criminal Responsibility: Ideas, Interests, and Institutions* (Oxford, Oxford University Press, 2016).

[83] *R v Vickers (John Willson)* [1957] 2 QB 664.

[84] [1975] AC 55, 59 (HL).

[85] SC 66.

[86] SC 58–59, *in arguendo.*

the old doctrines could not entirely be dispelled. Two of the five lords of appeal, Diplock and Kilbrandon, found that motive or purpose remained relevant due to two important modern reforms, namely the abolition of the concept of constructive or implied malice and the admission of a defendant's own testimony as to his or her mind state. Both reforms underlined the modern concern with subjective intentions as the hallmark of guilt – the point of controversy in the imbroglio over *DPP v Smith*.[87] The case of *Hyam* involved a person seeking to scare a rival away from her desired partner by setting the rival's house on fire, inadvertently killing two children who could not escape the flames. According to Lord Diplock, the defendant's evidence denying that she purposed to kill or grievously harm her rival could lead to a finding that she lacked the intention to kill or cause grievous bodily harm, even if that formation of intention was unreasonable; he therefore recommended a lesser finding of manslaughter. Perhaps an earlier judge like Holt CJ would insist that a person creating such a direct risk of death to others could not be heard convincingly to say she did not mean to cause or risk death; the conduct of setting a house on fire with people inside sleeping would normally establish malice prepensed, and only a lack of capacity to guide one's own actions, for example caused by disability, necessity, provocation, duress or mistake, could dispel the finding that such behaviour connoted evil intentions.

To conclude: the demise of historical malice prepensed occurred because the modern law by a series of steps fundamentally transformed both the forensics of intention and the onus of proof in crime. The prosecution must now prove a subjective criminal intent beyond reasonable doubt, and cannot read motive from bad conduct. A defendant can deny by showing a contrary innocent intent even if unreasonably held.[88] And only after guilty intention and actions are affirmatively established will the court shift the burden of proof to the defendant to show defences to criminal liability. Whether the new system is superior to the old is a question that goes beyond the task of the legal historian. Still, the history gives us some tools to form a judgement about perhaps the most basic task of the law – when to identify and punish serious crime.

[87] [1961] AC 290; and see text above, at n 15.

[88] *cf B (A Minor) v Director of Public Prosecutions* [2000] 2 AC 428 (HL).

11

Dogs, Dons and Monkeys: Legal Liability for Domestic Animals

WARREN SWAIN

I. Introduction

There was an Old Man of Dunrose;
A parrot seized hold of his nose.
When he grew melancholy, they said, 'His name's Polly',
Which soothed that Old Man of Dunrose.[1]

In the index to *A Historical Introduction to the Law of Obligations*,[2] 'Owl, lost', is a reference to *The Owl's Case*, a claim against the owner of a pet owl who had failed to pay the promised £1,000 for its safe return.[3] Several generations of bachelor dons were equally devoted to their pets. Bruce McFarlane's letters are full of remarks about his cats.[4] His friend, AL Rowse, sensibly preferred the company of cats to people.[5] Some law dons were also well-known animal lovers. Tony Weir who liked cats[6] and John Barton who favoured standard poodles and macaws[7] are obvious examples.

Not everyone is fond of domestic animals, nor is likely to be as forgiving as the old man of Dunrose if they are injured by one. The idea that the owners are liable for injuries that their animals cause is a very old one. Whilst Peter North's standard work on the modern law of animals covers the history of the subject very briefly,[8] Glanville Williams's older account contains more historical material.[9] The subject still merits a

[1] E Lear, *Complete Nonsense* (London, Folio Society, 1996) 203.

[2] DJ Ibbetson, *A Historical Introduction to the Law of Obligations* (Oxford, Oxford University Press, 1999).

[3] ibid 211. This decision is from the eighteenth century. In 1803 only 27,000 families had an annual income of £700 or more: H Perkin, *Origins of Modern English Society 1780–1880* (London, Routledge & Kegan Paul, 1971) 20.

[4] KB McFarlane, *Letters to Friends 1940–1966* (Oxford, Magdalen College, 1997).

[5] Rowse wrote a (very bad) poem about his cat, AL Rowse, *A Life – Collected Poems* (Edinburgh, William Blackwood, 1981) 282–84. There is a charming picture of Rowse and his cat on the cover of his published diaries: R Ollard, *The Diaries of AL Rowse* (London, Penguin, 2004).

[6] *The Times*, 9 February 2012.

[7] www.theguardian.com/uk/2008/jun/12/7.

[8] P North, *Civil Liability for Animals* (Oxford, Oxford University Press, 2012).

[9] G Williams, *Liability for Animals* (Cambridge, Cambridge University Press, 1939) 265.

second glance from legal historians. Although he may not be associated with a love of domestic animals, the history of liability fits very well with David's work on tortious liability from pre-Roman law[10] to the present day.[11] Existing accounts have underplayed the part of fault. As David has observed in relation to the English law of liability for animals: 'Whatever the language used by contemporaries, it is difficult in the twentieth century not to think of these situations in terms of questions of fault'.[12] What follows is a modest attempt to broaden and expand on his remarks in relation to domestic animals.

II. Domestic Animals in the Ancient World

Martial, described a Roman lapdog, Issa, as Publius' darling.[13] Publius was not the only Roman who was besotted by dogs, which were a popular pet especially amongst the wealthy.[14] The Ancient Greeks shared a love of dogs which appear extensively in iconography and literature[15] and were seen as possessing spiritual as well as human qualities.[16] There was also a recognition that domestic animals could be dangerous. Plutarch ascribes a law about dogs to Solon the Athenian statesman and poet who died in 580 BCE:[17]

> He also enacted a law concerning injuries received from beasts, according to which a dog that had bitten anybody must be delivered up with a wooden collar three cubits long fastened to it; a happy device this for promoting safety.[18]

It has been said that this law is apocryphal,[19] although it is evidenced in several sources.[20]

Oliver Wendall Holmes's influential account of liability for animals emphasised the role of noxal liability in which an owner was liable without fault.[21] The noxal remedy involved surrendering the animal to the person injured rather than, at first at least, paying compensation. Solon's code could be seen as a version of noxal liability, but a

[10] DJ Ibbetson, 'Wrongs and Responsibility in Pre-Roman law' (2004) 25 *JLH* 99; DJ Ibbetson, 'How the Romans Did for Us: Ancient Roots of the Tort of Negligence' (2003) 26 *UNSWLJ* 475.

[11] Ibbetson (n 2). Other references to Ibbetson's work are scattered in the footnotes.

[12] Ibbetson (n 2) 60.

[13] DR Shackleton Bailey (trans), *Martial Epigrams, Volume 1* (Cambridge (MA), Harvard University Press, 1993) 1.109.

[14] M Mackinnon, 'Pets' in GL Campbell (ed), *The Oxford Handbook of Animals in Classical Thought and Life* (Oxford, Oxford University Press, 2014) 269, 270–74; G Jennison, *Animals for Show and Pleasure in Ancient Rome* (Pennsylvania, University of Pennsylvania Press, 2005) 126–27.

[15] K Trantalidou, 'Companions from the Oldest Times: Dogs in Ancient Greek Literature, Iconography and Osteological Testimony' in LM Snyder and EA Moore (eds), *Dogs and People in Social, Working, Economic or Symbolic Interaction* (Oxford, Oxbow, 2006) 96–120.

[16] SH Lonsdale, 'Attitudes towards Animals in Ancient Greece' (1979) 26 *Greece & Rome* 146, 149–50.

[17] For Solon's legislation which has only survived in a fragmentary form, see DF Leão and PJ Rhodes (trans), *The Laws of Solon* (London, IB Tauris, 2016).

[18] B Perrin (trans), Plutarch, *Lives, Vol 1* (Cambridge (MA), Harvard University Press, 2016) ch 24.

[19] M Gagarin, *Early Greek Law* (Berkeley, University of California Press, 1989) 65, fn 58.

[20] C Brownson (trans), *Xenophon, Hellenica, Volume I: Books 1–4* (Cambridge (MA), Harvard University Press, 1918) Book II, ch IV, 41; J Henderson (trans), *Aristophanes, Clouds, Wasps, Peace* (Cambridge Mass., Harvard University Press, 1998) Wasps, 894–95.

[21] O Holmes, *The Common Law* (London, Macmillan, 1882) 7–8; Williams (n 9) 265 'the masterly Lectures of Justice O W Holmes'.

more natural reading is to treat the provision as an ancient version of health and safety law, ensuring dangerous dogs were chained up. In this respect, Solon's law is closer in character to the Talmud.[22] True noxal liability would require the dog to be removed from the owner and handed to the victim rather than be delivered to the authorities to be put in a collar.

Holmes referred to Exodus: 'If an ox gore a man or a woman, that they die: then the ox shall be surely stoned, and his flesh shall not be eaten; but the owner of the ox shall be quit.'[23] Oxen are a non-domestic animal and the passage might not reflect any broader principles. Nor is liability truly noxal. The ox was killed not handed over. Fault on the part of the owner also came to be treated as relevant.[24] A second passage from Exodus ignored by Holmes made this clear:

> But if the ox were wont to gore in time past, and it hath been testified to his owner, and he hath not kept him in, but that he hath killed a man or a woman; the ox shall be stoned, and his owner also shall be put to death.[25]

As a result of this later addition[26] the owner's fault in knowing that the ox had the potential to gore and failing to keep it locked up were treated as aggravating factors. This liability was still confined to an ox causing death by goring.[27] The main focus remained on the outcome (the injury) but consideration of blame had also crept in.[28] The practice of paying compensation (in preference to putting the owner to death),[29] and the animal's propensity both have echoes in the modern law. It has even been argued that Exodus might have influenced the development of the *scienter* action in England in the Middle Ages.[30]

Other ancient law codes placed greater emphasis on an owner's responsibility for their animals beyond mere ownership. The Laws of Eshnunna (circa 1770 BCE) stated:

> If a dog is vicious and the ward authorities so notify its owner, but he fails to control his dog and it bites a man and thus causes his death, the owner of the dog shall weigh and deliver 40 shekels of silver.[31]

A dog need not attack anyone before it was regarded as vicious. The owner's fault lay in failing to control the dog after a notification from the ward authorities that it was dangerous.[32] Fault may have been easy to establish by the fact that the biting occurred.

[22] N Solomon (ed), *The Talmud A Selection* (London, Penguin, 2009) 444.

[23] *The Holy Bible Revised Version* (Oxford, Oxford University Press, 1930) Exodus 21:28. Exodus formed the basis of the Covenant Code from the first third of the first millennium BCE, see R Westbrook, *Ex Oriente Lex* (Baltimore, John Hopkins University Press, 2015) 77–78.

[24] Williams (n 9) 274.

[25] Exodus 21:29.

[26] D Daube, *Studies in Biblical Law* (Cambridge, Cambridge University Press, 1947) 86.

[27] The provisions on damage to property caused by an ox to a slave or another ox were broader: Exodus 21:32, 35.

[28] A result orientated approach like this was common in ancient law, Ibbetson (n 10) 107.

[29] Exodus 21:30.

[30] BS Jackson, 'On the Origins of Scienter' (1978) 94 *LQR* 85, 100.

[31] M Roth, *Law Collections from Mesopotamia and Asia Minor*, 2nd edn (Atlanta, Scholars Press, 1997) 67–68, ¶ 56.

[32] For a discussion of the regulatory function of wards, see R Westbrook, *A History of Ancient and Near Eastern Law* (Boston, Brill, 2003) vol 1, 2.1.3.3.3.

The fact that the owner did everything they reasonably could to control the dog would not avail them. Compensation was payable if a dog attack results in a fatality.[33] Rather than an abstract principle, fault was linked to a failure to act in a particular manner having known of a particular danger. The Laws of Hammurabi (circa 1750 BCE) are silent on dogs but contain provisions on oxen.[34] Responsibility had its limits: 'If an ox gores to death a man while it is passing through the streets, the case is no basis for a claim'.[35] Assyrian and Hittite Laws contained provisions about oxen and a few on dogs,[36] but none concerned injury occasioned by an animal.[37]

III. Domestic Animals in Roman Law

Rather than general provisions, the earliest laws on liability for animals were limited to specific types of animals causing certain kinds of injuries, often in a particular way. The idea that fault on the part of the owner of the animal was a relevant consideration emerged slowly. Roman law was altogether more complicated. A man injured by a dog might bring a claim in *iniuria* against the dog's owner but only where the injury was caused intentionally rather as a result of negligence.[38] The *Lex Aquilia* imposed liability for damage to property (such as a slave) if the owner was negligent in handling their animal.[39] Only much later was it possible to bring a claim against the owner of an animal for negligently inflicted personal injury.[40] This left obvious gaps, especially in the earlier period, and the solution the Romans adopted fits well with Holmes' suggestion that: 'The liability of the owner was simply a liability of the offending thing',[41] and may explain the emphasis on noxal liability in accounts of the early history of liability for animals.[42]

There are several mysteries about the *actio de pauperie*, including the name.[43] The action first dates around the XII Tables (449 BCE). A text in the *Digest* attributed to Ulpian is much wider than earlier laws on liability for animals.[44] All quadrupeds were included, although at some point dogs may have come under a separate regime.[45]

[33] Similar rules apply to oxen: Roth (n 31) 67 ¶ 54.

[34] ibid 128 ¶ 251. Discussed in Ibbetson (n 10) 110–11. For a very detailed discussion see, JJ Finkelstein, 'The Ox that Gore' (1981) 71 *Transactions of the American Philosophical Society* 1.

[35] Roth (n 31) 128 ¶ 250.

[36] Herding dogs were treated as much more valuable than an ordinary dog and the penalty for injuring them was higher than for other dogs and livestock: T Bryce, *Life and Society in the Hittite World* (Oxford, Oxford University Press, 2002) 84.

[37] Save that in the Hittite Law it was a defence to a claim of bestiality that the ox or pig leapt on a man in sexual excitement, Roth (n 31) 237 ¶ 199.

[38] D 47.10.3 pr-3.

[39] D 9.2.8.1 which discusses mules running down a slave.

[40] D.9.2.13 pr. This may be a much later addition, see P du Plessis, *Borkowski's Textbook on Roman Law*, 4th edn (Oxford, Oxford University Press, 2010) 327.

[41] Holmes (n 21) 10.

[42] Williams follows Holmes in this respect, Williams (n 9) 265.

[43] For a discussion of this and other questions, see A Watson, *Legal Origins and Legal Change* (London, The Hambledon Press, 1991) 129–39.

[44] D 9.1.1 pr-3.

[45] The evidence on a special regime for dogs is not particularly strong and is post-Classical where it appears in Pauli Sententiae, www.ucl.ac.uk/volterra/texts/lrvps1 1.15.1 For a translation see, OF Robinson, *The Sources of Roman Law* (Abingdon, Routledge, 1997) 47.

No fault (or wrong) was required on the part of the animal's owner. There is no suggestion that the animal needs to have an existing propensity to cause injury. Liability was noxal with a focus on the animal rather than the owner, and the animal was handed over, or alternatively compensation was paid.[46]

Justinian's *Institutes* excluded animals that act according to their nature from the *actio de pauperie*.[47] In one text, Ulpian adopted the same approach.[48] Honoré's explanation is that Ulpian regarded an animal's nature as important because he viewed animals as rational.[49] Other passages attributed to Ulpian are more ambiguous on the issue of an animal's propensity.[50] In one text, Ulpian described the escape of a bear and implied that there is no liability because the bear is no longer owned, leaving open the possibility that the outcome might be different if the bear was in captivity.[51] If an animal was required to act contrary to its nature, then an owner of an aggressive guard dog that bites someone who comes onto the property would not be liable, but it would be different if the dog doing the biting was a small lap dog. More exotic animals were an obvious and very real problem. Monkeys and snakes were popular pets with the Romans,[52] and some of the very wealthy kept even more dangerous animals.[53]

Noxal liability attributes responsibility to the animal but fault crept in once fault on the part of the victim was used to deny liability. For example, when the animal is provoked[54] or when a horse lashes out after being struck or wounded.[55] A man fleeing from the magistrate who runs into a shop and is injured by a ferocious dog cannot bring a claim.[56] The man who has put himself in harm's way when there was no need to do so, perhaps because there is no right to enter the shop,[57] fits with Paul's observation that the outcome would be otherwise if the dog were at large.[58] Sometimes Roman law attributed responsibility for the injury to the owner more directly. When a mule driver is responsible for the mule overturning the cart, then he and not the mule is treated as responsible.[59] Take the case of a Roman dog walker. A dog breaks free on account of its wildness and causes injury, Ulpian tells us: 'If it could have been better restrained by

[46] D 9.1.1 pr. Compensation might be given for medical treatment, loss of employment or even for the loss of opportunity of employment, see D 9.1.1.3.

[47] Inst 4.9 pr.

[48] D 9.1.1.7.

[49] T Honoré, *Ulpian* (Oxford, Oxford University Press, 1982) 31.

[50] D 9.1.1.4; D 9.1.1.11.

[51] D 9.1.1.10.

[52] Jennison (n 14) 127–29, 130; F Lazenby, 'Greek and Roman Household Pets' (1949) 44 *Classical Journal* 245; W McDermott, *The Ape in Antiquity* (Baltimore, John Hopkins Press, 1938). Snakes are adept at killing vermin.

[53] Jennison (n 14) 132.The Emperor Nero kept a large menagerie: JC Rolfe (trans), KR Bradley (revd), *Suetonius, Lives of the Caesars, vol II* (Cambridge (MA), Harvard University Press, 2014) XXXI, 131. The Emperor, Caracalla, supposedly kept a tame lion called 'Rapier' which slept in his bedroom and shared his meals: E Cary (trans), D Cassius, *Roman History, Books 71–80* (Cambridge (MA), Harvard University Press, 1927) Epitome of Book LXXIX, 353.

[54] D 9.1.1.6.

[55] D 9.1.1.7.

[56] D 9.1.2.1.

[57] See Frier's suggestion that the man was a trespasser: BW Frier, *A Casebook on the Roman Law of Delict* (Atlanta, Scholars Press, 1989) 141.

[58] D 9.1.2.1.

[59] D 9.1.1.4.

someone else or if it never should have been taken to that particular place, this action will not lie and the person who had the dog on the lead will be liable'.[60] The owner escapes liability because they did not cause the injury. On the surface, liability was strict. But as with the English medieval action of trespass, fault was indirectly relevant under the cover of causation.[61] The example of the dog breaking free also suggests the possibility of a more direct consideration of fault.

Justinian's *Institutes* included a later edict forbidding keeping a dog, bear, boar, wild boar, or a lion near a public road.[62] Compensation was payable for death or injury.[63] The edict included some dangerous animals that have the potential to act according to their nature. Fault beyond keeping particular animals near the highway was irrelevant. Where a chained dog or caged bear bites a passer-by, the owner, who has done all they reasonably can, is still liable. This is the opposite situation to the man who runs into a shop to escape the magistrate. There is little option to avoid using a highway and no one can be blamed for doing so.

IV. Liability for Domestic Animals in the Post-Roman World

Elements of Roman law survived in Europe.[64] The *Lex Romana Visigothorum* of 506 CE contained a version of noxal liability for dogs killing sheep.[65] In other respects it diverged. Propensity was more central. An animal known to be vicious was required to be killed. If it was allowed to live, compensation was payable when the animal killed or injured its victim when under the owner's control.[66] The fault in this situation lay in keeping an animal known to be dangerous. The Roman idea that the victim's behaviour might absolve the owner of liability was preserved and extended.[67] Special provisions about dogs meant an owner was only liable when they incited the dog, in which case it was as if the owner had inflicted the injury themselves, unless the dog injured or killed a thief or other criminal.[68]

Noxal liability mainly fell out of use and was replaced by compensation. Fault was also closer to the surface. The Laws of Alfred, circa 890 CE, also contained special rules for dogs. Six shillings after the first attack becomes 30 shillings on the third occasion someone is bitten by a dog.[69] On a fourth occasion, the owner is required to pay compensation reflecting the seriousness of the injury.[70] A dog owner was liable without

[60] D 9.1.1.5.

[61] On this general point in relation to trespass see Ibbetson (n 2) 61.

[62] Inst 4.9.1. The *Digest* adds a panther and wolf to the list, D 21.1.

[63] D 21.1.

[64] For the continued influence of Roman law during this period generally see: K Shoemaker, 'Germanic Law' in H Pihlajamäki, M Dubber, M Godfrey (eds), *The Oxford Handbook of European Legal History* (Oxford, Oxford University Press, 2018) 249–62.

[65] SP Scott (trans), *The Visigothic Code* (Boston, The Boston Book Company, 1910) Title IV, XX, 291.

[66] ibid Title IV, XVI, 289; Title IV, XVII, 290. By implication this passage suggests that there is no liability for a vicious animal which escapes.

[67] Scott (n 65) Title IV, XVIII, 290.

[68] Scott (n 65) Title IV, XIX, 291.

[69] S Jurasinski and L Oliver, *The Laws of Alfred* (Cambridge, Cambridge University Press, 2021) [27].

[70] ibid [27.2].

fault. Compensation was payable even if the dog had no previous propensity to bite. One bite was enough. But propensity was reflected in the fact that a greater penalty was payable with each attack. This made fault of the owner indirectly relevant because the owner had failed to properly secure a dog after it had already bitten someone. The Laws of Alfred were still relatively lenient on dog owners because for compensation to reflect the amount of harm suffered, three earlier incidents were required.

Although there was no noxal liability for dogs,[71] Williams referred to another passage in the Laws of Alfred which he suggests is closer to noxal liability:[72]

> If a beast should wound someone, let [the owner] turn that beast over [to the wounded person] or let him settle [with the wounded person].[73]

It was not particularly unusual to treat dogs separately which may reflect the nature of the injuries caused by dogs. A dog bite whilst painful is likely to be less serious than other common animal related injuries such as being gored by an ox or kicked by a horse.[74] It is unlikely that most victims of these potentially more serious injuries would choose to be handed the animal when the level of compensation, outside minor injuries, was set at a higher level in the Laws of Alfred than the likely value of the animal.[75] The century after Alfred's laws, the laws of Hywel in Wales,[76] contained a provision on dogs killing livestock which included the phrase: 'it is proper for everyone to keep his animal from doing wrong'.[77] The way that propensity was relevant echoed the Laws of Alfred.[78] The consequences were different.[79] There were limits on an owner's responsibility when liability for a rabid dog was excluded.[80]

Evidence of early Scots law is found in *Regiam Majestatem* and *Liber de Iudicibus*.[81] It was possible to see a Roman influence in the way that the owner of an animal was liable irrespective of fault. Yet as the example of a horse that kills a pedestrian demonstrates, fault on the part of the victim may also be relevant when it came to the size of compensation.[82] Scots law required the payment of compensation but noxal surrender of the animal may also have survived.[83]

[71] On this point see, S Jurasinski, 'Noxal Surrender, the "Deodand", and the Laws of King Alfred' (2014) 111 *Studies in Philology* 195, 205–12.

[72] Williams (n 9) 271–72.

[73] Jurasinski and Oliver (n 69) [28].

[74] Which is not to say that there is no risk of a dog bite leading to serious problems or even death if it became infected. On the treatment of wounds in Anglo-Saxon England see: D Banham and C Voth, 'The Diagnosis and Treatment if Wounds in the Old English Medical Collections: Anglo-Saxon Surgery' in L Tracey and K De Vries (eds), *Wounds and wound repair in medieval culture* (Leiden, Brill, 2015) 153–74.

[75] Jurasinski and Oliver (n 69) [47]–[80].

[76] For the context see, TG Watkin, *The Legal History of Wales*, 2nd edn (Cardiff, University of Wales Press, 2012) 44–71.

[77] D Jenkins, *Hywel Dda The Law* (Llandysul, Gomer Press, 1990) 206.

[78] For the influence of Alfred on Hywel Dda see, Watkin (n 76) 45.

[79] Jenkins (n 77) 182.

[80] ibid.

[81] P Stein, *The Character and Influence of the Roman Civil Law* (London, Hambledon Press, 1988) 279–88; A Simpson and A Wilson, *Scottish Legal History Volume One 1000–1707* (Edinburgh, Edinburgh University Press, 2017) 322–26.

[82] BS Jackson, 'Liability for Animals in Scottish Legal Literature: From the Auld Lawes to the Sixteenth Century' (1975) 10 *Irish Jurist (NS)* 334, 334–35; K Reid and R Zimmermann (eds), *A History of Private Law in Scotland II. Obligations* (Oxford, Oxford University Press, 2000) 551–52. Lower compensation was payable when someone is killed walking behind a horse rather than in front of it.

[83] Jackson (n 82) 347–48 where he refers to Sir J Balfour, *The Practicks* (circa 1595).

Rothair's Edict in Lombard of 643 CE states that the owner of a four-legged animal is liable to pay compensation if it causes damage or injury.[84] The next provision nevertheless makes clear that no blame should attach to the animal's owner: 'he whose animal it is shall pay compensation for the killing or damage, but the feud, that is the enmity, shall cease since the thing was done by a dumb animal without any intent on the part of its owner'.[85] There is no liability if the animal is shown to be insane and propensity is otherwise irrelevant.[86] The owner is also absolved in the case of a dog incited by the victim.[87] In the European codes of this era, liability was imposed without fault for injuries caused by domestic animals and the payment of compensation largely replaced handing over the animal. But neither of these features was universal. In Norwegian law, an owner was required to hand over a dog that causes injury provided a victim makes a claim within five days.[88] Failure to hand over the animal ran the risk of compensatory payment assessed as if the animal's owner had caused the same injury. The Laws of the Salian Franks have been described as 'the most Germanic of the barbarian law codes (with the exception of the Anglo-Saxon)'[89] and date from between 507 and 511 CE. The remedy for someone killed by a domestic animal involved payment of compensation and handing over of the animal to the victim's estate.[90] Fault was also required. Fault was not something that went to the level of compensation or causation – it was a core feature. Witnesses were called to prove that the owner had not taken proper care of the animal before it killed its victim.[91]

V. English Law: Injury by Domestic Animals in the Common Law

The origin of liability in the English common law for injury caused by domestic animals has been described as 'obscure'.[92] It is relevant to the wider debate about the writ of trespass and the origins of the action on the case. Williams, and later Milsom, described a writ of trespass for a dog chasing sheep.[93] As well as the standard form allegation of *vi et armis*, the writ contained an allegation that the dog was incited. Incitement is also alleged in a writ from the early fourteenth century when a dog bites a man.[94] Milsom

[84] KF Drew (trans), *The Lombard Laws* (Philadelphia, University of Pennsylvania Press, 1989) ¶ 325, 115.
[85] ibid ¶ 326, 115.
[86] Drew (n 84) ¶ 324. 115.
[87] Drew (n 84) ¶ 322. 115.
[88] L Larson (trans), *The Earliest Norwegian Laws* (New Jersey, Law Book Exchange, 2011) V. [Miscellaneous Provisions] ¶ 16, 288.
[89] KF Drew (trans), *The Laws of the Salian Franks* (Philadelphia, University of Pennsylvania Press, 1991) 29.
[90] ibid ¶ XXXVI, 98.
[91] Drew (n 84) ¶ XXXVI, 98.
[92] Williams (n 9) 276.
[93] An example is: (1329) 3 Edw III pl 7 fo. 3a-3b, see Williams (n 9), SFC Milsom, 'Trespass from Henry III to Edward III Part I: General Writs' (1958) 74 *LQR* 195, 216. Incitement might also appear in cases of dogs biting people: *Simon and Emma Hunt v Richard Rowley* (1391) in M Arnold (ed), *Select Cases of Trespass From the King's Courts 1307–1399 Volume II* (London, Selden Society, 1987) 37.3.
[94] E de Haas and GDG Hall, *Early Registers of Writs* (London, Selden Society, 1970) 177 [297].

suggested that 'incitement sounds artificial, and an incitement to bite can hardly ever have been genuine'.[95]

There was no indication in the early writs that an owner needed to be aware that the animal was potentially dangerous. By the late fourteenth century, a new writ in the action on the case had emerged known as the *scienter* action. Milsom thought that this form of liability was older but hidden in trespass behind a fictitious allegation of incitement.[96] Palmer argued that liability was genuinely novel in the late 1350s.[97] The *scienter* allegation in his account first appeared alongside incitement as an aggravating factor before various forms of *scienter* writ emerged later.[98]

The *scienter* action would be the primary remedy for injuries caused by animals until the Animals Act 1971. The *scienter* writ was general in form. There was no restriction to particular species of animals or types of injuries.[99] Early cases contained allegations of biting, infections caused by a bite, and loss of work as a result of the injury.[100] The allegation of *vi et armis*, which is most associated with trespass, could still be found as late as the sixteenth century.[101] If strict liability meant liability without fault, then liability in *scienter* was not strict. The fact that the animal caused an injury was not enough to make the owner liable. The animal was required to have a propensity to cause injury and the owner was required to have knowledge of this characteristic. Fault was of a particular kind which involved keeping the animal knowing that it could cause injury. An owner who was ignorant of an animal's propensity escaped liability.[102] Fault of this sort did not present plaintiffs with a particularly high threshold. Where for example the owner of a dog did everything that they reasonably could to restrain the animal – such as chaining it up or keeping it inside a property – and it still bites someone, the owner was liable if they knew its character. The fact that the owner may not be negligent does not absolve them. The way that an animal's propensity is used was the opposite of Roman law: the fact that an animal is by its nature ferocious condemns rather than absolves the owner.

A good summary of English law by the eighteenth century can be found in a short judgment of Strange CJ:

> [An] action will lie against him at the suit of a person who is bit, though it happened by such person's treading on the dog's toes, for it was owing to his not hanging the dog on the first notice.[103]

[95] SFC Milsom, *The Historical Foundations of the Common Law* (London, Butterworths, 1981) 310.

[96] Milsom (n 93) 218.

[97] RC Palmer, *English Law in the Age of the Black Death 1348–1381* (Chapel Hill, The University of North Carolina Press, 1993) 228–51.

[98] ibid 238–44.

[99] Palmer suggests that it was originally limited to dogs but then had wider application, Palmer (n 97) 244. By the 1390s there are examples of damage or injuries caused by horses: *Sir Thomas Fogge v Robert Brigham* (1385), Arnold (n 93) 36.1. Palmer describes local court cases of liability for dogs which did not use the scienter form: Palmer (n 97) 245–50.

[100] Examples in Palmer (n 97) include, A160, A16l, A16n.

[101] JH Baker, *The Oxford History of the Laws of England Volume VI 1483–1558* (Oxford, Oxford University Press, 2003) 765.

[102] This requirement of knowledge was reiterated on several occasions: *Anon* (1537) Dyer 25 b § 162; *Kinnion v Davies* (1636) Cro Ca 487; *Buxendin v Sharp* (1696) 2 Salk 662.

[103] *Smith v Pelah* (1746) 2 Stra 1265.

A few decades earlier a note in Salkeld's Reports had stated that '[t]he owner of a mastiff is not bound to muzzle him, unless he be found to be mischievous',[104] which was closer to the type of rules that applied in some ancient legal systems. English law operated on a different assumption. Owners of domestic animals were free to take any or no measures as they saw fit but would still find themselves liable if they had knowledge of the animal's propensity.

Knowledge was something to be demonstrated in evidence under the general issue in response to a defendant's not-guilty plea.[105] According to Holt CJ in *Mason v Keeling*, the assumption was that 'a dog is not of a fierce nature, but rather the contrary',[106] by which he meant that knowledge of the propensity of the dog by the owner was required. Knowledge that the animal was vicious as opposed to, more narrowly, that it was accustomed to engaging in the act complained of was required, although the two pieces of evidence may sometimes amount to the same thing.[107] Gould J agreed that it was necessary to show that the dog was fierce but also seemed to suggest that the breed of dog might also be relevant and he compared a mastiff and a spaniel.[108] He also made the point that the dog in question had bitten someone when going unmuzzled on a public street when 'the law takes notice of highway', suggesting an idea a little like the Roman edict on animals near the highway. Although in the end, one report suggested that Gould J changed his mind and gave a judgment for the defendant.[109]

It was enough for a dog to have bitten one other person. It need not 'show a disposition to snap and bite everybody'.[110] However a dog need never have bitten anyone as opposed to having a propensity to be dangerous. Darling J said that '[i]t was a misapprehension on the part of many people to suppose that in order to make the owner of a dog liable the dog must, with the knowledge of the owner, actually have bitten someone before'.[111] It was sufficient that there was knowledge that a dog was ferocious which Darling J defined as 'likely to bite without provocation'.[112] At the same time, the fact that a dog was 'in the mere habit of bounding upon and seizing persons' to the extent that it damaged their clothes was insufficient to sustain a claim.[113] Erle CJ observed that Lord Campbell had allowed a dog to be presented to a jury in such cases and he had no objection to such an approach even if it is difficult to see what this exercise would have achieved beyond showing that the dog was boisterous.[114]

Holt CJ had asked the question: 'can it be imagined a man would keep a fierce dog in his family wittingly?'.[115] All dogs have the potential to bite in some situations and certain breeds of dogs may have a greater likelihood of biting than others. A generalisation of

[104] 2 Salk 140.
[105] *Gerard v Dickenson* (1590) 4 Co 18; *Sneade v Badley* (1615) 3 Bulst 76; *Cokeram v Davies* (1641) 1 Ro Abr 4.
[106] (1699) 12 Mod 332, 335.
[107] See Williams (n 9) 303.
[108] (1699) 12 Mod 332, 335.
[109] (1699) 12 Mod 332. According to a different report (1699) 1 Ld Raym 606, the case was settled.
[110] *Charlwood v Creig* (1851) 3 Car & K 46, 48.
[111] *Barnes v Lucille Ltd* (1907) 23 TLR 389, 390.
[112] ibid.
[113] *Line v Taylor* (1862) 3 F & F 731, 732.
[114] ibid 732.
[115] *Mason v Keeling* (1699) 12 Mod 332, 335.

this kind had not historically been regarded as sufficient to fix an owner of domestic animals with knowledge that the animal is vicious,[116] although there were a handful of decisions to the contrary.[117] Actual knowledge of propensity was required but the owner need only have knowledge that the animal was vicious. There was no need to witness it[118] and knowledge could even be imputed from an employee[119] or a spouse.[120]

VI. Scienter and Negligence

In the seventeenth century, Hale drew a distinction between animals like dogs where a *scienter* action was required and animals which were *ferae naturae* such as a lion, bear, wolf, ape or monkey where it was unnecessary to show knowledge that the animal 'did any such thing before'.[121] Hale referred to *Andrew Baker's Case* in which he said a child had been bitten by a monkey that had broken its chain.[122] As in the ancient world, exotic pets were popular with the very wealthy. In the eighteenth century, a growth in consumerism, combined with easier access to exotic animals through trade, fuelled an increase in these kinds of pets including monkeys and parrots.[123] Monkeys were already a well-established feature of popular entertainment.[124]

By the nineteenth century, the question of liability for domestic animals was at the heart of the debate surrounding the merits of fault-based liability, including negligence and strict liability. In *May v Burdett*,[125] the plaintiff had been attacked by the defendant's monkey.[126] The count was in the usual *scienter* form alleging that the monkey had previously attacked people to the knowledge of the owner. Counsel for the defendant referred to animals acting according to their nature as discussed by Justinian and suggested that the owner needed to be negligent before they could be liable.[127] Denman CJ disagreed: 'The gist of the action is the keeping the animal after knowledge of its mischievous propensities'.[128] He seemed to suggest that in cases like this, 'a person keeping a mischievous animal with knowledge of its propensities is bound to keep it secure at his peril,

[116] See the comment of Atkins LJ: *Manton v Brocklebank* [1923] 2 KB 212, 230.

[117] For these authorities see Williams (n 9) 289–91.

[118] *Soames v Banardiston* (1676) 1 Freem 430, 431–32.

[119] *Stiles v Cardiff Steam Navigation Company* (1864) 33 LJQB 310, albeit that there was insufficient knowledge on the part of the company on the facts. For other examples see Williams (n 9) 306–307.

[120] *Gladman v Johnson* (1867) 36 LJCP 153 – although it was noted that mere knowledge of a wife or servant was not sufficient to impute knowledge to the husband or master.

[121] M Hale, *Historia placitorum coronæ. The history of the pleas of the Crown*, vol 1 (London, E and R Nutt, 1736) 430.

[122] ibid.

[123] I Tague, *Animal Companions Pets and Social Change in Eighteenth-Century Britain* (Pennsylvania, Pennsylvania State Press, 2015) 14–49.

[124] Samuel Pepys describes seeing monkeys on ropes at Bartholomew Fair, 'which was strange, but such dirty sport that I was not pleased with it'; R Latham (ed), *Pepys's Diary*, vol 1 (London, Folio Society, 1996) 307, 4 September 1663.

[125] (1846) 9 QB 101, 16 LJQB 64.

[126] It was alleged that the monkey was 'at large' but it was customary to keep monkeys on a chain: Tague (n 123) 41–42.

[127] ibid 105–108.

[128] (1846) 9 QB 101, 111.

and that, if it does mischief, negligence is presumed, without express averment'.[129] This passage can be read as endorsing a standard *scienter* action in which liability is based on fault in keeping an animal knowing that it is dangerous. At the same time, Sir John Comyns's *Digest*, referred to in argument and in Denman CJ's judgment, listed situations in which someone might be liable for *negligent* conduct which included taking care of his cattle or dog.[130] At one point, Denman CJ seemed to be attempting to square negligence and the *scienter* action when he said that 'the negligence is in keeping such an animal after notice.'[131]

Denman CJ was speaking at the start of the period when negligence was becoming established as a tort in its own right constructed around a duty of care.[132] If these claims were properly considered as falling within negligence, then it was easy for owners of dangerous animals to find themselves liable without much in the way of fault because of how the standard of care was defined.[133] Within a few years, liability for dangerous animals could be more confidently described as strict in a true sense. In *Besozzi v Harris*,[134] a bear attacked the plaintiff and Crowder J directed the jury that the allegation of knowledge of propensity must be taken as proved because everyone knows bears are savage. The fact that the bear had never attacked anyone before did not absolve the defendant of liability although it was suggested that it might reduce the amount of damages. In the case of animals of this kind, '[a] person who keeps such an animal is bound so to keep it that it shall do no damage'.[135] Liability for dangerous animals as emphasised in subsequent authorities was strict.[136] If the animal fell within the class of *ferae naturae*, the owner was seemingly liable even without the need to demonstrate that they had knowledge of the animal's propensity – knowledge in these cases was presumed. Fault on the part of the victim remained a complete defence.[137]

In contrast the general form of *scienter* liability was not strict, but nor was it absorbed into negligence either and as a result, it was difficult to classify. Writing in the 1880s, Frederick Pollock suggested that 'the necessity of proving the scienter … is often a greater burden on the plaintiff than that of proving negligence would be'.[138] Pollock placed dangerous animals in a section of his treatise that contained a rather miscellaneous collection of what he termed, 'duties of insuring safety'.[139] Whilst Pollock

[129] ibid 112.

[130] Sir J Comyns, *A Digest of the laws of England*, vol 1 (London, Woodfall and Strahan, 1762) Action upon the Case for Negligence (A, 5), 226. For the importance of this passage more generally, see DJ Ibbetson 'The Tort of Negligence in the Common Law in the Nineteenth and Twentieth Centuries' in EJH Schrage (ed), *Negligence The Comparative Legal History of the Law of Torts* (Berlin, Duncker & Humblot, 2001) 229.

[131] *May v Burdett* (1846) 9 QB 101, 112.

[132] Ibbetson (n 2) 169–87.

[133] DJ Ibbetson, 'The Tort of Negligence in England' in N Jansen (ed), *The Development and Making of Legal Doctrine* (Cambridge, Cambridge University Press, 2010) 46, 58.

[134] (1858) 1 F & F 92.

[135] ibid 93.

[136] *Wyatt v Rosherville Gardens Company* (1886) 2 TLR 282; *Filburn v People's Palace and Aquarium Company* (1890) 25 QBD 258, 6 TLR 402; *Marlor v Ball* (1900) 16 TLR 239.

[137] *Wyatt v Rosherville Gardens Company* (1886) 2 TLR 282, 283 (equated with contributory negligence); *Marlor v Ball* (1900) 16 TLR 239, 240 (a matter of 'common sense').

[138] F Pollock, *The Law of Torts: A Treatise on the Principles of Obligations Arising from Civil Wrongs* (London, Stevens and Sons, 1887) 406.

[139] ibid 393–428.

noted that these situations, which included the rule in *Rylands v Fletcher*,[140] might have been brought within the general law of negligence,[141] they have remained distinct because, 'the law takes notice that certain things are a source of extraordinary risk'.[142] Pollock accepted the general division between strict liability, intentional wrongs, and negligence[143] as a fact but he was never totally at ease with the idea of strict liability.[144]

VII. Rationalising Liability for Domestic Animals

Liability for animals beyond those classified as dangerous does not fit very easily within Pollock's tripartite division. Whilst there was no need for intent or negligence, it is difficult to argue that in a standard *scienter* action fault is completely absent. Fault involves knowledge of propensity. Fault was more obviously marginalised, and liability more truly strict, where the animal was of a kind that was inherently dangerous. Difficulties in rationalising liability for animals may be one of the reasons why the two leading writers on tort law of the period, Pollock[145] and Thomas Beven,[146] were driven to examine *Baker v Snell*.[147] A dog that was incited by a servant had bitten the plaintiff. One issue was whether the master was vicariously liable. But there was also some discussion about the nature of liability for domestic animals. The issue was summarised by Cozens-Hardy MR, who said:

> If a man keeps an animal whose nature is ferocious, or an animal of a class not generally ferocious, but which is known to the owner to be dangerous, is the owner of that animal liable only if he neglects his duty of keeping it safe or is negligent in the discharge of that duty, or is he bound to keep it secure at his peril? In my opinion the latter is the correct proposition of law, and I think that it is not open to the Court to decide the other way.[148]

Beven expressed his objections in rather colourful language[149] and was particularly upset by the suggestion of Farwell LJ that 'anyone who keeps [a dangerous animal] does a wrongful act and is liable for the consequences'.[150] Pollock was also uneasy, because, as he explained, there was nothing wrong in keeping dangerous animals per se when 'damage is the gist of the action'.[151] Although Pollock was able to accept the fundamental distinction between dangerous animals and other kinds of animals,[152] in his mind these cases certainly fell at the outer limits of the proper reach of tort liability.[153]

[140] (1865) 3 H & C774, (1866) 4 H & C 263, LR 1 Exch 265; (1868) LR 3 HL 330.
[141] Pollock (n 138) 393.
[142] Pollock (n 138) 394.
[143] N Duxbury, *Frederick Pollock and the English Juristic Tradition* (Oxford, Oxford University Press, 2004) 238.
[144] For his attitude towards *Rylands v Fletcher* for example, see ibid 254–57.
[145] F Pollock, 'The Dog and the Potman or "Go it, Bob"' (1909) 25 *LQR* 317.
[146] T Beven, 'Responsibility at Common Law for the Keeping of Animals' (1908–1909) 22 *HLR* 465.
[147] [1908] 2 KB 825.
[148] [1908] 2 KB 825, 828.
[149] Beven (n 146) 468.
[150] [1908] 2 KB 825, 833.
[151] Pollock (n 145) 317.
[152] Whilst agreeing with Beven that not all animals which are *ferae naturae* should be classed as dangerous, see Pollock (n 145) 317. Both writers use the example of rabbits as wild animals which are not dangerous.
[153] Pollock (n 145) 321.

The Animals Act 1971 continued to describe the existing form of *scienter* liability as 'strict', which is only correct in so far as it relates to animals that are dangerous[154] and in the secondary sense that the term 'strict' is used to convey the idea that there is liability without negligence as opposed to without fault. The legislation largely preserved the essence of the old law with some differences in detail. The distinction between dangerous and non-dangerous animals was retained,[155] with all non-dangerous animals (which would include dogs but probably not monkeys) falling under a general provision.[156] The requirement of actual knowledge of the animal's character also survived. This is distinct from negligence liability. A defendant can do everything expected of a reasonable person and still be liable if their dog bites someone. The requirement of knowledge prevents liability from been truly strict. This important distinction is illustrated by a decision under the old law where a dog had bitten the same victim twice, once in a trivial way and then half an hour later more seriously. It was knowledge of the first bite combined with a failure to control the dog that resulted in liability for the owner.[157] Whilst it may usually be easier to prove knowledge than negligence, an owner lacking knowledge may potentially be liable in negligence.[158] General liability in the Animals Act can be contrasted with a special provision that makes dog owners strictly liable, without knowledge, for dogs that kill or injure livestock and highlights the fault-based nature of liability for personal injury caused by domestic animals.[159]

The history of the subject would suggest that there are good reasons for demanding an even higher level of care from owners of animals beyond negligence. One reason for treating liability for domestic animals differently could be that they present an abnormal risk.[160] Pollock seems to have been thinking in these terms. This explanation is most convincing in the case of dangerous animals. It works less well for more standard domestic pets. And it still leaves us with the more general problem of rationalising strict liability which is so troubling to some tort theorists.[161] Even for dangerous animals, culpability has a small role given that a victim who suffers injury 'due wholly' to their fault has no claim.[162] It is harder to argue that the standard household dog is an abnormal risk to anyone, which is where knowledge or propensity comes in. Liability in these cases falls somewhere between strict liability and negligence. It is a pragmatic

[154] Animals Act 1971 c 22, s 1(1)(a).

[155] With dangerous animals defined in s 6(2).

[156] Animals Act 1971, s 2(2). The application of various elements of this part of the legislation has proved problematic and the drafting has been criticised: *Mirvahedy v Henley* [2002] QB 769, 777 (Hale LJ).

[157] *Parsons v King* (1891) 8 TLR 114, 115.

[158] *White v Steadman* [1913] 3 KB 340 (owner of a horse ought to have known the likely reaction of a horse to motor vehicles).

[159] Animals Act 1971, s 3. The dog owner may however escape liability if the damage was 'wholly the fault of the person suffering it', see Animals Act 1971, s 5(1). There is a long history of statutory liability for dogs that attack livestock: Dogs Act (871 c 56; Dogs Act 1906 c 32; Dogs (Amendment) Act 1928 c 21.

[160] R Stevens, *Torts and Rights* (Oxford, Oxford University Press, 2007) 113.

[161] For a well-known attempt to explain strict liability for abnormally dangerous activities within corrective justice, see EJ Weinrib, *The Idea of Private Law* (Cambridge (MA), Harvard University Press, 1995) 187–90.

[162] Animals Act 1971, s 5(1).

compromise which recognises that animals can be unpredictable and that all dogs can bite, and all horses can kick. Perhaps in the end, liability for domestic animals is an anomaly, albeit one with longstanding historical and comparative precedents.[163] Or as Lord Simonds put it rather more elegantly, 'beasts have travelled in a compartment of their own'.[164]

[163] Williams (n 9) v, 'the very precocity of this kind of liability gave it a character of its own'.
[164] *Read v J Lyons & Co Ltd* [1947] AC 156, 182.

PART III

Comparative Legal History

12

Peer Reviewing Cujas

ALAIN WIJFFELS

I. An Unusual Request

'Do you ask me, Conrad Paullus, to give you my opinion on Cujas's consultations? Believe me, until now I never looked at that work, as I was determined not to study any further the writings by either this or any other recent author'. Thus, the opening sentence (in Latin) of a letter in the form of a reasoned opinion by Alberico Gentili to his correspondent Conrad Paullus,[1] dated 5 August 1586.[2] Gentili then explains that he reluctantly relented, partly because the brevity of that work allowed him to do so despite his current workload, partly because exposing Cujas's alleged mistakes could be of interest to a larger readership of scholars.[3] Why Paullus was interested in Gentili's opinion on that particular work, which had already been published in Germany,[4] is not mentioned. A few passages merely suggest that he was seeking Gentili's assessment of

[1] Whom I have not identified. Possibly related to a homonym, a jurist (I.U.D.) from Brunswick who was a councillor to Friedrich (1530–52) and Sigismund (1538–66) von Brandenburg, who were both (in succession) elected at a young age archbishop of Magdeburg and bishop of Halberstadt, and credited with a book on usury, which was published with a preface by Ph. Melanchton (*De usuris libri tres* (Francofurti, C. Egenolphus, 1561)). That Conrad Paulus died in 1577, if the entry is correct in Guillielmus Budaeus's *Thanatologia*, 252, in Johann Michael Heineccius and Johann Georg Leuckfeld, *Scriptores rerum germanicarum* (Francofurti ad Moenum, Ex officina Christiani Genschii, 1707). I have kept the (Latin) spelling of the letter's addressee used by Gentili. I am very grateful to Mathias Schmoeckel (Bonn University) for his willingness to assist me in trying to identify Paullus.

[2] Bodleian Library, MSS D'Orville 574, f. 360v : '*... iam vale ex hospitio VII. Kal. Aug. 1586*' (presumably following the Julian calendar).

[3] ibid f. 356r: 'Et vero cum multas, reliquorum, Cuiaciique erroneas commentationes libris editis aperuerim, forte neque id male accidit, si et in consultationibus hunc operam infoelicem narasse, tibi et, si tibi placet, omnibus studiosis ostendo'.

[4] The 60 consultations (preceded by a '*consultatio veteris cuiusdam iurisconsulti*') had been published in the 1577 edition of Cujas's collected works (*Opera Iacobi Cuiacii I.C. quae de iure fecit in hunc diem ab ipso auctore disposita et recognita, & aucta libro singulari Consultationum, & libr. XV. XVI. XVII. Observationum* (Parisiis, Apud Sebastianum Nivellium sub Ciconis, 1577) T. I, 269–332). The consultations were published separately the same year (*Cuiacii I.C. Praeclarissimi Consultationum Liber singularis, Recens in lucem editus* (Coloniae Agrippinae, Apud Ioannem Gymnicum, sub Monocerote, 1577), and reprinted the following year (same title, same printer, 1578) and in 1590 (by the same printer in Cologne, with a slightly more detailed subtitle). They were included in later editions of Cujas's *opera omnia*. I refer in this chapter to the 1578 edition. Gentili's letter was probably written while he was staying in Germany (a note in D'Orville MSS 617 indicates that he was in Wittemberg on 1 July 1586).

the collection's qualities ('virtus'). The result, as far as the surviving manuscript sources tell us, was an overall damning review of Cujas's consultations. Following a mannerism not uncommon among sixteenth-century scholars who sought to break away from the late-medieval speech styles, Gentili resorted to a broad register of disparaging phrases and rhetorical devices in order to criticise the individual consultations and their author. From the very beginning, he warns his correspondent that Cujas's approach fails to meet the elementary standards of legal methods.

Alberico Gentili's support, at an early stage of his career, in favour of the late-medieval civil law tradition and his criticism of more recent legal scholarship (vaguely identified by conventional historiography as 'legal humanism') is well documented. Gentilian studies[5] have nonetheless emphasised that as a mature scholar, he sought to combine features of both the traditional and the modern approaches. Far from undergoing an instant Pauline conversion to the new learning, Alberico Gentili's incorporation of a neo-classical scholarly language and historicising jurisprudential methods was the fruit of sustained, painstaking research, of which his copious informal reading notes bear witness. At the same time, he continued his efforts towards consolidating the traditional learning of his early legal education at Perugia. During the (early) 1580s, his initial attitude towards much modern legal learning was often critical and antagonistic. He may even at some point have envisaged a publication specifically intended to criticise systematically Cujas's work.[6]

Cujas's relatively short collection of consultations occupies a modest place in his *opera omnia*. Yet, they illustrate how the scholar was also involved in the legal practice of his day.[7] In his opinions, Cujas departed in many ways from the traditional format of the *consilia* literature, which, at the time, remained hugely popular and influential in different jurisdictions throughout Europe. Notwithstanding the stark differences in style and methods, some similarities with the traditional *consilia* genre are evident.[8]

[5] This is not the place for an overview of current Gentilian studies. Giovanni Minnucci's studies are all compulsory reading, I simply pinpoint his fundamental monograph, essential for understanding Gentili's concept of a jurist's purpose: *Alberico Gentili iuris interpres della prima età moderna*, Archivio per la Storia del diritto medievale e moderno; Studi e Testi, 16 (Bologna, Monduzzi, 2011); a recent synthesis, which focuses as the title suggests on Gentili's reputation as an early contributor to international law is the monograph by V Vadi, *War and Peace: Alberico Gentili and the Early Modern Law of Nations*, Legal History Library 37; Studies in the History of International Law 14 (Leiden, Brill, 2020).

[6] I Maclean, 'Alberico Gentili, his publishers, and the vagaries of the book trade between England and Germany, 1580–1614' in I Maclean, *Learning and the Market Place: Essays in the History of the Early Modern Book* (Leiden, Brill, 2009) 291–337, at 337. Among Gentili's copious unpublished notes on various works by Cujas, D'Orville 609, f. 127 ss. contains several critical remarks, including one marked in the margin in capital letters 'ANTICUIACIUS' (f. 129r): 'Instituo Anticuiacium, in quo antiquorum sententias antiquis reddam ab isto plagiario; suas, si quae sunt, discutiam, ad emendationes, que maiorem partem suorum operum habent, dicam et quod facilius nihil quam de incolumitate scripturae dubitationes movere, et confingere etiam aut invenire aliqua, quibus emendationes tuas approbasse videris: sed interim nihil ad determinationem caussarum ; stultus enim ille patronus qui sic vel ex suis manuscriptis sive his etiam multo magis sententias suas confirmare nitatur in variis exemplaribus quis negabit stari oportere Florentino contextui, si sit de lectione quaestio?'.

[7] X Prévost, 'Between Practice and Theory: Succession Law According to Jacques Cujas (1522–1590)' in MG di Renzo Villata (ed.), *Succession Law, Practice and Society in Europe Across the Centuries* (Cham, Springer International Publishing, 2018) 359–79. At the conference *Jacques Cujas (1522–2022). La fabrique d'un 'grand juriste'* (Collège de France 28–29 March 2022), some speakers mentioned that Cujas's consultations were frequently referred to in later legal literature.

[8] Not least in France, the genre was undergoing substantial changes during the sixteenth century: see the Introduction by the editors in G Cazals and S Geonget (eds), *Les recueils de plaidoyez à la Renaissance entre droit et literature* (Genève, Droz, 2018) 7–18.

In most consultations, Cujas starts with a concise and mostly abstract outline of the case (recalling the *species facti*), then formulates, again in the briefest of terms, the abstract legal question raised, immediately followed by a sentence starting with *Respondi, Dixi …*, or a similar term,[9] in which he states his conclusion. This statement is followed by a more or less elaborate reasoning, including references to authorities. A consultation may consist of several questions and responses. In some consultations, one may also recognise an echo of the 'Nec obstat' counter-arguments which occur in traditional *consilia*, in Cujas's collection typically introduced by a phrase such as 'Nec moveor …'. In contrast to a stock-device in many late-medieval *consilia*, Cujas does not give any elaborate *sic et non* reasoning, starting with arguments against his conclusion, followed by arguments in support of his thesis, and possibly ending with a refutation of the first arguments.

Cujas's collection deals mostly with cases on issues of family property law.[10] It was an area which at the time fuelled a large portion of the caseload in higher courts, precisely where (on the continent) civil lawyers often occupied prominent roles as advocates and judges. It was also an area which presented a significant challenge to civil law, because of the complexities and unresolved issues which characterised Justinian's compilations and his later constitutions, but also because everywhere in continental Europe, particular laws (customs and statutes) had strongly developed specific family property concepts and rules, which were more resilient to any reception of a *ius commune* modelled by civil law.

II. Gentili's Autographs

A synopsis of Gentili's handwritten notes on Cujas's consultations in different manuscripts is presented in the Appendix.[11]

(1) A draft of the letter to Paullus (or consultation, as Gentili styles it) is kept in the Gentili Papers at the Bodleian Library, D'Orville Ms. 574 (hereafter: '574'). It is a small-sized volume[12] which contains notes and drafts by Alberico's brother Scipione, but also, from fol. 356r to 360v (ie in the modern pencil folio numbering), the first four sheets and the last sheet of Alberico's letter. The letter includes general remarks at the beginning and at the end. The discussion of Cujas's opinions follows the numbered sequence of the consultations in the printed editions, though some consultations are passed over. Because the paper format used for the letter is larger than that of the volume in which it has been bound, the sheets are folded twice, and the reader has the impression of a 'pop-up' book when unfolding the letter. The first four sheets have in the right upper corner a page number in ink, possibly added in Gentili's time: fol. numbers 1 to 4 (now ff. 356–359); followed by a fifth sheet numbered 13

[9] Occasionally, the response is written in the third person singular.

[10] The standard work of reference is now X Prévost, *Jacques Cujas (1522–1590) jurisconsulte humaniste* (Genève, Droz, 2015). For the topics dealt with in the present contribution, see especially, in the second part of that monograph, the first chapter (on inheritance law), and the second chapter (on feudal law) 355–500.

[11] In addition to the notes mentioned in the Appendix, a few references with annotations occur in MSS D'Orville 613, ff. 15rv (cons. 1, 4, 5, 40) and 126v (14, 23, 15) among notes on other works by Cujas.

[12] Outer dimensions of the bound volume: 17 x 22cm; the sheets of the letter measure 21.5 x 32.3cm.

(now fol. 360rv). This, together with the interrupted sequence of consultations by Cujas under discussion, suggests that this version of the letter lacks the ff. 5 to 12, roughly coinciding with the discussion of the consultations between Nos. 43 and 57. Fol. 356 is clearly the beginning of the letter, with a formal headpiece and title as if announcing a distinct scholarly work. It is addressed to Conradus Paullus.[13] Fol. 360rv contains Alberico's remarks on Cujas's *consilia* 57, 58 and 59, some concluding remarks, and a final salute with the date. After the bottom line of each page on ff. 356–357, the use of a catchword indicates the continuity with the following page. Such a catchword also occurs on fol. 357v, but the practice is discontinued from fol. 358r onwards, where the handwriting also becomes slightly different. On the right bottom corner of fol. 358r, the page is marked with a capital 'B.' Marginal notes and corrections (in Alberico's hand) appear on some pages, parts have been summarily crossed out (including the four lines discussing consultation 3). In the left margin, Roman numerals indicate the consultation discussed in the main text. The same watermark appears on ff. 356, 359, 360.

(2) A second batch of handwritten notes, also in Alberico's hand, appear in the volume D'Orville Ms. 616. At first sight, these notes reflect at least two different stages of Gentili's reading. The first (hereafter referred to as 616A), is written in Gentili's informal, quick handwriting. The second (hereafter: 616B) is similar to the handwriting in 574, and has the same presentation with Roman numerals in the margin indicating the consultations.

616B runs from fol. 136r to 143v. The ff. have in the upper right corner (on some sheets partly lost due to torn corners and edges) an old numbering from 5 to 12. At the bottom right of the odd folio numbers (5r, 7r, 9r and 11r), the page (or quire of four pages) has been marked with capital letters (respectively: C. D. E. and F.). It would be tempting to recognise this batch as the missing part in 574. The old folio numbering and quire marking may indeed suggest that at some stage, those two batches were put together, but the sequence of the consultations in 616B (*cf* the Appendix) and some of its contents show that this batch probably reflects (at least two) different (advanced) stages of Gentili's drafting. The B quire in 574 appears to have been transferred from a batch now partly incorporated in 616B, where the quire C seems to be its original sequel. However, in 616B, the subsequent quires[14] may partly reflect a distinct drafting (No. 52 appearing twice, in different versions, on fol. 137r and fol. 143v).[15] The watermarks on ff. 136, 138, 141, 143 are different from those in 574. Moreover, as the sequence of consultations in the quires C and D refers to the Nos. 45 to 60, and in the quires E and F to the Nos. 1 to 56, the old folio numbering and quire marking do not match the numerical order of the consultations. The Appendix shows that even for those fragments of 574 which have been preserved, the text in 616B does not systematically select and omit the same consultations as in the 574 version.

[13] 574 356r: 'ALBERICI GENTILIS / De consultationibus Jacobi Cuiacii / Consultatio / Ad Conradum Paullum '. In the opening sentence, Gentili has added, as an explicit address, 'Conrade Paulle', an address repeated *passim* in the drafts.

[14] D: covering consultations among Nos. 54–60, is still apparently a continuation of C; E: covering Nos. from 1 to 26, and F: Nos. from 30 to 56.

[15] On f. 143v, the remarks skip from cons. 48 to 52; however, on ff. 136v-137r, they deal with cons. 47, 51 and 52. At least part of 616B was drafted as an opinion addressed to Paullus: f. 150v.

616A on ff. 130r–135v and 144r–151v (bound, as the synopsis shows, in some disorder) comprises different annotations by Alberico on most of Cujas's consultations. The handwriting is quick (as in most of his numerous annotations on different legal and non-legal works in several volumes of the D'Orville Mss.), including marginal additions and passages crossed out. In the margins, Gentili has added, as elsewhere in his notes, brief remarks or keywords. Most of these refer to some disagreement with Cujas's opinion on a specific question ('*contra Cuia.*'), more rarely in support of the latter's opinion ('*pro Cuia.*'). Occasionally, the marginal note seems to remark on some argument by Gentili himself ('*contra me*'). The keyword '*condicio*' appears frequently, probably in order to retrieve some passages for a projected work on the topic.[16]

The three batches therefore reflect at least four different readings of (parts of) the consultations. Although none of them discusses the full range of Cujas's 60 consultations, the combination of the three shows that Gentili read and annotated all 60 at some stage. 616B contains a passage in which Gentili lists those consultations which he deemed totally below standards.[17] Almost all the consultations from that 'blacklist' are omitted in the versions 574 and 616B, but 616A shows that at some (presumably, earlier) stage, he had read and (however briefly) annotated the consultations which he then decided to disregard. For practical purposes, it will be assumed that 616A reflects Gentili's initial reading of the consultations; 616B an intermediate attempt at drafting his comments; and 574 a substantially revised version of his opinion. The corrections and additions in 574 either indicate that it was not yet the final version, or that Gentili afterwards revised the final version which he may eventually have sent (or not) to Paullus.

III. Gentili's Explicit Methodological Yardstick: Definitions

At the outset of his letter, Gentili refers to the *ars definiendi* for assessing whether a legal opinion is sound or not. Cujas's consultations, in Gentili's view, fail the test repeatedly, because his 'definitions' in approaching a case are all too often wrong (*falsae*) or useless (*inanes*).[18] Perhaps Gentili's insistence on the *ars definiendi* in this particular context echoes the association in classical dialectics between a definition as a preliminary to a reasoned inquiry and the determination of the issue at the beginning of legal proceedings ('*ea res agetur*'), as notably in Cicero's *De finibus* 2.3–4.[19]

[16] 616 contains several drafts of his treatise *De condicionibus* (published in London in 1587), some obviously at an advanced stage (*cf* Maclean, Alberico Gentili, his publishers, o.c., p. 328, No. 8).

[17] 616B 140r: 'Eae autem sunt VI. VII. IX. XVI. XVIII. XIX. XXI. XXII et ridicula illa XXIII. XXVII. XXIX. XXXII. XXXV. XXXVI. XXXIX. XL. ne quid praeterea de multis dicam, quae adiuncta aliis sunt, et sunt huius generis puta in prima, in secunda, in decimaseptima, in vigesima quincta, aliis consultationibus'.

[18] 574 356r : ' … ita definitiones Cuiacii multas, quae falsae, aut inanes sunt, adnotabo, et in arte definiendi quanta hominis sit virtus expediam. Falsas definitiones dixero, quae a iure alienae sunt : inanes appello, quibus prudentia civilis nihilo auctior existit. Ars definiendi fuerit, aptas, firmas, plures rationes et ad suam definitionem constabiliendam, et ad evertendam diversam proferre : in qua Cuiacium fere nullibi bonum comperiemus. Sed age, a falsis definitionibus incipiamus … '. Gentili was familiar with that angle when dealing with Cujas's work: *cf* his *Lectionum & Epistolarum quae ad ius civile pertinent Liber II* (Londini, Excudebat Ioannes Wolfius, 1583) ch 5, 88–93.

[19] On Cicero's perhaps intentionally disingenuous discussion of the Epicurean rejection of definitions: B Taylor, 'Definition and Ordinary Language' in Cicero *De finibus* 2, *Classical Philology* 111 (2016): 54–73.

That association seems reinforced if one looks at the introductory remarks preceding the discussion of the individual consultations in 616B. After discussing the last consultation (No. 60), Gentili rhetorically addresses Cujas with some general critical remarks, including, at the very end of that fragment, the objection of false and useless definitions. The manuscript ends abruptly, leaving most of the page blank, with the beginning of an unfinished sentence. However, the same words are repeated, on the following page, which, in the 616B version, appears as the continuation of what seems to have been an earlier draft of Gentili's introduction to his own consultation, immediately preceding his discussion of the first consultations by Cujas. The effect is therefore that of a loop, where the end of one draft runs without interruption (except for the blank space on the page) into the beginning of another draft. Compared to the introduction in 574, and although the central theme (*viz* the censure directed at false and useless definitions) is the same, the wording and style are different. The introduction in 616B is written as a long tirade in which Gentili complains that although in practice, a consultant may occasionally have to deal with settled legal issues (*de iure aperto*), there is no need to drag such consultancies into (published) scholarly debates. The rhetorical flourish of this version is highlighted by cropped quotes from Cicero and the Digest.[20] Both quotes make the point of the futility of arguing (in public) settled law. The quote from *Pro Murena* provides in context the principle of addressing the issue ('*qua de re agitur*') at the outset of legal proceedings. Gentili keeps hitting the nail (as he sees it) by accusing Cujas of accumulating far more than others empty consultations and, more generally, trifling contributions to legal literature.[21]

While the *ars definiendi* is formally presented as the paramount methodological tool for assessing Cujas's opinions in 574, Gentili's first-hand notes (616A) show that occasionally, he already criticised Cujas's approach through the angle of the latter's definitions at the earliest stages of his reading.[22] However, even at the later stages of his review, Gentili did not systematically deal with an opinion's definitions, or rather,

616 ff. 79v-82v contain Gentili's brief reading notes on the five books *De finibus*, without recording in particular the association between definitions and the framing of legal proceedings.

[20] 616 f. 140r : ' … sed ut eiusmodi responsa ad praelum quoque, et in studiosorum manus ducantur, cui bono ? Ut aliquis nos merito videat Cicero. Non tenes illa? Peritus ideo haberi nemo potest etc. [see Cicero, Pro Murena 28] ut aliquis meritissime rideat Claudius ? num illa non succurrunt ? Magno ingenio, de iure aperto respondit [D. 35.1.109]. Quod si quaestiones illae tuae vel tyroni proponantur, et is dissolvere queat, quod nuda tantum lectione legum cognosci possunt, quî tuae illae consultationes ?' (underlining added, the same passages are underlined in the ms.).

[21] ibid 'Nihil mihi ex aliorum consultationibus regeras, tu enim vir singularis de vulgarium et plebeiorum consultorum facto digne patrocinium sumere nequis, et habent praeterea illi, si sit opus, excusationem quam tu non habes : quod scilicet in magno responsorum numero latere unum aliquod possit vel inanissimum ; tuae autem consultationes quot? Tot, ut viceris Hotomanum : cui nec in eo concedis, quod et tu ex aliis libris tuis aliquam repetis consultationem, sicut ille < ex suis repetiit> [crossed out : fecit]. Hoc illud vitium est, ut exposita manifeste, dicas <tu> tamen, scribasque, et inculces iterum'. Gentili continues by recalling that Hippocrates refused to write 'de rebus non admodum arduis', a fresh opportunity for haranguing Cujas directly: 'Quam putas, Cuiaci, caussam ? putes, quam velis : divini illius viri testimonio et consultationes hae tuae, et tua omnia, quae de iure scripta sunt, et aliorum opera inania, aut levia condemnantur'.

[22] For example, on cons. 30, Gentili (in 616A, 149r) says that Cujas's definition of the case is unsustainable, because Cujas bypassed the main argument: 'omittit praecipuum argumentum, quo ostenditur eam donationem non fuisse causa mortis, quod est, quia tantum exactio post mortem collata est, ergo non est donatio causa mortis, ipse tamen nugator in argumentis pro altera parte <dubitandi scilicet> hoc utitur ut ostendat causa mortis donationem. Ait, donationis exactio collata est in tempore mortis, ergo censetur esse causam mortis. Immo non censetur esse causam mortis. Certe nisi hoc unum argumentum esset, quod ipse non notat, consultationis definitio non posset sustineri […]'.

it appears that it was an angle which gave him much latitude for focusing his critical remarks. A *definitio* is used by Gentili as a peg for circumscribing the central issues of a case. To a large extent, the *definitio* or *definitiones* of a case coincide with the questions explicitly addressed in the opinion, or at least by Cujas's response and reasoning in support of his response. Gentili also frequently challenges a *definitio*, even when he sometimes agrees with Cujas's conclusion, because he considers that the latter's argument is (eg) inconsistent, incomplete, wrongly or insufficiently reasoned, or because the authorities adduced do not support the argument.[23]

IV. Moving Targets

For all his sharp criticism, the various layers of the notes show that Gentili repeatedly changed tack in writing his opinions. Not only is the list of Cujas's *consilia* which he discusses in 616B and 574 not identical, but the gist of the criticism also often varies, targeting different issues. In some cases, even at the stage of the version in 574, the documentary evidence betrays Gentili's change of tactics, whether by reverting to questions already addressed in 616A, but disregarded in 616B, or by bringing up fresh arguments.

Cujas's Cons. 1 illustrates the point. In that case, Cujas had opined that the testament *inter liberos* of an heir burdened by a *fideicommissum* was invalid because of the absence of witnesses, but that the heir's choice (*electio*) of the child who would benefit of the *fideicommissum* was nevertheless valid, while a condition attached to the choice ('provided he did not marry Maevia') was also invalid. Cujas also outlined the division of the succession, whereby he allocated half of the estate to be transferred to the chosen beneficiary of the *fideicommissum*, and the other half shared in three equal parts by the sons of the testatrix. A fourth child, a daughter, was left out because of her renunciation at the time a dowry had been provided in her ante-nuptial agreement.

On the first issue, Cujas insisted that despite Roman law authorities allowing the upholding, in some cases, of an imperfect testament, the requirement of witnesses could not be bypassed altogether. At a first stage of reading that opinion,[24] Gentili (in addition to notes merely copying or closely paraphrasing Cujas's text) questioned the effects Cujas had granted to the choice of the beneficiary. He wondered why, if the *electio* was valid notwithstanding the lack of witnesses, it was, in Cujas's reasoning, not fully applicable. Regardless, Gentili considered that the mother's choice was not valid: apart from the difficulty of splitting up her act of will, he took objection to Cujas's argument that the granting of a choice was not to be regarded either as akin to a *legatum*, nor to a *fideicommissum* (an argument derived by analogy from D. 38.4.7), a corollary not warranted in

[23] The watchwords '*inepta*' and '*falsa*' for Cujas's 'definitions' provide a convenient (though oversimplified) signpost to the broad range of his criticisms levelled at the *consultationes*. Inept are those which Gentili deems futile (as also the frequent charge of 'levity') because, typically, Cujas's argument expresses no more than what a lex says, or than what can be read in the gloss, or in scholars' works. The phrase also appears to refer to issues which Gentili considers to be no longer controversial. Those are the opinions which he says are '*de re non dubia*', '*de re exploratissima*' and the like. The 'wrong' definitions may cover a broader range of criticisms, including alleged flaws in the (logical) reasoning, the legal assessment of the facts, including the omission of case-sensitive facts, or the mishandling of authorities.

[24] 613 115rv.

Gentili's view by Scaevola's reasoning. He was also critical of the lack of precision with regard to the exact form of the document, but considered that in any event, none of its purpose was valid. In the 616B draft, Gentili focused on three issues. First, he objected to Cujas's reading of the Novella 107 with regard to the mischief which Justinian had intended to redress. Secondly, Gentili argued that Cujas's dictum linking the substance of a testament to the intervention of witnesses (*testes*) is both controversial and incorrect. Finally, Gentili chided Cujas for not properly differentiating, with regard to the daughter's exclusion, between a renunciation to the succession and the renouncement of a remedy against an imperfect testament. In the last draft (574), Gentili originally developed a brief argument denying the validity of the mother's exercise of the *electio*, for which Cujas, in his view, had all too easily ruled out the requirement of witnesses. As in his original notes, Gentili questions the precise form (and nature) of the document. However, this whole argument in the last version has been crossed out and hastily replaced in the lower and left margins (in stark contrast to the neat lay-out of the letter's format) by putting forward a substantially different argument, on the validity of a testament *inter liberos* in the absence of any witnesses. This new argument, which flatly contradicts Cujas's main response to the principal question of his consultation, is supported by a reference to the '*communes opiniones*', for which Gentili cites Giulio Claro.

Gentili may have upheld in version 574 his assertion that Cujas's *definitio* in Cons. 1 was off the mark in legal terms ('*aliena a iure*'), but this brief outline of the successive stages of his critical comments tends to show that he was himself unsure about the issues on which to focus his own challenges to Cujas's opinion.

V. Skirmishes Around Authorities

Cujas's arguments are mainly buttressed by direct references to Roman law texts.[25] His historical understanding of Roman law is at times expressed through his differentiation of different layers in the development of the law, most obviously when he distinguishes between *ius vetus* (as pre-Justinian law) and *ius novum* (also referred to as '*hodie*') for legislative changes introduced by Justinian. Cujas occasionally refers to late-medieval legal scholarship, quoting an author's opinion approvingly or criticising it. In some cases, the prevailing or common opinion on an issue is referred to. Contemporary legal literature appears only exceptionally. Non-legal literature, mainly drawn from the ancient classics, is often adduced in order to reinforce the understanding of a term or rule in ancient law. Inevitably in the context of contemporary litigation, Cujas refers to particular laws: French customs and royal ordinances, but also in a few cases to foreign law.

Gentili picks up on the full array of authorities referred to by Cujas, though not comprehensively or systematically. On several occasions, he also chides Cujas for failing to mention a particular authority when dealing with a specific question. In spite of Gentili's antagonistic approach to Cujas's consultations, these controversies about the

[25] Inevitably, cases on feudal law may entail references to the *Libri Feudorum* (eg Cons. 17, but not Cons. 54; Cons. 56). Cujas seems to draw very little on his canon law expertise (eg Cons. 35, 36, 52, 56).

use of authorities provide a degree of common ground between the consultations and Gentili's comments, as both engage with textual authorities gathered from the same legal and literary traditions. Both Cujas and Gentili, when referring to Roman law, rely on their reading of the text, in most cases without referring explicitly to the filter of commentaries. Cujas's reasoning and Gentili's criticism do not reflect, in spite of the latter's quasi-constant disagreements, a systematic methodological dichotomy, although in some cases, Cujas's inclination for preferring his understanding of the historical Roman law against a different doctrine in later traditional legal learning appears to be stronger than Gentili's commitment to ancient Roman law in the light of prevailing legal scholarship.

VI. Roman Law

When Cujas emphasises a change in Justinian's legislation, departing from the earlier law, the argument appears to back the new law.[26] In Cons. 24, he advocates a restrictive view on cases where gifts have to be accounted against the legitimate portion. For example (he argues), whereas before (*olim*), witness the Codex Gregorianus, a dowry and a gift *propter nuptias* were not accountable, this was changed by constitutions incorporated in Justinian's Code,[27] an explanation which did not satisfy Gentili.[28] However, the presumption behind those statutory changes should not be extended to all donations *inter vivos*: only those are accountable, for which a specific law has been introduced to that purpose. This is a case of a *definitio* in Cujas's own words, which is to be understood as a qualification.[29] In many cases, of course, no such disparity is apparent and Cujas can gracefully go along the opinions of the earlier Roman jurist. For some questions, he points out how those ancient jurists responded, in the same vein as he does in his consultation, in a similar case.[30]

Cons. 9 is a brief opinion on the question whether for applying the *ius retractus*, the degree of kinship has to be calculated according to the canon or civil law. Cujas rejects the argument that the claim originated in the Mosaic law, and was therefore governed by canon law. The computation has therefore to follow the civil law, as Cujas mentions as the claim's origins statutes 'by Frederick in the West and Romanos Lekapenos in the East' (without any further details). In his initial notes, Gentili criticised the lack of references to either authors or legal authorities, while suggesting – with some caution ('*ni fallor*') and without offering himself a textual basis – that the claim can already be found in the Digest, but he did not pursue the issue in his later drafts.[31]

[26] See eg Cons. 16.

[27] Cons. 24, p. 65 (referring to C.3.28.29.1 and C.5.13.1.12).

[28] 616B f. 141v (pursuing his earlier notes in 616A f. 147v), all crossed out: 'Consultatio vigesima quarta habet rationem ineptam ne donatio inter vivos imputetur <explicat minus bene, cur dos et donatio propter nuptias in legitimam hodie imputentur> quia scilicet vivente patre ea in ipsius bonis non [erat, cedo?], enim et dos, et donatio propter nuptias, et militiae casus an nec imputabitur? Responde de uno militiae casu. Ratio est, quod illa a suo patrimonio aliena pater voluerit'.

[29] Cons. 24 p. 65 ('quae definitio summe notanda est […] Donatio igitur inter vivos non ea lege facta, quoniam legibus non est nominatim annumerata his, quae computari debet in legitimam, non computabitur').

[30] See eg Cons. 28, 34, 38 and 45.

[31] 616A f. 133ar : after summarising Cujas's argument, Gentili adds: 'qua nec legem, nec auctorem citat. Levissima consultatio. Falsum etiam puto eum dicere de origine, nam in Digestis ni fallor'.

Commenting on Cons. 34, Gentili questioned, not without doubts ('*Cogito*'), Cujas's interpretation of the widow's choice in selecting the beneficiary of a *fideicommissum* entrusted by her husband in favour of their children. In Cujas's interpretation, the widow was bound by the sequence of substitutions ordained by her late husband. Even an apparent degree of discretion in the testament's clause ('*idoneis potius quam non idoneis*') is restricted by Cujas according to objective (though in its formulation somewhat gendered) standards: '*etiam et libera matri electio non datur, sed pro boni viri arbitratu*'. In that respect, the testament's clause instructing the mother instituted as heir to proceed to the *fideicommissum* '*cum moreretur, vel cum ipsa vellet*', would seem to rule out the issue whether, after having designated the beneficiary, she could still change her mind (at least with regard to the daughters mentioned in the testament). Gentili wondered how this could be reconciled with the clause '*cum moreretur, vel cum ipsa vellet*'[32] and questioned whether Cujas's argument '*ea verba tractum temporis habent*' applied in general or, referring to D. 38.17.6 and D. 45.1.112, in the consultation's particular case.[33]

In Cons. 49, Cujas offers an argument for exempting extensively the formal requirements in the case of a soldier's testament. Apart from the *corpus iuris*, he refers to Greek sources (Xenophon, Theophilos's Paraphrasis, the Theodosian Code, the Basilica).[34] This is a case where Gentili, in his initial reading (the opinion is absent from the later drafts), supports the opinion,[35] but not without qualifications. In a preliminary question, Cujas had stated that the production of six witnesses before a notary (and a seventh before a judge) by the pretended heir of a soldier was void. Gentili challenges that view by arguing that some laws appear to give notaries (quasi-)judicial authority, though he also notes that the standard gloss negates that claim.[36] Cujas's opinion, however, considers more at length how the testator's intention may be proved, and whether the exemption of formal requirements applies in long-term soldiers' quarters. In favour of a fairly broad interpretation of such places where soldiers may make a valid will without observing all the formalities, he refers to his Greek sources. Gentili duly copied most of the argument, including the references, yet also checked them critically in editions available to him.[37]

[32] 616A 130r: '… itaque videatur non ad tempus mortis hoc referendum. Cogito'.

[33] 574, 359v : 'nam non de omnibus verbis tractum habentibus nec de his, quae in casu tuo admittis, illud dicitur, sed de quibusdam. d. l. filii. Ad Terty. [D.38.17.6] et l. si quis stipulatus 112 de verb. oblig. [D. 45.1.112]'.

[34] Though probably not the Suda, even if the term Suidas is printed with a capital initial: Cujas here more likely uses the word in the litteral sense of a stronghold (p 121).

[35] 616A f. 150r (in the margin: both '*pro Cuia.*' and '*contra Cuia.*'): '… si excipimus quae in principio <ad alteram q.> dicit, probo maxime et in definitione, et in rationibus'.

[36] 616A f. 150r : 'Nam tabelliones iudices Chartularii, et non uno casu funguntur iudicis officio in proposito [referring to Nov. 85, C. 1.3.31, C. 5.37.24, 'cum similibus'], itaque fidem tabellio vel iudici faciet. [in a smaller handwriting:] Tamen dicit gl. in l. hac consultissima in §. Si quis autem C. de testa. [gl. 'Depositiones' ad C. 6.23.21.5] quod numquam reperitur ut notarii possit recipere [crossed out: istas depositiones] <talia sacramenta>. Vide diserte contra me'.

[37] 616 f. 150r, in reaction to Cujas stating 'nec ex §. 1. Institu. De testament. milit. [I. 2.11pr.: sedibus in the Krueger ed., with edibus as alternative reading] puto recte quosdam sedes interpretari stativa, & malim, aedes …': 'Sed ego lego in d. §. 1 in aedibus in impressione Tinghi Lugd. 79, consultationes edite anno 76', presumably a reference to the Lyons edition Sumptibus Philippi Tinghi, 1579, *loc. cit.*, col. 191; Gentili may have mentioned 1576 on the strength of the dedication to Jacques de la Guesle, reproduced in the Cologne editions, if he had not seen the 1577 edition of Cujas's collected works.

Those are examples where Roman law texts are adduced or discussed by Gentili in order to buttress a more general diverging opinion. Consultations 14 and 37 illustrate how Gentili upholds his own argument in such cases.

Cons. 14 deals with a case where a party had offered a toll-right as a pledge, with the proviso that the secured creditor could not dispose of the pledge, nor use it as security himself. Later, the creditor offered all his property as a general pledge to a third party. Cujas argued that (after a lapse of three years)[38] the pledgor could not prevail himself of an *actio utilis*, referring to D. 20.5.7.2. Gentili took exception to Cujas's reference to that *lex*, which he said dealt with a different case: '... dico eam legem loqui de diverso pacto, ne scilicet debitor vendere depossenti, ne scilicet creditor, loquitur l. 4 <et seq.> de pi. act. Et ex utraque lege colligo ego distractionem tantum non valere contra pactionem, contra paciscentem, adeoque contra alios bene valere, itaque et contra tertium [...]'.[39]

In Cons. 37, a testator had provided for a *fideicommissum* in favour of his wife's granddaughter, who was to be instructed in the true religion. She would benefit from the *fideicommissum* provided her parents had returned to the true religion. If the granddaughter died childless, a *fideicommissum* of the estate was provided for a grandson, who was also to be instructed in the true religion; if the latter were to die without having married, the testator had provided for a substitution '*sub eadem conditione*' on behalf of a third beneficiary. Cujas had been asked whether the condition of the parents recanting was also applicable to the *fideicommissum* on behalf of the grandson. Cujas had answered affirmatively, because the testator's will had been to prevent the property or its income from ending up in the hands of the heretical parent. Cujas also extended his reasoning to the case of the third beneficiary of the testament. Gentili brought against Cujas's opinion both legal arguments and social policy considerations. As regards his legal dissent, Gentili objects against driving too much of a wedge between an heir's institution and a substitution, against the point of D. 28.5.74.[40] Gentili also censures severely Cujas's policy argument in his construction of the testator's intention (*sc.* that the father of the testament's beneficiary should not derive any benefit from the testament while remaining a heretic), apparently because Cujas had not questioned the capacity of a heretic. Gentili then adds another non-legal (but gender-based) consideration, suggesting that the condition made more sense with a daughter than a son, who may be less inclined to be influenced than his sister.[41]

[38] The case was more complex and raised other issues, which were also picked up by Gentili. One complication (following Cujas's argument, at 43) stemmed from the fact that the toll-right seems to have been under Saxon jurisdiction, where restrictions applied to offering securities charging immoveables to anyone outside Saxony.

[39] 616A 146r. Comp. 574 357rv : '... non probo : quia l. si creditor §. ult. de distr. pig. de pacto loquitur, ne debitor pignus distrahat : species autem Cuiaciana de pacto, ne creditor distrahat, est autem inter speciem et speciem differentia, quia creditor rem sibi oppignoratam oppignorare aliis potest [...]'.

[40] 'Consultatio trigesima septima mihi sane vera est in eo, ut condicio imposita primo substituto repetita et alteri videatur, nam et docui, condicionem instituto adiectam substituto repetitam videri, sed Cuiacio vera vix esse potest, qui ab opinionis suae iugulo amovere nescit, l. sub condicione de her. inst., ait enim non obstare huius legis definitionem, quia non eadem continuo in substitutionibus admittenda sit, cum sit latius inter substitutionem, et institutionem discrimen, quam inter substitutionem et substitutionem. Id ait, sed non ostendit, nec ostendere potest ad speciem d. l. sub condicione, ubi institutio sub condicione erat concepta. Age Cuiaci, quid est substitutio nisi condicionalis quaedam institutio? Sane non illud discrimen invenies, si mature deliberaveris. Ego mature alibi' (626 142r).

[41] 'Venio ad tuam coniecturam, qua istam repetitionem introducere tentas. Dicis condicionem repetitam videri, quia mens testantis ea fuerit, ne ad ullum, quam ad orthodoxum bona sua perveniant, aut ex bonis

On the third question of Cons. 51 (a donation confirmed by testament, with both instruments including several conditional substitutions), whether the use of the word *liberi* extends infinitely to further descendants, Cujas as usual highlights the intention of the gift's or *fideicommissum*'s author, though as always backing up his interpretation of that intention by referring to different texts of Roman law (including a quotation drawn from Ulpian's fragments 25.1). In his original notes, Gentili wrote down Cujas's arguments and references in favour of a broad understanding of the word *liberi* in the gift and testament. His dissent from Cujas is mainly based on a different reading of some of the same textual authorities mentioned by the Frenchman, including a restrictive construction of the sequence of statements in D. 50.16.220.2[42] and adding (possibly on the strength of Alciato's *Paradoxes* III.14) an argument drawn from I. 1.14.5.[43]

suis emolumentum ullum: et pervenisset utique emolumentum ususfructus ad patrem nepotis, si non intelligeretur condicio repetita. Euge, quid scripsisti? Capax istius beneficii, quod ius civile in bonis filiorumfam. patri tribuit, haereticus est? In tanto errato ubi te oviculae viderint tuae quid ipsae <agnellis> suis balabunt? Iam quod non videatur condicio repetita, profero ego, quod non tanta in filio ratio, quanta in filia, est, ut ea insit condicio: quoniam corrumpi filius minus potest, honeste magis a patre abest, suus, in summa, est magis, quam illa sua' (*ibidem*).

[42] 'Ego non falso ad filios <hoc Cuiacii casu> restringi adsero, et dico fideicommisariam odiosam esse. Et primum primo. Debet restringi ad filios, nam ut introducitur condicio, si sine liberis, et latissime accipitur in d. §. ult. [C. 6.25.7.1-3] ne liberi institutorum a substitutis excludantur, ita ne iidem excludantur, latissime non accipietur, illa eadem ratione etiam in uno nepote, pronepote, etiam in uno postumo, quominus adhuc liber dici potest, condicionem, si sine liberis, deficere aiunt d. §. pe. et d. l. i. [C. 6.49.6.2; C. 6.46.1]. Ergo eodem argumento non utimur contra eos, pro quibus est inductum. Nec moveor l. liberorum [D. 50.16.220.2] quum illa in contrarium stare potius videtur: si quidem loquitur aperte in legum dispositionibus usque ad §. Sed et Papirius, usque quo scilicet dicitur latissima liberorum significatio, mox ad testamenta trahit I.C. et ait, sed et etc., hoc est, non in legibus tantum ea significatio habetur, sed et in testamentis iuxta hanc Papirii speciem, que scilicet specialem caussam habet' (616 150v).

[43] [...] Caeterum et illud dixerim, probatam omnibus de nomine liberorum, et filiorum nomine sententiam esse penitus falsam: nec enim a Callistrato ea est in l. liberorum de ve. sig. [D. 50.16.220] qui uno tantum casu excepto facit immo pacem utriusque nominis potestatem, et facit illam, ut interpretatione potius, quam significatione propria utrunque nomen alios deinceps a primo gradus contineat. Et quid constituetur differentia, si auctores alii, si ipsi iurisconsulti, et Callistratus met usurpant nomina ista promiscue? 'Filii appellatione omnes liberos intelligimus', inquit Paulus eo. ti. de ve. sig. [D. 50.17.12]. An hic Alciatus elegantiae affectatae praetextu illud responsum eludit, et nobis illudit? 'Qui liberorum procreandorum animo uxores ducunt', ait Callistratus, hic an non liberorum nomen pro filiorum adsumptum? Eccur praeterea intermixtum Divi Marci rescriptum, nisi ut ostendatur promiscua definitio? Non admiscetur (quod doctores autumant) ut definiatur, etiam in uno constare liberorum nomen, qua enim arte? Sed ut lata illa significatio et rescripto divi Marci probata ostenderetur liberorum significatio? Ineptissime dum agit de nomine filiorum, et postquam longe ultra nepotem produxerat prius, ad quem tantum producit rescriptum Marci. Igitur de filiis accipit ilic Calistratus liberorum nomen. Ecquid tandem ea in lege iste I.C. pro nomine liberorum scribit, quod non etiam de filiorum nomine adiungat? Excepto illo cognationis enumeratae casu nihil, cuius quidem casus ratione, atque exemplo fatemur et nos liberorum nomen facilius aliquando produci posse, quam filiorum possit, ut in §. ult. Inst. qui tes. tu. [I. 1.14.5], ubi extensionem factam, aio ex adiuncto verbo 'videantur', quod non propriam significationem notare, receptum est. Alias et, subtilem illam legem distinctionem vulgo homines nec observare, traditur [added in the margin: a gl. et Bal. in l. 6. de test. tu. (D. 26.2.6, glossa 'non continebuntur'; Baldus ad leg. cit., ed. Venice 1599, f. 26rb, on the communis usus loquendi, which is said to depart from the interpretatio iuris)] atque mirum non est, siquidem et nominum casus novos, et nominum differentias novas, et nova etiam nomina, quo quodque distinctius esset, leges invenerunt, ut de casu (si memoria non fallor), filiabus Charisius notat, et de aliis multa cum apud Ciceronem, tum apud alios habeantur. Itaque si ratio, si verba, si mens testatoris Cuiacium refutat in ista consultatione, alii qui excipient ?' (616 137r, passages between quotation marks are underlined in the manuscript).

VII. Civil Law Doctrine

Cujas sparingly referred to modern legal literature, and somewhat more frequently to traditional legal scholarship, though definitely not as frequently as that traditional scholarship itself. In the dedicatory letter of his consultations, and in the chapter where he criticises what he considers malpractices of many legal professionals,[44] he expresses what he considered an inept tendency to accumulate (doctrinal) authorities in legal arguments. The Accursian gloss is referred to in several consultations, usually with approval,[45] occasionally on a critical note.[46] On very few occasions, Cujas departs explicitly from the *communis opinio*, but without any systematic bias against that traditional learning: for example, in one case, he states that he sides with Raphael Fulgosius against the common opinion.[47]

Gentili does not systematically pick up on those doctrinal references and discussions. Sometimes, he points out that the issue under discussion is dealt with by other authors, which may sometimes reinforce his remarks about redundant arguments. Only in a handful of cases is Cujas's use of doctrinal references the target of a more specific criticism.

In the case of Cons.19, a woman, urged by her mala fide husband, had waived her real surety rights on the dowry, and the husband had sold all the property. The central question was whether the woman did nonetheless have a remedy against the buyers on the strength of her surety. Cujas argued along Roman law authorities that the woman could not rely on any remedies, although Bartolus (ad D. 4.29.1)[48] and many others ('*alii plerique*') professed that the law had to provide some remedy to her. Cujas cautiously acknowledges that Bartolus's opinion may 'nowadays' prevail, and then continues the argument by stating that if the husband's fraud was established,[49] an *actio in factum* could be given to the woman, the result of which would be to restore her surety and provide her with an *actio utilis*. Gentili briefly ridicules Cujas's argument, who fails to discuss or counter Bartolus's and the prevailing opinion.[50] In Cons. 17, on the status of a fief which had returned to the lord, Cujas briefly mentions that Bartolus's statement ad C. 10.10.5 on derelict goods (*bona vacantia*) was not applicable in the case at hand, also because the rationale for fiefs was different. Gentili understands Cujas's reference as if Bartolus's opinion was censured, and proceeds to show that the parallel between the situations with regard to the fief and *bona vacantia* is sustainable. In Cons. 57, Gentili considers that, on two different issues (questions 2 and 6), Cujas's reference to the gloss is wrong: in the first case because he misrepresents what the gloss says, in the second case because in Gentili's view, Accursius had dealt with a different situation.[51]

[44] This kind of criticism was rife in sixteenth-century legal discussions, eg S Geonget, 'Contre 'les rabules & impudens criards, vrais pestes des barreaux' in Cazals and Geonget (n 8) 167–85.

[45] See eg Cons. 11, 19, 25, 34, 35, 40, 42. See also approving references to Bartolus, eg Cons. 4, 60.

[46] See eg Cons. 16.

[47] *cf* infra Cons. 25.

[48] *Super prima Codicis* (Venice 1526), 159ra-va.

[49] At the beginning of the consultation, the husband's fraud is included in the *species facti.*

[50] 616 147r ('*ridicula prorsus*') and 141r ('*An praevaricatur*?').

[51] 616 144v (q. 2: glossa '*Petat*' ad D. 18.3.7, *jo.* D.18.3.6.2; q. 6: glossa '*non fieri*' ad D. 29.2.6.7); Gentili reiterates his point on q. 2 in 616 139r, and on q. 6 in 574 360r ('aio … abuti Cuiacium Accursii auctoritate, qui nihil ad rem dicit, sed ad casum longe diversum, quoniam ad hereditatem illam adeundam non compellebatur

Ten questions are raised in Cons. 25, most of which are ignored by Gentili because he turns down the arguments as insignificant. In the seventh question, which deals with issues of conflicts of laws, Cujas disagreed with the *communis opinio doctorum*. The testator's estate comprised lands, property and assets in different jurisdictions (somewhat loosely referred to as Austria, Carinthia, Alsace, the Burgundian Free-County, and Antwerp), but mostly in Austria, which was the jurisdiction of the deceased's *ius patriae*. Cujas's opinion was that the rules governing the testament and the succession to all the estate's property was subject to Austrian customary law, even though in some jurisdictions (the opinion refers here to Alsace and the Free-County), *ius commune* applied. Cujas asserted his thesis in accordance with Raphael Fulgosius against the prevailing doctrine.[52] The latter, he protested, would have resulted in the absurd situation (by Roman law standards) of dealing with a succession partly intestate, partly governed by the testament. In subjecting the whole succession to one jurisdiction's law, Cujas relied also on an opinion by Paulus de Castro applying Florentine law to a succession composed of properties in different jurisdictions. Gentili, in addition to criticising Cujas for failing to take duly into account some restrictions imposed by the testator in his will, wonders whether he should discuss at all an argument which is not even Cujas's own original position. He then nevertheless launches into an argument along civil law authorities justifying the possibility of a diversity of legal regimes.[53]

Modern doctrine, despite the polemics they often generated, seem to provide far less opportunities for crossing swords. As for traditional learning, Gentili occasionally points out that some argument may be found in the works of recent authors.[54]

VIII. Canon Law

Canon law authorities do not appear very frequently in Cujas's consultations, and then mostly closely related to issues which were still (in France) to some extent governed by the law of the Roman-Catholic Church. In very general terms, Gentili reasons on

ullo iure, qui compulsus proponitur: at hic noster debitor omnino solvere tenebatur id, de quo transegit. Non sunt casus dissimiles, et dissimiles casuum rationes?').

[52] Referring to Raphaël Fulgosius ad C. 1.1.1 (Lyons 1547, Nos. 21–24, f. 4va–5ra).

[53] 'Ad septimam quaestionem eiusdem consultationis an quid dicam dubito, disputat cum Fulgosio contra communem opinionem, quae est, ut eidem intestato defuncto varie succedatur pro iure vario locorum, in quibus illius sita sunt bona, atque cum ea sit disputatio, quae a multis habeatur, fortassis fecero rectius, si hic ego non resumo, ne suis videar respondere argumentis, quae non sunt sua. Facerem sane rectius : sed libet tamen respondere. Patriae uno iure succedendum contendunt, quia eidem homini nec succeditur partim ex testamento, partim ab intestato : nec partim civili, partim praetorio. Nos dicimus argumento a non simili tanquam a simili ductum, quoniam causae testati et intestati contrariae et pugnantes, ut simul stare non possint. Sed et nec uno casu, nec una ratione aliquando etiam stant, ut bene explicatum a nostratibus est in l. ius nostrum de reg. iur. [cf civil law doctrines on D. 50.17.7] alibique, ex quo consequitur, ut magis ista diversi iuris successio admitti in casu nostro et possit, et debeat. Age vero, eidem per contra tabulas succeditur, et per secundum tabulas l. 6. de bo. poss. [D. 37.1.6 ?] iure civili ex testamento, et iure praetorio per contra tabulas l. si duobus de bon. poss. cont. tab. [D. 37.4.14] ab intestato iure civili, et iure praetorio. l. filium. eo. [D. 37.4.20] cum similibus, unus et idem ex pluribus partibus institutus : itaque et ius accrescendi in uno et eodem l. i. cum seq. de acq. her. [D. 29.2.1-2] multa supersunt, et fortiora forte : sed non mihi otium quaerere. Atque si eidem diverso iure succeditur cur idem succedere non possit, ratio nulla est. Caeterum an non idem filius iure naturae quaedam, quaedam civili sibi vendicare de paternis bonis solet ?' (574 358v).

[54] See eg Cons. 2 and 4 (referring to F Hotman and U Zasius).

common grounds with Cujas in a few cases where 'the true religion' or 'heresy' are at stake (for example in relation to conditions imposed by testators), since, in theory, the same rules can operate either way in Protestant and Roman-Catholic jurisdictions. Very occasionally, the potential ambivalence of the term 'catholicon' may have been played upon by Gentili in a more personal jibe.[55]

IX. Feudal Law and *Iura Propria*

A few consultations are published under the caption *De feudis*, as, inevitably, feudal rights played a major role in legal practice and (family) property. In his discussion of Cons. 20, Gentili claims that Cujas omits the *summa ratio* that prevails in assessing feudal succession, which he identifies as the *servitium*.[56]

In Cons. 54, Cujas apparently suggests in a brief obiter that general principles of feudal law can be departed from by particular regional customs and statutes which would then prevail. *Iura propria*, which dominated the life of the law outside the academic sphere, are routinely referred to in consultations which proceeded from litigation. Following the well-established principles of *ius commune* doctrine, those particular laws prevail over civil law, though at the same time, they are systematically articulated and construed according to the standards of civil law scholarship, for which Cujas has a bias to refer directly to texts from the Roman law compilations. Customary law, through the prism of Cujas's consultations, is French customary law, which Cujas acknowledges in its regional variety,[57] although in some cases, but without swelling the ranks of the French literature championing the construct of a 'common custom of the realm', he refers to the custom of France (*mos Galiiae*).[58] A few consultations refer to customary principles which tend to be wide-spread in France.[59] The custom of Bourges is specifically referred to in litigation anchored in that region.[60] In a few major consultations involving foreign interests, Cujas focuses on the application of foreign customs and laws.[61] Specific customs are those linked to a family or common practices attributed to testators.[62]

The increasing importance of royal ordinances in France during the sixteenth century is also reflected through several consultations.[63] In one instance, Cujas even notes that since he wrote his opinion, the law had changed as a result of a royal ordinance which had been enacted.[64]

[55] See Gentili's comments on Cons. 26 and 31.

[56] '... non dicit summam rationem, cur in feudis masculi filiorum nomine veniant tantum, quae est, quoniam masculi servitia feudi praestare rectius possunt' (616 141rv).

[57] Cons. 3.

[58] Cons. 32 ('Le mort saisit le vif').

[59] See eg Cons. 9 (on the *droit de retrait*), 32, 56. Custom or practice is also referred to in order to construe specific terms in testaments or contracts: Cons. 10, 52. Cons. 7: the *leges* may have inspired legal scholars to construe customary principles applicable in different places.

[60] Cons. 5, 8.

[61] Cons. 14 (Saxony), Cons. 25 (Austria, Carinthia, Alsace, Free County of Burgundy).

[62] Cons. 35 (*consuetudo domus*), 42 (*usus testatorum*).

[63] See eg Cons. 3, 12, 41, 49.

[64] Cons. 12 *in fine*, p 42 (probably a reference to the ordinance of Fontainebleau 1560; see J Hilaire, 'L'arbitrage dans la période moderne (XVIe-XVIIIe siècle)' (2000) *Revue de l'Arbitrage* 187–226, esp. p 221, No 32).

On issues of customary law, Gentili does not commit his expertise. However, indirectly, through issues of interpretation, and assisted by civil law authorities, he criticises some of Cujas's opinions. Thus, in Cons. 10, on the application of a clause '*paterna paternis, materna maternis*' in a codicil, although he apparently approves Cujas's remarks on the importance of the *usus loquendi* with regard to a testator's intention, he dissents on the portion of goods which qualify as maternal goods. In Cons. 52, the issue was whether a son born out of wedlock from a relationship between an unmarried man and an unmarried servant and who had been legitimised through a rescript of the prince, was to be regarded as a legitimate child with regard to his father's testamentary succession. Cujas had considered the civil and canon law authorities, but also, in his time ('*hodie*'), the extensive use of the term 'natural' for children, even regarding issue from fornication. Gentili, who brings up the issue that such an extensive use could open the path to surreptitiously obtained rescripts, questions the blurring of the legal distinction between (ordinary) natural children and *spurii*. Civil law authorities are also used in order to discuss the style of proceedings: in Cons. 12, Cujas had guardedly argued that when parties had submitted to arbitration under a penal arbitration clause prohibiting them to appeal against the sentence, the party who lost and appealed to the Parliament of Paris did not incur the penalty because the practice in France (*mos Galliae*) allowed such appeals (despite authorities to the contrary which Cujas refers to with some emphasis). Gentili objected (referring himself to civil law)[65] that the practice did not preclude that a party could waive his right.

X. The Difficulty of Mixing Scholarly and Forensic Reasoning

While scholarly reasoning is supposed to remain above the fray and pursue an ideal of abstract justice – the 'common good' being the interest it is supposed to use as its yardstick for sorting out conflicts of interests – *consilia*, at least the most common type of *consilia pro parte*, merely propose a model of legal reasoning which argues the case of a litigant, usually the client of the consultant. Cujas's consultations are mostly drafted (in their printed version), following a long-standing tradition in that genre of legal literature, as if stating an objective assessment of how to resolve the legal issues of the case. The author does not give the appearance of intervening as the advocate of a particular litigant, although in practice, the consultations inevitably support the interests of one party against the other in a real-life case. Gentili, in his critical notes on these consultations, does not take into account the cases' conflicts of interests, but subjects Cujas's arguments to a test of scholarly aptitude, just as if the consultations were to be treated as scholarly literature – which, of course, the late-medieval *consilia* literature had to a large extent become. That approach was legitimate, but it entailed that Gentili's criticisms inevitably did not reflect a level playing field, as he was not, as Cujas, constrained by the case of a particular litigant in the proceedings. Later on in his career, when he was himself involved in consultancy, Gentili would be confronted with

[65] D. 31,1,77,20.

the need to justify that his arguments did not contradict the positions he had earlier defended in his own scholarly publications.

A fuller assessment of Gentili's critical reading of Cujas would therefore require a detailed examination of his annotations on Cujas's doctrinal works – annotations which are scattered over several volumes of the D'Orville manuscripts. The '*consultatio*' on Cujas's opinions shows that, beyond the general aim of writing a relatively short review discrediting the authority of these opinions, Gentili used an array of different devices within the general framework of the opinions' '*definitiones*' to censure Cujas's reasoning. The criticism is levelled at the identification of the issues, the use of authorities, the coherence of the arguments and their corollaries. It does not, however, reflect any fundamental methodological or ideological contrast, but seems to target Cujas's reputation as an eminent jurist. The agenda behind the exercise remains uncertain, unless it fitted in the at the time fashionable genre of focusing scholarly works around prominent figures.[66]

Appendix

		D'Orville 574	**D'Orville 616 (A) & 613**	**D'Orville 616 (B)**
01	De testamento inter liberos	356rv	*cf* 613: 115rv	140v
02	De legato a Presbytero filiae suae spuriae relicto	356v	132r	praeteritum
03	De insinuandis donationibus	356v	132r	140v
04	De successione ab intestato	praeteritum	*cf* 613: 114v	140v
05	De legatis	praeteritum	*cf* 613: 114v	140v–141r
06	De querela inofficiosi testamenti	praeteritum	132v	praeteritum
07	De Communione inter coniuges	praeteritum	[132v]	praeteritum
08	De iure retractus	356v	132v–133ar	*cf* cons. 9
09	De eodem iure	praeteritum	133ar	141r
10	De bonis paternis et maternis	356v	133ar	praeteritum
11	De beneficio abstentionis	356v–357r	133av	praeteritum
12	De poena compromissi	357r	133av	praeteritum
13	De vectigali fundi	357r	133av	141r

(continued)

[66] A reference to the abundant sixteenth-century literature in different fields where the preposition or prefix 'anti' was used in the titles of polemical tracts: in religious matters, the many writings on the 'Anti-Christ', and writings railing against Calvin, the Huguenots ('anti-Hugues'), Guisart, Osiander, Sturmius, Sanderus etc., and also in political literature (eg the Anti-Spaniard, and against Machiavelli) and to some extent in the broader legal literature (J.Hotman's *Anti-Choppinus*, published in 1592).

(Continued)

		D'Orville 574	D'Orville 616 (A) & 613	D'Orville 616 (B)
14	De nominis hypotheca	357r	146r; 613: 126v	141r
15	De substitutione precaria	357r–358r	146rv	praeteritum
16	De usuris dotis	praeteritum	146v	praeteritum
17	De feudis	358r	146v–147r	praeteritum
18	De remissione pignoris a muliere facta	praeteritum	147r	141r
19	De substitutione precaria	praeteritum	147r	praeteritum
20	De fideicommissis	358rv	[144v], 147rv	141rv
21	De legatis	praeteritum	147v	141v
22	De substitutione precaria	praeteritum	147v	praeteritum
23	Variae et satis leves quaestiones et opiniones advocatorum	praeteritum	[147v ?] 613: 126v	praeteritum
24	De imputatione in legitimam	praeteritum	147(r)v	[141v, crossed out]
25	De testamentis	358v–359r	148rv; 616: 126v	141v
26	De donationibus	359rv	148v–149r	141v–142r
27	De testamentis	praeteritum	149r	praeteritum
28	De substitutione precaria	praeteritum	149r	praeteritum
29	De societate	praeteritum	149r	praeteritum
30	De donationibus inter virem et uxorem	praeteritum	149r	142r
31	De substitutionibus fideicommissariis	359v	149rv	praeteritum
32	De institutione heredis Arriani	praeteritum	149v	praeteritum
33	De donatione inter coniuges facta contemplatione matrimonii	praeteritum	149v	142r
34	De hereditate restituenda uni ex liberis	359v	[130r]	praeteritum
35	De liberis in conditione positis	praeteritum	130r	praeteritum
36	De testamentis	praeteritum	130v	praeteritum
37	De fideicommissis	praeteritum	130v	142r
38	De evictionibus	praeteritum	134r	praeteritum
39	De conditione coelibatus	praeteritum	[134r]	praeteritum

(continued)

(Continued)

		D'Orville 574	D'Orville 616 (A) & 613	D'Orville 616 (B)
40	De portionibus coheredum	praeteritum	[134r], 616: 114v	praeteritum
41	De constitutione regia, quae vetat testamento dari quicquam tutori et curatori	praeteritum	134r	142rv
42	An nepotum appellatione, continenatur pronepotes	praeteritum	613: 114v	142v
43	De donationibus	359v–	134v	praeteritum
44	De donationibus	fol. deest	134v, 151r	142rv–143r
45	De testamento caeci et legatis	fol. deest	151rv	136r
46	An substitutus substituto sit substitutus instituto	fol. deest	151rv	136r
47	De pactis dotalibus	fol. deest	151rv	136v
48	De rescindenda transactione	fol. deest	[149r], 150r	143v
49	De militari testamento	fol. deest	150r	praeteritum
50	De substitutionibus	fol. deest	150v	praeteritum
51	De substitutionibus	fol. deest	150v, 145r	136v–137r, (138r)
52	De naturalibus liberis	fol. deest	145r	137rv & 143v
53	De substitutionibus	fol. deest	(151v)	(137v)
54	De feudis	fol. deest [360r ?]	145v	138rv
55	De testament[o] holographo	fol. deest vel praeteritum ?	144r, 145v	138v
56	De adoptionibus et de nobilitate	fol. deest vel praeteritum ?	144r	143v
57	De oblatione et depositione pecuniae debite et aliis articulis	360r	144v	139r
58	An substitui possit filio in bonis, quae ex donatione capit facta in nuptiis contrahendis inter patrem et matrem	360r	144v	praeteritum
59	De conventione adversa iuri publico et praescriptionibus	360r	[133av]	139r
60	De persecutione portionis debitae liberis	praeteritum		139rv

13

Star Chamber and the Civil Law

IAN WILLIAMS*

In the 1607 edition of his *Britannia*, William Camden explained that in the Star Chamber 'causes here are debated and decided … after the course of the civill Law'.[1] The relationship between the Star Chamber and the civil law has also been considered by Professor Ibbetson, discussing Edward Coke's report *De Libellis Famosis*,[2] and other scholarship has highlighted links with civilian material and ideas in the important decision in *Twyne's Case*.[3] This chapter goes beyond particular decisions and reports, taking a broader view by examining the practice of the court, as well as discussions both in and about it. In doing so, the chapter raises questions about how references to the civilian tradition should be understood in early-modern England, especially distinguishing between the European *ius commune* and the law of classical Rome.

There are some important preliminary issues which need to be addressed. The first is that perennial evidential problem when dealing with accounts of early-modern cases, that not all reports cover the same ground in the same way. For example, in the *Countess of Rutland's Case*, only one of the two reports includes any material from the speaker who referred to the civil law.[4] Second, attributions to the civil law are not always clear, if they are made at all. The report of *Short and Silo v Nudick* includes a civilian *sententia*,[5]

* The year is taken as beginning in January. Thanks to Paul Cavill for his advice, to participants at the Oxford Legal History Seminar and all the participants at the conference which led to this volume. Much of the research into Star Chamber manuscripts was supported by a British Academy/Leverhulme Trust Small Research Grant (SRG151808). Original spelling has been retained, translations from law-French are my own.

[1] W Camden, *Britannia, sive Florentissimorum regnorum Angliae, Scotiae, Hibernaie, et insularam adiacentium* (George Bishop and John Norton, 1607) 131. This remark is not present in earlier editions.

[2] DJ Ibbetson, 'Edward Coke, Roman Law, and the Law of Libel' in L Hutson (ed), *The Oxford Handbook of English Law and Literature, 1500–1700* (Oxford, Oxford University Press, 2017) 487–506. It has since been shown that Coke's main source was William West's *Symboleography* (W West, *Three treatises of the second part of symbolaeographie* (Charles Yetsweirt, 1594), itself borrowing from Hermann Vulteius, *Jurisprudentiae Romanae a Justiniano compositae libri II* (Paul Egenolph, 1590): J Mansky, 'Edward Coke, William West, and the Law of Libel' (2021) 42 *JLH* 328.

[3] C Willems, 'Coke, Collusion, and Conveyances: Unearthing the Roots of *Twyne's Case*' (2015) 36 *JLH* 129.

[4] *Isabell, Countesse de Rutlands Case* (1605) Moore KB 765, 769; 72 ER 892, 894, per Henry Howard, Earl of Northampton. See text at n 61 below. The account in J Hawarde, *Les Reportes del Cases in Camera Stellata 1593 to 1609* (WP Baildon (ed) (London, privately printed, 1894) 237 does not include Howard's speech.

[5] '*vendens eandem rem duobus falsarius est*': *Short and Silo v Nudick* (1627) Lambeth Palace Library (hereafter LPL) MS 1253, fo 109v.

but without a citation it cannot be determined whether this was taken directly from a civil law source or from Coke's report of the case of *Alton Woods*, which includes the same phrase and does attribute it to the civil law.[6] Similarly, it is in only one of the reports of *Twyne's Case* on fraudulent conveyances where an attribution of a point to the canon law, specifically the work of William Lyndwood, is included.[7] There is therefore the possibility that more civilian material was used than is visible in surviving accounts. Third, sometimes it cannot always be determined whether a point has been drawn from the civil law tradition or the wider Latin culture of the Renaissance. John Cowell's discussion of *crimen stellionatus*, for example, cited Jacques Cujas,[8] but John Hawarde relied upon a sixteenth-century Latin dictionary, yet they are very similar.[9] These evidential issues create considerable uncertainty about whether the civil law was consciously used, how that knowledge was acquired, and how thorough that knowledge was.

All that said, in common with another paper on Roman law in early-modern England, in relation to the Star Chamber and the civil law there is '[j]ust about enough … to justify this one paper'.[10] All types of people who sat in the court can be seen referring to the civil law. Perhaps unsurprisingly, the small number of judges with civilian training did so: Sir Julius Caesar[11] and Henry Howard, Earl of Northampton.[12] Several of the common law judges mentioned the civil law, such as Edward Coke and his successor Henry Montagu. Privy Councillors who were not professional lawyers also did so, although all had spent some time at the Inns of Court: William Cecil,[13] John Egerton[14] and Richard Weston.[15] Finally, even the bishops can be found, very occasionally, raising the civil law: John Williams (who presided over the court as Lord Keeper) and William Laud. The civil law was a resource used by judges from a range of professional and educational backgrounds. Knowledge of the civil law was gained from personal experience[16] and conversations with civilians,[17] as well as from texts from both England and continental Europe. It should also be noted that some of the civilian material used in the Star Chamber which can be identified was relatively recent.[18] A case in 1619 used a civilian work published between 1594 and 1614,[19] and judicial papers from the reign of Charles I refer to a work first printed in 1618.[20]

[6] *Case of Alton Woods* (1600) 1 Co Rep 40b, 45a; 76 ER 89, 103.

[7] Willems (n 3) 136.

[8] J Cowell, *The Interpreter or Booke Containing the Signification of Words* (John Legate, 1607) s.v. 'Cosening', citing Jacques Cujas' *Paratitla* (J Cujas, *Paratitla in Libros Quinquaginta a Digestorum seu Pandecta* (Maternum Cholinum, 1570) 326). Cowell's text includes a reference to Pliny, *Natural History*, book 30.10 which may be taken from S Schardius, *Lexicon Iuridicum* (Basel, 1582), s.v. 'Stellionatum' (col 2138).

[9] Hawarde, *Les Reportes del Cases*, 124 cites A Calepinus, *Dictionarium Latinae Linguae* (Paulus Manutius, 1558), s.v. 'Stellionatus Crimen', a definition which refers to what is said by jurists.

[10] JH Baker, 'Roman Law at the Third University of England' (2002) 55 *CLP* 123, 123.

[11] A Wijffels, 'Caesar [formerly Adelmare], Sir Julius' in ODNB, doi.org/10.1093/ref:odnb/4328.

[12] P Croft, 'Howard, Henry, Earl of Northampton' in ODNB, doi.org/10.1093/ref:odnb/13906.

[13] T McCaffrey, 'Cecil, William, first Baron Burghley' in ODNB, doi.org/10.1093/ref:odnb/4983.

[14] LA Knafla, 'Egerton, John, first earl of Bridgewater' in ODNB, doi.org/10.1093/ref:odnb/8587.

[15] B Quintrell, 'Weston, Richard, first earl of Portland' in ODNB, doi.org/10.1093/ref:odnb/29126.

[16] See text at n 75 below, for Archbishop Laud's recollection of hearing about the civil law when a student.

[17] See text at n 79 below.

[18] Confirming an observation by Helmholz in relation to *ius commune* literature and English civilian practice (RH Helmholz, *Roman Canon Law in Reformation England* (Cambridge, Cambridge University Press, 1990) 146).

[19] See n 24 below.

[20] See n 50 below.

The more interesting question is not whether the civil law was mentioned, but how and why it was used. Here, an important distinction needs to be drawn between the use of the civil law in relation to matters of procedure, evidence and proof, and the civil law in relation to the substance of matters addressed in the Star Chamber. It is also necessary to distinguish between these uses of the civil law to provide procedural and substantive norms and the role of the civil law in legitimising Star Chamber proceedings.

I. Procedure, Evidence and Proof

The Star Chamber's procedure was similar to that of the Chancery, itself informed by the procedural and evidential rules of the *ius commune*.[21] The most frequent references to the civil law are found in the contexts of procedure and proof.[22] For example, in 1605 Lord Ellesmere addressed the question of whether costs could be awarded to a relator when the relator had made libellous allegations against various defendants. Ellesmere referred to the practice of the court and the observation that such costs 'by the Civill Law are not in any case allowed'.[23] In 1619, in the important and very high profile proceedings brought against English goldsmiths and various Dutch merchants for transporting gold out of England, Julius Caesar's notes include a section entitled 'What proofes are required to the condemnation of an accused person for such transportation', which is answered by extracts from *ius commune* authors such as Farinacius.[24]

The tone of reports also suggests that a degree of civilian knowledge was taken for granted among the judges of the court. In the early-1590s case of *Parsons v Herne*, William Cecil could simply observe that perjury allegations, such as that in the case, were very serious and so no sentence should be given without 'witnesses *omni exceptiones maiores*',[25] a civilian idea found in Vulteius and others.[26] So far as can be seen from the report, Cecil did not need to explain the point any further and could assume

[21] MRT Macnair, *The Law of Proof in Early Modern Equity* (Berlin, Duncker and Humblot, 1999). Macnair's study is mainly focused after the abolition of the Star Chamber, when printed sources for equity courts become more common. However, there are significantly more Star Chamber reports in manuscript for the earlier period than for other courts (I Williams, 'Learning the "New Law of the Star Chamber": Legal Education and Legal Literature in Early-Stuart England' (2022) 43 *JLH* 243, 255). The material covered here suggests that the more limited printed sources showing earlier evidence of *ius commune* influence discussed by Macnair were not atypical.

[22] It is important to note that there is no evidence that the Star Chamber adopted the full *ius commune* system of criminal procedure. In particular, there is no evidence of the Star Chamber using torture as a mode of proof (on this aspect of *ius commune* criminal procedure, see JH Langbein, *Torture and the Law of Proof: Europe and England in the Ancien Régime* (Chicago, University of Chicago Press, 2006) 3–16), although as the Star Chamber could not impose the death penalty, torture would not have been permitted as part of its process under the *ius commune* rules (ibid 13).

[23] *Nicholas v Hichecocke et al* (1605) 244–6 in Hawarde, *Les Reportes del Cases*, 246.

[24] BL MS Add 12497, fo 45r, referring to, eg, P Farinacius, *Praxis et theorica criminalis* (1594–1614). For the background and proceedings, see S Healy, 'Star Chamber and the Bullion Trade, 1618-20' in KJ Kesselring and N Mears, *Star Chamber Matters: An Early Modern Court and Its Records* (London, Institute for Historical Research, 2021) 175–94.

[25] *Parsons v Herne* (1594) 7–10 in Hawarde, *Les Reportes del Cases*, 9.

[26] Vulteius, *Jurisprudentiae Romanae*, fo 507v.

the other judges would understand it. This was also the case when the same language was used over three decades later, suggesting the civilian knowledge was well-established amongst those working in the court.[27]

The ambiguity of a civilian *sententia* found in a circulating collection of Caroline reports also suggests familiarity with civilian sources. Thomas Coventry LK observed that if a poor man will not pay costs, 'he shall not be discharged excepete he wilbe whipte'.[28] This is then immediately followed by '*[q]ui non luit ere luat corpore*', a sententia which was soon to be described by Edward Coke simply as an 'old rule', and which ends the report of the case.[29] It is not clear whether the *sententia* was spoken by Coventry, or if the reporter inserted it as an explanation or elegant summary of Coventry's remark, but it appears that no further explanation or elaboration was necessary.

This material therefore suggests that Shapiro's argument that material on witchcraft, ultimately derived from continental sources, was the source for civilian influences on the wider development of ideas of proof and presumptions should be qualified.[30] Lawyers and others participating in Star Chamber proceedings were aware of the civilian ideas, seemingly independently of the witchcraft material. There were three issues of proof in the Star Chamber where civilian ideas and material appear repeatedly: the two witness rule; the role of presumptions; and the identification of suspicious documents.

A. The Two Witness Rule

A requirement that, absent a confession, there were two witnesses to provide full proof was a key part of the *ius commune* law of evidence,[31] including in criminal proceedings in the English church courts.[32] The rule was adopted in the Star Chamber and discussion of the rule appears in reports. Cases sometimes turned on whether there was sufficient proof in terms of the number of witnesses.[33] John Egerton's judicial notes on cases also highlight where there were two witnesses in a case, showing its importance for decision-making in the court.[34]

[27] *Wollaston v Harecourt and Ayleworth* (1626) BL MS Add 48057, fo. 14. This is only true for the original law-French versions of these reports. Most of the English translations obscure the civilian origin of the language by translating to the witnesses as being 'above all exception' (eg LPL MS 1253, fo 21v).

[28] *Cannon v Flower* (1627) LPL MS 1253, fo. 162v.

[29] 2 Co Inst 173. By the early-seventeenth century the *sententia* was linked to the Twelve Tables (J Godefroy, *Fragmenta XII. Tabularum, suis nunc primum tabulis restituta: probationibus, notis, & indice munita* (Heidelberg, Typis Johannis Lancelloti, 1616) 'Index ad XII Tabul', s.v. 'Poenae', sig b2). The civilian rule was not limited to procedure, but could apply to replacing financial penalties with corporal punishment.

[30] B Shapiro, *Beyond Reasonable Doubt and Probable Cause: Historical Perspectives on the Anglo-American Law of Evidence* (Berkeley, University of California Press, 1991) 51–54, 209.

[31] Macnair (n 21) 249–54.

[32] RH Helmholz, *The Oxford History of the Laws of England, vol. I, The Canon Law and Ecclesiastical Jurisdiction from 597 to the 1640s* (Oxford, Oxford University Press, 2004) 605.

[33] See eg *Needham v Salisburie* (1626) LPL MS 1253, fo 33r.

[34] Henry E Huntington Library (hereafter Hunt Lib) Ellesmere MS 7880, fo 1r.

The rule was rejected by common lawyers in criminal trials at common law,[35] but known to common lawyers as a statutory rule for some criminal offences,[36] in the context of writs of prohibition issued to the church courts,[37] and was encountered in *Bracton*. Thomas Egerton, the future Lord Ellesmere, specifically linked his reading of *Bracton* with the Star Chamber in his personal notes.[38] Sometimes the rule and its modification or exceptions were considered with no mention of civilian ideas.[39] However, other discussions of the two witness rule and associated civilian ideas suggest more familiarity with civilian ideas. In *Remington v Allen*, for example, discussion of the two witness rule moves into consideration of whether there were sufficient half proofs to support a conviction, a very civilian approach which can be seen when Edward Coke used the civilian language of '*semiprobaciones*'.[40] In *Sir John Bennet's Case* in 1622, Lord Keeper John Williams accepted the role of the two witness rule in the Star Chamber, but asserted that there were exceptions to the rule, including that a single witness could be relied upon if there were an order from the court, expressly referring to that as a rule of the civil law.[41]

B. The Role of Presumptions

Francis Ashley observed in 1616 that in the Star Chamber 'the great part of the nature of the suit is … for matter that is secret'.[42] Presumptions and signs were particularly useful means of resolving cases concerning such hidden offences. As noted in an undated manuscript work on the court, some of the judges in the Star Chamber 'say that in cases of fraude and the like workes of darknes presumptions and slight proof will serve for noe man will take witnesses with him when hee goeth to doe such facts'.[43] William Hudson

[35] B Shapiro, 'Presumptions and Circumstantial Evidence in the Anglo-American Legal Tradition 1500–1900' in RH Helmholz and WDH Sellar (eds), *The Law of Presumptions: Essays in Comparative Legal History* (Berlin, Duncker & Humblot, 2009) 163–64, although Shapiro's claim that Thomas More 'made no reference to the need for a two witness requirement' at his trial is incorrect (RH Helmholz, 'Natural Law and the Trial of Thomas More' in HA Kelly, LW Karlin and GB Wegemer (eds), *Thomas More's Trial by Jury* (Suffolk, Boydell Press, 2011) 59–63).

[36] This was the case for several statutory misdemeanours triable by justices of the peace (see the list in R Chamberlain, *The complete justice being a compendious and exact collection out of all such statutes and authors as may any ways concern the office of a justice of peace* (R Atkins and E Atkins, 1681) 450, which includes statutes from the reign of Henry VIII onwards) and for treason, albeit with some uncertainty for the latter (on which see LM Hill, 'The Two Witness Rule in English Treason Trials: Some Comments on the Emergence of Procedural Law' (1968) 12 *AJLH* 95).

[37] CM Gray, *The Writ of Prohibition: Jurisdiction in Early-Modern English Law* (New York, Oceana Publications, 1994) 2 vols, *passim*, but especially vol 2, 207–91.

[38] I Williams, 'A Medieval Book and Early-Modern Law: *Bracton's* Authority and Application in the Common Law c.1550–1640' (2011) 79 *Tjidschrift voor Rechtsgeschiedenis* 47, 66.

[39] See eg *R v Moodie* (1627) LPL MS 1253, fo 98v.

[40] *Remington v Allen* (1625) LPL MS 1253, fo 5r; *R v Henry Percy, Earl of Northumberland* (1606), in Hawarde, *Les Reportes del Cases*, 294.

[41] *Sir John Bennett's Case* (1622) Cambridge University Library MS Ii.6.51, fo 94v. As Helmholz observes, the number of exceptions to the two witness rule was extensive and 'a question of the greatest complexity in the *ius commune*' (Helmholz, 'Natural Law' (n 35) 62).

[42] BL MS Harley 4841, fo 52r.

[43] BL MS Hargrave 482, fo 13v.

also asserted in *AG v Vaughan* that presumptions could serve another purpose: 'circumstances & presumptions must controll disperate wittnnesses', presumptions providing a means to resolve conflicting witness evidence.[44]

This role of presumptions was particularly visible in the prosecution of the Earl of Northumberland for his alleged involvement in the Gunpowder Plot. There was little direct evidence of the Earl's involvement in the plot, so Coke lacked a smoking fuse for his prosecution. Instead, Coke needed to persuade the judges through presumptions which Coke described as coalescing and growing.[45] Coke invoked the traditional *ius commune* categories of presumptions '*levis aut temerariae*', '*probabiles, aut veresimiles*' and '*violentae aut necessariae, aut vehementes*', as well as to '*semiprobaciones*'.[46] Like William Cecil, Coke appears to have assumed his audience would understand his point and civilian language and saw no need to elaborate further.[47]

C. Suspicious Documents and Conveyances

A particularly important role for presumptions came in relation to a major component of the Star Chamber's jurisdiction: cases concerning fraud and forgery. This was particularly visible in the various accounts of *Twyne's Case*, which set out an approach to identifying fraud using badges, or *indicia*, of fraud which was linked to that described by the fifteenth-century English canonist William Lyndwood and through him to the medieval *ius commune*.[48]

Cases about forgery and suspicious documents also seem to have piqued judges' interest in other issues of proof. The notes of Thomas Egerton, Lord Ellesmere, on the forgery case of *AG v Sir Thomas Palmer* include brief extracts from three civilian books, all suggesting that Ellesmere saw the civilian law of proof as highly relevant in this particular field, one where witness evidence was unlikely to exist.[49] The papers of Ellesmere's son, John Egerton, Earl of Bridgewater, include a collection of passages from Johannes Althusius' *Dicaeologicae*, all of which include citations from civilian jurists,

[44] *A-G v Vaughan* (1630) Hunt Lib Ellesmere MS 7900, fo 35v.

[45] *R v Henry Percy, Earl of Northumberland*, 297.

[46] *R v Henry Percy, Earl of Northumberland*, 294. For these civilian categories, see Macnair (n 21) 270. Macnair identifies medieval and early-modern English canon law sources which refer to these categories, but none describe the categories in the same language as Coke. Coke referred to the same classes of presumptions over 20 years later in E Coke, *The First Part of the Institutes of the Lawes of England. Or, A Commentarie Upon Littleton* (Societie of Stationers, 1628) fo 6v.

[47] See text at n 26 above. *Presumptio violenta* is mentioned in *Bracton* (GE Woodbine (ed), SE Thorne (trans), *On the Laws and Customs of England*, vol 2 (Cambridge (MA), Harvard University Press, 1968–77) 186, 386) and a yearbook case from 1496 ((1496) YB Mich 12 Hen VII, fo 29b (of 11 Hen VII), pl. 1, fo 3a (of 12 Hen VII) per Bryan CJCP). Neither appears to be a technical usage and I have not found the other forms of presumptions in common law sources before this case.

[48] Willems (n 3).

[49] Hunt Lib Ellesmere MS 2779. Extracts are taken from: R Maranta, *Aurea Praxis* (Theodorum Baumium, 1580) 265 nos 148 and 149 (Ellesmere cites these extracts as p 256, but they match p 265 in this edition); P Decius, *De regulis iuris* (Jean David, 1528) fo 98v '*Que dubitationis*' (Ellesmere owned a copy of this book: Hunt Lib Rare Book 120081); and P Peck, *Ad regulas Iuris Canonici Commentaria* (Jacobus Lucius, 1588) fo 200r.

mostly linked to the question of establishing whether a document was genuine or not and the relationship between documents and witness evidence.[50]

II. Norms in the Star Chamber

Questions of proof and presumptions are not always clearly distinct from points of substantive law. The civilian-inspired badges of fraud approach taken in *Twyne's Case* can be presented as 'one of proof, not of definition' of fraud.[51] However, the badges of fraud approach may at times have created almost irrebuttable presumptions of fraud. The approach came close to providing a list of situations in which fraud would be found to have occurred, in effect providing a definition of fraud.[52]

There is evidence that the offences prosecuted in the Star Chamber were understood in civilian terms. The anonymous preface to Richard Crompton's *Star-Chamber Cases* sets out definitions of offences commonly tried in the Star Chamber. The common law material in these definitions is mostly taken from the Cambridge regius professor of civil law John Cowell's *Interpreter*, itself providing something of a civilian perspective.[53] The preface included civilian understandings of the same offences, principally taken from Mattheus Wesenbecius' *Paratitla*.[54] Wesenbecius is sometimes cited,[55] but there are other uncredited uses to define offences too.[56] Similarly, an undated text setting out the 'five kindes of causes' which 'principally are handled' in the Star Chamber discussed the offence of perjury.[57] The text set out a definition of perjury: '*Periurium est liciti iuramenti violatio*',[58] a definition which is very close to that in the sixteenth-century *Reformatio Legum Ecclesiasticarum*, itself informed by the *ius commune*.[59]

From the perspective of these two texts, it appears that the Star Chamber was at least a court in which offences could be understood in civilian terms, potentially one in which the substance of the offences prosecuted was defined by the civil law. However, the texts should be treated with caution. The two major Star Chamber treatises of the

[50] Hunt Lib Ellesmere MS 7900, fo 39r, extracts from J Althusius, *Dicaeologicae Libri Tres, Totum et universum Ius* (Christopher Corvinus, 1618) 692, 743–46.

[51] H Mares, 'Fraud and Dishonesty in King's Bench and Star Chamber' (2019) 59 *AJLH* 210, 217.

[52] A point made by Foster (D Foster, 'Legal Demands Against the Beneficial Interest under a Trust, c.1590–1759' (PhD thesis, Queen Mary University of London, 2020) 39). Although *cf* John Egerton's note that 'presumptions geeve place to positive proof' (Hunt Lib Ellesmere MS 7900, fo 18r).

[53] See eg R Crompton, *Star-Chamber Cases, shewing what causes properly belong to the cognizance of that court* (John Grove, 1630) 3 (on riot) and Cowell, *The Interpreter*, s.v. 'Riott (*Riottum*)'. Crompton's work is an English translation of the section on the Star Chamber in R Crompton, *L'Authoritie et Jurisdiction des Courts de la Maiestie de la Roygne* (Charles Yetsweirt, 1594) fos 29r–41r, but the preface was a new addition in the 1630 text.

[54] M Wesenbecius, *Paratitla in Pandectarum* (Ioannem Oporinum, 1563).

[55] Crompton (n 53) 6–7, 10.

[56] Crompton (n 53) 10–11 (for libel, *iniuria* and *crimen extraordinaria*), taken from Wesenbecius, *Paratitla*, 429, 425 and 430 respectively.

[57] BL MS Harley 1576, fos 19r–20r. The text is undated and anonymous, although the collection of which it is part includes material from James I to the Restoration, suggesting this is a Jacobean or Caroline text.

[58] BL MS Harley 1576, fos 19v.

[59] G Bray (ed), *Tudor Church Reform: The Henrician Canons of 1535 and the Reformatio Legum Ecclesiasticarum* (Suffolk, Boydell Press, 2000) 550.

reigns of Elizabeth I and James I did not define the offences prosecuted there in that way.[60] It would equally be a mistake to take the evidence of those two treatises at face value and claim that the civil law was never relevant in relation to the substantive norms applied in the court.

There is one example of a case where, as reported, a single judge did rely solely upon the civil law to explain the wrongfulness of the conduct in the case. The *Countess of Rutland's Case* concerned an 'unlawful, riotous and uncivil arrest and detention' of the widowed Countess of Rutland upon a *capias ad satisfaciendum* in relation to debt proceedings in the Common Pleas. Much of the case concerned the manner in which the arrest was performed, but an important issue was whether it was in fact lawful to arrest the widow of a peer or not. It was clear that had the proceedings been against the Earl of Rutland, arrest would have been impossible. Henry Howard, the civilian educated Earl of Northampton, is reported as making only one contribution to the court's discussions, that 'by the civil law a widow woman shall have the privilege of her husband'. The countess therefore could not be arrested and the arrest was consequently unlawful and criminal.[61] This reliance solely on the civil law was highly unusual. The other judges in the case did not take the same approach. Even in the case against the Dutch merchants, the civilian-educated Julius Caesar used the civil law when considering questions of proof, but not when considering the wrongfulness of the conduct in question.[62] His notes on that issue refer only to the law of England.[63]

This does not mean that the civil law was irrelevant for questions of substantive wrongdoing, but that it was not a primary point of reference. The wrongfulness of conduct in the civil law was sometimes mentioned once the conduct had already been explained as unlawful using English legal sources. For example, in the *Earl of Suffolk's Case*, Henry Montagu explained that the alleged conduct of the Earl, corruption and abuse of the office of Lord Treasurer, was unlawful in English law, before also setting out its wrongfulness in the civil law and its harmful effects to the commonwealth.[64] The same approach, of establishing the unlawfulness of the conduct and then referring to the civil law, can be seen in other cases.[65] The civil law here appears to have a confirmatory role, showing that the conduct was widely (perhaps even universally) seen as wrongful. Something similar can be seen in the prosecution of several defendants for defaming the Lord Deputy of Ireland, Sir Thomas Wentworth. There was no question that the defamation would amount to an offence (one or both of seditious libel and *scandalum*

[60] W Lambarde, *Archeion or, a Discourse upon the High Courts of Justice in England* (CH McIlwain and PL Ward (eds), Cambridge (MA), Harvard University Press, 1957) 96–116 and W Hudson, 'A Treatise of the Court of Star Chamber' in F Hargrave (ed), *Collectanea Juridica*, vol 2 (E and R Brooke, 1792) 62–107.

[61] *Isabell, Countesse de Rutlands Case* (1605) Moore KB 765, 769; 72 ER 892, 894. The remark is so short compared to those seen in other reports that it is possible more was said but not reported.

[62] See text at n 24 above.

[63] BL MS Add 12497, fos 42r and 45r. There is a heading 'The custom & lawes of Spain' in Caesar's notes, but no substantive material about them (ibid fo 43r).

[64] *Earl of Suffolk's Case* (1619) BL MS Stowe 159, fos 3r and 10v.

[65] *Dr Benet's Case* (1622) Folger Shakespeare Library (hereafter FSL) MS V.a.622, fo 64v per Sir Richard Weston and James I's speech on duelling (BL MS Harley 1576, fo 79r). On James's speech, see I Williams, 'James VI and I, rex et iudex: One King as Judge in Two Kingdoms' in W Eves, J Hudson, I Ivarsen and SB White (eds), *Common Law, Civil Law, and Colonial Law: Essays in Comparative Legal History from the Twelfth to the Twentieth Centuries* (Cambridge, Cambridge University Press, 2021) 95, 108 and 111–12.

magnatum), but the Archbishop of Canterbury, William Laud, explained that the Star Chamber had an obligation to maintain the position of those in authority, '& that from the example of the Roman Empire in the 12. lib of the Codes Ius Senatorum', then quoting from C.12.1.8.[66] Like Montagu, Laud used the civil law to confirm the need for the Star Chamber to act, although less clearly linking this to the wrongfulness of the conduct.

The civil law was also involved in finding that an offence was aggravated. A simple example is in Thomas Egerton's papers, a list of cases which were at least nominally about riot, but include a quote attributed to Peckius that hiding the offence would merit a harsher punishment.[67] More typical is the use of the civil law in *AG v Sir John Yorke*, in which the defendant was prosecuted for an entertainment performed in his home. The players put on a mock disputation between a Catholic priest and an English minister, which the Catholic priest won. The devil took the minister but an angel came for the Catholic priest, all before a recusant audience.[68] One of the chief justices explained that bringing matters of religion and state into disrepute was inherently criminally libellous, but that the offence was aggravated because the wrongful conduct was committed by actors, a class who were 'rogues by statute' and intestible by both civil law and common law.[69] Here the civil law, paired with the common law, was one of the means by which the offence was held to be an aggravated one. Similarly, in the prosecution of musicians for performing libellous songs about the Duke of Buckingham, Richard Weston referred to the Roman legal past. As the Star Chamber judges referred to the growth and danger of libels, Weston referred to Roman libellers as 'excommunicated' persons subject to legal prohibitions, a means of showing that libellers deserved particularly stringent punishment.[70]

This mixture of the civil law with other sources to aggravate an offence is also visible in a speech by the Archbishop of Canterbury, George Abbott, in *Thaire v Jones*.[71] One of the allegations in the case was of false claims of misconduct made against an office-holder by the reversioner to that office. The reversioner would have been entitled to take on the office in the event the current holder were dismissed. This conduct was aggravated by the reversioner being the son of the office-holder. All the judges, many of them fathers, were disgusted by this behaviour, and Abbott set out quite how atrocious the actions of the son were by first referring to the Bible, then to a passage in Ovid's *Metamorphoses*, and finally to the civil law, observing that the son would be subject to *infamia* for such conduct.[72] Of these sources, it seems likely that the civil law was the

[66] BL MS Hargrave 489, fo 11v.

[67] Hunt Lib Ellesmere MS 2781, fo 1r. I have not found the relevant passage in Peck, *Ad regulas Iuris*.

[68] On the case and the scholarship about it, see P Jensen, 'Recusancy, Festivity and Community: The Simpsons at Gowlthwaite Hall' (2002) 6 *Reformation* 75.

[69] *A-G v Sir John Yorke* (1614) BL MS Harley 1330, fos 16r–16v.

[70] (1627) *R v Mosley, Markhall and Greene* BL MS Add 48057, fo 78v. The description of libellers as 'excommunicate' is perhaps an attempt to convey the idea of *infamia*, to which libellers were subject in Roman law (D.47.10.5.9–10). Weston continues to say that under the civil law it was not lawful to have 'commerce' with libellers, something which does not seem to represent the Roman law. Libellers could be barred from testifying in court (D.47.10.5.9), but that does not seem to be Weston's meaning.

[71] *Thaire v Jones* (1626) LPL 1253, fo 24r.

[72] *Thaire v Jones*, fo 30r, referring to a combination of Genesis 9:22 and Proverbs 30:17 and Ovid, *Metamorphoses*, bk. 1, l.148 (Ovid, *Metamorphoses*, vol 1 (FJ Miller (trans)) (Cambridge (MA), Harvard University Press, 1916) 12–13).

least important, given the passage in Ovid described the breakdown of society and the first coming of war to the world.

When determining liability, the civil law was also used to reject arguments against conviction raised by defendants. In the trial of William Prynne for the writing and publication of *Histriomastix*, Prynne was tried for his book about the unlawfulness of plays, in which he denigrated actors, and especially women performing. This was seen as a libel of the queen, who had herself performed at court.[73] Prynne tried to argue that his text was derived from the work of other scholars and present a consensus against the performance of plays.[74] Archbishop William Laud rejected Prynne's argument, recalling a dispute in his time at Elizabethan Oxford when the theologian John Rainolds argued against plays, but 'doctor Gentilis, at the same tyme defended them in the Lawe Schooles and wee that were of the younger sort thought that doctor Gentilis had as good reasons in defence of the plaies as doctor Reynolds had arguements against them'.[75] Laud's argument appears to be that Prynne was wrong to defend himself by arguing that plays were unlawful and the claims in his book clearly correct. Laud approached the issue by reference to arguments made by a civilian.

In *Sir John Bennet's Case*, Bennet was accused of receiving bribes as a judge in the prerogative court of Canterbury. Bennet argued that he had taken no bribes, but received gifts which were permitted under the civil law.[76] Lord Keeper Williams accepted the possibility of a defence based on the civil law, but rejected Bennet's argument, referring to the prosecution of Julius Bassus in Rome as showing that the receipt of gifts was unlawful according to the civil law.[77] By contrast, in *Doctor Barker's Case*, a claimed defence to a prosecution in the Star Chamber on the basis of the lawfulness of conduct in the *ius commune* was acceptable. One of the issues in the case was that Barker had taken commutation of ecclesiastical cases in 'undue manner' and 'abused the authority of the Highe Commission Courte to advance his Corruption'.[78] On the issue of commutation, Barker argued that his conduct was permissible under ecclesiastical law. The Archbishop of Canterbury, George Abbott, accepted this defence. Abbott explained that he had 'advised with some Masters of the Civil Lawe, It agrees with Custome, used in the Ecclesiastical Lawe'.[79] In this case a defence based on the practice of the ecclesiastical courts was successful, although it did not convince all of the judges in the Star Chamber.

[73] On this allegation and the case, see CS Clegg, *Press Censorship in Caroline England* (Cambridge, Cambridge University Press, 2008) 164–78.

[74] For the longer tradition of debates and formal disputations about plays, actors and acting in early-modern England, see, eg, D Blank, 'Actors, Orators, and the Boundaries of Drama in Elizabethan Universities' (2017) 70 *Renaissance Quarterly* 513, especially 513–32.

[75] *R v Prynne and Sparkes* (1634) BL MS Stowe 159, fos 52r–52v. Laud's speech is not included in the printed account of the speech in 3 St Tr 561–86.

[76] *Dr Benet's Case* FSL MS V.a.622, fos. 45r–78r. For a discussion of the earlier parliamentary petition and proceedings against Bennet, see JP Ferris and S Healy, 'Bennet, Sir John (c.1553–1627), of London and Uxbridge, Mdx.; formerly of York' in A Thrush and JP Ferris, *The History of Parliament: The House of Commons 1604–1629*, vol 3 (Cambridge, Cambridge University Press, 2010) 200.

[77] *Dr Benet's Case* FSL MS V.a.622, fo 76r.

[78] *Doctor Barker's Case* (1623) BL MS Hargrave 16, fos 111v–114v.

[79] BL MS Hargrave 16, fo 113v.

III. Legitimising Proceedings in the Star Chamber

A third role for references to the civil law in the Star Chamber was to use them not just to establish the law of procedure or proof, or to determine conviction, but to legitimise the court's proceedings. When prosecuting the Dutch merchants for the illegal transportation of gold, the crown may have hoped to use the case as leverage in international negotiations, while avoiding a diplomatic rift with the Dutch.[80] Showing that the proof in the case would have been sufficient to convict the merchants in their home, *ius commune*, legal system may have been an attempt to reassure both foreign governments and other foreign merchants that the case was not a political show trial and that the convictions were justified.

A more unusual form of legitimation might be seen in the prosecution of Henry Percy. One account of Coke's speech suggests that Coke perceived some unhappiness on the part of other peers that the earl was being treated differently, and more publicly, to other peers in 'matters of great contempt'.[81] Coke was therefore concerned to stress the legitimacy of the approach taken both in the investigation of the earl and the arguments in his prosecution, which he did by relying upon the *ius commune* law of presumptions.[82] If this is correct, the prosecution of Henry Percy is a very unusual example of the civil law alone acting as the means of legitimising a trial and conviction.

In *Sir John Bennet's Case*, the defendant observed that he was the first 'Ecclesiastical officer ever questioned in this court'.[83] The Star Chamber's jurisdiction over such officials does seem to have been in doubt, as another account focused on this as the only issue to be reported.[84] There clearly was concern to demonstrate the legitimacy of the Star Chamber's proceedings, something exacerbated by Bennet's attempted reliance on the claimed lawfulness of his conduct in ecclesiastical law as a defence. As Coventry AG put it in his argument, 'It seems hee would flye to the protection of another Law'.[85] References to the Star Chamber applying the civil law in the case were a means by which the Star Chamber could show that not only was Bennet guilty and without defences, but that he was only being subjected to the law he professed to know and apply.

IV. Star Chamber: *Ius Commune* or Civil Law?

The civil law was certainly present in the Star Chamber, and in the field of procedure and proof could sometimes be decisive. But the role of the civil law in the Star Chamber also provokes questions about the status of the civil law tradition in early-modern England.

[80] Healy (n 24) 176, 182.

[81] M Nicholls, 'The "Wizard Earl" in Star Chamber: The Trial of the Earl of Northumberland, June 1606' (1987) 30 *Historical Journal* 173, 178.

[82] See text at nn 45–47 above.

[83] *Sir John Bennett's Case* (1622) Cambridge University Library MS Ii.6.51, fo 92r.

[84] *R v Sir John Bennett* (1622) Cambridge University Library MS Dd.6.57, fos 471r–471v.

[85] *Dr Benet's Case* FSL MS V.a.622, fo 48r.

When Lord Keeper Williams rejected Sir John Bennet's defence based on ecclesiastical law in the *ius commune*, he did so by asserting that Bennet's 'distinction is not of the civill law, but of the Lawyers'.[86] Williams distinguished between the civil law identified from a classical literary source and the law developed by 'the lawyers', impliedly the *ius commune*. Similarly, Sir Richard Weston, again in *Sir John Bennet's Case*, referred expressly to 'the *old Romane* Law' [emphasis added], rather than the contemporary *ius commune*.[87] The *ius commune* based-defence on which Bennet relied had to give way to the law of ancient Rome itself.[88] A difficult, but important, point is what this might tell us about attitudes to the civil law tradition in Renaissance England. Williams's approach appears particularly odd, in that a bishop judging in a secular court preferred the law of pagan Rome to that of the church, rejecting the application of the law which was asserted to apply in the church courts.

The rejection of Bennet's defence may well have been entirely opportunistic. Bennet had in fact already been subject to parliamentary proceedings in 1621 and his prosecution was an opportunity for the king to show that he could respond to the concerns of subjects about the abuse of power by officials without needing to go through Parliament.[89] However, even if that is correct, Williams's argument suggests that in a high profile case it was more acceptable to refer to the law of ancient Rome than to the *ius commune*.

When lawyers trained in the *ius commune* reverted to the original sources of the *ius commune* tradition, they used the *Corpus Iuris Civilis* of Justinian. Only one reference to the *Corpus Iuris* itself has been found in the accounts of Star Chamber cases.[90] Williams's likely source was instead Pliny the Younger's *Letters*.[91] It may be more appropriate to think of Williams's reference to a trial in ancient Rome as intellectually closer to Archbishop Abbott's citation of Ovid, or John Cooke's mention of the ostracising of Aristides from Athens, than to Sir Julius Caesar's use of Farinacius.[92] Professor Ibbetson described some of the language in Coke's *De Libellis Famosis* linking to classical Roman

[86] *Dr Benet's Case* FSL MS V.a.622, fo 76r.

[87] *Dr Benet's Case* FSL MS V.a.622, fo 64v.

[88] Such a distinction might be associated with continental legal humanism (eg P Stein, *Roman Law in European Legal History* (Cambridge, Cambridge University Press, 1999) 76–79), but there is no evidence of legal humanism having this kind of influence in England (DJ Ibbetson, 'Humanism and Law in Elizabethan England: The Annotations of Gabriel Harvey' in PJ du Plessis and JW Cairns, *Reassessing Legal Humanism and its Claims: Petere Fontes?* (Edinburgh, Edinburgh University Press, 2016) 282–84).

[89] For the parliamentary concern, see n 76 above. This was not the first occasion on which James I used the Star Chamber to respond to concerns raised in parliament. The same occurred in 1605 in relation to purveyors. Purveyance was a subject of major controversy in the parliamentary sessions of 1604 and 1606 (see EN Lindquist, 'The King, the People and the House of Commons: The Problem of Early Jacobean Purveyance' (1988) 31 *Historical Journal* 549). Lindquist observes that the 1605 Star Chamber cases were 'the council's own exercise in public relations' (ibid 562). Some of the cases are reported in *AG v Stockwell* (1605) Moore KB 760, 72 ER 888 and *AG v Richard Richards* (1605) Moore KB 762–64, 72 ER 890–91.

[90] Laud's citation of C.12.1.18, see text at n 66 above.

[91] Pliny the Younger, *Letters: Books 1–7* (B Radice (trans)) (Cambridge (MA), Harvard University Press, 1969) 258–67.

[92] See n 24 above. For Cooke's mention of Aristides, see *AG v Bonham Norton* (1629) Cambridge University Library MS Dd.9.61, fo 34r, probably drawn from Plutarch's *Life* (Plutarch, *Lives, vol II: Themistocles and Camillus. Aristides and Cato Major. Cimon and Lucullus* (B Perrin (trans)) (Cambridge (MA), Harvard University Press, 1914) 231–33). The case was a prosecution for the defamation of Lord Keeper Coventry by a disgruntled litigant, alleging he made decisions because of bribery or corruption.

sources as 'verbal cues of a sort that was very common in legal argument and text in the early modern period: nothing of real substance flowed from them'.[93] Should this kind of classical material and language be seen as something distinct from the influence or role of the *ius commune* and not so readily dismissed?[94]

We might see this use of Roman material linked to Roman legal proceedings as a specific example of the recourse to Roman examples in early-modern English discourse on which there is a large historiography, but not related to judicial and curial reasoning.[95] This seems plausible, but does need to be treated with some caution. While non-legal sources were being used to establish the Roman law, the events and norms which were extracted were explicitly legal, such as trials. The same can be seen in a citation of the bible by Richard Neile, bishop of Durham. The case concerned a justice of the peace ordering the plaintiff to be whipped without cause. Neile observed that 'when in the Acts of the Apostles [the capteine of the guard] heard that Paul being a free Cittizen of Rome was to be whipt hee trembled at it', a reference to Acts 22, where Paul asked whether it was lawful to whip a Roman.[96] Neile's normative point was taken from the bible, but the point was not a religious one. Instead, Neile used the bible to establish the Roman law of the first century, law which Neile considered could be extended to a free Englishman of the seventeenth century.

When John Egerton made notes from Althusius' *Dicaeologicae* for his work in Star Chamber, he used a work replete with *ius commune* citations which Althusius brought together with Jewish law.[97] The *Dicaeologicae* has been described as one of Calvinist natural law.[98] Egerton's reading for the case was eclectic.[99] The other (unattributed) Latin extracts in his notes appear to come from the Accursian gloss,[100] Juan Luis Vives's popular collection of *sententiae*, the *Satellitum sive symbola* (itself attributing the *sententia* to Cicero's *De Legibus*, although it is not a direct quote)[101] and John of Salisbury's *Policraticus*.[102] When brought together, we may see these works as part of wider English

[93] Ibbetson (n 2) 497.

[94] For another example of this in the law of treason, see Williams (n 38) 76–77.

[95] On this literature, see P Kewes, 'Introduction: Ancient Rome in English Political Culture, ca.1570–1660' (2020) 83 *Huntington Library Quarterly* 401, 403–405 for further references.

[96] *Fawsett v Grice* (1627) LPL MS 1253, fo 104r. 'The captaine of the guard' is missing in this copy of the reports, but present in all other copies, eg Cambridge University Library MS Ll.3.2, fo 158v. The reference is to Acts 22:24–29.

[97] See text at n 50 above.

[98] J Witte Jr, 'A Demonstrative Theory of Natural Law: Johannes Althusius and the Rise of Calvinist Jurisprudence' (2009) 11 *Ecclesiastical Law Journal* 248. We may wonder whether John Egerton turned to the *Dicaeologicae* because it was described on its titlepage as 'a work useful in theory and practice for scholars in *other* faculties' [emphasis added] ('*Opus tam theoriae quam praxeos aliarumque Facultatum studiosis utilissimum*' (Althusius, *Dicaeologicae*, titlepage)).

[99] Hunt Lib Ellesmere MS 7900, fo 20v.

[100] '*testis causam sui testimonii dicere debet*' from *Digestum Vetus* (Hugonem a Porte, 1549), 147, col 1 gloss (i).

[101] '*Qui mercede est vir bonus, mercede erit malus*' from JL Vives, *Satellitium sive symbola* (Simon Vermeulen, 1526), no 208 (citing book 1 of Cicero's *De Legibus*, probably book 1.18 (Cicero, *On the Republic, On the Laws* (CW Keyes (trans) (Cambridge (MA), Harvard University Press, 1928) 352–53). On the popularity of Vives, see L Casini, 'Juan Luis Vives [Joannes Ludovicus Vives]' (2021) *The Stanford Encyclopedia of Philosophy*, plato.stanford.edu/archives/spr2021/entries/vives/.

[102] '*Jurat credere minus non juret credere noli / Juret non juret hostis ab hoste cave*'; JA Giles (ed), *Joannis Saresbeniensis Opera Omnia*, vol 3 (JH Parker, 1848) 9. Continental printings of this work in 1513, 1595 and 1622 are noted ibid vi.

intellectual culture, perhaps in a similar manner to the attention devoted to Pufendorf from around 1700.[103]

While questions of procedure were closely linked to the *ius commune*, consideration of normative ideas in the Star Chamber shows a wider range of sources being used, sources which were part of wider intellectual culture in early-modern England. This provides an explanation for the diversity of references to the longer civil and Roman law tradition. Those sources might be Calvinist natural law, classical literary sources, or a reference to a public debate involving both theologians and a civil lawyer. However, there was a clear emphasis on sources which revealed expressly legal norms. In this way the civil law was part of early-modern English culture[104] and relevant in the Star Chamber, but it was not limited to the usual sources of its academic study.

[103] DJ Ibbetson, 'Natural Law and Common Law' (2001) 5 *Edinburgh Law Review* 4, 5.

[104] Something confirmed by the civil law's occasional appearance in Shakespeare's plays (RH Helmholz, 'Shakespeare and the *Ius Commune*' in M Lobban and I Williams (eds), *Networks and Connections in Legal History* (Cambridge, Cambridge University Press, 2020) 262–84).

14

The Law of Treason in Britain's Roman-Dutch Colonies

MICHAEL LOBBAN

In 1851, in the aftermath of the Kat River Rebellion, the mixed-race 'Hottentot' leader Andries Botha was charged with high treason, for levying war and insurrection against the Queen.[1] When the question was raised during the trial whether he could enjoy procedural rights introduced in England after the Glorious Revolution, the presiding judge, Chief Justice Sir John Wylde, asked 'whether treason can vary … in any part of the British dominions?'[2] The question was an important one for imperial and colonial officials. If all Her Majesty's imperial subjects owed her allegiance, and if the 1351 English statute of treason bound them all, was it possible also to have different laws of treason in different parts of the empire? In an empire of pluralism, when local laws relating to property, marriage or inheritance remained in place, what was to be the view taken of public law, and the most important public offence?

In what follows, we will examine the experience of British colonies acquired during the Napoleonic wars which retained Roman-Dutch law as their common law. As shall be seen, while in each case the British assured their newly conquered subjects that existing legal rights would be recognised, it was not evident from the outset that Roman-Dutch law would remain the common law of these colonies, particularly in the area of criminal law. In colonies where a new body of judges educated in the common law tradition was given jurisdiction, there was an impetus to adopt English rules. As shall be seen, in Ceylon, an English conception of treason became dominant by the middle of the nineteenth century, and Roman-Dutch criminal law was ultimately replaced by a code modelled on that of India. By contrast, in the Cape, where the basis of the law of treason was long ambiguous, Roman-Dutch law was confirmed as the clear basis of the law of treason by the era of the Anglo-Boer war, when this more expansive law was used to punish as traitors those who had engaged in activities which were much easier to view as treasonable through Roman lenses than English ones.

[1] *The Trial of Andries Botha for High Treason* (Cape Town, Saul Solomon & Co, 1852) 1–5.

[2] This major constitutional point was left undecided, for the objection had been raised too late even to have been effective in England: *R v Frost* (1840) 9 C & P 129, 173 ER 771; 2 Moody 140; 169 ER 56; State Trials, New Series 85.

I. The Law of Treason in English and Roman-Dutch Law

According to the English statute of treason of 1351, there were three central forms of treason: compassing and imagining the king's death; levying war against the king in his realm; and giving aid and comfort to the king's enemies, either in his realm or elsewhere.[3] If the wording of the act was very precise, the ambit of treason had been expanded by constructive interpretations during the early modern period. Under these, compassing and imagining the king's death embraced not merely plots to kill him, but also conspiracies to depose or imprison him until he 'yielded to certain demands'.[4] Furthermore, although a mere conspiracy to levy war or rebellion was not itself treason, there was authority that suggested that it could be taken as an overt act of compassing and imagining the king's death.[5] The treason of levying war against the king had also been extended by constructions. As a result of early modern case law, it included not merely resorting to arms in the manner that a foreign enemy might, but also any general armed attack aimed to effect changes 'of a publick and general concern'.[6]

'Constructive' treasons were controversial. In the 1794 treason trial of the London Corresponding Society leaders, Thomas Erskine had persuaded a jury to acquit defendants accused of compassing and imagining the death of the king by virtue of a political conspiracy, since they had not in any way conspired against the king's own life.[7] The government's response was to pass legislation to put some of the constructions on a statutory basis. The 1795 Treasonable Practices Act made it treason to compass to deprive or depose the monarch 'from the style, honour or kingly name of the imperial crown' in any of his dominions. It also became treason to compass the levying of war 'within this realm' in order to compel him to change his measures or to overawe parliament.[8] In 1848 the Treason Felony Act defined these political treasons to be felonies, not punishable by death. By the mid-nineteenth century, English law therefore had two forms of treason: the capital treason of taking arms against the sovereign or plotting his death; and the non-capital treasons of conspiring to depose the monarch or to use force to compel a change of measures.[9]

The Roman-Dutch law of treason was founded on the *Lex Julia Majestatis*. This defined treason in general – *majestas* – as a crime 'committed against the Roman people

[3] 25 Edw 3 s 5 c 2. It included other treasons, including counterfeiting the king's seals or money, or killing the Chancellor or judges in the execution of their duty. I have explored the wider history of the law of treason in the nineteenth century British Empire in M Lobban, 'The Travels of Treason' (2024) 87 *Modern Law Review* 24.

[4] E Coke, *The Third Part of the Institutes of the Laws of England* (London, E & R Brooke, 1797) 12.

[5] See the differing views of Coke (n 4) 15 and M Hale, *The History of the Pleas of the Crown*, 2 vols (London, E & R Nutt and R Gosling, 1736) vol 1, 122–23. See also H Hallam, *The Constitutional History of England from the Accession of Henry VII to the Death of George II*, 5th edn, 2 vols (London, John Murray, 1846) vol 2, 316–17.

[6] Sir M Foster, *A report of some proceedings on the commission of oyer and terminer and goal delivery for the trial of the rebels in the year 1746 … to which are added Discourses upon a Few Branches of Crown Law* (Dublin, Sarah Cotter, 1767) 211. See the case of *Daniel Dammaree* in TB Howell (ed), *A Complete Collection of State Trials*, vol 15 (London, Longman et al, 1812) 522.

[7] See J Barrell, *Imagining the King's Death: Figurative Treason, Fantasies of Regicide, 1793–1796* (Oxford, Oxford University Press, 2000).

[8] 36 Geo III c 7. It was made permanent in 1817: 57 Geo 3 c 6.

[9] In theory, these latter forms might still be prosecuted as constructive treasons under the 1351 Act, but they never were.

or against their safety' (D.48.4.1.pr). A variety of examples of the offence followed. Many related to aiding enemies, as by giving them information, or supplying them with arms, money 'or any other thing' (D.48.4.4.pr). It was treason to bear arms against the state, or to raise a private army without authorisation. Seditious activity fell within the law, such as plotting to assemble armed men 'against the interests of the state' or calling men together 'for seditious purposes' (D.48.4.1.1). Texts also suggested the crime might be committed by those who usurped the authority of the emperor in some way, as where a private citizen purported to act as a magistrate. There were also examples of dishonouring the emperor, as where consecrated likenesses were melted down.

The rather vague and often outdated set of examples found in the *Digest* was classified and explained by early modern writers. Following Hotman, Antonius Matthaeus distinguished between *perduellio* and other less important forms of *majestas*, considering the former to deal with offences which threatened the stability of the state, and the latter to deal with matters pertaining to its dignity.[10] Johannes Voet[11] and Johan Moorman[12] invoked Gothofredus's threefold division, which distinguished '*perduellio*', the high treason – or *Hoogverraad* – committed with hostile intent against the Roman people or the prince, from two forms where there was no hostile intent.[13] In Johannes van der Linden's much-quoted definition, '[t]his crime is committed by those who, *with a hostile intention*, disturb, injure, or endanger the independence or security of the state'.[14] It could only be committed against a state with *majestas*. Following Bodin, Dutch jurists defined this as an attribute of a sovereign, who was above all law – *legibus solutus* – and who acknowledged no other power as superior.[15] Such sovereignty could lie in different places, according to the constitution of the state, in the prince, nobility or people.[16] Although treason could only be committed by subjects of the state, the Roman-Dutch view of treason did not contain the notion of personal allegiance to the sovereign found in English law.[17] *Perduellio* was a crime committed against the state and its agents. Even where supreme power lay with an emperor, it could be committed by targeting other magistrates.[18] Some jurists even argued that it could be committed against the East and West India Companies, at least in their capacity as 'vicars of the sovereign' who chartered them.[19]

[10] *On Crimes: A Commentary on Books XLVII and XLVIII of the Digest by Antonius Matthaeus JC* (ML Hewett and BC Stoop (ed and trans)), vol II (Pretoria, University of South Africa Press, 1993) 220 (48.2.2.2).

[11] J Voet, *Commentariorum ad Pandectas libri quinquaginta*, vol 6 (5th Venetian edn, Venice, Milesi, 1827) 227–28 (48.4.2).

[12] J Moorman, *Verhandelinge over de Misdaden* (Dordrecht, Abraham Blusse en Zoon, 1772) 56 (1.3.2).

[13] These two forms were '*laesae venerationis*', where the sovereign was treated with disrespect, and unauthorised exercises of public power.

[14] J van der Linden, *Institutes of Holland, or Manual of Law, Practice and Mercantile Law*, 3rd edn (Sir H Juta (trans)) (Cape Town, Juta and Co, 1897) 202 (2.4.2). Moorman's definition of *perduellio*, adapted from D.48.4.1.1, was to do something to the detriment of the state or supreme government, from a hostile intent: 'Hoogverraad … is, uit een vyandlyk opzet, iets doen of ondernemen, ten nadele van den staat, of van's Lands Hoge Overigheidt' (Moorman (n 12) 56 (1.3.2)).

[15] Voet (n 11) 229 (48.4.5); Matthaeus (n 10) 212 (48.2.1.3), Moorman (n 12) 42–43 (1.2.1).

[16] Voet (n 11) 227 (48.4.2).

[17] Matthaeus pointed out that vassals, who received lands from a private person, or from a prince who did not make them subjects of his *majestas*, could not commit treason. Matthaeus (n 10) 218 (48.2.1.10).

[18] Matthaeus (n 10) 224 (48.2.2.7).

[19] Moorman (n 12) 49 (1.2.7).

As the examples in the *Digest* suggested, *perduellio* could be committed both by assisting an enemy, or by rebellious acts which made the rebel himself akin to an enemy.[20] To amount to the higher form of treason, the act had to have been committed with a hostile intent.[21] In Matthaeus's view, a hostile intent could be presumed in some of the enumerated instances.[22] For instance, it could be presumed from the very act of allowing hostages to escape without the emperor's command, since that endangered the security of the state.[23] Similarly, explaining why it was *perduellio* to kill anyone exercising *imperium* or *potestas* (such as a magistrate), Matthaeus commented that 'anyone who endangers the security of the Roman people is a *perduellis*'.[24] Where enemies of the state were assisted, the presumption of hostile intent was very high. However, not all acts which might endanger the state constituted *perduellio*, if it was clear that the actor had no hostile intent against the state. If a magistrate was killed out of personal enmity, this would not count as *perduellio*.[25] Those who acted under duress could not be guilty of the offence.[26] Equally, those whose actions were only the occasion for war or rebellion to break out were not guilty of treason. A soldier whose complaints about conditions in the army provoked a mutiny, or a man whose assault of an ambassador provoked a war, would not be guilty of treason.

There was less room to presume hostile intent when it came to internal commotions.[27] As Matthaeus explained, not all risings constituted *perduellio*: those aimed at killing officials or altering the government were so traitorous but those aimed against private citizens were not. Second, not all those who took part in insurrections were guilty of the crime, but only those who instigated the insurrection.[28] Furthermore, as Moorman explained, in treason the intention could be taken for the deed. While jurists did not consider mere thoughts to constitute treason, they did hold them to be punishable if they had been followed by some preparations. Just as it was an act of treason to buy poison after planning to kill the prince, so it was treason to have entered into a criminal faction, with the aim of damaging the state, even though nothing had been put into effect.[29]

The examples in the *Digest* gave jurists much material to comment on. Matthaeus explained that the treason of betraying state secrets could be committed by anyone who gave useful information to an enemy, as when the emperor's physician betrayed news of his imminent death to the enemy.[30] Explaining the meaning of the text dealing

[20] Matthaeus (n 10) 220 (48.2.2.2).

[21] As Voet pointed out, the various acts listed in the *Digest* as treason might or might not constitute *perduellio*, depending on whether or not they were committed in order to overthrow the state: Voet (n 11) 228 (48.4.3).

[22] Not all jurists agreed: see in particular his disagreements with Hotman in Matthaeus (n 10) 220 (48.2.2.3).

[23] Matthaeus (n 10) 221 (48.2.2.4). *cf* Moorman (n 12) 57 (1.3.3).

[24] Matthaeus (n 10) 224 (48.2.2.7).

[25] Moorman agreed with Matthaeus on these points, supplementing his argument with examples from Dutch military law: Moorman (n 12) 59 (1.3.6–7).

[26] In Matthaeus's view, those who surrendered a city out of cowardice should not be held guilty of *perduellio*: Matthaeus (n 10) 230 (48.2.2.15). Contrast Moorman's more sceptical position: Moorman (n 12) 70–71 (1.3.15).

[27] See the discussion in HH Gonin, 'Perduellio' (1951) 14 *Tydskrif vir Hedendaagse Romeins-Hollandse Reg* 1.

[28] Matthaeus (n 10) 222 (48.2.2.5–6). Moorman agreed with this: Moorman (n 12) 57–58 (1.3.4–5).

[29] Moorman (n 12) 93 (1.6.4). *cf* Matthaeus (n 10) 241 (48.2.3.4).

[30] Matthaeus (n 10) 226 (48.2.2.10). Moorman also agreed it could be committed by private citizens: Moorman (n 12) 61 (1.3.8). He also argued that it was treason for officials to give state secrets to allies: ibid 74–75 (1.3.19).

with supplies given to the enemy, Matthaeus distinguished between goods which were only of use in war (such as weapons), those which were of use in both war and peace (such as money), and luxuries which were only of use for pleasure (such as wine). It was *perduellio* to supply the first two sorts, but not the third (which would enervate rather than strengthen the enemy).[31] Where forbidden goods were supplied, it was irrelevant that the merchant had simply intended to make a private profit: his hostile intent could be presumed from his action which directly promoted the destruction of the state.[32] Turning to whether it would be treason for the wife of a traitor to supply him with food or money, Matthaeus stated that in such cases, one should look at her intention. If the wife acted out of a treacherous intention, to assist her husband as a traitor, she would be guilty, but not if she acted out of humanity.[33]

When it came to punishment, Matthaeus stated that every crime of *majestas* was capital, but since the crime of *perduellio* was more serious, not only were *perduelles* capitally punished, 'but their memory is also damned after their death'.[34] Moorman pointed out that the penalty of forfeiture only applied to those who committed the more serious form of treason.[35] However, by a *Placaat* of 1778, the States General of the United Provinces abolished the confiscation of the property of criminals in all of its colonies, including in cases of '*crimen perduellionis* or *laesae majestatis*'.[36]

The Roman-Dutch law of treason was therefore potentially much more expansive and wide reaching than the English law (at least when shorn of its more controversial constructions). It was also potentially more usable in a colonial context, since it did not purport to protect the body of a sovereign who was never physically present but protected a state and its personnel in a more general way. This feature of the Roman law might have raised an objection to its use. It was clear from the writings of the jurists that for a state to have *majestas*, it could not be subject to any other state. Since it was the British crown which was sovereign within the empire, this might have suggested that the relevant law of treason would be a pan-imperial one, based on English law. However, as shall now be seen, how far it was thought that local law must follow an imperial model varied according to context and colony.

II. Ceylon

When the British acquired the Dutch-held coastal parts of Ceylon in 1796, the articles of capitulation provided that all civil suits in progress would be determined by Dutch law.[37] Three years later, Governor Frederick North issued a proclamation stating that the courts would operate 'according to the Laws and Institutions that subsisted under

31 Matthaeus (n 10) 233 (48.2.2.19).
32 Matthaeus (n 10) 233 (48.2.2.19).
33 Matthaeus (n 10) 235–36 (48.2.2.20).
34 Matthaeus (n 10) 240 (48.2.3.2), citing D.48.4.11.
35 Moorman (n 12) 95–96 (1.6.5).
36 *Statute Law of the Cape of Good Hope, comprising the Placaats, Proclamations and Ordinances enacted before the establishment of the Colonial Parliament* (Cape Town, Saul Solomon and Co, 1862) 9.
37 *A Collection of the Legislative Acts of the Ceylon Government*, vol 1 (Colombo, William Skeen, 1853) 3.

the ancient Government of the United Provinces', subject to such deviations as would be proper and beneficial to introduce. One change immediately introduced was the abolition of torture against those suspected of crimes, as well as 'barbarous' punishments.[38] While the existing criminal procedure was reformed to strengthen the rights of defendants, the Dutch system was reformed rather than being replaced.[39] Nonetheless a proclamation of 30 January 1800 explained punishment in explicitly English terms: High Treason was to be punished by death, while 'Petty Treason, Murder, Sacrilege, the Crime against Nature, Rape, Robbery on the King's Highway, Burglary and Arson shall not be entitled to Clergy, but shall receive Capital punishment'.[40] Furthermore, English forms of criminal procedure were slowly introduced. As Chief Justice Richard Ottley explained, '[a]fter the abolition of Torture as a mean of obtaining confession of guilt in Criminal cases, the English laws of evidence were adopted'.[41] Trial by jury was also introduced in 1810.[42] In 1801, a Charter of Justice created a Supreme Court for the maritime provinces, with two judges who were to be taken from the English or Irish bar. Although it made separate provision for some indigenous communities, the charter did not specify which law was to apply to Europeans.[43] However, general phrases indicating that the Supreme Court was to follow the 'law as already declared' suggested that Roman-Dutch law was to remain the general law in the maritime provinces.[44] When the British later acquired sovereignty over the Kandyan provinces in the interior in 1815, it was agreed by a Convention that the administration of justice would be exercised according to the existing forms and by the established authorities there (though with a right reserved to the British to alter repugnant laws).[45] In 1833, a new Charter of Justice was issued, which introduced a uniform system of judicial administration for the whole island. However, it made no change to the substantive law, and the local customary law continued to apply in Kandy. Not until 1852 was an ordinance passed to introduce the law as administered in the maritime provinces to Kandy, where the local law was silent.[46] If Roman-Dutch law was the 'lex loci' in matters of civil law,[47] Ceylon was in

[38] Proclamation 23 September 1799, *Collection* (n 37) 6.

[39] Proclamation of 23 September 1799, *Collection* (n 37) 6; T Nadaraja, *The Legal System of Ceylon in its Historical Setting* (Leiden, Brill, 1972) 57; A Schrikker, *Dutch and British Colonial Intervention in Sri Lanka, 1780–1815: Expansion and Reform* (Leiden and Boston, Brill, 2007) 144.

[40] Proclamation of 30 January 1800, *Collection* (n 37) 13.

[41] T[he] N[ational] A[rchives, Kew, London] CO 416/16 F41, fo 421.

[42] Charter of 6 August 1810, section X, *Collection* (n 37) 124. The 1810 Charter of Justice followed a protracted quarrel between the Governor and the Chief Justice, which led to the latter's powers being increased: Nadaraja (n 39) 62.

[43] It did however confirm that the Dutch and British inhabitants were to follow distinct rules on testamentary and matrimonial matters.

[44] Clause XXIX of the Charter of 18 April 1801: *Collection* (n 37) 36.

[45] See KM de Silva (general ed), *University of Ceylon, History of Ceylon* (Colombo, Ceylon University Press, 1973) 321.

[46] Ordinance No 5 of 1852, *A Revised Edition of the Ordinances of the Government of Ceylon: volume 1 – 1799–1882* (Colombo, GJA Skeen, 1894) 125. This also applied the maritime criminal law in the Kandyan provinces.

[47] Report of the Committee of the Executive Council on the Fixed Establishments of the Island of Ceylon, P[arliamentary] P[apers] 1852 (568) XXXVI.120, p 35. It may be noted that at the same time the Chief Justice Sir Anthony Oliphant noted that 'The Roman-Dutch law not necessary to be retained as the law of the island': ibid 145.

practice ruled by a *mélange* of laws.[48] Roman-Dutch law was also the basis of criminal law, but (as William Empson pointed out in 1841), 'English innovations during the last forty years have made it doubtful'.[49] Since only the Supreme Court had jurisdiction over serious crimes, and since all its judges were trained in England, it was no surprise that (as Ottley put it in 1829), the criminal law in Ceylon had been 'materially changed in practice by assimilation to the Laws of England'.[50]

There were many calls for criminal law to be codified. An early attempt was made in 1801 by James Dunkin, on the basis of a 'Parcel of Regulations' prepared by the Dutch Governor Falck.[51] Dunkin proposed modifying Dutch law in a number of ways. First, he made significant modifications in the definition of crimes. Having followed the arrangement of Blackstone's *Commentaries*, he made use of some of Blackstone's definition of offences.[52] Alongside making provision for the punishment of drunkenness and adultery, following the Roman-Dutch model,[53] he defined as distinct the offences of burglary, housebreaking, larceny and private stealing from the person, borrowing from Blackstone's enumeration of English offences defined by statute.[54] The combination of English and Dutch sources is also evident in his treatment of treason, which combined some elements from the statute of 1351 (such as compassing and imagining the death of the king or adhering to his enemies) and others from civilian sources (such as communicating with the enemy or betraying forts to them).[55]

Dunkin's second modification came in the definition of punishments. In common with other English officials, he found the Dutch code too sanguinary.[56] However, he did not wish to introduce punishments modelled on the English notion of 'Clergyable Felonies'.[57] Instead, he favoured a combination of corporal punishments and fines, which would be determined according to the nature of the crime. Dunkin's code was not introduced, but his concern with a proper definition of punishments was shared by later jurists. In 1829, Chief Justice Ottley and Justice Marshall bemoaned the fact that the Charter of Justice did not 'direct what code of criminal law is to be taken as the guide' when it came to punishments.[58] Out of their revulsion for the 'great severity of the Dutch criminal law', the judges (they argued) had stopped imposing the death penalty,

[48] See, eg, PP 1852 (568) XXXVI.120, p 129. See also William Empson's call for a code in 1841, TNA CO 54/191, fos 475–77, and see Sir Richard Ottley CJ's comment to the Commissioners of Eastern Inquiry in 1829-30: TNA CO 416/16 F41, fo 420.

[49] TNA CO 54/191, fo 477. Compare the remarks of Marshall PJ in TNA CO 416/17, F 42 fos 181–82.

[50] TNA CO 416/16, F41, fo 441a–b.

[51] Letter to Supreme Government respecting the introduction of a criminal code for the island of Ceylon [from F North to Mornington] B[ritish] L[ibrary] IOR G/11/6, fo 1584.

[52] For instance, he defined manslaughter as 'the unlawful killing of a man but without deliberation or malice either expressed or implied' (BL IOR G-11-6, fo. 1036, following 4 *Comm.* 191, itself drawing on Hale (n 5) vol 1, 466). See also his definition of 'petty treason', where one owing 'a special obedience' (such as a wife) killed another: fo. 1037, *cf* 4 *Comm.* 203.

[53] See BL IOR G-11-6, fo 992.

[54] See BL IOR G-11-6, fos 1045-7. Eg compare his definition of privately stealing 'as by picking his pocket or the like' with Blackstone's: 4 *Comm.* 241.

[55] James Dunkin to Frederick North, 15 January 1801, BL IOR G/11/6, fo 997.

[56] James Dunkin to Frederick North, 15 January 1801, BL IOR G/11/6, fo 975.

[57] Punishments for such felonies in England were 'much too gentle for the first offence, and by far too sanguinary for the second offence'.

[58] Richard Ottley and Charles Marshall to Governor 29 May 1829, TNA CO 416/13 F1, fo 3.

save for murder.[59] They felt that the criminal law had become too lenient. Ottley and Marshall consequently recommended introducing the punishments set out by recent English legislation.[60] Although they omitted the technical distinction between felony and misdemeanour which was unknown in Ceylon, they followed English terminology when recommending the introduction of new capital offences, such as 'robbery' and 'burglary'.[61]

There continued to be some debate in the middle of the century over whether to introduce a code of punishments.[62] By then, Chief Justice Oliphant was sceptical about codification, thinking that punishments should vary according to the circumstances of the case. However, he was not sceptical about English influence, for he said he would 'take the punishments of England … those laid down by Archibald, for instance'.[63] The criminal law of Ceylon would be codified, but not until 1883. By then, the idea of importing English criminal law wholesale had lost its attraction. When in 1871, the Colonial Office suggested the adoption by Ceylon of the criminal code recently drafted for Jamaica by R. S. Wright, the Queen's Advocate, F.A. Corgan, argued that 'the body of our law is still taken from the Roman Dutch law books, the rules of which are simpler and less unbending than are those of the English law'. In contrast to the approach taken by the judges in 1829, he noted the simplicity and flexibility of the Roman-Dutch concept of 'furtum', when compared with the English 'offence of theft, with its divisions of simple larceny, embezzlement, burglary &c'. In his view, replacing the broad categories of the Roman-Dutch common law with 'detailed statutory provisions' from English law would be to the colony's disadvantage. At the same time, like his predecessors, he stressed the need for a code to give a clear definition of punishments.[64] When a code was finally introduced in 1883, it was based on the neighbouring Indian Penal Code, which had itself been shaped by commissioners familiar with English law. Section 3 of the code abolished Roman-Dutch criminal law in Ceylon.[65]

Given this fluid legal background, it was not clear which law should be used when the colonial authorities faced rebellions. Rebellion or the threat of it was frequent enough in the first half of the century in Ceylon, which saw open rebellions in 1817–18, 1823 and 1848, as well as plots uncovered in 1816, 1834 and 1843, which had resulted in treason trials.[66] When dealing with these challenges – all of which occurred in the

[59] Ottley told the Commissioners of Eastern Inquiry that 'Sentence of death is never pronounced, except in cases of Murder, Bestiality and Sodomy.' TNA CO 416/16, F41, fos 420–21.

[60] 9 Geo IV c 74.

[61] TNA CO 416/13 F1, fo 9-v. The English definitions were adapted to Ceylonese conditions: burglary was thus defined as 'any stealing in a dwelling house by day or by night any person being therein, by one or more persons, either of them being armed with a deadly weapon, or either of them using violence to any person in the house'.

[62] See HC Selby's comments in PP 1852 (568) XXXVI.120, p 120.

[63] PP 1852 (568) XXXVI.120, p 145. The Chief Justice's reference (indirectly reported) was presumably to JF Archbold's *Summary of the Law relating to Pleading and Evidence in Criminal Cases*, 11th edn (ed WN Welsby) (London, S Sweet, V and R Stevens and G S Norton, 1849).

[64] Report of FA Corgan, enclosed in WH Gregory to Kimberley, 10 April 1872, TNA CO 54/475, fo 380 at fo 383.

[65] Ord. 2 of 1883 in *A Revised Edition of the Ordinances of the Government of Ceylon, volume 2 – 1883–1889* (Colombo, HC Cottle, 1895), 3.

[66] For Colonial Secretary Sir James Emerson Tennent's count of plots and insurrections, see PP 1851 (36) 162–63, q. 2541.

Kandyan provinces – the authorities resorted to customary law, martial law and English law, but do not at any stage seem to have drawn on the Roman-Dutch idea of *perduellio*. The British faced the first challenge to their rule in the year after the conquest of Kandy, when they identified a plot against their rule, which led to Madugalle, Disāva of Dumbara, being tried for 'treasonable practices'.[67] As provided for in the Convention, this trial was conducted under Kandyan law. It was the Kandyan chiefs who determined that Madugalle was guilty of disloyalty 'according to the laws and institutions of the Kandyan provinces'[68] and the Governor who determined the penalty, in this case a sentence of two years' imprisonment, soon followed by a pardon.[69]

In September 1817, another rebellion broke out in support of a pretender to the Kandyan throne. On this occasion, Governor Brownrigg's response was to proclaim martial law.[70] Brownrigg turned to martial law to punish the rebels 'as the Forms of Kandyan Judicature cannot be had resort to, in so disturbed a state as the country now presents'.[71] Numerous rebel chiefs were tried for treason before martial law courts, including the leaders Kāppitipola and Madugalle, who were executed in November 1818. Other rebel chiefs tried for treason had their death sentences commuted by the Governor to banishment or imprisonment.[72] In dealing with these cases, the martial law courts did not have to consider closely what constituted treason, since they were dealing with those engaged in armed insurrection, rather than the kind of conspiracy charged in 1816.

In the aftermath of this rebellion. Brownrigg made changes to the administration of the Kandyan provinces. Most of the judicial powers hitherto enjoyed by the chiefs was transferred to British officials.[73] Cases of treason and homicide were now to be tried in the court of a new Judicial Commissioner sitting with assessors, with their decision being referred first to the Board of Commissioners and then to the Governor for his determination.[74] However, the judicial system of Kandy was not integrated with that of the Maritime Provinces, and the local substantive law was still applicable. The operation of this law can be seen in the response to another rebellion, which broke out in Kandy in May 1823. As in 1816, the plot appeared to have been organised by priests, who put up a pretender to the throne of Kandy.[75] The conspirators were tried under the new system,

[67] Another one of those suspected of involvement, a Malay called Mohandiram, was banished to Batavia under powers given in the royal instructions to the Governor to remove dangerous persons from the island. Brownrigg to Bathurst, 5 November 1816, TNA CO 54/61, fo 182v.

[68] James D'Oyly to James Sutherland, 16 September 1816, TNA CO 54/61, fo 228, 245v.

[69] Brownrigg to Bathurst, 25 Sept. 1817, TNA CO 54/66 fos 162, 168v.

[70] Brownrigg to Bathurst, 7 November 1817, TNA CO 54/66, fos 205, 215v. Proclamation 1 November 1817, TNA CO 54/66, fo 217. See further KM de Silva, 'The Kandyan Kingdom and the British – the last Phase, 1796 to 1818', in de Silva (n 45) 12–33.

[71] Brownrigg to Bathurst, 29 February 1818, TNA CO 54/70, fo137 at fos 150v–151.

[72] Brownrigg to Bathurst, 24 July 1818, TNA CO 54/71, fo 245; 8 January 1819, TNA CO 54/73, fo 3; id. to id. 8 July 1819, TNA CO 54/74, fo 147. Twenty-six rebels were banished to Mauritius 'under authority vested in me by my Instructions', though a regulation had to be passed to prevent their return: Brownrigg to Bathurst, 8 February 1819, TNA CO 54/73, fo 349 at 350. See also J Wilson, 'Reappropriation, Resistance, and British Autocracy in Sri Lanka, 1820–1850' (2017) 60 *Historical Journal* 62.

[73] Nadaraja (n 39) 65.

[74] Nadaraja (n 39) 66, Proclamation 21 November 1818, s 4 (on the mode of proceeding in treason and homicide), TNA CO 54/73, fo 84v.

[75] This 'disturbance bore no very dangerous character' and was quickly suppressed. Governor Campbell to Bathurst, 12 May 1823, TNA CO 54/84, fo 223.

before the Judicial Commissioners at Kandy, with 'the most distinguished Kandyan chiefs' acting as assessors.[76] Following the course of the ancient Kandyan procedure, as modified by the Proclamation, the chiefs again determined the guilt of the accused, and the Governor passed sentence.[77]

By the time the next treasonable conspiracy had been uncovered, the 1833 Charter of Justice had been issued, and the Supreme Court had jurisdiction over Kandy. In 1834, six defendants were charged with treason as a result of a conspiracy to remove the British.[78] In this, the first occasion on which the Supreme Court would deal with a treason case, the law which was applied was neither Kandyan nor Roman-Dutch, but the law of England. The three main counts charged were compassing the death of the king; conspiring to levy war against him in his dominions; and 'conspiring to depose him from his royal style and kingly name in this his Isle of Ceylon and to subvert his Government therein'.[79] Addressing the jury of 13, the presiding judge, W. Norris, explained the English law of treason and how it applied to this case. He began by noting that it might seem strange to bring a charge of compassing the death of a king 'who is never perhaps likely to set his foot in Ceylon'. However, drawing on Sir Michael Foster, he explained the English doctrine of constructive treason.[80] He noted that it had been repeatedly decided that 'a *conspiracy to rise in rebellious war* against the King's Government is one *overt act* of compassing the King's death', since the king was bound by his coronation oath to resist, which would place his life in danger. Norris admitted that the risk to his life would be 'certainly remote' in the present case. However, he told the jury it was needless to dwell on that matter, since the charges also included a count of compassing to depose him from his royal style and kingly style – and '[a]lmost the whole evidence tends to the establishment of this charge'. The core accusations were therefore founded on the 1795 Act, an Act which was widely thought in the metropolis only to apply in England.[81] Although the judge clearly thought the defendants guilty, the accused were acquitted by the jury.[82]

English law and martial law continued to be the preferred tools to deal with rebellions in early nineteenth century Ceylon.[83] In 1848, Ceylon saw another rebellion, with martial law proclaimed for the first time since 1818. Within a week the rebellion was effectively crushed, though martial law remained in place. In dealing with the rebels,

[76] Campbell to Bathurst, 16 August 1823, TNA CO 54/84, fo 341.

[77] Kahawatte Unnanse, a Priest of Matele, who was considered the principal organiser was executed, along with Koswatte Ratteralle, who had been pardoned for his part in a previous disturbance. Thirteen more were banished to Mauritius for life.

[78] Wilson (n 72) 63.

[79] *Trial of the Kandyan State Prisoners* (Colombo, [1835]), in TNA CO 54/137, p 84.

[80] He quoted passages from Foster (n 6) 195–96: *Trial of the Kandyan State Prisoners*, 85.

[81] The 1848 Treason Felony Act was introduced partly because it was thought the 1795/1817 Act did not apply in Ireland: Sir G Grey, *Parl. Debs.*, third ser, vol 98, col 23 (7 April 1848). See also the discussion of the 1817 Act in *William Smith O'Brien v The Queen* (1848–49) 3 Cox CC 360.

[82] See dispatch TNA CO 54/140: 9 Feb 1835.

[83] In 1843, when 13 were tried for treason, Chandragotty Selewanse Sareinkere Unnanse was convicted after admitting to preparing a rebellion, but 12 others were acquitted. His confession is in PP 1849 (1018) XXXVI.1, p 370. See also the evidence of Sir JE Tennent, PP1851 (36), q. 2642, p 175. Torrington thought the 12 were acquitted because of the corruption of the jury: Torrington to Grey, 14 August 1848, PP 1849 (1018) XXXV.1, No. 22, p 168 at 173.

Governor Torrington turned to both civilian and martial law courts. He asked Chief Justice Oliphant to preside at a special sitting of the Supreme Court at Kandy to deal with prisoners held for crimes committed before martial law was proclaimed.[84] The area around the court was 'cut out of martial law'.[85]

Thirty-four faced civilian trials for high treason, accused of endeavouring to take Kandy and the Central Province from the Queen of England, by means of putting forward a pretender to the throne.[86] The high acquittal rate in the civilian trials – where half were acquitted – irritated Torrington, but he consoled himself with the thought that 'the wholesome terror inspired by martial law' would counteract the 'inefficiency … of a trial by jury before a civil court'.[87] The acquittal rate before the military courts was much lower – only three of 47 tried.[88] The military men running the courts martial were far less scrupulous when it came to matters of procedure than the civilians. Prisoners did not have counsel, and the charges against them were simply of 'high treason' without specifying what it consisted of.[89] The military did not use any particular definition of treason when handling cases before them. As Capt. Albert Watson explained, 'The crime for which those persons were tried, viz. personal conflict with our troops, was plainly sufficient in itself to constitute high treason'.[90] The continuation of martial law, and the use of martial law courts to try rebels, led to a conflict between the Governor and his lawyers, Queen's Advocate Selby and Chief Justice Oliphant, which would lead to a parliamentary inquiry in England.[91]

The concept of treason in this colony where Roman-Dutch civil law had taken root was not a Roman one. When the Colonial Secretary, Sir James Emerson Tennent, sought to trace a line of filiation between the rebels of 1834 and those of 1848, he invoked the precise English charges of which the former had been acquitted.[92] Both Chief Justice Oliphant and Advocate General Selby were experienced in Roman-Dutch law, the former having been in practice at the Cape (including being Attorney General) for over a decade and the latter having been his articled clerk.[93] However, there is no sign that they thought of the charges brought in 1848 as being ones of *perduellio*. Indeed, the commencement of the trials in Kandy was postponed for ten days after Oliphant's arrival in Kandy on 25 August, since Selby informed him that it was necessary to serve the indictments on the defendants ten days before trial.[94] In taking this view, Selby was

[84] Torrington to Grey, 14 September 1848, PP 1849 (1818), No. 32, p 217 at 219; *cf* Evidence of Oliphant, PP 1851 (36), p 586, qq 6841-3, and the explanation of Sir JE Tennent, ibid 236, q. 2934.

[85] PP 1851 (36), p 587, qq 6848, 6856.

[86] PP 1851 (36), p 588, q 6873–74. 'You have all been found guilty of various acts, all conducing to the same general end, that of deposing Her Majesty of her right and title to the Kandyan country'. PP 1851 (36-II), pp 206-07.

[87] Torrington to Grey, 14 September 1848, PP 1849 (1818), No. 32, p 217 at 220.

[88] Statement of Col. T.A. Drought, PP 1851 (36), p 204.

[89] Evidence of Capt. A. Watson, PP 1851 (36), p 46 q. 1007, p 47 q. 1025.

[90] Evidence of Capt. A. Watson, PP 1851 (36), p 54 q. 1173.

[91] See RW Kostal, 'A Jurisprudence of Power: Martial Law and the Ceylon Controversy of 1848–51' (2000) 28 *Journal of Imperial and Commonwealth History* 1. For Selby's view that civilian courts should have been used, see his evidence in PP 1851 (34), p 73, qq. 1429–30.

[92] PP 1851 (36), p 174, q. 2640.

[93] PP 1851 (36), pp 584–86. Selby was untrained in English law: ibid 104–105.

[94] PP 1851 (36), p 588, q. 6871.

applying the procedure required by the English treason law. *Perduellio* would not flourish in Ceylon. When Ceylon finally introduced its code, it imported an Indian definition of offences against the state, borrowed from the Indian Penal Code, which had itself been influenced by an English project of codification.

III. The Cape of Good Hope and Natal

The Cape Colony was also conquered from the Dutch during the Napoleonic wars. Although the Dutch burghers were guaranteed their property rights under the articles of capitulation of January 1806,[95] it was no more certain that Roman-Dutch law would remain the ruling law in the colony than it was in Ceylon. Commissioners appointed in the 1820s to consider judicial reforms favoured the introduction of English law.[96] However, since the Colonial Secretary, Goderich, feared that an abrupt alteration of the civil law would be disruptive, he decided that the Supreme Court created under the Charter of Justice of 1827 should 'commence [its] career by continuing to administer the ancient Law of the settlement'. At the same time, he wanted the judges to propose changes to make the local law 'adhere as far as may be practicable to the spirit of the Law of England'.[97]

When it came to criminal law, there was also much debate over possible reform. During the first period of British control, in 1797, the use of torture in criminal proceedings and extreme punishments were abolished, as in Ceylon.[98] However, procedure remained rooted in the Dutch law derived from the criminal ordinance of Philip II of 1570. An inquisitorial procedure was maintained by the code introduced in 1819, known as the 'Crown Trial'.[99] After commissioners appointed to investigate criminal law proposed to assimilate criminal procedure at the Cape to the English forms, these rules were modified significantly. Between 1827 and 1830, jury trial and English rules of pre-trial procedure and evidence were introduced.[100] Looking at substantive law, the commissioners noted that the crimes defined by the Roman-Dutch writers 'were all punishable by English law', with the exception of adultery and concubinage;[101] though they also felt that the definition of crimes in treatises on Roman-Dutch law such as Van

[95] CG Van Der Merwe et al, 'Republic of South Africa' in VV Palmer (ed), *Mixed Jurisdictions Worldwide: The Third Legal Family*, 2nd edn (Cambridge, Cambridge University Press, 2012) 110.

[96] 'Report of JT Bigge, Esq, to Earl Bathurst upon Courts of Justice' in GM Theal (ed), *Records of the Cape Colony*, vol 26 (London, William Clowes, 1905) 16–19.

[97] Viscount Goderich to Maj. Gen. Richard Bourke 5 August 1827 in GM Theal (ed), *Records of the Cape Colony*, vol 32 (London, William Clowes, 1905) 256, 258.

[98] 'Report of the Commissioners of Enquiry to Earl Bathurst upon Criminal Law and Jurisprudence' in M Theal (ed), *Records of the Cape Colony*, vol 33 (London, William Clowes, 1905) 29.

[99] *Crown Trial: or, Mode of Proceeding in Criminal Cases, at the Cape of Good Hope* (Cape Town, 1819) in Sir R Plaskett and T Miller, *Proclamations, Advertisements and other official Notices published by the Government of the Cape of Good Hope from January 10th 1806 to May 21st 1825* (Cape Town, Cape of Good Hope Government Press, 1827) 709.

[100] Theal, *Records* (n 98) 283; Ordinance No. 40 of 1828; Ordinance No. 72 of 1830. For a survey of the history of criminal procedure in this era, see J Dugard, *South African Criminal Law and Procedure. Vol 4: Introduction to Criminal Procedure* (Cape Town, Juta & Co, 1977) 19–28.

[101] Theal, *Records* (n 98) 95.

Leeuwen's 'are general and vague, and evidently leave great latitude to the Judge in the application of the law as well as of punishment'.[102] In their view, the principal differences between English and Roman-Dutch law centred on the punishments inflicted, and they made some proposals (informed by recent English legislation) regarding the appropriate punishments for certain crimes. Roman-Dutch remained theoretically the core of the substantive criminal law of the Cape, though it was increasingly influenced by English ideas.[103]

As in Ceylon, British rule extended to areas where Roman-Dutch law did not apply. When in 1835, the new – and short-lived – Queen Adelaide Province was proclaimed in the Eastern Cape, most criminal matters were to be left to native customary law, but a limited number of offences – including treason – were to be dealt with by 'British laws'.[104] This area would come under British formal rule again after 1847 as 'British Kaffraria'. After 20 years under martial law, it was incorporated into the Cape Colony in 1865, when it became notionally subject to Cape laws. However, as the Cape's Commission on Native Laws and Customs reported in 1883, 'although legally subject to Colonial law, [they] have been only nominally so; and to a very considerable extent they are still actually under their own traditional laws and usages'.[105] Appointed in 1880 to codify law for the Transkeian territories, the commissioners did not propose introducing the uncodified Roman-Dutch criminal law of the Cape. Instead, they modelled their draft on the Indian Penal Code and on the code drawn up by JF Stephen which failed to be enacted at the metropolis in 1879 and 1880. The provisions in the code on offences against the state were borrowed directly from the Indian Penal Code.[106] The law of treason against the crown in these 'native' areas therefore reflected the law in India and Ceylon, rather than that in England or early modern Holland.

Which law was to apply at the Cape? Answering Chief Justice Wylde's question in Andries Botha's case whether the law of treason could vary in the empire, Attorney General Porter stated that English law 'determines what is the sovereign, but in a colony the law of the colony determines what are the functions and powers of the Crown'.[107] This was to suggest that the Roman-Dutch law of treason should apply. However, there appeared to be some ambiguity over the relevant law. The first occasion when British rule was challenged by their new subjects came in 1815 with the Slagter's Nek rebellion, when a group of farmers in the Eastern Cape squared up against the military in rebellion. Twenty were tried in Uitenhage for treason, with five being executed for the

[102] Theal, *Records* (n 98) 5.

[103] See EM Burchell and PMA Hunt, *South African Criminal Law and Procedure. Vol I: General Principles of Criminal Law* (Cape Town, Juta & Co, 1970) 23–29.

[104] 'Report and Proceedings with Appendices of the Government Commission on Native Laws and Customs' (Cape Town 1883) Cape Parliamentary Papers G.4 – '83, p 15.

[105] 'Report and Proceedings' (n 104) 18.

[106] Draft code in 'Report and Proceedings' (n 104) section 88. These provisions were enacted as law in Act No. 24 of 1886.

[107] *The Queen v Botha* (1852) 6 Searle 150 at 153. Porter cited the Canadian appeal case of *Donegani v Donegani* (1834-35) 3 Knapp 63; 12 ER 571, in which the Judicial Committee of the Privy Council (in a case concerning the applicability of the *droit d'aubaine* in Quebec) held that the prerogative powers of the crown in relation to the property of aliens was determined by the law of the particular colony where the question arose, even though the question of who was an alien was to be determined by English law.

crime. In setting out his case, the prosecutor, JG Cuyler, defined treason in the following manner:

> If a man do levy war against our Lord the King in his realm, while as on the one side to make the crime of *High treason* appear, it is not required to prove that a person was actually in arms against the State, but is sufficient that he had excited hostilities against the State, so on the other side by being found in an Armed Rebellion, the crime of High treason is not constituted, when it does not appear that he had a part in the hostile design or conspiracy; and which is the distinguishing mark between the crime of High treason and that of High misprision or *laesae Magestatis*.[108]

Although this appears to be a Roman-Dutch definition of treason, Cuyler (wrongly) claimed that he was quoting from the section in Blackstone's *Commentaries* on the offence of levying war against the king.[109] In Botha's own case, the indictment echoed those brought in England: it charged that, 'not regarding the duty of his allegiance', he 'most wickedly, maliciously, and traitorously did levy and make war and rebellion against our said Lady the Queen'.[110] Given that raising arms against the sovereign was treason in both systems, it may not have seemed important exactly how the charges were framed. As Porter told the jury, 'English laws and Dutch laws alike regard what has happened in the Kat River as treason, – and there is no difference upon this subject between Matthaeus and Voet upon the one side and Hale and Foster upon the other'.[111]

In the second half of the nineteenth century, by which time the Roman-Dutch law of treason had fallen away in Ceylon, South African lawmakers confirmed that the *crimen perduellionis* was to be seen as the basis of treason law in their jurisdictions. This can be seen from the reaction of the South African colonies to the Colonial Office's circular letter of December 1867 asking colonies to pass legislation on the lines of the English 1848 Treason Felony Act.[112] The English statute included a clause stating that nothing in it should affect the force of the 1351 statute. The Colony of Natal, where Roman-Dutch Law had been introduced as the common law in 1845,[113] dutifully followed the instructions from London, passing the requested legislation, but modified the saving clause to read that nothing in the ordinance should 'affect the Law of this Colony in regard to the crime of High Treason, or *Crimen perduellionis*'.[114] This was to confirm that Roman law, and not the statute of 1351, was the basis of the law.

The Cape Colony did not introduce legislation, after a number of objections were raised by the Attorney General, William Downes Griffith. First, he pointed out that the law at the Cape did not recognise the technical distinction between treason, felony and misdemeanour. This was significant, since in the Cape, 'no offence involves a forfeiture of goods or attainder of blood'. It would not be until two years later, in 1870, that the

[108] HCV Leibbrandt, *The Rebellion of 1815 generally known as Slachters Nek* (Cape Town, Juta & Co, 1902) 48.
[109] The passage he claimed to be quoting is 4 *Comm*. 81–82. The criminal law commissioners assumed that the case was brought under the Roman-Dutch law of treason: Theal, *Records* (n 98) 13.
[110] *Trial of Andries Botha* (n 1) 2.
[111] *Trial of Andries Botha* (n 1) 151. Botha's conviction was controversial, since the evidence of his active participation in a rebellion he had sought to restrain was slender.
[112] Circular despatch, 11 December 1867: TNA CO 854/8, fo 631.
[113] 1845 Ordinance No. 12 (Cape).
[114] Law No. 3 of 1868 (Natal).

penalty of forfeiture for treason and felony was abolished in England.[115] Secondly, in contrast to England, there was very little criminal statute law at the Cape. Since its criminal law was rooted in common law rather than technical statutes, he thought it 'much more consistent with real justice than that of England'. Thirdly – identifying problems which his counterpart in Natal had not seen – he argued that introducing a measure based on the 1848 Act would also require the Cape to codify the 1351 Act and later English treason law. Finally, he argued that even if all these changes were made, 'I still do not see that practically the law of the colony would be much altered'. For good measure, he advised officials in London to consult their copy of Van der Linden's treatise, to see how similar the laws were.[116] The permanent under-secretary at the Colonial Office, Sir Frederick Rogers, conceded that 'that it w[oul]d be most injudicious to patch on to the Dutch Law of the Cape of Good Hope a statute based on the peculiarities of the English Law',[117] though he apparently had no qualms about the same being done in the neighbouring colony of Natal. Griffith's objections were not those of a died-in-the-wool Roman-Dutch lawyer: he was an Irish barrister of the Inner Temple, who would return to be a county court judge in England in 1877. His objections were rather rooted in his preference for common law over statute, and his feeling that the two laws were substantially the same.

The understanding that Roman-Dutch law was the underlying law in South Africa, but that it overlapped with English law, can be glimpsed in the 1888 trials of the Zulu king Dinuzulu and some other Zulu leaders, who were charged as a result of an armed conflict which broke out between his followers and a rival faction backed by the colonial forces. They were tried in a special court in the newly annexed colony of Zululand, presided over by the senior puisne judge of Natal, sitting without a jury, using the law of Natal.[118] Outlining the capital charge, Attorney-General Michael Gallwey referred to Van der Linden's treatise. Turning to the non-capital charge, he invoked the 1868 law, which he thought embraced the lesser *crimen laesae majestatis*.[119] The indictment charged Dinuzulu with 'treason, rebellion and public violence',[120] but specified that, 'not regarding the duty of his allegiance, he did maliciously and traitorously conspire, consult, consent, and agree with divers false traitors … unknown, to raise, levy and make insurrection and war … against Her Majesty the Queen.'[121] During the trial itself, the question was debated whether the warlike activity engaged in by Dinuzulu's followers was treason. Rather than drawing on the rich Roman-Dutch literature on the distinction between armed risings aimed at overthrowing the state (which constituted treason), and those which did not (where were not treason),[122] Dinuzulu's lawyer, Harry

[115] See 33 & 34 Vict c 23 and K Kesselring, 'Felony Forfeiture in England, c.1170–1870' (2009) 30 *Journal of Legal History* 201.

[116] 'Report on Circular from Her Majesty's Principal Secretary of State': TNA CO48/441/7899, fo 216.

[117] Minute, 28 July 1868, TNA CO 48/441/7899, fo 213.

[118] Proclamation No IV of 1888, PP 1890 (c. 5982), enc. in No. 61, p 91; Proclamation No. 2 of 1887 (Zululand) in Sir E Hertslet, *A Complete Collection of the Treaties and Conventions*, vol 18 (London, Butterworth, 1893) 778. See further M Lobban, *Imperial Incarceration: Detention without Trial in the Making of British Colonial Africa* (Cambridge, Cambridge University Press, 2021) ch 3.

[119] PP 1890 (C. 5892), enc. in No. 24, p 33.

[120] For public violence, see van der Linden (n 14) 318.

[121] TNA CO 879/30/2, enc. 2 in No. 141, p 194.

[122] See eg Moorman (n 12) 57 (1.3.4).

Escombe cited Foster's treatise, as quoted in *R v Frost*, as 'unquestionably the highest authority on the subject of high treason'.[123] The trials ended in convictions, with the presiding judge Wragg declaring (in Roman-Dutch terms) that the defendants had 'a settled intention hostile to the Queen'.[124]

In the trials considered so far, it might have made little difference whether English or Roman-Dutch law was used, since the core charges were of armed rebellion. During the Anglo-Boer war, however, it became evident that the Roman-Dutch law of treason was better suited to deal with the kinds of cases which now came to court. This can be seen from the comments of Justice Finnemore, in one of the first cases to come before the Natal Supreme Court during the war. Finnemore began by stating that there was very little difference between the law of Natal and England on treason: '[t]he law of England corresponds to a considerable extent with Roman law, upon which our Roman Dutch law is based, so that both the English law and the Natal law have the same origin'. Turning to the Roman-Dutch law of treason, he soon showed that the Roman-Dutch law was significantly broader than the English. As he put it, '[i]t is a crime of a very wide scope under our common law'. Provided there was a hostile intent, it could be committed not only by resort to arms, but by helping the enemy with provisions, giving them counsel or assistance, or not disclosing any matters affecting the safety of the state. Trading with the enemy, or harbouring enemies could also constitute treason, and it might also extend to 'attempts to excite feeling of disaffection to the Government'.[125]

Finnemore stressed that Roman-Dutch law was also flexible when it came to punishment. There had been some debate about this in 1896, when four leaders of the 'Jameson Raid' who pleaded guilty to charges of *perduellio* in the South African Republic for having attempting to trigger an uprising of disfranchised English-speaking workers were sentenced to death.[126] Although the presiding judge, Reinhold Gregorowski, thought he was bound to impose the sentence suggested by the Roman-Dutch writers, James Rose Innes, who had been sent by the Cape Government to observe the trials, thought that judges had a discretion to impose 'any lesser sentence'.[127] This was also Finnemore J's view, who told the jury that he had a wide discretionary power when it came to sentencing.[128] If Roman-Dutch law could catch a much wider group of traitors, it could also punish them more leniently.

During this war, most of the treason cases which came before the courts – as opposed to the much more draconian military tribunals – were not heard by ordinary courts, but by special tribunals created by legislation in both the Cape and Natal in

[123] Address of Harry Escombe, in Bodleian Library MSS Brit Emp s 22 – G 12, p 135.

[124] Judgment against Ndabuko: TNA CO 879/30/5, enc. in No. 84, p 163.

[125] *Reg v Gert, Arnold and Hendrik Boers* (1900) 21 NLR 116, 120–22.

[126] See the report of *The State v Lionel Phillips and sixty three others* in (1900) 17 *Cape Law Journal* 15 and *S v Phillips, Rhodes and Others* (1896) in *The Official Reports of the High Court of the South African Republic* (London, Stevens and Haynes, 1903), vol III, p 216.

[127] TNA CO 879/30/2, enc. 2 in No. 141, p. 194. Innes's report on the law of treason was reprinted in (1896) 13 *Cape Law Journal* 182-5. After intense lobbying by the British government, the sentences were commuted to prison sentences.

[128] *Reg v Gert, Arnold and Hendrik Boers* (1900) 21 NLR 116,t 123. He sentenced each of the men to 5 years imprisonment with hard labour, and a £250 fine, with the prison sentence extended by a year if it could not be paid.

1900.[129] The legislation in both colonies was passed to provide a mechanism for dealing with the very large number of subjects who had joined the invading Boers in the first phase of the war. The courts were created specifically to deal with treason. This was defined in Natal to include *crimen perduellionis*, *crimen laesae majestatis*, offences under the law of 1868, sedition and every attempt or solicitation to participate in treason.[130] By contrast, the Cape's Act defined the applicable law more narrowly, as that administered by the Supreme Court, and stated that the court's jurisdiction was to cover 'high treason' and any 'political offences' certified to be such by the Attorney General.[131] In the event, although the Cape's court dealt with far more cases than Natal's, it was the latter court which generated more reported case law. Although Natal's act gave a broad statutory definition of treason which might have made it hard to generate precedents on particular areas of doctrine, in practice the questions which arose largely centred on the meaning of *perduellio*.

When the court was set up, the Colonial Office recommended that the colonial judge Sir William Smith be appointed president, since he had been a judge in the Roman-Dutch jurisdiction of British Guiana.[132] In fact, Smith's Guyanese experience would not help him in understanding Natal's criminal law. When Demerara, Essequibo and Berbice had been captured from the Dutch during the Napoleonic Wars, the articles of capitulation guaranteed – as they did in the case of other Dutch acquisitions – to respect the laws in force, which included the same system of criminal procedure derived from Philip II which applied in the Cape. Even after they had been consolidated in 1831 into one colony, the local prosecutor – still called the First Fiscal – turned to writers such as Voet when evaluating the seditious conduct of protesters.[133] However, in 1846, an Ordinance introduced the English law of treason into the colony.[134] Furthermore, in 1868, the colony dutifully passed an act introducing the British Treason Felony Act, with its saving provision mentioning the 1351 statute as already introduced into the colony.[135] Finally, in 1891, the colony adopted the code R.S. Wright had drafted for Jamaica, which confirmed the English law of treason to be applicable.[136]

If Smith's previous experience would not be of help, he was happy enough once in Natal to draw on the Roman-Dutch writers to define what counted as treason in periods of occupation, such as that experienced in Northern Natal early in the war, when much of the region was occupied for more than seven months. Many cases which came before the court involved activities by defendants who had never taken up arms, but who had assisted the occupying forces in various ways. For instance, William Bester was accused of treason for taking his family across the border into the Orange Free State when war broke out, and then acting as a guard on the border with Basutoland. Drawing on the

[129] See further Lobban, *Imperial Incarceration* (n 118) 333–39.

[130] Act No. 14 of 1900 (Natal) in PP 1902 (Cd. 981) 50.

[131] Act No. 6 of 1900 (Cape) in PP 1902 (Cd. 981) 58. For the creation of these courts, see Lobban (n 118) 333–39.

[132] TNA CO 179/213/21333.

[133] See eg, PP 1831-2 (733) XLVI.297, enc. 2 in No. 16, p 233.

[134] Ordinance No. 20 of 1846 (British Guiana).

[135] Ordinance No. 6 of 1868 (British Guiana).

[136] Ordinance 18 of 1893 (British Guiana). See ML Friedland, 'RS Wright's Model Criminal Code: A Forgotten Chapter in the History of the Criminal Law' (1981) 1 *Oxford Journal of Legal Studies* 307.

works of Matthaeus and Carpzovius, Smith held this to be treason, since it had assisted the enemy: for if he had not acted as a guard, the Boers would have had to use one of their men for the task, detracting from their war effort.[137] John William Gowthorpe was accused of supplying the occupiers from his chemist's store, of entertaining the Boer general Joubert at his home, of giving refreshments to the troops and of volunteering to help police in Newcastle to protect property (including his own) on four occasions.[138] In deciding this case, Smith drew on Roman-Dutch ideas of what was acceptable and what unacceptable hospitality to an enemy. In Smith's view, Gowthorpe had committed no treason by selling goods from his shop, nor by hosting Joubert; but his giving refreshments to the troops and helping police the town were traitorous. It was treason to act as a policeman, since if he had not done so, the occupiers would have had to do it themselves. As for the matter of hospitality and supply, Smith later explained that Gowthorpe and his wife were friends of the occupying officials: 'the giving of tea or similar small acts of hospitality extended to such friends was not an assistance to the King's enemies from which a hostile intent against the State could be presumed to exist'. By contrast, 'the voluntary giving of food to the rearguard of the force when evacuating the town was held to be an act of high treason and of this the prisoner was convicted.'[139] Wynand Adendorff was similarly convicted of treason for acting as a Native Commissioner in Newcastle, and thereby assisting the enemy, but got no penalty for entertaining a Boer official by the name of Meintjes at his home.[140]

In 1902, the Privy Council confirmed that there did not have to be a common law of treason throughout the empire. It had been acknowledged by the Colonial Laws Validity Act of 1865, that local laws were not void for being repugnant to English law, unless the English law in question specifically extended to the colony. The Privy Council could therefore confirm that cases in Natal might be heard under Roman-Dutch rules rather than English ones.[141] No South African defendant raised the objection that the local polity under whose laws he was prosecuted had no *majestas*, being a colony of a greater imperial power. It was perhaps a difficult argument to make, since the *majestas* which was protected by the law was that of the imperial crown: and if the crown chose to protect itself in its Roman-Dutch empire with Roman-Dutch law, it was free to do so. In any event, constitutional developments within the empire soon settled this question: for after the establishment of the Union of South Africa, this self-governing dominion was perceived to have its own sovereign status sufficient to allow it to prosecute traitors against the state.[142]

[137] *Reg v W A L Bester* (1900) 21 NLR 237, 239.

[138] *Reg v John William Gowthorpe* (1900) 21 NLR 221.

[139] Smith's explanation is given in *The Trial of Dinuzulu on Charges of High Treason at Greytown, Natal, 1908-09* (Pietermaritzburg, Times Printing and Publishing Co, 1910) Judgment, xv.

[140] *Reg v Wynand Peter John Adendorff* (1900) 21 NLR 230. John Henry Randelhoff was convicted of treason for acting as a clerk and interpreter of the Native Commissioner Lodewyk de Jager (whose acceptance of that post was one of the charges of treason against him). *R v John Henry Randelhoff* (1901) 22 NLR 59.

[141] *In re The Queen v Marais* [1902] AC 51.

[142] See *S v Christian* 1923 AD 101.

15

Rome in the Antipodes: *Emphyteusis* and the Australian Perpetual Lease

PAUL BABIE

I. Introduction

In Australian idiomatic usage, 'squattocracy' describes a nineteenth-century class of unlawful colonial occupiers of vast tracts of Crown waste land used to produce wool, generating enormous wealth for the fledgling colonies.[1] Near the end of the century-long adaptation of English land law to meet increasing demands by the squatters for security of tenure, colonial legislators created a curious, hybrid interest: the perpetual leasehold. As any common lawyer knows, however, a perpetual lease is a conceptual impossibility. The fee simple alone endures in perpetuity, while the leasehold confers exclusive possession for a defined term. Still, parliament can create such hybrids, including the perpetual lease.[2]

Less clear is how the perpetual lease came to be. Here I examine whether this paradoxical tenure bears the impress of the Roman contract of *emphyteusis*. Unlike that best known of Roman transplants in English law, the easement,[3] little direct evidence supports a Roman inspiration for the perpetual lease. Still, circumstantial though it is, the evidence points towards Rome, in two ways. First, that a social imaginary which included Roman law was operative in the work of the early colonial legislators. And, even if it played no direct role, looking at the story through a Roman lens reveals important information about this hybrid.

The chapter contains four sections. Section II provides a brief overview of nineteenth-century Crown land management in colonial New South Wales. Section III examines the introduction of the perpetual lease as a means of resolving problems created by the occupation of squatters. Here I suggest that while a direct connection to *emphyteusis* cannot be shown, it seems likely that the social imaginary held by colonial legislators included it as part of the toolbox of concepts which could be used in addressing the

[1] 'Squatter', *Meanings and Origins of Australian Words and Idioms* (2017) slll.cass.anu.edu.au/centres/andc/meanings-origins.

[2] *Taff Vale Railway Co v Amalgamated Society of Railway Servants* [1901] AC 426 (HL) 429–30 (Farwell J).

[3] B Nicholas, *An Introduction to Roman Law* (Oxford, Clarendon, 1962) 141–44.

problems associated with squatting. Section IV reflects upon the achievements of the lease of Crown land. Whether Roman or not, the solution demonstrated a mind-set very like the Roman experience with such leases; and if we see the story this way, we might also see how Roman law can, if used expressly, provide the foundation for novel solutions to novel problems. We might see both new ways of understanding the perpetual lease, but more than that, we might see how, when seen through Roman eyes, it might be interpreted, understood, and applied to modern challenges.

II. Squattocracy

A. Pastoral Lease

While Australia's Aboriginal and Torres Strait Islander peoples have inhabited Australia for around 65,000 years,[4] permanent European occupation began on 22 August 1770, when James Cook took possession of the east coast for England.[5] We know now that the acquisition of sovereignty conferred a radical title upon the Crown.[6] At the time, though, sovereignty was equated with absolute ownership and that, combined with the abhorrent doctrine of *terra nullius*, not only allowed England to ignore the claims of Aboriginal and Torres Strait Islander peoples,[7] but also allowed colonial administrators to issue grants of land to settlers.[8] And settlers brought livestock.[9] By 1820, numbers of merino sheep – with 'wool the equal of any Spanish wool', and therefore very valuable[10] – tripled from the initial flock of 1000 in 1798.[11]

Sheep need land for grazing, and eastern Australia seemingly had plenty.[12] Its allocation to settlers, though, came about through 'a gradual process of evolution, each situation being met as it developed.'[13] Early instructions gave governors wide discretion to issue grants of any land.[14] A Government Order issued in 1829 fixed 'limits of location' comprising about one-ninth of the total area of New South Wales, beyond which settlement was prohibited;[15] a Colonial Office Circular concerning lands in Western Australia provides added clarification as to the nature of the grants within the limits of location: 'land … granted will belong in perpetuity to the grantee, his heirs and assigns,

[4] C Clarkson et al, 'Human occupation of northern Australia by 65,000 years ago' (2017) 547(7663) *Nature* 306.
[5] CMH Clark, *A History of Australia I: From the Earliest Times to the Age of Macquarie* (Melbourne, Vic., Melbourne University Press, 1962) 42–56.
[6] TP Fry, *Freehold and Leasehold Tenancies of Queensland Land* (Brisbane, University of Queensland, 1946) 18–20.
[7] S Banner, 'Why Terra Nullius? Anthropology and Property Law in Early Australia' (2005) 23(1) *Law and History Review* 95.
[8] TP Fry, 'Land Tenures in Australian Law' (1946) 3 *Res Judicatae* 158.
[9] Clark (n 5) 62, 79, 80, 85, 223, 286.
[10] ibid 151, 331.
[11] AG Lang, *Crown Land in New South Wales* (Sydney, Butterworths, 1973) [102].
[12] Clark (n 5) 200, 299, 370.
[13] HC Carter, 'Land Settlement in New South Wales' (1933) 5(19) *The Australian Quarterly* 64, 64.
[14] Lang (n 11) (1973) [102].
[15] Government Order, No 50 (NSW), *Sydney Gazette* (17 October 1829).

to be held in free and common socage, subject, however, to such reservations and conditions as may be stated in conveyance.'[16] An inflated minimum price combined with the decrease of available land as each grant was made within the limits[17] fuelled a hunger for land that led squatters illegally to occupy land beyond the limits.[18]

From 1836, as a means of placating the burgeoning squattocracy, Governor Bourke issued 'annual licences to occupiers of runs of "indefinite extent", outside the bounds of settlement, at 10 pounds per run' and, in consequence, 'the squatter ceased to be a trespasser[;] his occupation of land in unsettled areas … recognized.'[19] But with no long-term security or pre-emptive right to purchase, licensees had little incentive to erect homesteads or make improvements.[20] A great welter of complex legislation followed in an attempt to redress this imbalance.[21] The original legislation, enacted in 1847,[22] established novel 'pastoral leases', unknown in English law, to be held on 8 or 14-year terms at an annual rent and subject to a Crown right of resumption.[23]

Prior to 1855, the legislative power to deal with Crown land was vested in the Legislative Council of New South Wales, established in 1823, which could deal only with legislation submitted to it by the Governor (who was appointed by the Imperial Government).[24] In 1855, however, the Constitution Act 1855 (Imp) vested responsible government in the New South Wales Parliament (consisting of the lower Legislative Assembly and the upper Legislative Council), which thereafter held 'the entire management and control of [Crown] waste lands'.[25] Exercising that power in 1861,[26] the Parliament replaced the 1847 legislation with a new system of pastoral leases carrying one-year terms in settled districts and five-year terms beyond. In 1884, the Parliament consolidated the system of pastoral leases in the Crown Lands Act 1884 (NSW).[27]

Beginning in the 1880s, many pastoral leases began to expire. The New South Wales Parliament faced a choice: renew the tenures and, if so, for how long? Put another way, the Parliament sought a means of retaining maximum public control over land with its corresponding revenue providing 'for schools, police and other social services, and public works'[28] while simultaneously guaranteeing security of tenure for the squattocracy, the primary driver of the colonial economy. If the Parliament had looked explicitly to Roman law, it would have found the perfect solution: *emphyteusis*.

[16] Fry (n 8) 159, n 5 (citation omitted).

[17] Lang (n 11) [103].

[18] CMH Clark, *A History of Australia III: The Beginning of an Australian Civilization* (Melbourne, Vic., Melbourne University Press, 1973) 252.

[19] Lang (n 11) [104]–[106].

[20] Crown Lands Unauthorized Occupation Act 1836 (NSW); Crown Lands Unauthorized Occupation Act 1839 (NSW).

[21] Lang (n 11) [101]–[111].

[22] Sale of Waste Lands Act 1846 (Imp) (9 & 10 Vic c 4); Order-In-Council 1847 (NSW) (7 October 1847).

[23] AC Millard and GW Millard, *The Law of Real Property in New South Wales* (Sydney, Halstead Press, 1905) 5–6.

[24] New South Wales Act 1823 (Imp) (4 Geo 4 c 96) s 24.

[25] Constitution Act 1855 (Imp) (18 & 19 Vic c 54) s 2.

[26] Crown Lands Alienation Act 1861 (NSW); Crown Lands Occupation Act 1861 (NSW).

[27] Crown Lands Act 1884 (NSW).

[28] Fry (n 6) 28.

B. *Emphyteusis*

The Roman *locatio conductio* created a lease of land[29] under which, as long as rent was paid, a lessee held rights to land, including possession and an *in rem* claim.[30] Municipalities often held substantial landholdings leased perpetually, the rent called a *vectigal* and the land known as *ager vectigalis*. In the third century, two specialised forms of contractual letting of land entered the Roman law:[31] *superficies* – a right to build on land belonging to another – and *emphyteusis* – a perpetual proprietary interest in state or public land.[32] The *ager vectigalis* served as the prototype of the codified contract of *emphyteusis*,[33] under which *fundi patrimoniales* (private property of the emperor) or *fundi rei privatae* (state or municipal land)[34] was 'assigned to an emphyteutic possessor, *emphyteuticarius*, on a perpetual basis, in exchange for an annual rent'.[35]

Emphyteusis thereby equated the possessor to an owner holding secure rights, including rights of possession and an entitlement to fruits, to alienate the *emphyteutic* rights to others, to leave them to heirs, and to create servitudes.[36] Barry Nicholas elaborates that rights were 'inheritable and alienable. And the holder had a "real" relation to the land in that … he had possession … By th[e time of Justinian], the … *emphyteuta* … had not merely possession, but also … an *actio in rem*, so that, where the *emphyteusis* was perpetual, he was for all practical purposes an owner'.[37] The rights were therefore predicated upon payment of rent, and could be lost if rent went unpaid for three consecutive years, for irremediable damage, or if their holder died without heirs.[38] By the Roman emperor Zeno's time, *emphyteusis* was 'recognized and accepted … as an institution *sui generis*, creating a *ius in rem* and being distinct from both *locatio conductio* and transfer of ownership subsequent to a contract of sale'.[39]

C. Perpetual Lease

Throughout the first half of 1894, the opposition Free Trade Party made repeated calls in New South Wales Parliament for perpetual tenure to replace expiring pastoral leases.[40]

[29] R Zimmerman, *The Law of Obligations: Roman Foundations of the Civilian Tradition* (Oxford, Oxford University Press, 1996) 338–412.

[30] DP Kehoe, 'Tenure of Land and Agricultural Regulation' in PJ du Plessis, C Ando and K Tuori (eds), *The Oxford Handbook of Roman Law* (Oxford, Oxford University Press, 2016) 646–59, especially 655–56, citing D 6.3.1, 3; D 6.3.2.

[31] P du Plessis, *Borkowski's Textbook on Roman Law*, 4th edn (Oxford, Oxford University Press, 2010) 170.

[32] L Capogrossi Colognesi, 'Ownership and Power in Roman Law' in P du Plessis et al, *Oxford Handbook of Roman Law* 524–36, especially 534.

[33] WW Buckland and AD McNair, *Roman Law and Common Law*, 2nd edn (FH Lawson ed, Cambridge, Cambridge University Press, 1952) 83.

[34] Zimmerman (n 29) 358–59.

[35] Kehoe (n 30) 656.

[36] Du Plessis (n 31) 170.

[37] Nicholas (n 3) 148–49.

[38] Kehoe (n 30) 656, citing C 4.66.1 (476–484 CE); Inst 3.24.3; C 4.66.2 (529 CE); du Plessis (n 31) 170, citing Paul, *Edict*, Book 21, Ulpian, *Sabinus*, Book 17[2] (D 6.3.1.1, 2.).

[39] Zimmerman (n 29) 359, citing C. 4.66.1; *cf* Inst 3.24.3.

[40] New South Wales, *Parliamentary Debates*, Legislative Assembly, 6 February 1894, 427 (T Rose); 7 February 1894, 484 (G Cruickshank); 27 February 1894, 1038 (A Rae), 1050, 1051 (EW O'Sullivan), 1051–52

While the Protectionist Party government stood implacably opposed to the suggestion,[41] strong public sentiment opposing the alienation and calling for the retention of Crown land as a source of revenue dominated the ensuing election of 17 July 1894.[42] It came as little surprise, then, when the Free Trade Party, riding the populist wave to power,[43] led by the Secretary for Lands, Sir Joseph Carruthers, proposed the Crown Lands Bill 1894 (NSW).

Introduced in the Lower House on 13 September,[44] the 1894 Bill, intended to be read with the Crown Lands Act 1884 (NSW),[45] contained clause 15, which read in part:

> The Governor shall issue a ***grant in fee-simple*** of the homestead selection … to an applicant …
>
> The grant of a homestead selection shall contain provisions for –
>
> (a) The annual payment by the grantee, his heirs, and assigns ***for ever of a perpetual rent*** …; and
> (b) The performance by the grantee, his heirs and assigns ***for ever*** of an obligation to live upon the homestead selection …; and
> (c) Forfeiture to the Crown of the lands granted in case the obligation to live thereon or to pay any sums due as rent be not duly performed.
>
> The obligation to live on the lands granted, and the liability to pay rent shall be ***incidents in perpetuity of the tenure of the lands*** (emphasis added).[46]

In the First Reading speech, Sir Joseph said of the proposed homestead selection:

> I cannot … use the term 'perpetual leasehold', but I will tell you what I do. I give them perpetual leasehold in all its incidents, in perpetual rent, which must be paid year by year. I give them the incidents and obligations of a leasehold tenure. Always having the Crown as the landlord I preserve the old title of freehold. Why? There is [sic] very erroneous ideas of what a freehold is. Some think that a freehold is held independent of any landlord; but every freehold title in the British dominions, every freehold in this country, is held from the Crown as its landlord. We have no need to change the name of freehold to leasehold in order to gain greater power under the one than is given under the other. Whilst I attach to these holdings the elements and incidents of perpetual leaseholds, I keep the old name of freehold because it will be more valuable to the holder, and it will be less likely to lead to complications which must arise in conveyancing if there is introduced a strange and hitherto unknown tenure, which may become a fertile source of litigation by its operation.[47]

According to Sir Joseph, while the alienee would hold a proprietary tenure, the Crown would retain a form of control over the lands not possible following the grant of a

(W A'Beckett), 1056 (A Hutchison); 21 March 1894, 1761 (R Jones); 29 March 1894, 1880 (H Chapman), 1887 (A Rae).

[41] ibid 27 February 1894, 1038, 1050, 1057; 21 March 1894, 1761; 29 March 1894, 1886–87 (H Copeland).

[42] ibid 4 October 1894, 1106 (J Morgan); 23 October 1894, 1572 (J Hayes); 6 November 1894, 2040 (WC Wall).

[43] A Green, '1894 election totals', *New South Wales Election Results 1856–2007* (2007) www.parliament.nsw.gov.au/electionresults18562007/1894/Totals.htm.

[44] New South Wales, *Parliamentary Debates*, Legislative Assembly, 11 September 1894, 301; 12 September 1894, 359; 13 September 1894, 433–59 (J Carruthers).

[45] Crown Lands Act 1895 (NSW), s 1.

[46] New South Wales, *Parliamentary Debates*, Legislative Assembly, 25 October 1894, 1689.

[47] ibid 13 September 1894, 436; 19 September 1894, 547 (J Carruthers).

common law fee simple. Sir George Simpson, Solicitor-General (later a judge of the New South Wales Supreme Court), responsible for the Bill's passage in the Upper House, said much the same:

> The settler, instead of becoming a free selector, will be, in name … a leaseholder; he will have to pay a certain portion of the rent for a certain time, and after the expiration of a certain number of years he will have perpetually to pay a small rent to the Crown. Practically it is a freehold … but actually [the holder] will be called a leaseholder, although the amount of rent which he will have to pay will be comparatively nominal. We know that in the old days in England, people always had to pay for many years, and under a great many old grants here people had to pay a certain sum.[48]

Despite the effort to show that clause 15 created nothing more than a statutory fee simple, it was not long before members of both Houses, including Carruthers and Simpson, slipped into the habit of calling it a perpetual lease. Unsurprisingly, in addition to the Opposition's outright hostility,[49] all members who spoke during debate of the Bill expressed uncertainty about the meaning of perpetual incidents coupled with a fee simple.[50] Thus, with little discussion, an amendment proposed in the Upper House omitted the words 'in fee-simple',[51] so that it read: 'the Governor shall issue a grant of the homestead selection … to an applicant'. The Bill, with the amended clause 15 now renumbered section 17, received Royal Assent on 3 May 1895, coming into force as the Crown Lands Act 1895 (NSW).[52]

There is no doubt, of course, that the perpetual lease ensured Crown control over the demised lands in a way not possible under a fee simple;[53] conditions imposed on a lessee related to residence, fencing, payment for existing improvements, conversion to other forms of tenure, and restrictions on transfer.[54] While Crown control of these lands ensured ongoing revenue and the productive capacity and economic value of land, and prevented absentee owners possessing undeveloped lands,[55] any hope that section 17 as enacted would avoid litigation over its meaning was misplaced. Scholarly opinion was, at best, divided, one commentator writing 'it appears the clearly expressed legislative intention, that perpetual lease grants confer a leasehold title',[56] and another that the '"lease in perpetuity," which cryptic expression, so far as it has any meaning, appears to connote a sort of bastard freehold, subject to a perpetual rent'.[57] And while

[48] ibid Legislative Council, 29 November 1894, 2862–63 (GB Simpson).

[49] ibid 4 December 1894, 2967–68 (HE Kater); 5 December 1894, 3035 (HC Dangar); 13 March 1895, 4368 (E Webb).

[50] ibid Legislative Assembly, 26 September 1894, 774 (J Ashton), 781 (EW O'Sullivan), 796 (H Copeland); 27 September 1894, 831 (T Waddell); 4 October 1894, 1040 (CA Lee), 1064 (J Abbott), 1074 (WP Crick), 1095–96 (RA Price), 1104 (J Haynes); 23 October 1894, 1572–73 (J Hayes); 25 October 1894, 1689–90 (ED Millen, J Carruthers, RA Price), 1690–91 (J Carruthers, RA Price), 1700 (D Storey), 1703 (H Copeland); Legislative Council, 13 March 1895, 4371 (HC Dangar).

[51] ibid Legislative Council, 13 March 1895, 4370–71 (HC Dangar).

[52] ibid 3 May 1895, 5897.

[53] *Wilson v Anderson* (2002) 213 CLR 401, 481 (Callinan J).

[54] AD Hargreaves and BA Helmore, *An Introduction to the Principles of Land Law (New South Wales)* (Sydney, The Law Book Co, 1963) 92–93.

[55] Fry (n 8) 165.

[56] Lang (n 11) [409].

[57] H Wheeler, 'The Method of Registering Statutory Titles to Land in New South Wales' (1935) 8 *The Australian Law Journal* 366, 367.

judges might have been certain about the effect of section 17 when called upon to interpret it, that did nothing to prevent litigation.[58]

The High Court issued its first pronouncement in 1915, in *Fisher v Deputy Federal Commissioner of Land Tax*, which found a perpetual lease to be 'in its nature inherently distinct from a fee simple'.[59] In 1939, the New South Wales Supreme Court, in *Nolan v Willimbong Shire Council*, wrote that 'on the question whether titles conferred by the Perpetual Lease Grants are fees simple, I feel considerable doubt; but I am inclined to the view that they are not';[60] in 1949, the same Court came to the same conclusion in *Re Hawkins*,[61] which the High Court affirmed on appeal.[62] And between 1960–2002, the High Court dealt with the matter in three separate cases: in 1960, *Walsh v Minister for Lands* affirmed *Re Hawkins*;[63] in 1996, *Wik Peoples v Queensland* stressed that a lessee's rights and obligations must be determined by reference to the applicable statutory provisions;[64] and, in 2002, in *Wilson v Anderson*, the Court wrote that 'the incidents of a statutory lease are not exhaustively defined by statute, and may include the incidents of a lease as provided by the common law'.[65] Far from preventing litigation, section 17 of the 1895 Act seemed only to encourage it.

III. Inspiration

On the surface, the fundamental components of the perpetual lease seem to bear a strong resemblance to *emphyteusis*. Of course, a resemblance, even a strong one, is not proof of causality. Rather, as Sir William Holdsworth once said of trusts:

> [T]he existence of an analogy is one thing: the proof that the later in date of these two analogous things is derived from the earlier is quite another. Everyone is now agreed that these institutions of Roman law are merely analogies of a superficial kind; and that, though some of them may have had some slight influence on the development … we must look elsewhere for its origin.[66]

Is it possible, then, that in the case of the perpetual lease there is more than mere resemblance? The legislative debates during passage of the 1894 Bill offer little guidance. While one member of the Legislative Council suggested that 'I know of no British colony where the Crown parts with its land on a perpetual lease',[67] it seems likely that such a tenure did already exist in South Australia[68] and in New Zealand.[69] But that only takes the story one step back from New South Wales.

[58] Hargreaves and Helmore (n 54) 91–92.
[59] *Fisher v Deputy Federal Commissioner of Land Tax* (1915) 20 CLR 242, 248 (Isaacs and Gavan Duffy JJ).
[60] *Nolan v Willimbong Shire Council* (1939) 14 LGR (NSW) 89, 90 (Roper J).
[61] *Re Hawkins* (1949) 49 SR 117, 123 (Jordan CJ).
[62] *Hawkins v Minister for Lands* (1949) 78 CLR 479, 485, 487–88 (Latham CJ), 492 (Dixon J), 496 (McTiernan J).
[63] *Walsh v Minister for Lands* (1960) 103 CLR 240, 248 (Dixon CJ, McTiernan, Fullagar and Menzies JJ).
[64] *Wik Peoples v Queensland* (1996) 187 CLR 1, 115 (Toohey J).
[65] *Wilson v Anderson* (2002) 213 CLR 401, 421 (Gleeson CJ).
[66] WS Holdsworth, *An Historical Introduction to the Land Law* (Oxford, Clarendon Press, 1927) 141.
[67] New South Wales, *Parliamentary Debates*, Legislative Council, 5 December 1894, 3027 (J Hoskins).
[68] Crown Lands Act 1888 (SA) ss 15, 16, 25, 32, 34, 37, 40, 140.
[69] Land Act 1877 Amendment Act, 1882 (NZ), ss 20–22; Land Act 1885 (NZ), ss 3, 30, 70, 89, 113, 130, 163, 167.

Two facts, though, may provide evidence for concluding that Rome provided some, admittedly slight, inspiration. First, colonial legal education included Roman law, and second, Victorians as well as colonial Australians had a general familiarity with Roman history and law. Together, these two sources of background knowledge may constitute what Charles Taylor has called a 'social imaginary':

> [T]he ways in which [people] imagine their social existence, how they fit together with others, how things go on between them and their fellows, the expectations which are normally met, and the deeper normative notions and images which underlie these expectations.[70]

Specific knowledge of Roman law and a broader general familiarity may have formed part of the colonial legal social imaginary. But even if Rome was not its inspiration, demonstrating the resemblance with *emphyteusis* opens the possibility of using long Roman experience with that tenure as a means of better understanding the perpetual lease.

A. Legal Education

English legal education at Oxford and Cambridge dates to the late Middle Ages, when law – meaning Roman law (Regius Professorships of Civil Law were later established at both universities)[71] – was taught principally to those seeking a career in diplomacy or the ecclesiastical courts. The modern form of legal education is generally accepted to have emerged from the time of Blackstone in the eighteenth century, although Roman law continued to form a core part of the curriculum well beyond that time.[72] Indeed, by the nineteenth century, and well into the twentieth, the law curriculum at Oxford and Cambridge remained the two great statements of law – Justinian's *Institutes* for Roman, and Blackstone's *Commentaries* for English.[73] The 1876 Oxford syllabus provided that Roman Law was 'to be studied in the Institutes of Gaius and Justinian. Candidates are expected to be acquainted with the History of Roman legislation and Roman Judicial Institutions'.[74] Similarly, the 1948 statute for the Honour School of Jurisprudence provided that the examination 'shall always include … such departments of Roman Law … as may be specified from time to time'.[75] The study of Roman law, Buckland and McNair explained, allowed a student to 'examin[e] the independent approach of [England and Rome] and their lawyers to the same facts of human life, sometimes with widely different, sometimes with substantially identical results'.[76]

What of the Australian colonies? John Waugh writes that 'England was the most influential reference-point for Australian lawyers, providing features either to emulate

[70] C Taylor, *A Secular Age* (Cambridge (MA), Harvard University Press, 2007) 171.

[71] FH Lawson, *The Oxford Law School 1850–1965* (Oxford, Clarendon Press, 1968) 1; J McConica (ed), *The History of the University of Oxford: The Collegiate University* (Oxford, Clarendon Press, 1986) 358–61.

[72] PH Birks, 'Roman Law in Twentieth-century Britain' in J Beatson and R Zimmermann (eds), *Jurists Uprooted: German-Speaking Emigré Lawyers in Twentieth Century Britain* (Oxford, Oxford University Press, 2004) 249–68.

[73] Lawson (n 71) 4, 22–23.

[74] ibid 39, 40, 66, 132, 134, 139, 146–47, 149–57.

[75] ibid 36.

[76] Buckland and McNair (n 33) x.

or avoid'.[77] When it came to Roman law, the Australian colonies clearly sought to follow the Oxbridge model.[78] Australia's first law school, established in 1857 at the University of Melbourne, taught Roman Law as a core subject from its inception until at least 1946.[79] As late as 1937 it remained 'the university's preference for history, Roman law and jurisprudence [to be taught]'.[80] The same was true of Australia's second law school, established in 1883 at the University of Adelaide – there, Roman law remained a part of the core curriculum well into the 1970s.[81]

There is no doubt, then, that the colonial legal social imaginary at the time during which the perpetual lease was introduced was based upon both English and Roman law. But more importantly, *emphyteusis* very likely formed an explicit part of that social imaginary. The 1922 Roman Law I examination paper of the Oxford Honour School of Jurisprudence, for instance, contained a question dealing expressly with *locatio conductio* and the contract of *emphyteusis* of municipal land.[82] It can be assumed that similar *foci* existed in Australian colonial law schools, many of the faculty members having been Oxbridge trained. And of the 25 members of the New South Wales Parliament (20 members of the Legislative Assembly and five members of the Legislative Council) who spoke regularly during the debates of the Crown Lands Bill 1894, seven, or one-quarter, were legally trained, either at a law school or by articles of clerkship.[83] Most importantly, the Secretary of Lands, Sir Joseph Carruthers, and the Solicitor-General, Sir George Simpson, were both lawyers, the former educated at the University of Sydney, and the latter having completed articles of clerkship.[84] If *emphyteusis* formed part of the colonial legal social imaginary, it might be assumed that colonial legislators, and certainly the two ministers responsible for the Bill's passage, brought that knowledge to the task of establishing the perpetual lease.

B. Familiarity with Roman History and Law

Some evidence points to a broader familiarity with Roman history among colonial legislators – this, too, may have formed part of the legal social imaginary. During the Second Reading debate of the New Zealand Land Bill 1887, the first colonial legislation to introduce a perpetual lease, James Menzies, Legislative Councillor (and not a lawyer),[85] said, in relation to water rights,[86] that 'in old Roman legislation … water was the property

[77] J Waugh, *First Principles: The Melbourne Law School 1857–2007* (Carlton, Vic., Miegunyah Press, 2007) 4.
[78] ibid 1–3.
[79] ibid 94, 171.
[80] ibid.
[81] J Waugh, *Adelaide Law: A History of the Adelaide Law School* (Adelaide, Australia, Wakefield Press, 2024) 16, 17, 20, 30, 41, 43, 62, 85–6, 90, 98, 108–10, 115, 118, 126, 136, 151–2, 183–86.
[82] Lawson (n 71) 225.
[83] See *Australian Dictionary of Biography* (2023) adb.anu.edu.au; *Obituaries Australia* (2023) oa.anu.edu.au; AW Martin and P Wardle, *Members of the Legislative Assembly of New South Wales 1856–1901: Biographical Notes* (Canberra, Australian National University, 1959).
[84] JM Ward, 'Carruthers, Sir Joseph Hector (1856–1932)' (2023) *Australian Dictionary of Biography*; JM Bennett, 'Simpson, Sir George Bowen (1838–1915)' ibid.
[85] J Hall-Jones, 'Menzies, James Alexander Robertson' (1990) *Dictionary of New Zealand Biography* teara.govt.nz/en/biographies.
[86] New Zealand, *Parliamentary Debates*, Legislative Council, 16 December 1887, 770 (JAR Menzies).

of the State, and its use was given by way of lease, revocable at any time that it could be shown that other interests were injured'.[87] And during the Second Reading debate of the New South Wales Crown Lands Bill 1894, William Chandos Wall (not legally trained), noted a possible Roman connection concerning perpetual incidents of tenure:

> I do not know where [Sir Joseph Carruthers] got his inspiration when he introduced this provision of perpetual residence; but it occurs to me that he must have been reading Gibbon's 'Decline and Fall of the Roman Empire'. I remember that Gibbon depicts the Roman peasants as reduced to such a state, by the importation of cheap grain from Egypt, that it was found necessary to chain them to the plough to compel them to cultivate the soil. That seems to me very much what the hon. member proposes to do under this bill.[88]

Nothing more is said about sources, Roman or otherwise, in either House, during the debate of the Bill. And, of course, neither of these references is evidence in itself that Rome was the inspiration for the perpetual lease. But both statements point to a wider familiarity with Roman history and law.

It seems at least plausible, then, that those who enacted the Crown Lands Act 1895 (NSW), rather than turning directly to Roman law, carried with them a legal social imaginary that included Roman history and law, and that that was operative in their work. Indeed, that was the very point of including Roman law as part of common law legal education: to inform lawyers in their thinking about the common law and in finding novel solutions to new challenges. As David Johnston suggests, lawyers trained in this way can 'learn … from legal history and from [the] methods and approaches of our predecessors';[89] we need not

> trac[e] a direct line from modern rules of law back to Roman ones, but [rather, look for] the recurrence in quite different social and legal contexts of problems which call for similar legal analysis and so for the employment of tools and rules developed in quite different contexts.[90]

Roman analysis and its tools are available for exploitation in any era.[91] That was the basis on which Roman law was included as part of the curriculum of colonial legal education – we can therefore assume that colonial legislators would have at the very least been influenced by it. Legislators influenced by education that included *emphyteusis* would have been aware that a perpetual lease would allow a degree of state (Crown) control over the land not afforded by the fee simple, and that such control could be ensured in perpetuity by grant of a perpetual term.

IV. Conclusion

The statutory perpetual lease may not be a direct descendant of *emphyteusis*; rather, it may be the inadvertent return of an ancient rule through the colonial legal social

[87] ibid.
[88] New South Wales, *Parliamentary Debates*, Legislative Assembly, 19 September 1894, 587 (WC Wall).
[89] D Johnston, 'Renewal of the Old' (1997) 56(1) *Cambridge Law Journal* 80, 81 (citation omitted).
[90] ibid 89–90 (citation omitted).
[91] ibid 95.

imaginary.[92] But even that conclusion is significant, for the close similarities between the two can prompt us to look to our ancient forebears as a means of better understanding what the pastoral lease achieved. Two lessons follow.

First, *emphyteusis* might have resolved a century of scholarly and judicial perplexity about the nature of the perpetual lease. Close to a century ago, Buckland and McNair concluded that the status of the *emphyteuta* was that of an owner akin to what we understand as a freeholder.[93] This is unsurprising. As Johnston notes, Roman law plays a 'clarifying function [because] it provides a structure, a taxonomy of rights and the ways in which they arise, a guiding framework to cling to when rights, wrongs and remedies all seem deeply obscure'.[94] The Roman *emphyteuta*, therefore, provides clarity concerning the closely analogous perpetual tenant that the legislation itself failed to provide: as the holder of state land, the perpetual lessee, like the *emphyteuta*, enjoys rights *in rem*, perhaps tantamount to, if not in fact, ownership.

Second, and perhaps more importantly, the perpetual lease played a part in the survival of something entirely unknown not only to the Romans, but also to colonial legislators: Aboriginal and Torres Strait Islander native title to land. It would be another 100 years before the High Court recognised that the British acquisition of sovereignty failed to extinguish native title (only the grant of fee simple could have that effect).[95] And it would take another four years for the High Court to find that unlike the fee simple, a statutory lease, including a perpetual lease, did not as a matter of law extinguish native title; rather, any extinguishing effect could be assessed only through a comparison of the incidents of native title and a competing statutory tenure – if the two could co-exist, native title was left intact.[96] The statutory perpetual lease, new to Australia, but long-known to the Romans, very likely allowed native title to survive extinguishment. Regrettably, what colonial legislators did not do, their modern counterparts did: in 1998, responding to the High Court's decision, the Commonwealth Liberal government amended the Native Title Act 1993 (Cth) to provide that all statutory tenures had the automatic effect, from their creation, of extinguishing native title.[97]

The colonial statutory perpetual lease – the return of an ancient rule in modern guise – left untouched the underlying native title on those vast tracts of land held by the squattocracy. One might wonder what the perpetual lease might still make possible if seen through the lens of *emphyteusis*. How, as Johnston has put it, might the old yet become new again; how might Rome yet still be found in the Antipodes?

[92] ibid 82–85.
[93] Buckland and McNair (n 33) 83.
[94] Johnston (n 89) 90.
[95] *Mabo v Queensland [No 2]* (1992) 175 CLR 1.
[96] *Wik Peoples v Queensland* (1996) 187 CLR 1.
[97] Native Title Act 1993 (Cth) pt 15; sch 1.

16

Specific Performance and the Indian Contract Act: History, Theory and Politics

STELIOS TOFARIS

> It is the province ... of Substantive Law to define the rights and liabilities of parties arising out of their contracts, and in so doing to specify what contracts may and what shall not be specifically enforced ... The proper province of procedure is to point out the mode by which effect is to be given to rights already defined, and not itself to define those rights.[1]

> [T]he Law of Specific Performance .... [is] *cognate to* Procedure rather than to Substantive Law ... the right to Specific Performance [is] a right arising out of the actual or threatened violation of the rights created by contract – ... a 'right of action,' which as Austin says ... 'cannot be completely distinguished from the action of procedure which enforces it' ... I do not think it could be very incorrectly described as being, not a primary right, but a mere limitation of a primary right, arising out of the necessary or artificial imperfections of Procedure.[2]

Where does specific performance conceptually belong – as part of substantive law or procedure? This is a question fit for scholarly debate. One might be forgiven for thinking that the statements above originate in academic writing on legal taxonomy or the law of remedies. They are not. Both feature in the debate on the enactment of the Indian Contract Act in the late 1860s. The underlying question is important: for lawyers, taxonomy matters. In legislative law-making, however, politics matter too. What might appear as an abstract legal question can have far-reaching social, economic, and political consequences.

One of the lessons that David's work teaches us is not to take legal phenomena at face value, but to inquire what lies behind them, how and why they developed; in short, to question them as a way of understanding them more fully. Another lesson is to engage

[1] 'Fourth Report of Indian Law Commissioners, 18 December 1867', Parliamentary Papers (PP), House of Commons (HC), vol XLIX (1867–68) 702.

[2] 'Minute of 9 April 1868' in *Minutes by the Honourable Sir HS Maine (1862–69): With a Note on Indian Codification* (Calcutta, Government of India, 1889) 139, British Library (BL) IOR/V/27/100/3.

in the historical exploration that this might entail with an open mind which accepts the capriciousness of legal change[3] and that dots can be joined in different ways.[4]

The present chapter revisits an episode in the making of the Indian Contract Act 1872 with those lessons in mind.[5] It first aims to describe how and why a disagreement arose between the Indian law commissioners and Henry Maine, the law member of the Indian government, over the classification and scope of specific performance. In doing so, it shows how questions of legal theory and colonial policy were closely intertwined. While the disagreement over specific performance was not the only one, it was central, and significantly the first. It set in motion a process of conflict that escalated into a constitutional crisis and threatened to derail the project of codification. The second aim is to explore through this episode the nature of legislative law-making; in particular, to illustrate how it can be appropriately seen as a complex interplay of factors which are 'internal' and 'external' to the law.[6]

I. The Codification of Contract Law

Anglo-Indian codification as a centralised policy of colonial law-making originated in the 1830s, following widespread dissatisfaction among colonial officials with the existing legal order.[7] The Government of India Act 1833 provided for the creation of a uniform body of codified law for the whole of India.[8] The first concrete result was a draft Penal Code prepared in 1837 by Thomas Macaulay. This, however, was not enacted until 1860, around the same time as the Codes of Civil and Criminal Procedure.[9] By that time, the framework of prospective Anglo-Indian codification had become established.[10] The codes were to be as far as possible universal, based on English law, but adapted to suit local conditions.[11]

The codification of contract law was born out of the need to address the fragmentary and complex state of contract law in mid-nineteenth century India.[12] The law

[3] DJ Ibbetson, 'Comparative Legal History: A Methodology' in A Musson and C Stebbings (eds), *Making Legal History* (Cambridge, Cambridge University Press, 2012) 131–45; DJ Ibbetson, 'The Challenges of Comparative Legal History' (2013) 1 *Comparative Legal History* 1.

[4] DJ Ibbetson, 'What is Legal History a History of?' in A Lewis and M Lobban (eds), *Law and History* (Oxford, Oxford University Press, 2004) 33–40; DJ Ibbetson, 'Milsom's Legal History' (2017) 76 *CLJ* 360.

[5] The chapter is based on a PhD thesis undertaken under David's supervision: S Tofaris, *A Historical Study of the Indian Contract Act 1872* (PhD thesis, University of Cambridge, 2011).

[6] For these terms, see eg RW Gordon, 'Introduction: J Willard Hurst and the Common Law Tradition in American Legal Historiography' (1975) 10 *Law and Society Review* 9; DJ Ibbetson, 'Historical Research in Law' in P Cane and M Tushnet (eds), *The Oxford Handbook of Legal Studies* (Oxford, Oxford University Press, 2003) 863–79.

[7] See eg 'Appendix to the Report from the Select Committee on the Affairs of the East India Company', PP, HC, vol VI (1831) 465. Anglo-Indian codification was at core undemocratic and imperialistic: see eg N Hussain, *The Jurisprudence of Emergency* (Ann Arbor, University of Michigan Press, 2003); E Kolsky, 'Codification and the Rule of Colonial Difference: Criminal Procedure in British India' (2005) 23 *LHR* 631.

[8] 3 & 4 Wil IV, c 85, s 53.

[9] These were based on drafts by the second Indian law commission. Some of its members, including its chair, Sir John Romilly, also served in the third law commission which drafted the contract code.

[10] MP Jain, *Outlines of Indian Legal and Constitutional History*, 6th edn (New Delhi, LexisNexis Butterworths, 2009) 417–89; GC Rankin, *Background to Indian Law* (Cambridge, Cambridge University Press, 1946) 22–160.

[11] 'Second Report of Commissioners, 13 December 1855', PP, HC, vol XXV (1856) 206.

[12] Tofaris (n 5) ch 2.

administered by the colonial courts was diversified on regional and religious grounds. The courts in the presidency towns of Calcutta, Bombay and Madras had to administer English, Hindu, and Muslim laws of contract. As a matter of fact, in most cases the courts applied English rules,[13] although there were several examples where native law was used. The courts in the *mofussil* (the Indian countryside) were directed to resolve contract disputes according to 'justice, equity and good conscience'. By the 1860s, the formula was employed by the higher appellate courts to import English rules,[14] although at lower level most decisions were guided by common sense. The result was a complicated body of law which generated uncertainty in a subject that afforded 'the most frequent occasion for litigation in all parts of [India]'.[15] This was perceived as impeding trade,[16] at a time when growing numbers of European capitalists were coming to India, and improved means of transportation were shortening distances across India, and between India and the rest of the British Empire. Against this background, the case for a standardised contract code was increasingly viewed by colonial administrators and the mercantile community as overwhelming.[17]

The role of translating theory into practice fell to the law commission in London and the Indian government in Calcutta. Established in December 1861, the third Indian law commission consisted of some of the most eminent English lawyers of the time: Sir John Romilly, Master of the Rolls, as chair, Sir William Erle, Sir Edward Ryan, Robert Lowe, Sir James Willes, and John Macpherson Macleod.[18] The commission submitted a draft code of contract law in July 1866.[19] The draft came at a time when English jurists and judges were reworking the rules on contract law, previously fragmented across the forms of actions, into a conceptually uniform body on the basis of general principles.[20] The commission's draft was part of these efforts. Working outside the confines of common law and equity, the commissioners were able to analyse doctrinal threads from across the two systems within a common theoretical framework to formulate a single law of contract. Most of the rules were taken from English law, but the underlying analytical framework bore the influence of a treatise on contract law by William Macpherson, the secretary of the law commission, and through him of the French Civil Code and Pothier.[21]

[13] 'Letter from L Peel CJ to H Hardinge, July 1845', PP, HC, vol XVI (1864) 434; 'Evidence by D Hill, 10 March 1853', PP, HC, vol XXXI (1852–53) 209.

[14] 'Statement of Objects and Reasons, 9 July 1867', PP, HC, vol XLIX (1867–68) 686; *Dada Honaji v Babaji Jagushet* (1865) 2 BHCR 36, 38 (Bombay High Court).

[15] 'Second Report of Indian Law Commissioners, 28 July 1866', PP, HC, vol XLIX (1867–68) 603.

[16] 'Meeting of 9 April 1872', Abstracts of the Proceedings of the Council of the Governor-General of India, Assembled for the Purpose of Making Laws and Regulations, vol IX (1872) 342, BL IOR/V/9/12.

[17] 'Meeting of 6 December 1867', Abstracts of the Proceedings of the Council of the Governor-General of India, Assembled for the Purpose of Making Laws and Regulations, vol VI (1867) 378, BL IOR/V/9/9–11.

[18] Erle and Willes were replaced by WM James, J Henderson, and when the last died, Robert Lush.

[19] 'Second Report of Indian Law Commissioners' (n 15) 603.

[20] This occurred under the influence of Civilian sources: DJ Ibbetson, *A Historical Introduction to the Law of Obligations* (Oxford, Oxford University Press, 1999) 220–44; AWB Simpson, 'Innovation in Nineteenth Century Contract Law' (1975) 91 *LQR* 247.

[21] W Macpherson, *Outlines of the Law of Contracts as Administered in the Courts of British India* (London, RC Lepage, 1860) borrowed heavily from *The Code Napoleon; or, The French Civil Code* (London, Hunter, 1824) and Pothier's work (*A Treatise on the Law of Obligations, or Contracts, by M. Pothier* (trans WD Evans) (London, Butterworth, 1806)). For the view that Macpherson was the draftsman of the commission's draft code, see W Stokes, *The Anglo-Indian Codes* (Oxford, Clarendon Press, 1887) xxviii.

According to the institutional framework in place, the law commission's draft was to be cast in the form of a Bill by the legislative department in India under the law member of the government. It was then introduced to the legislative council, circulated for opinion to the local governments, discussed in a select committee, and then brought back to the legislative council for a decision. The Secretary of State for India had power to disallow it.[22]

The early steps in the codification of contract law gave the impression that a smooth legislative process lay ahead. Maine gave the commission's draft the stamp of approval, preparing a Bill in July 1867 that reproduced the commission's draft in its entirety minus sections 51–59, which dealt with the specific performance of contracts. In the 'Statement of Objects and Reasons' that was to accompany the Contract Bill's introduction to the legislative council, Maine suggested that the Bill's adoption would give India 'a body of contract law which leaves nothing to be desired, in point of simplicity and comprehensiveness, in respect of the essential equity of its provisions, and in respect of the perspicuity with which those provisions are set forth'.[23] At first glance, the omission of the relevant sections looked inoffensive, a minor difference of legal opinion. It was not.

II. Theory: The Classification of Specific Performance

The first ground of disagreement over specific performance concerned its classification. 'Between law and procedure', Maine wrote, there is 'a debateable land'.[24] Maine was in no doubt on which side of the boundary specific performance lay. He asserted that civil remedies applicable in contractual disputes belonged in a code of procedure and not of substantive law.[25] The relevant sections were therefore omitted from the Bill partly because they were 'out of place'.[26]

Maine's criticism prompted an official reply from the law commissioners.[27] They affirmed that the proper place for the rules on specific performance was in a code of substantive law. This was because 'it is the province of the Code of Substantive Law to define the rights and liabilities of parties arising out of their contracts, and in so doing to specify what contracts may and what shall not be specifically enforced;'[28] in contrast, the province of procedure is 'to point out the mode by which effect is to be given to

[22] JF Stephen, 'Legislation under Lord Mayo' in WW Hunter, *Life of Earl Mayo*, 2nd edn (London, Smith, Elder & Co, 1876), vol II, 144–52; AC Banerjee, *English Law in India* (New Delhi, Abhinav Publications, 1984) 139–59.

[23] 'Statement of Objects and Reasons' (n 14) 689.

[24] 'Minute of 14 August 1867' in *Minutes* (n 2) 134. The term 'debatable land' was coined to describe territory between the kingdoms of England and Scotland whose possession was disputed in medieval times.

[25] 'Statement of Objects and Reasons' (n 14) 689.

[26] 'Note by Maine, 26 July 1867', PP, HC, vol XLIX (1867–68) 696. Maine also believed that the sections should be introduced after the new contract code operated for some time, thereby remedying any confusion about the contract rules that existed in the *mofussil* courts ('Statement of Objects and Reasons' (n 14) 689). On the contemporary state of the law, see 'The Specific Performance of Contract' *Calcutta Review*, vol LII (1866) 301. (The author was CD Field: 'Note by CD Field, 14 January 1868', BL IOR/L/PJ/5/15).

[27] 'Fourth Report of Indian Law Commissioners' (n 1) 701.

[28] ibid 702.

rights already defined, and not itself to define those rights'.[29] The law commissioners cited Field's New York Civil Code,[30] Justice Story's treatise on equity jurisprudence[31] and John Austin's work[32] to support their view.[33]

The disagreement divulged into the finer points of abstract legal thinking with Maine's response.[34] Maine's principal riposte was that the law commissioners misunderstood Austin's thesis and were therefore wrong to quote Austin against him.[35] Maine noted that the distinction between rights and the methods of enforcing them originated with Bentham, who used it to arrange the law into substantive and adjective (procedural).[36] However, Austin, who was 'the only writer on Jurisprudence whose opinion outweighed Bentham's in the few instances in which they differed',[37] shared Maine's opinion that it was impossible to establish a complete distinction between substantive and procedural law or to make it the basis of strict classification. Maine explained that Austin drew a different distinction, one between: (a) rights which do not arise from injuries or wrongs, and (b) rights which arise from injuries or wrongs. According to Maine, a code corresponding to (a) would largely resemble a code of substantive law and a code corresponding to (b), in which Austin would have included procedure, would not widely differ from a code of civil procedure.[38] Maine then asked: 'Now, in which Code … would Austin have placed the Specific Performance of Contracts? His language

[29] ibid 702. Robert Lush, one of the law commissioners, subsequently judicially discussed the distinction between procedural and substantive law along similar lines: *Poyser v Minors* (1881) 7 QBD 329, 333.

[30] *The Civil Code of the State of New York* (Albany, Weed, Parsons & Co 1865), ss 1887–1898. Originally drafted by Dudley Field in 1862, it was never enacted in New York, although versions of it were adopted in other US jurisdictions. An earlier code of civil procedure, also drafted by Field, was enacted in New York in 1848 (see eg SN Subrin, 'David Dudley Field and the Field Code: A Historical Analysis of an Earlier Procedural Vision' (1988) 6 *LHR* 311). What is important for present purposes is that Field placed specific performance in the civil code and not the code of civil procedure.

[31] J Story, *Commentaries on Equity Jurisprudence as Administered in England and America* (Boston, Hilliard, Gray & Company, 1836). The treatise ran into many editions, including the 8th edition in 1861 and the 9th in 1866.

[32] On Austin, see below. The position in Continental law, not explicitly cited in the debate, was not uniform. French law treated specific performance as a matter of substantive law, while Austrian and Prussian laws dealt with it under procedural law: H Dondorp, 'Specific Performance: A Historical Perspective' in J Smits et al (eds), *Specific Performance in Contract Law: National and Other Perspectives* (Antwerp, Intersentia, 2008) 280.

[33] The distinction between substantive and procedural law had been accepted in reports of earlier Indian law commissions (see eg Jain (n 10) 428–47). The Code of Civil Procedure 1859 included rules on when specific performance may be decreed (s 192). Although the code was based on a draft by the second law commission, it was revised in India under Sir Barnes Peacock (W Stokes, *The Anglo-Indian Codes* (Oxford, Clarendon Press, 1888), vol II, 384–85). The relevant provisions originated during the revision. The commission's draft referred only to how the decree was enforced, not when it could be granted: 'First Report of Commissioners', PP, HC, vol XXV (1856) 58 (clause CLIII).

[34] 'Minute of 9 April 1868' in *Minutes* (n 2) 136–42.

[35] Maine was less concerned about the position in English treatises, having decried their 'confused arrangement' ('Minute of 14 August 1867' in *Minutes* (n 2) 135).

[36] See eg *Principles of Judicial Procedure* in J Bowring (ed), *The Works of Jeremy Bentham* (Edinburgh, William Tait, 1843), vol II, 5–6; *Introductory View of the Rationale of Evidence* in Bowring, *Works*, vol VI, 7.

[37] 'Minute of 9 April 1868' in *Minutes* (n 2) 138. Maine described Austin as 'an authority to whom all who have bestowed the least thought on this class of enquiries will bow' (ibid 140). Maine's general approach to jurisprudence, based on historical and comparative methodology, was at odds with Bentham's and Austin's analytical jurisprudence (P Schofield, 'Jeremy Bentham and Nineteenth-Century English Jurisprudence' (1991) 12 *JLH* 58). Yet on codification, all three broadly belonged in the same camp (Tofaris (n 5) 182–87). See further, WE Rumble, *Doing Austin Justice* (London, Continuum, 2005) 132–77.

[38] ibid 138.

appears to me not to leave room for a doubt … He describes the right to compel Specific Performance as a "right arising from a civil delict which is an infringement of a right *in personam*." He would therefore have placed it in [the Code] in which he would also have placed mere procedure'.[39]

It is tempting to ask who was right. How would Austin classify specific performance? And, going a step further, where does specific performance truly belong? Interesting as these questions are, they are of secondary importance here. The chapter is not concerned with the correct taxonomical answer, but with why Maine and the law commissioners engaged in an in-depth debate about it; in other words, with what the debate itself can tell us about the process of legislative law-making. Yet in another sense, exploring the taxonomical questions can be informative of the range of answers that are available, their foundations and their wider significance.

Austin's answer was equivocal. This is no surprise: a key insight of Austin's analysis was to problematise the distinction between substantive and procedural law itself.[40] Austin distinguished between primary rights and duties which arise from events which do not involve a wrong, and secondary or sanctioning rights and duties which arise from the violation of primary rights and duties, ie, from events which involve a wrong.[41] At first glance, Austin's classification appears to resemble Bentham's. As Austin wrote, 'if I adopted the language of Mr. Bentham … I should style the law of primary rights and duties, *substantive law*; and the law of sanctioning or secondary rights and duties, *adjective* or *instrumental law*. In other words, I should divide the … bulk of the legal system, into law conversant about rights and duties which are *not* means or instruments for rendering others available; and law conversant about rights and duties which are merely means or instruments for rendering others available'.[42] In fact, Austin's scheme was a rejection of Bentham's. For Austin, secondary rights and duties were means or instruments for making the primary rights and duties available, but many primary rights and duties were of the same nature.[43]

Austin's classificatory concerns went beyond misgivings about substantive and procedural law. Austin believed that there was no logical distinction between primary and secondary rights and duties. In his view, 'a primary right or duty is not of itself a right or duty, without the secondary right or duty by which it is sustained; and *e converso*'.[44] The distinction was based on convenience rather than analytical truth. If one had to attach to the description of every primary right and duty a description of the rights and duties arising from its breach, the acts which constitute its violations, and the procedure by which it was enforced, there would be 'endless repetition'.[45]

Austin's conception of secondary rights and duties included remedies but also procedure.[46] This related to the way secondary rights and duties were enforced. In his

[39] ibid 139.

[40] See further, M Lobban, *The Common Law and English Jurisprudence 1760–1850* (Oxford, Clarendon Press, 1991), 239–41.

[41] J Austin, *Lectures on Jurisprudence* (London, John Murray, 1863), vol II, 451, 453–54.

[42] ibid 451–52.

[43] ibid 452–53.

[44] ibid 457.

[45] ibid 462.

[46] ibid 454.

view, it was 'impossible to distinguish completely a *right of action* from the action or procedure which enforces it'.[47] Bentham was guilty of 'double inconsistency' in calling rules of procedure instrumental and limiting the epithet to them.[48] For Austin, everything connected. Although it was appropriate for analytical convenience to separate primary and secondary rights from violations, and each from procedure, 'all these parts ought to be considered as *members of one whole*, and bear a common name: whereas the plural "Codes," would seem to oppose them'.[49]

Austin's discussion of specific performance was based on rational principles.[50] He divided rights arising from civil delicts that were infringements of rights *in personam* into: (i) rights of compelling the specific performance of such obligations as arose from contracts (and quasi-contracts); (ii) rights of obtaining satisfaction in lieu of specific performance; (iii) rights of obtaining partly specific performance and partly satisfaction.[51] He then explained, under a separate heading, that 'having classed and described civil injuries, and treated of the rights and duties which civil injuries engender, I shall consider the *modes* wherein those rights are exercised, and wherein those duties are enforced. In other words, I shall consider *civil procedure*'.[52] That was principally concerned with 'the pursuit of rights of *action*' and involved consideration of topics such as pleading, evidence, decrees, appeals and execution of judgments.

Austin's distinction between secondary rights and civil procedure was a concession to the need for convenience of exposition and not an abandonment of his reservations about the distinction's validity. That he drew it, however, suggests that the distinction, with its caveats and imperfections, was one that Austin might have been willing to accept given that 'the arrangement of a *corpus juris*' could not be 'constructed with logical rigour'.[53] Maine was right to state that Austin opposed a strict division between substantive and procedural law. He was also right to note that Austin included aspects of procedure within secondary rights. Nonetheless, he was wrong to assume from these that, had Austin faced a choice as a matter of practical reality between the codes of substantive and procedural law, he would have definitely placed specific performance in the latter. Austin's language leaves plenty of room for a doubt.

Beyond Austin, the question of whether specific performance belongs in substantive or procedural law cuts across several scholarly inquiries, many of which rely on his scheme. First, the theoretical nature of specific performance has been scrutinised by contract scholars. According to a common view, specific performance operates at the primary level.[54] The starting point is that performance is inherent in the contractual

[47] ibid 455.

[48] ibid 454.

[49] ibid 463.

[50] J Austin, *The Province of Jurisprudence Determined*, 2nd edn (London, John Murray, 1861) cii. In contrast, the 'caprices of English law' were to be explained 'historically' (ibid cii). The book, first published in 1832, was also included in volume I of *Lectures on Jurisprudence*.

[51] ibid ci–cii.

[52] ibid cii.

[53] ibid ciii. Maine thought this passage might count against him 'if Austin had written nothing more. But it is only part of a syllabus of lectures' ('Minute of 9 April 1868' in *Minutes* (n 2) 139).

[54] In *Photo Production Ltd v Securicor Transport* Ltd [1980] AC 827, 848, and *Sudbrook Trading Estate Ltd v Eggleton* [1983] 1 AC 444, 478, Lord Diplock analysed specific performance as a remedy for the enforcement of primary obligations. See further, B Dickson, 'The Contribution of Lord Diplock to the General Law

right. An order of specific performance gives direct effect to the primary contractual right and, unlike an award of damages, is not based on a breach of contract.[55] Secondly, the classification of specific performance has featured in writings on remedies.[56] These have produced no uniform answer on the taxonomy of remedies or the place of specific performance within it. For some authors, the law of remedies falls somewhere between substance and procedure,[57] but that of course depends on what one understands by those terms. That has provided a third area of scholarly analysis.[58] Substance and procedure are contested labels whose dividing line has been variously drawn in different contexts. For example, the identification of remedies (including specific performance) with procedural law, influentially adopted by Dicey in private international law,[59] was jurisprudentially rebuked by Salmond.[60] All of this suggests that the taxonomical question addressed by Maine and the law commissioners admits no definite, and definitely no easy, answer. It cautions against the reification of taxonomical schemes and indicates the importance of appreciating their purpose and practical limits.[61]

Why then did Maine and the law commissioners found it necessary to engage in such a theoretical discussion? This did not appeal to everyone. Other members of the legislative council viewed the correct classification of specific performance as a technicality, 'a point of minor moment'[62] that 'ought not to have much weight'.[63] Maine was apologetic that he had to prolong the jurisprudential discussion,[64] but not enough to refrain from doing so. For him, the question was not merely one of classification, but

of Contract' (1989) 9 *OJLS* 441; D Foxton, 'How Useful is Lord Diplock's Distinction Between Primary and Secondary Obligations in Contract?' (2019) 135 *LQR* 249.

[55] See eg C Webb, 'Performance and Compensation: An Analysis of Contract Damages and Contractual Obligation' (2006) 26 *OJLS* 41; R Stevens, '*Damages and the Rights to Performance*: A Golden Victory *or Not?*' in JW Neyers, R Bronaugh and SGA Pitel (eds), *Exploring Contract Law* (London, Hart Publishing, 2009) 171–98.

[56] See eg DM Walker, *The Law of Civil Remedies in Scotland* (Edinburgh, W Green, 1974); FH Lawson, *Remedies of English Law*, 2nd edn (London, Butterworths, 1980); MJ Tilbury, *Civil Remedies* (Sydney, Butterworths, 1990). For more theoretical work, see R Zakrzewski, *Remedies Reclassified* (Oxford, Oxford University Press, 2005); SA Smith, *Rights, Wrongs, and Injustices: The Structure of Remedial Law* (Oxford, Oxford University Press, 2019). For general discussion, see R Halson and D Campbell (eds), *Research Handbook on Remedies in Private Law* (Cheltenham, Edward Elgar, 2019).

[57] See eg D Laycock, *Modern American Remedies: Cases and Materials* (Boston, Little, Brown and Company, 1985), 1; Lawson (n 56) 10.

[58] See eg A Kocourek, 'Substance and Procedure' (1941) 10 *Fordham LR* 157; DM Risinger, 'Substance and Procedure Revisited with Some Afterthoughts on the Constitutional Problems of Irrebuttable Presumptions' (1982) 30 *UCLA LR* 189; TO Main, 'The Procedural Foundation of Substantive Law' (2010) 87 *Washington University LR* 801.

[59] AV Dicey, *A Digest of the Law of England with Reference to the Conflict of Laws* (London, Stevens and Sons, 1896), 711–14. In private international law, the question continues to attract judicial and scholarly interest and has a dispositive effect: eg *Harding v Wealands* [2007] 2 AC 1; R Garnett, *Substance and Procedure in Private International Law* (Oxford, Oxford University Press, 2012).

[60] JW Salmond, *Jurisprudence*, 4th edn (London, Stevens and Haynes, 1913) 437. Salmond placed specific performance within substantive law. In contrast, Pollock took the view that specific performance belonged in a code of civil procedure (F Pollock and DF Mulla, *Indian Contract and Specific Relief Acts*, 4th edn (London, Sweet & Maxwell, 1919) 841).

[61] Salmond (n 60) 439. Birks thought that 'specific performance functions on the primary plane' but 'could, with little enough trouble, be represented as a response to the wrong of breach' (P Birks, 'Rights, Wrongs, and Remedies' (2000) 20 *OJLS* 1, 27).

[62] 'Note by H Durand, 29 July 1867', PP, HC, vol XLIX (1867–68) 699.

[63] 'Note by Governor-General, 25 July 1867', ibid 696.

[64] 'Minute of 9 April 1868' in *Minutes* (n 2) 137, 140.

of re-classification. Rules on specific performance already existed in the Code of Civil Procedure 1859. The law commission's proposal was not to legislate from scratch, but to remove the law from the existing code and transfer it to a new one.[65]

For Maine and the commissioners, the classificatory question was consequential. Today's lawyers are accustomed to viewing taxonomy as important,[66] but this was not always true of common lawyers.[67] Yet since the late eighteenth century, legal writing in the common law evidenced a growing concern for systematic arrangement of the law, especially in contract law.[68] By the mid-nineteenth century, many English lawyers and judges viewed law as a science, whose principles could be expounded in a rational form.[69] Maine was very much part of this group. By the time he went to India in 1862, he had already established himself as a leading Victorian jurist.[70] He had been a Regius Professor of Civil Law at Cambridge, a Reader at the Council of Legal Education and in *Ancient Law* had written the only legal best seller of the nineteenth century.[71] He had also written an essay on 'Roman Law and Legal Education', in which he supported the reorganisation of English law on the basis of sound principles of legal classification.[72] When Governor-General John Lawrence suggested that the classificatory question was technical, Maine replied that 'scientific faults are of great importance in our codes'.[73] For him, this went to the heart of the project.

What's more, Maine had strong views on the precise question that was debated, having previously expressed them 'both as a writer and as a teacher of law'.[74] Like Austin, Maine thought that the boundaries between substance and procedure could be blurred, and historically had been so. He captured this point most famously in later work when he wrote: 'so great is the ascendancy of the Law of Actions in the infancy of Courts of Justice, that substantive law has at first the look of being gradually secreted in the interstices of procedure'.[75]

The law commissioners were also attentive to classificatory questions. Between them, they sat on the bench, but also attended Austin's lectures in London,[76] participated in

[65] ibid 137, 140.

[66] See eg *Attorney General v Blake* [2001] 1 AC 268, 290 (Lord Steyn); E McKendrick, 'Taxonomy: Does it Matter?' in D Johnson and R Zimmermann (eds), *Unjustified Enrichment: Key Issues in Comparative Perspective* (Cambridge, Cambridge University Press, 2002) 627–57.

[67] AWB Simpson, 'The Rise and Fall of the Legal Treatise: Legal Principles and the Forms of Legal Literature' (1981) 48 *University of Chicago LR* 632.

[68] S Waddams, 'Nineteenth-Century Treatises on English Contract Law' in A Fernandez and M Dubber (eds), *Law Books in Action: Essays on the Anglo-American Legal Treatise* (Oxford, Hart Publishing, 2012) 127–44.

[69] See eg RCJ Cocks, *Sir Henry Maine: A Study in Victorian Jurisprudence* (Cambridge, Cambridge University Press, 1988) 14–17.

[70] G Feaver, *From Status to Contract: A Biography of Sir Henry Maine 1822–1888* (London, Longmans, 1969); Cocks (n 69).

[71] AWB Simpson, 'Contract: The Twitching Corpse' (1981) 1 *OJLS* 265, 268. The reference is to HS Maine, *Ancient Law* (London, John Murray, 1861).

[72] Originally published in 1856, it was reprinted in HS Maine, *Village-Communities in the East and West*, 3rd edn (London, John Murray, 1876) 330–86.

[73] 'Note by Maine, 27 July 1867', PP, HC, vol XLIX (1867–68) 698.

[74] Minute of 9 April 1868' in *Minutes* (n 2) 142.

[75] HS Maine, *Dissertations on Early Law and Custom* (London, John Murray, 1883) 389.

[76] See eg as regards Romilly, 'Letter from JS Mill to Sarah Austin, 10 February 1860' in FE Mineka and DN Lindley (eds), *The Collected Works of John Stuart Mill, Vol XV – The Later Letters of JS Mill, 1849–1873, Part II*

various commissions for the reform of English law[77] and tried their hand in treatise-writing. As a group, they were not insular common lawyers, though they were successful members of the legal fraternity. They had both the respect and critical approach of an internal observer but were willing to look more broadly for jurisprudential ideas.[78] They symbolised a growing group of common lawyers in the 1850s and 60s, who saw law as a science and were searching outside the confines of technical ability for underlying principles. Drafting codes involved identifying the underpinning principles from the existing rules and presenting them methodically;[79] as such, it was part of the intellectual enterprise of treating law scientifically.[80] Like Maine, the commissioners were serious when they protested that the rules in the codes should be scientifically devised.[81]

Codification forced Maine and the law commissioners to confront the taxonomical dichotomy between substance and procedure and the place of specific performance within it. The ensuing debate was not gratuitous. For both, classification on scientific principles was an inherent facet of codification. At the same time, Maine and the commissioners were no servants of conceptualism: both understood that the essence of the matter lay elsewhere. Classification was neither intended nor allowed to control reality.

III. Politics: The Reality of Specific Performance

The second ground of disagreement over specific performance concerned its substance. That this was the principal ground was plain to all participants. As Maine declared, 'if there were no question at issue except that of arrangement, it would be easy to give practical effect to the Commissioners' conclusions', but there was a 'question of substance whether their sections constitute a good and fitting law for India'.[82] That question raised complicated issues going to the root of colonial politics. It related to the peculiar circumstances of Indian agriculture and in particular indigo cultivation. The crux of the matter was whether specific performance ought to apply to contracts made between European planters and Indian peasants for the cultivation of specific crops. 'It would be very uncandid', Maine wrote, not to acknowledge that the relevant sections were framed with indigo contracts in mind or the 'grave political difficulty' involved in considering them.[83] The regulation of those contracts had been a thorny subject of colonial

(Toronto, University of Toronto Press, 1972) 674. Erle was a close friend of Austin: J Ross, *Three Generations of English Women* (London, Fisher Unwin, 1893) 201.

[77] For example, Willes took part alongside Maine in the Digest of Law commission, whose ultimate goal was the codification of English law: 'Second Report of the Digest of Law Commission', PP, HC, vol XVIII (1870) 231. Willes encouraged Pollock to approach 'the law of obligations methodically' (F Pollock, *The Law of Torts* (London, Stevens & Sons, 1887) viii).

[78] See further, Tofaris (n 5) ch 5.

[79] C Ilbert, *The Government of India*, 2nd edn (Oxford, Clarendon Press, 1907) 341; Simpson (n 67) 666.

[80] The Duke of Argyll, Secretary of State for India, referred to 'the highly scientific work of drawing up codes of substantive law and procedure' ('Legislative Despatch (no 47), 24 November 1870', PP, HC, vol LVI (1876) 26).

[81] 'Letter from W Macpherson to MEG Duff, 16 January 1869', BL IOR L/PJ/5/428.

[82] 'Minute of 14 August 1867' in *Minutes* (n 2) 135.

[83] 'Minute of 9 April 1868' in *Minutes* (n 2) 140. He described revisiting indigo contracts as an 'irritating political question' ('Remarks by Maine, 26 July 1867', PP, HC, vol XLIX (1867–68) 696).

policymaking for years. The Contract Bill provided a new battleground for fighting old ideological battles.

A. Legal Regulation of Indigo Contracts, 1830–62[84]

In early nineteenth century, indigo was a major Indian export and a prime source of investment for European capitalism. An indigo plantation industry was established in Lower Bengal. Cultivation of indigo was carried out by ryots (Indian peasants) on land belonging to zamindars (Indian landholders) after they entered into contracts with European planters (factory owners) for delivery to the latter's factories. The ryots were given an advance when the contract was made; if the value of the plant subsequently delivered exceeded the advance, the ryot received additional payment. The system, however, was open to abuse. The ryot often accepted an advance out of necessity or was forced to take it by the planter. The factory kept account of the advances and the delivered indigo, but the ryot seldom knew the figures. After a year's cultivation, the ryot typically owed the factory money. The balance mounted until it was deemed unrecoverable. The planter used the debt as an instrument of pressure on the ryot to cultivate indigo. Yet indigo cultivation was unpopular with ryots due to its poor return in comparison with other crops. Ryots often sowed food crops instead of indigo after receiving an advance and planters resorted to violence to force them to grow indigo.[85]

The colonial government tried to regulate indigo contracts via legislation. The first attempt took place in 1830, at a time when it was firmly on the side of the planters and the Calcutta merchant houses who financed them. The starting point was that civil justice was ineffective because the courts could not compel specific performance of the contract but only award damages for its breach, which were worthless given the ryots' finances. Following lobbying from the planters, Governor-General William Bentinck passed Regulation V of 1830, under which ryots who broke indigo contracts were made criminally liable. The Regulation faced scepticism from the Company's Court of Directors and was repealed in 1835 on the ground that it unjustly treated only one of the parties as a criminal for breach of contract. The government considered re-enacting some of the Regulation's provisions in the mid-1850s,[86] but the plan was dropped after criticism by district officials.

In 1859, major disturbances broke out between the ryots and the planters.[87] Having received their advance, many ryots refused to sow indigo. Under pressure from the planters and Governor-General Lord Canning, the Lieutenant-Governor of Bengal,

[84] T Roy, 'Indigo and Law in Colonial India' (2011) 64 *Economic History Review* 60. For details on indigo planting, see B Kling, *The Blue Mutiny: The Indigo Disturbances in Bengal 1859–62* (Philadelphia, University of Pennsylvania Press, 1966); A Rao and B Rao, *The Blue Devil: Indigo and Colonial Bengal* (Delhi, Oxford University Press, 1992); GA Nadri, *The Political Economy of Indigo in India, 1580–1930* (Leiden, Brill, 2016).

[85] 'Report of Indigo Commission', PP, HC, vol XLIV (1861) 357; 'Minute by Lieutenant-Governor of Bengal on the Report of the Indigo Commission, 17 December 1860', PP, HC, vol XLV (1861) 77.

[86] 'Letter from F Beaufort to Commissioner of the Rajshahye Division, 26 October 1854', PP, HC, vol XLIV (1861) 17.

[87] This came shortly after the Indian Rebellion of 1857 when tensions were high.

John Grant, reluctantly agreed to pass legislation making a breach of contract to cultivate indigo criminally punishable. The Bill provided that if a ryot wilfully delayed or omitted to cultivate indigo according to his agreement for which a cash advance was made, the magistrate could make the ryot pay high damages and, in case the ryot failed to do so, imprison him for up to three months.[88] Sir Barnes Peacock, Chief Justice of the Calcutta Supreme Court, introduced amendments to the Bill, including allowing the magistrate to decree specific performance.[89] While the Secretary of State for India, Sir Charles Wood, was 'uneasy' about basing a criminal prosecution on a civil contract,[90] he consented to the Act as it dealt with the emergency of that year and expired after six months.[91] Pursuant to that Act, an enquiry of the whole system was commissioned. The ensuing report condemned the system of advances,[92] having found evidence of abuse by the planters, and opposed any special legislation on indigo contracts, partly because the magistrate's 'bias has been unconsciously towards his countrymen, whom he has asked to his own table, or met in hunting fields'.[93]

Notwithstanding these criticisms, a new Bill 'to provide for the punishment of breaches of contract for the cultivation, production, gathering, provision, manufacture, carriage and delivery of agricultural produce' was prepared in 1861.[94] Unlike its predecessors, this was not limited to indigo contracts but dealt with agricultural contracts in general. The Bill applied to fraudulent breaches of written contracts of no more than a year's duration and a specified value. In essence, it provided that any ryot, labourer or other person, who had received money in advance and had wilfully and without lawful and reasonable excuse neglected or refused to perform his side of the contract, was liable to pay damages or be ordered to perform the contract. If he failed to do so, he could be imprisoned with hard labour for up to three months.[95] Canning threw his weight behind the Bill,[96] but it was withdrawn in the face of strong opposition by Wood.[97] A similar proposal resurfaced in 1862, when a Bill, prepared by the law member William Ritchie, gave civil courts the power to order damages at penal rates where the breach of contract was made in 'bad faith' and, where that was not possible, to imprison with hard labour.[98] The new Bill was shelved after Wood[99] and Maine,[100] by now the law member, spoke against it.

[88] 'Meeting of 24 March 1860', Proceedings of the Legislative Council of India, vol VI (1860) 289–308, BL IOR V/9/3–6.

[89] 'Meeting of 31 March 1860', ibid 328–52. For the final form of the Bill, see PP, HC, vol XLIV (1861) 206.

[90] 'Letter from Wood to Canning, 3 May 1860', BL MSS Eur F 78; R Moore, *Sir Charles Wood's Indian Policy 1853–66* (Manchester, Manchester University Press, 1966) 78.

[91] 'Despatch (No 71), 18 April 1861', PP, HC, vol XLV (1861) 200.

[92] 'Report of Indigo Commission' (n 85) 362 (majority report).

[93] ibid 364.

[94] 'Meeting of 2 March 1861', Proceedings of the Legislative Council of India, vol VII (1861) 84, BL IOR V/9/6–9.

[95] For the Bill, see PP, HC, vol XLV (1861) 190–91.

[96] 'Letter from Canning to Wood, 18 March 1861', BL MSS Eur F 78.

[97] 'Despatch (No 71), 18 April 1861', PP, HC, vol XLV (1861) 199–201.

[98] For the Bill, see PP, HC, vol XL (1862) 4–5.

[99] 'Letter from Wood to Elgin, 10 May 1862', 'Letter from Wood to Maine, 26 January 1863', BL MSS Eur F 78; 'Legislative Despatch (No 16), 9 June 1862', PP, HC, vol XL (1862) 1–4.

[100] 'Speech of 17 December 1862' in G Duff, *Sir Henry Maine: A Brief Memoir of his Life, with some of his Indian Speeches and Minutes, selected and edited by Whitley Stokes* (London, John Murray, 1892) 85–91.

B. Earlier Debate on the Specific Performance of Agricultural Contracts

Maine's concurrence with Wood on Ritchie's Bill masked a discord of views on how to deal with indigo contracts. While they agreed that criminal law should not be used for that purpose, they disagreed on the role of specific performance. Maine believed that Indians had two standards of morality: a fairly high one among themselves, and a low one between themselves and Europeans. He objected to this on two grounds. At a practical level, he felt that the habit of breaking contracts with Europeans, after having received advanced payment, generated lack of certainty in contractual relations, something that seriously impeded the conduct of Anglo-Indian commerce and agriculture.[101] At a theoretical level, he thought that 'one of the most efficient means of moral education – the exact performance of contracts' had to be secured, even 'if exceptional measures had to be resorted to'.[102] Contractual relations based on trust were necessary in a state of 'completest freedom of contract', with which 'all the modern progress of society seemed to be intimately connected' and 'in some way almost mysteriously dependent on it'.[103] Maine viewed the award of damages for breach of contract as 'barbarous' and, in India, 'illusory':[104] 'there is no country in which damages afford practically so imperfect a redress for breach of contract as they do in India, and none in which the prospect of having to pay damages operates so slightly to compel the performance of agreements'.[105] For Maine, neither criminal law nor damages could offer protection against irresponsible contractors.[106] The solution lay in the use of specific performance.

The existing Code of Civil Procedure of 1859 provided in section 192 that 'if it appear that the defendant is able to perform the contract, the Court, with the consent of the plaintiff, may decree the specific performance of the contract ... and in such case shall award an amount of damages to be paid as an alternative if the contract is not performed'.[107] This made specific performance the primary remedy for breach of contract.[108] Although its language was wide enough to embrace all contracts, procedural difficulties meant there were large numbers of contracts to which the remedy could not be effectively applied. Hence, decrees for specific performance of contract were comparatively rare.[109] In an effort to simplify the application of specific performance,

[101] Feaver (n 70) 80.

[102] 'Speech of 17 December 1862' in Duff (n 100) 91.

[103] ibid 90. In *Ancient Law* (n 71), Maine famously argued that societies progressively move from 'status' to 'contract'. The link between Maine's views in *Ancient Law* and legislative activity in India is complicated and nonlinear. This is variously discussed in eg Feaver (n 70); S den Otter, 'Freedom of Contract, the Market and Imperial Law-making' in M Bevir and F Trentmann (eds), *Critiques of Capital in Modern Britain and America* (New York, Parlgrave, 2002) 49–72; K Mantena, *Alibis of Empire: Henry Maine and the Ends of Liberal Imperialism* (Princeton, Princeton University Press, 2010).

[104] 'Note by Maine, 15 July 1867', PP, HC, vol XLIX (1867–68) 692.

[105] 'Statement of Objects and Reasons' (n 14) 689.

[106] 'Speech of 11 November 1864' in Duff (n 100) 167.

[107] See also s 93 on injunctions.

[108] For case law, see LPD Broughton, *The Code of Civil Procedure being Act VIII of 1859*, 2nd edn (Calcutta, Wyman Bros, 1867) 133.

[109] The difficulty was that those wishing to obtain specific performance had to file a regular suit in the civil courts which was appealable. The remedy was often useless by the time it was awarded ('Statement of Objects and Reasons' (n 14) 689).

Maine drafted a Bill to revise section 192 of the Code. Maine's scheme was designed to enable the courts to order the performance of a legal promise where it could be ascertained that the defendant was in a position to do so and had not contracted under false impressions. Maine saw this as exhibiting neither the timidity of English Chancery Courts, nor the full freedom of French law, which ordered Dumas to write a novel in six volumes, or of the Code of Civil Procedure, which could be used to order one person to marry another.[110] Importantly, Maine's scheme covered contracts for the cultivation of specific crops. Maine was aware of the problems with indigo contracts and the possibility that any remedy of compulsion could be abused, but he was not willing to 'keep the whole procedure of India in a backward condition because unjust contracts are made in a corner of Bengal'.[111]

Maine's proposals met with the disapproval of both the Secretary of State and the Governor-General. Unsurprisingly, the discussion centred on the politics of planter-ryot relations. Although not opposed to specific performance 'on principle'[112] and admitting that damages were an 'imperfect remedy',[113] Wood affirmed his position against any legislation which could work in the planters' interests and at the peasants' expense. In a letter to Maine, he wrote: 'I cannot help having before my eyes … the old indigo contracts, & the system of fraud & force which characterised the system. I am a little bit afraid of an enactment which would put such a weapon in the hands of the English Planter wherewith to coerce the ryot'.[114] Sir John Lawrence, the new Governor-General, opposed Maine's scheme for similar reasons.[115] In reply, Maine thought that his superiors were blinded to the advantages of his scheme by a form of dogmatic sentimentalism that overlooked the recently improved relations between planters and ryots in Bengal.[116] In truth, Maine did not attach to the policy of protecting Indian peasants the same significance as Wood and Lawrence.[117]

Between 1863 and 1865, Maine and a select committee produced successive drafts of the specific performance clauses in an attempt to overcome the objections of Wood and Lawrence. When Wood received the final draft, he referred it to the third Indian law commission which had already submitted its report on contract law. The commissioners objected to Maine's proposals since they potentially allowed the courts to award specific performance in the case of agreements for the cultivation of land in a particular manner or for the growth of specific crops. In their view, not only were the conditions in the Bill under which the power could be exercised inadequate to prevent its abuse, but the provision of adequate conditions for that purpose was not generally possible.[118] The commissioners' response effectively put an end to Maine's proposals.

[110] Rankin (n 10) 79.

[111] 'Speech of 11 November 1864' in Duff (n 100) 169.

[112] 'Letter from Wood to Trevelyan, 25 February 1864', BL MSS Eur F 78.

[113] 'Letter from Wood to Maine, 2 January 1865', BL MSS Eur F 78.

[114] 'Letter from Wood to Maine, 3 December 1863' BL MSS Eur F 78.

[115] See the letters from Lawrence to Wood, dated 30 July 1864, 19 October 1864, 4 May 1865, 16 July 1865, 21 October 1865, BL MSS Eur F 78.

[116] 'Letter from Maine to Lawrence, 2 April 1864' BL MSS Eur F 90.

[117] It would be wrong to think that Maine unequivocally supported European settlers. He officially clashed with them on several issues: Feaver (n 70) 84–85, 91–98.

[118] 'Legal Opinion taken in England, 27 November 1866', PP, HC, vol L (1867) 355.

C. Disagreement Over the Specific Performance Clauses in the Commission's Draft

Against this background, it is not hard to understand Maine's disagreement with the merits of the commission's proposals on specific performance. The scope of specific performance in India was in theory wide, in that it applied to contracts of every type, but in practice limited, in that it was rarely exercised due to procedural difficulties. The commission's draft narrowed the scope of the remedy by limiting the types of contracts to which it applied. Section 52 of the draft provided that the extraordinary remedy of specific performance was restricted to agreements for the creation or transfer of any interest in immoveable property, or the delivery of any specific article of moveable property, but it excluded agreements to cultivate land in a particular manner or grow particular crops.[119]

Maine protested that the proposed law was too narrow: narrower than English law, which was the narrowest in the world.[120] His objection centred on two points. The first was one of policy and concerned indigo contracts. Maine argued that the commission's sections would produce little practical benefit in respect of those contracts for two reasons. First, whatever the evils of indigo planting, they no longer arose from a complicated system of contracts since the indigo planting in Bengal, which depended on those contracts, was now 'virtually extinct'.[121] Second, the proposed sections did not alter the provisions in the Code of Civil Procedure 1859 which required the filing of a regular suit before a decree for specific performance could be obtained. Those provisions acted as an absolute bar to using specific performance in indigo matters, because by the time the process and any appeals were completed, the crops would have been sold or consumed.[122] Overall, the new sections would add nothing in practice but stir up political controversy by putting 'a perfectly needless and useless affront on the European community'.[123]

Maine's second point was that the commission's proposals were not suited to India. Directed at the wrong target (of indigo contracts), they missed the real problem – 'the greatest evil' of civil procedure in India – which was the system of unexecuted decrees for pecuniary damages.[124] Such decrees were rarely executed against small debtors in view of their limited moveable property and the value of their land depending on their labour. The result was that those decrees were hoarded and sold to richer villagers, typically moneylenders, who used them as a means of oppressing the debtors. The commission's draft did nothing to address this problem.

Maine's suggested omission of the relevant sections was resisted by Governor-General Lawrence. A strong opponent of the application of specific performance to

[119] The same was true of s 59 on injunctions ('Note on the Second Report of the Indian Law Commissioners by W Stokes, 6 May 1867', 5, BL MSS Eur F 86/111).

[120] 'Statement of Objects and Reasons' (n 14) 689.

[121] ibid 692.

[122] 'Note by Maine, 23 July 1867', PP, HC, vol XLIX (1867–68) 694.

[123] 'Note by Maine, 15 July 1867', PP, HC, vol XLIX (1867–68) 692.

[124] 'Note by Maine, 27 July 1867', PP, HC, vol XLIX (1867–68) 697.

indigo contracts, he applauded the substance of the commission's proposals. For him, the inequality of power between indigo planters and ryots meant their contracts could never be voluntary and equitable to justify a law enforcing their specific performance. At the same time, he believed that although unfair indigo contracts had become less common in Bengal, they were by no means extinct.[125] Lawrence eventually consented to the omission of the disputed sections from the Bill,[126] after Maine had offered to reinstate them on the basis that he could oppose them later,[127] and referred the discussion to London.

The law commissioners reiterated the soundness and expediency of the proposed law. They contended that that law was founded on legal principles of universal application and was consonant with the practice of English Chancery Courts[128] to refuse the specific performance of a contract where it required a succession of acts,[129] the exercise of skill, or the application of personal labour.[130] In their view, there was nothing in the local circumstances to justify giving Indian judges greater powers than those enjoyed by their English counterparts.[131]

The key issue was not what English law prescribed, since that could be modified, but what India 'needed'. And what India 'needed' depended on social and economic factors on the ground. 'Need' was not an objective category waiting to be discovered, but a contested space constructed and given content by real people with different outlooks. Maine had one understanding of 'need'; the Governor-General and the law commissioners had another. Both were rooted in colonialism but were refracted through different ideological lenses. Colonial minds did not all think alike.[132]

The disagreement over specific performance in the Contract Bill focused the discussion of policy within a more confined framework. Nonetheless, old causes of ideological friction reappeared. On the one hand, there was the 'need' to enable better contract-making and contract-enforcing practices in a world dominated by small contracts where trust was missing and awards of damages were ineffective. On the other hand, there was the 'need' to protect Indian peasants from contracts with European capitalists which were made within a relationship of great inequality of power.[133] Fundamental to understanding the disagreement is appreciating how the decision makers perceived the 'problem' and its 'solution' and how, in the process of doing so, law and colonial politics intertwined.

[125] 'Note by the Governor-General, 19 July 1867', PP, HC, vol XLIX (1867–68) 693.

[126] 'Note by the Governor-General, 16 August 1867', PP, HC, vol XLIX (1867–68) 701.

[127] 'Note by Maine, 25 July 1867', PP, HC, vol XLIX (1867–68) 695.

[128] For details, see M Lobban, 'Contract' in W Cornish et al (eds), *The Oxford History of the Laws of England, Vol XII, 1820–1914: Private Law* (Oxford, Oxford University Press, 2010) 548–62.

[129] J Berryman, 'The Specific Performance Damages Continuum: An Historical Perspective' (1985) 17 *Ottawa LR* 295, 316–18.

[130] E Fry, *A Treatise on the Specific Performance of Contracts* (Philadelphia, Johnson & Co, 1858) 44–45. For the view that indigo contracts fell within this category, see 'The Specific Performance of Contract' *Calcutta Review*, vol LII (1866) 328.

[131] 'Fourth Report of Indian law Commissioners' (n 1) 702.

[132] See eg, TR Metcalf, *Ideologies of the Raj* (Cambridge, Cambridge University Press, 1995); DM Peers and N Gooptu (eds), *India and the British Empire* (Oxford, Oxford University Press, 2012); T Roy and AV Swamy (eds), *Law and the Economy in Colonial India* (Chicago, University of Chicago Press, 2016).

[133] Although much of the debate focused on indigo, similar issues could arise in respect of the cultivation of other produce such as opium, cotton and sugar ('Note by Sir H Durand, 29 July 1867', PP, HC, vol XLIX (1867–68) 699).

IV. Later Developments

A. Constitutional Crisis, Resignations, and the Indian Contract Act 1872

The disagreement over specific performance was followed by one over the *nemo dat* rule in the sale of goods.[134] The select committee responsible for scrutinising the Contract Bill and the local governments objected to the law commission's clauses on the ground that they were unsuitable to the conditions of trade in India.[135] The matter was referred to the Home government so that the commission could consider the objections.

Maine's relationship with the law commissioners became increasingly antagonistic. He openly questioned their role by criticising the practice of drafting codes in England without consultation with the government in India and by suggesting its replacement with a new process under which preliminary drafts prepared by the commissioners would be considered in India by a committee with power to adapt them to local conditions.[136] Maine was warned that his plan might cause offence to the commissioners and lead to their resignation.[137] Undeterred, he offered his resignation in 1868 but Secretary of State Stafford Northcote refused to accept it.[138] Writing candidly to Grant Duff, his friend and Under-Secretary for India, Maine remarked: 'the general question which has arisen is one of great seriousness … [it] is whether the decision of certain grave points of policy shall or shall not be shifted from the Indian government to the Indian law commissioners, a perfectly irresponsible body, sitting once a week for two hours and including only two gentlemen who have ever been in India, both of those having been 30 years out of the country'.[139]

Maine's critique and the limited progress with the contract draft caused discontent to the law commissioners and the new Secretary of State, the Duke of Argyll. What began as 'a difference of opinion about a technical point of law, was elevated to the dignity of a grave constitutional controversy'.[140] London and Bengal became involved in a dispute over the extent of the Indian government's legislative independence and its role in shaping the codes. Following consultation with the law commissioners on the disputed points, Argyll sent a despatch to the Indian authorities in 1869, instructing them to adopt the draft in the essential form sent by the commissioners and enact it without

[134] For details, see G Pearson, 'A Cattle Lifter's Bill: Nemo Dat Rule and the Indian Contract Act' (2015) 89 *Australian LJ* 31.

[135] Similar concerns were raised about the provisions on liquidated damages and penalties: 'Letter from Maine to Lawrence, 18 February 1868', BL MSS Eur F 90.

[136] 'Letter from Maine to Lawrence, 31 July 1868', BL MSS Eur F 90; 'Letter from Maine to Mayo, 13 July 1869', Cambridge University Library (CUL) Add 7490/121.

[137] 'Letter from Perry to Maine, 3 July 1868' in Feaver (n 70) 103.

[138] Maine eventually left India in 1869, having served as law member for seven years: G Johnson, 'India and Henry Maine' in A Diamond (ed), *The Victorian Achievement of Sir Henry Maine* (Cambridge, Cambridge University Press, 1991) 376–88.

[139] 'Letter from Maine to Grant Duff, 22 December 1868' in Feaver (n 70) 101–02. In the same letter, Maine accused the commissioners of forming 'a radically false notion of the India of the present day' as a 'field of application of a diluted Benthamism' (ibid 102–03). See also 'Letter from Maine to Lytton, 2 April 1878', BL MSS Eur E 218. For the view that the disagreement over the adaptability of codified law was a matter of degree, see Tofaris (n 5) ch 5.

[140] C Ilbert, 'Indian Codification' (1889) 5 *LQR* 347, 351.

further delays. Argyll further indicated that in the future the Indian government could consult local officials regarding the commissioners' drafts and raise concerns with the Secretary of State, who would discuss them with the commissioners, before sending the drafts back to India with the expectation that, subject to strong unforeseen objections, they would be enacted.[141] The Indian government under Governor-General Lord Mayo resisted the suggested course and reiterated its opposition to the sale of goods provisions in the commission's draft.[142]

The commissioners objected that their reports were treated as mere drafts, with rules being criticised in public and being subject to revision by the select committee and the legislative council.[143] In their view, if the latter was the 'fitter body to decide', then 'the existence of the Indian Law Commission cannot be justified'.[144] The commissioners officially resigned in 1870 in protest over systematic inaction in relation to drafts they had prepared at the expense of considerable time and labour.[145] Their resignation had two effects. First, it helped to quell the disagreement between the Home and Indian governments. A compromise was reached by accepting that the Secretary of State had the last saying, but that it would be exercised only in rare cases.[146] Second, the Indian government was allowed to pursue its own course with the Contract Bill. James Fitzjames Stephen, the new law member, felt that he was 'practically & substantially … a sort of king in my own department for nobody interferes with me'.[147] He reworked the existing draft,[148] making structural changes and inserting new sections under the influence of Field's New York Civil Code.[149]

When the Indian Contract Act was passed in 1872, specific performance was left out.[150] Stephen explained that specific performance was part of 'what, by a strange misnomer, is called equity' in England, but 'might perhaps be not quite inappropriately described as the law of relief'.[151] That branch of law lay between substantive law and procedure. Nevertheless, the issue of agricultural contracts, including indigo ones, resurfaced under a different doctrinal guise during the final discussion in the legislative council. Sir George Campbell, the Lieutenant-Governor of Bengal, sought to introduce amendments that aimed to protect the poorer classes of Indian society by giving courts

[141] 'Legislative Despatch (No 8) of 18 March 1869', PP, HC, vol LVI (1876) 22; National Archives of India (NAI), Legislative Department, A Proceedings, May 1872, No 600.

[142] 'Legislative Despatch (No 1) of 22 March 1870', PP, HC, vol LVI (1876) 24; NAI, Legislative Department, A Proceedings, May 1872, No 601.

[143] 'Letter from W Macpherson to MEG Duff, 16 January 1869', BL IOR L/PJ/5/428.

[144] ibid.

[145] For the details, see 'Resignation of Third Indian Law Commission 1870', BL IOR L/PJ/5/438; 'Letter to Duke of Argyll, 2 July 1870' in Ilbert (n 140) 351–52. Stephen described their resignation as being 'in disgust of our obstructiveness' ('Letter from Stephen to Lytton, 6 March 1876', CUL Ms Add 7349/14/1). See further, G Pearson, 'The Resignation of the Third Indian Law Commission: Who Makes Law?' (2020) 41 *Adelaide LR* 575.

[146] 'Legislative Despatch (No 47) of 24 November 1870', PP, HC, vol LVI (1876) 24; 'Legislative Despatch (No 2) of 1 February 1871', ibid 26.

[147] 'Letter from Stephen to Venables, 4 July 1870', CUL Ms Add 7349/12.

[148] Stephen was able to 'reap where others had sown' (JF Stephen, 'Codification in India and England' *Fortnightly Review*, vol XVII (1872) 653).

[149] Tofaris (n 5) ch 5. F Pollock and DF Mulla, *The Indian Contract Act*, 2nd edn (London, Sweet & Maxwell, 1909) described Field's code as the 'worst piece of codification ever produced' (at vii).

[150] 'Report of Select Committee, 4 April 1868', BL IOR/L/PJ/5/15.

[151] 'Meeting of 9 April 1872' (n 16) 329.

broad powers to strike down hard bargains. For example, Campbell moved the insertion of the following illustration to section 16 on undue influence: 'A, a rich and powerful zamindar, induces B, C and D, poor and ignorant ryots holding under him, to engage to grow certain produce and to deliver it to him for a term of twenty years, in consideration of an inadequate price for which no independent ryot would have so engaged. A employs undue influence over B, C and D'.[152] With characteristic self-assurance, Stephen retorted that it would be no more unobjectionable to replace the illustration with the following: 'C, a rich and powerful Lieutenant-Governor, of remarkable force and character, induces S, a Member of the Council of feeble intellect, to sell him a horse for a totally inadequate price. C employs undue influence'.[153] Stephen's objection was that contractual expectations ought to be protected: the zamindar might have advanced a large amount of capital to the ryots and performance of the contract might have been vital to him as the fulfilment of a series of contracts depended on it. Campbell's paternalistic concern for the poor was countered by the competing concern of the mercantile members for sanctity of contract,[154] which Stephen embraced albeit to a lesser extent.[155]

B. The Law of Specific Relief: Betwixt and Between

The law of specific performance developed outside the Indian Contract Act 1872. Yet it did so, not as part of procedure, but of a separate body of law in the Specific Relief Act 1877. The Act arose in connection with the reform of the Code of Civil Procedure in 1875.[156] Whitley Stokes, the secretary of the legal department, and Arthur Hobhouse, the new law member, took the view that by including specific performance in the Code of Civil Procedure, its framers 'overstepped the boundary, and had passed over into substantive law'.[157] It was therefore appropriate to remove it from that code while under revision. Although this was a clear rejection of Maine's taxonomical view,[158] it was not a full endorsement of the commissioners'. The Specific Relief Act 1877 was designed 'to occupy a middle place between the Civil Procedure Code … and the Indian Contract Act',[159] 'touching both but not encroaching upon either'.[160] The Act's structure was modelled on

[152] ibid 351. The illustration was clearly directed against contracts between European planters and Indian ryots for the cultivation of indigo.

[153] ibid 362.

[154] ibid 345–50.

[155] ibid 361–63. See further, Tofaris (n 5) 218–20.

[156] 'Statement of Objects and Reasons, 25 October 1875' in SC Banerji, *The Law of Specific Relief in British India*, 2nd edn (Calcutta, Cambray & Co, 1917), Appendix B, 13.

[157] 'Specific Relief Bill, 23 November 1875', Abstract of the Proceedings of the Council of the Governor-General of India, Assembled for the Purpose of Making Laws and Regulations, vol XIV (1875) 276.

[158] Stokes served in the same role under Maine, by whom he was taught and with whom he became friends (R Cocks, 'Who Attended the Lectures of Sir Henry Maine: And Does it Matter?' in JA Bush and A Wijffels (eds), *Learning the Law: Teaching and the Transmission of Law in England 1150–1900* (London, Hambledon Press, 1999) 391).

[159] 'Specific Relief Bill, 7 December 1875', Abstract of the Proceedings of the Council of the Governor-General of India, Assembled for the Purpose of Making Laws and Regulations, vol XIV (1875) 279. See also, Stokes (n 21) 938. This was probably inspired by Stephen's view: see n 151.

[160] 'Specific Relief Bill, 22 November 1876', Abstract of the Proceedings of the Council of the Governor-General of India, Assembled for the Purpose of Making Laws and Regulations, vol XV (1876) 305. See also, Law Commission of India, *Ninth Report: Specific Relief Act, 1877* (1958) 1–2.

Field's New York Civil Code,[161] but the rules on specific performance closely adhered to English law.[162]

The Act effectively reversed the working premise of section 192 of the Code of Civil Procedure 1859 by making damages the primary remedy for breach of contract. Contracts which could be specifically enforced in the discretion of the court included those whose non-performance could not be adequately relieved by monetary compensation,[163] whereas contracts which could not be specifically enforced included those whose non-performance could be adequately relieved by monetary compensation.[164] The official minutes suggest that agricultural contracts were not at the forefront of the discussion. An illustration made clear that there could be no specific performance of a contract under which B would cultivate particular crops for three years and deliver them to A in consideration of an annual advance by A to B. This was understood as falling within the English-based rule that contracts could not be specifically performed where they were dependent on the personal qualifications or volition of the parties.[165]

The Act of 1877 remained in force until its replacement by the Specific Relief Act 1963, whose main effect was to weaken some of the bars to specific performance.[166] A more substantial change was introduced by the Specific Relief (Amendment) Act 2018, which intended to enhance India's ranking in 'Ease of Doing Business'.[167] Following this amendment, section 10 of the Specific Relief Act 1963 provides that specific performance of a contract 'shall be' enforced by the court subject to the subsequent provisions. This contrasts with the previous language, traceable to the original Act, of 'may, in the discretion of the court, be enforced'. Additionally, the bar based on the adequacy of damages has now been removed.[168] In effect, the recent amendments have made specific performance yet again the primary remedy for breach of contract.[169]

V. Concluding Thoughts

Historical description can shed light on the mechanisms of legal change.[170] The present chapter has set the disagreement over specific performance in the Indian Contract Act against the background of jurisprudential theory, real life problems and colonial ideology. In doing so, it has sought to illustrate the variety and complexity of factors which

[161] Stokes (n 21) 938. Pollock and Mulla (n 60) referred to the 'unhappy imitation' of Field's code (at iii).

[162] 'Specific Relief Bill, 7 December 1875' (n 159) 279; Stokes (n 21) 931, 938. Sections 14–15 of the Act were taken from the draft code of contract law prepared by the law commissioners: Stokes (n 21) 954–55.

[163] Specific Relief Act 1877, s 12(c).

[164] ibid s 21(a).

[165] ibid s 21(b).

[166] See further, V Niranjan, 'Specific and Agreed Remedies for Breach of Contract in Indian Law: A Code of English Law?' in M Chen-Wishart et al (eds), *Studies in the Contract Laws of Asia: Remedies for Breach of Contract* (Oxford, Oxford University Press, 2016) 58–83.

[167] *Global Music Junction Pvt Ltd v Shatrughan Kumar* 2023 SCC OnLine Del 5479, [32]–[33] (Delhi High Court).

[168] *Katta Sujatha Reddy v Siddamsetty Infra Projects* (2023) 1 SCC 355, [50] (Supreme Court of India).

[169] *Global Music Junction* (n 167) [38]–[42].

[170] J Baker, 'Why the History of English Law Has Not Been Finished' in J Baker (ed), *Collected Papers on English Legal History* (Cambridge, Cambridge University Press, 2013), vol III, 1544–45.

underpin the process of legislative law-making. That process can be profitably analysed in terms of a dynamic interplay between factors which are 'internal' and 'external' to law.

The inescapably paramount context within which the codification of Indian contract law took place was colonialism. As a prime example of official policy, codification was first and foremost a *colonial* project. Yet colonial policy was not a monolithic structure. Within the Anglo-Indian administration, there was a variety of governing philosophies and views on social and economic issues. Conflicting ideas were often held simultaneously in tension with one another. The regulation of contracts between European capitalists and Indian peasants for the cultivation of specified crops offers but one example.

Law, however, did not collapse into colonial politics. Anglo-Indian codification was a colonial *legal* project. The classification of specific performance was not mere window dressing; for the lawyers involved, it was an important question. Code drafting was an exercise in doctrinal formulation and classification, an example of the scientific study of law that was becoming more prominent in the nineteenth century. While the Indian contract code was not designed to serve juristic needs, it was nonetheless a juristic project. As such, it formed part of broader conversations regarding analytical structures and rules, and operated within a framework of professional terms of reference from which it derived much of its meaning. The accompanying concepts were multifarious and potentially at odds. The taxonomical question of whether specific performance is part of substantive law or procedure is again but one example.

Codified law at core possessed an autonomous intellectual nature. The autonomy was 'relative' because the law did not respond only to forces inside the legal community, but also to those located in the outside, 'non-legal' world.[171] The influence of 'external' factors was for the most part refracted through the inward practices and conventions of the code's drafters and legislators. To the extent that 'external' factors moulded the law, they did so within the confines of an intellectual tradition with its own language, norms, and peculiar forms of rationalisation, and within an institutional framework in which the identity and ideology of the decision-makers played a vital role.

'Internal' and 'external' factors can be composite, diverse, and contradictory, and their interaction complex and contingent. It is ultimately dependent on the configuration of individual factors in particular historical contexts. While the model of interaction can be sketched at a level of generality, its details can only be filled by undertaking in-depth studies of those contexts. The present study is one of many inspired by observing a master at work.

[171] See further, J Bell and DJ Ibbetson, *European Legal Development: The Case of Tort* (Cambridge, Cambridge University Press, 2012) 1–50.

17

Path Dependence and French Administrative Law

JOHN BELL

In an earlier work, written as part of collaboration with David Ibbetson, I tried to define the concept of 'path dependence'. I suggested that

> established legal approaches from the past to the solution of issues will determine the way in which new situations or new problems are handled in the present and in the future. Legal development is explained not simply by the effect of social and economic pressures operating on the law from the outside at the current time, but also by the internal dynamic of the law, the pressure of established ways of dealing with issues.[1]

It seems to me that French administrative law provides a very good illustration. Why? Well, French administrative law barely existed before 1799. The Revolution in 1790 reinforced the Edict of St-Germain-en-Laye of 1641 and forbade the private law judges from interfering with the administration. The creation of the Conseil d'Etat in 1799 began the process of building a body of law which would regulate the administration in a manner distinct from private law. In 1799, there was no thought of a code of administrative law in parallel to the codes being elaborated in private law, commercial law and criminal law. There were no university or other courses to train lawyers in administrative law and there were no textbooks to which they could refer. It is the nearest you can get to a *tabula rasa*. Jean-Louis Mestre has argued that many of the ideas and values found in modern administrative law have roots in Roman law, medieval canon law and the law of the Parlements.[2] While he does show that certain ideas and practices did exist before the Revolution, this does not demonstrate an organised and coherent body of knowledge and legal principle at the eve of the Revolution that could parallel private law at the hands of Domat and Pothier. What emerges over the following century is a distinct set of institutions, some distinct legislation, distinct bodies of

[1] J Bell, 'Path Dependence and Legal Development' (2013) 87 *Tulane Law Review* 787.

[2] J-L Mestre, *Introduction Historique au Droit Administratif Français* (Paris, PUF, 1985) and J-L Mestre, 'Juridictions Judiciaires et Annulation des Actes Administratifs dans la France d'Ancien Régime et en Angleterre' in EV Heyen (ed), *Administration and Administrative Law in France and England (18th/19th Century)* (Baden-Baden, Nomos, 1996) 37.

judges, distinct law courses and distinct academic and judicial professions devoted to this branch of law. These distinct features of separate court institutions, separate legal personnel, and separate legal procedure gave rise to a distinct body of legal doctrine which shaped what we now understand as 'French administrative law'. They provide the subject-matter for examining the origins and development of a self-contained sub-system of law.

In very many ways, France of the nineteenth and twentieth centuries had very similar social conditions to other western European countries. Transport and communications became easier, liberal politics developed in many periods, as did capitalist economic conditions. There was also the internationalisation of the economy and of intellectual and cultural life. France was certainly not isolated from currents of legal, political and social ideas. All the same, France developed and continued with a distinctive model of administrative law. That distinctive model involved a sharp separation between public and private law in terms of courts, personnel, universities and educational programmes, published works and journals, substantive rules of property, contract, liability and judicial review, as well as rules of litigation procedure.

Path dependence suggests that the development of the field of 'administrative law' in the nineteenth and twentieth centuries was shaped significantly by key choices and practices at the turn of the nineteenth century and the years that immediately followed

I. Factor 1: Court Institutions

The Law of 16–24 August 1790 established a prohibition on the ordinary civil and criminal courts interfering with the administration. The establishment of the Conseil d'Etat in 1799 provided the positive side in that someone could potentially control the administration. The establishment of the conseils de préfecture in 1800 provided the potential vehicle for controlling local government. It was not that either court was commissioned explicitly to control the administration. Formally, the power lay with the consuls, later the ministers, or with the local prefect. Complaints made against the administration were to be judged by a senior member of the administration. But, as in the English Privy Council, the role of providing advice to the person with formal power became the vehicle through which principles of lawful administration were developed and sanction for inappropriate decisions or unjustified harm could be secured.

In the febrile atmosphere of frequent revolutions, the very existence of these institutions was frequently under threat. Particularly in 1815 and 1870, there were moves to abolish the institution of the Conseil d'Etat altogether. The Bourbons and the Republicans at each of those dates were hostile to the relics of the Empire. It was too much associated, particularly in its advisory capacity, with the regime which had just been overthrown. But it did not take much to recognise the value of its function of dealing with complaints. The institution was reinstated, often with many of the same members as under the previous regime. Indeed, the Republicans passed the Law of 24 May 1872 which provided that the Conseil d'Etat would rule 'sovereignly' on complaints against the administration and on applications to quash decisions of administrative authorities. This provision was not controversial at the time.

Formally, through the first three-quarters of a century, the legislator adopted the idea of 'retained justice' – that the administrative courts merely advised the minister, rather than having judicial authority. But the topic of giving the courts an independent power of decision had been debated for many years. Macarel and Cormenin argued for formal independence of the Conseil since 1818 and 1822 respectively. In 1828, Macarel discussed the separation of judicial and administrative powers in the light of Montesquieu and concluded that ministers should not be judges.[3] He argued that the Conseil d'Etat should be autonomous, a view which a government bill proposed in 1833, but which was not included in the Law of 1845. It was briefly accepted under the Second Republic (from 1849 to 1852), but then dropped in the Second Empire. The legislative basis was only established in 1872 (after an earlier interlude) and the case law confirmed this in *Cadot* in 1889.[4] It was long recognised as a legal fiction, but it retained political importance.

More problematic was the political control over appointments. The instability of regimes led to a political control of membership which was still present in the Third Republic which gave the power of nomination to the National Assembly. The failure of the MacMahon coup attempt in 1879 led to a major purge of the Conseil d'Etat's members.[5] Indeed, further purges in 1944 and 1963 demonstrate the continued controversiality of the role the Conseil d'Etat played as both a major institution of the governmental regime and as a judge over the administration. All the same, a strong sense of an independent identity of those involved in litigation had already been established and was developed further. Judicial independence emerged gradually as a necessity for getting public acceptance. The fully-fledged constitutional recognition of the independence of administrative judges waited until 1980.[6]

An important feature within the Conseil d'Etat was the creation of a distinct unit dealing with litigation. It went under different labels in the early years and its original task was to prepare decisions for the administrative section to which the complaint related. Typical of a bureaucracy, a complaint was assigned to a junior official to prepare papers that would summarise the decisions more senior people would have to take. But the very fact that there was a group of people who regularly dealt with complaints from across the different areas of the administration and examined their legality provided the basis from which consistent principles could be developed.

The development of the conseils de préfecture was slower. They were institutions of limited jurisdiction and only had the competence assigned to them by the legislature. The Law of 28 Pluviôse An VIII gave them competence over tax, contracts and damage relating to public works and matters relating to the major public roads. There was no legislative basis for their procedure until the decree of 30 December 1862 and an institutional Law of 21 June 1865 created a standard pattern of composition. That Law of 1865 established the role of the Vice-President of the conseil de préfecture as the effective presiding judge, which recognised that the prefect had far too many other

[3] L-A Macarel, *Des Tribunaux Administratifs ou l'Introduction à l'Etude de la Juridiction Administrative* (Paris, Roret, 1828) 141–44.

[4] CE 13 December 1889, Leb. 1148 concl. Jagerschmidt.

[5] See *La Revue Administrative 1998 numéro spécial: Le Conseil d'État et les crises*, 23–24, 47–49.

[6] CC decision n° 80119 DC, 22 July 1980, *Validation of Administrative Decisions*, Rec. 46, para 6.

activities to be fully involved in resolving litigation.[7] This created a clear demarcation between administrative and judicial roles. The legislation of 1862–1865 formalised what had already been accepted by Macarel in 1828 that there was effectively a judicial hierarchy in administrative courts. The bulk of complaints went to the conseils de préfecture and then by way of an appeal to the Conseil d'Etat. A smaller number of complaints against decisions of ministers, such as decrees, went directly to the Conseil d'Etat. The formal recognition of the status of the conseils de préfecture as lower courts had to await caselaw at the beginning of the twentieth century and the reform of the conseils de préfecture in 1953.

The conseils de préfecture were re-organised by reducing their number and increasing their geographical area in 1926. They were renamed *tribunaux administratifs* in 1953 when a fully-fledged two-tier system of courts was established, the lower tier being courts of general jurisdiction.[8] The creation of a three-tier system of appeal to regional *cours administratives d'appel* with the Conseil d'Etat as predominantly a cour de cassation on top, parallel to the private law courts, had to wait until the reform of 1987.[9] The interesting feature of these various reforms was that they maintained a distinction between the members of the highest administrative court, the Conseil d'Etat, and the members of the lower courts. Even at the time of writing, Art R233-1 of the Code de la Justice Administrative identifies a separate body of the 'magistrats des tribunaux administratifs et des cours administratives d'appel' with its own Conseil supérieur, which is both distinct from that of private law judges under its conseil supérieur de la magistrature and also distinct from the Conseil d'Etat. Once established, the institutional framework has just carried on.

The distinctiveness of the administrative courts from the private law courts was enforced by the Conseil d'Etat until 1850, when the Tribunal des Conflits was established. From an order of 13 Brumaire An X (4 November 1801), prefects were able to raise a conflict before the ordinary courts. Three particular areas of litigation required such a procedure. First, Art 75 of the Constitution of 22 Frimaire An VIII (13 December 1799) actions against public officials in the course of their functions were only permitted by order of the Conseil d'Etat. Only with that permission (and thus when the acts were outside their official duties) would civil or criminal actions be possible. So private law rules on vicarious liability did not apply. Secondly, debts of the administration were paid from a central fund (including a special fund for local authority debts) and payment from the funds required the order of an official or the administrative court. Thirdly, most of the competence of the conseils de préfecture related to public land – public works and public highways. The Law of 28 Pluviôse An VIII had given considerable protection from litigation to those who had acquired land from the state (Art 4). The aim was to prevent private law litigation (and private law principles of ownership) being used to undo transactions entered into during the Revolution. The amnesty of 6 Floréal An X (26 April 1802) specifically prevented the amnestied émigrés from challenging the validity of transactions entered into by the Republic and private individuals before that date. This would include both outright sales and rights to use public land

[7] G Bigot, *Introduction Historique au Droit Administratif Depuis 1789* (Paris, PUF, 2002) 132–33.
[8] LN Brown, 'The Reform of French Administrative Courts' (1959) 22 *MLR* 357.
[9] LN Brown and J Bell, 'Recent Reforms of French Administrative Justice' (1989) 8 *CJQ* 71.

which the Republic had confiscated. It is from this third area of concern that the classical distinction between acts of authority (which are public law) and management acts (*actes de gestion*, which may be private law) emerges.[10] The expropriation of land and the decision to undertake public works are public law, but nuisance caused to neighbours from public land may be private law. In reality the distinction was between the state as public power and the state as property owner, and the Conseil d'Etat wanted to police this.[11] The preoccupations of the early nineteenth century ensured firm policing of the boundary between public law and private law, even if the private law courts did try to recover more work relating to contracts and harm caused by the public administration during the Restoration and the July Monarchy.[12] The creation of the Tribunal des Conflits which had equal numbers of members from the Conseil d'Etat and the Cour de cassation pacified disputes between the administrative and civil courts. In particular, it rejected the application of the Civil Code to the administration, especially Art 1384 on liability for others, since this would undermine the immunity of public officials.[13] Once put in place, this separation of public law and private law courts has become entrenched. In 1987,[14] the Conseil constitutionnel found that the judicial review of decisions of bodies exercising executive power belonged to the administrative courts, so a Law conferring such powers on the ordinary courts was unconstitutional. The decision consecrated the separation of administrative and ordinary courts by way of a fundamental principle recognised by the laws of the Republic (even if the best statement was in a law of the Bourbon monarchy in 1790).

So, in one sense, the system of court institutions developed early, and this formed the context in which administrative law developed. But only the Conseil d'Etat had general competence over any subject-matter. All the same, the vast bulk of work was in the conseils de préfecture. In 1862, the Minister of Justice estimated that there were over 200,000 cases a year, whereas the Conseil d'Etat dealt with barely 1000 cases.[15]

At the same time, it is worth remembering that the workload of the administrative courts was not predominantly review of administrative decisions. For example, in 1880, of the 352,070 decisions handed down by the Conseils de préfecture, 98 per cent of cases were on tax matters, and other large matters (less than 0.5 per cent) were damages for harm caused by public works, fines for wrongs on public highways and waterways, and elections. Matters concerning the governance of the commune amounted to merely 0.16 per cent of cases.[16]

The continuity that the existence of the institutions provided was the base for developing legal principles and ideas. Administrative law was the institutional memory of the Conseil d'Etat, the more influential institution dealing with a smaller number of significant cases than the lower courts. In more recent years, the Conseil has been active in its own publicity. The *Etudes et Documents du Conseil d'Etat* started after World War II

[10] Bigot (n 7) 70–71.
[11] ibid 72.
[12] ibid 90–91, 105–108.
[13] TC 17 July 1850, *Letellier*, Leb. 493.
[14] CC decision nº 86-224 DC, 23 January 1987, *Competition Law*, Rec 8, para 15.
[15] Bigot (n 7) 131–32; T Fortsakis, *Conceptualisme et Empiricisme en Droit Administratif Français* (Paris, LGDJ, 1987) 250.
[16] E Laferrière, *Traité de la Juridiction Administrative*, 1st edn (Paris, Berger-Levrault, 1887) 259.

and offer not only an annual report, but a publication where members of the Conseil (and invited others) write with greater freedom and at more length on general issues facing the Conseil, eg, its activity under Vichy, and the challenges to French law posed by Europe. Even more so, the internet permits the Conseil to project itself, its judgments and its opinions in distinctive ways.

Institutions form the core of path dependency in this aspect of French law.[17] With the same institution being seized of problems during decades, it was possible to build an incremental response which can be seen as reliable and predictable for both the legal profession and for litigants. The existence of the institutions enabled the development of personnel who spent significant time on its work and shaped its response. The distinctive combination of advisory and judicial functions enabled ideas to shape the administrative processes and objectives through legislation and administrative decisions as well as in the judicial review of administration: 'juger l'administration, c'est aussi administrer'.[18] There is a distinctive character of the people involved.

A. The 'Administration'

The other important feature of judicial activity was the coherence of the notion of 'the administration'. The Revolution had destroyed the church and the education, health and other services it provided. The Napoleonic settlement not only reached an accommodation with the church in the 1801 Concordat with the Pope. It established a state system of public education in 1802 and regulated medicine in 1803. Ministers could determine the school curriculum and acted through the prefect and the recteur de l'Académie. So, in France, the state undertook not only defence and public order but, under the Empire, public education, hospitals and the state-supported religion. Even more than under Louis XIV, local government was under the supervision of the state inspector, the prefect, who could annul its decisions for illegality (and whose decision could then be challenged before the Conseil d'État). Subsequently state inspectors of factories or work would report to ministries. There was an organisational reality to the unified idea of 'the administration', which was subjected to administrative law.

II. Factor 2: Personnel

The continuity of the institutions is supported by the existence of a body of individuals working within them.

When the administrative courts started, there were no previous judges to be called upon.[19] No one had expertise in handling complaints against the administration. Within the Conseil d'Etat, the conseillers were appointed as trusted advisors to the Consuls and

[17] On the place of institutions in legal development more generally, see J Bell, 'The Importance of Institutions' in M Adams and D Heirbaut (eds), *The Method and Culture of Comparative Law. Essays in Honour of Mark Van Hoecke* (Oxford, Hart Publishing, 2014) ch 15.

[18] Henrion de Pansey (1827) cited in Bigot (n 7) 42.

[19] In 1814, the Restoration monarchy was able to appoint as conseillers d'Etat some people who had served in the pre-Revolutionary Conseil du Roi, but they had no significant impact on the development of

then to the emperor. The roles were generalist. The Conseil was conceived as a kind of training school for public administration – people would serve within the Conseil at *auditeur* level and then move to other branches of the public administration.[20] The Conseil d'Etat was planned for 30–40 conseillers 'in ordinary service' split over the five administrative sections and these were given a wide range of roles. In addition, other members undertook 'extraordinary service' as prefects or ambassadors. The conseillers as a class were too busy to spend a lot of time on complaints. In 1803 some lower-level civil servants, *auditeurs*, were appointed to prepare the file on complaints for decision by the conseillers. In 1806, more senior civil servants were appointed to oversee the work of the *auditeurs* and to prepare the judgments. These were the *maîtres de requêtes*, the masters of requests, a name familiar to historians of the Conseil du Roi under the Ancien Régime and of the English Privy Council. But, like the conseillers, they were appointed to a wide variety of administrative roles. The appointment of *auditeurs* and *maîtres des requêtes* marked an effective separation of administrative and judicial functions within the Conseil d'Etat and was part of a formalisation of procedures. All these officials involved in resolving litigation had to learn on the job. An apprenticeship model emerged.

By the time of the July Monarchy, when frequent purges ceased, a career structure emerged. Bigot reports that in the 1840s, three-quarters of the *maîtres de requêtes* were drawn from the *auditeurs* and, overall during that Monarchy, half the conseillers and two-thirds of the *maîtres de requêtes* were drawn from inside the Conseil d'Etat itself. The basic pattern of career progression was established, continued in the Third Republic,[21] and endures in a very similar form today. More pedantically, Monnier argues that the formal existence of a career really only dates from 1923 when an entitlement to a pension was established,[22] this provided a *cadre* of experts in administrative law who were able to develop consistent and coherent principles in deciding cases (and advise on their application in the formulation of legislation and administrative practice). Most of the *auditeurs* would have had a law degree from the universities, whose role in teaching administrative law is discussed below.

There was no specific prior training for those wishing to join the Conseil d'Etat. In the period 1815 to 1870, most entrants were either lawyers or members of the *corps* of prefects before they passed the examination.[23] Appointment was by the head of state or, in the Second Republic, by the National Assembly. Those who specialised in litigation were predominantly trained in private law in the universities. Indeed, that continued to be the case until the creation of the *Ecole Nationale d'Administration* in 1945. They would thus understand the conceptual structure of law and concepts of legality in procedure (particularly important in the early years). But their understanding of distinctive public law approaches was learnt only within the Conseil d'Etat.

administrative law: J Imbert in R Drago, J Imbert, J Tulard and F Monnier (eds), *Dictionnaire Biographique des Membres du Conseil d'Etat 1799–2002* (Paris, Fayard, 2004) 127.

[20] V Wright, 'Le Conseil d'Etat et les Changements de Régime: Le Cas du Second Empire' (1998) *Revue Administrative Spéciale* 13, 14.

[21] R Drago in Drago et al (n 19) 385.

[22] *La Revue Administrative* (n 5) 66–68.

[23] See J Imbert in Drago et al (n 19) 127, 129.

The members of the conseils de préfecture were appointed by the head of state, just as the prefect was. But the members in effect became more protected against interference. They were initially officials who heard complaints along with their other duties. Gradually, they became focused on the hearing of complaints. As noted above, the Law of 21 June 1865 provided a legislative basis for the organisation of the courts. Appointment to the conseils was restricted to those who had a *licence* degree in law and had ten years of judicial or administrative experience. It was thus possible to make use of expertise as a private law judge. There was no career progression. Even the subsequent creation of the tribunaux administratifs in 1953 maintained the separation of their judiciary from the Conseil d'Etat.

The career role of the *commissaire du gouvernement* was very important. As Drago points out, most of the senior figures in judicial work of the Conseil d'Etat (Vice-President or President of the Section du Contentieux) had been *commissaires du gouvernement.*[24] It is a role in which a person's brilliance is allowed to shine because he or she offers a single personal speech, unconstrained by the formal character of the terse judgment of the Conseil, and it is delivered in public. The most obvious contribution of a great administrative lawyer like Romieu (1858–1953) was during his period as *commissaire du gouvernement* where his ideas on the role of administrative law in controlling the administration and in the economy came out, even though he had many subsequent illustrious roles within the Conseil.[25]

The significance of the role is also helped by the small number of these posts. Originally 3 in number (now 20) with an expectation that they would deliver observations, even briefly, on most cases before the Conseil d'Etat, they had the opportunity to offer ideas on a wide range of administrative law issues. Even when they were not followed, they could sow the seeds of future legal development. Particularly when the Conseil d'Etat itself provided very short, if not cryptic judgments, then the *commissaire* provided the explanation of what was going on and why a solution had been adopted – 'to the silence of the judge replies the eloquence of its *commissaire*'.[26] The names of the *commissaires* are well known and are frequently cited. Indeed, more of the conclusions of the *commissaires* are published than those of their counterparts in private law.

There was a large body of members of the Conseil d'Etat, but a few specialised in developing the principles of administrative law. Already in the period 1800 to 1815, some 121 conseillers, 74 *maîtres de requêtes* and 435 *auditeurs* had been appointed.[27] Of course most did not deal with litigation. The judicial function was an adjunct to the general work of being the motor of government and so it had an easy route to influence the approach of the wider administration. But it is an indication of the large number of people who would have been involved at some stage in litigation compared with the English courts of the period. The importance of promotion within the membership of the Conseil, especially to senior roles in litigation, ensured a body of expertise could develop the principles of administrative law.

[24] Drago et al (n 19) 385.

[25] See F Rolin, 'Jean Romieu: Une Pensée en Action au Service d'un Projet pour le Droit Public' (2021) *Revue Française de Droit Administratif* 1151.

[26] N Rainaud, *Le Commissaire du Gouvernement près le Conseil d'Etat* (Paris, LGDJ, 1996) 6.

[27] J Tulard in Drago (n 19) 13.

The first distinctive feature of the administrative judges, particularly in the Conseil d'Etat, is that they are not simply career judges, as in the private law courts. The pattern established in 1799 has continued with the Conseil d'Etat being a relatively tight group of career civil servants. Even those who are predominantly involved in litigation have often undertaken other roles in politics and the public service. Service within government ministries has been a characteristic of the work of members. So the distinctive feature is of judges who are typically recruited early in their career, but will spend some significant time in the 'active' administration.

The second distinctive feature of the judges is that they deal with a lot of cases and so have a broad sense of administrative law. The early litigation fed into the five administrative sections who then formally made decisions on problems in their area. These days, there are specialist sub-sections of the Section du contentieux which deal with specific types of problem – tax, public contracts, education, etc. But they still needed a broad knowledge of administrative law principles and procedures to deal with the problems in their area. This is even more important the higher the judge goes within the court, since appeals are heard by multiple judges sitting as a panel.

Whilst the distinctiveness of the personnel in the administrative courts is significant, it is worth recalling that the avocats and the avocats au Conseil d'Etat et à la Cour de cassation play a significant role. In the absence of an administration school before 1945, most of the administrative judges would have undertaken a law degree and many would have been avocats.[28] The great Laferrière practised as an avocat before 1870 and was appointed to the Conseil d'Etat in its reformed state precisely because he was from outside. The avocats practise public and private law. So it is natural for them to suggest solutions drawn from private law when considering problems in public law, if they are helpful. There are numerous examples of the creation of public law rules which mirror those which existed already in private law, not least in the areas of public law employment and public contracts. So the separation of courts, judges and caselaw is not watertight because the legislator and practitioner lawyers straddle the public law-private law divide.

All the same, the significance of distinct judges and (as we will see) distinct academics is that they have attention focused on administrative law. They have the cohesion necessary to advance the subject in a clear way.

III. Factor 3: Procedure

The continuity of institutions has enabled the incremental development of procedure. There was no code of administrative court procedure before 2000 (though there was a code for the lower administrative courts from 1990). This was in contrast to private law which had a code of civil procedure from 1807. So, for the first 200 years, the rules of procedure were developed piecemeal in response to particular situations. In the early days, the Conseil d'Etat and the conseils de préfecture operated in a way similar to

[28] On the influence of legal practitioners, see eg A Morillot, 'La Collaboration de l'Ordre avec le Conseil d'Etat' in *Le Conseil d'Etat. Livre Jubilaire* (Paris, Sirey, 1950) 367.

institutions of the Ancien Régime. Complaints would be received and resolved by office procedures, not by judicial procedures as before the Parlements. A file would be prepared by a junior official so a decision could be taken by superiors. A more judicial approach arrived with the July Monarchy. The ordinance of 2 February 1831 on the Conseil d'Etat provided for public hearings and to allow lawyers to argue on behalf of parties. It also introduced the equivalent of the *parquet*, a public advocate who would advise the court in the name of the law, rather than on behalf of litigants. This *commissaire du roi* became in 1849 the *commissaire du gouvernement* and is since 2009 the *rapporteur public*. These procedural innovations really borrowed a model from the private law courts.

As has been mentioned, the equivalent procedural reforms at the level of the conseil de préfecture had to wait until the decree of 30 December 1862. It also provided for public hearings and lawyers to represent parties. The secretary-general of the court was to be the *commissaire du gouvernement*, a practical measure when the court only had three or four judges. More detailed procedural rules were prescribed by a decree of 12 July 1865 which thus made these bodies of similar standing to the lower civil courts. The public acceptability of administrative courts relied largely on them mirroring the model of procedure found in the private law courts, which was the paradigm of 'judicial' process.

The implications of these reforms were significant. In the first place, the procedure of the administrative courts became recognisably judicial and not just an administrative inquiry. They involved findings of fact and arguments based on the law, even if proceedings were more based on written documents, rather than oral pleadings. Secondly and significantly, the short, impersonal judgment of the court gave away merely the barest of the reasons for a decision. But the discursive, advisory opinion of the *commissaire du gouvernement* provided the opportunity to articulate ideas on public law principles which could then be inspected and debated by lawyers and by doctrinal writers. Because individuals occupied this role continuously for several years and because they had the opportunity to pronounce on a large number of cases, they became, as we shall see, key actors in legal development.

The procedural principles were developed by fragmentary legislation and by judicial decision. There were common ideas of what should count as 'legal' and 'judicial' proceedings, and administrative law typically borrowed these from private law, not least under the influence of the avocats who pleaded before them. But the fundamentally written procedure and the flexibility this gave to the administrative judges enabled a distinctive administrative law procedure to be sustained. Among the distinctive procedural features which were developed were a range of complaints which did not need the complainant to employ an avocat, especially when challenging the legality of a decision. This made litigation relatively cheap. There was also the development of the collective action at the beginning of the twentieth century, well in advance of private law.[29] On the other hand, administrative law was weak on enforcement of judgments

[29] See CE 21 December 1906, *Syndicat des propriétaires et contribuables du Quartier de Croix-de-Seguey-Tivoli*, n° 19167, D. 1907.3.41 concl. Romieu.

against the administration except where a judgment amounted to an order to pay money. This seemed to provide a special privilege to the administration.

In more recent times, the French model of judicial proceedings has come under scrutiny from the European Court of Human Rights which has forced the French to change it in a variety of areas. In administrative law, the most contentious was the way the Strasbourg Court required changes to the way the *commissaire du gouvernement* operated, eventually forcing a change of name to 'rapporteur public' in 2009 (now also feminised as 'rapporteure publique'). In 1995, the Strasbourg Court ruled that members of the Conseil d'Etat of Luxembourg who had been involved in advisory functions related to legislation governing milk quotas could not sit as judges over a legal challenge to the validity of the decisions made under them.[30] The key point was that 'the mere fact that certain persons successively performed these two types of function in respect of the same decisions is capable of casting doubt on the institution's structural impartiality'.[31] While this did not directly challenge the operation of the French Conseil d'Etat, it was a warning that Art. 6 of the Convention required that justice must not only be done, but must appear to be done.

This emphasis on appearances came to a head with the operation of the *commissaire du gouvernement*. When I observed proceedings extensively in the mid-1980s, the *commissaire* would see the draft judgment, produce a public comment after the parties had presented their arguments on how the case should be decided, and then retire with the judges while they made their decision, even if he or she did not have a vote. During the judicial deliberations, the *commissaire* would frequently be invited to clarify points in his argument or to express views on the implications of a possible solution. This did not happen in the private law courts or in the European Court of Justice, which was modelled on the French system. In a series of decisions, these various aspects of the operation of the *commissaire* were challenged in relation to various French courts.[32] But it became clear that the *commissaire* had to operate more like an independent party, an amicus curiae, rather than as a member of the judiciary albeit performing a different role to that of the sitting judge.

This saga demonstrates that, whereas the influences on French administrative court procedure were largely internal to France in the first 200 years, involvement in Europe has been an increasing influence in the last 25 years. As I have noted elsewhere, the reforms to the procedure of the administration, especially ideas of 'good administration', have also been very strongly influenced by European ideas.[33] All the same, in the area of procedure administrative law is not self-contained, even if many rules were developed by the administrative courts on their own.

[30] ECHR 28 September 1995, *Procola v Luxembourg*, Application 14570/89 (1995) 22 EHRR 193.

[31] ibid, para 45.

[32] See generally, J Bell and F Lichère, *Contemporary French Administrative Law* (Cambridge, Cambridge University Press, 2022) 16–19; *Kress v France*, 7 June 2001, App. n° 39594/98, AJDA 2001, 675 (ECHR); J Bell, 'The Role of the Commissaire du Gouvernement and the European Convention on Human Rights' (2003) 9 *European Public Law* 309; *Martinie v* France, 12 April 2006, App. n° 58675/00, AJDA 2006, 986, (2007) 45 EHRR 15 (ECHR Grand Chamber).

[33] Bell and Lichère (n 32) 221–31.

IV. Factor 4: Legal Doctrine

The development of 'administrative law' as a body of legal doctrine did not arise from the reception of an inheritance of Roman law or even canon law ideas, as in private law. Rather it emerges from the activity of institutions: courts, education institutions, and the publishers of scholarly works. Although it is conventional to distinguish today between 'administrative law' (*le droit administratif*) and 'administrative litigation' (*le contentieux administratif*), decisions of the courts (as in the English common law) were a key factor in the development of legal doctrine in relation to both.

In France, doctrinal legal writing is considered as a collective, not just an individual activity. As Hakim suggests, 'doctrine is thus a body made up of independent personalities working together in the direction of a community of lawyers'.[34] Scholarly writing is not simply a mass of wise monologues.[35] In France, the institutional lead role of the *Conseil d'État* has been significant not only because it has provided leading judicial decisions, but also because its senior members have provided leading contributions to scholarship, and also because they have served within the academy either as teachers or as members of the *jury d'agrégation* in selecting future professors. There is an administrative law legal community which operates in comfortable dialogues between leading judges and academics teaching across the universities and civil service schools. The Conseil holds its own events in which it invites participation from academics.[36]

A. Law Reporting

The pre-Revolutionary Conseil du Roi had handed down decisions without reasons. That was the initial pattern when the Conseil d'Etat was created. But it was necessary for the wider administration to know of the results of complaints so that future problems could be avoided. Under the Bourbon Restoration (1814–30), the caseload of the Conseil d'Etat averaged 400 cases a year; in the 1850s, this rose to 1,000 cases a year, and by the end of the century, the caseload was over 4,000 cases.[37] Law reporting aided both communication and the coherence of caselaw was helped by consistency of reporting. Initially reports were produced in a commercial journal edited by one of the *conseillers d'État*, Macarel, from 1819; but an official collection was published regularly (what is now known as the *Recueil Lebon*) from 1831. Sirey was also encouraged to report decisions which were occasionally the subject of notes. Earlier commentaries were published in journals such as the *Revue Thémis* (1819–24) and the *Revue de Législation et de Jurisprudence de Wolowsky* in the 1820s.[38] As a result, there was a significant body of case law that could be known. Even in the 1820s, case law was being seen as a complement to legislation because so few points were resolved by the texts.

[34] N Hakim, *L'Autorité de la Doctrine Civiliste Française au XIXe Siècle* (Paris, LGDJ, 2002) 374.
[35] ibid 340.
[36] See www.conseil-etat.fr/Actualites/Colloques-Seminaires-Conferences.
[37] Fortsakis (n 15) 250.
[38] M Touziel-Divina, *La doctrine Publiciste 1800–1880* (Paris, Memento du Droit, 2009) 57.

Later in the century, Serringy wrote in 1865 that 'case law is the most abundant and most certain source of administrative law.'[39] In the pivotal work on administrative law, Laferrière wrote in 1887:

> Case law is one of the essential sources of doctrine because it alone can form the bridge between permanent principles and contingent provisions, establish a hierarchy between texts, make up for their silence, their obscurity, their insufficiency by drawing inspiration from general principles of law and of justice.[40]

The existence of reports from judicial proceedings (at least in the highest court) and the status accorded to them flowed from the importance of the institution and the respect given to the work of individuals. The case law made available became the key reference point for the development of administrative law.

B. Legal Education

If you need people to staff institutions and legal advisers to guide litigants, then legal education is an important feature in the development of a branch of the legal system. Universities were closed from the beginning of the Revolution. They were re-opened under the Empire with a very clear, centrally dictated programme of study. The Loi du 22 Ventôse XII (2 March 1804) prescribed the study of various aspects of the civil code including 'the civil law as it relates to public administration'. The problem was there simply were no people trained at university level to deliver this programme. Unlike in civil law, there had been no university programmes on the topic before the Revolution, and so they were really starting from scratch. As a result of the absence of a code or of a coherent set of rules, and it took time for the teaching of administrative law to happen in practice. The term 'administrative law' first appears in 1807, and the very first course was delivered in 1808.[41] But it took until 1819 for the Minister of Education to appoint a professor in Paris, Gérando, who was a conseiller d'Etat with eclectic interests.[42] From the 1830s, there was regular teaching across the country in the universities, leading to the permanent foundation of administrative law chairs in all universities in 1838.[43] But by appointing professors of an ill-defined subject, it was more like having an author in search of a subject. It is for that reason that following the case law of the Conseil d'Etat became a natural way of shaping the subject. A national programme for university courses in administrative law was imposed by decree in 1862 justified by the need to ensure equality for all students![44] From 1855, there was a national recruitment of university professors (the *agrégation*), including in public law. So there was a gradual development of a body of academics able to teach administrative law, though they

[39] D Serrigny, *Traité de la Compétence Administrative*, 2nd edn (Paris, Durant, 1865) vol 1, vi.

[40] Laferrière (n 16) 5.

[41] As part of the proposals drawn up by the inspectors of the faculties: J-L Mestre, 'Aux Origines de l'Enseignement du Droit Administratif: Le *Cours de Législation Administrative* de Portiez de l'Oise (1808)' (1993) *Revue Française de Droit Administratif* 244.

[42] Touzeil-Divina (n 38) 263.

[43] Fortsakis (n 15) 44–48.

[44] Touzeil-Divina (n 38) 237–40.

themselves had no formation in it. The separation of public and private law was thus not simply an issue between different courts. It also was embodied in the universities which had distinct student courses, distinct academic jobs and distinct routes leading to those jobs.

The teaching of students resulted from government requirements and from student demand. As has just been noted, there was a government requirement of administrative law teach from 1808 which gradually produced a prescribed programme of study over the next half century. The centralisation of policy in the hands of the Ministry of Education ensured that the needs of the administration and the views of academics could be brought together. Student need for education was stimulated by the requirement to obtain a law degree in order to become an avocat from 1810. In practice, the *auditeurs* and the *maîtres de requêtes* in the Conseil d'Etat and the members of the conseils de préfecture were drawn from law graduates. In addition, the training of senior civil servants started after 1830. Teaching in administrative law was established in 1831 at the *École des Ponts-et-Chaussées*, the leading college for the administration's engineers. Law was part of the formation of civil servants, even if they were not intending to specialise in the litigation. The teachers were leading members of the *Conseil d'État*, such as T.-A. Cotelle, L. Aucoc and E. Laferrière.[45] After 1872, the *École Libre des Sciences Politiques* followed the same pattern for generalist administrators with teachers such as J. Romieu, R. Odent and G. Braibant, all major leaders in the development of administrative law. Typically, this would be undertaken by the *maîtres de requêtes*, especially the *commissaires de gouvernement*.

So, we have a national programme of instruction in administrative law developing over the first half of the nineteenth century. This was then followed by professorial appointments often imposed by the Ministry of National Education and a national curriculum for administrative law studies. This central direction gave the subject a clear place in the law curriculum and encouraged a systematisation which did not occur in England until much later.

C. Scholarly Literature

Legal education created demand for textbooks. The body of teachers across the country were required at least to produce their courses, often in printed form. The written versions of the courses taught in universities and colleges teaching aspirant administrators became the major texts of administrative law scholarship (and the work of their successors remains such today).[46] At the beginning of his treatise in 1828, Macarel wrote: 'There was no book which dealt particularly with administrative litigation and

[45] ibid 116–20; P Gonod, *Édouard Laferrière, un Juriste au Service de la République* (Paris, LGDJ, 1997) 38–39.

[46] See P Gonod, 'Les Membres du Conseil d'État, Auteurs de Manuels de Droit Administratif' in J Caillosse (ed), *Le Conseil d'État et l'Université* (Paris, Dalloz, 2015) 1–27. She states that the three 'Bibles' of administrative law are all by *conseillers d'État*: *Les Grands Arrêts de la Jurisprudence Administrative* by Long, the course of Odent (1970) and the treatise of Laferrière (1887). As J Rivero put it, 'le juge écrit et le juge enseigne': 'Jurisprudence et Doctrine dans l'Elaboration du Droit Administratif' (1955) *Etudes et Documents du Conseil d'État* 27, 29.

the courts which exercise it: it appeared to me that such a work would be useful and I undertook it.'[47] It is clear from this preface that the work was written to defend the idea that administrative courts based decisions on legal principle against criticism that they simply defended the administration. The interesting feature of the work is that it is predominantly about the work of the *conseils de préfecture*, which were the main bodies dealing with administrative litigation. The advantage of this focus was the clear legal texts on which their jurisdiction was based, notably the Law of 28 Pluviôse An VIII. Its theme is to demonstrate that there are organised rules on which the courts take decisions. The style of this early work was to organise the law under subject headings which could be found in legislative texts. The principle of organisation was reflected in his earlier compilation of case law of the Conseil d'Etat, which grouped cases according to subject headings.[48]

This need for teaching materials required original attempts to put together different rules applying to the administration in terms which were based on some general principles. Many of the early professors presented pedestrian summaries of legislation and cases as their structure of administrative law. This was certainly the case with Gérando.[49] Many aimed to provide students with summaries of the work of others. But Touzeil-Divina shows that this was not the case for all.[50] The writing of summaries needed to be principled, and this led to reflection on underlying principles, a process which was really only fully developed in the last fifteen years of the nineteenth century. To a great extent, this picture of administrative law mirrored that of private law. The approach of the early teachers and writers adopted a legalistic view of interpretation, as guardian of the Civil Code and thus of legal certainty, a service thus of synthesis and dissemination of the law.[51] It is only in the 1880s with the influence of German scholarship that private law doctrinal writing becomes fully developed.

The difficulty of producing an insightful synthesis was noted by Aucoc in his lectures on judicial review in 1878:

> The theory of judicial review for acting beyond one's powers (*excès de pouvoir*) is even more a creation in the proper sense of the word. Here, it is no longer a matter of offering a commentary on a text, it was more or less a matter of making the text emerge from nothing, and in that they succeeded.[52]

The absence of a code, or even directly applicable legislation in certain areas led to an appeal to general principles in both case law and doctrinal writing.[53]

[47] Macarel (n 3) v.

[48] LA Macarel, *Élémens de Jurisprudence Administrative, Extraits des Décisions Rendues par le Conseil d'État en Matière Contentieuse* (Paris, Dondey-Dupré, 1818).

[49] M Touzeil-Divina, 'Gérando et L'Enseignement du Droit Administratif' (2013) *Revue d'histoire des Facultés de Droit* 395 gives a more positive account of Gérando's work.

[50] Touzeil-Divina (n 38) 122–35. He also argues that even those producing summaries had some theoretical ideas which provided structure to their work.

[51] Hakim (n 34) 61–69.

[52] L Aucoc, *Des Recours pour Excès de Pouvoir devant le Conseil d'Etat* (Paris, Académie des Sciences Morales et Politiques, 1878) 11.

[53] M Deguergue, *Jurisprudence et Doctrine dans L'Elaboration du Droit de la Responsabilité Administrative* (Paris, LGDJ, 1994) 44. See also G Jèze, *Les Principes Généraux du Droit Administratif*, 3rd edn (Paris, Marcel Girard, 1926); G Jèze, 'Collaboration du Conseil d'Etat et de la Doctrine dans L'Elaboration du Droit Administratif Français' *Livre Jubilaire* 347.

It is worth remembering the disruption caused by changes of regime and purges. It is true that many key figures, eg, Cormenin, Macarel and Aucoc, served several regimes and developed ideas over time with an important degree of continuity. But it is significant that Cormenin and Aucoc were eventually purged. The recurring need to justify the institution of a distinct form of judicial control in relation to complaints against the administration did not encourage the reflection on the system as a whole. It is therefore not surprising that the golden age of administrative law scholarship begins in the 1880s and continues until World War I.

To some extent, the dawn of the golden age of administrative law happened by chance. The French Ministry of Education appointed Laferrière, President of the Section du Contentieux in the Conseil d'Etat, to give the inaugural course of lectures on administrative law to doctoral students in Paris (about 40 a year) in 1883–84. This course of lectures subsequently became his path-breaking *Traité de la Juridiction Administrative et des Recours Contentieux* of 1887, which is considered one of the masterpieces of French administrative law.[54] It was his vision of the formation of administrative law, notably the place of case law, which shaped the further development of the subject.[55] He organised the search for principle around the different areas of administrative litigation: review for the abuse of power, appeal (*plein contentieux*), control of legality and sanctioning. Significant development of doctrinal writing would come out of published theses (the most common form of French legal monograph), and this forum provided a greater impetus to reflection than undergraduate teaching. Nevertheless, the economics of publication made the student textbook a vehicle through which major scholarly writing from university professors developed legal doctrine. The most famous example is the *Précis de droit administratif* of Maurice Hauriou, published first in 1892.

The demand for study materials that the place of a subject within the law curriculum creates provides a major impetus to systematisation. If you have to write about a subject simply and clearly, this encourages thought about the general principles which underpin the subject.

In addition, the creation of academic positions focused on a subject (often as a result of it being significant to education) creates a critical mass of scholars who can debate with each other and refine legal thought. It is that notion of debate which is seen as central to French conceptions of legal doctrine. The creation of a body of scholars was given stimulus by the national competition, the *agrégation*, in 1855. Public law formed a distinct part of the *agrégation* in 1895 and that has continued ever since. Professors of public law are recruited separately from those in private law and thereafter appoint their successors. Since programmes of teaching follow the existence of teachers, there are distinct programmes of public law teaching at masters and doctorate level. That community is reinforced by the presence of doctoral students who contribute extensive study to the mix of arguments within the legal community. Although the practitioner professions are important, both as writers and readers, the existence of a developed place for education in a subject as part of legal education is a significant driver both to the demand for scholarly works and for writing them.

[54] E Laferrière, *Traité de la Juridiction Administrative*, 1st edn (Paris, Berger-Levrault, 1887). A second edition was published in 1896–1897: see Gonod (n 45) 38–39.

[55] ibid 44–48.

Those writing on French administrative law had no prior education in the subject and no models of pre-Revolutionary writing to copy. There were two established models available. On the one hand, there was the long tried and tested scholarly model of Roman law. Many of the early writers used the framework and structure of Roman law to present administrative law: persons, things and actions.[56] All lawyers were educated on the (then) new Civil Code, and so it provided the obvious reference point to organise the law governing the administration, not least in areas of contract and liability for wrongs. Both of these provided *structure* rather than *content* to the presentation of administrative law.

The great *principled content* of administrative law and judicial review came with the work of Laferrière in 1887 and with those academics such as Hauriou, Jèze and Duguit who wrote at the turn of the twentieth century. Indeed, Jèze argued that earlier writers were bound far too much in the thinking of private law to see the distinctiveness of public law.[57] On the other hand, Touzeil-Divina argues that distinctive principles did underpin the structure of the earlier summaries of caselaw and legislation, or of presentations of specific areas of law, such as public works. Some libertarians wanted to restrict the role of the state. There was thus a strong emphasis on express competences.[58] Others, such as Foucart (1834), emphasised the importance of protecting the civil liberties of citizens against public power.[59] The rule of law meant something more than just ensuring respect for the competences given by the legislator. Indeed, Laferrière spent his early career as a journalist and civil rights avocat before being appointed to the Conseil d'Etat. These different ideas served as the beginning of a theory of administrative law. The contribution of Laferrière's *Traité de la Juridiction Administrative* (1887) and Hauriou's *Précis de droit administratif* (1892) was to present a much greater and more principled systematisation of administrative law and judicial review.[60] The serious analysis of public law was helped by the founding of *La Revue de droit public* in 1894 with the deliberate policy of counter-balancing private law by having a journal dedicated to public law.[61]

D. Commissaires du Gouvernement

Furthermore, *commissaires du gouvernement* (as they were then known) would not only teach, but would develop legal doctrine in their *conclusions* in judicial proceedings. These would provide the court with a dispassionate and extensive survey of the law, together with clear recommendations as to its development. Their role in negotiating the listing of cases for hearing enabled them to plan the grouping of decisions favourable to dealing with important issues of law and thus in shaping legal doctrine.[62]

[56] Touzeil-Divina (n 38) 160–62.

[57] G Jèze, 'Collaboration du Conseil d'Etat et de la Doctrine dans L'Elaboration du Droit Administratif Français' *Livre Jubilaire* 347, 348.

[58] Touzeil-Divina (n 38) 179.

[59] ibid 181, 197.

[60] Fortsakis (n 15) part 1, ch 2.

[61] F Larnaude, 'Notre programme' RDP 1894, 1.

[62] B Stirn, 'Les Commissaires du Gouvernement et la Doctrine' *La Revue Administrative 1997 numéro spécial: Le Conseil d'État et la Doctrine* 41. The nearest equivalent in the English common law was the lengthy judicial decision which, unlike the French judicial decision, is discursive and fully argued.

In one sense, the text of their *conclusions* (when published) provided a reference point for scholarly writing. They expounded principles at length and contributed original ideas. But, for much of the first 150 years, they did not explicitly engage with the views of scholarly writers.[63] They would refer explicitly to other *commissaires du gouvernement* and to decisions of the Conseil, only obliquely referring to the scholarship on which they were drawing. All the same, Deguergue argues that they maintained concordance between case law and scholarly writing.[64]

In more recent years, the writings of the commissaires have appeared in journals, not least the Conseil's own *Etudes et Documents du Conseil d'Etat*. They are also frequent participants in colloquia, organised either by the Conseil d'Etat or by universities. The rapporteur public (as the *commissaire* is now called) is very clearly a contributor to scholarly debate.

E. External Influence

Scholarly writing sometimes did take an interest in what happened in other countries (mainly in Europe and the US). The first issue of the *Revue de droit public* in 1894 deliberately had sections on foreign (European) legal and political systems. But, unlike in private law, there were few examples in the nineteenth century of French scholars making suggestions for the development of French law in the light of the law in other countries.[65] To a great extent, the doctrine of French administrative law was the product of internal forces and reflection. There were not the external models on which to draw. If anything, French administrative law was more a point of reference for other countries. German scholars like Mayer explained the French administrative law and offering it to the German scholarly audience as a model.[66] Dicey may not have wished to import it into English law, but he did write: 'On the whole it appears to be true that if administrative law is to exist it is seen at its best as French *droit administratif*.'[67]

The French system of administrative law contributed substantially to the European Court of Justice and the principles of administrative law that it recognised. But if this describes the initial position in the first century and a half, it is no longer accurate.

François Lichère and I have tried to document how France now operates within a European and an international environment. External influence existed after World War I,[68] but accelerated after the Second. Formally, since 1946, treaty law has prevailed over domestic law. France has committed itself to being part of an international legal community. In the case of the European Union, this was formally recognised by a

[63] Deguergue (n 53) 723–25 and 738ff.

[64] ibid 807.

[65] JL Mestre, 'The Vissitudes of a Tradition' in P Cane, HCF Hoffmann, EC Ipp and P Lindseth (eds), *The Oxford Handbook of Comparative Administrative Law* (Oxford, Oxford University Press, 2020) section 2.1.

[66] M Stolleis, *Public Law in Germany* (T Dunlap (trans)) (Oxford, Oxford University Press, 2017) 70–71. Strasbourg was a German territory at that time.

[67] AV Dicey, *Lectures on Comparative Constitutionalism* (J Allison (ed)) (Oxford, Oxford University Press, 2013) 314.

[68] See CE 5 July 1929, *Ministre du travail*, RDP 1931, 319; Bell and Lichère (n 32) 195 on influence from the International Labour Organisation.

constitutional amendment introducing a whole section on European Union law. In some areas, there have been clear European influences. I have already mentioned court procedure. But one can add administrative contracts, proportionality as a ground of review, as well as standards of good administration. Of course, the influence is not one-way and nor does it fail to meet resistance. France retains its distinctive legal doctrine, its legal values and its own way of doing things. But increasingly, it has to justify its choices not only internally, but also to wider audiences.

The external influences come in a number of directions. First, the political/constitutional context established commitments of France to the wider legal world. France was among the founders of many international and European bodies and so wanted to play its role. On the other hand, at the beginning of the European Economic Community, there was a tension between the commitments made by the Fourth Republic and the more hostile position adopted by the Gaullists in the early years of the Fifth Republic, which slowed down the willingness of the Conseil d'Etat to embrace the idea of the primacy of European Community Law. Secondly, personnel mattered. Members of the Conseil d'Etat took part in international judicial bodies. The earliest evidence of import was the idea of proportionality in civil service matters brought back by a participant in the International Labour Organisation.[69] Judges of the Conseil d'Etat played a prominent role as judges of the European Court of Human Rights, and also as judges, advocates general and référendaires at the Luxembourg court. In this way, they provided insider knowledge back to the Conseil d'Etat, particularly when they returned to take senior positions. Furthermore, their membership of these external bodies provided informal channels of communication facilitating understanding and sometime trying to influence developments.[70]

In addition, these developments provided topics for colloquia, journals and scholarly writing to which members of the Conseil, academics and practitioners participated. Because the topics were international, judges and academics from outside France also took part. The interest was no longer simply in disseminating the glories of French administrative law, but in examining how it could be involved reciprocally in the wider European and international legal worlds.

V. Factor 5: Circumstance

Much in legal development is down to chance events. Development occurs by way of reaction to them. An example would be the development of judicial review. The growth of the economy at the beginning of the French industrial revolution led to a large increase in the numbers of appeals and complaints coming to ministers from local authorities. In 1852, the Second Empire sought to 'decentralise' decision-making by conferring on prefects powers to make final decisions. This meant that the ministers (and thus the Conseil d'Etat as advisor) no longer saw these matters on appeal. As Aucoc explained, the result was that the Conseil d'Etat expanded the *recours pour excès de pouvoir* in order

[69] ibid.
[70] Bell and Lichère (n 32) 305.

to provide a control over the new powers.[71] In the past, the decisions of an administrator would have been considered a matter of 'pure administration' which was not reviewable. Aucoc was well placed to comment, because his *conclusions* in the *Bizet* case of 1867 were considered to be the new charter of judicial review.[72]

The failure of the constituent assemblies of 1945–46 to produce a clear statement of fundamental rights left the Conseil d'Etat with the task of articulating these. To achieve this within the existing sources of law, the Conseil drew on the established idea of 'general principles of law' on which the Conseil d'Etat and scholars had drawn since the early nineteenth century.[73] The term first appeared in judgments from 1945 and was significant until the 1970s when the Conseil constitutionnel articulated general principles at constitutional level.[74]

VI. Conclusion

The basic argument has been that path dependence is not merely doctrinal but involves a cumulation of features, notably institutional features such as courts, professions and universities. Path dependence is not a one-off feature, but the result of a series of choices and actions over time. The implications of these choices and actions may not have been anticipated or planned in advance. They are often incremental and pragmatic responses to specific situations and needs that build together into a pattern. As a result, path dependence is easier to see retrospectively rather than looking from the moment of the initial decision.

French administrative law was created more or less from scratch at the beginning of the nineteenth century. It was created largely through case law of the Conseil d'Etat by a relatively small pool of people who specialised in resolving litigation. Its decisions formed the basis for public understanding and for university teaching on administrative law. These early beginnings shaped the development of the substantial body of doctrine and activities which we now describe as 'French administrative law'. Similar values, but different institutions have led other countries along different paths.

[71] Aucoc (n 52) 26–27.

[72] CE 13 March 1867, *Bizet*, S 1868.2.91 concl. Aucoc, note Choppin.

[73] Macarel (n 3) 231, 459.

[74] B Jeanneau, *Les Principes Généraux du Droit dans la Jurisprudence Administrative* (Paris, Sirey, 1954) 3; Bell and Lichère (n 32) 210–19.

PART IV

History and Modernity

18

Law in Henry James's Early Fiction

PAUL MITCHELL*

I.

At the age of 19, Henry James travelled from Newport, Rhode Island, to Cambridge, Massachusetts, on what he would later describe as 'one of the oddest errands … that, given the several circumstances, I could possibly have undertaken'.[1] He was entering Harvard Law School. The 'Law School experiment', as James later dubbed it, lasted only one academic year. In the following year, 1864, he would publish his first criticism, a review of Nassau Senior's *Essays on Fiction*, and, soon afterwards, his first fiction, 'A Tragedy of Error'. His career as a critic and writer soon took off.

When, very much later, in *Notes of a Son and Brother*, James came to look back at this year at Harvard, he gave an uninspiring account of his motivation:

> it had seemed to me for some time past that some such step as my entering for instance the Harvard Law School more or less urgently concerned what I could but try to help myself out by still putting forward as my indispensable education – I am not sure that the claim didn't explicitly figure, or at least successfully dangle, as that of my possibly graceful mere 'culture'.[2]

At best, it seemed, the Law School would buy him some time; 'though I hasten to add', James continued,

> that my approach to the Law School can scarcely, as a means to this end, in the air of it that comes back to me, have been in the least deceptive. By which I mean that my appearance of intentions, qualifications, possibilities, or whatever else, in the connection, hadn't surely so much as the grace of the specious.[3]

Who it was that might have been deceived – whether his father, family, social circle, perhaps even himself – is left open. But the basic message is clear enough: James retrospectively saw himself as transparently unsuited to legal study. To judge from the autobiography, the determining influences in James's decision to become a law student

* I am grateful to Steve Fender, Anthony Julius and Marco Wan for their comments on an earlier draft.

[1] H James, 'Notes of a Son and Brother' in H James, *Autobiographies* (P Horne (ed)) (New York, Library of America, 2016) 434.

[2] ibid 434.

[3] ibid 434–35.

were the outbreak of the Civil War, and his inability to enlist for active service. There was, in other words, nothing intrinsically appealing for him about legal study.

Once he had entered the Law School, James found many things to enjoy about Harvard.[4] But law, apparently, was not one of them. He preferred to read fiction, literary criticism or history;[5] and though, looking back, he was impressed by his diligent attendance at lectures, the diligence was all the more impressive as he understood 'not a word'. What kept him coming back was the opportunity to observe his classmates and their interactions. James wrote with far greater enthusiasm about attending lectures on literature by James Russell Lowell and Francis James Child. It was hardly surprising, then, that James lasted only a year in the Law School; indeed, we might feel that he did well to stick it out that long. Above all, there is nothing in James's autobiography to suggest that the legal ideas to which he was exposed offered any possibilities for his literary work. If the autobiography tells the whole story, the Law School experiment produced no literary results.

II.

It is, however, well known that James's late retrospective work has a tendency to rewrite his own history. As one critic has put it, 'in these books dealing with his early years, [he] gives us his mature self rather than his younger'.[6] It has also been noticed that the autobiographies 'characteristically tend to obscure the ideological and political content of his Harvard experience'.[7] A suggestive contrast with the autobiographies' rather categorical rejection of any connection, for James, between law and literature, is provided by an earlier passage from his notebooks. A friend had remarked to James, presumably with a significant look, that every man's life had its 'turning-point'. James's initial response was 'blank and unrecognising', but he then realised what his friend was suggesting:

> It so happened that I had in the deepest depths of the past spent a year at that admirable institution the Harvard Law School, and that, withdrawing from it prematurely – though under no precipitation that I may not now comfortably enough refer to; – I brought away with me certain rolls of manuscript that were quite shamelessly not so many bundles of notes on the perusal of so many calf-skin volumes. These were notes of quite another sort, small sickly seed enough, no doubt, but to be sown and to sprout up into such flowers as they might, in a much less trimmed and ordered garden than that of the law.

The friend had read two or three of these early stories, and suggested to James

> the inference that, since [this work] had, in principle forced its way up through a soil that so little favored it, I must there, in the cold shade of queer little old Dane Hall, have stood at

[4] H Hutchinson, 'Just Literary: Henry James and "the Law School Experiment"' (2013) 15(1) *Literary Imagination* 36.

[5] RK Martin, 'Henry James and the Harvard College Library' (1969) 41(1) *American Literature* 95 sets out James's library borrowing record. No equivalent records exist for the Harvard Law Library (I am grateful to Robin G McElheny of the Harvard Archive Service for this information).

[6] CP Kelley, *The Early Development of Henry James*, revised edn (Urbana, University of Illinois Press, 1965) 12.

[7] SB Blair, 'Changing the Subject: Henry James, *Dred Scott*, and Fictions of Identity' (1992) 4(1) *American Literary History* 28, 33.

> the parting of my ways, recognised the false steps, even though few enough, already taken, and consciously committed myself to my particular divergence. Let me say at once that I welcomed that suggestion – for the kindly grace of it, the element of antique charm and bedimmed romance that it placed, straight away, at the disposal of my memory; by which I mean that I wondered whether I mightn't find, on ingenious reflection, that my youth *had* in fact enjoyed that amount of drama. I couldn't, I felt, be sure …[8]

Here James is consciously and comically resisting the temptation to rewrite his own history. He could not bring himself to say that in practice the soil had been quite so barren as it had, 'in principle', first appeared. The notebook entry thus gestures towards a more complicated, and nuanced – we might say, a more Jamesian – relationship between James's literary development and his legal studies.

III.

What makes these autobiographical materials particularly intriguing is that, if we did not have the benefit of James's own interpretations, and judged purely by his interests as a novelist and critic, his choice to study law would not seem in the least 'odd'. As a novelist one of his great themes is the conflicting demands of duties, obligations and rights, and characters' attempts to ameliorate or resolve these clashes. Legal rules often provide one strand of a complex situation in which duty, morality, self-determination and love are interwoven. As a critic James consistently emphasised questions of form, regularity and convention. The opening sentence of his first published critical article, for instance, expressed the hope that Senior's *Essays on Fiction* would 'attempt to codify the vague and desultory canons, which cannot, indeed, be said to govern, but which in some measure define, this department of literature'.[9] He was also much concerned with the question of a novelist's '*locus standi*'.[10] He is, in other words, pre-eminently a writer we might expect to be interested in, and stimulated by, law.

James's protestations that the Law School experiment was just a way to fill the time are perhaps most effectively problematised by his creative use of law in the fiction, particularly the short stories, that he published in the decade or so after his time at Harvard. He declared in his essay on Senior that 'For our own part, we would like nothing better than to write stories for weary lawyers and school-masters'.[11] As the essay continues, James seems to be making a rather playful and provocative general point about the imaginative freshness and energy of busy people, as contrasted with idle readers, but the fact that he visualised his ideal reader as a lawyer is very striking, and, significant. As we shall see, the early fiction is rich in characters with whom lawyers, whether weary or otherwise, could identify, with allusions to legal texts and points that lawyers would appreciate, and with situations in which the antinomies between law and other systems of rules create

[8] H James, 'The Turning Point of My Life' in *Autobiographies* (n 1) 704–705.The friend is probably William Dean Howells (ibid 830).

[9] H James, 'Nassau W Senior' in H James, *Literary Criticism Volume One: Essays on Literature; American Writers; English Writers* (L Edel (ed)) (New York, Library of America, 1984) 1196.

[10] H James, 'Anthony Trollope' in ibid 1330, 1342–43. See further, Blair (n 7).

[11] James, 'Nassau W Senior' (n 9) 1197.

problems for the characters. I shall also argue that in three of his early short stories James went further, and used legal doctrine as the germ of his narrative. These stories are reflections on, and responses to, fundamental legal ideas.

IV.

James's use of law was sometimes comedic. In *Roderick Hudson*, for instance, everyone apart from Roderick's mother can see that Roderick is not cut out for legal practice. We hear that he is 'reading law, at the rate of a page a day'; and the lawyer in whose office he has been apprenticed describes Roderick 'sitting by the hour with the page unturned, watching the flies buzz, or the frost melt on the window-pane'.[12] There is here, perhaps, a note of rueful, autobiographical self-satire – it was only recently, after all, that James had been attempting to toil through legal treatises himself. Just how little those treatises offered to a visual artist is nicely suggested in the narrator, Rowland Mallet's, comment when shown one of Roderick's early sculptures and told it is by a law student: 'He has found something in Blackstone that I never did'.[13] It is a nice comic moment, but we should also notice two points about it. First, you only really get the joke if you have (attempted to) read Blackstone – it is a little in-joke for the lawyer readership. Second, it tells us that the narrator, who will come to have a very significant, indeed, pivotal, role in the novel, has been a law student, possibly even a lawyer, himself.[14]

Reading Blackstone has not been the narrator's only involvement with law. Before the action begins in *Roderick Hudson*, he has been involved in litigation over an inheritance:

> [His father] left but a third of his property to his son, and devoted the remainder to various public institutions and local charities. Rowland's third was an easy competence, and he never felt a moment's jealousy of his fellow-pensioners; but when one of the establishments which had figured most advantageously in his father's will bethought itself to affirm the existence of a later instrument, in which it had been still more handsomely treated, the young man felt a sudden passionate need to repel the claim by process of law. There was a lively tussle, but he gained his case; immediately after which he made, in another quarter, a donation of the contested sum. He cared nothing for the money, but he had felt an angry desire to protest against a destiny which seemed determined to be exclusively salutary.[15]

This vignette hints at the complex mixed motives of Rowland as litigant. Rowland tells himself that he is protesting 'against a destiny', but there is surely a more personal antagonist here: the father. As the passage immediately preceding this summary of the litigation explains, Rowland's wealthy father had imposed utter parsimony in his son's upbringing.

[12] H James, *Roderick Hudson* in H James, *Novels 1871–1880* (WT Stafford (ed)) (New York, Library of America, 1983) 185, 207.

[13] ibid 178.

[14] James came to see Rowland Mallet's 'view and experience' of Roderick as the 'subject' of the book: 'Preface to *Roderick Hudson*' in H James, *Literary Criticism Volume Two* (L Edel (ed)) (New York, Library of America, 1984) 1039, 1049–50.

[15] *Roderick Hudson* (n 12) 176.

The inheritance litigation represents the first time that Rowland has been able to fight back against this paternal financial sadism. As the novel unfolds, Rowland will become less and less in control of situations in which neither law nor money will help him to express or channel his anger and frustration. And the vignette is also an ironic anticipation of how uncooperative Roderick himself will be when he feels that he is being required to act. Rowland, we might be tempted to think, would do well to remember how he himself had responded when told to do something that he would, otherwise, have been perfectly content to undertake voluntarily.

The inheritance story also states a theme to which James would frequently return and elaborate on: law has no presumptive moral authority; it does not determine characters' valuations or their conduct. The law decides that Rowland is entitled to the money, and his response is to dispose of it in a way that (for all we are told) is indistinguishable from the claim he has just repelled. When the character at the centre of the situation is a lawyer, the antinomies between law and moral assessment are particularly sharp. In *The Europeans*, for instance, Mr Wentworth is a semi-retired lawyer whose niece has contracted a morganatic marriage with a German prince. Wentworth is worried: 'Was it right, was it just, was it acceptable? He always slept badly, and the night before he had lain awake much more even than usual, asking himself these questions'.[16] A little later, Wentworth's perplexity remains undiminished: 'He could not even bring himself to attempt to measure her position in the world. She was the wife of a foreign nobleman who desired to repudiate her. This had a singular sound, but the old man felt himself destitute of the materials for a judgment'.[17] James here affectionately mocks the excessively earnest and serious mindset of a traditional New England head of the family. Wentworth seems to be turning everything over in his mind, but the one question he never seems to ask is whether the arrangement is legally effective. It is implicit that mere legal validity would not settle the point one way or the other.

V.

James was particularly skilful in exploiting the gap between legal and moral obligations in contractual contexts. One early example is 'A Landscape Painter', in which a marriage comes about through mutual, and complementary, misrepresentations by both bride and groom.[18] It is a nice question who is more blameworthy, but there is no doubt that the marriage is legally binding. In 'The Story of a Masterpiece', another early story about a painter, the gap between legal and moral is explored systematically.[19] The tale revolves around the commission of a portrait. The commission is given to the artist, Baxter, by Lennox; the subject of the portrait is to be Lennox's fiancée, Marian Everett. It transpires that Baxter already knows Marian; they have been engaged, but Marian broke it off.

[16] *The Europeans* in *Novels 1871–1880* (n 12) 873, 905.

[17] ibid 929.

[18] H James, 'A Landscape Painter' in H James, *Complete Stories 1864–1874* (J Strouse (ed)) (New York, Library of America, 1999) 67.

[19] H James, 'The Story of a Masterpiece' in H James, *Complete Stories 1864–1874* (J Strouse (ed)) (New York, Library of America, 1999) 209.

Baxter paints the picture – it is his masterpiece, and part of its achievement is to hint at aspects of Marian's character which Lennox would rather not face. Here is an exchange between Lennox and Baxter as the portrait is nearing completion:

> 'I hardly know how to formulate my objections. Let me, at all events, in the first place, say that I admire your work immensely. I'm sure it's the best picture you've painted'.
>
> 'I honestly believe it is. Some parts of it', said Baxter, frankly, 'are excellent'.
>
> 'It's obvious. But either those very parts or others are singularly disagreeable. That word isn't criticism, I know; but I pay you for the right to be arbitrary. They are too hard, too strong, of too frank a reality. In a word, your picture frightens me, and if I were Marian I should feel as if you'd done me a certain violence'.[20]

Once it is finished, things are no better, and Baxter presses Lennox to say exactly what is wrong with it:

> 'If you were not the gentleman, Mr Lennox … I should believe you simply bent on cheapening the portrait … If the picture really offends you, I'll rub it out. Say the word', and he took up a heavy brush, covered with black paint.
>
> But Lennox shook his head with decision and went out. The next moment, however, he reappeared, 'You *may* rub it out', he said. 'The picture is, of course, already mine'.
>
> But now Baxter shook his head. 'Ah! now it's too late', he answered. 'Your chance is gone'.[21]

What is 'wrong' with it, of course, is that it confronts Lennox with the devastating truth. For our purposes what is particularly striking is that James mediates the revelation through the legal relations of the parties. In the first passage Lennox self-consciously relies on his contractual 'right to be arbitrary' (which, we take it, must be an implied term). In the second passage, the price is now due, and, at least on Lennox's understanding, he has become the owner of the work. As a matter of legal analysis, this probably reflects the parties' intentions; but it is also true in a different sense – having once seen the truth about Marian, Lennox cannot now unsee it, he has internalised the picture forever. Lennox's contractual rights, however, do not extend to having the artist destroy his own work. He will have to do this for himself, which eventually, the day before the wedding, he does with disturbing violence. The story ends with a terse final paragraph including the following passage:

> It is not necessary to relate how he explained his exploit to Marian and how he disclosed it to Baxter. He at least put on a brave face. There is a rumor current of his having paid the painter an enormous sum of money. The amount is probably exaggerated, but there can be no doubt that the sum was very large.[22]

James's original version of the story did not include this final paragraph, it ended with the destruction of the painting.[23] Whatever James's reservations about its merits, the conclusion serves to reiterate his creative use of the friction between law and morals.[24]

[20] ibid 229.

[21] ibid 236.

[22] ibid 241–42.

[23] CK Fish, 'Indirection, Irony, and the Two Endings of James's "The Story of a Masterpiece"' (1965) 62(3) *Modern Philology* 241.

[24] See James's letter of 23 October 1867 to Francis Pharcellus Church, co-editor of the *Galaxy* (which had accepted the story for publication) in H James, *The Complete Letters of Henry James 1855–1872* (PA Walker and GW Zacharias (ed)) (Lincoln, University of Nebraska Press, 2006) vol 1, 187.

Lennox, of course, owes Baxter nothing as a matter of law. What we might, perhaps, feel, is that he owes Baxter an explanation; but here James is careful to distinguish – Marian (his now wife) receives Lennox's explanation; to Baxter the fact of destruction is merely 'disclosed'. The rumoured large payment remains ambiguous – it is not an agreed price, nor is Lennox guilty of any legal wrong by destroying his own property; so is it an apology, a solace for injured feelings? Perhaps Lennox is buying Baxter's future silence? The law cannot explain the source of this obligation.

VI.

'Guest's Confession' sees James continuing to explore the legal, social and moral aspects of making and breaking contracts. Guest is a businessman who, it seems, has been guilty of some sharp practice that has caused loss to the narrator's half-brother, Edgar Musgrave. We are never given exact details, but Guest seems to have exceed his authority in his dealings with Edgar's bonds. Guest does not deny his guilt, but is unable to make good the loss immediately. Edgar threatens litigation, to avoid which, at the narrator's suggestion, Guest writes a humiliating confession, in terms dictated to him by Edgar:

> I have on my bended knees, in the presence of Mr Musgrave and his step-brother, expressed my contrition; in consideration of which Mr. Musgrave forfeits his incontestable right to publish his injury in a court of justice. Furthermore, I solemnly declare myself his debtor in the sum of twenty thousand dollars; which, on his remission of the interest, and under pain of exposure in a contrary event, I pledge myself to repay at the earliest possible moment.[25]

Guest sells all his possessions, and pays off the debt relatively promptly. Both Guest and the narrator expect Edgar to return the written confession to Guest, but Edgar refuses to do so: 'Where else would be his punishment? … Is it set down in the bond that I'm to give it up to him? The thing's mine to have and to hold forever'.[26] As a strict matter of interpretation, Edgar is, of course, correct; but, as the narrator points out to him, this insistence on his strict rights makes him 'a veritable Shylock'.[27] Edgar then falls ill, and soon dies; on his deathbed, as he is fanatically burning his papers, he comes across the confession, which the narrator saves from destruction. The narrator then proceeds to use the confession to pressurise Guest into dropping his objections to the narrator's marrying Guest's daughter. The story concludes with the narrator stopping just short of revealing Guest's earlier wrongdoing.

'Guest's Confession' is an unsettling work – Guest's humiliation is carried out in a systematic, relentless way, which is hard to watch. But what makes this story particularly disturbing is the way that events spiral out of all proportion to Guest's initial act of exceeding his authority, and in the process basic moral distinctions are obliterated. What Edgar does out of self-righteous vengefulness is indistinguishable from what the

[25] H James, 'Guest's Confession' in *Complete Stories 1864–1874* (n 18) 669, 688–89.

[26] ibid 709.

[27] ibid. There are other allusions to *The Merchant of Venice* at 690 ('the vengeance of a very Shylock') and 721 ('His daughter and his ducats' – compare *The Merchant of Venice* 2.8.15: 'My daughter! O, my ducats! O, my daughter!').

narrator does for love. As the narrator self-incriminatingly puts it, 'In a holy cause – and holy, you may be sure, I had dubbed mine – were not all arms sanctified?'[28]

We might hope that the law could restore some kind of order, or proportion, but that is not how law affects events. As a matter of legal analysis, it does seem that Guest has exceeded his authority. The legal right thus conferred on Edgar, combined with Edgar's character as 'perpetually affirming, and defining and insuring himself, insisting upon a personal right or righting a personal wrong',[29] generates toxic consequences which the law cannot prevent. It is trite law that a threat to litigate to vindicate your own legal rights cannot found a plea of duress; it is similarly trite that blackmail requires a demand *for money* with menaces. Nor, as a matter of legal right, does Guest have any entitlement to the return of the document. Law, unhappily, is complicit in Guest's humiliation and emasculation. Indeed, it is precisely because Edgar and (implicitly) the narrator have taken the strict legal position as licensing them to act on their unchecked emotions that events unfold in the way that they do. By the end of the story, the only person who has committed a legal wrong is Guest; but both Edgar and the narrator have behaved far worse than him. 'Guest's Confession' is a powerful, disturbing portrait of what happens when law is allowed to count for too much.

VII.

If 'Guest's Confession' has too much law, *Watch and Ward* has troublingly too little. James's first novel – although he would later effectively disown it by excluding it from the New York edition – is a sinister and strange story. It perhaps gives a sufficient sense of its strangeness that Roger Lawrence, a middle-aged man who adopts a twelve year old girl and trains her (more accurately, grooms her) to become his wife is the hero: the novel ends with their marriage. The 'adoption' is as informal as it could possibly be. Roger happens to be staying at the same hotel as Nora and her father. The father commits suicide, and Roger is the first on the scene; the destitute Nora accepts Roger's offer to look after her. There is never any suggestion that the law might disturb this cosy arrangement.

As Nora grows up, she registers that something is not quite right:

> 'Roger … has it never struck you as very strange that we should be living together in this way? … What are you? Neither my brother, nor my father, nor my uncle, nor my cousin, – nor even, by law, my guardian.'
>
> 'By law! My dear child, what do you know about law?'
>
> 'I know that if I should run away and leave you, you couldn't force me to return.'
>
> 'That's fine talk! Who told you that?'
>
> 'No one; I thought of it myself. As I grow older, I ought to think of such things.'[30]

[28] ibid 723.
[29] ibid 676.
[30] H James, *Watch and Ward* in *Novels 1871–1880* (n 12) 1, 41.

Roger's dismissal of law here represents an ironic contrast with his earlier reflections on Nora's future:

> Ought he not, in the interest of his final purpose, to force home to her soul in her sensitive youth an impression of all that she owed him, so that when his time had come, if imagination could lead her a-wandering, gratitude would stay her steps? A dozen times over he was on the verge of making this point, of saying, 'Nora, Nora, these are not vulgar alms; I expect a return. One of these days you must pay your debt. Guess my riddle! I love you less than you think, – and more! A word to the wise'. But he was silenced by a saving sense of the brutality of such a course, and a suspicion that, after all, it was not needful. A passion of gratitude was silently gathering in the young girl's heart: that heart could be trusted to keep its engagements.[31]

What makes these thoughts so peculiarly nauseating and repulsive is the attempt to legitimise them by co-opting the legal framework of debts, obligations and – most sickeningly – 'a return'. It wilfully fictionalises a consent to a transaction that the girl could never have imagined.

Nora's perception that, if she ran away Roger 'couldn't force [her] to return' signals that Nora knows she is not a slave. But, disturbingly, the other characters, and even Nora herself, think of her as property, to be possessed. Thus, when Nora's long-lost cousin appears, 'Nora was not slow to perceive that Roger had no love for their guest, and she immediately conceded him his right of judgment … Fenton's presence was a tacit infringement of Roger's prescriptive right of property'.[32] And another character's flirtation with Nora is arrested by 'the thought that all this was Roger's, – Roger's investment, Roger's property!'[33] The force of the legal language here lies, paradoxically, in its being an outrageous misdescription. In *Watch and Ward* there is no law where it is needed; and where there is law it takes the form of provocatively obnoxious legal fictions.

VIII.

On three occasions, James seems to have put legal doctrine at the centre of a story. The first of these cases was his first published fiction, 'A Tragedy of Error', in which an unfaithful wife plots to have her husband murdered. The story is in four parts of unequal length, with the longest and most developed being the wife's negotiations with a boatman whom she hopes will carry out the killing. The wife asks to be taken to the cemetery:

> 'Straight across?' he asked.
>
> Hortense looked around her. 'It's a fine evening', said she; 'suppose you row me out to the lighthouse, and leave me at the point nearest the cemetery on our way back'.

[31] ibid 33.
[32] ibid 48.
[33] ibid 93. For recent critical explorations of the more disturbing aspects of this novel see P Walker and J Spina, "Introduction" in H James, *Watch and Ward* (P Walker and J Spina (ed)), (Cambridge, Cambridge University Press, 2023) lvi–lvii.

> 'Very well', rejoined the boatman; 'fifteen sous', and began to pull lustily.
>
> '*Allez*, I'll pay you well', said Madame.
>
> 'Fifteen sous is the fare', insisted the man.
>
> 'Give me a pleasant row, and I'll give you a hundred', said Hortense.
>
> Her companion said nothing. He evidently wished to appear not to have heard her remark. Silence was probably the most dignified manner of receiving a promise too munificent to be anything but a jest.[34]

The sense of uncertainty, mystery and mutual mistrust here is at least in part created by contractual ambiguities. Has Hortense promised 15 sous? Can her remaining in the boat signify acceptance (even though she is in no position to disembark)? And what of the promise to pay one hundred? What Hortense means by 'a pleasant row' could extend to the boatman accepting the commission to commit murder – in that case, as we shall see, she is, indeed happy to pay more than one hundred. In other words, the offer of one hundred could be serious, if cryptic. And, in that case, whose assessment of whether the promise is made 'in jest' is decisive, the offeror's or the offeree's? Can a contractual offer be accepted if the offeree initially believes it to have been made in jest, but later realises that it was serious? Furthermore, does it make a difference that the offeror was led to believe that the offer had not been communicated? In a less exalted literary context this would be an excellent contract problem question.

The inconclusive discussion about the fare is only a precursor to the real business of negotiating a contract for murder. The sticking point is, of course, the price. Hortense's opening gambit is to offer to pay 'ten times the weight in gold of every grain by which your conscience grows heavier in my service'.[35] Perhaps unsurprisingly, the boatman is not tempted by this. Hortense's next ploy is to leave the final price open –

> 'This watch is a pledge of what I shall be able and glad to give you afterward. There are two thousand francs' worth of pearls in the case'.
>
> '... *Il faut fixer la somme*', said the man, leaving the watch untouched.

The parties finally agree on 25,000 francs. Here, as in the negotiations about the fare, the legal analysis complements the parties' uneasy, uncertain relationship. Hortense's first suggestion has the look of a formula for calculating a price, but one of its terms – the additional weight of the boatman's conscience – is impossible to measure; a price to be fixed afterwards is also too inherently uncertain to be effective. The boatman's insistence on the price being fixed is, of course, a sensible protection of his interests, but it also, intriguingly, echoes the default Civil and Roman law rules about the price in consensual contracts.[36] James's peripatetic childhood had included long periods in Europe, and this story is set in France; might he, here, in the assertion that '*Il faut fixer la somme*', be giving the boatman an authentically forceful and legally grounded position? Obviously,

[34] H James, 'A Tragedy of Error' in *Complete Stories 1864–1874* (n 18) 1, 8–9.

[35] ibid 16.

[36] R Zimmermann, *The Law of Obligations Roman Foundations of the Civilian Tradition* (Oxford, Oxford University Press, 1996) 254–55; French Code Civil 1804, Art 1589 ('La promesse de vente vaut vente, lorsqu'il y a consentement réciproque des deux parties sur la chose et sur le prix') and Art 1591 ('Le prix de la vente doit être déterminé et désigné par les parties').

there is no question of this kind of contract being legally enforceable, but the parties' skirmish over the price is conducted as if general contractual principles applied.

James's achievement in this story is to have harnessed legal analysis to his literary interests. The 'weary lawyers' for whom he imagined himself writing would have registered that the dialogue gestured towards a backdrop of legal principles, and an appreciation of those principles undoubtedly deepens a reader's enjoyment of the story. But there is never any danger of a descent into the exposition of legal doctrine. The contractual material reveals the characters' motivations and power struggle – it operates as a double discourse, both legal and psychological.

IX.

James's continuing interest in the fictional and psychological possibilities of contract doctrine can be seen in the later story 'Adina'. Two Americans are riding in the countryside just outside Rome when they come across a young man who is fast asleep and clasping a gemstone in his hand. The young man wakes, and, when asked about the gem, says he has found it while out hunting. One of the Americans, who narrates the story, observes that 'There was something very simple, – a trifle silly, – in his smile, and I wondered whether he was not under-witted'.[37] Meanwhile, the narrator's companion, Sam Scrope, has almost immediately recognised that the gem is a hugely valuable topaz; he has also recognised that the young man, Angelo, has no idea of its true value. As Scrope puts it, in an aside to the narrator, 'He don't know a topaz from a turnip'.[38] Scrope detects an opportunity – 'He must sell it as a turnip'[39] – and, being careful not to intimate its value to Angelo, he flings down eleven silver *scudi*.

> 'Are you satisfied?' said my companion, curtly.
>
> The young fellow gave a strange smile. 'Have *you* a good conscience?' he demanded.
>
> 'Hang your impudence!' cried Scrope, very red. 'What's my conscience to you?'[40]

The Americans ride away in silence. The narrator has found the transaction troubling:

> I was wondering over [Scrope's] off-hand justice. I was youthful enough to shrink from being a Puritan or a casuist, but it seemed to me that I scented sophistry in Scrope's double valuation of Angelo's treasure. If it was a prize for him, it was a prize for Angelo, and ten *scudi* – and one over, – was meagre payment for a prize. It cost me some discomfort to find rigid Sam Scrope, of all men, capable of a piece of bargaining that needed to be ingeniously explained. Such as it was, he offered his explanation at last – half angrily, as if he knew his logic was rather grotesque. 'Say it out; say it, for Heaven's sake!' he cried. 'I know what you're thinking – I've played that pretty-faced simpleton a trick, eh? – and I'm no better than a swindler, evidently. Let me tell you, once for all, that I'm not ashamed of having got my prize cheap. It was ten *scudi* or nothing! If I had offered a farthing more I should have opened those sleepy eyes of

[37] H James, 'Adina' in *Complete Stories 1864–1874* (n 18) 904, 908.
[38] ibid 909.
[39] ibid.
[40] ibid 911.

> his. It was a case to pocket one's scruples and *act*. That silly boy was not to be trusted with the keeping of such a prize another half hour; the deuce knows what might have become of it. I rescued it in the interest of art, of science, of taste. The proper price of the thing I couldn't have dreamed of offering; where was I to raise ten thousand dollars to buy a bauble? … What does he want of money? Money would have corrupted him!'

Scrope is momentarily triumphant, but he has set in motion a chain of events that will inflict on him far greater losses than his gain, and will ultimately destroy his happiness. The story ends with him flinging the topaz into the Tiber.

As in 'A Tragedy of Error' the legal analysis perfectly complements the psychological interest of the story. For all the farrago of flimsy self-justification he offers the narrator, the real reason behind Scrope's desire to purchase the topaz so cheaply is unwittingly revealed by his description of Angelo as 'pretty-faced'. Scrope is oppressed by the grace and beauty of Italy, and acquiring the topaz for a fraction of its true value is his way of hitting back, of asserting himself against the feelings of inadequacy that the country has engendered in him. Crucially Scrope is committing no clear legal wrong – but that, as Angelo's devastatingly direct question to him highlights, is because sale transactions at even an extreme undervalue are not automatically set aside; on the Anglo-American law as it stood in the mid-nineteenth century the disproportion of price was at best evidence of fraud or imposition.[41] Rather like Edgar Musgrave in 'Guest's Confession', Scrope has conflated what is legally permissible with what is morally acceptable.

Where 'Adina' moves beyond 'Guest's Confession' is that in 'Adina' the self-serving self-righteousness is given an international, cultural significance. For, the simple common law contractual doctrine that a price need not be adequate was by no means universally accepted. The Civil Law had a long tradition of requiring a just price in principle, which stemmed from imperial Roman rescripts introducing a rule of *laesio enormis* whereby a sale of land for less than half of its true value was liable to be set aside.[42] The scope of the legal doctrine had expanded beyond sales of land at an undervalue, but had then been cut back for ideological and pragmatic reasons, and had almost disappeared by the mid-nineteenth century. When 'Adina' was published, in 1874, however, the position was not clear-cut. The 1804 French Code Civil had, on Bonaparte's personal intervention, retained a provision to invalidate sales of land entered for less than 5/12th of the land's true value.[43] Italy in 1865 had enacted its own Codice Civile, very largely modelled on the French code, but providing for rescission of sales of land in cases of 'lesione', which was defined as a price of less than half of the true value.[44] Italian law thus exactly reinstated the Roman law doctrine of *laesio enormis*. The doctrine would not, of course, have assisted Angelo (he had not sold land), but its reaffirmed presence suggested a broader general principle of equality of exchange. As Civilian writers put it, transactions involving inequality of exchange which fell outside

[41] See eg the sophisticated comparative analysis by Joseph Story (at that time Dane Professor at Harvard) in *Commentaries on Equity Jurisprudence as Administered in England and America* (Boston, Hilliard, Gray and Co, 1836) 239–54.

[42] For the history and development of the rule see Zimmermann, *The Law of Obligations* (n 36) 259–70.

[43] Code Civil 1804, Art 1674. J Gordley, 'Equality in Exchange' (1981) 69 California Law Review 1587, 1593. The fraction has been described by Zimmermann, *The Law of Obligations* (n 36) 264 as 'charmingly extravagant'.

[44] Codice Civile 1865, Arts 1529–1537.

the protection of positive legal rules should be dealt with in the 'internal forum' – that is to say, the parties' consciences.[45] When Angelo asks Scrope about his conscience, therefore, he is asking the question that the Civilian tradition regarded as precisely the right one. It gives Angelo's speech at this point something of the doubleness typical of pastoral: the simple rustic character puts an implausibly astute point.

Whether James was aware of the legal and philosophical underpinnings of the Civil law is difficult to say. He was perhaps most likely to have come across them in Joseph Story's *Commentaries on Equity Jurisprudence*, although equity was a second-year subject; at any rate, some of his lawyer readers would inevitably have known about the Civilian approach.[46] Whether legally informed or not, James's decision to stage the initial confrontation between Scrope and Angelo as a sale of a historical Roman artifact at an undervalue was a particularly happy one. Behind the individual characters' personal antipathy, they can be seen to embody irreconcilable cultural and legal traditions, the one focused on individualism and acquisitiveness, the other on mutuality and fair dealing. Scrope imposes his values; and the basic common law contractual tenet that a price need not be adequate thus becomes an instrument of oppression, and a legal variation on one of the great themes of James's early work – the clash between the New World and the Old.

X.

In 'My Friend Bingham', James's focus moves to tort. The narrator is one of James's imagined ideal readers – a weary lawyer, who meets his friend Bingham at a seaside resort in summer. Bingham, we are told, 'was *par excellence* a moralist, a man of sentiment'. 'I know', the narrator continues, '– he knew himself – that, in this busy Western world, this character represents no recognized avocation; but in the absence of such avocation, its exercise was nevertheless very dear to him'.[47] Bingham's moral insights are not, however, immediately obvious. He and the narrator go out shooting for something to do – 'languidly disposed towards the slaughter of wild ducks', as it is described.[48] They pass a woman with a child on their way. As they return, empty-handed, a large seagull lands on a cliff nearby.

> 'I wonder if I could put a shot into him', said Bingham.
>
> 'Try', I answered; and as he rapidly charged and levelled his piece, I remember idly repeating, while I looked at the great bird,
>
> 'God save thee, ancient mariner

[45] J Pothier, *A Treatise on the Law of Obligations, or Contracts* (WD Evans (trans)) (London, Strahan, 1806) vol 1, 21 (discussed by Story, *Commentaries on Equity Jurisprudence* (n 41) 252–53).

[46] On Story's use of Civil law in his commentaries, see MH Hoeflich, *Roman Law and Civil Law in the Development of Anglo-American Jurisprudence in the Nineteenth Century* (Athens (GA), University of Georgia Press, 1997) ch 1. On the interest in Civil law more generally, see the later chapters in Hoeflich, *Roman Law* and P Stein, 'The Attraction of the Civil Law in Post-Revolutionary America' in P Stein, *The Character and Influence of the Roman Civil Law: Historical Essays* (London, Hambledon, 1988) 411.

[47] 'My Friend Bingham' in *Complete Stories 1864–1874* (n 18) 126, 128.

[48] ibid 130.

> From the fiends that plague thee thus!
> Why look'st thou so? "With my cross-bow
> I shot the albatross"'.[49]

Bingham shoots, but the seagull has taken flight. The narrator continues,

> I cannot express our relation to what followed … better than by saying that it exposed to our sight, beyond the space suddenly left vacant, the happy figure of the child from whom we had parted but an hour before. He stood with his little hands extended, and his face raised towards the retreating bird. Of the sickening sensation which assailed our common vision as we saw him throw back his hands to his head, and reel downwards out of sight, I can give no verbal account, nor of the rapidity with which we crossed the smooth interval of sand, and rounded the bluff.[50]

The men find the boy's mother, holding her child in her arms. 'I turned from this spectacle to my friend, as to an image of equal woe. Bingham, pale as death, bounded over the stones …'[51] The 'equal' woe, and the jarring description of *Bingham* being as pale as death when the victim of the shooting lies dying in front of him, begins to alert us to the narrator's loyalties here.

The woman allows Bingham to take her child out of her arms.

> 'Did it strike his head?' cried Bingham. 'What the devil was he doing up there?'
>
> 'I told him he'd get hurt', said the young woman, with harrowing simplicity. 'To shoot straight at him! He's killed!'
>
> 'Great heavens! Do you mean to say that I saw him?' roared Bingham. 'How did I know he was there? Did you see us?'
>
> The young woman shook her head. 'Of course I didn't see you. I saw you with your guns before. Oh, he's killed'.

The narrator, who fully realises that the boy is dead, then intervenes, '"He *may* not be killed", I said, turning to Bingham; "keep your senses. It's not your fault. We *couldn't* see each other"'.

That evening, after a couple of hours of soul-searching, Bingham asks the narrator to go and see the child's mother, Lucy Hicks. He has been admiring the sky.

> 'I wish she could come out here and look at that sky', he said at last. 'It's a sight for bereaved mothers. Somehow, my dear boy', he pursued, 'I never felt less depressed in my life. It's none of my doing'.
>
> 'It would hardly do for me to tell her that', said I.[52]

Nevertheless, the narrator does see Lucy the next day, when we learn from her that she 'shall be able to avoid an inquest'. 'Mr Bingham has attended to that',[53] we are told. There will be no legal proceedings.

[49] ibid 131–32.
[50] ibid 132.
[51] ibid 132.
[52] ibid 137–38.
[53] ibid 139.

James here presents us with a shocking, tumultuous sequence of events. One way to begin to make sense of them is to consider the narrative point of view. Critics have observed that this story is an early example of James's use of a minor character as narrator, a technique he may have learned from Mérimée.[54] But the really crucial point is that he is a lawyer – for that makes the intervention when he tells Bingham 'It's not your fault. We *couldn't* see each other' particularly telling. The narrator is here, of course, applying the objective standard of reasonable care. '*Couldn't*' rather than 'didn't', italicised in the original, makes even the weary lawyer reader sit up.

It may well be that James's decision to have a lawyer narrator, who could interject in this way, was prompted by his legal studies. Torts as a distinct academic subject was slow to emerge in American law schools, and there was no lecture course specifically on torts offered at Harvard in James's time there; nor, apparently, were students referred to the recently published treatise on the subject by Hilliard.[55] Any coverage of torts would have been in the lectures on the Commentaries given by the Dane Professor, Theophilus Parsons, and, although it is difficult to get a sense of how much time could have been devoted to torts, there had been a relatively recent, fundamental case on negligence which no competent lecturer (particularly at Harvard) could have overlooked. This was *Brown v Kendall*,[56] decided by the Supreme Court of Massachusetts, which had very authoritatively laid down the general principle of 'ordinary care'. As Shaw CJ explained:

> what constitutes ordinary care will vary with the circumstances of cases. In general, it means that kind and degree of care, which prudent and cautious men would use, such as is required by the exigency of the case, and such as is necessary to guard against probable danger. A man who should have occasion to discharge a gun, on an open and extensive marsh, or in a forest, would be required to use less circumspection and care, than if he were to do the same thing in an inhabited town, village or city.[57]

'My Friend Bingham' can be read as a literary response to, and critique of, this concept.

The facts of *Brown v Kendall* were very simple. The parties' dogs were fighting; the defendant was trying to separate them by hitting them with a stick. Not realising that the claimant was behind him, the defendant lifted the stick over his head to strike another blow and hit the claimant in the eye. The injury was held to be 'the result of pure accident'.[58] Similarly, at the moment of firing the gun on the beach, Bingham '*couldn't*' see the boy. But James, as if playing with the idea of 'pure accident' complicates matters. There was no necessity to have gone out shooting in the first place; the potshot at the seagull was completely gratuitous; Bingham and the narrator have already seen

[54] Kelley (n 6) 70.

[55] On the late emergence of torts generally see GE White, 'The Intellectual Origins of Torts in America' (1977) 86 *Yale Law Journal* 671; for factors peculiar to Harvard, see R Pound, 'The Law School' in SE Morison (ed), *Development of Harvard University 1869–1929* (Cambridge (MA), Harvard University Press, 1930) 472, 491. For the lecture courses and books recommended to students see *A Catalogue of the Officers and Students of Harvard University for the Academical Year 1862–1863. First Term* (Cambridge, Sever and Francis, 1862) 62 (lectures) 66–69 (books). The first American torts treatise was F Hilliard, *The Law of Torts* (Boston, Little, Brown and Co, 1859).

[56] (1850) 60 Mass 292.

[57] ibid 296.

[58] ibid 297.

Lucy and her son going to the beach, so this is not quite like firing the gun in a marsh. It is, in other words, only by zooming in on the precise moment at which the damage was inflicted that it is possible to preserve the illusion of blamelessness.

Average attentiveness in the moment is all that can be demanded of the reasonable man, it seems, a point which James delights in satirising and probing. The narrator is busy recalling lines from *The Rime of the Ancient Mariner* when a less literary person might have said 'Ah, don't shoot it', or might have spotted the boy. And both Bingham and the narrator are very confident, to the point of complacency, about the limited extent of their responsibility. Their taste for moralising, we cannot help noticing, enables self-exculpation.

For all their confidence, however, it becomes clear that elsewhere different ideas of blame and responsibility are in play. Lucy seems to be genuinely grateful to be spared the publicity, and public investigation, of an inquest. It is never spelt out why this is, but there must be a lurking suggestion that a mother who showed 'ordinary care' in protecting her child would not have met the exacting standards of a judgmental public. Societal standards of blame are particularly brought out in later events. Bingham visits Lucy, at first to offer his condolences and inquire after her health, but soon his visits become romantic. Lucy is a poor widow who is living with her cousin, Miss Horner, but she then becomes homeless. Bingham explains to the narrator what has happened:

> Miss Horner has seen fit to resent, in no moderate terms, what she calls the 'extraordinary intimacy' existing between Mrs Hicks and myself. Mrs Hicks, as was perfectly natural, has resented her cousin's pretension to regulate her conduct. Her expression of this feeling has led to her expulsion from Miss Horner's house.[59]

What Bingham calls Miss Horner's 'incurable vulgarity of feeling' seems to be widely shared. Bingham presses his suit, and when Lucy hesitates, he accuses her of being 'afraid of the world'.[60] There is also a certain defensiveness in the narrator's comment when Lucy eventually accepts: 'the simple utterance of a solemn and intelligent choice; and as such, the whole phalanx of the Best Society assembled in judgment could not have done less than salute them'.[61] The Rest of Society, we can infer, would be less than delighted. And how much of a 'choice' is it, when Lucy's alternative is destitution? Outside the circle of society moralists, James seems to be hinting, the fact that Bingham caused the death of Lucy's child makes him unforgivably culpable. This is an intuitive model of responsibility, in which key terms are causation and directness, not individual fault; it is, in fact, a model of responsibility which had some support prior to *Brown v Kendall*. The court, however, insisted on the centrality of personal fault, and it is an intriguing thought that, reading 'My Friend Bingham' as a response to the decision, James is suggesting that the court was thereby detaching legal rules from widely held social values.

The conclusion of the story is, at first sight, the conventional happy ending: Lucy and Bingham marry, and their marriage proves 'truly happy'. When we hear in the next

[59] 'My Friend Bingham' in *Complete Stories 1864–1874* (n 18) 144.
[60] ibid 146.
[61] ibid 147.

sentence that Lucy is now 'in the fullness of her bloom', we might take this as the conventional, indeed clichéd, code for pregnancy. But we would be mistaken:

> She has made a devoted wife; but – and in occasional moments of insight it has seemed to me that this portion of her fate is a delicate tribute to a fantastic principle of equity – she has never again become a mother.[62]

Here, yet again, is a form of words that specially resonates with lawyers. If we think of principles of equity in the classic, technical sense, as doctrines that modify, ameliorate or adjust common law rules, the common law rule most obviously relevant here is the standard of reasonable care. Under this rule, Bingham is blameless, and Lucy, therefore, equally blameless for marrying him. Equity has other ideas, and withholds the blessings that a happy marriage would normally bring. We should notice on whose conscience the equitable principle fastens: it is not Bingham's, nor 'the couple's', but specifically Lucy's. We do not know exactly what the narrator has in mind here. It might conceivably be Lucy's failure to keep her son away from the cliff top, as a known source of danger, in the first place; but it seems more likely to be her willingness to listen to Bingham's post-accident overtures. Lucy's forgiveness and acceptance of Bingham is tainted – the 'principle of equity' seems to be that Lucy does not deserve to have a second child if she is prepared to betray her first child's memory by marrying his killer.

For 'equity' to be imagined in this way as a kind of cosmic retributive justice is already rather disturbing; but for our lawyer narrator to acknowledge its workings in 'moments of insight' retrospectively throws the whole narrative point of view into doubt, for it sharply exposes the limits of his rational, legal-analytical persona. Ostensibly universal tests of responsibility, it turns out, are only to be applied selectively: the narrator sympathises with, and is ready to exonerate his 'friend' by appealing to classic legal principles, but he judges Lucy by completely different standards. Thus, while Bingham is allowed to assert, without contradiction from the narrator, that the death is 'none of his doing', Lucy has brought her lack of a child on herself, it serves her right. The narrator's commitment to law and moral reasoning is ultimately revealed as partial, gendered and all too easily displaced by atavistic attributions of blame. What had, until its conclusion, seemed to be a story of lawyers, rationality and responsibility has, at the very last moment, been turned upside down, and taken on a moral complexity that embraces elements of one of James's famous tales of the supernatural.

XI.

It is simply impossible to accept that James's early fiction is the work of a writer who understood 'not a word' of law lectures, and took nothing of intellectual value worth mentioning from his year at Law School. On the contrary, it shows James living up to the exhortation he would later address to aspiring novelists, to be 'one of the people on whom nothing is lost'.[63] For James, it can be seen, made an extraordinarily extensive,

[62] ibid 147–48.
[63] 'The Art of Fiction' in James, *Literary Criticism Volume One* (n 9) 44, 53.

imaginative and varied use of law in his early fiction. There was much here for a lawyer to appreciate and enjoy, and much to admire in the way that James beautifully integrated the legal material so that it made telling points about character, motivation and psychology. At its most interesting, the fiction took legal rules as a point of departure for probing, ironical and critical responses. The stories positioned themselves at an oblique angle to the law, creating tensions and revealing inconsistencies, which makes them particularly rewarding to read with an alert legal eye.

The work considered here all belongs to what is generally regarded as James's 'apprenticeship' period: the latest story, 'Adina', was published in 1874, and the 'middle period' only begins with *The Portrait of a Lady* in 1882. But James's later work continues a lively engagement with law: *The Spoils of Poynton* (1897), for instance, interweaves legal rights with moral duties and loyalties to brilliant psychological effect; *What Maisie Knew* (also 1897) explores the repercussions of divorce. It is perhaps significant that both of these law-focused later works followed a disastrous experiment with drama, and represented an attempt by James to 'take up my own old pen again'.[64]

[64] H James, *The Complete Notebooks of Henry James* (L Edel and LH Powers (eds)) (Oxford, Oxford University Press, 1987) 109.

19

English Student Legal Periodicals, 1842–1922: Peculiarly Applicable to English Law Students

CATHARINE MacMILLAN

Little has been written about legal periodicals in England. This omission is curious for several reasons: the scholarly examination which exists of nineteenth century periodicals other than the legal;[1] the sheer mass of legal literature; and the unique perspectives offered in professional legal literature into law, legal culture and legal development in the common law. Much of what we do know, though, was published by Professor Ibbetson in an examination of the history of this literature between 1820 and 1870.[2] Ibbetson divided legal journals into four types on the basis of their purpose. The objective of this chapter is to examine in greater depth the one type least considered in Ibbetson's earlier study: pedagogical journals. Student legal periodicals he quickly covered in a couple of paragraphs, partly because of the short lived nature of these journals in the half century from 1820 and partly because '[f]rom a legal point of view their content is uniformly dismal'.[3] Ibbetson's assessment of the content of student legal periodicals was shared by Professor Vogenauer, who wrote that the only value of the periodicals lay in the 'conclusions to be drawn about the curricula of the organisations which carried out legal training'.[4]

It must be conceded at the outset that a great deal of the content published in student legal periodicals was concerned with examination questions and answers. This is not a subject which readily captivates readers. However, there is more to student legal periodicals than meets the eye. It is argued in this chapter that student legal periodicals

[1] A King, A Easely and J Morton (eds), *The Routledge Handbook to Nineteenth-Century British Periodicals and Newspapers* (Abingdon, Routledge, 2016); J Don Vann and RT VanArsdel (eds), *Victorian Periodicals and Victorian Society* (Toronto, University of Toronto Press, 1994).

[2] DJ Ibbetson, 'Legal Periodicals in England 1820–1870' (2006) *Zeitschrift für Neuere Rechtsgeschichte* 175. See also RA Cosgrove, 'Victorian Legal Periodicals' (1975) 8 *Victorian Periodicals Newsletter* 21; RA Cosgrove, 'Law' in Don Vann and Rosemary (n 1) 11–21; S Vogenauer, 'Law Journals in Nineteenth-Century England' (2008) 12 *Edinburgh Law Review* 26.

[3] ibid 189.

[4] Vogenauer (n 2) 41.

are essential to understanding the legal education, training and professional culture of attorneys and solicitors in the nineteenth century. These are important issues in their own right and for the role they play in in the development of the common law. They have also had a very long lasting impact upon English legal education and professional training.

The English common law developed in different ways than its civilian counterparts in continental Europe. A significant nineteenth century difference is that, unlike continental Europe, English universities offered little by way of formal legal education and had little impact upon the professions. The common law emerged from the courts, a product of barristers and judges educated within the Inns of Court. Recent scholarship has, however, challenged the assumption that law was necessarily created through the decisions of judges. English Commercial Law, Professor Cranston has convincingly argued, was largely created by the practices of commercial parties and not by the decisions of commercial judges.[5] Although this research did not consider the solicitors who advised – or did not advise – these commercial parties, it is clear that solicitors will frequently have played a part in these commercial practices. The role of solicitors in the structure of transactions and the advice they gave their clients is hard, though, to study in relation to the development of the common law because their records are not public ones. And yet the legal knowledge and practices of these solicitors had a role in shaping the common law of the nineteenth century. The early legal education of these solicitors, based in practical apprenticeships of articled clerks and their individual legal studies, is obscure and little studied. Student legal periodicals are a means of understanding the nature of this legal education, and in so doing, to understand more of the forces which shaped the common law.

I. Reasons Behind the Mid-nineteenth Century Emergence of Student Legal Periodicals

Why did student legal periodicals emerge in mid-nineteenth century England? A number of factors contributed to the creation of these publications. One was financial. The repeal of taxes on advertisements, newspapers and paper between 1849 and 1869 enabled the creation of a mass circulation of all kinds of journalism.[6] A second was that technological changes in nineteenth century printing and typesetting transformed the production of printed materials.[7] A third lay in the establishment of railways: railway lines created a 'perfect road'[8] and provided a far quicker and more efficient means to distribute periodical publications than mail coaches. Railway transportation was utilised by the post office from 1838 in England. The result was to substantially increase

[5] R Cranston, *Making Commercial Law Through Practice 1830–1970* (Cambridge, Cambridge University Press, 2021).

[6] See M Hewitt, *The Dawn of the Cheap Press in Victorian Britain: The End of the 'Taxes on Knowledge,' 1849–1869* (London, Bloomsbury, 2014).

[7] SR Smith, 'Technologies of Production' in King, Easely and Morton (n 1) ch 2.

[8] W Schivelbusch, *The Railway Journey: The Industrialization of Time and Space in the Nineteenth Century* (Oakland, University of California Press, 2014) 20–21.

the speed of delivery from the metropolis to provincial towns and cities, to expand the postal network and to lower the cost of the delivery.[9] A periodical published early in the morning in London could be read by individuals in towns hundreds of miles away that same evening.

While all these general factors had a role in the rise of the student legal periodical, two specific changes spurred the publication of student legal periodicals: the introduction of mandatory examinations as necessary qualifications to practise law for both barristers and solicitors and the concomitant development of a professional ethos and culture during the nineteenth century. The lower branch of the legal profession led the way in introducing a system of examinations. Ever-driven by the quest for professional and social respectability,[10] solicitors introduced a written examination for all articled clerks in 1836. The Solicitors Act 1860[11] required articled clerks to undertake two further examinations. The first was required to become an articled clerk, a preliminary examination in general knowledge, largely of the sort of matters of which a gentleman was knowledgeable. The purpose of this preliminary examination was to exclude entrants who were not gentlemen and it appears to have altered the social character of the profession.[12] The second was the requirement of an intermediate examination in legal knowledge undertaken during a clerk's articles. An unintended effect of the two new examinations mandated by the Solicitors Act 1860 was an explosion in the number of student periodicals. Some were short-lived, unable to survive the editorial and financial demands generated in this suddenly crowded market: *The Law Students' Debating Society's Journal and Reporter* (1865–66) and *The Law Examination Reporter* (1866–69) are two such examples.[13] It was not uncommon for some of the journals in this period to narrow their focus closely to examination questions and suggested answers, published regularly but infrequently, such as *The Telegram: containing the Questions and Answers in Common Law, etc* (1859–79). The Solicitors Act 1877[14] created certain exemptions for university graduates and those who passed certain matriculation examination with regard to their articles. In 1879 the Law Society introduced a separate honours examination with a different paper to the final examination.[15] The Bar was much slower in introducing professional examinations. While the Inns of Court established a form of examinations in 1844, Bar students were able until 1872 to either attend lectures or submit to the examination. When the Bar final became a mandatory written examination in 1872 the new requirement did not generate the same number of student legal periodicals.[16] Bar students were, however, clustered within the London

[9] RM Schwartz, 'Mail, Rail, and Legwork: State and Nation Building through Postal Service in France and Great Britain, 1830–1914' (2021) 45 *Social Science History* 291, 302–307.

[10] D Sugarman, 'Bourgeois Collectivism, Professional Power and the Boundaries of the State. The Private and Public Life of the Law Society, 1825–1914' (1996) 3 *International Journal of the Legal Profession* 81, 108.

[11] 23 & 24 Vic, c 37. The Rules and Regulations for conducting these examinations are reproduced in (1861) 1 *The Law Students' Examination Chronicle* 175–77; the content of the preliminary examination appears in the same issue at 76–78.

[12] B Abel-Smith and R Stevens, *Lawyers and the Courts* (London, Heinemann, 1967) 187.

[13] To these can be added: *Legal Inquirer* (1869–72); *Law Students' Review* (1886); and *The Jurist* (1887–91).

[14] 40 &41 Vict, c 25.

[15] These rules are set out in 3 *The Law Examination Journal and Law Students' Magazine* 398.

[16] An exception was the *Bar Examination Journal* from 1871, continued from 1893 until 1899 as the *Bar Examination Annual.*

Inns of Court. Most student legal periodicals were aimed primarily at articled clerks, who represented both a bigger and more geographically diffuse number of students than those at the bar.

II. Hemings' Legal Science and a National Student Network

Who published and edited these student legal periodicals and to what end? The earliest, *Weekly Law Magazine*, appeared briefly in 1842, as an experiment by an editor who followed it with the *Law Students' Magazine* in 1844. Under various titles,[17] the periodical survived until 1868. The success of this periodical, in terms of the range of its coverage, its literary qualities and the scope of its intellectual ambition, meant that it was the legal periodical the editors of all others mimicked in style and approach. Frequently copied, it was never surpassed in its efforts. The editor, William Hemings, was a Middle Temple conveyancing and equity barrister. While some London lawyers must have known Hemings' identity, he deliberately withheld it from his readers, refusing even to confirm whether or not he was a barrister.[18] Two decades after commencing his publications, Hemings, without explanation, placed his name on the publication as editor.[19] Little is known about conveyancers and equity draftsmen generally and of Hemings himself we know even less. He was a remarkable figure. Born in Stratford upon Avon in 1815, in modest circumstances as an architect's second son, he made his way to London where he appeared on the 1841 census as a solicitor's clerk. He may already have lived abroad as his wife Josephine, then still a teenager, was from Brussels. Hemings studied at University College without taking a degree before being admitted to Lincoln's Inn in 1847; he was then admitted to Middle Temple in June 1850 and called to the bar in 1851. At the time of his call he had been publishing materials for law students for close to a decade: whether or not this was the sole occupation from which he supported his wife and (then) six children is uncertain.

Hemings was the anonymous author of *Key to the Examination Questions* and he only launched the *Law Students' Magazine* once he had solicited 300 subscribers.[20] Existing legal periodicals, he realised, were unconcerned with articled clerks and their needs. In defending his journal, he emphasised its purpose: '[c]an the Articled Clerks obtain, for one shilling, as much *information, peculiarly applicable to his situation*, in any other legal

[17] The title changes signalled slightly new offerings designed to increase revenue. The titles are: 1845–49, *The Law Students' Magazine and Library* (edited and abridged works were sent to subscribers a fortnight after each *Magazine*); 1849–54 *The Law Students' Magazine with Abridgments of Practice Cases and Supplement*, new series (with emphasis on practice cases, in an attempt to appeal to solicitors, with student material included in a supplement); 1854–59 *The Law Chronicle* (a fortnightly publication with a name designed to obtain greater circulation); 1859–60 *The Law Chronicle and Law Students' Magazine* (an attempt to return to the original format); 1861–66 *The Law Students' Examination Chronicle* (with a greater emphasis on examinations following the Solicitors Act 1860); and *The Examination Chronicle* 1866–68.

[18] Anon (Hemings), 'Address to Our Readers' (1860) 2 *The Law Chronicle and Law Students' Magazine*, new series, 161, 164.

[19] (1866) 6 *The Examination Chronicle* (November).

[20] Advertisement 'To Articled Clerks and Law Students' (1844) 8 *The Justice of the Peace* 240.

periodical as he can in ours?'[21] Hemings had identified a new audience in articled clerks and sought to bring to them a broader vision of legal education than existed elsewhere. His publication motives were profit combined with a desire to improve legal education. Existing studies of legal education are largely focussed upon London and Oxford.[22] Such studies overlook the cohort Hemings saw: the thousands of articled clerks[23] who studied law '[f]rom the Land's End to the banks of the Tweed, throughout every county, every town and village'.[24] The monthly *Law Students' Magazine* was sold directly to subscribers and through booksellers and newsmen in town and country. Clerks in the country, often articled to a sole practitioner, lacked the easy access to other lawyers and students possessed by young men in the metropolis. Clerks were young: most began their articles at the age of 16 or 17 and completed them in five years. As one articled clerk, ET Payne, testified before the 1846 Select Committee on Legal Education, there was no prescribed course of legal studies and the principals of most articled clerks were so busy with their own legal practice that they could not attend to the education of their clerks.[25] Even in the cities there were few libraries or legal lectures open to articled clerks. The legal treatises of the day were, in any event, not aimed at the beginner and the beginner's guides tended to the simplistic. Many guides were also aimed at potential barristers rather than solicitors. Samuel Warren, for example, devoted only two brief and unhelpful chapters to attorneys and solicitors.[26] One might employ a 'crammer', a solicitor or barrister who attempted, with varying degrees of ability and success, to prepare a clerk for his final examination. Such services, though, meant that the clerk was located in an urban environment of sufficient size for the crammer to operate. In these circumstances articled clerks were desperate for the legal knowledge necessary to pass the final examination upon which their professional qualification was dependent.

Advertised as an 'Educational Magazine',[27] published monthly and 32 pages long, the foundation of *Law Students' Magazine* lay in the provision of advice and guidance to its readers as to how to study law. Various approaches were taken to this provision. The questions from the final examination papers, given four times annually, were printed. Initially, Hemings did not provide model answers to these questions but gave an indication of 'what amount of knowledge would be required of a candidate, in order to be able to answer them satisfactorily'.[28] The demand of his subscribers, though, was for more complete answers and although Hemings was reluctant to compromise potential sales of his *Key to the Examination Questions*, he went to great lengths to meet this demand in his periodical. In these answers, he was at pains to explain the issue posed by the

[21] 'Notice to Subscribers' (1844–45) 1 *Law Students' Magazine* ii (June).

[22] See, though, W Wesley Pue, 'Professional Legal Education at Queen's College, Birmingham, in the 1850s' in W Wesley Pue, *Lawyer's Empire: Legal Professions and Cultural Authority, 1780–1950* (Vancouver, UBC Press, 2016).

[23] ET Payne, in his evidence before the Select Committee, estimated that there were 2,000 articled clerks in London alone (Select Committee on Legal Education, Parliamentary Papers, 1846 (686), x, 1, Minutes of Evidence, q2606) while Heming's conservatively estimated 2,000 articled clerks across the country required assistance in their studies: 'Notices to Subscribers, &c.' (1846–47) 3 *Law Students' Magazine* ii.

[24] W Hemings, 'Exhortatory Address to Law Students' (1844–45) 1 *Law Students' Magazine* 1, 4.

[25] Select Committee on Legal Education (n 23) q2545–46.

[26] S Warren, *A Popular and Practical Introduction to Law Studies* (London, A Maxwell, 1835) chs 13–14.

[27] ibid.

[28] Anon (Hemings) 'Preparative Study for the Examination' (1844–45) 1 *Law Students' Magazine* 67.

question, to set out all the applicable legal authorities and to do so in an orderly and rationale manner. After two decades he introduced a more detailed approach he labelled 'Legal Reasons Why'. To facilitate the reader's further comprehension, Hemings added references to previous issues of his periodical in which the same point had already been considered. The answers gave readers the practical application of principles extracted from often bulky treatises. In addition to these answers, Hemings was keen to provide students with advice on how to study. This took the form of often detailed suggestions and plans of action. But *Law Students' Magazine* adopted novel approaches to study advice and sought, also, to present various systems of study recommended by prominent lawyers because no one person 'can pretend to lay down a course of study which shall be suitable to everyone'.[29] This method of imparting of advice also made it both interesting and authoritative. Bearing in mind the youth of many of his readers, Hemings supplemented this with practical suggestions on matters such as to how and when to approach their principal for guidance on legal points.

Hemings had higher ambitions, both for himself and his readers, than mere examination answer guides. As he explained the law was an 'interesting and noble science'.[30] An attorney and solicitor needed to study even harder than a barrister for this not only emphasised the growing importance of his profession but because it was the attorney who first met with the client, who organised the client's affairs and who briefed the barrister. The attorney needed to know the law to understand the probable consequences 'before he dares to pull the string which shall set the whole legal machine in motion'.[31] To that end, the *Magazine* provided short discussions on recent leading cases, in which Hemings was concerned to emphasise the principles upon which the case had been decided rather than the facts. The *Magazine* also concerned itself with providing reviews of new law books the editor thought most helpful to an understanding of the law. The scholarly criticisms of one thinker upon another were presented.[32] A wide variety of articles on different topics were published, many well beyond what was needed to simply pass the final examination.[33] Hemings sought to provide his readers with an understanding the forces and the men who had shaped English law. He expressed scepticism of the uninspiring topics and lectures provided by the Incorporated Law Society because they were inferior to the excellent ones delivered within University College.[34] In these endeavours he should be recognised as one who was both shaped by the reforming zeal regarding legal education then present in the Middle Temple[35] and also one who disseminated these new and changing ways of thinking about law and legal education beyond London.

[29] Anon (Hemings) 'Suggestions and Directions for Study: Advice of CJ Reeve, Lord Hale, and others' (1844–45) 1 *Law Students' Magazine* 16.

[30] Hemings (n 24) 6.

[31] ibid.

[32] Anon, 'Notices of Blackstone's Commentaries – Opinions of Bentham, Austin, Ritso, Carey, &c.' (1844–45) 1 *Law Students' Magazine* 10.

[33] See eg Anon, 'The Arguments and Proofs of the Law' (1844–45) 1 *Law Students' Magazine* 49.

[34] 'Law Lectures' (1844) 1 *Law Students' Magazine* 126.

[35] See eg R Cocks, 'The Middle Temple in the 19th Century' in RO Havery (ed), *History of the Middle Temple* (Oxford, Hart Publishing, 2011); R Cocks, 'That Exalted and Noble Science of Jurisprudence: The Recruitment of Jurists with Superior Qualifications by the Middle Temple in the Mid-Nineteenth Century' (1999) 20 *Journal of Legal History* 62.

The first issue of *Law Students' Magazine* began with an allusion to Horace's *Ars Poetica*, promising that the *Magazine* would 'not forget to mingle, occasionally, the "dulce" with the "utile" so as not to disgust the student by a too forbidding prospect'.[36] To that end general articles appeared on topics such as 'Legal Characters – the Pettifogger described'[37] and 'The Study of Anglo-Saxon'.[38] There were initial experimentations with an advice column in which 'Punch' dispensed advice to his 'Son-in-law' on law and legal practice. On the advice of readers, though, the column was dropped. Hemings' capacity to introduce new approaches in his periodical remained a constant. In the 1860s, for example, he introduced a new column, 'Chamber Jottings', in which he discussed legal points relating to Conveyancing and Equity as they arose in his chambers. The column 'will give our readers almost all the advantages of being in Counsel's chambers, without the inconvenience of paying the usual fee'.[39] 'Chamber Jottings' both saved Hemings the need to write copy from scratch and reinforced the practical and contextual legal education provided to his readers.

Law Students' Magazine not only reached articled clerks around the country but also brought them into contact with each other to create novel interactive learning experiences. These systems also worked to save the sole proprietor having to create material himself. They depended upon the newly introduced uniform penny post. Hemings set 'Moot Points', questions on different heads of law, to allow those subscribers to return answers to be published. They were encouraged to support their position with authorities to allow readers to test their accuracy. The purpose behind Moot Points was to 'draw our readers insensibly to study thoroughly … there is nothing so useful as the endeavouring to answer questions, especially when those questions relate to matters of practical utility, and call for the application of general principles'.[40] While some readers questioned the utility of student answers, which they regarded as less authoritative than those provided by the Editor, the column remained.[41]

'Moot Points' also served to support another of Hemings' innovations, the mutual correspondence of articled clerks with each other. At regular intervals, *Law Students' Magazine* published the names and addresses of articled clerks desirous of communicating with others through the post. 'Moot Points', Hemings explained, acted as an icebreaker to open correspondence between these previously unknown parties. They were then free to exchange information about readings, points of law, practice and so forth. While it is impossible to gauge how many articled clerks participated in this form of mutual correspondence, articled clerks from around the country offered to correspond with each other. A list of correspondents' addresses from 1859 demonstrates the extent to which articled students were engaged in legal endeavours beyond the metropolis:

[36] Hemings (n 24) 6.
[37] Anon (1844–45) 1 *Law Students' Magazine* 101.
[38] Anon (1845–46) 2 *Law Students' Magazine* 325–29, 387–90.
[39] 'Chamber Jottings' (1865) 5 *Law Students' Examination Chronicle* 320.
[40] 'Moot Points' (1844–45) 1 *Law Students' Magazine* 19.
[41] 'Answers to Moot Points' (1854) 6 *Law Students' Magazine*, new series 314, 315. Hemings' reply included specific directions on what was required in the answers: ibid.

> Luton, Huddersfield, Reading, Hadleigh, Great Coggeshall, Worcester, Deal, Llandovery, Bruton, Stafford, Thorpe Hamlet, Worksop, Witham, Cambridge, Abergavenny, Bradford, Launceston, Market-rasen, Tygwynne, Shrewsbury, Tipton, Gillingham, Hull, Chatham, Chesterfield, Market Harborough, Rochdale, Much Woolton, Lincoln, Durham, Tunstall, Barnard Castle, Billericay, Halesowen, Wootton Bassett, Birmingham, Aylesbury, Exeter, Brampton Moor, Bristol, Newcastle-upon-tyne, Lowther, Manchester, Sandwich, Llanelly, Sandwich, Louth, Boston, Huddersfield, Whitby, Carnarvon, Leicester, East Grinstead, Bristol, Ellesmere, Liverpool, Honiton, Plymouth, Mansfield, Norfolk, Colchester, Swindon, Sherborne, Burnley, Carlisle, Norwich, Hexham, Bilston, Plymouth, Yeovil and Northampton.[42]

At a time when even solicitors lacked a national professional body, this was a clever means of facilitating the development of networks between clerks nationwide and independent of the metropolis. A sense of community was further strengthened by the practice of publishing the names, with their firm, of articled clerks who passed their examinations. Those with distinctions or prizes were particularly singled out, no doubt to act as an incentive to others.

Over time, the various iterations of *Law Students' Magazine* became more tightly focussed upon the legal examinations, recent legal decisions and statutes, and points of legal practice. This arose for a number of reasons. First, the publications had to pay for themselves and Hemings was always optimistic that he could retain as subscribers those solicitors who had begun as articled clerks. To include solicitors required a more practical focus to the periodical. Second, Heming worked as a sole editor and publisher, while simultaneously conducting a legal practice. His observations indicate that his practice was often busy, particularly from the 1860s. A publication averaging 400 pages a year was a time-consuming side line. Third, after 1860, three examinations were given four times annually and dealing with each of these took up space.

Money was a constant worry for Heming. There are no records as to the number of his subscribers, each of whom paid a shilling an issue. It seems probable that he had at least 500 subscribers because, in one of his frequent pleas for subscribers to clear their arrears, he stated that he had nearly 300 in arrears.[43] While he attempted to run his periodical on a pre-payment basis he was almost constantly hectoring individuals to clear their arrears. The many changes to the periodical were at least partly driven to ensure subscribers paid up and also in attempts to increase the subscription base. In 1861 he lost a Queen's Bench suit brought by his printer to recover £222 for printing the *Law Chronicle*.[44]

Why did Hemings write, edit and publish these periodicals for nearly twenty-five years? A zeal for reform in legal education was no doubt a part of his initial impetus. He described his efforts as 'a labour of love'[45] and the embellishments, creativity and originality that are presented in the journal give credence to this claim. There is

[42] 'List of Correspondents' (1859) 1 *The Law Chronicle and the Law Students' Magazine*, new series 31–32. Larger cities had multiple correspondents, including two men named Peerless in East Grinsted.

[43] 'Notices to Subscribers, &c – Subscriptions – Arrears – Pre-payment' (1846–47) 3 *Law Students' Magazine* ii (October).

[44] Anon, 'Hoist by his own Petard', *The Luton Times and Dunstable Herald*, 8 June 1861, 2.

[45] 'Notice to Subscribers' (1844–45) 1 *Law Students' Magazine* ii (June).

also an empathy exhibited to young articled clerks who are trying to learn the law, to acquire professional skills and to improve not only their education but also their social status. There are, also, undoubtedly financial considerations present. Hemings wrote and published a detailed examination answer guide[46] and his editorship allowed him promotion opportunities for that work. So, too, did his creation of what he called first the Law Students' Library, in which he produced a version of *Littleton's Tenures* which omitted material now irrelevant but added explanatory notes. The Law Students' Library came to include other titles providing a more detailed knowledge of the subjects of the final examination before it was discontinued, only to be revived years later as the Small Law Library. The journal gave him authority as an author in relation to these publications and also a platform from which they could be sold. When his *Modern Law Dictionary* failed to attract sufficient support, it was stopped (at 'Decree').[47] There are indications that some subscribers, once they were solicitors, engaged him as counsel.[48] It is more likely, though, that the acquisition of clients who read the periodical was a happy by-product of the publication rather than a reason for it. What is clear, and sets Hemings apart from other student periodical publishers, is that he neither coached nor crammed students in preparation for their examinations. He expressed scepticism over the ability of another 'to be able in a few weeks to cram the necessary amount of knowledge into candidates'.[49]

Hemings managed the business on his own, working from his home address rather than his chambers. To judge by his constant pleas for subscribers to pay their arrears he was less successful as a businessman than as a lawyer. He 'suspended' his publication after the December 1868 issue of what was then *The Examination Chronicle.* Complaining that he had been 'most unfairly dealt with by persons who ought to have been above such conduct',[50] he appears to have again struggled to pay his printer. Once again, substantial arrears of subscriptions had arisen and he warned his 'so-called *subscribers*' that if they did not clear their arrears he would, reluctantly, be forced to cease publication.[51] While he was optimistic that he might begin anew with a quarterly periodical in 1869 it never emerged.

When Hemings withdrew from the periodical market, his fellow barrister and younger neighbour on Chancery Lane, Herbert Newman Mozley began his *The Law Examination Journal and Law Student's Magazine*. Published between 1869 and 1885, it followed Hemings' final plan of issuing a periodical quarterly around the Law Society examinations. Mozley, for all his early success at Cambridge and Lincoln's Inn, produced a publication lacking Heming's intellect and imagination. While some of this undoubtedly arose from its less frequent appearance it was not helped by the occasional addition of sterile essays and a near barren correspondence section. The digests of recent cases and statutes lacked Hemings' insight into legal principle and the works reviewed would

[46] The Editors of the Law Students' Magazine, *The Key to the Examination Questions containing the Examiners' questions from 1835–1849*, 2nd edn (London, Robert Hastings, 1849).

[47] Anon, 'Notices to Correspondents' (1867) 7 *Law Students' Examination Chronicle* xv.

[48] 'Address to Our Readers' (1860) 2 *Law Chronicle, new series* 161, 164.

[49] 'Results of the Examinations' (1867) 7 *The Examination Chronicle* 192, 193.

[50] 'Suspension of the Chronicle' (1868) 8 *The Examination Chronicle* 326.

[51] ibid.

appear to have been of more interest to the editor than his readers. Even the answers to the, admittedly dull, examination questions were less than insightful:

> Q. – What is an implied contract?' A. – A contract presumed by law from the acts of the parties, in cases where no express contract has been made between them.[52]

Mozley also took pupils for all legal examinations in his chambers on Chancery Lane. His periodical obviously supported his coaching. His heart, however, does not seem to have been in the publishing endeavour. By the fourth volume, covering the years 1881–85, the periodical had become a law examination journal, with the questions and answers for the intermediate, the final and the honours examination forming the bulk of the publication. While some digests and a handful of reviews appeared, little else and nothing of real interest appeared in the journal itself. One suspects that Mozley's career had developed elsewhere at this point, leaving him less time for his journal.

III. Student Legal Periodicals and the Rise of the Law Coaches

The disappearance of one student periodical opened an opportunity for another, which explains the publication of Mozley's *Law Examination Journal* on the demise of Hemings' *Examination Chronicle*. It was also the case that student periodicals competed with each other for market share. In the last quarter of the nineteenth century, the two student legal periodicals with the longest existences began publication: *The Law Students' Journal* (1879–1917) and *Law Notes* (1882–1994). Their domination of the student periodical market meant that few other editors were able to publish for long. They contributed to the demise of both Mozley's *Law Examination Journal* and Henry Purkis' *Telegram*. While Cosgrove states that the *Telegram's* 'demise indicated its success' as articled clerks no longer needed encouragement and assistance by 1880,[53] in reality clerks had switched to the *Students' Law Journal*. Far from abandoning the quest for encouragement and assistance students pursed it with greater zeal. The dominance of these two new journals marks a new phase in student legal periodical: the publication as voice of the law coach.

While much consideration has been given to the teaching of law in nineteenth century universities, little attention has been given to the crammers and coaches who provided most lawyers, particularly solicitors, with their legal education.[54] Student legal periodicals give us an insight into the activities of the two biggest firms of coaches: Indermaur and Thwaites; and Gibson and Weldon. John Indermaur, a Londoner, was a solicitor and the Clifford's Inn Prizeman, Michaelmas Term 1872. From the outset of his career as a practising solicitor on Chancery Lane he also took students to prepare

[52] (1869–73) 1 *The Law Examination Journal and Law Students' Magazine* 62. The question was drawn from the Intermediate Examination for Michaelmas Term, 1869; the answer is Mozley's.

[53] Cosgrove (n 2) 13.

[54] See, though, P Leighton, 'The LLB as a Liberal Degree' (2015) 22 *International Journal of the Legal Profession* 87, 90–96; RH Kersley, *Gibson's 1876–1962: A Chapter in Legal Education* (London, Law Notes Lending Library, 1973).

for the various examinations administered by the Incorporated Law Society. As was not uncommon for coaches he made an early start to writing study guides,[55] from which the publication of the monthly *Law Students' Journal* in 1879 was a natural progression.[56] Indermaur's printer was George Barber, he began with a twelve-page journal for which he charged sixpence, a price maintained for the life of the journal. Indermaur was a better businessman than Hemings and the publication of a student legal periodical combined neatly with the business of coaching law students. It is likely that much of the material in the *Students' Law Journal* was also used in the classroom and the preparation of teaching materials. Indermaur never wrote all the articles himself and he always had the assistance of others in the preparation of the examination related materials. In 1884 Charles Thwaites, Indermaur's former student, became his partner in the coaching business. Thwaites, like Hemings, rose from humble circumstances. Born to a Yorkshire stonemason who died when Thwaites was still a child, he excelled in his own examinations as the First Prizeman in June 1880 and the winner of the Reardon Prize, the Broderip Prize, the Scott Scholarship and Sheffield District Prize. He, too, practised law, not though with Indermaur who had a separate partner for his practice as a solicitor. From 1903, Thwaites took over the editorship of the *Journal* and Indermaur contributed occasionally but regularly for the remainder of the periodical's existence.

The Students' Law Journal was aimed at articled clerks attempting to pass their intermediate and final examinations (and honours examination for the more ambitious clerks) although consideration was also given to Bar pupils. Indermaur estimated that there were over 4,000 articled clerks[57] and *Law Students' Journal* was a way of promoting his coaching services, which were conducted not only in person on Chancery Lane but also by post and a combination of post and personal attendance to conclude the studies. From 1895, the *Journal* also addressed those students sitting the University of London LL.B. examinations. The interest in the LL.B. examinations was not focussed upon any perceived benefit of university study but because they provided certain exemptions to the service and examinations required of articled clerks by the Law Society. The preparation for these various examinations took a number of forms. At its core was the reproduction of the examination papers with answers prepared by Indermaur and others. All of the papers were practical ones, the divisions being Common Law, Equity and Conveyancing, Bankruptcy, Criminal Law, Admiralty and Ecclesiastical Law for solicitors with a slightly wider range for the Bar Final. Indermaur did not provide answers to the Bar's Roman Law examination, explaining that there was an insufficient interest in the topic.[58] The wide ranging and detailed nature of the practical questions set[59] encouraged students to study very widely; the examination paper coverage in the *Students' Law Journal* facilitated this form of study. In addition,

[55] John Indermaur, *Self-Preparation for the Final Examination*, 2nd edn (London, Stevens and Haynes, 1874).

[56] It was also seven years after the introduction of the Bar Final, two years after the Solicitors Act 1877 defined the examinations required of solicitors and coincided with the establishment of an Honours examination for finalists.

[57] 'Notes of the Month' (1880) 2 *Law Students' Journal* 1, 2.

[58] 'Questions in The Roman Law' (1880) 2 *Law Students' Journal* 56.

[59] Some samples from the June 1880 Solicitors' Final (Pass) Examination indicate the challenge: 'What is the effect of non-entry of a demurrer, no order for leave to amend having been obtained and served?'; 'What

Indermaur also provided a form of reports on the examination papers. In these he analysed the papers, observed on the fairness (or hardness) of particular papers, and explained what had occurred where there was an unusually high failure rate. Dire warnings were continually provided to readers on the necessity of regular study, ideally utilising not only the *Students' Law Journal* but also Indermaur's guides and coaching services.

Further examination support was provided through the provision of regular digests of student cases. These were short summaries, thematically organised and referenced to the texts set for the examinations and to Indermaur's various subject guides. Complementing these digests were epitomes of recent statutes, accompanied with instructions as to how to incorporate them into the student's larger study programme. An annual summary of the recent cases in those areas of examination staples, common law, equity and conveyancing, were also provided by Indermaur. In common with the editors of all student periodicals, Indermaur emphasised the importance of active learning, the application of knowledge to the resolution of problems and questions. To this end, *Law Students' Journal* regularly provided its readers with practice questions drawn from the texts and the cases.

The Law Students' Journal provided its readers with the usual fare of legal periodical literature. Short articles on a variety of topics were regularly published. The subject matter was usually practical and related to examination topics: C. Swinfen Eady, 'The Personal Liability of Trustees in Bankruptcy';[60] B. Morris, 'Priority of Incumbrances';[61] and Chandos H. Parry, 'Incidents of a Criminal Trial'[62] are all examples. These articles rarely aspired to more than setting out the existing law, usually without criticism or recommendation. The appearance of an article both criticising *Stephen's Commentaries on the Laws of England* and of its choice by the Law Society as the treatise all articled clerks would be examined upon was an unusual departure.[63] *Law Students' Journal* adopted a doctrinal approach to the common law. Law existed to solve problems and students were expected to have a very broad, but not necessarily critical, approach to the law. There was little room for scientific jurisprudence or even a critical approach to legal principles in the pages of the *Journal*. The narrow nature of this approach is explicable when one realises that the *Journal* delivered what its readers sought. Articled clerks generally served five years of articles, a period in which they largely worked during the day with little time for study. In the time they did have available to study they were anxious to focus upon what was directly necessary to passing their professional examinations.

Indermaur did provide his readers with a wider sense of professional legal culture. He began each issue with 'Notes of the Month' in which he covered matters he thought

evidence is required on an application for appointment of guardians of infants and allowance for maintenance?'; 'Where the donee of a power to appoint new trustees is a lunatic, what course is followed, and under what Act?'; 'What is 'stoppage in transit,' and how may it be lost?' and 'Is an atheist capable of giving evidence in a Court of Justice? Give a reason for your answer': (1880) 2 *Law Students' Journal* 96–98.

[60] (1879) 1 *Law Students' Journal* 15.

[61] (1881) 3 *Law Students' Journal* 102.

[62] (1909) 31 *Law Students' Journal* 141.

[63] DA Stroud, 'Strictures on Stephen: Being a Short Criticism of the Method and Arrangement of *Stephen's Commentaries on the Laws of England*' (1898) 20 *Students' Law Journal* 56.

of interest to students. While Indermaur adopted a rather breezy tone in these Notes, Thwaites brought an altogether different approach in providing the details of legal developments in England and drawing upon a wide range of other legal periodicals to summarise legal events from a variety of other jurisdictions. 'Notes of the Month' was also used to advance the various campaigns taken up by the *Journal*. Most of these campaigns were critical of the Incorporated Law Society and the way in which it dealt with articled clerks. There was, for example, a long running campaign, raising several petitions from readers, for the Law Society to award honours at the Intermediate examination.[64] Another ongoing concern was that the Law Society should do more to use the large income it derived from articled clerks to support their legal education, particularly with the improvement of the lectures offered by the Society. Indermaur supported the cause of women, particularly with regard to their admission to the legal profession and used the *Journal* to report on societies and individuals who supported this cause.[65] Thwaites, in contrast, did not support women entering the legal profession and, in a rare agreement with action by the Law Society, supported its opposition to the 1917 Bill which proposed to qualify women for admission as solicitors.[66]

Law Students' Journal encouraged its readers to support each other in their learning. The approach was not the correspondents' network developed by Hemings but upon student law societies. Observing that 'they now exist very extensively throughout the kingdom' they were recommended as the most useful means of educating students.[67] They stimulated reliance and self-confidence and enabled students to contact each other to exchange information and ideas. Students were encouraged to join a society or to participate in forming one. The secretaries of these societies were urged to send in reports of their society's activities and these were published in each issue. Another regular feature of the *Journal* was the Correspondence column. Here students could both address remarks to each other, which were published, and also pose questions to the editor. Editorial responses to these questions were published. These responses give an indication of student concerns, from how best to profit from their articles to what they should do upon the death of their principal to what texts and guides would be best for particular examination papers. An innovation of the *Journal* was the introduction, early on, of holding annual prize essay competitions amongst its readers as a means of both stimulating their legal studies and the circulation of the *Journal*. The publication of the winning essay also provided students with an indication of the sort of answers they might wish to produce.

The last issue of the *Journal* was published in 1917. The issues between 1914 and 1917 make for grim reading as the articled clerks and bar students who made up the *Journal's* subscribers were largely engaged in military service. As Thwaites noted, many 'have laid down their lives in the defence of the realm'.[68] As the number of articled clerks

[64] Anon, 'Notes of the Month' (1910) 32 *Law Students' Journal* 111, 112.

[65] See eg Anon, 'Association to Promote Women's Knowledge of Law' (1879) 1 *Law Students' Journal* 34; 'Notes of the Month' (1880) 2 *Law Students' Law Journal* 1–2; J Indermaur, 'Anomalies in the Position of Married Women' (1899) 21 *Law Students' Journal* 74.

[66] 'Notes of the Month' (1917) 39 *Law Students' Journal* 49.

[67] J Indermaur, 'The Study of the Law for the Profession of a Solicitor' (1879) 1 *Law Students' Journal* 5, 6.

[68] 'Notes of the Month' (1915) 37 *Law Students' Law Journal* 141, 143.

substantially diminished the honours exam was removed in 1916 and the Solicitors Examination Act 1917 allowed the Law Society to reduce the sittings of intermediate and final examinations to two rather than four occasions in the year. The decision was made to suspend publication of the *Journal* until peace was restored. Not only were there far fewer examinations to prepare readers for but '[t]hose who are interested in the topics dealt with in this Journal are mostly diverted form the Law to national service of one kind or another connected with the War'.[69] The suspension was permanent.

The second student legal periodical closely associated with law coaching is *Law Notes*, a publication produced and edited first by Albert Gibson in 1882 and from 1886 with his partner in the coaching business, Arthur Weldon. Both also practised law as solicitors. Gibson and Weldon, again based on Chancery Lane, were the most successful and long-lived of the law coaching firms. They were ultimately acquired by the Law Society to form the College of Law in 1962. Their history was written by one of its later members, Kersley.[70] Gibson was an early pupil of Indermaur's, who described him, rather tartly, as 'a most industrious and indefatigable "coach," and producer of student literature, which, if not destined to leave a permanent mark, is at any rate much approved of in the present'.[71] Gibson and Weldon, to judge by their advertisements, was a larger and more successful (at least in the number of candidates who obtained distinctions) law coaching business than Indermaur and Thwaites. It also operated in conjunction with the Law Notes Lending Library formed by Weldon in 1886 to provide law books to all.[72]

Gibson and Weldon as editors of *Law Notes* employed the various tutors within the coaching business to work on the publication from time to time. Because of this, *Law Notes* is written with greater detail and reference than the *Law Students' Journal*. The format and editorial approach between the two were remarkably similar. *Law Notes*, too, began with general prefatory notes on the state of the law and the legal profession within the wider events of the day: from 1887 it was called 'De Minimis'. The foundation of the periodical was preparation for various Law Society examinations and a staple feature were the editors' observations on the results of these examinations. In a sharp contrast to the *Law Students' Journal* the editors of *Law Notes* did not publish answers to the examination questions. While this must have diminished the comparative desirability of their publication it probably worked to increase the students who attended their law coaching business.

Law Notes, in common with the *Law Students' Journal*, published the practical material necessary to support examination preparations: digests of recent cases; epitomes of recent statutes; a wide range of articles on practical and examinable subjects; articles concerned with the practice of law (and the conduct of articles) written by experienced solicitors; and book reviews of titles thought useful to students. At times it produced works of prose and that late Victorian peculiarity, leading cases in rhyme. Students were featured in *Law Notes*, both in the usual manner of publishing pass and honours' lists, but also in a regular feature, 'Chats with an Articled Clerk'. The publication also featured

[69] Anon, 'Editorial Notice' (1917) 39 *Law Students' Journal* 117.
[70] Kersley (n 54).
[71] 'Reviews – *Aids to Equity*' (1882) 4 *Law Students' Journal* 5.
[72] Kersley (n 54) 11.

those of its students who obtained particular honours in the Law Society examinations with a short biography and photograph.[73]

In common with the *Law Students' Journal*, *Law Notes* was often critical of the operation of the Law Society, particularly with regard to its interactions with articled clerks. At times its campaigns spurred the Law Society into action. In 1886, for example, it conducted what began as a novel investigation into the practice of law by unqualified persons by surveying first its professional correspondents around the nation and then through the invitation to its subscribers to forward detailed individual instances of such practices.[74] The investigation, and resulting campaign, was undertaken to protect young solicitors who were most at risk of losing clients to the unqualified.

Law Notes survived the first world war and continued, remarkably, until 1994. After the first world war, though, a changed approach to legal education for solicitors emerged. By the Solicitors Act 1922[75] the Law Society made attendance at an approved university law school compulsory. The Society of Public Teachers of Law was formed in 1908 around the emerging system of legal education in the universities. Law coaches were pointedly excluded from joining this new Society. While student legal periodicals continued to be produced their role in legal education was a changed one.

IV. Conclusions

What conclusions can be drawn from this study? One is that student legal periodicals between 1842 and 1922 provided a critical means by which legal knowledge, professionalism and legal culture were transmitted from Chancery Lane throughout England and Wales. The nature and the approach of this legal knowledge was relentlessly practical and doctrinal because this was what subscribers, primarily articled clerks, would pay for in a periodical. These periodicals give an insight into how solicitors learned their law and these early influences were enduring ones. The shape of the Law Society's examinations worked to reinforce the practical nature of English law. Student legal periodicals also managed to bring together students around the country, albeit in print. The reading of these student legal periodicals provides us with an insight into how law was practised and shaped outside the metropolis.

[73] See eg Anon, '"Law Notes" Prizeman–Ewan Gibson Davies, Esq' (1912) 31 *Law Notes* 21.
[74] Anon, 'Unqualified Practitioners' (1886) 5 *Law Notes* 327.
[75] 12 & 13 Geo 5, c 57.

20

Historical Insights into Contemporary Legal Problems: The 2020 Reforms to the Law of Civil Contempt

DAVID FOXTON[1]

I. Introduction

When introducing David Ibbetson's valedictory lecture on his retirement from the position of Regius Professor in Civil Law at the University of Cambridge on 22 November 2022,[2] I observed that one of the (many) things I had learned from David was how often an understanding of what the law is, and what it could be, can be informed by an understanding of its history, and how it came to assume its present form. As always, David put it so much better, observing in the introduction to *A Historical Introduction to the Law of Obligations* that 'if we are to make sense of today's law we have to understand its history, and it is only when we make sense of it that we can confidently begin to reform it'.[3] There is a particular irony when the problem which it requires an understanding of the past to resolve arises from a reform intended to wipe the slate clean and start again. On 1 October 2020, a new Part 81 of the Civil Procedure Rules, addressing the issue of committal for contempt of court, was brought into force. Undeterred by Lord Salisbury's reputed warning, 'Reform, reform: aren't things bad enough already?', the Civil Procedure Rules Committee introduced the changes with a view to making the 'rules simpler, easier to operate and more succinct'.[4]

The new version of Part 81 ('the 2020 Reforms') is undoubtedly much clearer and simpler, reducing the number of rules from 38 to 10, absorbing two Practice Directions and a Practice Guidance statement, and reducing the number of forms from 24 to four.[5] However, two of the provisions omitted in the process were any express requirement

[1] A judge of the King's Bench Division, Judge of the Commercial Court, and a student of David Ibbetson's between 1983 and 1987 when David was a Fellow and Tutor in Law at Magdalen College, Oxford.

[2] 'Roman Law, Comparative Law, Legal History' (25 November 2022). For the lecture, see ch 2 above.

[3] DJ Ibbetson, *A Historical Introduction to the Law of Obligations* (Oxford, Oxford University Press, 1999) vi.

[4] Minutes of Civil Procedure Rules Committee (CPRC) 4 October 2019 [35].

[5] Minutes of CPRC, 5 June 2020 [24].

for personal service of an order before there could be committal for breach, and a rule addressing the position of directors when there had been a breach of an order by a company. Inevitably, issues soon arose as to whether these omissions were intended to change the law. In *MBR Acres Limited and other v Maher and another*,[6] Nicklin J held that the 2020 Reforms had not removed the requirement for personal service of the order for breach of which committal was sought. In *Olympic Council of Asia v Novans Jets LLP*,[7] I held that the 2020 Reforms had not removed or altered the court's power to commit directors or officers for non-compliance with orders made against bodies corporate, a conclusion upheld by the Court of Appeal in *ADM International SARL v Grain House International SA*.[8] All three judgments referred to the historical development of the relevant principle in justifying their conclusions. This chapter reviews the historical development of the law as it relates to both issues, before returning to the challenges which the 2020 Reforms raised, and how they were resolved. A draft of this chapter was provided to the Court of Appeal in the course of argument in *ADM International SARL v Grain House International SARL*, and was relied upon by the court in reaching its conclusion.[9]

II. The Contempt Jurisdiction

In *King v Almon*,[10] Wilmot J described the power of courts to vindicate their authority through the contempt jurisdiction as 'coeval with their first foundation and institution; it is a necessary incident to every court of justice … It is as ancient as any other part of the common law; there is no priority or posteriority to be discovered about it'.[11] In introducing one of many attempts to reform the law of contempt of court, the Contempts of Court Bill, in 1883,[12] the Earl of Selborne offered his own taxonomy of contempts, dividing them 'into two distinct classes'. In the first class were 'contempts of the Court itself, not consisting in disobedience to its orders', which 'might be committed either by persons who were entirely strangers to any proceedings pending, or by persons who were parties to those proceedings'. The second 'consisted of disobedience to the orders of a Court, and was necessarily confined to the parties to proceedings before the Court'. He sub-divided the former category into contempts in the face of the court, and those

[6] *MBR Acres Limited and other v Maher and another* [2022] EWHC 1123 (QB); [2023] 1 QB 186.

[7] *Olympic Council of Asia v Novans Jets LLP* [2023] EWHC 276 (Comm); [2023] 1 WLR 1462.

[8] *ADM International SARL v Grain House International SA* [2024] EWCA Civ 33; [2024] 1 All ER (Comm) 1194.

[9] *ADM International SARL v Grain House International SA* [2024] EWCA Civ 33; [2024] 1 All ER (Comm) 194, [101].

[10] *R v Almon* (1765) Wilm 243; 97 ER 94 (published in 1802).

[11] For *R v Almon* see JC Fox, 'The King v Almon' (1908) 24 *LQR* 184, (1908) 24 *LQR* 266. The judgment was prepared but never delivered, the attempt to commit being abandoned before a procedural defect had been overcome. The draft judgment in Mr Justice Wilmot's notebook was published by his son, and referred to in various cases from 1813 onwards before acquiring greater prominence when it was cited by Lord Lyndhurst in *Ex parte Van Sandau* (1844) 1 Phil 454; 41 ER 701. The unorthodox provenance of the case led Fletcher J in *Taafe v Downes* (1813) 3 Moo PC 30, in the full version of the judgment, to question why he should follow a case which 'rested in undisturbed repose … for the twenty-one years of the compiler's life, after his retirement from the bench, and for ten more years after his death' and which had only been published as an act of filial piety. TJF take note.

[12] Hansard 3rd series Vol 276 cols 1708–1709. The Bill did not pass.

outside of court. It is that last sub-category which proved the most controversial, not least when this jurisdiction was used to punish those who were alleged to have libelled the judiciary, as in the alleged libel of Lord Mansfield which gave rise to the decision in *Almon*.

The Earl of Selborne's second class – which became known as civil contempt –was originally enforced through the writs of attachment and committal. The writ of attachment originated as the means generally used to ensure that a defendant appeared to answer a charge, but it survived as a mechanism for enforcing certain types of court orders after it had been abolished as a means of compelling appearance.[13] The writ *per vadium et salvos plegios* was directed to the sheriff, requiring him to seize goods of the respondent by way of gage as security for his appearance. If the respondent failed to appear, not only was the gage forfeit, but the writ of *distringas* could be issued, allowing the sheriff to distrain the respondent's goods and the proceeds of his land until he appeared.[14] If necessary, the sheriff was required to attach the respondent himself by the writ of *capias ad respondendum*.[15] Where the defendant was called upon to answer a contempt, the sheriff could proceed to an immediate attachment of the offender, and lodge him in the county gaol.[16] The defendant was then brought to court, and either committed to prison or put on bail, to answer on oath interrogatories directed to the alleged contempt.[17]

In contrast, the writ of committal was executed by the tipstaff who brought the prisoner to the Court Prison at Holloway. The distinction between the two forms of writs was explained in a very learned memorandum by Mr Registrar Lavie reported as a note to *In re Evans, Evans v Noton*.[18] As Lavie explained, 'a man was committed for doing what he ought not to do and attached for not doing what he was ordered to do'. Certainly, this was the case in the Chancery Division, and the difference in approach is likely to have influenced the distinction drawn between breaches of prohibitory and mandatory injunctions in the law of contempt. Committal was available not simply against a party to an existing cause who had been ordered to do something and failed to do it, but also against non-parties whose behaviour constituted contempt.

The use of attachment as a mechanism for enforcing court orders appears to have originated in the courts of equity, Blackstone noting that 'the whole process of the courts of equity, in the several stages of a cause, and finally to enforce their decrees, was, until the introduction of sequestrations, in the nature of a process of contempt; acting only

[13] *Harvey v Harvey* (1884) 26 Ch D 644, 653.

[14] W Blackstone, *Commentaries of the Law of England*, 1st edn (London, Clarendon Press, 1765–1769) vol III 280–81. All references to the *Commentaries* are taken from the facsimile of the 1st edn (Chicago, University of Chicago Press, 1979).

[15] The Court of Appeal in *ADM International SARL v Grain House International SA* [2024] EWCA Civ 33; [2024] 1 All ER (Comm) 1194, [105], referred to two forms of writ, *per valium et salvos plegios* (by security and sureties) and *per corpus suum* (arrest), citing Bracton, *De Legibus et Consuetudinibus Angliae* Folio 149.

[16] Blackstone (n 14) vol IV, 282.

[17] ibid 283. This was the position which had evolved by the sixteenth century. Before that, attachment led to the respondent being brought to court to be tried in the ordinary course of law and punished on conviction: JC Fox, 'Eccentricities of the Law of Contempt' (1920) 36 *LQR* 394, 400. The defendant was generally permitted to answer the interrogatories 'at large and not in custody': *Danby v Lawson* (1700) Prec Ch 110; 24 ER 53.

[18] *In re Evans, Evans v Noton* [1893] 1 Ch 252, 259 (CA) ('the Lavie Note'). In *Hem Bala Dassi vs Sundar Shaw and ors* AIR 1953 Cal 627; 57 CWN 179, the Lavie Note was described as 'the best statement of the distinction'.

in personam and not *in rem*'.[19] It also reflected the fact that the power of the Chancellor to commit for contempt was clearly established before the position at common law.[20] In the Court of Chancery, it was possible for one party to obtain a writ of attachment as an administrative act, and without any judicial decision, by filing an affidavit attesting to non-performance.[21] By contrast, committal required an order of the court.[22]

Amercement and fines developed as the sanctions for non-compliance with court orders. Amercement, imposed for minor defaults in procedure, involved the seizure of property on a provisional basis, as security for an amount the party in 'mercy' would be required to pay which was fixed by the offender's neighbours according to his means, failing which the amount would be recovered from the property seized.[23] A fine, for more serious contempts, involved a voluntary payment made as an alternative to imprisonment, in an amount fixed by the court (which came to be determined by reference to a scale). By the seventeenth century, the distinction had all but dissolved, and the imposition of a fine had come to be recognised as a sanction in its own right, which could be imposed in addition to imprisonment, rather than a voluntary alternative to indeterminate detention, with the amount of the financial penalty being determined by the court.[24]

Imprisonment and fine were later supplemented by the writ of sequestration, which seized the respondent's personal estate, and the rents, issues and profits of their real estate. The origin of this particular sanction for non-compliance has been the subject of controversy. It has been attributed to an order made by Lord Coventry, the Lord Keeper under Charles I, against Sir John Read,[25] or to Lord Nottingham when Lord Chancellor from 1675–82.[26] However, there are references to such orders having been made by Francis Bacon when Lord Chancellor in his *Ordinances*.[27] A writ of sequestration is said to have first been made by a common law court on 14 June 1687, in *Fountain and Wavers*.[28] Sequestration could be imposed in addition to imprisonment, as in *Pope v Ward*[29] where the writ was issued against Benjamin Pope, detained in the Fleet, who was in contempt of a writ of attachment issued in relation to the non-payment of a costs order made in Chancery. It soon became the default sanction for corporations who failed to comply with court orders.[30]

[19] Blackstone (n 14) vol IV, 284–85. See also W Holdsworth, *A History of English Law* (*HEL*), vol V. References to Holdsworth's *HEL* are taken from AL Goodhart and HG Hanbury (eds), 7th edn (London, Sweet and Maxwell, 1964).

[20] Holdsworth (n 19) vol I, 458.

[21] Fox (n 17) 401.

[22] The Lavie Note (n 18).

[23] See generally JC Fox, *The History of Contempt of Court: The Form of Trial and the Mode of Punishment* (Oxford, Clarendon Press, 1926) ch VIII and Holdsworth (n 19) vol III, 391–92.

[24] Fox (n 23) 164–65, 174–77, 200; *Selden's Case* Gow St Tr iii, 267.

[25] See generally Holdsworth (n 19) vol IX, 350.

[26] So attributed in *Whitehead and Harrison* (1730) 1 Barn KB 431; 94 ER 290.

[27] *Ordinances made by the Right Honourable Sir Francis Bacon*, (London, Mathew Walbanke and Lawrence Chapman, 1642) Orders 29 and 30.

[28] *Whitehead v Harrison* (1730) 1 Barn KB 431; 94 ER 290; 'Of Reviving a Sequestration' (1744) 2 Eq Ca Abr 712; 22 ER 600.

[29] *Pope v Ward* (1785) 1 Cox Eq Cas 194; 29 ER 1125.

[30] *Agar v The Regent's Canal Company* (1815) 19 Ves Jr 379, 380; 34 ER 558.

III. Service

English procedural law developed from a starting point that all legal process had to be served personally.[31] If a defendant did not attend, and a writ of attachment was sought to procure appearance, the plaintiff had to file an affidavit 'containing positive and certain averments of the time, place and manner of service'.[32] It is scarcely surprising that this was also the case for orders or injunction, before the respondent could be attached or committed for non-compliance. However, exceptions began to emerge in the eighteenth century. In *Skip v Harwood*,[33] Lord Hardwick held that those who were present in court when a decree was pronounced were guilty of contempt and could be punished if they contravened the order, even though it had yet to be drawn up 'otherwise it would be extremely easy to elude decrees, some of which in their nature require a considerable length of time before they can be completely drawn up'. This was not initially extended to a respondent who had attended the hearing but was not in court when the decree was pronounced,[34] but Lord Eldon held that this was sufficient to proceed to committal in *Hearn v Tennant*,[35] observing 'I cannot attend to a distinction so thin, as that persons, standing here until the moment the Lord Chancellor is about to pronounce the Order, which from all that passed, they must know will be pronounced, can by getting out of the Hall at this instant avoid all the consequences'. In *James v Downes*,[36] the court found that 'a party who has full notice, in any way, that an injunction has issued against him, is guilty of a contempt if he do any act prohibited by such injunction, although the order may not have been regularly served upon him'. In *Kimpton v Eve*,[37] Lord Eldon observed:

> I have heard some of my Predecessors in this Place treat as a great Abuse of Justice and want of Consistency the Refusal to apply that practice, which is applied to a Person, present in Court, and hearing the Order, to a Man, standing outside of the Court, and informed by some one who heard it, that the Order was pronounced.

These cases all concerned prohibitory injunctions, with the court's concern being that the thing prohibited might be undertaken between the making of the injunction and the service of the order – as Lord Eldon noted, 'if it was against marrying a ward of the Court, the Marriage might be had by the next morning'.[38] That particular concern did not arise with a mandatory injunction – if the act had not been done prior to service, it could be done afterwards, and in any event, the respondent needed to know the time by which the act had to be done. The only mandatory injunctions where personal service

[31] As Chitty J noted in *Harvey v Harvey* (1884) 26 Ch D 644, 653.

[32] See eg Holdsworth (n 19) vol IX, 258; E Daniel, *A Treatise on the Practice of the High Court of Chancery* (London, J & WT Clarke, 1837) 579.

[33] *Skip v Harwood* (1747) 3 Atk 564; 26 ER 1125.

[34] *Pengree v Jonas* (1786) 2 Bro CC 141; 29 ER 81 (Lord Thurlow).

[35] *Hearn v Tennant* (1807) 14 Ves Jr 136; 32 ER 73. See also *Osborne v Tennant* (1809) 2 Ves Jr 360; 34 ER 1132;*Scott v Becher* (1817) 4 Price 352; 146 ER 485; *Vansandau v Rose* (1820) 2 Jac and W 265; 37 ER 628.

[36] *James v Downes* (1809) 2 Ves Jr 547; 34 ER 1220.

[37] *Kimpton v Eve* (1813) 2 V & B 349, 350; 35 ER 352. See also *Vansandau v Rose* (1820) 2 Jac and W 265; 37 ER 628.

[38] *Kimpton v Eve* (1813) 2 V & B 349, 351; 35 ER 352.

does not appear to have been essential was in relation to orders for disclosure or inspection of documents, where service on the party's attorney was sufficient.[39]

There was rather greater controversy as to whether personal service was required of the notice of motion seeking to sanction the breach, on which the question of what constituted sufficient service varied as between attachment and committal. By Lord Eldon's period of office as Lord Chancellor, it was clear that a notice of motion for committal had to be served personally on the defendant.[40] This was so even if counsel had undertaken to appear for the respondent on the hearing of the motion,[41] or had in fact appeared.[42] The result was that where a notice of attachment, served on a solicitor, was turned into a notice of motion, there had to be personal service.[43] Kekewich J acknowledged the distinction in *Mander v Falcke*,[44] but observed 'why that should be, I do not pretend to know or guess … and in matters of practice even more than in matters of law …. it is more important that practice should be uniform and certain than that it should be right'.

The distinction is likely to have reflected two factors. First, the object of an attachment was already subject to a court order, attachment arising from a failure to comply with it, whereas committal did not always involve a breach of an order directed to the respondent. Second, attachment could be issued as a matter of course, without any order, on production of the order directing the act to be done, and evidence it had not been done.[45] By contrast, committal required an order either made against a respondent in court, or on a notice of motion which had to be personally served.[46]

IV. Bodies Corporate

English law came to recognise two categories of legal person – corporations aggregate, defined by Blackstone as consisting 'of many persons united together into one society and are kept up by a perpetual succession of members, so as to continue for ever' and corporations sole, which 'consist of one person only and his successors in some particular station, who are incorporated by law in order to give them some legal capacities and advantages particularly that of perpetuity, which in their natural persons they could not have had'.[47]

Enforcement against a corporation sole did not present particular difficulties – the corporation was constituted by a single individual, against whom the remedies of attachment and sequestration could be levied. A successor was bound to respond to a writ of sequestration levied against his predecessor.[48]

[39] *In re Tuck* [1906] 1 Ch 292, 696 (CA) (memorandum of the registrar).
[40] *Angerstein v Hunt* (1801) 6 Ves Jr 488; 31 ER 1158; *Hope v Carnegie* (1868-69) Lr 7 Eq 254.
[41] *Ellerton v Thirsk* (1820) 1 Jac & W 376; 37 ER 419.
[42] *Nelson v Worssam* (1890) WN 216.
[43] *Callow v Young* (1887) 56 LT (NS) 147, and Oswald's submissions in *Mander v Falcke* [1891] 3 Ch 488, 489.
[44] *Mander v Falcke* [1891] 3 Ch 488, 492.
[45] The Lavie Note (n 18): 'whether the person attached had or had not done what he was ordered to do was a simple question'.
[46] The Lavie Note (n 18).
[47] Blackstone (n 14) vol I, 437.
[48] *Phelps v St John* 10 Ex 895; 156 ER 705, *Powell v Hibbert* (1850) 15 QB 129; 117 ER 407.

Corporations aggregates presented greater challenges. There were numerous statements to the effect that they could not be attached,[49] and suggesting that sequestration was the appropriate course.[50] In *Mayor, Commonalty and Citizens of the City of London v Mayor and Burgess of the Borough of Lenne Regis*,[51] Lord Loughborough rejected the contention 'that process of contempt would issue against the acting part of a corporation for disobeying a *mandamus*', responding that 'supposing an attachment of contempt would issue, it must be against the individual members of the corporation and not against the defendants in their corporate character'. Blackstone, in the first edition of his *Commentaries*, stated that 'the process against a body corporate is by *distringas*, to distrain them by their goods and chattels, rents and profits, till they obey the summons or directions of the court'.[52] Blackstone identified 'the major and commonalty of a city, the head and fellows of a college, the dean and chapter of a cathedral' as examples of corporations aggregate against whom enforcement could be procured by distraint of goods.[53]

The various means of enforcing court orders against corporations in the Court of Chancery are discussed in *Harvey v East-India Company*.[54] The first step after the writ of execution was issued was the writ of *distringas*, which was intended to compel an appearance. In that case, the corporation still failed to appear, and the court issued a writ of sequestration. At that point, the defendant sought to enter an appearance, and discharge the writ of sequestration, and the issue arose as to whether it was entitled to do so. The court rejected the attempt to do so, the sequestration order having been made absolute. While Sir Jack Jacob was probably mistaken in later suggesting that sequestration was 'no doubt designed … to provide machinery for proceeding against a corporation guilty of contempt',[55] the writ was particularly useful in that context, and there was a view that the writ was only available to enforce a negative injunction against a corporation.[56] Thus in *R v Doctor Windham, Warden of Wadham College*,[57] a bill was issued against the Warden in Chancery, to compel him to fulfil an agreement to execute a lease. Lord Mansfield noted that 'in the Court of Chancery, when a bill is brought against a corporation in contempt, there is no remedy by way of proceeding for contempt personally against the real parties who offend, but the mode of compulsion

[49] *Approved Men of Guildford v Mills* (1665) 2 Keb 1; 84 ER 1: Attachment for not obeying award 'per Keeling CJ cannot be granted against a corporation; contra if the rule were between A, B and C who comprise the corporation'; *Morgan v The Corps of Carmarthen* (1673) 3 Keble 350; 84 ER 760: 'An attachment will not lie against a corporation'.

[50] See eg *United Company of Merchants of England Trading to the East Indies v Kynaston* (1832) 3 Bli 153, 163; 4 ER 561: 'If the East India Company should refuse to permit inspection, they will be guilty of a contempt of Court, in which case, being a corporation which cannot be affected by personal process, a sequestration issues against their goods, to compel obedience to the order'.

[51] *Mayor, Commonalty and Citizens of the City of London v Mayor and Burgess of the Borough of Lenne Regis* (1789) 1 H BL 206; 126 ER 119.

[52] Blackstone (n 14) vol III, 445.

[53] Blackstone (n 14) vol I, 437.

[54] *Harvey v East-India Company* (1700) Prec Ch 128; 24 ER 62.

[55] J Jacob, 'Sequestration for Contempt of Court' (1986) *CLP* 219, 220.

[56] This was the position taken in J Oswald, *Contempt, Committal, Attachment and Arrest upon Civil Process in the Supreme Court of Judicature*, 1st edn (London, W Clowes, 1892) 61.

[57] *R v Dr Windham, Warden of Wadham College* (1776) 1 Cowp 377; 98 ER 1139.

is by sequestration'.[58] The case came before Lord Mansfield because the Warden had refused to apply the College's seal to the answer to be filed in Chancery, leading the majority of the Fellows to seek (and obtain) a writ of *mandamus* from the King's Bench Division compelling him to do so, which was duly granted.

In *Salmon v The Hamborough Company*,[59] a bill was brought in the Court of Chancery to enforce a debt, but the company did not appear, and could not be forced to appear by *distringas*, 'they having nothing by which they may be distrained'. A number of members of the company were also sued in their personal capacities, and they obtained the dismissal of the bill on a demurrer. However, a petition of appeal was allowed by the House of Lords. It was admitted 'that in the ordinary Course of Proceedings in Chancery that Court could not help the Plaintiff', but noted that 'in Causes of this Nature the Lords House had given special directions to the Chancery to relieve'.[60] The precedents provided in those directions required process to be issued in the usual way, and for decrees (either in default of appearance or on the merits) to be served upon the company's 'Deputy-Governor, Treasurer, Clerk or Secretary for the Time being'. If the decrees were not complied with, the Lord Chancellor was 'to order and decree, that the Governor or Deputy-Governor and the twenty-four Assistants of the said Company, or so many of them as by the Tenor of their Charter do constitute a *Quorum* for the making of Leviations upon the Trade, or Members of the said Company, for the Use of the said Company … as shall be sufficient to satisfy the said Sum to be decreed to the Plaintiff in that Cause, and to collect and levy the same, and to pay it over to the Plaintiff as the Court shall direct.' If no such levy was imposed, then 'the Lord Chancellor or Lord Keeper may issue Process of Contempt against them, as is usual against Persons in their natural Capacities'.[61]

The process of attachment, therefore, was brought into play by making an order – usually through the mechanism of the writ of *mandamus* – requiring those officers or directors able to perform their duty of ensuring that the corporate body complied with the order against it to take the steps necessary to ensure compliance, with the writ of attachment then being issued against them personally if they failed to do so.[62] Where a particular officeholder was required to take the step – eg where it was the mayor of a rown who was obliged to admit the applicant to the office of town-clerk – the writ of *mandamus* could be directed to the mayor,[63] and the writ of attachment could be issued against the mayor in the event of non-compliance. Difficulties arose, however, in the case of decisions which had to be taken collectively, and where it was unclear who was able to undertake the relevant act and who was not. In *Sir Joshua Sharp v Major'*

[58] ibid 377.

[59] *Doctor Salmon v The Hamborough Company, by the Name of the Governor, Assistants and Fellowship of Merchant Adventurers of England, and divers particular Members of that Company by Name, in their natural Capacities* (1671) 1 Ch Cas 204; 22 ER 763.

[60] ibid 205.

[61] ibid 207.

[62] See eg *Corpe v Glyn* (1832) 3 B & Ad 801; 110 ER 294.

[63] *R v The Mayor of Hereford* (1705) 2 Salk 701; 91 ER 593. The Court of Appeal in *ADM International SARL v Grain House International SA* [2024] EWCA Civ 33; [2024] 1 All ER (Comm) 1194, [110] refer to a further example, *R v The Mayor, Sheriffs, Citizens and Commonalty of the City of Norwich* (1830) 1 B & Ad 809; 109 ER 802, in which the writ was directed to the mayor, sheriff and entire citizenry of Norwich to perform their obligations to appoint 20 persons as guardians of poor for the city.

Co'itat' et Cives London,[64] a writ of *mandamus* was directed to the Mayor, Commonalty and Citizens of London, to swear and admit the plaintiff to the position of common councilman for the Cheap ward. An application was made to quash the writ because it should not have been 'directed to the whole body by the corporation name'. Justices Powis and Littleton Powys were willing to uphold the writ, the former referring to the 'great variety in the cases of directions of these writs, some being to the persons amoving, others to the corporation, some to the commissioners for regulating corporations on the Corporations Act'.[65] Mr Justice Eyre and Chief Justice Parker wanted to quash the writ which 'ought to have been directed to the lord mayor, and not to the corporation'. In *R v Mayor &C of Hereford*,[66] the writ of *mandamus* was quashed because it had been addressed too widely, in an attempt to capture the right target. In *Queen v Chapman*,[67] when a writ of *mandamus* had been issued in relation to a command to proceed with the election of a town clerk, Chief Justice Holt said that the writ of *mandamus* was to be delivered to the mayor, but that the action for a false return could be made against the whole corporation, and if the election had not taken place because votes were equally split, 'they shall [be] brought up as in contempt and laid by the heels until they do agree'.

Francis Buller explained in his influential treatise on trial at *nisi prius* that 'where a *mandamus* is directed to a corporation to do a corporate act, the attachment is granted only against those particular persons who refuse to pay obedience to the *mandamus*',[68] or as it was put in another text, 'those members of the corporation who are responsible for the disobedience'.[69] Thus in *R v Ledgard and others*,[70] where the peremptory *mandamus* required the corporation to pay compensation to its former town clerk who had been dismissed from his office, the objection was taken that the individuals should have been named. Lord Denman CJ interjected in argument that 'where no return is made, a peremptory *mandamus* issues against those persons to whom the *mandamus* was directed; but it should seem that an attachment ought to be granted only against those particular persons who refuse to pay obedience', later observing that 'if the town councilman have decided not to obey the writ, that might be prima facie evidence on a motion against all of them; but … the present application, which includes the burgesses, cannot be supported'.[71] The objection that 'it would be inconvenient if writs of *mandamus* were directed to the town council, which is a carrying body, instead of the corporation, which is permanent'[72] did not prevail.

[64] *Sir Joshua Sharp v Major' Co'itat' et Cives London* (1714) Gilb KB 255; 93 ER 321.

[65] ibid 257.

[66] *R v Mayor of Hereford* (1705) 2 Salk 701; 91 ER 593.

[67] *Queen v Chapman, late Mayor of Bath* (1704) 6 Mod 152; 87 ER 910.

[68] F Buller, *An Introduction to the Law Relative to Trial at Nisi Prius*, 5th edn (London, A Strahan and W Woodfall, 1790) 201–02. The Court of Appeal in *ADM International SARL v Grain House International SA* [2024] EWCA Civ 33; [2024] 1 All ER (Comm) 1194, [113]–[114] noted that this account conflated the separate steps of issuing *mandamus* against the corporation and against its officers. While the process of enforcement and attachment could be directed to those corporators who refused to comply with the order for *mandamus*, no action would lie for damages against those individuals, at least without proof of malice: *Harman v Tappenden* (1801) 1 East 555; 102 ER 214.

[69] J Grant, *A Practical Treatise on the Law of Corporations in General as Well Aggregate as Sole* (London, Butterworths, 1854) 240.

[70] *R v Ledgard and others* (1841) 1 QB 616; 113 ER 1268.

[71] ibid 619.

[72] ibid 621.

As has been said, the solution arrived at by the courts to enforce compliance with orders made against bodies corporate – at least for decisions of a kind which would fall to be taken collectively – was to ensure the process of attachment was available against those directors who had used their offices for the purpose of opposing compliance with the injunction, or had omitted to take such steps as they could take to procure compliance. James Stephen summarised the position as follows:

> With respect to enforcing a peremptory *mandamus* against a corporation aggregate, the law seems to be to the following effect. Where the corporation at large have the power and duty to perform the act in question, the writ is directed against the corporation by its name of incorporation, and may be enforced by attachment against those members who actually, at a corporate meeting, voted against obeying the writ; or, who having been duly summoned, stayed away from such meeting without adequate excuse.[73]

This reflected the fact that 'the absentees are considered in law to have voted with the majority', and that 'it ought not to be tolerated that a party, by shirking from his duty, should thus relieve himself from liability'.[74]

The process proved a cumbersome mechanism for enforcement of court orders against corporations.[75] There had to be a default in compliance with the order which could be attributed to the acts or omissions of those against whom the writ of *mandamus* was to be issued. The court would generally issue a writ to show cause against those still in office and able to procure compliance with the court's order,[76] requiring them to show cause to why the writ of *mandamus* should not be issued. The 'show cause' writ had to be directed to those against whom the writ of peremptory *mandamus* would later issue, which raised difficulties given the often floating membership of the governing bodies of corporations aggregate.[77] A writ of peremptory *mandamus* would issue if an insufficient return was made to the requirement to show cause, and a writ of attachment only when the writ of peremptory *mandamus* was issued and not complied with. All of this delayed the enforcement process considerably.[78]

V. Reform in the Nineteenth Century

The complete codification of the law of contempt for which many devoutly hoped eluded even the zeal of Victorian law reformers, Lord Selborne's 1883 Contempts of Court Bill failing to pass. However, the law of contempt, both generally and with regard to bodies corporate, was altered in significant respects by legislation passed in the second half of the nineteenth century.

[73] J Stephen, *The Common Law Procedure Act 1860 with Notes and Introduction* (London, Butterworths, 1860) 68.

[74] Grant (n 69) 241 and *Charitable Corporation v Sutton* (1742) 2 Atk 404; 26 ER 642.

[75] See also R Kerr, *The Common Law Procedure Act 1854 with Practical Notes* (London, Butterworths, 1854) vii–vii referred to by the Court of Appeal in *ADM International SARL v Grain House International SA* [2024] EWCA Civ 33; [2024] 1 All ER (Comm) 1194, [114].

[76] *King v University of Cambridge* (1765) 1 Wm Bl 547, 548; 96 ER 316.

[77] Buller (n 68) 199–202.

[78] See eg Campbell's submissions in *Corpe v Glyn* (1832) 3 B & Ad 801, 803; 110 ER 294: 'The objection to a *mandamus* is the delay'.

So far as the position of bodies corporate is concerned, section 3 of the Railway and Canal Traffic Act 1854 empowered the court to grant injunctions against companies in respect of any acts or omissions contrary to the Act, and provided that 'in case of disobedience of any such writ of injunction or interdict it shall be lawful for such court or judge to order that a writ or writs of attachment, or any other process of such court incident or applicable to writs of injunction or interdict, shall issue against any one or more of the directors of any company, or against any owner, lessee, contractor'. This avoided the need for an order first to be made against the directors to take a particular step before proceedings could be brought against those directors for non-compliance. However, the statute did not identify the circumstances in which it would be appropriate to issue a writ of attachment, and against which directors.

The problem of contumelious corporations was addressed more generally in section 33 of the Common Law Procedure Act 1860, a section which emerged unheralded by any work on the part of the Common Law Commissioners or a Select Committee. This provided:

> Writs of injunction against a corporation may be enforced either by attachment against the directors or other officers thereof, as in the case of a *mandamus*, or by writ of sequestration against their property and effects, to be issued in such form and tested and returnable in like manner as writs of execution and to be proceeded upon and executed in like manner as writs of sequestration issuing out of the Court of Chancery.

The assumption behind section 33 appeared to be that an order for *mandamus* made against a company could already be enforced by writ of attachment against a director or officer, and that henceforth injunctions could similarly be so enforced. A contemporary commentor[79] observed that an order for *mandamus* against a company (as opposed to one made against its directors) could not be enforced by writ of attachment against the directors. However, he noted that the words 'as in the case of *mandamus* may, however, be construed as not descriptive of something pre-existing but as operative', a construction which 'though utterly ungrammatical, may further what would seem to be the intentions of the legislature'.

The Common Law Procedure Act 1852 made provision for the service of proceedings on the officers of corporations aggregate,[80] abolished the writ of *distringas*[81] and provided that the an order of *mandamus* could be enforced by attachment.[82] Section 16 and schedule 1 of the Supreme Court of Judicature Act 1875 brought new rules of court into force, with provision for subsequent amendment by Order in Council.[83] The new Order 11 Rule 2 provided for personal service as the default mode of service, with power to order substituted service where this could not be done promptly. However, when an order was made against a party in the course of proceedings, service on a party's solicitor was a sufficient basis for an application for attachment for non-compliance,[84] with provision for attachment of a solicitor who neglected without reasonable cause

[79] JCFS Day, *The Common Law Procedure Acts* (London, H Sweet, 1863) 290–91.
[80] Common Law Procedure Act 1852, s 16.
[81] Common Law Procedure Act 1852, s 24.
[82] Common Law Procedure Act 1852, s 73.
[83] Issued pursuant to s 16 of the Supreme Court of Judicature (1873) Amendment Act, 38 & 39 Vict.
[84] Order 21 Rule 21.

to pass on the order to his client.[85] Order 43 Rule 5 blurred the traditional distinction between attachment and committal, by providing that 'a judgment requiring any person to do any act other than the payment of money, or to abstain from doing anything, may be enforced by writ of attachment, or by committal.' Order 44 Rule 1 provided that a writ of attachment would have the same effect as the writ previously issued out of the Court of Chancery, but Rule 2 provided that 'no writ of attachment shall be issued without the leave of the Court or a Judge, to be applied for on notice to the party against whom the attachment is to be issued.' The effect of the change in practice in the Chancery Division was explained in *Abud v Riches*[86] in the following terms:

> Formerly, when a contempt of the Court of Chancery was committed, an attachment was often issued as an order of course at the applicant's wish; and if he who got the attachment was wrong, he took the consequences. The intention of the present rule … was that the suitor shall not have the power of imprisoning anybody, but the Court only. That, once for all, deprives the suitor of the right he formerly had of imprisoning his opponent, if he chose to do it, at his own risk. The suitor acting thus might be a pauper, and unable to pay the costs, or might do it maliciously. It is now an order of Court, to be made upon notice, and therefore in many cases after discussion. That is the new position of matters.

The result was that the writ was not generally issued until after the contempt had been adjudicated upon, such that the order for the writ to issue became, in effect, an order for punishment of the offender.[87] Notwithstanding this, the writ retained its traditional form, and continued to direct the sheriff to bring the offender before the court. Further, the position was different for sequestration. Order 47 provided that where there had been non-compliance with a mandatory order which was subject to a fixed time for compliance, the plaintiff could issue a writ of sequestration without the need for further order of the court.

In 1883, a new set of rules of court was issued for the newly constituted High Court of Justice, several of which touched on the consequences of non-compliance with court orders. Order 41 Rule 5 provided that a judgment or order requiring an act to be done had to stipulate a time for compliance. The order had to be served personally, and be indorsed with a warning 'if you the within-named A.B., neglect to obey this judgment [or order] by the time therein limited, you will be liable to process of execution for the purpose of compelling you to obey the same judgment [or order]'. There was no equivalent provision for prohibitory injunctions. Order 42 Rule 30 provided that, as an alternative to enforcing specific performance by 'proceedings against the disobedient party for contempt', the court might order the act to be done by the party who obtained the order at the disobedient party's expense. Order 42 Rule 31 provided that judgments or orders against a corporation which were wilfully disobeyed could, with the court's leave, 'be enforced by sequestration against the corporate property, or by attachment against the directors or other officers thereof, or by writ of sequestration against their property'. As was noted at the time, 'this is taken from Common Law Procedure Act 1860, s.33. and in addition to that section allows sequestration against

[85] Order 21 Rule 22.
[86] *Abud v Riches* (1876) 2 Ch D 528, 529. See also *In re Evans, Evans v Noton* [1893] 1 Ch 252, 267.
[87] JC Fox, 'The Summary Process to Punish Contempt (2)' (1909) 25 *LQR* 354, 354.

the corporate property'.[88] It was subsequently held that there had to be personal service on any director before the writ of attachment could be issued against them, even though the rules did not expressly provide for this,[89] and that this was an alternative remedy only available when the order had also been appropriately served on the company.[90] Order 52 rule 4 provided that a notice of motion for attachment had to identify in general terms the grounds of the application, and be served with the supporting evidence. It was later noted that this rule 'was framed expressly for the purpose of protecting persons threatened with attachment … What the order means is that a person whom it is sought to send to prison should know, not only why the application is made, but also the evidence on which it is to be made, and that he may have the opportunity of considering such matters together.'[91] Service of orders was addressed by Order 67, which provided that service of a copy of the order would suffice 'except in the case of an order for attachment', and that service at the address for service given by the respondent in the proceedings was sufficient for orders 'in respect of which personal service is not requisite.'

There are a number of notable features of these reforms. The first is how little they sought to engage with the substantive law of contempt of court, which was largely left to the common law. Sir John Fox, writing in 1922,[92] noted that "Process of contempt' is nowhere defined in the rules, nor is the punishment for contempt provided for … The framers of the rules left the definition of contempt and its punishment where they stood, perhaps with an ultimate view to the codification of the law by Act of Parliament.' Second, the separate concepts of attachment and committal were maintained, but the distinction, if any, between them was in large measure obscured. This led to confusion as whether the requirement to serve a copy of the affidavit evidence together with the motion applied to a motion for an order for committal, as well as one for a writ of attachment. In *Harvey v Harvey*,[93] Chitty J suggested that the effect of the Rules of Court was that 'attachment and committal are apparently placed on the same footing,' and referred to an unreported observation of Sir George Jessel in a case in which Chitty had appeared as counsel[94] that 'the distinction between committal for contempt and attachment for contempt was practically abolished.' However, the ghosts of the past continued to rattle their chains. In *Taylor Plinston Bros & Co Ltd v Plinston*,[95] Warrington LJ was troubled by 'the general impression that there is now no difference between attachment and committal.' The Master of the Rolls, Sir Herbert Cozens-Hardy, held that 'the distinction between attachment and committal is recognized in the Rules of the Court' and was 'not an old-fashioned distinction,' and rejected the attempt to

[88] FP Tomlinson, *The Judicature Acts and Rules of the Supreme Court 1883* (London, William Clowes & Son, 1883) 268.

[89] *McKeown v Joint Stock Institute Limited* [1899] 1 Ch 671; *Iberian Trust, Limited v Founders Trust and Investment Company, Limited* [1932] 2 KB 87, 97–98.

[90] *Iberian Trust, Limited v Founders Trust and Investment Company, Limited* [1932] 2 KB 87, 98; *Benabo v William Jay & Partners Ltd* [1941] Ch 52, 55.

[91] *Taylor v Rowe* (1893) XLVIII LT (NS) 213, 214.

[92] JC Fox, 'The Practice in Contempt of Court Cases' (1922) 38 *LQR* 185, 189–190.

[93] *Harvey v Harvey* (1884) Ch D 644, 653–54.

[94] *Sprunt v Pugh* (1878) 7 Ch D 567.

[95] *Taylor Plinston Bros & Co Ltd v Plinston* [1911] 2 Ch 368.

apply Order 52 Rule 4 to committals. In *Re Evans*,[96] Lindley LJ held that there was no requirement for personal service of the notice of motion for a writ of attachment, as opposed to one for a writ of committal, because 'this being an application for a writ which under the old practice would have issued without any order, I do not see any ground on which we can say that personal service is required.'

Finally, the differential treatment of mandatory and prohibitory orders had evolved in a very different manner from that accorded by the distinct processes of attachment and committal. A party was able to procure the issue of a writ of attachment simply by filing evidence of the making and service of the order and non-compliance, without the need for any judicial determination, until the 1875 Rules, and that remained the position so far as issuing the writ of sequestration was concerned under the 1883 Rules. Committal required an order of the court. The effect of the 1883 Rules was that the enforcement of mandatory injunctions was made subject to more exacting requirements than prohibitory injunctions, with a requirement of personal service and the inclusion of a penal notice. Finally, the law relating to enforcement of orders made against directors or officers was brought into the domain of rules of court for the first time, even though section 33 of the Common Law Procedure Act 1860 remained in force until repealed by paragraph 1 of Schedule 1 of the Statute Law Revision Act 1950. This remained the case until the 2020 Reforms.

VI. The Position Up to the 2020 Reforms

The process of enforcing orders directed to corporations against directors or officers remained the subject of confusion, in particular as to who had to be served, and which directors were appropriate objects of writs of attachment. An 1890 commentary suggested that 'when the writ is directed to companies, corporations, justices etc a quorum should be served – that is as many as are competent to do the act required to be done …'[97] In *R v Corporation of Worcester*,[98] a peremptory writ of mandamus was issued against the mayor and councillors of a local corporation, in respect of the corporation's failure to implement a statutory scheme. The writ was served on the mayor and nine of 48 council members, but by the time the case reached court, only seven of those nine were still councillors. Wills J brushed aside a miscellany of objections as to the number of councillors served, their change in status before the hearing and the mode of service, stating the purpose of his order was 'to bring these gentlemen to their senses and … to show them that there are means by which the court can make itself obeyed, even by a reluctant and recalcitrant corporation.' There were similar difficulties in *R v Council of the Metropolitan Borough of Poplar*,[99] in respect of writs of mandamus made to enforce the contributions which the Poplar council had refused to make to the

[96] *Re Evans* [1893] 1 Ch 252, 265.
[97] F Short and F Mellor, *The Practice on the Crown Side of the Queen's Bench Division of Her Majesty's High Court of Justice* (London, Stevens and Haynes, 1890) 52.
[98] *R v Corporation of Worcester* (1904) JP 130, 132.
[99] *R v Council of the Metropolitan Borough of Poplar* [1922] 1 KB 72; [1922] 1 KB 95 (No 2).

London County Council and the Metropolitan Asylum Board.[100] Once again, attempts to rely on defects in service, the failure to serve all of the councillors and the changing composition of the council were to naught, Lord Sterndale MR observing that 'it is quite clear according to the practice of the Courts and the cases which have been cited to us that where a writ of this kind is addressed to a corporate body which can only act by the persons who compose it, if it is not obeyed those persons can be attached for not obeying it and if it be not obeyed, the individual members who have control of the corporation are liable to be attached.'

There was a major revision of the Rules of the Supreme Court in 1965.[101] Enforcement by attachment was abolished, the commentary to *The Supreme Court Practice* noting that this revision 'happily terminates a long and unfortunate history, in the course of which distinctions developed and multiplied in the decisions of the courts, and in the rules, and contempt of court was punishable in some circumstances by attachment and in others by committal.'[102] A new Order 45 Rule 5 provided for the enforcement of both mandatory and prohibitory injunctions made against a body corporate, 'with the leave of the court [by] a writ of sequestration against the property of any director or other officer of the body' and by 'an order of committal … against any such officer'. Order 45 Rule 7(2) required personal service of both mandatory and prohibitory injunctions, and in the case of orders against corporations, personal service on the officer against whom an order for sequestration or committal was sought. The order to be served had to be endorsed with a notice providing that the person so served was 'liable to process of execution' to compel compliance.[103] It was possible, under Rule 7(6), to enforce a prohibitory injunction in cases in which those service requirements had not been complied with, but no equivalent provision for mandatory injunctions, alongside a more general power to dispense with service. These rules were substantially reproduced in the new CPR Part 81 brought into force on 1 October 2012.[104]

The precise basis on which a director could be committed for an order made only against the company was yet to be settled when the issue arose in *Director General of Fair Trading v Buckland*.[105] Anthony Lincoln J rejected the suggestion that the director's mere failure to procure compliance was sufficient, as opposed to an allegation 'of a failure to supervise or investigate or of wilful blindness.'[106] He noted that Order 45 Rule 7:

> occupies a place once occupied by section 33 of the Common Law Procedure Act 1860 … The statute was repealed in 1950 and the provisions of section 33 were incorporated in the former RSC Order 42 r 31, itself replaced by the present RSC Order 45, r 5. All these provisions,

[100] For the background to the Poplar litigation see D Foxton, *The Life of Thomas E Scrutton* (Cambridge, Cambridge University Press, 2013) 227–33, a book which would never have been published without Professor Ibbetson's support.

[101] Rules of the Supreme Court (Revision) 1965, 1965 No 1776. This followed, somewhat belatedly, the *Final Report of the Committee on Supreme Court Practice and Procedure* Cmd 8878 (1953). That report said very little about the enforcement of orders through the contempt jurisdiction, beyond recommending the retention of the writ of sequestration as a means of enforcing injunctions against companies ([422]).

[102] *The Supreme Court Practice 1967* (London, Sweet & Maxwell, 1967), commentary on Order 52.

[103] Something which had previously only been required for mandatory inunctions: *In re Tuck* [1906] 1 Ch 692, 696.

[104] SI 2012/2208.

[105] *Director General of Fair Trading v Buckland* [1990] 1 WLR 920.

[106] ibid 923.

> whether in the statute or the Rules of Court, were procedural in the sense that they provided methods of enforcing the law against bodies and persons who otherwise were liable for contempt of court under the general law.[107]

He held that a director who adopted a purely passive position, failing to procure the company's compliance, was not liable under the substantive 'common law' of contempt. That conclusion would have made the enforcement of injunctions, and particularly mandatory injunctions, against bodies corporate a challenging process, and it did not survive long. In *Attorney-General for Tuvalu v Philatelic Distribution Corporation Ltd*,[108] the Court of Appeal held that 'where a company is ordered not to do certain acts … and a director of that company is aware of the order … he is under a duty to take reasonable steps to ensure that the order … is obeyed, and if he wilfully fails to take those steps and the order … is breached, he can be punished for contempt'. It was not wholly clear from the decision whether that conclusion rested on the wording of Order 45 Rule 7, or a wider principle of the substantive law of contempt, although the latter seems more likely.[109] However, the effect of the decision was that 'a director can be liable for civil contempt without necessarily being in contempt under the general law',[110] and this was so because of a principle of judge-made law.

VII. The 2020 Reforms

Prior to the 2020 Reforms, CPR 81.5(1) provided that 'unless the court dispenses with service under CPR 81.8, a judgment or order may not be enforced under rule 81.4 unless a copy of it has been served on the person required to do or not to do the act in question'. CPR 81.6 similarly emphasised the requirement of personal service ('copies of judgments or orders … must be served personally'). The omission of both rules in the 2020 Reforms led the applicant in *MBR Acres Ltd v Maher*[111] to submit that the court should proceed with its application to commit the respondent, notwithstanding the fact that the order alleged to have been breached had only been served on the respondent's solicitors, and not on the respondent personally. However, CPR 81.4(2) provided that a contempt application must provide 'confirmation that any such order was personally served, unless the court or the parties dispensed with personal service'. In rejecting the assertion that the requirement of personal service had been removed, Nicklin J drew heavily on the history of the law of contempt to show that, for mandatory orders, the requirement that the order be personally served on the respondent before enforcement by attachment or committal could be undertaken was established at common law 'well before efforts were made to codify them in procedural rules'.[112]

So far as bodies corporate were concerned, CPR 81.4(3) had provided that in the case of breach of an order made against a company, 'the committal order may be made

[107] ibid 924.

[108] *Attorney-General for Tuvalu v Philatelic Distribution Corporation Ltd* [1990] 1 WLR 926, 936 (CA).

[109] *ADM International SARL v Grain House International SA* [2024] EWCA Civ 33; [2024] 1 All ER (Comm) 1194, [144].

[110] *Templeton Insurance Limited v Motorcare Warranties Limited* [2012] EWHC 795 (Comm), [24].

[111] *MBR Acres Ltd v Maher* [2022] EWHC 1123 (QB); [2023] QB 186.

[112] ibid [73].

against any director or other officer of that company or corporation'. This was removed by the 2020 Reforms, although, as with the treatment of personal service of the order, there were parts of the new CPR 81 which proceeded on the basis that the position of directors and officers had not changed. Thus, the definition of 'penal notice' in CPR 81.2 was 'a prominent notice on the front of an order warning that if the person against whom the order is made (and, in the case of a corporate body, a director or officer of that body) disobeys the court's order, the person (or director or officer) may be held in contempt of court and punished by a fine, imprisonment, confiscation of assets or other punishment under the law'. CPR 81.4(2)(e) required a penal notice in those terms to have been placed on the order when an application for committal was made. Further one of the transitional provisions, Rule 81.20, provided that where an injunction was made against a corporation, 'the writ of sequestration may in addition be issued against the property of any director or other officer of that company or corporation'. On that basis, I concluded in *Olympic Council of Asia v Novans Jets LLP*[113] that the 2020 Reforms had not altered the law of contempt so far as the directors and officers of body corporate respondents to injunctions were concerned, holding that the statement in the 2020 Reforms that they were not intended to alter the substantive law of contempt included 'the principles and case law which determine the circumstances in which an application for committal may be made against a director or officer in respect of a breach of a court order by a body corporate'.[114] I noted that, given that conclusion, it was not necessary to determine whether there was any special rule of liability of the directors of corporations for contempt at common law, but noted the support for such a view in James Stephens' *The Common Law Procedure Act 1860*[115] and I concluded that 'it cannot be assumed that, prior to the Common Law Procedure Act 1860, the courts lacked means to commit those natural persons who were responsible for the non-compliance by a corporation with an injunction'.[116]

Following a detailed review of the history of the relevant legal principle, the Court of Appeal in *ADM International SARL v Grain House International SA*[117] came to the same conclusion. Popplewell LJ held that the principle whereby those persons responsible for the conduct of legal persons could be answerable in the law of contempt for the legal person's failure to comply with a court order:

> is a matter of substantive law, not procedural law, which was not dependent upon the 1860 Act, the Rules of the Supreme Court prior to 2012, or the Civil Procedure Rules prior to 2020, and remains unaffected by the 2020 Revision.

The 1860 Act had not created that principle, but merely made 'some procedural changes to give more streamlined effect to its enforcement.'[118]

[113] *Olympic Council of Asia v Novans Jets LLP* [2023] EWHC 276 (Comm); [2023] 1 WLR 1462, [33].
[114] ibid [33(iii)].
[115] Stephen (n 73) 68.
[116] *Olympic Council of Asia v Novans Jets LLP* [2023] EWHC 276 (Comm); [2023] 1 WLR 1462, [36]. I hope the failure to research the historical position further at that point will be excused by the fact that the hearing concluded on 31 January 2023, written submissions followed on 1, 2 and 3 February 2023 and the draft judgment was provided to the parties on 6 February 2023!.
[117] *ADM International SARL v Grain House International SA* [2024] EWCA Civ 33; [2024] 1 All ER (Comm) 1194, [138].
[118] ibid [141].

VIII. Conclusion

The interaction between substantive and procedural law, and the difficulties in distinguishing between the two, has long been one of David Ibbetson's interests. In 'Milsom's Legal History', he noted Professor Milsom's 'use of court records, of plea rolls, as a source of data to explicate the development of substantive law',[119] and much the same can be said of David's work. David noted that procedural innovations – 'the presence of those quick and cheap remedies' – 'served to accelerate the proprietisation of the feudal relationship'.[120] In Part One of *A Historical Introduction to the Law of Obligations*, 'Form and Substance in Medieval Law', David noted that the formalism of medieval common law 'tends to conceal substantive principles',[121] and in his conclusion he noted both that 'really significant shifts in the law commonly resulted from the conceptual recharacterization of claims by litigants … trying to avoid some irksome procedural rule or to take advantage of some more favourable legal process available elsewhere',[122] and the 'very long-term effect of … relatively minor procedural changes'.[123] The core theme of the Twentieth British Legal History Conference, which David chaired was 'all aspects of interaction between legal practice and legal doctrine'.[124]

The ambit of the 2020 Reforms was delineated by reference to the distinction between substantive and procedural law. In his foreword to the consultation document proposing the 2020 Reforms, Coulson LJ stated that 'the procedural aspects of contempt proceedings are causing frequent difficulties', and that the reforms had the aim of 'simplifying, shortening and strengthening the procedural rules' by 'omitting 'nearly all the substantive law'.[125] The new CPR 81.1(2) provided that 'this Part does not alter the scope and extent of the jurisdiction of courts determining contempt proceedings' and CPR 81.1(4) that 'this Part has effect subject to and to the extent that it is consistent with the substantive law of contempt'.

However, the determination of which parts of the law of contempt were procedural, and which were substantive has, as ever, offered scope for dispute. Nicklin J identified the key issue in *MBR Acres* as whether 'the requirement personally to serve the injunction order is a requirement of the substantive law of contempt or is merely a procedural requirement'. The difficulty of separating those concepts is apparent in his conclusion that 'the substantive requirements of the law of contempt … designed to ensure procedural fairness in an area where the liberty of the subject was at stake … were established by the common law rules well before efforts were made to codify them in procedural rules'[126] and that 'the general requirement of personal service of an injunction order is

[119] DJ Ibbetson, 'Milsom's Legal History' [2017] *CLJ* 360, 361–62.

[120] ibid 368.

[121] Ibbetson (n 3) 11.

[122] ibid 296.

[123] ibid 297.

[124] M Dyson and DJ Ibbetson (eds), *Law and Legal Process: Substantive Law and Procedure in English Legal History* (Cambridge, Cambridge University Press, 2013) Preface.

[125] Civil Procedure Rule Committee Consultation, 'Proposed Rule Changes Relating to Contempt of Court: Redraft of CPR Part 81' (March 2020).

[126] ibid [73].

a substantive requirement of the law of contempt that existed well before it was codified in procedural rules'.[127] A similar tension is apparent in my conclusion in *Olympic Council of Asia* that 'there is some scope for argument as to whether the rule that was CPR 81.2(3) was part of 'the substantive law of contempt, or a procedural provision addressing how an order is to be enforced' but that 'the better view is that it is a legal principle which was substantive in content, but one which took effect via procedural statutes and rules'.[128] In *ADM International SARL v Grain House International SA*,[129] Popplewell LJ noted that 'reference is often made to matters of substantive law in procedural rules of court, but that does not provide any indication that the rules are the sources of such law; nor does it render the rules the source of that law.'

The result of overlaying a 'procedural' reform on the 'substantive law' may not be conceptually tidy, but it has allowed significant reforms to be undertaken through a process and with a speed which any wholesale attempt to restate the law of contempt could never have achieved. As David Ibbetson has noted, 'the common law has many virtues; tidiness is not among them',[130] an observation perhaps as true of a great common lawyer, as of the subject he has illuminated to such effect.

[127] ibid [102].
[128] *Olympic Council of Asia v Novans Jets LLP* [2023] EWHC 276 (Comm); [2023] 1 WLR 1462, [31(i)].
[129] *ADM International SARL v Grain House International SA* [2024] EWCA Civ 33; [2024] 1 All ER (Comm) 1194, [140].
[130] Ibbetson (n 3) 294.

21

Tort and Stability

MATTHEW DYSON AND EMILY GORDON

I. Introduction

David has, for decades, been an example of the scholarship to which so many of us aspire. He is the standard against which we judge our own work, and by which we both duly find it wanting and are inspired to make it better. He brought us into the academic community, showed us where things were and invited us to play with them.

This chapter picks out a theme from David's work: how to understand legal change. In particular, it explores what the modern history of tort law might show us about *stability* in legal rules. We begin by considering the idea of stability itself, before turning to look at some practical examples, particularly the duty of care in negligence, breach of duty and the directness requirement in tort. From there we theorise about some of the processes involved in the stability of legal objects over time.

II. In Stability

We sketch here a working definition of stability, its application to law, and what is in stability that helps us understand the law and its development.

A. Stability in General: Issues, Processes, Outcomes

Stability could describe many phenomena, and that variety helps us understand *legal stability*. The *Oxford English Dictionary* offers:

> Fixity of position in space; freedom from liability to changes of place.
>
> Ability to remain in the same relative place or position in spite of disturbing influences; capacity for resistance to displacement; the condition of being in stable equilibrium, tendency to recover the original position after displacement. Also, of a body in motion: Freedom from oscillation, steadiness.

Key themes emerge as resistance to change in location or trajectory, or the return to an original position after deviation, and as resistance to external forces, rather than describing an internal state. We can also see that an object might be stable in some regards, even if that is not its commonly described characteristic. For example, that '[t]he stability of colour consists in its power of resisting the action of acids, alkalis, etc'.[1] Finally, stability might be temporary. For instance, scaffolding is meant to be fixed and stable for a limited time, until it is disassembled into smaller units and moved elsewhere. A patient might be in a stable condition, but with a poor prognosis in the absence of further options for treatment.

The importance of stability often turns on *what* is stable. The examples just given are generally about *physical objects*: structures and bodies, colours, patients in medical care. Stability is not limited to such objects. It can also be used to describe states of other *objects* such as animate agents, and the constructs of those agents: everything from the emotions, motivations, ideas, and values of humans, through to their rules, prohibitions, concepts. These might be thought of as 'issues' to their human agents.

Most significantly, stability might be used to describe *processes* and *outcomes*, not just *issues* such as physical things, constructs or issues within human minds. For example, a river flows through a valley: it erodes the land by the same process, regardless of the different forms of the land, and the outcome is the same small particles carried downstream and broadly predictable long-term movements in the shape of the river. In that way, over a long period of time the precise location of the river is not stable, but the processes shaping it are, as are the results of those processes at particular times. *Object* must be understood broadly, to include not just human rules, but the processes by which rules are created, applied, reformed and removed, and the outcomes of these processes.

Building from this, as a working definition, we use stability to mean:

> an object's resistance to a specified form of outward change or movement in the face of external pressure; or an object's propensity to return to its prior form or position after external pressure caused a change or movement.

B. Stability in Law

The range of objects, and their forms, becomes particularly important as we now turn to consider *legal stability*.

The most obvious objects are legal rules and related phenomena. For example, we might examine how the law on 'nervous shock' became the law on 'psychiatric harm' and the law allowed greater recovery over the last 150 years, seeing periods of stability cut by periods of change.[2] We might also consider the stability of one tort compared to another. One example is the tort in *Rylands v Fletcher* being (re-)categorised under nuisance,[3] or absorbed within negligence (in Australia).[4]

[1] C-L Berthollet (transl. W Hamilton), *Elements of Art of Dyeing* (England, S Couchman, 1791) vol I, i.i.iii.45 and see generally www.oed.com.

[2] See most recently, for a path to change not taken, *Paul v Royal Wolverhampton NHS Trust* [2024] UKSC 1.

[3] *Cambridge Water v Eastern Counties Leather* [1994] 2 AC 264.

[4] *Burnie Port Authority v General Jones Pty Ltd* (1994) 120 ALR 42.

To understand legal stability we would need to understand the form law can be found in, and that takes us first to some comparative law methodology for examining legal objects. One useful formula is to consider law as being found in three states: law in the books, law in action and law in minds. Each describes a form for legal constructs used in society. Stability across all three states is needed for the law in fact to remain stable, but it might be stable in different ways and for different reasons in each state. We also learn something useful about the law if we see where instability starts, and what effects that has.

The law in the books is that recorded in formal sources, from statutes and cases to the work of official bodies and academics and practitioners. It represents the conventional component of the law as captured in transmissible sources. It is commonly the most accessible, and has the most apparent force; to many laypeople and some lawyers it is assumed to be the only source of law needed.

The law in action is the way the law has an effect in the real world. It is the implementation of the law in the books, covering everything from whether the law is enforced, or even if a valid claim is in fact pursued, to how its formal rules or their enforcement shape lived realities for laypeople.

The law in minds captures the conception and perception of law in the minds of legal actors. It provides the space where human involvement understands and develops the law in the books, and the means by which it is expressed in the law in action. It therefore mediates and explains the other two levels. This significance was noticed by Ewald, who has forcefully sought to reshape comparative law as a discipline for investigating law in minds rather than law in the books or law in action:

> What comparative law should aim for is an understanding of the conscious ideas at work in the foreign legal system; that is, the principles, concepts, beliefs, and reasoning that underlie the foreign legal rules and institutions.[5]

One of Ewald's examples to support this, putting rats and other pests on trial, is discussed in some depth in perhaps his most famous article:[6] 'The sixteenth century courts that placed weevils and locusts on trial plainly had some outlandish beliefs; but the most striking of those beliefs were about insects, and not about legal philosophy'.[7]

We are particularly interested in the reasons for stability, and the 'law in minds' approach seems key here. The reasons behind stability seem to be mediated through legal actors' applications of real life to the law and the law to real life. Put at its least controversial, as Watson did in one formulation, the 'cause' of legal rules 'is commonly, but not always, rooted in social, economic, or political factors important to the life of society or its leaders'.[8] This is part of the processes that the law is under, and just as

[5] W Ewald, 'Legal History and Comparative Law' (1999) *ZEuP* 553, 557; J Stapleton, 'Benefits of Comparative Tort Reasoning: Lost in Translation' in M Andenas and D Fairgrieve (eds), *Tom Bingham and the Transformation of the Law: A Liber Amicorum* (Oxford, Oxford University Press, 2009) 773–814.

[6] W Ewald, 'Comparative Jurisprudence (I): What Was it Like to Try a Rat?' (1995) 143 *University of Pennsylvania Law* Review 1889.

[7] Ewald (n 5) 557.

[8] A Watson, 'Legal Change: Sources of Law and Legal Culture' (1983) 131 *University of Pennsylvania Law Review* 1121, 1135; see also A Watson, *Society and Legal Change* (Edinburgh, Scottish Academic Press, 1977).

stability could describe objects, processes and issues, so should *legal* stability also look not only at legal objects, but also at the processes and outcomes of legal phenomena.

Understanding how human reasoning and practices are linked to the law is beyond the scope of the current project, but one argument about that relationship does merit some consideration. Some have argued, in more or less strong forms, that the law is a mirror of the society in which it is based. This 'mirror thesis' can take many forms, from 'law is explicable only in terms of X' to 'law and X are closely related'; and 'X' there might be wider or narrower, covering many parts of cultural phenomena, or just one part, like economics or psychology.[9] This argument might have much intuitive appeal, at least in to modern audiences, who might view their law as something linked to their identity. It is also hard to argue that factors relating to the wider context of legal actors do not influence their involvement with the law. However, even a weak version of the mirror thesis has difficulties explaining significant phenomena like legal transplants, where legal objects are copied from one society into another, a potentially significantly different society.[10] Other critiques have acknowledged the role of the external environment to the extent it is channelled through legal elites.[11] A powerful counter to the mirror thesis was set out by Tamanaha, highlighting that wherever there is a difference between legal rules and what people in the community actually do, there is evidence of the mirror thesis being incorrect.[12] For our purposes, we do not assume that there is a mirror between society and its law, but would acknowledge both diversity in the society, and the possibility that the law could, depending on the situation, be deliberately, or knowingly, imperfectly reflecting the society it is in. The value then is identifying the asymmetry, and explaining it.

The chapter starts from the traditional entry point of the law in the books, picking out some examples of stability, and hopefully in due course, instability. It then tries to explore what made those features in those cases, and from there draw out some general themes. To do so we need to understand stability in time, which is what we turn to next.

C. Stability in Time

Stability presents an interesting opportunity to explore when, how and why change occurs, and when it does not. In this context, the change that interests is in law, and hence, stability is a window on the nature of law itself. Two related points arise immediately: that law is responsive to 'external' pressures, and it is predominantly found in the minds and works of lawyers and those bound by it. These two threads pick up the

[9] See particularly W Ewald, 'Comparative Jurisprudence (II): The Logic of Legal Transplants' (1995) 43 *American Journal of Comparative Law* 489, 492–96.

[10] See particularly the work of Alan Watson in making this argument: A Watson, *Legal Transplants: An Approach to Comparative Law* (Edinburgh, Scottish Academic Press, 1974).

[11] See eg G Teubner (ed), *Autopoietic Law: A New Approach to Law and Society* (New York, W de Gruyter, 1988) and N Luhmann, *The Differentiation of Society* (New York, Columbia University Press, 1982).

[12] BZ Tamanaha, *A General Jurisprudence of Law and Society* (New York, Oxford University Press, 2001) ch 5.

perspectives of stability in law just described, and have been neatly captured by two leading English lawyers.

First, Harold Dexter Hazeltine, Downing Professor of the Laws of England, captured the nature of law as a changeable response to forces inside the legal community or outside:

> No body of law is ever, even for a single moment, in a state of absolute repose; for it is of the nature of law to be restless. Law is continually moving, changing, in response to the pressure of the forces that arise in the inner life of the community or that penetrate from outside.[13]

Second, Lord Goff, writing as a Law Lord but having served as an academic as well at the start of his career, highlighted the element of instability of law as a construct of human thought:

> Seen in the perspective of time all statements of the law, whether by the legislature, or by judges, or by jurists, are no more than working hypotheses. They are, quite simply, temporary approximations which some people in their wisdom have found to be convincing at certain points of time.[14]

Lord Goff neatly describes how law can be seen at each point of time it is examined, to be a temporary approximation of an answer convincing to legal actors. This is subject to change and incapable of definitive and permanent proof as true. The convincingness of a particular statement, and audience, and that audience's openness to be convinced, might change over time; it is mediated through those people's social, economic, political and philosophical positions, and given expression in recognition as law.

Legal development might therefore be marked by moments of stability and moments of transition. These reflect when legal actors conceive of the object moving from one working hypothesis to something else. Moments of stability describe an object showing no change in position or its characteristics despite the application of force to it.

Moments of transition cover the point at which an object comes out of stability and moves, changes or is replaced. More than just describing legal change, it speaks to the reasons for why the object's stability ceased to be sufficient. It also reminds the researcher of both the range of possible paths when an object is no longer stable, and that an object might remain on a path until further forces are applied to it. A famous example, discussed below, is *Donoghue v Stevenson*. In short, the question was whether the ultimate purchaser, made ill by an unsafe drink, could bring an action in negligence against the manufacturer. This landmark of English tort law is known the world over for Lord Atkin's 'neighbour principle', informing the extent of the duty to take care now fuelling the 'staggering march' of negligence.[15]

[13] HD Hazeltine, 'The Study of Comparative Legal History' (1927) *Journal of the Society of Public Teachers of Law* 27, 33.

[14] Lord Goff, 'Judge, Jurist and Legislature' (1987) *Denning Law Journal* 79, 80.

[15] *Donoghue v Stevenson* [1932] AC 562; T Weir, 'The Staggering March of Negligence' in P Cane and J Stapleton (eds), *The Law of Obligations: Essays in Honour of John Fleming* (Oxford, Oxford University Press, 1998) 97–138.

However, for some years after the decision it was not clear whether Lord Atkin's view or Lord Macmillan's more restricted view would win out. This doubt persisted for some years, even after further Privy Council decisions.[16]

Thinking in terms of moments of stability and transition highlights the ongoing forces on an object: there must be reasons why an object of study is not changing and there must be forces underlying when it does. Until a moment of transition occurs, the legal system is operating within a restricted legal space. It is in one sense true that with each judicial or non-judicial application of the object of study, 'new' law is being created. Nonetheless, this is a restricted and particular meaning of 'new'. There must be reasons why this restricted space remains. In other words, legal non-change is just as much a part of legal development as legal change; legal historians should be just as interested in why an object remained unchanging. By considering what forces are keeping the object where it is, the researcher will also then be in a better position to explain any eventual moment of transition. An example might help show this clearly.

English tort law had, between 1933 and 2003, a rule of impecuniosity. It began when the *Liesbosch*, a dredging ship, was tortiously sunk and because the owners could not afford immediately to buy a new one, they hired a replacement at a high cost to finish a contract. The House of Lords confirmed that any claim for the sinking could not extend to the expensive hire, holding that it was the owners' lack of funds that caused this loss, not the tort that sank their ship.[17] The extra hire was treated as related to the duty on the victim to mitigate harm, and so the normal rule that you take your victim as you find him, that is, with empty pockets or with full ones, did not apply.[18]

The impecuniosity rule was overturned in *Lagden v O'Connor* in 2003. Lagden's car was tortiously damaged and while his car was being repaired, his lack of funds meant he had to use an expensive credit hire firm.[19] This increased the hire charge payable by the tortfeasor at the end as the claimant could not afford to pay up front. All three courts who heard the claim allowed recovery for the £659 that it cost for Lagden to hire a car (increasing the total claim by about two-thirds[20]). The House of Lords argued that the distinctions on which *The Liesbosch* was founded were wrong and that in any case it had been overtaken by a focus on reasonable foreseeability as the core of the scope of the defendant's liability.[21]

The impecuniosity rule moved from stability to transition and now to a new rule. One interesting question is why it took 70 years to leave the *Liesbosch* at the bottom of the judicial ocean? In fact, *Lagden* was the last in a series of cases, largely involving defendants' insurers facing large sums for credit hire cars. After some initial success

[16] See eg *Grant v Australian Knitting Mills, Limited, and Others* [1936] AC 85, 88–89 per counsel for the defendant knitting mill.

[17] *Liesbosch Dredger v SS Edison* [1933] AC 449, 460 per Lord Wright. The case builds on *British Westinghouse Electric and Manufacturing Co Ltd v Underground Electric Railways Co of London Ltd* [1912] AC 673. On the *Liesbosch*, see in particular B Coote, 'Damages, *The Liesbosch*, and Impecuniosity' (2001) 60(3) *CLJ* 511.

[18] *Liesbosch Dredger v SS Edison* [1933] AC 449, 460–461 per Lord Wright.

[19] [2003] UKHL 64.

[20] *Lagden v O'Connor*, Official Transcript, Oxford County Court, 14 September 2001, [34].

[21] *Lagden v O'Connor* [2003] UKHL 64, Lord Hope [49]–[61], Lord Scott [82], Lord Walker (in dissent on the appeal) [90]–[102].

on contractual grounds,[22] *Lagden* was a clear reversal for the insurance industry. It is unclear what caused the shift, but perhaps it was the number of cars getting damaged, the role of the car in English culture, and the long-term view of insurers meaning they wished to preserve and enforce the rule so, unfortunately for them, litigated. It is also unclear why litigation grew from the 1990s only.[23]

Stability is also understood in part as an antithesis: stable as opposed to malleable, brittle, inconsistent, and changeable. It sits at a junction of purposes within a legal system, between permanence and adaptability. Stability is not necessarily wedded to a particular theory of law-making, such as common law precedent or civilian code-based approaches. It can be used in any context, and commonly suggests a positive: the value in resilience and resistance to change. We use it here particularly as a tool to understand what makes something resist external influence, and what that stability means to the law and to perceptions of it.

III. Tort's Development

We turn now to apply this understanding of stability in the development of tort law in England in the last 150 years, using case studies from the law of negligence.

A. Duty of Care

Though much has been written on the duty of care and how courts have approached the question of whether or not a duty is owed in any given situation,[24] the focus here will be on a period of development which has generally received less attention than others: the time immediately before *Donoghue*. We will then turn to some observations from its later development.

The concept of the duty of care emerged in the early nineteenth century, as plaintiffs wishing to bring an action in tort rather than contract claimed that a duty existed beyond contract.[25] Negligence law for the majority of the nineteenth century was characterised by pockets of liability, governed by recognised categories of duty.[26]

[22] See eg *Giles v Thompson* [1994] AC 142 on the credit hire agreements not being void for champerty, but they were drafted in breach of the Consumer Credit Act 1974: *Dimond v Lovell* [2002] 1 AC 384.

[23] See eg A Tettenborn, 'Compensating the Cash Strapped: The Sinking of the Liesbosch' [2004] *LMCLQ* 135.

[24] See eg J Plunkett, *The Duty of Care in Negligence* (Oxford, Hart Publishing, 2018).

[25] See MJ Prichard, 'Scott v Shepherd (1773) and the Emergence of The Tort of Negligence' in S Thorne et al (eds), *The Selden Society Lectures* (Buffalo (NY), William S Hein & Co, 2003) 442–47. For discussion of the development of the law of negligence and the duty of care, see eg DJ Ibbetson, *A Historical Introduction to the Law of Obligations* (Oxford, Oxford University Press, 1999) (hereafter: *HILO*) 169–201; M Lobban, 'Negligence'in WR Cornish et al (eds), *The Oxford History of the Laws of England, Vol XII: 1820–1914 Private Law* (Oxford, Oxford University Press, 2010) 903–57.

[26] For example, surgeon-patient was a recognised duty situation: see eg *Pippin v Shepherd* (1822) 11 Price 400, 147 ER 512. On the idea of 'pockets' of liability for negligence in the nineteenth and into the twentieth century, see J Stapleton, 'Duty of Care and Economic Loss: A Wider Agenda' (1991) 107 *LQR* 249.

Famously, *manufacturer to ultimate consumer* was not a recognised duty situation until *Donoghue v Stevenson* in 1932. The privity rule, a principle of contract law brought into the law of tort in the mid-nineteenth century, stood in the way of such a duty.

How courts in the twentieth century analysed when a duty of care might be owed by manufacturers or vendors of goods to the ultimate consumer is a useful example of legal stability and transition. It echos one of Milsom's key insights, as identified and elaborated upon by Ibbetson: '… that legal change commonly comes about as a result of lawyers, especially plaintiffs' lawyers, framing their cases in such a way as to maximise the chances of winning in the actual litigation, not with a view to developing the law in a particular direction'.[27] Ibbetson explains further:

> If some way of achieving a result works, other lawyers will follow the same route and a new rule may in time be seen to have been born. Its history can be reconstructed, even if no-one at the time knew that they were creating a new rule. We might add that the flexibility in framing cases may equally stand in the way of the law changing.[28]

In fact, before the House of Lords in *Donoghue* ousted the privity rule from the law of negligence, there was an alternative path in the law of tort (and outside of the law of contract) available to those injured by defective products: an exceptional category concerning the supply of 'dangerous' things. This legal argument was used to achieve outcomes similar to that in *Donoghue*, but before that case's formal change in the law.[29] The development of this alternative argument allowed a circumvention of the formal rule in *Donoghue*, and is likely to have added to the pressure for change in 1932. These repeated instances of circumvention created instability in the law in minds, if not in the books, and thereby weakened the rigid rule.

This rigidity of the formal privity rule prior to *Donoghue* is significant. Some judges lamented that it precluded a finding in favour of deserving plaintiffs.[30] Such a rule necessarily encouraged plaintiffs' lawyers to try to find a way around it. We also see the other side of the coin, to which Ibbetson referred in the final line quoted above, in the decades after *Donoghue*. It is the flexibility of the later twentieth century approach to duty of care that has led to a period of stability in the twentieth century – at least if we look at the formal rules 'in the books'.

i. Pre-Donoghue: 'Dangerous Things' and the Pressure for Change

It is well-known that in 1932 the House of Lords in *Donoghue* recognised a duty of care in tort between the manufacturer of goods and the ultimate consumer.

Before *Donoghue* it is generally understood that injured consumers would find it difficult, without a contract, to sue the supplier or manufacturer of the injury-causing

[27] DJ Ibbetson, 'Milsom's Legal History' (2017) 76 *CLJ* 360, 370. See eg SFC Milsom, *Historical Foundations of the Common Law*, 2nd edn (Oxford, Oxford University Press, 2009) 7.

[28] ibid.

[29] This argument has been made more comprehensively in E Gordon, 'Blacker v Lake and Elliot: (Closing and Opening) a Path for Injured Consumers in Tort before Donoghue' in J Gardner and I Ramsay (eds), *Landmark Cases in Consumer Law* (London, Hart Publishing, 2024) 135–52.

[30] See eg *Mullen v Barr* 1929 SC 461, 471.

goods. Though some few cases, like *George v Skivington*,[31] could be interpreted as recognising a duty more generally, this possibility was firmly rejected in 1912 in *Blacker v Lake and Elliot*[32] – the privity rule precluded any such general duty. However, there was an exceptional category of case in which a duty might exist between consumer and supplier/manufacturer: cases involving 'dangerous' things. A duty would be owed where a supplier or vendor knew an item to be unsafe and fraudulently represented it as safe, or for the supply or sale of something known to be dangerous because of some quality or defect.[33]

Looking only at the 'law in the books' in the 20 years before *Donoghue*, the law appears settled and stable. There were certain categories of relationship giving rise to recognised duties of care in tort, and manufacturer/consumer was not yet one. The privity rule prevented claims by third parties if a contract existed. Exceptionally, the supply of 'dangerous things' could give rise to a duty.

However, incomplete law reporting hides a swathe of successful claims by consumers in tort against vendors and manufacturers at the time. These are visible in newspaper reports. A small sample will be set out here, but further instances have been noted elsewhere[34] and there are likely more examples yet to be uncovered. While missing legal detail, these reports provide a glimpse into the law as seen in actions by ultimate consumers.

In the 1920s, there was an 'epidemic' of dermatitis caused by cheap fur garments.[35] Unsurprisingly, this resulted in claims against vendors – most of which appear to have been successful – in county courts and before single judges of the King's Bench.[36] This is, at first glance, uninteresting: vendors at this time might be sued under the Sale of Goods Act 1893. However, at least with *married* female claimants, it is likely that there was no privity of contract between the defendant and the party injured. Wives did not yet have full contractual capacity.[37] They would also often be contracting as agent for their husband in buying items like clothing.[38] Sometimes husbands are joined in these actions and seek recovery for expenses, but, at least in some cases, the married women are clearly seeking a sum for their injuries.[39]

[31] (1869) LR 5 Ex 1. See also *Heaven v Pender* (1883) 11 QBD 503. For a detailed discussion of *George*, see DJ Ibbetson, 'George v Skivington (1869)' in C Mitchell and P Mitchell (eds), *Landmark Cases in the Law of Tort* (Oxford, Hart Publishing, 2010) 69–94.

[32] (1912) 106 LT 533.

[33] See M Lobban, 'Personal Injuries' in WR Cornish et al (eds), *The Oxford History of the Laws of England, Vol XII: 1820–1914 Private Law* (Oxford, Oxford University Press, 2010) 958–1000, 986–90; *Langridge v Levy* (1837) 2 M & W 519, 150 ER 863; *Clarke v Army and Navy Co-operative Society* [1903] 1 KB 155 *Langridge* concerned an unsafe gun held out to be safe, while in *Clarke* the 'dangerous thing' was a tin of chlorinated lime with a tendency to explode if not opened very carefully. Conversely, in *Blacker*, it was held that a cheap brazing lamp which had burst and burned its user did not fall within the exceptional category.

[34] Gordon (n 29).

[35] 'Fur Poison: Doctor Thinks It Due to Arsenic' *Nottingham Evening Post*, 16 March 1923.

[36] See eg 'Skin Trouble from Fur' *The Scotsman*, 18 July 1923; 'Dermatitis From Fur: £ 100 Damages Against a Shopkeeper' *Northern Daily Mail*, 22 July 1926.

[37] Any contract entered into by a married women would bind her 'separate property' and would not bind her personally: see Married Women's Property Acts 1870, 1882, 1893. 'Separate property' would come from work, a gift or an endowment, and most married women at this time did not work.

[38] See, eg, *Paquin v Beauclerk* [1906] AC 148.

[39] For a clear example, see 'Story of a Fur Coat: Dermatitis Alleged in County Court Case' *Norwood News*, 21 June 1929.

Claims for painful skin conditions were also successfully brought by women against hair dye manufacturers. These must have been in tort, rather than contract: the manufacturer had no direct relationship with the injured claimants. In 1922, the manufacturer of 'Inecto Rapid', Inecto Limited, was successfully sued in the King's Bench by Miss Rivette for injuries caused by her use of the dye.[40] Rivette was awarded £200 in damages against Inecto. Other similar claims were made throughout the 1920s.[41]

Perhaps the most striking successful claim was brought by a seven-year-old boy against a manufacturer of soft drinks. The boy and his father brought an action in 1920 in the King's Bench against White and Sons Ltd.[42] Mr Camelo had purchased bottled drinks from the defendants, one of which contained a dead mouse which apparently caused serious illness in his son. Salter J found for the plaintiffs, awarding £11 7s. 6d. to the father for expenses incurred, and £15 to the son for 'pain, suffering, and sickness due to the defendants' negligence'.[43] According to the 'law in the books' at the time, the son should have no claim by reason of the privity rule since only the father was a party to the contract.

The newspaper reports are sparse, but the most likely explanation for this apparent anomaly is the 'dangerous things' exception that offered a route to success for the plaintiffs – in the hands of a sufficiently sympathetic court. Some reports make it clear that the claim is being brought an exceptional case of the supply of 'dangerous things'. The report in *The Times* of Ms Rivette's successful claim contains the following detail:

> In opening the case for Inecto, Limited Mr. Giveen said … [t]he plaintiff had to show that the company sent out, without adequate warning, a substance which was dangerous. It could not be said that this dye came within the category of dangerous things, as it had been used in thousands of cases without ill effects. He cited Blacker and Lake v. Elliot … in support of this contention.[44]

The fact that this dye was a popular product generally used without problems does suggest a more expansive understanding of the term 'dangerous' than might be expected. The existing exception thus appears to have been applied more loosely at this lower court level. Dyed furs causing dermatitis would also fall fairly comfortably within this (loosened) category. More difficult to understand is the *Camelo* case. Were food and drink considered sufficiently 'dangerous' in the days before effective refrigeration and stringent food safety practices? Claims failed with respect to defective ginger beer bottles, when these exploded and caused lacerations,[45] though this was not a hygiene or contamination problem; but, more importantly, an attempt to apply the exception failed

[40] 'Injury Caused By a Hair Dye' *The Times*, 28 February 1922.

[41] See, eg, 'Hair-dye claim' *The Chemist and Druggist*, 14 January 1922; 'The "Inecto" action: £500 damages' *The Times*, 19 May 1926.

[42] See eg 'Dead Mouse in Lemon Squash: Bottled Shock for Thirsty Boy' *The Globe*, 24 June 1920; 'Mouse in Bottle of Lemon Squash' *The Leeds Mercury*, 25 June 1920; '£26 For a Dead Mouse Found in Lemon Squash' *The Daily Herald*, 25 June 1920. 'Dead Mouse in Lemon Squash' *The Edinburgh Evening News*, 24 June 1920.

[43] See eg 'Mouse in Bottle of Lemon Squash' *The Dundee Evening Telegraph*, 24 June 1920; 'Mouse in Bottle of Lemon Squash' *Leeds Mercury*, 25 June 1920.

[44] ibid.

[45] *Bates v Batey* [1913] 3 KB 351.

with respect to a mouse in a child's drink on appeal before the Scottish Court of Session in *Mullen v Barr*.[46]

The contractually-derived privity rule was rigid, unable to accommodate the delicate balance of fairness in every case. This, of course, had led to the creation of an exceptional category in the first place. However, the 'dangerous things' exception to this rule was from its inception lacking in a stable identity. Its characteristics were not clearly defined – what did it mean to say that an item was 'dangerous'? The knowledge requirement was also inconsistently applied.[47] Related to its lack of persistent and clear characteristics, it was also *too* adaptable – *any* object causing harm could potentially be squeezed into the category of 'dangerous', which rendered the 'exceptional' category as something capable of undermining the privity principle.

Of course, it is not true that any and all uncertainty in the application of a rule necessarily creates legal instability, such that a formal change is inevitable. However, where a rule is central in determining the outer boundaries of a particular legal principle, here the existence of a duty of care in negligence, then uncertainty and inconsistency in application of the rule makes it less likely that there is stability across all three states of the law concerning duty in negligence – stability in the law in action and the law in minds are at risk, even if the official law reports and textbooks remain unchanged until formal amendment.

The Law Lords in *Donoghue* did not address, in detail, many of these successful claims. It is probable that they were unaware of many, as a result of selective and incomplete law reporting at this time. However, there is a hint in Lord Macmillan's speech that he was dissatisfied with claimants' use of the 'dangerous things' exception, and he noted the lack of clarity in its operation, which is likely to have been important in the ultimate decision.[48]

There were also other factors at play, in the time before *Donoghue*, which created an environment making it more likely that uncertainty and inconsistency in application of the privity rule would lead to a moment of transition in the law of negligence. The continued challenges posed by married women's legal status – their limited ability to hold property and enter into contractual relationships – is one such factor.[49] It was only in 1935 that married women were given the same rights as single women with respect to property, and that married women's liability under contract became personal rather than proprietary.[50] That this happened shortly after *Donoghue* is indicative of a broader societal shift around this time which would favour discarding a rule that might stand in the way of women's actions in tort.

A second feature of the 1920s and 30s is that a 'consumer culture', which had been developing in the nineteenth and early-twentieth centuries, had reached all parts of society.[51] Cheaper goods and mass-produced luxuries were available to all. This meant

[46] *Mullen v Barr* 1929 SC 461.

[47] Compare *White v Steadman* [1913] 3 KB 340 and *Bates v Batey* [1913] 3 KB 351. See also discussion in WTS Stallybrass, 'Dangerous Things and Non-Natural User of Land' (1929) 3 *CLJ* 376.

[48] See *Donoghue* (n 15) 611, 616.

[49] See eg Law Revision Committee, *Fourth Interim Report*, Cmd 4770, December 1934.

[50] See Law Reform (Married Women and Tortfeasors) Act 1935.

[51] See eg P Gurney, *The Making of Consumer Culture in Modern Britain* (London, Bloomsbury, 2017) 135–38 and chs 2, 5, 6. See also B Lancaster, *The Department Store: A Social History* (London, Leicester

more goods circulating and it became increasingly likely that goods causing harm would not have been bought directly from their maker. This is likely to have put pressure on laws restricting access to legal remedies – including the privity rule. Several speeches in *Donoghue* referred to changed times.

Finally, this period also saw the rapid rise in availability of liability insurance.[52] While liability insurance does not *necessarily* mean a more expansive approach to liability in negligence, it does mean that policy arguments that may have swayed courts to reduce the burden on commercial parties in the nineteenth century were no longer convincing.[53] Large-scale producers are better able to spread their costs anyway, and liability insurance meant that the burden could be more easily managed.

As a result, then, developments both inside and outside the legal system came together to create an environment in which a change in the law was more likely. The resulting moment of transition brought about the outcome in *Donoghue* and marked the beginning of an important change in direction for the law of negligence.

ii. The 'Formless' Twentieth Century after Donoghue

The history of courts' approaches to the duty of care concept in the later twentieth century has been considered in detail elsewhere.[54] However, some broad observations about stability may be made concerning the twentieth century developments.

As we noted earlier, the time after *Donoghue* was marked by a period of continued uncertainty. The effect of *Donoghue* was unclear; was Lord Atkin's approach to be followed, whereby the 'multiplicity of duties'[55] approach was abandoned in favour of a general test based on reasonable care and neighbourhood? Or were courts to follow the more conservative approach adopted by Lord Macmillan, whereby the categories still dominated?

The categories approach initially appeared resistant to change.[56] The slow acceptance by courts of an approach based on the application of a generalised test may, in part, have been because of the element of flexibility introduced by Lord Macmillan's approach. Before *Donoghue*, it seemed as if the 'categories of negligence', to amend Lord Macmillan's famous assertion to the contrary, were in fact closed:[57] attempts to add new categories, like the duty owed by manufacturers to consumers in *Blacker*, fell flat. However, the suggestion that new duties of care might be recognised in appropriate cases, even if a close eye had to be kept on the boundaries set by precedent, would have added sufficient flexibility into the law to accommodate some novel situations. Litigants and their lawyers need not search for alternative pathways or press for amendment to

University Press, 1998); C Wildman, *Urban Redevelopment and Modernity in Liverpool and Manchester, 1918–1939* (London, Bloomsbury, 2016) 96–97, 101.

[52] See eg 'Third Party Insurance: Development of Third Party Insurance', *The Policy-Holder: An Insurance Journal*, 25 August 1937, 1388; 'Insurance that Shields!' *The Northern Whig and Belfast Post*, 29 November 1924.

[53] See *Winterbottom v Wright* (1842) 10 M&W 109, 152 ER 402.

[54] See Plunkett (n 24).

[55] See discussion in Ibbetson, *HILO* (n 25) 191.

[56] See discussion in ibid 190–92. On Stapleton's analysis, this was still the approach into the 1980s: see Stapleton (n 26).

[57] See comments by Lord Reid in *Home Office v Dorset Yacht Co Ltd* [1970] AC 1004, 1026.

the law; they need only draw connections to existing precedent. Nevertheless, change did finally arrive by the 1970s.

Ibbetson has argued that it was partly the 'general principle' articulated by Lord Atkin in *Donoghue* and partly the move away from jury trials in England that transformed negligence law in the twentieth century.[58] An approach based on the recognition of narrow, specific duties of care was replaced by 'a more or less empty rule that one should take reasonable care to avoid injuring one's neighbour'.[59] This was the next moment of relative stability at which the law of negligence arrived – and specifically, duties of care in negligence. It was also the beginning of a long period of stability in legal rules associated with finding a duty of care, in large part because of the malleability, adaptability and flexibility in the dominant approach. This approach based on the Atkinian construct of neighbourhood, as Ibbetson suggests, created the 'all-embracing but largely formless tort of negligence' of the early twenty-first century.[60] The application of a general test based on reasonable foreseeability and proximity began in earnest (after its attempted introduction by Lord Atkin) in the 1970s in cases including *Home Office v Dorset Yacht Co Ltd*[61] and *Anns v Merton*,[62] then apparently[63] refined in *Caparo Industries plc v Dickman*[64] to an approach (not test) centred on consideration of the concepts of reasonable foreseeability, proximity and whether or not a duty would be 'fair, just and reasonable'. This tripartite formula was widely used until the late 2010s (but is not given the same prominence by the current UKSC[65]).

It might therefore be argued that the duty of care in negligence during the twentieth century is an example of a stable set of legal rules. There are several features that have remained unchanged. The duty of care concept has, since its inception, been used as a gatekeeping device to distinguish situations in which remedies in tort might be sought by the injured party from situations in which the loss must either lie where it falls or follow the scheme agreed between the parties. Looking at the *process* courts have adopted in identifying situations in which negligence law might operate to provide a remedy, the law in the books also remained largely the same for almost 50 years during the twentieth century. The *Caparo* approach consisted of vague labels or concepts to guide courts' consideration; they are inherently adaptable, malleable and flexible, at worst becoming close to meaningless.

On the other hand, there was, for the same time period, some lack of predictability as to the *outcome* when courts are confronted with a novel situation.[66] This difficulty ultimately led to the introduction of further rules in situations where courts were reluctant to see through the potential expansiveness of the general approach – that

[58] DJ Ibbetson, 'How the Romans Did for Us: Ancient Roots of the Tort of Negligence' (2003) 26 *UNSWLJ* 475, 479.

[59] ibid.

[60] ibid.

[61] [1970] AC 1004.

[62] [1978] AC 728 (HL). See discussion in Plunkett (n 24) 146.

[63] The Supreme Court has recently been at pains to emphasise that *Caparo* did not, in fact, lay down a general test and is, instead, to be understood as authority for incremental expansion by analogy with existing categories: see, eg, *NRAM Ltd v Steel* [2018] UKSC 13. However, it has done so expressly because *Caparo* had been widely understood as laying down such a test.

[64] [1990] 2 AC 605 (HL).

[65] *Robinson v Chief Constable of West Yorkshire Police* [2018] UKSC 4.

[66] Professor Ibbetson has also commented on this problem: Ibbetson (n 58) 475.

is, situations involving psychiatric injury not consequent on personal injury (ie 'pure' psychiatric injury), 'pure' economic loss, omissions and public authority liability. Several of these additional rules or principles proved controversial and much-criticised; particularly the introduction of restrictive rules concerning claims for pure psychiatric injury by those who were not themselves in physical danger,[67] and (at least in academic circles), the jack-of-all-trades device of 'assumption of responsibility'.[68]

What we have, then, is a period during which the function of the duty of care concept, and the formal 'on the books' approach to identifying duties of care, has not changed markedly. The adaptability of the core approach made it resistant to change. When this feature created some perceived uncertainty at the level of the law in action, exceptional categories with their own rules were used to create more certain boundaries in areas of concern to legal actors. These special rules did not undermine the core approach, which was sufficiently flexible to be made to reflect the reasons underpinning them. Any pressure for change was thus shifted to the periphery, to dissatisfaction with the special rules, and the core approach could remain – imperfect, perhaps, but functional in most cases.

B. Breach of Duty: Reasonable Care within Negligence

Between 1934 and 1949, breach of statutory duty was merged with the tort of negligence but this attempt at simplification did not prove stable. The context was industrial safety and an intellectual climate where duties to take care were being generalised. Indeed, *Lochgelly Iron v M'Mullan* came just after *Donoghue v Stevenson*, and featured three of the same judges.[69] The pursuer claimed damages at common law for the death of his son killed by a roof that fell in, in breach of a statutory duty that such areas 'shall be made secure'. Workmen's Compensation Act 1925, provided the exclusive remedy for a breach of that duty so a delict claim could only be brought if the statutory duty contained some notion of 'personal negligence' of the employer or his agent. This was, surprisingly, the first time the meaning of those terms had been debated even though a provision like it had been in the first Workmen's Compensation Act of 1897.[70] The claim succeeded. The standard of care had been determined by the legislature, but otherwise the duty was the same as any other duty in negligence.[71] Lord Wright was even more explicit:

> not only is the duty one which cannot be delegated but, whereas at the ordinary law the standard of duty must be fixed by the verdict of a jury, the statutory duty is conclusively fixed by the statute. But the duty is the same in kind in this respect, that it is a duty to take precautions and care for the safety of the workmen … Hence the breach of such a duty as that in question has been, I think, correctly described as statutory negligence.[72]

[67] See *Alcock v Chief Constable of South Yorkshire Police* [1992] 1 AC 310, and, eg, recent commentary in S Tofaris, 'Limping Into the Future: Negligence Liability for Mental Injury to Secondary Victims' (2018) 81 *CLJ* 452.

[68] See eg D Nolan, 'Assumption of Responsibility: Four Questions' (2019) 72 *Current Legal Problems* 123.

[69] *Lochgelly Iron, etc. Co Ltd v M'Mullan* [1934] AC 1 (Lords Atkin, Thankerton and Macmillan).

[70] ibid, 11; at least three House of Lords cases would have had to have been decided differently if it had succeeded here too.

[71] *cf Rudd v Elder Dempster* [1933] 1 KB 566.

[72] *Lochgelly Iron* [1934] AC 1, 23.

But this shifting of statutory duties into negligence was brief, especially for Lord Wright himself. It offered simplicity for statutory duties expressed in terms of taking reasonable care, the merger offered simplicity. However, statutory duties covered far more than that. Eight years after *Lochgelly Caswell v Powell Duffryn*, in 1940,[73] the victim was found dead inside a coal conveyor he was employed to clean when it was stationary. There had been no system of warning as to when the conveyor would start again. His mother sued under the Fatal Accidents Acts 1846 and 1864 and as his executrix. The House of Lords allowed the claim. The Coal Mines Act 1911 itself did not expressly grant a civil action on these facts. However, section 55 imposed a duty, that machinery 'shall be kept securely fenced', and the House of Lords treated that duty as if it were a common law negligence duty. Lord Macmillan found that the action must 'be based upon negligence and be subject to the general principles of law which govern actions of damages for negligence'.[74] But Lord Wright shifted the tone:

> I do not think that an action for breach of statutory duty such as that in question is completely or accurately described as an action in negligence. It is a common law action based on the purpose of the statute to protect the workman, and belongs to the category often described as that of cases of strict or absolute liability. At the same time it resembles actions in negligence in that the claim is based on a breach of a duty to take care for the safety of the workman. The cause of action is sometimes described as statutory negligence and it is said that negligence is conclusively presumed.[75]

Nine years later in *Galashiels v Millar*,[76] where a worker successfully claimed for being injured by an unsafe lift, further daylight was visible between the two forms of duty. Lord Morton[77] saw a clear statutory category of absolute duties established from at least the 1940s,[78] where no amount of care would avail the defendant;[79] this was obviously not the case for common law negligence.

The logical conclusion to this recognition of different fault components was *Upson v London Passenger Transport Board*,[80] at the end of 1949, when Lord Wright formally separated statutory duties out from negligence again. A regulation required that when a bus driver was proceeding past a pedestrian crossing with an obstructed view he should go only as fast as would allow him to stop if needed. The plaintiff was injured when she emerged from behind the taxi and walked onto the crossing. Lord Wright held:

> the authorities such as *Caswell's* case ... show clearly that a claim for damages for breach of a statutory duty intended to protect a person in the position of the particular

[73] [1940] AC 152.

[74] ibid 167.

[75] ibid 177–78. One of the only topical comments was (1940) 56 *LQR* 155, 155: 'This is a conclusion which will be heartily welcomed because at the present time an attempt to distinguish between these forms of action is entirely a matter of words and of no practical importance'. This was unattributed, but is believed to have been the editor, AL Goodhart. See similarly *Smith v Cammell Laird* [1940] AC 242, 264.

[76] [1949] AC 275. Affirmed in principle in *Latimer v AEC* [1953] AC 283, noted by G Williams, 'The Effect of Penal Legislation in the Law of Tort' (1960) 23 *MLR* 233, 238.

[77] ibid 283.

[78] [1940] AC 242; *Potts (or Riddell) v Reid* [1943] AC 1; *Carroll v Barclay (Andrew) & Sons, Ltd* [1948] AC 477.

[79] ibid 286 (Lord MacDermott) 289–90 (Lord Reid) to same effect.

[80] [1949] AC 155.

> plaintiff is a specific common law right which is not to be confused in essence with a claim for negligence … a claim for their breach may stand or fall independently of a claim for negligence.[81]

Keeping the negligence claim separate from the statute allowed the court to develop two separate tracks, with their own conditions, without distorting either.

Notably, this example highlights how stability can be context dependent. 'Statutory negligence' was much more successful in the country of its origin, the USA. The most notable proponent was Thayer, who, back in 1917, had argued that aside from omissions, criminal statutes should also set the standard for relevant negligence actions.[82] Lord Wright was well acquainted with both the North American literature, where 'statutory negligence' was well established, and the Scottish literature. In defining the duty in *Lochgelly*[83] he had veered towards the Ontario case of *Thompson v Wright* in 1892,[84] though this was also very similar to a Scottish case, *Kelly v Glebe Sugar Co* in 1893.[85] It may also be merely coincidence that the decision in *Lochgelly* followed so closely on the heels of an article by Morris in the Harvard Law Review in 1933[86] where the debate over 'statutory negligence' was re-opened. It might also have been coincidence that Morris' second article on the topic came out at exactly the same time as the decision in *Upson*.[87] Morris, in both articles, favoured of a modified form of statutory negligence, but the second pointed out how often the legislative standards in a criminal provision were more exacting, and that trying to incorporate those standards was effecting substantive change to tort law.

What we see from this example is the stability of negligence in its flexible standard of reasonable care: an experiment with a related cause of action distorted that core meaning, causing its originator, Lord Wright, to end it. This did not stop some later writers trying to reinstate that approach. Glanville Williams, for example, writing in 1960, statutory negligence was the best way to conceive of duties of care under statutes.[88] Williams' work did not lead to further changes in the law.

C. Direct and Indirect

The distinction between damage that has been caused by a defendant *directly* and damage that has been caused *indirectly* is one with significant longevity in the law of tort. This once held an important place as the deciding principle in identifying cases for which the action of trespass was appropriate from those caught by the action on the case. Particularly interesting for the present enquiry is the fact that it has endured

[81] ibid 168.

[82] ER Thayer, 'Public Wrong and Private Action' (1914) 27 *Harvard LR* 317, though not cited in *Lochgelly*.

[83] [1934] AC 1, 27.

[84] *Thompson v Wright* (1892) 22 Ont Rep 127, 130 (Boyd C) describing a failure to guard dangerous machinery as 'per se evidence of negligence'.

[85] *Kelly v Glebe Sugar Refining Co* (1893) 20 R 833, 835 (Lord Adam).

[86] C Morris, 'Relation of Criminal Statutes to Tort Liability' (1933) 46 *Harvard LR* 453.

[87] C Morris, 'The Role of Criminal Statutes in Negligence Actions' (1949) 49 *Columbia LR* 21.

[88] Williams (n 76).

as a rule in one corner of tort law, the law of nuisance, but proved unstable and was superseded in the law of negligence.

From the second half of the fourteenth century, there were two trespass actions in the common law: trespass *vi et armis* and trespass 'on the case'.[89] The former was, at least in principle, concerned with forcible breaches of the king's peace. The latter came to fill a gap that existed in the law: however ingenious the pleader, trespass *vi et armis* could not be made to cover certain types of wrong. But eventually it was decided that plaintiffs had to choose, and not plead in the alternative.[90] This was an early example of a moment of transition, towards the flexibility of the descriptive portion of case, and driven by a pleading and litigation strategy that pushed the boundaries of trespass *vi et armis*.[91] By contrast, the action on the case was sufficiently flexible to accommodate a vast array of wrongs, including nuisance.[92]

However, this did not mean that trespass *vi et armis* died away in the fourteenth century. Despite the flexibility of the action on the case, these two trespassory actions apparently existed alongside one another for several hundred years.[93] However, this period of stability was undone following the introduction by legislation of stricter rules for costs in trespass actions, thereby driving some plaintiffs to try to bring their claim within the ambit of the action on the case.[94]

The perceived need to find the boundary between the two actions resulted in much litigation. However, it took a long time for finer grained analysis of fault to be relevant to the definition of trespass and case.

The gateway issue of 'breach of the peace' had given way in the nineteenth century to the concept of 'directness': that injuries were done directly rather than consequently.[95] By 1833, it was settled that distinction between trespass and case was concerned with the directness or indirectness of the damage caused.[96]

However, the rule had developed in a stuttering fashion, and was not impregnable, as the famous thrown firework case of *Scott v Shepherd* showed.[97] The defendant had thrown a squib into the marketplace, and two stall owners had in sequence thrown it on until it hit the plaintiff and exploded, causing serious injury. The question of law, hidden by the pleadings, was probably in the defendant's favour on a conventional understanding, however the plaintiff won, probably as a deserving case not to be lost to

[89] See Ibbetson, *HILO* (n 25) ch 3.

[90] ibid 55. For example, the enraged husband could not at the same time sue for chattels stolen as his wife and the defendant eloped: *Battley v Faulkner* (1820) 3 B & Ald 288, 106 ER 668; *Fraser v Swansea Canal Navigation Co* (1834) 1 Ad & El 354, 110 ER 1241. Similarly, limitation was initially longer for a case action, but later became (and remains) twice as long, at six years, for a trespass action than one for breach of duty causing personal injury: the Limitation Act 1623 initially, but then see the Limitation Act 1939, s 2; See now Limitation Act 1980, s 11 *cf* s 2. Lord Justice Tucker, *Report of the Committee on the Limitation of Actions*, Cmd. 7740 (London, HMSO, 1949), esp [22] and [23].

[91] This is the view taken by Ibbetson, and probably the majority of legal historians. For an alternative interpretation, see RC Palmer, *English Law in the Age of the Black Death, 1348–1381* (Chapel Hill, UNC Press, 2001).

[92] Ibbetson, *HILO* (n 25) 103.

[93] ibid 156.

[94] ibid.

[95] See eg *Reynolds v Clark* (1724) 2 Ld Raym 1399, 92 ER 410.

[96] *Williams v Holland* (1833) 2 LJCP (NS) 190.

[97] (1773) 2 Blackstone W 892, 96 ER 525; see generally, Prichard (n 25).

a technicality. Blackstone J dissented, reiterating the 'settled distinction' by nuancing the forms of loss: trespass was for the immediate injury, and case for consequential loss.[98]

It instead took a shift in scale and context for fault to enter into the trespass/case distinction. Negligence in the performance of an undertaking, calling or office had been known to the common law for some time but it was cases where there had been no prior contact, particularly running down cases, which really shifted the focus of trespass and case. Industrialisation and the significant expansion of the roads in England, moving from local turnpikes to something approaching a national system, dramatically increased the number of people using what were still gravel roads. It has been estimated that between 1790 and 1830, 15 times more people were using stagecoaches, and journey times between major cities were halved in the same period.[99] With much greater numbers of people, and much greater speeds, accidents came before the courts with greater regularity. Most accidents involved servants driving the vehicles; case was the form for suing the employer for these injuries caused indirectly through their servant, and case actions grew. However, examples grew in the 1820s where the employer had in fact been driving. To fit into case it was argued that directly caused injuries could be brought through case, so long as they were not 'wilful'.

The first such driving case, *Lloyd v Needham* in 1823, permitted non-wilful injuries in case by a bare two to one majority, with only the dissent highlighting how the settled distinctions on directness were being dismissed. This was soon followed, with the Court of Common Pleas in 1833 in *Williams v Holland*[100] giving what is commonly seen as the definitive statement. The defendant negligently drove his gig against the plaintiff's cart. As Tindal CJ put it, 'where the injury is occasioned by the carelessness and negligence of the Defendant, the Plaintiff is at liberty to bring an action on the case, notwithstanding the act is immediate, so long as it is not a wilful act'.[101] Subject to some uncertainty about what wilful meant, the overall position was clear: case was widening while trespass was narrowing: case could not involve wilfulness, while it could involve directness or indirectness; trespass required wilfulness and directness.

Yet even this position was unstable. Only 40 years later, wilfulness was joined by negligence as a reason for the act to be *wrongful*, a prerequisite of the tort of trespass. This happened in *Holmes v Mather* in 1875,[102] another running down case. A servant was endeavouring to guide unruly horses and, without negligence, managed to injure the plaintiff in the highway. Bramwell B held that 'if the act that does an injury is an act of direct force *vi et armis*, trespass is the proper remedy (if there is any remedy) where the act is wrongful, either as being wilful or as being the result of negligence'.[103] It was clear that the burden of proving fault was on the plaintiff, and no claim was made out on the facts. Fault was increasingly used, first as 'wilfulness' and then as 'negligence', both gatekeepers to liability in trespass, but ultimately showing the decline in division between trespass and case.

[98] (1773) 2 Blackstone W 892, 897, 96 ER 525, 528.
[99] PS Bagwell, *The Transport Revolution*, 2nd edn (London, Routledge, 1988) 27–31.
[100] (1833) 10 Bing 112, 131 ER 848.
[101] ibid 115, 849.
[102] (1875) LR 10 Ex 261.
[103] ibid 268–69.

In summary, fault was slowly being teased out of the interstices of procedure and into a definitional role. In earlier tort law, this kind of discussion of fault was relevant to the facts, but not to the law, being a matter left to juries to decide according to the mores of the time and place. Fault was probably as relevant to trespass as to case. According to Baker:

> It seems from these occasional discussions that, although negligence played no overt role in the action of trespass *vi et armis*, a person was only considered guilty of a trespass if he was to blame for it, in the sense that he had caused the damage and with due care could have averted it. There is no reason to suppose that the standard of liability was any different in trespass on the case, since in either action it was left to the jury to decide according to the current notions of culpability. Plaintiffs would hardly have switched to actions on the case for negligence if it was a harder case to prove.[104]

And plaintiffs did indeed shift over to negligence as the preferred action.[105] It was more flexible, simpler and better represented reality.

IV. Structural Fig Leaves

We turn now to consider some of what these tort examples inspire us to think about stability more generally, and in particular, to consider some of the rich mechanisms at play in stability. They suggest three classes of these 'structural fig leaves', processes that both hide instability and/or structurally support the object to make it more stable. They are *Form*, *Location* and *Development*. The theme running through them is how much change is accommodated internally, with flexibility of some kind in the object resulting in stability for its effects in law. Each is connected to the working definition of stability which began the chapter: 'an object's resistance to a specified form of outward change or movement in the face of external pressure; or an object's propensity to return to its prior form or position after external pressure caused a change or movement'.

A. Form

As highlighted in our working definition, stability is linked to the internal shape of the object, in the face of external pressure. Some mechanisms have been evidence in tort law for internal changes to give the effect of stability. We saw some above, and one more, perhaps the most well-known, has been the 'legal fiction'. This is well-known from Henry Maine's *Ancient Law*,[106] which called it one of the three main instrumentalities of legal change. Fictions, along with 'equity' and 'legislation', were said to be necessary to prevent settled systems of law or legal practices from stagnating. For Maine, legal fictions signified 'any assumption which conceals, or affects to conceal, the fact that a

[104] J Baker, *An Introduction to English Legal History*, 5th edn (Oxford, Oxford University Press, 2019) 432. See also PH Winfield, 'The Myth of Absolute Liability' (1926) 42 *LQR* 37.
[105] See eg PF Winfield and AL Goodhart, 'Trespass and Negligence' (1933) 49 *LQR* 359, esp 365–66.
[106] H Maine, *Ancient Law* (London, John Murray, 1861).

rule of law has undergone alteration, its letter remaining unchanged, its operation being modified'.[107] The history of the development of tort law appears not to offer examples of legal fictions of precisely the same nature as, for example, the fictitious lessors (many of whom were 'John Doe') who facilitated enquiry into title.[108] While misleading pleading also involves an element of untruth, it is not the same as all parties pretending that dogs are cats. Nevertheless, the pleading device in the action of trespass revolving around careful re-framing of facts is closely related to legal fictions, and was certainly used to expand – without changing it on the face of the record – the ambit of trespass to situations of misadventure not in reality properly describable as forcible breaches of the king's peace.

Perhaps less well-known is what might be called constructively ambiguous rendering, or perhaps 'rugging': where the layout is messy enough to permit difficult questions or instability in processes to be 'swept under the rug'. The very nature of the reasonable person standard within negligence raises rugging to an entire motif, with the flexibility of that standard becoming totemic of negligence but also entirely necessary to cover the diverse cases being put underneath it. The rug has become structural.

The third example is where internal parts harden or soften in a way that is less perceptible to the outside, but which ultimately provides the flexibility needed for stability. A clear example of this in operation is the use of the tripartite approach to consideration of novel scenarios for duties of care, often called the *Caparo* approach, which was introduced above. This involves consideration of whether or not: (1) the harm suffered by the claimant was reasonably foreseeable, (2) the parties were in a relationship of sufficient proximity, and (3) recognition of a duty would be 'fair, just and reasonable' in the circumstances. As has been emphasised in recent years by the Supreme Court, these factors are imprecise and vague. Lord Reed, in the 2018 case of *Robinson*,[109] was at pains to point out that Lord Bridge in *Caparo* had, in setting out these factors, warned against using the factors as a test: they were 'not susceptible of any such precise definition as would be necessary to give them utility as practical tests but amount … to little more than convenient labels to attach to the features of different … situations which, on a detailed examination of all the circumstances, the law recognises pragmatically as giving rise to a duty of care'.[110] Using this approach allows courts to select for emphasis any specific features of the case before them, the factors often acting as little more than an *aide-mémoire* for the courts as to relevant issues for consideration. Their lack of precise content also means that they can be made to perform the task of creating or excluding a duty of care, depending on where the balance of justice lies. For example, 'proximity' has been given rigid requirements in the field of pure psychiatric injury, whereby secondary claimants must demonstrate relationship proximity and proximity in 'time and space'.[111]

[107] ibid 16.

[108] Professor Baker explains the device: 'The fictitious form of the action of ejectment … enabled freehold title to land to be tried in an action designed for leaseholders, [and] involved the freeholder making a fictitious lease to a non-existent person called John Doe, who brought the action on his behalf': JH Baker, *The Law's Two Bodies* (Oxford, Oxford University Press, 2001) 34.

[109] *Robinson v Chief Constable of West Yorkshire Police* [2018] AC 736, [24].

[110] *Caparo Industries plc v Dickman* [1990] 2 AC 605, 617–618.

[111] See *McLoughlin v O'Brian* [1983] 1 AC 410; *Alcock v Chief Constable of South Yorkshire Police* [1992] 1 AC 310.

'Proximity' has also been said to be lacking where a visitor to a pub was injured from sliding down its bannisters, despite the relationship of occupier-visitor and the obvious spatial-physical proximity.[112] On the other hand, a generous approach to proximity was taken by the majority in *White v Jones*,[113] allowing disappointed beneficiaries of a will to sue the testator's negligent solicitor.[114]

Finally, we might consider the process of applying force to the object, in effect, considering the pressure points within its form. The plaintiff frames the action in tort law. The courts will then decide whether the action is viable. That process used to, and on rare occasions still does, involve a jury deciding questions of fact. In any case, tort cases will almost always involve a defendant contesting the claims of fact and/or law made by the plaintiff. The result is that the stability of an object, and the chance of new legal solutions, may be driven by different legal actors. Often, but by no means always, plaintiffs might generate new pressure by adapting causes of action. Most commonly plaintiffs will try to apply a cause of action in a situation with facts which have not be litigated under that cause of action before. In return, a process of feedback responds, with defendants challenging that change in the cause of action, and/or seeking to develop defences. The role of the bench is also important here: judges must respond to pressure exerted by plaintiffs' framing of claims in new situations, and in doing so can also apply pressure where the law is perceived as inadequate or ill-adapted. One cannot help but feel that the days of the privity rule were numbered after it was described in the Scottish Court of Session in *Mullen* as, essentially, an obstacle to justice in the case before the court.[115]

B. Location

Stability is connected to the form of the object, but also its location. One of the prime examples of this explored above was the levels on which law operate: it appears that the rules with respect to privity and 'dangerous things' were applied by some county courts and by single judges in the King's Bench, on numerous occasions, in a way that was out of synch with the formal legal sources. There appears to have been a 'high law' of product liability in tort, exemplified by cases like *Mullen* and outlined in detail by the Law Lords in reaching a decision in *Donoghue*, and a 'low law', which was not the subject of discussion in that seminal case. The 'high law' was apparently stable before *Donoghue*; the inconsistency in application occurred in a different location and largely beyond the view of the Law Lords in *Donoghue*. This is likely to be related to the incomplete law reporting during this period, to which reference was made above – even significant numbers of successful claims in lower courts might be hidden to all but the most committed newspaper-comber. Looking only at the 'high law' might lead to a conclusion that the law was more stable – at least as to the law in the books and law in action – than the 'low law' position might suggest.

[112] *Geary v JD Wetherspoon plc* [2011] EWHC 1506 (QB) [58], [67]–[72].
[113] [1995] 2 AC 207.
[114] See eg ibid 295, per Lord Nolan.
[115] *Mullen v Barr* 1929 SC 461, 471.

A second form of location-stability is in outsourcing work to contain it elsewhere. Tort law ultimately adopted this by returning breach of statutory duty into a separate tort from negligence. Keeping the function within negligence would have distorted the negligence rules beyond taking reasonable care; the attempt to do so proved unstable.

C. Development

Finally, stability can, as noted at the beginning, involve the acceptance of movement, but the anticipated return towards the original, or expected continuation of core features. The 'flex' might not just be a shift in location, such as whether the rule in *Rylands v Fletcher* should: (a) expand to be a general tort of liability for ultra-hazardous activities,[116] (b) fold into negligence,[117] or (c) should continue to eke out a rare existence.[118] Indeed, it might not even be 'movement' alone that is in issue. For example, legal development can 'lag' behind the reasons for it to change. In lag, the processes leading to legal change have been set in motion but the rule appears stable for a period of time. On the other hand, that movement might end up being circular. 'Tail-eating' describes a formal legal change where the nature and/or process of making the change involves picking out part of the earlier formulation of the object and elevating it to the key element.[119] A powerful example of this was most evident in vicarious liability in *Lister v Hesley Hall*[120] in 2001, where the 'close connection test' was pulled out of the tail-end of the older '*Salmond* test' for deciding whether or not a tortfeasor's wrong was committed within the 'course of employment'.

V. Conclusion

Understanding legal development is, as David implied in his valedictory lecture in Cambridge in November 2022, something for which one needs a long and distinguished career followed by an equally long and productive retirement. Stability, in tort at least, seems to draw not on ideas of immobility, resistance to forces to change, but to utility, or, in some cases, non-disutility. That is, the law is often not, and David's offices never are, influenced by Marie Kondo. The question is not whether an object sparks joy, and only if it does should you retain it. The issue is what the law is being used to achieve and how far our conceptual limits can be pushed to do so.

[116] As happened in the USA, see eg s 520 of the Restatement (Second) of Torts.
[117] See eg *Burnie Port Authority v General Jones Pty Ltd* (1994) 120 ALR 42.
[118] *Transco v Stockport Metropolitan Authority* [2003] UKHL 61.
[119] And not only in tort, see eg Case C-267/91 and C-268/91 *Keck and Mithouard* ECLI:EU:1993:905, [1993] ECR I-6097.
[120] [2002] 1 AC 215.

22

'Unofficial Law', Doctrinal Change, and Judicial Review of Prerogative Powers

DAVID FELDMAN

I. The GCHQ Case

It is a pleasure to offer this case-study of twentieth-century common-law development to honour David Ibbetson, an inspiring colleague, friend, and scholar. For centuries, courts settled the scope of the Crown's prerogative powers, but would not examine the manner of its exercise. On 22 November 1984, however, that changed when the House of Lords decided *Council of Civil Service Unions v Minister for the Civil Service*[1] (the GCHQ case). At Government Communications Headquarters (GCHQ), a branch of the intelligence services, most staff had been allowed since 1947 to belong to national trade unions, and government had consulted unions when considering changing terms and conditions of service. In 1982, following industrial action at GCHQ as part of a bitter struggle between trade unions nationally and Mrs Thatcher's government, the government had made the Civil Service Order in Council under the royal prerogative. Article 4 provided that the Minister for the Civil Service (at that time, the Prime Minister) 'may from time to time make regulations or give instructions … (ii) for controlling … the conditions of service of' civil servants. Without consulting the unions, in December 1983 the Prime Minister issued an instruction imposing new conditions of service for staff at GCHQ, including a prohibition on membership of national trade unions. The unions sought judicial review. Their main argument was that there was a duty on the Minister to act fairly by honouring the unions' expectation of prior consultation before changing terms and conditions of service. The Minister argued that the use of a prerogative power was unreviewable.

At first instance, Glidewell J held that the exercise of the power was reviewable, and agreed that the minister had breached the duty of fairness, so the instruction was invalid and of no effect. On appeal, the minister tendered an affidavit made by Sir Robert Armstrong, the Cabinet Secretary, asserting that previous industrial action by unions had disrupted the work of GCHQ and damaged national security, so it had

[1] [1985] AC 374, [1984] 3 All ER 935, HL.

been necessary to act without prior consultation to prevent further damage to national security. The Court of Appeal accepted that national security considerations justified departing from the legitimate expectation of consultation.

The House of Lords (Lords Fraser, Scarman, Diplock, Roskill and Brightman) held that the exercise of prerogative powers was not absolutely immune to the courts' supervisory jurisdiction. Their Lordships noted that the challenge was to the exercise of a power delegated to the Minister by the Order. Lords Fraser and Brightman saw no reason why a power delegated under Order in Council should not be judicially reviewable in the same way as a power delegated by statute in order to ensure that the bounds of the power were not exceeded, but they left open an issue as to whether a direct exercise of the prerogative, such as the making of an Order in Council, would be reviewable.[2] Lords Scarman, Diplock and Roskill held that exercises of all powers were in principle reviewable as long as the subject-matter was justiciable, regardless of the source of the power. All the Law Lords further accepted that procedural fairness was a legal principle to be applied generally to administrative decisions, and that a past practice of consulting could give rise to a legally enforceable legitimate expectation of consultation. The unions lost, however, when the House held that, once credible evidence was led that the government had considered there was a threat to national security, the executive's assessment of national security and its requirements was not justiciable. Lord Roskill suggested that the nature of a power might also make it non-justiciable. He gave as examples treaty-making, defence, mercy, honours, dissolution of Parliament, but subsequently the prerogative of mercy has been regarded as justiciable.[3] Louis Blom-Cooper QC, leading counsel for the unions, found himself in the not unfamiliar position of achieving victory on important points of law without ultimately benefiting his clients.[4]

II. The Question

Why was it in 1984 that the House of Lords finally accepted that the manner of exercising prerogative powers was in principle subject to judicial review? Partly, of course, it was because that was when the question was litigated. But doctrinal change does not happen suddenly. I suggest that two factors had produced conditions in which members of the legal profession, including judges, were receptive to an invitation to open a new field to judicial scrutiny. A consensus predominantly deferential to political authority

[2] The question left open by Lords Fraser and Brightman was eventually settled 24 years later in the Chagos Islanders litigation, *R (Bancoult) v Secretary of State for Foreign and Commonwealth Affairs (No. 2)* [2008] UKHL 61, [2009] AC 453, HL, holding that a direct exercise of the prerogative in making Orders in Council to remove Chagos Islanders from their islands was reviewable.

[3] [1984] AC at 718 *per* Lord Roskill; *R v Secretary of State for the Home Department, ex parte Bentley* [1994] QB 349, DC.

[4] D Feldman, 'The Life and Work of Sir Louis Blom-Cooper' in G Drewry and C Blake (eds), *Law and the Spirit of Inquiry: Essays in Honour of Sir Louis Blom-Cooper* (London, Kluwer, 1999). For discussion of the GCHQ case by one of Blom-Cooper's juniors, see R Drabble (one of the junior counsel for the unions), '*Council of Civil Service Unions v Minister for the Civil Service* [1984]: Reviewing the Prerogative' in S Juss and M Sunkin (eds), *Landmark Cases in Public Law* (Oxford, Hart Publishing, 2017).

was cracking in response to a changing social and moral climate. Alongside that, a line of thought which elevated the search for conceptual consistency and practical effectiveness in law and procedure became more popular and influential among academics, practitioners and judges. Together, these trends made it easier for some to question old ways, even when cases were brought by trade unions trying to bring down an elected government.

Sir John Baker has shown that one needs to understand a body of professional practice and wider expectations of the law to make sense of the way the common law works. Changing professional and lay values and the conditions of life help to make possible the development of formal law in new directions.[5] This is part of a 'common learning' which forms a type of what Milsom called 'unofficial law'.[6] Baker gives as an example the 'more or less universal belief that capital punishment should not be automatic for all felonies …', which 'surely originated outside the courtroom and outside the chambers of the special pleader', finding expression in several legal systems not because they borrowed doctrine from each other 'but because lawyers are not isolated from other people'.[7] Such ideas influence legal practice and formal legal development because '[l]awyers have to keep the law in touch with the realities of life, or at least have to consider how the changing realities of life may be accommodated with the law which they profess'.[8]

Judicial review of the manner of exercising prerogative powers shows how, in a relatively modern context, 'official' law as expounded in judicial decisions responded to a developing consensus in the profession and society, or perhaps more accurately fragmentation of an earlier consensus, expressed in various ways in different places, so that the exercise of the prerogative should lose the aura of inviolability which it had when it was exercised directly by the sovereign.

III. Changing Attitudes to Political Authority

Social attitudes to authority were changing by the 1960s and 1970s. The Labour victory in the 1945 General Election had shown that many people were determined that society, politics and economics should work in the interests of the majority rather than those in entrenched positions of superiority. To that end, the electorate was ready for greater state intervention in people's lives, but did not necessarily trust people in positions of authority. If anything, the war had alerted many people to the capacity of officials to be small-minded, incompetent and unreflective. Radio comedy programmes reflected this. Popular series *The Navy Lark* was broadcast between 1959 and 1977 on the BBC's Light Programme, making fun of the accident-prone crew of HMS Troutbridge;

[5] JH Baker, *The Law's Two Bodies: Some Evidential Problems in English Legal History* (Oxford, Oxford University Press, 2001) especially 2–9 and Lecture 3.

[6] SFC Milsom, 'Law and Fact in Legal Development', reprinted in SFC Milsom, *Studies in the History of the Common Law* (London, Hambledon Press, 1985) 176–79 and 188–89, cited by Baker (n 5) 62.

[7] Baker (n 5) 62.

[8] ibid 63.

The Men from the Ministry, broadcast between 1962 and 1977, did a similar job on incompetent civil servants. In print, *Private Eye* was first published in 1961.

Governmental misjudgements and misbehaviour had revealed professional and ethical shortcomings in government. In 1954, serious deficiencies were uncovered after the Government refused to sell over 700 acres of land at Crichel Down, Dorset, compulsorily purchased for war purposes, back to the descendant of the original owner when the war ended, breaching an undertaking which had been given by the then Prime Minister, Winston Churchill. The resulting public inquiry, led by Sir Andrew Clark QC, 'was probably the first instance of close and very public scrutiny being directed at a Minister of the Crown in the execution of his duties'.[9] The Secretary of State for Agriculture and Fisheries, Sir Thomas Dugdale, resigned. The affair stuck in the collective memory, and was one of the influences leading to the establishment of the Parliamentary Commissioner for Administration in 1967.

Then there were sex and security scandals. Judicial inquiries into how homosexual civil servant John Vassall had succeeded in spying for the Soviet Union for 18 years, and what had occurred between minister John Profumo, model Christine Keeler, her friends Mandy Rice-Davies and osteopath Stephen Ward, and Yevgeny Ivanov, a Soviet spy under cover as a naval attaché, whitewashed the government, but prurient interest in the details reinforced a sense that all was not squeaky-clean in government.[10]

It is hard to know how widely disillusionment spread and how far it undermined traditional deference to authority. There were some very conservative young people,[11] while some older people were very critical of the exercise of authority. Generations are no more monolithic than societies. Nevertheless, new outlets emerged for criticism of the government, sometimes using satire to point out absurdities in previously barely questioned institutions. The BBC first broadcast *That Was The Week That Was* on television in November 1962. Its social and political satire divided its audience. Some, like Dennis Potter, welcomed 'a topical show written by people "with chips rather than pips on their shoulders"'; others found it either distasteful in its 'knocking' of institutions and allies or too cosy. 'Still,' comments David Kynaston, 'undeniably something was stirring ...'[12]

When Robin Day on ITN, in February 1958, conducted the first live interview on air with a Prime Minister, he asked Harold Macmillan about the position of the much-criticised Foreign Secretary, Selwyn Lloyd. Macmillan answered, but privately thought the questions impertinent. Many people shared his view,[13] but it was becoming the way

[9] R Gibbard, 'Whose Land Was it Anyway? The Crichel Down Rules and the Sale of Public Land', *Working Papers in Land Management and Development No. 2002-01. Reading: University of Reading: Department of Land Management and Development* (2002) 3, accessible at centaur.reading.ac.uk/24237/1/0102.pdf. See further JAG Griffith, 'The Crichel Down Affair' (1955) 18 *MLR* 557–70.

[10] *Report of the Tribunal Set Up to Inquire into the Vassall Case and related matters* (Lord Radcliffe (Chair), Mr Justice Barry and Milner Holland QC) (London, HMSO, 1963); *Lord Denning's Report* (on the Profumo affair), Cmnd 2152 (London, HMSO, 1963).

[11] I myself was (surprisingly, in retrospect) generally conservative and deferential as a youth, but felt myself to be outside the mainstream of my contemporaries.

[12] D Kynaston, *A Northern Wind: Britain 1962–65* (London, Bloomsbury, 2023) 24–25, quoting Dennis Potter writing in the *Daily Herald*. See further B Levin, *The Pendulum Years: Britain in the Sixties* (London, Jonathan Cape, 1970).

[13] D Kynaston, *Modernity Britain: Opening the Box, 1957–58* (London, Bloomsbury, 2013) 119–20.

of the world, reflecting a wider, though not universal, shift away from deference. We can speculate that some lawyers and even judges felt the mood. It is probably not a coincidence that, in the 1960s and 1970s, lawyers found it hard to behave as if governmental institutions should be subjected to less robustly critical scrutiny than other people and bodies.

IV. Growing Interest in Conceptual Coherence in Law

In the second half of the twentieth century, rationalism, linked to principled conceptualism, enjoyed a resurgence in public law. As legal education expanded in universities, academic authors sought organising principles to make legal thinking systematically coherent, for purposes of both pedagogy and advocacy. Academics contributed greatly to discussion in the pages of *Public Law*, launched in 1956 under the editorship of JAG Griffith of the London School of Economics. The Clarendon Law Series, published from the 1950s by Oxford University Press, had a role in this. Its main aim was to provide an introduction to the main subjects of the Law curriculum for students and, as Professor FH Lawson wrote in the Preface to his *Introduction to the Law of Property*,[14] 'non-lawyers who wish to obtain a rapid and summary view of what is usually regarded as a highly technical and obscure part of English law. Hence it is an explanatory, not a learned book.' That last sentence undersold the Series. Stripping back the detail of a subject to present a set of comprehensible and reasonably coherent basic rules and principles is a creative process. Fundamental elements sometimes have to be sought by inductive reasoning from the mass of details with which scholars and practitioners are often preoccupied and which sometimes obscure, rather than clarify, principles and values which underpin them and the shape of the structure. As Professor HLA Hart observed in the Preface to *The Concept of Law*,[15] his book on jurisprudence in the Series, published in 1961, he wanted to 'discourage the belief that a book on legal theory is primarily a book from which one learns what other books contain'. Choosing what to regard as fundamental involves judgements which may be both liberating and controversial: Hart's short book stimulated a major realignment in Anglo-American legal theory, for better or worse.

A search for structure struck a chord with some counsel and judges. Lord Diplock, for example, was fascinated by classifying legal concepts in the search for coherent structures in law. It shaped the resurgence in interest in constitutional and administrative law among academics and practitioners which had begun in the 1930s. Lord Hewart, a notoriously illiberal Lord Chief Justice, had complained about what he regarded as abuses of power by Labour governments and local authorities in his book *The New Despotism*,[16] and in response the Government had established the Donoughmore Committee on Ministers' Powers to review the use of executive power and legal controls

[14] FH Lawson, *Introduction to the Law of Property* (Oxford, Clarendon Press, 1958) vii.
[15] HLA Hart, *The Concept of Law* (Oxford, Clarendon Press, 1961) viii.
[16] G Hewart, *The New Despotism* (London, Ernest Benn, 1929).

on it in the UK.[17] It stimulated left-leaning academics to reassess the idea of the rule of law. Under the influence of lawyer Sir Ivor Jennings and political scientist Professor Harold Laski, a generation of academics began to give serious attention to the law as it affected government and public administration.

Jennings was more willing than Hewart to embrace collectivism and the changing decision-making and administrative processes which were needed to make it work. Jennings wrote that administrative law 'determines the organisation, powers and duties of administrative authorities'.[18] But the powers could give rise to great hardship for individuals as well as general benefits, and the administration could not entirely be trusted to police itself. To keep it running well and limit harm, it was necessary to have regard not only to the structure and powers of the administration but also to ways of keeping it within its legal bounds. John Griffith and Harry Street gave proper respect to the importance of non-court adjudication, inquiries and in due course parliamentary and local government commissioners of administration, the 'ombudsmen' whose functions were then adapted to and adopted by private or privatised enterprises. Courts and tribunals were of secondary importance, a long-stop for those (hopefully few) cases in which the administration had unfortunately been unable to regulate itself effectively and had failed to implement its legal obligations. In 1951, Griffith and Street's *Principles of Administrative Law* recognised this role: while the book's structure examined the legislative, administrative and judicial powers of the administration (chapters 2 and 4) and public corporations (chapter 7), it also considered control of the powers of the administration and suits against the administration (chapters 3, 5 and 6). Their book, they wrote, was primarily concerned with three questions. 'First, what sort of powers does the Administration exercise? Secondly, what are the limits of those powers? Thirdly, what are the ways in which the Administration is kept within those limits?'[19]

Some other public lawyers, perhaps less collectivist in outlook, viewed remedies for individuals against the administration as the core of administrative law. In the first half of the twentieth century, judges had tended to defer to governments' expanding of the role of the state, understandably in view of the prevalence of existential threats to the existence of the state; what we now call judicial review had retreated behind formal, increasingly inflexible restrictions on the availability of remedies. There was, however, a rich seam of older cases encapsulating a more flexible approach, and even in the half-century to 1950 a number of important judgments had been made concerning procedural protections for individual rights in the face of administrative interference. Professor Stanley de Smith's magisterial work, *Judicial Review of Administrative Action*,[20] concentrated on deriving coherent principles from an exhaustive analysis of centuries of caselaw on the key 'prerogative orders' – certiorari, prohibition, and mandamus – and the grounds on which they might be issued. It immediately became a bible for practitioners, being reprinted in 1960 and 1961, before going into two new editions before de Smith's untimely death.

[17] Committee on Ministers' Powers, *Report*, Cmd 4060 (London: HMSO, 1932).
[18] I Jennings, *The Law and the Constitution*, 5th edn (London, University of London Press, 1964) 217.
[19] JAG Griffith and H Street, *Principles of Administrative Law*, 5th edn (London, Pitman, 1973) 4.
[20] S de Smith, *Judicial Review of Administrative Action* (London, Sweet & Maxwell, 1959).

Professor HWR Wade was equally influential in the development of the law. Like de Smith, he was a powerful exponent of attempting to draw out broad principles from the mass of case-law and tribunal decisions across different areas of administration governed by many different statutes and statutory instruments. In his concise introductory text in the Clarendon Law Series, *Administrative Law*, first published in 1961, he defended his view that principles of administrative law

> can only be found by studying the ways in which the courts interpret many different statutes, and looking for the logical connexions between different types of cases .... Many general principles thus emerge. Although some writers criticize analytical study as 'conceptualism', this seems to be meaningless. All law is 'conceptual' in that it demands synthesis of concepts and inductive logic. Administrative law, in particular, is in special need of clear analysis in some of its most important parts, as later chapters will make plain. Its fundamental ideas are often by-products of the process of statutory interpretation, and it is only by comparison and analysis of numerous cases, often arising under very different statutes, that a coherent picture of the law can be drawn.[21]

Wade started from the idea that at its heart administrative law was concerned with

> the nature of the powers of public authorities and, especially, with the manner of their exercise ... Most of all, we are concerned with general principles which apply to public authorities of every kind, and which equally come into play whether a minister is confirming a slum clearance scheme or a chief constable is dismissed from the police force .... For the citizen it is vital that all power should be used in a way conformable to his ideas of liberty, fair dealing, and good administration. This is a matter of great consequence and some difficulty, for social needs and traditional liberties are frequently hard to reconcile. The courts have, on the whole, evolved a body of sound and valuable rules for effecting this reconciliation. But they have sometimes failed to recognize their own achievements. There is a special need for presenting the subject in simplified form, so that its principles may stand out clearly.[22]

Wade's approach, backed by the authority of an Oxford Chair, spread by personal acquaintance and correspondence with senior judges. Elected an Honorary Bencher of Lincoln's Inn in 1964, Wade brought his ideas to bear on those he met at the Inn and developed an extensive correspondence with senior judges and practitioners in England and abroad,[23] increasingly stressing the need to tackle legal chaos and advocating a principled approach to executive privilege and administrative law generally.

One area of public law which did not fit well into a principled structure was the royal prerogative. The reaction of some leading writers on administrative law was to minimise its scope and importance. Griffith and Street did not mention prerogative powers in relation to administration except to note in passing that the powers could not be used when the space had been occupied by statute; in relation to legislative powers, they noted that parliamentary control was of the same kind as applied to administrative acts and decisions.[24] Wade wrote: 'There is little left of the prerogative in our domestic

[21] HWR Wade, *Administrative Law*, 3rd edn (Oxford, Clarendon Press, 1971) 10.

[22] ibid 2–3.

[23] J Beatson, 'Henry William Rawson Wade 1918–2004' (2007) 150 *Proceedings of the British Academy* 287–310, 295.

[24] Griffith and Street (n 19) 78–79, 99–100.

administrative law …. The one drastic internal power of an administrative kind is the power to intern enemy aliens in time of war.'[25] He suggested that the power of the Crown to appoint, dismiss, and set terms and conditions of service of its servants without being subject to recourse in ordinary courts and tribunals (the power in issue in the GCHQ case) was probably not a prerogative power, but an aspect of the general law of master and servant but without judicial remedies.[26] This avoided the need to decide whether the manner of exercise of prerogative powers was reviewable, the issue which later became central to the arguments in the GCHQ case. Similarly, he regarded the Crown's power to prevent production of evidence in civil or criminal proceedings, then known as 'Crown privilege', not as part of the prerogative but probably a rule of evidence based on the public interest.[27]

Despite not classifying it as a prerogative power, Wade's treatment of the evidential privilege exemplified the development of 'unofficial law' in respect of special governmental immunities. Before World War II, there had been a long-standing 'special privilege of being able to prevent evidence from being given in court if its disclosure would be contrary to the public interest', but it had been confined to the content of particular documents, and in exceptional cases it might be possible for a judge to review the material in question and decide whether its non-disclosure would be contrary to the public interest.[28] But this changed in a wartime judgment, *Duncan v Cammell Laird & Co Ltd*.[29] Relatives of civilian workers among 99 people killed when the submarine HMS Thetis sank on its first dive sued the builders and designers of the submarine, alleging negligent design and construction. They sought discovery of the designs for the vessel. The Government intervened to assert Crown privilege. The House of Lords held that the courts could not look behind a suitably worded certificate claiming privilege against disclosure. Lord Simon LC, delivering the leading speech, decided that a minister could – indeed, must – claim Crown privilege when either: (a) a particular document could not be released without damage to the public interest because, for instance, it would threaten national security; or (b) the document fell into a class of documents which could not be released without harming the operation of public services, including the working of central government.[30]

Extending class claims to privilege in this way was not universally welcomed, although the outcome was regarded as sensible in wartime. It was later held, in peacetime, that the wide rule did not apply in Scotland, where judges might reject a claim.[31] The decision in *Duncan* was also criticised by some influential people,[32] including Wade. He never minimised the defects flowing from the Crown's ability to stop courts from

[25] Wade (n 21) 16.

[26] HWR Wade, *Administrative Law*, 1st edn (Oxford, Clarendon Press, 1961) 19.

[27] ibid 13.

[28] Wade (n 21) 306-8. The quotation is from 306.

[29] *Duncan v Cammell Laird & C, Ltd* [1942] AC 624. On the background, M Spencer, 'Bureaucracy, National Security and Access to Justice: New Light of *Duncan v Cammell Laird*' (2004) 55 *NILQ* 277–301.

[30] [1942] AC 624, 636.

[31] *Glasgow Corporation v Central Land Board* 1956 SC (HL) 1.

[32] Jocelyn (Jack) Simon, later a government minister and then judge, rising to the House of Lords as Lord Simon of Glaisdale, published a critical article, 'Evidence Excluded by Consideration of State Interest' (1955) 13 *Cambridge Law Journal* 62–79.

admitting evidence which might be of great probative value. In 1961, he wrote, 'Of all the questions affecting the Crown's part in litigation, none is more difficult than how far this privilege ought to be allowed to go .... The real problem is whether the present law is right, and whether it gives ministers too much power in a matter which is very much the concern of courts of law.'[33] He noted that a different rule applied in Scotland. 'The contrast is important, for many people would like to see the courts given the last word in England also .... For a plaintiff with a perfectly good legal case may yet lose it if he cannot produce in court some vital document for which the Crown claims privilege.'[34] Wade regarded *Duncan v Cammell Laird* as 'a good example of the most genuine type, where it seems plain that there must be effective means of preventing the ventilation of state secrets, even though it may fall hardly upon a particular litigant.'[35]

Wade gave examples of cases in which the power had become a serious obstruction to justice, or an assertion of privilege had been rejected so as not to rule out in advance a witness's possible oral evidence,[36] and noted a governmental undertaking that the privilege would not be claimed in respect of reports of witnesses to road accidents or accidents on government premises or involving government employees, or medical reports concerning civilian employees or where the Crown or the doctor is sued for negligence, or for documents needed for defence against a criminal charge, statements to the police, and reports on matters of fact relating to claims in contract.[37] But he criticised remaining class claims, including communications between ministers and civil servants based on the supposed need to protect the conditions for candour in communications with and within the public service, which was thought to be unnecessarily wide in excluding the chance to balance that public interest against that in doing justice in each individual case. He argued that a judicial process for doing so was needed, as had been developed in the USA.[38]

After Wade's first edition, though not necessarily because of it, some judges were emboldened to limit the effect of class claims. Administrative concessions had made non-reviewability of class privilege claims more difficult to justify coherently. In two cases, the Court of Appeal, led by Lord Denning MR (never keen to allow the House of Lords to block what he regarded as the right result), held that it was not bound by the judgment of the Lords in *Duncan v Cammell Laird*. In *Merricks v Nott-Bower*,[39] Lord Denning MR, Harman and Salmon LJJ noted that the words regarding class claims in Duncan's case 'were not necessary for the decision' and so were, as Salmon LJ said, 'obiter'[40] and decided that a certificate of the Home Secretary did not sufficiently particularise the nature of the class of documents said to be privileged and so failed to make out a claim to class privilege. Salmon LJ considered that the executive tended to abuse class claims, doubted whether Lord Simon had been correct in *Duncan*, and

[33] Wade (n 26) 240.
[34] ibid 241.
[35] ibid 242.
[36] ibid 243–45, citing *Ellis v Home Office* [1953] 2 QB 135 and *Broome v Broome* [1955] P 190.
[37] Wade (n 26) 245, citing 197 HL Deb, 6 June 1956, col 741.
[38] ibid 246–48.
[39] [1965] 1 QB 57, CA; the quotation is from Lord Denning, 69; also Harman LJ, 71 and Salmon LJ, 75–76, regretting absence of reform.
[40] [1965] 1 QB, 69 *per* Lord Denning MR, 75 *per* Salmon LJ.

hoped in any case that the English system could be brought into line with the approach in Scotland.[41] *Wednesbury Corporation v Minister of Town and Country Planning*[42] was a decision to the same effect by the Court of Appeal in the same composition. In *Re Grosvenor Hotel (No 2)*,[43] the same judges insisted on deciding for themselves whether a class claim to privilege was justified on its merits (it was).

Other members of the Court of Appeal were more conservative in their approach both to precedent and to Crown privilege. Shortly before the publication of Wade's second edition, Lord Denning found himself dissenting in *Conway v Rimmer* in the Court of Appeal,[44] where the majority, Davies and Russell LJJ, held that the formulation of class privilege in *Duncan*'s case was not obiter and bound the Court of Appeal. The disagreement was mainly to do with approaches to stare decisis, not over the merits of the rule; consensus on the rule at the Bar (which saw clients' meritorious cases failing because of class claims even, sometimes, in cases to which the Crown was not a party) and on the bench was moving towards Wade's view. 'Official' law was out of line with developing 'unofficial law', causing doctrinal instability; the matter had been referred to the Law Reform Committee, established by the Lord Chancellor in 1952 to consider changes to law regarding matters referred to it by the Lord Chancellor, itself a sign of growing openness to systematic law reform.

By 1967, when the second edition of his *Administrative Law* was published, Wade observed that judicial attitudes to the privilege were becoming more critical and assertive. He described the privilege as 'a highly dangerous power, since it enables the executive to deprive a litigant of his legal rights'.[45] He strengthened his critique of *Duncan v Cammell Laird*, describing it as 'the source of much trouble because the House of Lords laid down the law in terms far wider than were required by the question before them', even though the outcome of the particular case was 'inevitable'.[46] He noted that the rule was thought to be 'so unsatisfactory in England that it has had to be mitigated administratively, has been three times denied by the Court of Appeal, and has been referred to the Law Reform Committee'.[47]

Wade commented, '[T]here is no reason why the law should aid and abet the suppression of "everything however commonplace that has passed between one civil servant and another behind the departmental screen"', accused the courts of producing a chaotic state of affairs by 'inability … to choose between the conflicting policies' of advancing justice and protecting secrecy,[48] and wrote that 'the position will never be satisfactory until the interests of justice and the interests of secrecy are weighted impartially in the balance, and unjustified claims of privilege are overridden'.[49]

[41] ibid 74–76 *per* Salmon LJ.

[42] [1965] 1 WLR 261, CA.

[43] [1965] Ch 1210, CA.

[44] [1967] 1 WLR 1031, CA.

[45] HWR Wade, *Administrative Law*, 2nd edn (Oxford, Clarendon Press, 1967) 283.

[46] ibid 284. In relation to administrative mitigation, he noted two further ministerial statements at 237 HL Deb col 1191 (1962) (referring to Wade's first edition) and 261 HL Deb col 423 (1964).

[47] ibid 283.

[48] Wade (n 45) 290, quoting from Lord Radcliffe in the Scottish case, *Glasgow Corporation v Central Land Board* 1956 SC (HL) 1, 19.

[49] Wade (n 45) 289.

We see here two aspects of friction within English judicial culture in the 1960s: first, emergence of a far less deferential attitude to governmental claims to immunity from judicial scrutiny among judges such as Salmon LJ and Lord Denning, both of whom were concerned to protect the liberty of individuals; secondly, a less rigid attitude to the demands of precedent than had been common, with Salmon LJ fated to sit later in the House of Lords in the GCHQ case. Of course, elements of the past continued to influence judges: Russell LJ was notably more concerned with legal certainty and accordingly less flexible than Denning in his approach to precedent, and was prepared to dissent vigorously on occasions; there were many other judges like him.

The class privilege rule in *Duncan v Cammell Laird* was finally overruled in the following year, when *Conway v Rimmer* reached the House of Lords.[50] The decision to depart from *Duncan* was an early exercise of the freedom of the House of Lords to depart from its previous decisions in accordance with the 1966 Practice Statement,[51] itself sign that senior judges were giving added weight to principled rationality when precedent led to what they regarded as absurdity. From then on, while it would be rare for a judge to reject a minister's assessment of the need to protect the contents of a particular document, when it came to classes of documents the courts had the responsibility to balance the public interest in good administration against the interests of justice on the facts of each case. This was the start of a series of cases in which the notion of 'public interest immunity' replaced that of Crown privilege: as Professor Wade had long proposed, 'the right way to regard it, probably, is not as a branch of the prerogative but as a rule of the law of evidence based on public policy and controlled by the courts'.[52] In due course, the House of Lords held it could therefore be invoked not only by the executive but by anyone acting in the public interest. It was henceforth the public interest, not the Crown, which had to be protected.[53] By the time he published the third edition of *Administrative Law* in 1971, he was able to conclude his discussion of this topic as follows: 'Primarily therefore the House of Lords has now destroyed the foundation of excessively wide 'class' claims. But by insisting upon the court's duty to weigh the two conflicting public interests it has put the whole subject on a far healthier basis. The essential dilemma remains. But a dangerous executive power has been brought back into legal custody.'[54]

Looking at the evolution of Crown privilege illustrates a number of things. First, academics who are able to forge close relations with practitioners and judges through Inns of Court can help to create an ethos which encourages scepticism about executive claims to special treatment and immunities. Secondly, the respect engendered in

[50] [1968] AC 910.

[51] *Practice Statement (Judicial Precedent)* [1966] 1 WLR 1234, HL.

[52] Wade (n 26) 16.

[53] See *D v National Society for the Prevention of Cruelty to Children* [1978] AC 171, HL. For analysis of *Conway v Rimmer* in the light of what they call 'administrative constitutionalism', arguing that courts since *Conway v Rimmer* have given too little weight to the views of public administrators as to their needs, see TT Arvind and Lindsay Stirton, 'Legitimacy and the Courts: the Forgotten Story of *Conway v Rimmer*' in TT Arvind, R Kirkham, D Mac Síthigh and L Stirton (eds), *Executive Decision-Making and the Courts: Revisiting the Origins of Modern Judicial Review* (Oxford, Hart Publishing, 2021) 85–113. See also M Spencer and J Spencer, 'Coping with *Conway v Rimmer* [1968] AC 910: How Civil Servants Control Access to Justice' (2010) 37 *Journal of Law and Society* 387–411.

[54] Wade (n 21) 312–13.

the process is not limited to single cases. Around the same time, Wade was an influential figure in relation to *Anisminic* as well, securing publication of the first-instance judgment of Browne J and galvanising public opinion through the press to guide parliamentarians in shaping the legislative response to *Anisminic*.[55] Throughout the rest of his career, when Wade spoke, the judiciary listened. Lord Denning MR, an admirer of Wade, acted as an advance guard for the judicial scrutiny of governmental prerogatives, and was supported by Salmon LJ, who later sat in the House of Lords in the GCHQ case, and some, but not all, other senior judges. In retrospect it can be seen as a harbinger of change that, in the fourth, much enlarged, edition of *Administrative Law*, Wade dealt more fully with the possibility of judicial review of the exercise of prerogative powers in the chapter on abuse of discretion. He noted that such powers were 'sometimes said to confer discretion which no court can question; and there has long been a dearth of authority to the contrary'. But, he continued, 'it may be that this is because the decided cases have involved discretions which are inherently unsuitable for judicial control, such as the disposition of the armed forces or the exclusion of aliens – though for the latter purpose the Crown's powers are now statutory'.[56] He went on to argue that the prerogative is as capable of being abused as any other power, 'and it may be rash to assume that the law would not find means of controlling it if necessary'.[57] Just before that edition went to press, he was able to add an appendix noting that Lord Denning MR had held that prerogative powers could be examined like any other power, and judges could control their exercise if used improperly or mistakenly.[58]

Other symptoms of declining deference included: applying standards of procedural fairness to all decision-makers in *Ridge v Baldwin* in 1963; extending the reach of the prerogative order of mandamus to a minister who had decided not to exercise a statutory discretion to refer a scheme of payment to milk producers to a special committee before implementing the scheme in *Padfield* in 1968; expanding development of the kinds of errors which could take a tribunal outside its jurisdiction in order to circumvent a statutory provision precluding the courts from exercising their supervisory jurisdiction over it in *Anisminic* in the same year, thereby increasing the usefulness of declarations as a public-law remedy to complement the prerogative orders;[59] and in 1976, following a reference to the Law Commission,[60] reforming the procedure of judicial review, making

[55] D Feldman, '*Anisminic Ltd v Foreign Compensation Commission* [1968]: In Perspective' in S Juss and M Sunkin (eds), *Landmark Cases in Public Law* (Oxford, Hart Publishing, 2017) 87–88.

[56] HWR Wade, *Administrative Law*, 4th edn (Oxford, Clarendon Press, 1977) 335.

[57] ibid 336.

[58] ibid 336 and 833–34, citing *Laker Airways Ltd v Department of Trade* [1977] QB 643, CA, at 705–706 *per* Lord Denning MR, Roskill LJ considered that the courts could not control the treaty-making power of the Crown (at 718), which according to the Department had been exercised in that case. Lawton LJ held that the prerogative in the international sphere could not be used to take away the rights of citizens, as the Crown had effectively done by revoking Laker Airways' designation under the Bermuda Agreement for regulating flights between the UK and the USA. The power of revocation was covered by the Civil Aviation Act 1971, and that displaced the prerogative: see 726–28. The case had been argued for 10 days in the Court of Appeal, after which judgment was delivered within 24 days.

[59] Wade noted in 1973, '… it is unfortunate that certiorari and the declaration each have advantages which the other lacks, and that they cannot be asked for in the alternative in one proceedings. The litigant is forced to make a choice at his peril. This is so obviously unreasonable that there is an urgent need for reform.' Wade (n 21) 142.

[60] Law Commission, Report No. 73, *Report on Remedies in Administrative Law* Cmnd 6407 (London, HMSO, 1976).

arguments about its reach focus on the types of matter to which public law applied rather than the juridical classification of sources of the powers being exercised.[61]

This was an essential stage in preparing the judiciary for review of the prerogatives themselves. There were still special situations in which the courts continued to refuse to review exercises of what might have been exercises of royal prerogatives. For example, in 1977 the House of Lords, reversing a Court of Appeal led by Lord Denning MR, held that courts must not review the Attorney General's decision, exercising the Crown's function as *parens patriae* regarding the enforcement of criminal law in the public interest, to refuse his *fiat* for a relator action by John Gouriet for an injunction to restrain an alleged breach by Post Office trade unionists of their legal duty to deliver post during their strike action.[62] The Law Lords regarded this as an exceptional power to be used in the public interest. Generally, however, judges tended to be uncomfortable when faced with claims to special immunities from judicial scrutiny.

V. Reason and the Authority of Tradition

A further indication that the profession preferred rational procedures to historical anomalies was the reform of procedures for judicial scrutiny of the executive was that many people, including some judges, were becoming less impressed by appeals to traditional dignity and pomp when it interfered with the effectiveness of democratic and effective aspects of the constitution. People were increasingly asking whether the rules, whatever they were, made sense and worked satisfactorily. David Kynaston has put his finger on a shift of attitudes when describing the television commentaries on BBC and ITV respectively for the first televised state opening of Parliament on 28 November 1957. On BBC, Richard Dimbleby was all solemn intonation as he painted 'a state occasion at its most magnificent'. On ITV, the younger Robin Day was 'crisper and more informal', but also more focussed on the practical than the symbolic: 'The crown will go back to the Tower of London. All the scarlet and ermine robes will go back to wherever they came from. And Parliament will go back to work.'[63]

In the context of prerogative powers, attempting to balance the appeal to history with the attraction of rationality was first seen in the Divisional Court in *R v Criminal Injuries Compensation Board, ex parte Lain*.[64] The case illustrates how the legal profession was working to bring 'official law' into line with the expectations changing 'unofficial law'. Mrs Lain challenged a decision of the Criminal Injuries Compensation Board, a non-statutory body established by the Home Secretary to adjudicate claims by victims of crime for compensation from a fund allocated by Parliament in the Appropriation Act 1966, to reduce her award to zero. For the Board, Nigel Bridge argued, applying a much followed dictum of Atkin LJ in *R v Electricity Commissioners, ex parte London*

[61] *Ridge v Baldwin* [1964] AC 40; *Padfield v Minister of Agriculture, Fisheries and Food* [1968] AC 667; *Anisminic Ltd v Foreign Compensation Commission* [1969] 2 AC 147, HL.

[62] *Gouriet v HM Attorney General and others* [1978] AC 435, HL.

[63] D Kynaston, *Modernity Britain: Opening the Box, 1957–59* (London, Bloomsbury, 2013) 199.

[64] [1967] 2 QB 864, DC.

Electricity Joint Committee Co (1920) Ltd,[65] that certiorari did not run to the Board because it lacked legal authority to determine the rights of subjects. Certiorari, he argued, only ran to statutory judicial bodies. Furthermore, certiorari would issue only if a body acted without lawful authority or made an error of law which appeared on the face of the record of its decision. Neither condition was met.

Geoffrey Howe QC, for Mrs Lain, argued that Atkin LJ's statement had not been intended to be, and should not be taken as, an exhaustive description of circumstances in which the High Court would issue certiorari. He pointed to the history of the writ, which showed that for hundreds of years it had run to bodies which had no statutory authority but nevertheless made decisions affecting people's rights. The Board 'determines matters in regard to which this court ought to intervene, otherwise it would be a remarkable oddity with a frightening scope';[66] 'it claims absolute power to act perversely and unjustly'.[67]

The Divisional Court's judgment, described later by Lord Roskill as 'a landmark in the development of this branch of the law',[68] unanimously held that the Board was subject to certiorari but had not acted unlawfully. Lord Parker C.J. started with the history of certiorari but it was not static but a history of gradual extension of its scope:

> … the exact limits of the ancient remedy by way of certiorari have never been and ought not to be specifically defined. They have varied from time to time being extended to meet changing conditions …. We have … reached the position when the ambit of certiorari can be said to cover every case in which a body of persons of a public as opposed to a purely private or domestic character has to determine matters affecting subjects provided always that it has a duty to act judicially.[69]

Ashworth J concentrated on the Board having been given limited authority, not the source of it:

> [I]t is a truism to say that the law has to adjust itself to meet changing circumstances and although a tribunal, constituted as the board, has not been the subject of consideration or decision by this court in relation to an order of certiorari, I do not think that this court should shrink from entertaining this application merely because the board had no statutory origin …. it acts with lawful authority, albeit such authority is derived from the executive and not from Act of Parliament.[70]

Lord Parker CJ and Ashworth J expressly said, and Diplock LJ implied, that the dictum of Atkin LJ was, read in context, not an exhaustive definition of when certiorari was to be available.[71] Diplock LJ grounded his conclusion firmly in certiorari's history: certiorari had run to courts established under the royal prerogative, royal charter, franchise and custom as well as Acts of Parliament, and as new tribunals

[65] [1924] 1 KB 171, CA, 205.
[66] [1967] 2 QB 864, 869.
[67] ibid 868.
[68] In the GCHQ case, [1984] AC 374, 418.
[69] [1967] 2 QB 864, 882.
[70] ibid 891.
[71] ibid 880–81 *per* Lord Parker CJ, 892 *per* Ashworth J.

had been established they became subject to supervisory jurisdiction of the High Court through certiorari. While the writ had not recently been directed to 'persons whose ultimate authority to decide matters is derived from any other source … I see no reason for holding that the ancient jurisdiction of the Court of Queen's Bench has been narrowed merely because there has been no occasion to exercise it. If new tribunals are established by acts of government, the supervisory jurisdiction of the High Court extends to them if they possess the essential characteristics upon which the subjection of inferior tribunals to the supervisory control of the High Court is based'.[72] In other words, the supervisory jurisdiction, and associated remedies, were generally applicable, regardless of the source of authority.

In this case, history tended to support a wide reach for certiorari. But the authority of history was on the wane when it could not support a proposition of 'official law' which seemed, in principle, to reflect a growing consensus in 'unofficial law' as to the right and rational rule as the judges now conceptualised it. When the House of Lords decided the GCHQ case, Lord Diplock (as he had become) regarded modern principles as more important than history.

> I intend no discourtesy to counsel when I say that, intellectual interest apart, in answering the question of law raised in this appeal, I have derived little practical assistance from learned and esoteric analyses of the precise legal nature, boundaries and historical origin of 'the prerogative,' or of what powers exercisable by executive officers acting on behalf of central government that are not shared by private citizens qualify for inclusion under this particular label.[73]

Lord Roskill, who had taken a first class honours degree in history at Exeter College, Oxford, quoted a letter from Maitland to Dicey in 1896:

> 'The only direct utility of legal history (I say nothing of its thrilling interest) lies in the lesson that each generation has an enormous power of shaping its own law'…[74] Maitland was in so stating a greater prophet than even he could have foreseen for it is our legal history which has enabled the present generation to shape the development of our administrative law by building upon but unhampered by our legal history.[75]

VI. Conclusion

In the decades leading to the GCHQ case, the legal profession, academic and practising, gradually felt its way from being highly deferential to executive decision-makers, especially in the field covered by prerogative powers, to a more questioning approach. Judges decided to conceptualise judicial review as being generally available against people and institutions affecting the public unless there was a very good reason to

[72] ibid 883, 884 *per* Diplock LJ.
[73] [1984] AC 374, 409.
[74] RA Cosgrove, *Rule of Law: Albert Venn Dicey, Victorian Jurist* (University of North Carolina Press, 1980) 177.
[75] [1984] AC 374, 417.

restrict it, not on the basis (as before) of the source of power but by reference to justiciability of the matter, rather than body, under review. This was made possible by a more conceptual approach to administrative law which could benefit clients as well as avoid anomalies. Judges, like many other people, were probably affected by a more robustly sceptical attitude to the establishment's claims to respect and privileges in the light of World War II and assorted scandals, spread by new kinds of journalism and comedy. The search for principle was influenced by eminent academics, adopted by enthusiastic counsel, and taken up with greater or lesser enthusiasm by some judges, including notably Lord Denning, Lord Diplock and Lord Salmon. There was a 'spirit of the age', directly affecting 'unofficial law' and indirectly, and more gradually, 'official law' through a process of osmosis tempered by judicial caution. The prerogative was often reviewable, but claims about national security (backed by some evidence) were not. The common law of judicial review was on the move, but where it went after the GCHQ case is another story. Is it history? Is it common law? I hope in any case that David will find it interesting.

23

Quackery, Care and Themes in Nineteenth-Century Legal Change

COLM PETER McGRATH

> From this time there grew up three regular, and many irregular, orders of medical practitioner.[1]

I. Introduction

Medical negligence presents a ubiquitous fact patten for legal systems. The universal nature of health needs amongst a population, the provision of relevant services – whether gratuitously or not, whether grounded in a particular claim to efficacy or not – by a select few, and the inherent risk of bodily injury combine to create a forum in which legal, medical, and lay conceptions of care inevitably collide. The account that follows explores the counterintuitive role of a particular influence on the English response to such collisions during the key formative period of the nineteenth century, offering a reflection on the drivers behind legal change in this area. The following section sets out the parallel nineteenth century medical and legal frameworks respectively. The subsequent section then considers liability for quack practice in this period, identifying three distinct themes in the law's development. In brief, an earlier position of neutrality gives way to an emphasis on patient choice before more actively enforcing a quasi-regulatory stance in relation to the quality of care.

Whilst the cases below often involve quackish defendants, the purpose of investigating this context is to shed light on the tension these cases created – or perhaps the fact that these cases created tension at all – between such practitioners and their orthodox brethren: by whose yardstick was care to be measured? The developmental themes below offer important insight into the broader construction of the standard of care for *orthodox* medical practitioners. English law's settled elevation of orthodox practice as the relevant measure by the late nineteenth century may plausibly have emerged in part

[1] JW Willcock, *The Laws Relating to the Medical Profession with an Account of the Rise and Progress of its Various Orders* (London, J and WT Clark, 1830) 8.

as a reflexive consequence of rejecting plurality as much as a decision to privilege this per se. The quasi-regulatory stance adopted by the courts and enforced by lay juries translated a formally abstract legal standard of care into an informal standard that favoured orthodox practice. In doing so, the idea that the legal consequences of injurious medical practice lay ultimately in the judgment of the regular profession was inescapably reinforced and, with it, the deferential imperative that would come to characterise the late nineteenth and early twentieth century.[2] That broader narrative of deference is often viewed as a means by which the law respects medical expertise. The account that emerges below explores a parallel counter-narrative grounded in a different way of approaching patient safety.

II. Constructing Medical Standards of Care

A. Law and the Contested Medical Marketplace

Medical practice in this era comprised a bewildering range of forms of practice and practitioner.[3] The ground here is well trodden by social historians of medicine and medical practice – it being entirely possible to fall outwith the bounds of accepted practice either through the form of treatment on offer, or on account of the status or behaviour of the practitioner themselves – and viewed from the vantage of disciplines beyond law, the messy reality of medical services may be assumed to provide impetus towards a plurality of legal standards. For our purposes, it is important to understand how such medical plurality was permitted to thrive.

In broad terms, the distinction between 'regular' and 'irregular' medical practice clearly persisted throughout the century.[4] The former most often described the classical triad of categories of practice: physicians, surgeons and, often regarded as the lowest of the three, apothecaries.[5] There was, put simply, no unitary orthodox profession against which were ranged serried ranks of hangers-on.[6] The picture on both sides, and the legal regulatory and practical division between them, was far less clear cut. Indeed, nor does the distinction necessarily capture individuated and distinct practitioners, given throughout much of this period orthodox practitioners may well have indulged in

[2] As Stein's survey notes, where the defendant practitioner led evidence of acceptance by regular practice between 1860 and 1900, they did not lose, MA Stein, CP Guzelian and KM Guzelian, 'Expert Testimony in Nineteenth Century Malapraxis Actions' (2015) 55 *American Journal of Legal History* 194. Likewise, there are plausible reasons to suggest the same unbroken chain stretched well into the twentieth century, see CP McGrath, 'Assessing (Divergent) Legal Development' in S Turenne (ed), *Reasons and Context in Comparative Law: Essays in Honour of John Bell* (Cambridge, Cambridge University Press, 2023) 148.

[3] The classic, comprehensive account is given in R Porter, *Quacks* (Stroud, Tempus, 2003).

[4] As is reflected in the legal tussles of the following section, even the very language itself chosen to describe different forms of practice and practitioner are freighted with meaning, R Jütte, 'Alternative Medicine and Medico-Historical Semantics' in R Jütte, M Eklöf and MC Nelson, *Historical Aspects of Unconventional Medicine* (Sheffield, European Association for the History of Medicine and Health Publications, 2001) 11.

[5] R Stevens, *Medical Practice in Modern England* (New Haven (CT), Yale University Press, 1966) 11ff.

[6] S Jacyna, 'Medicine in Transformation, 1800–1849' in WF Bynum, A Hardy, S Jacyna, C Lawrence and EM Tansey (eds), *The Western Medical Tradition, 1800–2000* (Cambridge, Cambridge University Press, 2006) 11, 29–31.

economically lucrative forms of more irregular practice alongside their usual practices.[7] By the early nineteenth century, these regular groupings either had their roots in long-settled institutional and guild-like structures such as a respective Royal Colleges, or had achieved sufficient occupational coherence to have raised themselves from the risk of irregular designation per se.[8] But the mere fact that a given type of practice might be regarded as irregular did not necessarily mean that it lacked its own internal organisational structures and capacity for self-organisation.[9] Often 'regular' practice carried with it – or, better, was in part identified by – access to some degree of legal privilege, with efforts to exclude other forms of practice from that marketplace the hallmark of many of the regulatory interventions or professional desiderata in the era, even if these were often limited to the metropolis and narrow environ.[10] This exclusionary impetus ultimately culminated in the statutory intervention of the Medical Act 1858, but even then this proved insufficient to regulate irregular practice out of contention.[11]

Beyond the boundaries of regular practice lay many forms of cognate practice that laid claim to some form of medical knowledge, whether rooted in alternative learning or practices, sheer empiricism, or, in nevertheless not purporting to, operating as a vector for downright charlatanry.[12] Indeed viewed broadly, the spectrum of available healers could encompass those whose practice had its roots in religious belief as easily as in another direction it could be thought (perhaps charitably) to stretch to those claiming access to magical intervention.[13] The notional classification as irregular of at least some of these practices, reflected only a failure to similarly institutionalise in the manner that others had, or the fact that they had been rejected en masse from existing professional structures. Likewise, as formal medical education coalesced over the nineteenth century, the fact that irregular practice could plausibly be characterised as being the province of those who were, '… despising or ignorant of the medical library of the schoolmen', kept a focus on the underlying characterisation of and claim to medical knowledge central to the division.[14] Likewise practices such as the use of secret or patent remedies or

[7] Porter notes top practitioners as being 'up to their chin in quackish practices themselves', Porter (n 3) 312.

[8] As in the case of those who benefitted from the Apothecaries Act 1815. Status as an apothecary under the Act was often combined in practice with a qualification in surgery to offer a nascent form of general practice.

[9] P Nicholls, 'The Social Construction and Organisation of Medical Marginality: the Case of Homeopathy in Mid-Nineteenth-Century Britain' in R Jütte, M Eklöf and MC Nelson, *Historical Aspects of Unconventional Medicine* (Sheffield, European Association for the History of Medicine and Health Publications, 2001) 163.

[10] As a later legal commentator bluntly observed, 'there was no control over provincial practitioners', F Bullock, *The Law Relating to Medical Dental and Veterinary Practice* (London, Ballière, Tindall and Cox, 1929) 90–91.

[11] W Swain, 'The Development of Medical Liability in England and Wales' in E Hondius (ed), *The Development of Medical Liability* (Cambridge, Cambridge University Press, 2010) 27, 37.

[12] Porter (n 3) ch 2; nor was this any sort of specific nineteenth century phenomenon. On the earlier position, see R Porter, 'The Patient in England c 1660–1800' in A Wear (ed), *Medicine in Society* (Cambridge, Cambridge University Press, 1992) 93–94.

[13] Willcock, thought nothing of including sorcerers and witches amongst the class of empirics alongside alchymists (sic) and astrologers. See Willcock (n 1) 19–20.

[14] As Willcock noted of the profession of medicine in the era, 'all men may be able to form a fair estimate of their comparative capacity' ibid 75. Similarly in America, deVille notes the view of a Connecticut doctor who lamented that the general population seemed to place little value on medical education, rooting this in a lay perception that individuals could achieve 'eminence in other professions by his own exertions', KA DeVille, *Medical Malpractice in Nineteenth-Century America: Origins and Legacy* (New York, New York University Press, 1990) 75.

promises of cure.[15] As a central means of justifying the validity of that claimed insight, the broad shift from the generalism that characterised earlier orthodoxy to the specialist forms of regular practice that emerged over the late nineteenth century – often involving advances in medical apparatus and technology to accompany the nascent respective form of specialist practice[16] – also played to the strengths of many forms of irregular practice, characterised as they were by the narrow, focused nature of many interventions.[17] From the archetype of the bonesetter and toothpuller onwards, more irregular forms of practice were often characterised by their pseudo-specialist nature and an interest in one particular aspect of the patient's health.[18] In the context of the numerous patent devices, remedies and treatments on offer at the irregular end of the spectrum, the increasing connection between the authority of medical orthodoxy and the specialist's perspective stood to unhelpfully blur the regular/irregular boundary.[19] As has been observed, it was all too easy for irregular practitioners to imitate the doctor in their affecting of '… pompous assumption of knowledge and authority' as a means of winning over patients.[20] The mysteries of technique and equipment clearly stood to bolster this emulation. Nevertheless, the unmistakably market-inflected nature of these nascent professional boundaries could be seen in the long-settled fact that, despite earlier efforts to formally bar unlicensed practice,[21] the *gratuitous* provision of medical services was generally not viewed as transgressing any regulatory boundaries.[22]

From the 1858 Act onwards, the nineteenth century saw these persisting occupational divisions settle into harder legal-regulatory boundaries.[23] Increasingly, remunerated practice required compliance with fixed markers of medical orthodoxy and with the instantiation of the Medical Register following the 1858 Act, the line between regular and irregular practice was overlain by the division between registered and unregistered practitioners (inapt as the latter was in that it would also capture those who had, by whatever route, simply lost registered status). But, having retained the multiplicity of existing examining bodies rather than introduce anything more radical,[24] the 1858 Act required supplementary intervention a few short decades later in 1886,[25] intended to

[15] See, famously, A Simpson, 'Quackery and Contract Law: The Case of the Carbolic Smoke Ball' (1985) 14 *Journal of Legal Studies* 345–89; More recently, A Rosenberg, 'Exaggeration: Advertising, Law and Medical Quackery in Britain, c. 1840–1914' (2021) 42 *Journal of Legal History* 202.

[16] See generally, G Weisz, *Divide and Conquer: A Comparative History of Medical Specialization* (Oxford, Oxford University Press, 2005).

[17] Stevens (n 5) 26ff.

[18] A situation that created particular suspicion and reticence amongst established practitioners in relation to the new, emerging specialities such as ophthalmology, urology and ENT diseases, see Stevens (n 5) 27. Yet even then, the overlapping relationship between regular and irregular practice in given categories of practice might be viewed a means by which the former could legitimise and then co-opt a given practice to their own benefit. See R Cooter, 'Bones of Contention? Orthodox Medicine and the Mystery of the Bone-Setter's Craft' in in WF Bynum and R Porter (eds), *Medical Fringe and Medical Orthodoxy 1750–1850* (London, Croom Helm, 1987) 158.

[19] SJ Reiser, *Medicine and the Reign of Technology* (Cambridge, Cambridge University Press, 1978) 144ff.

[20] AM Carr-Saunders and PA Wilson, *The Professions* (Oxford, Clarendon Press, 1933) 104.

[21] The Physicians and Surgeons Act 1511 (3 Hen VIII c11).

[22] A good early example can be found in the Herbalists Act 1542 (34&35 Hen VIII c8): 'Persons, being no common surgeons, may minister medicines, notwithstanding the Statute.'

[23] Swain (n 11) 37.

[24] Described by Stevens as merely consolidated the complexities of what had come before, Stevens (n 5) 25.

[25] Medical Act 1886 (49 & 50 Vict c 48).

tighten the requirements for education and registration, in an era that otherwise saw continual growth in the number of practitioners. It may only have been with the advent of the National Insurance Act 1911, and the connection between *registered* practice and employment under those structures, that regulars achieved long sought market dominance.[26] Throughout the nineteenth century however, two facts remained evident; there was money to be made from irregular practice and the developing architecture of legal regulation was neither appropriately empowered nor enforced so as to stamp out irregular practice.[27] Considerable variation in standards continued despite the 1858 Act. The fact that before the 1886 Act medical qualifications and licences could often be relatively easily obtained lent at least some patina of learning to many of the empiricists with whom the registered practitioners had to compete,[28] and if one practised beyond the scope of the often geographical privileges that licensure from one of the Royal Colleges might grant, the reality was that such qualification was seldom undertaken.[29]

But the persistence of irregular practice was not merely a matter of failing to draw the legal boundaries of permitted medical practice so narrowly as to exclude them, it was likewise a matter of brute practicality. Shifting perspective from the practitioner to the patient it was clear that for many in search of medical treatment, irregular practice might have provided the only or best means of access to healthcare. Certainly, in the form of contract clubs, Friendly Societies and other forms of mutual aid there was a patchwork of provision for the working classes before the steady expansion of centralised healthcare in the twentieth century,[30] but much of this, particularly from the 1860s on, was riven with disputes over pay and conditions of service for the practitioners that took on these roles.[31] Where patients directly engaged services, the contractual nature of that doctor-patient relationship throughout the century naturally characterises it as an era in which considerably greater power generally rested with the consumers rather than the provider of such services.[32] This stood to advantage the irregular, who could, relying on their own inscrutable claims to expertise, freely compete alongside their orthodox peers. Whilst the emergence of functional criteria for distinguishing between practitioners, whether to separate quack from regular or specialist from generalist, was steadily underway,[33] the nineteenth century saw considerable weight

[26] Such a close connection between national structures and medical orthodoxy was not a given in the era. Similar moves in Germany, in the developing framework of medical practice flowing from Bismarck's earlier reforms saw some health insurers take an ambivalent stance towards whether patients were required to only seek treatment from the orthodox equivalent, see CP McGrath, *The Development of Medical Liability in Germany 1800–1945* (Frankfurt, Vittorio Klostermann, 2019) ch 2.

[27] Looking back from the roots of our modern legal and medical practices, Bullock laid the blame squarely on the fact that medical education remained 'defective' for so much of the nineteenth century. As a result it was, he notes, 'as profitable to be an empiric', Bullock, 'Law Relating to Medical Practice' 90.

[28] ibid 91.

[29] Stevens (n 5) 17.

[30] See generally DS Green, *Working-Class Patients and the Medical Establishment* (Gower, 1985); WF Bynum, 'The Rise of Science in Medicine' in Bynum et al (n 6) 111, 217ff.

[31] Green (n 30) 18–19, going on to detail the 'battle of the clubs' that ensued.

[32] Bynum (n 30) 210. Indeed, the fervour with which quackery was identified and problematised often coincided in this era with the degree to which it was perceived as a threat to income as much as it was a crusade to stamp out dangerous practice, see I Loudon, 'The Vile Race of Quacks with which this Country is Infested' in in Bynum and Porter (n 18) 106.

[33] S Jacyna, 'Medicine in Transformation, 1800–1849' in Bynum et al (n 6) 19.

continue to be placed on the person and social status of the practitioner as much as their expertise.[34]

Moving from the person of the patient to the location of care itself, whilst entwined with the form and nature of practice on offer, the nineteenth century remained an era in which the geography of care was often centred in the home, again with the attendant power that vested in patient choice. The rise of the hospitals proved central to the eventual diminution of irregular practice in a number of ways.[35] As a baseline, they provided pressure towards encouraging regular practice.[36] It was expected that those physicians staffing the London hospitals would be required to hold the licence of the Royal College accordingly,[37] with some measure of qualification required for posts at many of the voluntary hospitals.[38] Equally, they provided the locus around which modern English medical education would come to centre itself,[39] grounding the means by which underlying knowledge claims could be justified and validated.[40]

To sum up, as much as the fight against quackery (and the self-interested advantages it would yield for orthodox practitioners) was a defining feature of nineteenth century medical life, it can appear remarkable how broadly indulgent legal regulation was towards irregular practices. Not only was there at no stage a fixed definition of irregular practice[41] – it was as possible that irregular practice described a heresy within a form of regular practice as something clearly distinct from it[42] – it was only with the arrival of the 1858 Act that any clear and distinct legal step was taken towards deploying the gatekeeping power of professional regulation against such practice and even then this could hardly be regarded as a success in practice, liberal as it was in its efforts to narrow the field of potential practitioners. As Porter suggests, quackery was clearly neither supressed nor silenced, characterising the state as unwilling to ban it when it could tax it, orthodox institutions as unable to drive it out, and both patients

[34] Jacyna notes for instance, ibid, the imperative in Britain and the United states against appearing too 'theoretical' lest it be thought this might outshine the practical needs of the patient. The advantage this might hand irregular practitioners is obvious.

[35] G Rivett, *The Development of the London Hospital System 1823–1982* (London, King's Fund, 1986).

[36] Bynum (n 30) 135, 150ff, noting their clearly medicalised nature, and the inseparable entwining of hospitals with medical education. As such, for present purposes, hospitals were institutions that drew from and in turn supported the development of the orthodox profession and their forms of practice; Stevens (n 5) 15–16.

[37] Stevens (n 5) 17.

[38] Bynum (n 30) 151.

[39] Stevens (n 5) 16.

[40] B Abel-Smith, *The Hospitals 1800–1948* (London, Heinemann, 1964). A Hardy, *Health and Medicine in Britain since 1860* (Basingstoke, Palgrave, 2001) 15, noting the common importance for private practice of some sort of institutional connection.

[41] A Tomkins, *Medical Misadventure in an Age of Professionalisation* (Manchester, Manchester University Press, 2017) 3–4. Albeit as the author later notes, where particular acts overlapped heavily in practice with the work of irregular practitioners, such as abortion, this could more easily be targeted, see 138ff. See also I Loudon, 'Medical Practitioners 1750–1850 and medical reform in Britain' in A Wear (ed), *Medicine in Society* (Cambridge, Cambridge University Press, 1992) 223. For that matter, what constituted orthodox practice could just as well, and did, develop, see PS Brown, 'Social Context and Medical Theory in the Demarcation of Nineteenth-Century Boundaries' in Bynum and Porter (n 18) 228–29.

[42] Brown (n 41) 216.

and practitioners themselves willing to use and exploit irregular practice for their own respective ends.[43]

Certainly it is true that irregular practice was not formally regulated out of existence, but as explored below, other legal means of censure were available and, it is suggested, actively deployed to that end. It is to the work of nineteenth century courts in constructing the standard of care for irregular practice that we now turn.

B. Malpractice and the Practitioner-Patient Relationship

Patients in this era could therefore find themselves treated through a broad range of practices depending on preferences, availability, and income. But when would a remedy be available for unintentional injurious practice? At least in the English common law tradition, the bulk of this task traditionally falls to the civil law, whether through breach of contractual or tortious duties to take reasonable care.[44] The general absence of a criminal offence penalising merely negligent injury falling short of death largely constrained the role of the criminal law. But that is not to say that analogous criminal practice can be overlooked or, indeed, that medical practitioners were not right to be wary of the potential use of the criminal law where a patient died under their care.[45] The generalised nature of the available actions, whether civil or criminal, would have ensured that judicial efforts to frame the required standard remained open to the vagaries of broader doctrinal influences. Likewise in both cases, any decision would ultimately rest with the jury and if there was plausible evidence, as there often would be where a patient had been injured at the hands of a treatment now known to be injurious, there were few procedural tools available to reopen those findings. To the extent that one can speak of court praxis here, this captures the collective response of these combined influences.

The following section weaves three themes into a narrative of the law's development here, but if one were approaching the question from first principles, the following options represent plausible responses from any legal system:

1. Fully plural. The standard of care is formally finely attuned to the type of practice undertaken. All types of practice can hope to avoid liability.
2. Fully monolithic. The standard of care is formally centred on a particular type of practice which acts as the dominant model against which all other models are judged. Compliance with this dominant model is required.
3. Bounded plurality. The standard of care is informally centred on a particular type of practice. A fuzzy degree of variance is permitted, but some forms of practice will, by default, fall outwith that practice.

[43] Porter (n 3) 259. See C Stebbings, *Tax, Medicines and the Law: From Quackery to Pharmacy* (Cambridge, Cambridge University Press, 2018); Carr-Saunders and Wilson (n 20) 69. As the latter sagely note, at 81, 'it may be that the idea of eliminating the quack is incapable of attainment …'.

[44] Swain (n 11) 36–37.

[45] Tompkins (n 41) 117ff or, as the author notes, where there were intentional wrongs, 157ff.

4. Court-centred. The standard of care is entirely divorced from the type of practice undertaken, with the court setting a standard of care appropriate to a given type of practice as they see fit.

III. Quackery and the Construction of Care

Much changed in English medicine, society and law during the nineteenth century. This section identifies three themes in the development of liability for quackery. From a surprising start, as the century progressed irregular practice appears to have increasingly fallen to be judged by the standards of their regular brethren.

A. Criminal Neutrality

Whilst there are very few cases in the early part of the century, there is evidence to suggest a more indulgent approach to irregular practice. In 1807 Lord Ellenborough presided over the prosecution of one John Williamson at the Old Bailey.[46] Williamson had been indicted for the murder of his patient, Ann Delacroix and charged with manslaughter by the coroner's inquisition. The former charge was dismissed; the focus was on the latter. Described as a '… person who had been in the habit of acting as a man midwife among the lower class of people'[47] he had returned to Delacroix a few days after delivering her to deal with what he mistook as retained placenta. In fact, medical witnesses testified, this was a prolapsed uterus and in attempting to remove it the accused had ruptured her artery, causing death. Describing Williamson as 'not a regularly educated accoucher', testimony from regular practitioners suggested he suffered from 'great want of anatomical knowledge'. It might be thought that such deficit would prove insurmountable, not least as Williamson's primary rebuttal was that he had acted 'according to the best of his judgment'. Yet two matters spoke to the contrary. The first was that 14 women who Williamson had previously delivered were called as witnesses in his defence, with six testifying to his kindness and skill. No less than their regular counterparts, irregular practice grounded in such empirical experience could still lead to errors, but did, likewise, provide an important service. The second was how this came to be characterised by Lord Ellenborough in summing up. Noting that what was required to substantiate the charge was 'the grossest ignorance or the most criminal inattention', he felt there had both been no want of attention, and the testimony from Williamson's previous patients spoke to the fact he possessed 'some degree of skill' in such matters. Suggesting that the mistake had arisen as a result of Williamson's shock at the situation, Lord Ellenborough stressed that guilt would 'tend to encompass a most important and anxious profession with such dangers as would deter reflecting men from entering into it'.[48] A verdict of not guilty followed. There is little sense here that the irregular nature of Williamson's practice

[46] *Rex v John Williamson* (1807) 3 Car & P 635; 172 ER 579.
[47] ibid.
[48] ibid.

stood to increase the likelihood of sanction and the plea over a deterrent effect might just as well have been treated as an opportunity to dissuade those with no formal training from taking on such delicate responsibility. Instead, Lord Ellenborough's approach hints that prosecution of a good faith irregular could risk being received as a general censure on *all* such shades of practice. Early in the century as it was, his focus was clearly on the nature of the treatment undertaken, not the status of the person undertaking it.

A pair of indictments for manslaughter in 1829 offer further insight into the importance placed in the years before 1858 on the need to preserve available medical services rather than police irregular practice and the relevance of patient knowledge and safety. On the somewhat eye-watering facts of *van Butchell* the accused was said to have caused the death of his patient, William Archer, through, 'the thrusting of a round piece of ivory into and up the fundament and against the rectum'.[49] Inserting such an ivory bougie was intended to relieve Archer of his symptoms, but instead he died seven days later from the perforation that had resulted.[50] Edwin van Butchell was himself the son of a notorious quack dentist (perhaps most famous for the donkey he would at times ride around Hyde Park touting for business, having painted the poor beast purple), and it was not established at trial whether Edwin had received a regular education himself.[51] Yet as Hullock B noted, this was not at all material to the case.[52] This characterisation was all the more surprising given *van Butchell* saw the prosecution lead evidence from the most eminent early treatise authors on the point. Blackstone, Hale and Coke's views were all put before the court in contest of the very matter Hullock B said to be immaterial. The stakes here were not inconsequential for irregular practitioners of all shades. If it were the case that injurious practice as an irregular was *itself* to be sanctioned, then such prosecutions were apt to become merely matters of factual dispute rather than substantive assessment. While this would have gold-plated regular status, the effect on the availability of irregular practice in the marketplace risked could have been substantial. Such concerns were certainly present in those earlier sources. Coke, reaching back to Britton, suggested that unlike a regular practitioner, one who was not, '… of the mystery of a physician or chirugeon', risked felony should a patient perish following treatment.[53] By contrast Hale rejected this proposition.[54] Instead he focused on the Henrician-era statutes regulating licensed practice.[55] Whilst those provided for regulatory sanction, Hale felt it imperative that this not bleed across into their assessment at law, favouring substance over rigid categorisation. As he poetically justified this, '… for physic and salves were before licensed physicians and surgeons', going on to lament that if it were otherwise many beyond London risked death in childbirth for lack of medical support.[56] Blackstone reflected both views, noting that Hale was correct to question the relevance

[49] *Rex v Edwin Martin van Butchell* (1829) 3 Car & P 629; 172 ER 576.

[50] ibid 631–32, 577. Adduced in evidence from a surgeon, one Mr Lloyd, who had examined the body and had himself interacted with the deceased in the days after van Butchell's ministrations.

[51] Albeit the parties appeared both prepared respectively to concede or presume, or show such in evidence, 632 578.

[52] ibid.

[53] Coke, *Fourth Institute*, 251.

[54] Hale, *History of the Pleas of the Crown*, vol 1, 429.

[55] See above n 22 including the Physicians Act 1523 (14 & 15 Hen VIII c5).

[56] Hale, 429.

of such a division tracking across to matters of liability.[57] In summing up, Hullock B was blunt. Adopting Hale and noting that no decision in support of the alternate proposition had been drawn on by those authors or, it appeared, since, a practitioner's status made no difference to their potential liability, which had to be assessed on the merits.[58] Again there was clear concern that any other approach might negatively impact the provision of healthcare in the wider country. The law was taken to be that bona fide and honest exercise of a practitioner's best skill could not sound as manslaughter.[59] That the operation had clearly failed was no more evidence that van Butchell had fallen foul of this rule than would have been the case for a regular practitioner, and in the absence of any such evidence prosecution could not stand and van Butchell was acquitted.[60]

Yet the concerns so vividly on display at the Old Bailey did not necessarily hold before other courts. In the same year at the Lancaster Assizes, one Nancy Simpson was indicted for manslaughter, having administered white vitriol (zinc sulphate) to a patient who had died as a result. There Bayley J was clear that if an irregular practitioner took it upon themselves to, '… hazard medicine of a dangerous tendency […] he does it at his peril'.[61] In a reversal of the concern not to dissuade provision of medical services in general, it was precisely the fact that such treatments were offered 'where medical assistance can be obtained' that appears to have motivated the result here.[62] How this was to be assessed is unclear. Likewise why it ought to override the patient's choice of practitioner, but at least some sense of this may be found in the indication that, despite conflicting testimony from regular practitioners on the point, Bayley J appears to have regarded the treatment itself as amounting to the administration of a noxious ingredient.[63]

In a high-profile case the following year, *Rex v John St John Long* saw one of the most notorious quacks of the day – who practised at 41 Harley Street and was a particular target of Thomas Wakeley and his *Lancet*[64] – prosecuted for the manslaughter of one Catherine Cashin, who succumbed following the administration of one of his patent remedies.[65] As in *van Butchell*, relied on by the defence, much turned on the relevance, if any, of his flagrantly irregular status. As in *Williamson* it became clear that St John Long had both administered the supposedly identical treatment to others without injurious outcome,[66] and that he could call a considerable number of satisfied patients to testify.[67] Whilst Park J was minded to withdraw the case entirely, Garrow B was not, and the issue went to the jury.[68] For Garrow, whether one was president of a Royal College or 'the humblest bone-setter of the village' the question was whether they had brought to the case 'ordinary care, skill and diligence'.[69] In summing up, Park J pithily

[57] Blackstone, *Commentaries on the Law of England*, vol 4, ch 14.
[58] *van Butchell* 633, 578.
[59] ibid 632, 578.
[60] ibid 634, 579.
[61] *Nancy Simpson's Case*, (1829) 1 Lewin 262, 263; 168 ER 1034.
[62] ibid.
[63] ibid 264.
[64] Porter (n 3) 308.
[65] (1830) 4 Car & P 397;172 ER 756.
[66] ibid 403, 758.
[67] ibid 404, 759.
[68] ibid 403, 758.
[69] ibid 404, 759.

endorsed Hale's position: 'licensed or unlicensed certainly does not signify'.[70] Unlike the earlier cases, in justifying this, Park J downplayed the potential practical impact of the alternative position, not least as he thought it without merit within London.[71] Rather, the focus lay on how *any* medical practitioner ought to be assessed given skill could be acquired empirically as much, it seems, as formal education.[72] The views of both Hullock B and Lord Ellenborough were recommended to the jury, with the question put being whether there had been gross ignorance or criminal inattention to human life.[73] Indeed, reflecting on the evidence adduced from a regular surgeon who had seen Cashin during treatment, Park J emphasised that this view was not the measure of the situation: '… it is not whether the act done is the thing that a person of Mr Brodie's great skill would do'.[74] Whilst it would be a different matter where someone who was grossly ignorant nevertheless took on the care of another with injurious results, what appeared to matter was the exercise of a method or practice aimed in good faith towards the cure of the patient. That so many others could positively attest to the accused's treatments appeared to bolster the impression that some skill was at play, even if regulars might decry that. If it came as any solace that St John Long was ultimately found guilty – fined £250 but avoiding prison – it cannot have consoled regulars that the courts' approach again hinged sanction on a substantive assessment of the quality of care provided over an assumption rooted in status.

B. Framing Patient Choice and Patient Safety

As the century progressed, an increase in the number of civil actions contextualises the early criminal position set out above. In bridging the two, it is useful to consider the foundations that had been laid for civil actions here. Reflecting the messy nature of legal development, many of the key principles were being laid out contemporaneously with the era of St John Long's prosecution. The aim here is to reflect on how such civil actions were framed in order to contextualise the cases that then conclude this section.

It was clear that to defeat a civil action, the defendant would be required to demonstrate the ordinary degree of skill that could be expected from someone undertaking that profession. In *Seare v Prentice*,[75] Lord Ellenborough had upheld an earlier direction to the jury that the mere want of such ordinary skill could not sustain an action in the absence of a finding that the defendant had been negligent. There was no formal allegation there that the defendant was an irregular practitioner but, having treated the plaintiff's broken arm with vinegar and paper, the surgeon called in evidence (who, as was often the case, had later remedied the situation) was scathing: '… an apprentice boy might have known better'.[76] Whilst Lord Ellenborough felt that the 'ordinary

[70] ibid 405, 759.
[71] ibid 406, 760.
[72] ibid 408, 761.
[73] ibid.
[74] ibid 409, 761.
[75] (1807) 8 East 348; 103 ER 376.
[76] ibid 350, 377.

qualification of skill' was required of anyone who undertook such treatment, and that liability could well ensue on those 'having rashly adventured upon the exercise of a profession', this was not clearly framed in terms of any distinction between regular and irregular practice.[77] In 1822 a strong court in *Pippin v Sheppard*, where the injury was to the plaintiff's wife, clarified that undertaking medical treatment carried with it the obligation to perform the treatment properly and skilfully whether this was made explicitly under contract or otherwise.[78] Garrow B emphasised the importance of clarifying this inherent responsibility not only in the context of the many patients who would be treated in public establishments, but more pointedly because particularly with surgery:[79]

> … the public are exposed to great risks from the number of ignorant persons professing a knowledge of the art, without the least pretentions to the necessary qualifications and they often inflict very serious injury on those who are so unfortunate as to fall into their hands.

If *Pippin* can be understood to confirm that undertaking treatment carried an inherent responsibility, it was again left unclear whether that prevented irregulars from pointing to their own practice, or merely acted to impose a minimum threshold of care *within* any such undertaking. Certainly, there was no suggestion that the defendant there was an irregular. This sense of undertaking as grounding both the duty owed outside contract and a threshold degree of skill and care returned in a pair of cases in the late 1830s, acting as the final foundation on which the modern law would develop.[80] Dealing with a surgeon-apothecary in *Lanphier v Phipos*, Tindal CJ confirmed that the standard expected from anyone who '… enters into a learned profession' was one of reasonable care and skill.[81] A practitioner could not be damned merely because there were persons of, '… higher education and greater advantages', nor because they had not used the highest possible care.[82] In setting a standard that would admit of reasonable divergences within regular practice, this nevertheless appeared to leave scope for irregular practitioners to rely on clarity about the nature the treatment on offer and whatever testimony they could produce as to its effectiveness in order to satisfy the jury. That regular practitioners might dispute such practices was not, at least formally, an obvious bar to avoiding liability. Indeed, the following year in *Gladwell v Steggall* the court confirmed in the context of a vicar-cum-surgeon-apothecary that this duty would be owed even in the absence of an explicit undertaking of a particular medical status, simply taking on employment as a surgeon would suffice.[83] Neither quacks nor regulars could avoid liability by denying a duty to take care altogether, but nor was it clear than in requiring due care that the standard was centred on one form of practice. As Ibbetson characterises them, some of these were hardly easy cases given there was much prevailing contemporary uncertainty about the boundaries between different

[77] ibid 352, 377.
[78] (1822) 11 Price 400; 147 ER 512.
[79] ibid 409, 515.
[80] J Bell and DJ Ibbetson, *European Legal Development: The Case of Tort* (Cambridge, Cambridge University Press, 2012) 86.
[81] (1838) 8 Car & P 475; 173 ER 581 (NP).
[82] (1838) 8 Car & P 479; 173 ER 583.
[83] (1839) 5 Bing (NC) 733; 132 ER 1283.

forms of action.[84] But in establishing its civil framework for assessing medical liability, English law implicitly appears to have favoured a unitary, abstract standard, focused on the quality of the practice, not the qualifications of the practitioner.

C. Civil Censure

Nevertheless, as a pair of later civil cases demonstrate, the formal neutrality practised in the criminal courts and seemingly reflected by the civil courts could nevertheless mask an informal reality. The application of that standard could operate as an ersatz form of regulatory censure for irregular practice. Here we consider two cases heard in 1865 at their respective summer Assizes. In the first, *Ruddock v Lowe*, Compton J directly considered the liability of an irregular, the proprietor of an 'Anatomical Museum' on the Strand.[85] This was one of a number of separate actions being brought against the defendant. The defendant had held himself out to be, as awkwardly described in the report, 'a duly qualified physician of the Royal College of Surgeons of England'.[86] In the classic mark of the quack, literature that he distributed to drum up business claimed his remedy was unique, eschewed the mercury and mineral cures notorious in the day, and that he never undertook treatment unless a perfect cure could be guaranteed.[87] After a course of treatment lasting months and costing a considerable sum of money, the patient's condition had merely worsened and – his teeth by now loose in his head – he finally sought further advice from a regular practitioner, one Dr Donoghue.[88] Donoghue's testimony was damning. The treatment in fact contained a considerable amount of mercury and, in any case, was entirely inappropriate for the plaintiff's condition. This was not helped by the fact the defendant's position, rather than contend that there was method at play here, was that they had not treated the patient at all. Little wonder the jury returned a verdict for the plaintiff.[89] An extensive note attached to the report rehearsed the totality of the key positions set out above, but framed English law's formal neutrality as a means of ensuring that the unqualified could not escape liability by pleading their own ignorance, rather than that such ignorance could provide grounds in itself for a finding of civil negligence or criminal inattention.[90] Yet *Ruddock* suggests that at least the more quackish species of irregular practitioner may in practice have struggled to take advantage of this. Where there was no basis on which the treatment undertaken could be defended as part of a broader method, irregular practitioners were clearly open to the scorn of their regular brethren through adversarial court process. In swaying the jury, regular practitioners could count not only on some claim to method, but all the influence that came with their orthodox status.

[84] DJ Ibbetson, 'George v Skivington (1869)' in P Mitchell (ed), *Landmark Cases in the Law of Tort* (Oxford, Hart Publishing, 2016) 69, 81.

[85] (1865) 4 F & F 519; 176 ER 672.

[86] ibid.

[87] ibid 520, 673.

[88] ibid 524, 675.

[89] ibid 524, 675.

[90] ibid 522 (a), 673.

A different form of irregular practice came under scrutiny in *Jones v Fay*, where a chemist who did not hold a licence from the Society of Apothecaries was retained as a surgeon-apothecary by the plaintiff painter.[91] Seeking relief from stomach pains ascribed to his trade, the plaintiff was prescribed pills of the defendant's own manufacture and continued to take these for some weeks, being repeatedly dissuaded from seeking medical advice by the defendant before resolving to do so as, inevitably, his condition worsened. The medical man consulted indicated that the tablets were mercury bluepill, as later analysis for the court would confirm. Further medical evidence suggested that although there was some case for the use of mercury in the patient's condition, such continuous use was improper and had served only to weaken the plaintiff, exposing him to the bronchitis and dropsy that currently afflicted him.[92] Again, Fay's defence was underwhelming. Rather than contest the basis on which the medication had been prescribed, counsel attempted to revisit the grounds on which the defendant had been retained – only to be rebuffed by *Gladwell* in response – or suggest the later diseases had innocently supervened.[93] In argument, Pigott B was clear that, on the authority of *Ruddock*, acting as a regular practitioner would leave one 'liable as such', and, having consulted with Crompton B, that it was unnecessary for the declaration to even require language specifying the type of regular practice that had been undertaken by the defendant.[94] There was no attempt to refute the evidence that a mercury treatment, were it given, would have been improper, leaving the jury with a purely factual question of whether this is what the defendant had prescribed.[95] It is little surprise that they awarded £100, subject only to Piggott B's mild rebuke to calculate this only in light of the defendant's negligence rather than the plaintiff's 'imprudence' in continuing the treatment.[96] Whilst patient choice was not under scrutiny per se, there was surely some – albeit unexplored – limit past which a patient could not be seen to complain that a 'cure' had proven anything but!

Whilst a more fulsome account of the law here is called for, the speculative narrative that emerges is this: The neutrality adopted in the criminal courts, seemingly justified in part by the need to avoid an overly stringent standard of care, permitted, at least formally, a plural approach to assessing medical liability. This neutrality was not wholly erased by the foundational civil authorities, but in time a standard that may have appeared neutral on the surface may have come in practice to rely on expert evidence from regular practitioners as to the bounds of appropriate treatment. Irregular practitioners could, informally, be held to the standards of their regular brethren. Whilst nothing ruled out quacks relying on evidence of their own method to challenge this, where they did not those standards would likely prove difficult to satisfy or rebut, and all the more so where a jury felt that true charlatanry was afoot.

[91] (1865) 4 F & F 525; 176 ER 675.
[92] ibid 528, 676.
[93] ibid.
[94] ibid 529, 677.
[95] ibid.
[96] ibid 530, 677.

IV. Reflections on Legal Change

Viewing that narrative alongside Stein's survey of the era highlights that it played out alongside the process of expert testimony from regular practitioners coming to overwhelmingly dominate the assessment of medical error for regular practitioners themselves,[97] a stance that continued undisturbed into the twentieth century.[98] Indeed, such was the grip of this approach that it took almost another century to challenge it,[99] or suggest that there could be plural standards of care in the medical context.[100] The idea that the law could ever have *begun* from such a proposition is, to the eyes of later lawyers, an absurdity: how else would one judge medical behaviours? Yet the narrative presented here suggests just that. A window in which it was open to the English law to truly reflect the plurality of medical behaviours with which patients engaged.[101] Indeed, it is clear that the law was willing to countenance for some period, at least formally, the idea that good medical practice was not the preserve of regular practitioners alone. If in practice that ultimately resolved in favour of such practitioners nevertheless, that was driven by informal court practice rather than a surface level change in the rule itself. In reflecting on legal change in this context, three points stand out.

To begin, tension between a formal rule and its informal application is not surprising here. Firstly, even increasing regulatory clarity after 1858 did nothing to formally privilege one form of medical practice *in relation to liability*. That English law had crystallised a unitary, abstract and objective standard of care rather than something more subjectively or contextually tailored left the law predisposed to think in broader not narrower terms, even if this smoothed over the blunt reality of different forms of practice. Ultimately the law acknowledged irregulars as providing a form of medical care even if the basis for that differed from regular practitioners. Secondly, the presence of the jury ensured a degree of uncertainty when assessing standards of care in practice. Juries were forums where lay and regular medical conceptions of patient safety collided. The absence of a formal rule distinguishing forms of practice from one another could naturally create tension where the former trumped the latter. Neither of the common forms of judicial control of the civil jury, usurpation through withdrawal or re-framing questions as a matter of duty,[102] would have been available to provide a counterweight in these cases, and control over the scope of liability would then largely rest with how the standard of care was framed. Indeed, the messy overlap between regular and irregular practice likely initially predisposed the law to focus on substantively assessing the quality of care rather than merely the status of the practitioner. As Ibbetson has suggested there is often 'a substantial measure of indeterminacy' in how the law is framed, and

[97] Stein et al (n 2).

[98] McGrath (n 2).

[99] *Bolitho v City and Hackney Health Authority* [1998] AC 232.

[100] *Montgomery v Lanarkshire Health Board* [2015] UKSC 11; followed now by *McCulloch v Forth Valley Health Board* [2023] UKSC 26.

[101] For a suggestion that such an approach could be identified in at least some US states see DeVille (n 14) 172–73.

[102] DJ Ibbetson, *A Historical Introduction to the Law of Obligations* (Oxford, Oxford University Press, 1999) 174–75.

even the same formal rule can be susceptible to different applications where not fixed in 'hard and fast terms'.[103] Here, we find a fine example of both conditions at play.

Secondly, there is clearly a connection between the civil and criminal responses here. Indeed, *Ruddock* would suggest later courts may have viewed a civil or criminal basis for liability as a matter of happenstance rather than an issue that made a profound analytical difference to the standard. Whilst the precise doctrinal question and consequences were radically different, the criminal and civil sources were often read together when framing the standard of care. In part this also reflects the balance of cases that were available to work with. Whilst inapposite, it is no surprise that the older institutional skeleton from Coke onwards was dredged up into the modern era. There had been a dearth of cases into the early nineteenth century and the treatise authors were a plausible source of legal thinking that could be used to give shape to the rather flabby forms of the respective criminal and civil actions. Criminal thinking then shifted across to influence civil thinking as the latter came to be the primary form by which medical liability was put to scrutiny. The law is made by the sources that are available for it to work with and work within. Here, whilst the doctrinal nature of these sources differed, the medical context with which they were concerned appears common and decisive.

Finally, exploring the liability of irregular practitioners casts a new and radical light on both the regulatory role of the courts in this era and existing explanations for how the standard of regular practitioners came to define the century. That the legal standard of care should play some role in this emerging dominance is perhaps surprising, not least given the forms of action involved were, as is clear above, general and abstract in nature. Whilst there was certainly no formal law of medical negligence in the nineteenth century, the narrative identified here suggests that medical liability was maturing into a plausible cryptotype within those structures far earlier than the broader literature might suggest.[104] Within that cryptotype, there was a persisting tension as to how the law parsed medical practice and whose standards were determinative. Far from the first or fourth models posited above, orthodox standards came to dominate through an informal, fuzzy model more akin to the third. But what the narrative identified here suggests is that in elevating regular practitioners, courts were plausibly motivated by active, if shifting, concerns in relation to healthcare provision throughout the century rather than simply acting as passive, permissive vehicles for deference to the occupational expertise claimed and increasingly demonstrated by regular practitioners. These concerns developed from seeking to ensure available healthcare options were not driven away entirely to holding irregular practitioners to account for a standard they purported to but could not meet. From the perspective of patients, working to ensure irregulars fell under the scrutiny of their regular brethren in matters of liability

[103] DJ Ibbetson, 'Comparative legal history: A methodology' in A Musson and C Stebbings (eds), *Making Legal History Approaches and Methodologies* (Cambridge, Cambridge University Press, 2012) 131, 136–39. The author gives assessment of reasonable care in particular contexts as an example of the latter.

[104] Whilst some treatises in the era were more expansive on the specific topic of medical liability, see T Beven, *Principles of the Law of Negligence* (London, Stevens, 1889) 827, it is only in the twentieth century that texts dedicated to the legal treatment of medical error emerge, see Bullock, 'Law Relating to Medical Practice', and indeed the first fully systematic modern treatment arguably does not emerge until the mid-twentieth century in R Nathan, *Medical Negligence Being the Law of Negligence in Relation to the Medical Profession and Hospitals* (London, Butterworth, 1957).

suggests concern for the vulnerability of patients and the risk of their exploitation, a risk that could, in the absence of formal legal means of doing so, be controlled in part through the standard of care such practitioners would be held to. From the perspective of regular practitioners, parsing the rise of orthodox standards as a feature of deep-rooted deference by courts and juries is a familiar explanation here.[105] Yet deference to the occupational, largely market-focused goals of such practitioners goes a step further than its customary framing as related to their expertise and seems unconvincing without concurrent patient-centred concerns to motivate the courts in the first place. It is one thing to privilege accepted regular practice in judgment over such practice itself, where deference to internal medical expertise may, if not inevitably, be expected. It is another matter altogether, through judicial practice, to define the category of medical practice itself so as to encompass all manner of medical intervention, only to then privilege one subset of those so captured as the means of assessing injurious practice. Likewise, given that nineteenth century regulatory architecture did not support any general, formal differentiation between regular and irregular practice until 1858, to first reject and then gradually import into such a highly differentiated medical marketplace a seemingly unitary approach to medical standards appears to be an effort to police a particular view of appropriate practice rather than seek to accommodate a plural, contextualised approach to good practice within abstract legal principles that were fully capable of doing so. This is, of course, not to suggest or quibble that there were not good reasons for doing so. In many cases quackery could obviously be flagrantly dangerous. Rather, the actions of the courts simply emphasise, from a different standpoint, a beneficent form of the paternalism with which patients were treated in this period, but far from enshrining orthodox practice through passive deference, here this self-same paternalism may have driven an active, instrumental choice to reach a particular and self-identified regulatory end.

V. Conclusion

In his defining work on quackery, Porter is unsparingly harsh on the courts: 'The law, civil and criminal, proved next to useless for those campaigning against quack practice [...] If anything, the law courts acted in favour of quacks.'[106] For the legal historian, this is, in turn, harsh judgement. It is certainly true that for a time English courts chose not to differentiate between forms of practice, and, as Porter suggests,[107] juries were willing to thumb their nose at outraged regulars who no doubt wished nothing more than to see injurious irregulars suffer swingeing legal consequence. But the courts did nothing more than fairly reflect the fact that entry into the marketplace was largely unconstrained and, as this situation changed, they can be seen to change with it. The fact of the jury was less mutable. It was always possible that they might take a dim view of a given practitioner regardless of occupational stripes, but even then, in practice as the

[105] See Stein et al (n 2) 205; Swain (n 11) 27.
[106] Porter (n 3) 54.
[107] ibid.

century wore on, expert evidence tended to win out, and that tended to be the preserve of the orthodoxy. Nothing here is to suggest that the law would have been normatively better had it embraced a truly plural approach to assessing the standard of care. Simply that this was a plausible path not taken. An alternative model of robust disclosure duties to help patients understand the nature of the treatment on offer and how it differed from other possible options would have provided one means of doing so, but English law was little equipped to require that of any practitioner in the era let alone those on the fringes. Indeed, the same refusal to formalise firm lines around a truly fixed, monist view of acceptable practice stood to benefit regulars as much as it damned them for a time to have to indulge their irregular competitors. English law's conception of medical error, fluid and abstract as it was, embraced a bounded form of plurality that protected those at the developing edge of medical technique as much as those whose practice was common in its own era, encouraging laggers to keep up as an old standard moved away from them. In the absence of a separate legal tool for policing injurious irregular practice, regular practitioners may well have come to rue the same sharper boundaries that would have left quacks clearly outside, and as the narrative identified here suggests, in time, for a time, their dominance would be assured in any case.

In the preface of his seminal monograph, David writes:

> Legal history takes many forms. This book is a history of legal categories, concepts and doctrines; the mechanisms used by lawyers to organize their thoughts. Such a work is of necessity both speculative and constructive.[108]

In approaching that task over his career, David has demonstrated a rare ability to understand the unusual angle, the overlooked vantage point. A glance at the end of the same work confirms this. Where else, amongst respected tomes of legal scholarship, might one find sequential index entries for, 'Ostrich, exhibition', and, 'Owl, lost'? Combined with his interest legal development this often allows him to see the currents *around* his central focus that proved decisive, to connect this focus with other movements within the law, and to situate all that in the wider world of the moment. He has a feel for the whole chessboard rather than, as lawyers too often do, just the individual moves. My hope here was to provide some small sketch of a familiar category from an unfamiliar starting point as a way to celebrate the man who has so often helped others grapple with categories, concepts and doctrines across time and national boundaries and, in doing so, opened a whole new world to explore. My own gratitude for that gift is boundless.

[108] Ibbetson (n 102) v.

24

Judges, Jurists and Style

JONATHAN MORGAN*

I open with an observation taken from Christopher Forsyth's inaugural lecture.[1] On promotion to a *personal* chair, there is no eminent predecessor to praise – but one must still acknowledge one's intellectual debts. Like Professor Forsyth I pay tribute to two 'giants of scholarship' – my earliest and so most influential teachers. Jane Stapleton was my tutor at Balliol. She set the pattern for how I have thought about law ever since. Also at Oxford, David Ibbetson taught me legal history – without which one cannot understand English law.[2] Particularly on this occasion, David must be singled out for thanks. He enticed me from the 'dark side' to the light – the light blue. Otherwise, I would not be standing before you in Cambridge today.

I. Style

One lecturing on style hazards appraisal of his oratory (stagey or stilted?), his writing (prose ornate – or *ordinaire*?), even his attire. I should clarify at once that my theme is styles of legal reasoning. I am unqualified to make *aesthetic* judgements. I can though report the verdicts of other *arbitri elegantiarum*. Judges, anyway *some* judges, have had a pretty good press. Benjamin Cardozo lauded the English judicial prose style. Significant, from a self-consciously epigrammatical judge.[3] Perhaps things have taken a turn for the worse. 'Longer judgments [now] cite more cases to settle smaller questions less clearly' (says Milsom)![4] Lord Rodger regretted, tongue in cheek, our 'decadent post-classical

* Inaugural lecture as Professor of English Law, University of Cambridge, 26 January 2024. References have been added but the text remains (almost) as delivered. I must thank Peter Cane and David Feldman, who will disagree with both the style and substance of what follows.

[1] CF Forsyth, 'Showing the Fly the Way out of the Flybottle: The Value of Formalism and Conceptual Reasoning in Administrative Law' [2007] CLJ 325.

[2] DJ Ibbetson, *A Historical Introduction to the Law of Obligations* (Oxford, Oxford University Press, 1999).

[3] AF Rodger, 'The Form and Language of Judicial Opinions' (2002) 118 *LQR* 226, 241.

[4] SFC Milsom, 'The Past and Future of Judge-Made Law' (1981) 8 *Monash Univ LR* 5, 13. Judicial pleas for brevity: MH Arden, 'Judgment Writing: Are Shorter Judgments Achievable?' (2012) 128 *LQR* 515, DE Neuberger, 'No Judgment – No Justice' (BAILII Lecture, 2012).

era' of judgment-writing.[5] But then, every Golden Age is always past. We may all lament the vanished epoch of Blackburn and Jessel, or Denning and Diplock – or now Bingham and Hoffmann.

When we turn to *jurists*, it appears there never was a Golden Age. At least not according to Fred Rodell:[6]

> There are two things wrong with almost all legal writing. One is its style. The other is its content. That, I think, about covers the ground … [It] seems to be a cardinal principle of law review writing … that nothing may be said forcefully and nothing … amusingly.

That was in 1936. But one still sees his point. From every sweeping generalisation come honourable exceptions. The first things that I heard 'said amusingly' about law were in the 1996 Clarendon Lectures. Jane Stapleton *insisted* the Balliol undergraduates must go (even if we hadn't studied the economic torts). The lecturer was, of course, Tony Weir.[7] I have always hoped that the authentic 'Cambridge Legal Style' is Weir's.[8]

Aesthetics aside,[9] what characterises judicial, and juristic, reasoning styles? Prepare, again, for sweeping generalisations. It is scarcely controversial, or novel, to see judges as problem-solvers, and jurists as system-builders. In the common law, great principles emerge and evolve – but obliquely, as a by-product of dispute resolution. For Lord Goff, 'pragmatism and gradualism' were the common law's 'sovereign virtues'.[10] Indeed, *cautious* judicial development is obligatory, not mere stylistic flourish. 'Gradualism' is the centri-petal force that keeps the common law – unwritten, customary law[11] – from spinning apart.

It would be foolish to attempt any general characterisation of legal *scholarship*. There is the doctrinal or 'black letter' tradition. Yet there are many various ways to approach a subject 'doctrinally'. Even a well-tilled field like contract shows a variety of perspectives.[12] One might divide scholars into 'pioneers', 'consolidators', and 'iconoclasts' – or in many other ways.[13] Quite legitimately, jurists may reject the doctrinal starting point. Philosophical, historical, or social-scientific approaches all enrich legal understanding. Or comparative law: we appreciate our own reasoning-style better by studying other systems.[14] And so on.

Senior scholars, including Professor Stapleton, have recently championed the doctrinal approach.[15] Yet in Professor Fentiman's rallying call to defend the 'citadel' one sees

[5] (2002) 118 *LQR* 226, 226.

[6] F Rodell, 'Goodbye to Law Reviews' (1936) 23 *Virginia LR* 38.

[7] T Weir, *Economic Torts* (Oxford, Clarendon Press, 1997).

[8] J Goudkamp and D Nolan (eds), *Scholars of Tort Law* (Oxford, Hart Publishing, 2019) 30, 39 ('devastating one-liners … sparkling prose and acerbic wit').

[9] *cf* Lord Burrows, 'Judges and Academics, and the Endless Road to Unattainable Perfection' (2022) 55 *Israel LR* 50, 62–63 (main stylistic difference from *academic* writing: that *judgments* must be 'decisive' and 'accessible').

[10] R Goff, 'Judge, Jurist and Legislature' (1987) 2 *Denning LJ* 79.

[11] See generally AWB Simpson, 'The Common Law and Legal Theory' in AWB Simpson (ed), *Oxford Essays in Jurisprudence: Second Series* (Oxford, Oxford University Press, 1973).

[12] J Goudkamp and D Nolan (eds), *Scholars of Contract Law* (Oxford, Hart Publishing, 2022).

[13] Goudkamp and Nolan (n 8) ch 1.

[14] BS Markesinis, 'A Matter of Style' (1994) 110 *LQR* 607 (inaugural lecture at UCL).

[15] J Stapleton, *Three Essays on Torts* (Oxford, Oxford University Press, 2021) ch 1. Also eg A Burrows in *Scholars of Contract Law* (n 12) at 291–93.

a tradition beleaguered, at least unfashionable.[16] Maybe a philosophical fashion catches on like a gastronomic fashion: one can no more refute an idea than a sauce.[17] However, for jurists viewing themselves as members of the wider academy, and not primarily as *lawyers*, the greater is theorisation's allure.[18] Systems win the academic palm: rigorously coherent, transformative theories. Scholars in all disciplines are praised for *innovation*, iconoclasm, the questioning of received wisdom. Nobel Prizes are awarded to those who shift paradigms, not for 'normal science' within existing ones.[19] Jurists who transform received understandings would be the closest equivalent. Yet the unfashionable treatise-writers have greater influence in law. Not in spite of their consciously un-theoretical style – but precisely because of it. Doctrinal writing embodies sympathy with the common law's gradualism.

Hear an exceptionally eminent jurist-cum-judge, Guido Calabresi.[20] The scholar's role (Calabresi says) 'is to tell and write the truth … fully and courageously'. It is also the scholar's lot 'for a time, to be ignored' by the courts. *They* apprehend 'infinite dangers' in 'wonderful, new, and seemingly correct theories'.[21] Ambitious scholarly claims are tested cautiously against the experience of precedent. For above all, judges must make rulings that 'work'. Judicial acceptance of deep theory, then, may be a long time coming.[22]

Still, English legal scholarship has significantly increased its influence.[23] Lord Goff argued that a judge's intense focus on the facts of disputes, and the academic's wider systemic view, are mutually complementary.[24] He envisaged judge and jurist joined as 'pilgrims … on the endless road to unattainable perfection'.[25] The combination seems irresistible: 'We think in generalities, but we live in detail' (Alfred North Whitehead). This said, Lord Goff still thought that judges should take the lead, or perhaps the wheel, on that 'journey'. Legal principles emerge from facts, through the common law process, in the good old-fashioned way. He insisted: 'Pragmatism must be the watchword'.[26]

I emphatically agree. Law can govern 'life in all its untidy complexity' only with a heavy dash of pragmatism. Rules and principles need to be developed *practically*.

[16] RG Fentiman, 'Citadels of the Law: Law Schools and the Defence of Doctrine' (Queens' College Cambridge, 12 October 2022).

[17] EM Cioran, *All Gall is Divided* (translated by R Howard, New York, Arcade Publishing, 1999) 23.

[18] N Duxbury, *Jurists and Judges: An Essay on Influence* (Oxford, Hart Publishing, 2001) 41 ('more or less every theoretical trend finds its place in the American law school').

[19] T Kuhn, *The Structure of Scientific Revolutions* (University of Chicago Press, 1962). (*cf* AWB Simpson, 'book review' (2008) 26 *Law & History Rev* 221, 222: 'I personally am deeply skeptical as to the possibility of there ever occurring, within a legal system, Kuhn type paradigm shifts in legal thinking so dramatic that they can usefully be viewed as revolutionary').

[20] G Calabresi, 'Reflections of a Torts Teacher on the Bench' (2018) 11 *Jo Tort L* 161.

[21] *cf* G Calabresi, *The Costs of Accidents* (Yale University Press, 1970); G Calabresi and D Melamed 'Property Rules, Liability Rules, and Inalienability: One View of the Cathedral' (1972) 85 *Harvard LR* 1089.

[22] *cf* DJ Ibbetson, 'Comparative Legal History: A Methodology' in A Musson and C Stebbings (eds), *Making Legal History: Approaches and Methodologies* (Cambridge, Cambridge University Press, 2012) 140 ('Law is largely backward-looking and heavily inertial: it stays the same unless and until it is changed; energy has to be expended in the deliberate introduction of any change and scholarly reformulations are sterile until and unless they become accepted').

[23] Duxbury (n 18) (comparing England, US and France). *cf* W Swain, *The Law of Contract 1670–1870* (Cambridge, Cambridge University Press, 2015) 278 ('scepticism is required before assuming that judges were, and are, widely influenced by legal literature … The influence of legal writing may be more subtle and less direct').

[24] R Goff, 'The Search for Principle' (1983) 69 *Proceedings Brit Acad* 169 (*cf* Duxbury ibid 102–105).

[25] *The Spiliada* [1987] AC 460, 488.

[26] Goff (n 24) 186.

I fear that sometimes, scholars under-emphasise practical constraints. These might seem tiresome obstacles on the broad, high road to general theories – and fancied academic immortality. Yet practicalities are central to understanding law.[27]

I cannot hope to substantiate these claims in any rigorous fashion here. But I shall exemplify them, using the law of contract, and then public law. Contract law's aim is 'satisfying the reasonable expectations of honest [contracting parties]'.[28] Pragmatism is inherent.[29] Both in identifying those 'reasonable expectations' and 'satisfying' them, practicality must be the 'watchword'. (By contrast, commercial contactors' desire for elegant, abstract theories is limited indeed). When I turn to *public* law, the point becomes more controversial and therefore important. Although here judicial reasoning has in my legal lifetime become more abstract-theoretical (and in that sense, more 'scholarly') in style, I suggest that in public law too, the courts approach their role with a practicality that scholars may under-appreciate.

II. Contract

But first, contract. For centuries, English courts have consciously aspired to *workable* commercial law – no more and no less. In my view, this is admirable, indeed inevitable. While it sounds intellectually un-exciting, the endeavour to satisfy parties' preferences can learn from scholarship about contract, as well as the factual 'data' of litigated disputes. Secondly, the 'pragmatic' law of contract still rests on intellectual underpinnings. Contract's theoretical basis is nineteenth century jurists' concealed legacy. I shall remind you of their forgotten achievements – but also their limitations. On occasion, foundational theories have contributed to doctrinal mis-steps. Mostly, however, the judges have remained breezily un-theoretical, setting about their pragmatic task.

Is 'satisfying commercial expectations' not vacuous – an empty category containing solely what parties, in fact, 'expect'? To some contract theorists it might seem *unambitious* ambition. There is something in this. But why should it matter? Contract is a *facilitative* department of law. Parties choose whether to enter legally-binding contracts – and choose *which* jurisdiction's law will govern. If a syndicate of morally-minded professors – Platonic Guardians – somehow enacted a contract code designed to punish breach, I predict it would attract the 'custom' of few well-advised commercial parties. Demonstrably, contractors prefer the opposite. English law, a very popular choice, contains absolute obligations with no defence of 'impracticability' (let alone 'reasonable care'); but it tempers these with relatively weak sanctions for breach.[30] If my hunch is correct, it would be pointless to institute a law of contract to gratify moral philosophers, while repelling the commercially savvy. They would flee to New York, or elsewhere, by exercising their Choice of Law.

[27] *cf* B Hale 'Principle and Pragmatism in Developing Private Law' (Cambridge Freshfields Lecture 2019) and B Hale, 'Principle and Pragmatism in Public Law' (Sir David Williams Lecture 2019).

[28] J Steyn, 'Contract Law: Fulfilling the Reasonable Expectations of Honest Men' (1997) 113 *LQR* 433.

[29] Hale ('Principle and Pragmatism in Developing Private Law' (n 27)): tort law also 'littered with concepts redolent of pragmatism'.

[30] Compare Civilian traditions with harsher penalties for breach, but more forgiving of unexpectedly onerous obligations: M Pargendler, 'The Role of the State in Contract Law: The Common-Civil Law Divide' (2018) 43 *Yale J Int L* 143.

Granting preference-satisfaction as commercial law's unavoidable goal,[31] what do 'commercial expectations' actually require? I have elsewhere tentatively advocated a 'minimalistic' set of default obligations.[32] But a rival view has force. In particular, long-term commercial relations may need rules modified to deter opportunism and support good faith. Judges and scholars whom I enormously admire have so argued. Unquestionably, different kinds of contracts need different rules. Perhaps the insistence that we have a law of *contract* (singular) is an over-simplification.

'Relational contract' equally concerns the accommodation of commercial preferences. Significantly, the debate flows from *theoretical* writing. The founding scholars were determinedly *not* doctrinal. Rather, Ian Macneil's and Stuart Macaulay's openness to sociological and economic research challenged contract *law's* assumptions about party expectations. Translating their work into concrete doctrinal recommendations is not straightforward.[33] The evolving law on relational contracts exemplifies Lord Goff's alliance between fact-focused adjudication, and broader scholarly research.[34]

At a deeper level, that partnership is nothing new. Although emerging from practical resolutions of commercial disputes, contract law appears as a tight, coherent theoretical whole. This structure was supplied by pioneering nineteenth century treatise-writers.[35] As Simpson noted, their work built on fully six centuries of contract litigation.[36] What was lacking was not (as it were) the raw materials, but systematic exposition underpinned by a coherent theory. Textbooks accounts enabled university education in English law.[37] While a novel form of English legal literature, these books were properly 'innovatory' only if we ignore their authors' 'plagiarism' (Simpson's word) of the civilian tradition. The treatise-writers understandably borrowed continental jurists' 'analysis, categories, and organising concepts'[38] – entirely absent from English law circa 1850.[39] To quote Professor Ibbetson,[40] the organising Will Theory's 'great merit

[31] *cf* Swain (n 23) 281 ('The extent to which judges were influenced by commercial considerations is also difficult to pin down … Most judges, including Lord Mansfield, were reluctant to allow commercial considerations to completely overturn established rules. A compromise was often required').

[32] J Morgan, *Contract Law Minimalism: A Formalist Restatement of Commercial Contract Law* (Cambridge, Cambridge University Press, 2013).

[33] See now D Campbell, *Contractual Relations: A Contribution to the Critique of the Classical Law of Contract* (Oxford, Oxford University Press, 2022).

[34] Since this lecture, Lord Briggs has identified a triumvirate: '[Common law] development is subjected to the refiners' fire of adversarial debate and testing before it is endorsed … The epithet "judge-made" [law] is a bit of a misnomer. In reality these step by step developments in the common law are the result, not merely of judicial decision, but also of academic analysis, coupled with the imaginativeness and wisdom of counsel's submissions': *Armstead v Royal and Sun Alliance Insurance Co Ltd* [2024] UKSC 6; [2024] 2 W.L.R. 632 [78].

[35] *cf* 18th century: Pufendorf's superficial influence on Henry Ballow's 1737 *Treatise on Equity* (actually a pioneering contract text): Ibbetson (n 2) 219 (Ballow 'little more than a veneer of Natural-law terminology and ideas, the mangled remnants of a once-coherent theory …'); *cf* Swain (n 23) 37 ('Ballow would not be the last English writer to struggle to reconcile a theoretical framework with the realities of the Common law').

[36] AWB Simpson, 'Innovation in Nineteenth Century Contract Law' (1975) 91 *LQR* 247.

[37] AV Dicey, *Can English Law be Taught at the Universities?* (inaugural lecture, Oxford, 1883) (Oxford had recognised the separate Honour School of Jurisprudence in 1872). (*cf* Simpson (n 36) 252: 'earlier doctrine lacked the abstract and speculative character of law evolved outside the court-room. There being no pedagogy of contract, its literature, such as it was, lacked the merits, and the demerits, of classroom law').

[38] (1975) 91 *LQR* 247, 254.

[39] *cf* Swain (n 23) 176 (Pothier 'proved unexpectedly useful in assisting English judges to fill the void' once questions of substance were no longer left to juries: Pothier 'full of examples for lawyers and judges looking for quick solutions to practical problems').

[40] Ibbetson (n 2) 221.

was … intellectual coherence that the traditional Common law had wholly lacked'. But 'to some extent [it was coherence] bought at the expense of practical common sense'. And as a model imposed on the common law from outside, 'considerable friction' arose.[41]

The text-writers' achievement may have been unrepeatable. Simpson describes also the 'fall' of the legal treatise. 'The great enterprise … [was] methodizing of disorderly traditional or customary law', and yet:

> once the job has been done … much of its intellectual excitement disappears. Later treatise writers are relegated to the laborious task of reworking the same materials or refining matters of detail.[42]

The treatises thus 'contain[ed] the seeds of their own destruction'.[43]

Milsom reflects on the same 'intellectual impulse' to fit rules into systems.[44] Nineteenth century jurists treated law as 'akin to mathematics', with 'intellectual coherence … a criterion in its own right'. Rules were 'captured' within an explicit theoretical framework; but this fixing-down marked 'the end of a cycle of legal development'.[45] Milsom draws a parallel with late-medieval land law.[46] It gained its remarkable first treatise in the fifteenth century (Littleton's *Tenures*).[47] But this early theorisation changed the courts' attitudes to feudal landownership: 'They were [now] making sense, not of people's lives, but of rules and concepts'. It obstructs *practical* laws, Milsom suggests, to 'embalm [them] in logic'.

With great respect, this seems overstated. Contract law evolves constantly despite the 'embalming' efforts of Pollock, Anson and their successors.[48] Perhaps there has been some decline in the status of treatise-writing. Professor Hedley argues that the vogue for private law *theory* is an attempt to recapture the subject's lost prestige.[49] Contract exemplifies a 'mature' subject where Simpson's 'laborious tasks' predominate. Yet 'black letter' texts like *Treitel on Contract* have more influence than abstract-theoretical treatments, however brilliant. Duxbury concluded of contract law's greatest 'pioneer', Sir Frederick Pollock, that his cautious, pedestrian style *enhanced* his influence.[50] The secret was Pollock's stamina, longevity, and unshowy persistence.[51]

[41] See further Ibbetson (n 2) 298 ('Little more than a century later the law of contract was recognized as an unsurprisingly confused mess').

[42] AWB Simpson, 'The Rise and Fall of the Legal Treatise: Legal Principles and the Forms of Legal Literature' (1981) 48 *Univ Chicago LR* 632, 674.

[43] ibid 675.

[44] SFC Milsom, 'The Past and Future of Judge-Made Law' (1981) 8 *Monash Univ LR* 1, 8.

[45] ibid 9.

[46] ibid 3.

[47] *cf* Swain (n 23) 31 ('anything approaching a contractual equivalent to *Littleton* took a long time to emerge').

[48] *cf* Swain (n 23) 201 ('coherence and uniformity were often more apparent than real, even within the covers of [19th century] contract treatises').

[49] S Hedley, 'Is Private Law Meaningless?' [2011] *Current Legal Problems* 89, 113 ('obligations theorists have been trying to revivify their subject, to give it a solid theoretical basis, to rebut the charge that they are simply the curators of mouldering piles of Victorian theory that would, in a more perfect world, have been legislated out of existence some time ago').

[50] *cf* A Burrows, 'Professor Sir Guenter Treitel' in *Scholars of Contract Law* (n 12): Treitel's contract textbook '*the* world authority' despite its determined avoidance of critical comment, uninterest in theory, and lack of engagement with academic writing!

[51] N Duxbury, *Frederick Pollock and the English Juristic Tradition* (Oxford, Oxford University Press, 2004) 326.

Simpson, however, describes *Pollock on Contract* as 'ostentatiously learned'.[52] (Certainly compared to Anson, whose derivative rival text deliberately omitted Pollock's theoretical discussion to appeal to a student audience).[53] Perhaps on occasion – as alleged of Pollock – scholarly accounts over-egg their 'logic'. In consequence, courts have sometimes abandoned pragmatism, tying themselves in conceptual knots. Judges are occasionally beguiled by academic theories that are, in truth, only half-baked.

I offer two examples. In my view, *Bell v Lever Brothers* was wrong to approve the doctrine of common mistake. *Attorney-General v Blake* wrong to introduce disgorgement of profits. As for *Bell*,[54] Catharine MacMillan persuasively argues that Pollock bears much of the blame.[55] His first treatise wholeheartedly accepted von Savigny's subjectivist Will Theory. Pollock gradually distanced himself in subsequent editions.[56] Eventually, he openly espoused an *objective* approach to formation. The late Professor Waddams argued that Pollock had found it impossible to impose 'simplicity, order and elegance' without 'undermining the historical *and pragmatic* … [characteristics] of English legal thought'.[57]

Pollock's first-edition discussion of mistake was discursive and even self-contradictory.[58] Pollock could not reconcile the drastic *theoretical* effect of 'subjective' mistakes with the actual English cases. Again, Pollock later repudiated views he'd come to think 'rather wide'. But, argues MacMillan, the damage had been done, so influential was Pollock's pioneering account.[59] *Bell v Lever* resulted, a leading case with essentially incomprehensible reasoning.[60] I suggest common mistake should be removed, and *Bell* overruled.[61]

Attorney-General v Blake introduced disgorgement of profits into the law of contract.[62] *Blake* engages English private law's youngest branch, restitution. We have seen a fully-fledged legal institution emerging here, academics no less influential than judges. In *Blake* itself, Lord Hobhouse warned that hard cases make bad law. The majority went on to make bad law, nonetheless. The merits were certainly against the defendant. But *contract* law should not have stripped his profits. The main intellectual justification was that as account is found elsewhere in the law, only rigid formalism could deny the

[52] AWB Simpson, 'Contract: The Twitching Corpse' (1981) 1 *OJLS* 265, 268. *cf* Swain (n 23) 19 (Pollock 'perhaps the most thoughtful of the nineteenth century contract writers').

[53] R Stevens, 'Professor Sir William Anson' in *Scholars of Contract Law* (n 12).

[54] [1932] AC 161.

[55] C MacMillan, *Mistakes in Contract Law* (Oxford, Hart Publishing, 2012). *cf* Goff (n 24) 173 (blaming Mackenzie Chalmers' codification of *Couturier v Hastie* (1856) 5 HLC 673 (Sale of Goods Act 1893, s 6) for English law's 'Romanist' doctrine of mistake).

[56] S Waddams, 'Nineteenth-Century Treatises on English Contract Law' in A Fernandez and MD Dubber (eds), *Law Books in Action* (Oxford, Hart Publishing, 2012). *cf* Duxbury (n 51) 197 ('[The] disjunction between theory and doctrine is apparent even in the first edition of *Principles of Contract*, when Pollock was still enthusiastic about the will theory').

[57] Waddams ibid 144 (emphasis added).

[58] J Gordley, 'Professor Sir Frederick Pollock' in *Scholars of Contract Law* (n 12) 167–171.

[59] *cf* Swain (n 23) 207, 211–12 (in producing a unified doctrine of mistake in the 19th century 'veracity was sacrificed on the altar of doctrinal coherence'; mistake 'perhaps the clearest illustration of the influence of the Will Theory on English law … in an undiluted form').

[60] Campbell (n 33) 327–28.

[61] J Morgan, 'Common Mistake in Contract: Rare Success and Common Misapprehensions' [2018] *CLJ* 559.

[62] [2001] 1 AC 268.

remedy in contract. Citing Dawson, Lord Nicholls ridiculed 'That well known ailment of lawyers, a hardening of the categories'.[63] He also approved Professor Birks's criticism of 'abusive instrumentalism', ie straining concepts to yield restitutionary remedies.[64] But the decision was a menace to English commercial law. There is no demand for innovative punishments of breach. Professor Campbell deplored *Blake's* elevation of 'abstract' reasoning about restitution over sound commercial sense.[65] Fortunately, the seed has not germinated.[66]

In the end, *Bell* and *Blake* cause relatively little disruption. Contract law has self-corrected, sidelining both common mistake and account of profits. But characteristically, failing to eliminate them entirely. Preventing these doctrines' invocation may involve expensive judicial ingenuity.[67] To quote Milsom again, such circumvention is not without cost. It leaves the rule 'formally unimpaired'; and

> Even when [the rule] is formally abolished or finally forgotten, its shape will be seen in the twisting route by which it was circumvented. And the ideas involved in the circumvention will prove their own strength.[68]

If my thesis is even half right, a significant contributory cause of these mis-steps was abstract, academic theorising: the subjective will theory of contract.[69] Unification of gain-based remedies, under the banner of restitution.

Fortunately, however, hard-headed commercial judges rarely succumb to the 'temptation of elegance' (Lord Goff).[70] The doctrine of consideration was always the heart of assumpsit.[71] Yet it has received remarkable disrespect from the judiciary. By this I mean, consideration has rarely proved an obstacle to enforcement of *commercial* agreements.[72] A near-irrebuttable presumption holds that in business dealings, what appears 'gratuitous' is *actually* reciprocal. See Lord Hailsham's comment that 'Business men know their own business best even when they *appear* to grant an indulgence' (hence there was 'no difficulty in discovering consideration').[73] It is a world away from selfless, affectionate gift-giving in the personal sphere.[74] Note also the Supreme Court's surprise that counsel could even contemplate the heretical point that *letters of credit are*

[63] ibid 284; J Dawson, 'Restitution or Damages' (1959) 20 *Ohio State LJ* 175.

[64] ibid 284; PBH Birks, 'Profits of Breach of Contract' (1993) 109 *LQR* 518, 520.

[65] D Harris, D Campbell and R Halson, *Remedies in Contract and Tort*, 2nd edn (London, Butterworths, 2002) 274–284.

[66] *Morris-Garner v One Step (Support) Ltd* [2018] UKSC 20, [2019] AC 649 [64]–[82].

[67] *cf* Ibbetson (n 2) 248 (complexity of the rules on mistake).

[68] SFC Milsom, *Historical Foundations of the Common Law*, 2nd edn (London, Butterworths, 1981) 6.

[69] *cf* Swain (n 23) 229 ('Mistake developed as it did [in the 19th century], not because of the case law, but in spite of it. It was the legal writers rather than the judges who were its handmaidens').

[70] Goff (n 24) 174.

[71] *cf* Ibbetson (n 2) 238 ('so strongly entrenched … that it could not simply be uprooted on the grounds of inconsistency with [19th Century] Will Theory'); Swain (n 23) 186 (consideration as the Common law's 'great' and 'inconvenient' survivor); *cf* 217 ('survival of … consideration after 1850 can in a large part be explained by the fact that its role was much diminished').

[72] *cf* Swain (n 23) 56 (development of bills of exchange under Holt CJ, circa 1700: 'Striking a balance between mercantile convenience and the Common law saw consideration downgraded in importance'); 90–94, 114 (Lord Mansfield CJ); *cf* 145–46 ('moral consideration').

[73] *Woodhouse AC Israel Cocoa Ltd SA v Nigerian Produce Marketing Co* [1972] AC 741, 757 (emphasis added).

[74] MA Eisenberg, 'The World of Contract and the World of Gift' (1997) 85 *California LR* 821.

unenforceable for want of consideration.[75] It was not so much that the point was wrong. It was theoretically *correct* – and for that reason could not be raised. Letters of credit, as Professor Goode explained, must be enforceable and so they *are* enforceable, *irrespective* of consideration.[76] Pragmatism beats doctrine.[77]

The judgment of Lord Wilberforce in *The Eurymedon* encapsulates commercial-law pragmatism.[78] Again, he dismissed the notion that relations within a commercial network were truly *gratuitous*. Yet in a technical sense the point had merit.[79] Parties may legitimately raise such technical objections (about privity or consideration).[80] A full-blown exception, even abolition, would be neater. But as noted, the common law eschews such decisiveness. The extraordinarily complex doctrine necessary to circumvent *Foakes v Beer* and *Stilk v Myrick* proves the point.[81] Nobody doubts its ingenuity.[82] Yet as Lord Sumption commented in *M. W.B. v Rock Advertising*, to reconcile this elaborate learning with *Foakes v Beer* is 'somewhat forced'.[83]

Intellectual purity demands a straight choice: either *Williams v Roffey* or *Foakes v Beer*.[84] Yet, characteristically, the common law retains both. In Professor Ibbetson's words its inventions are 'rarely combined with the discarding of the old'.[85] Principles live on, perhaps as 'quaint survivals', perhaps 'traps for the unwary' – and typically 'encrusted with exceptions'. The common law of contract is a glorious thing. But not literally the perfection of reason – given these 'legal hangovers' of outdated ideas, and the complex exceptions to them.[86] Some problems should even be left to the legislature – a recent example is *Phillip v Barclays Bank*.[87]

75 *Taurus Petroleum Ltd v State Oil Marketing Co of the Republic of Iraq* [2017] UKSC 64; [2018] A.C. 690 [25], [95], [100].

76 R Goode, 'Abstract payment undertakings' in P Cane and J Stapleton (eds), *Essays for Patrick Atiyah* (Oxford, Oxford University Press, 1991) (especially at 219 'any bank which sought to take the consideration point would destroy its commercial reputation overnight … [and] would be likely to receive short shrift at the hands of the judiciary'). See further Ibbetson (n 2) 203–205 (mercantile documents creating obligations in the absence of consideration, through 'the custom of merchants').

77 On 19th century similarly, Swain (n 23) 201 ('The so-called classical law of contract was developed using the Will Theory. But cracks in the edifice were already very apparent … In the courts, practical and pragmatic considerations mattered as much as they ever had').

78 *New Zealand Shipping Co Ltd v AM Satterthwaite & Co Ltd* [1975] AC 154.

79 ibid 172 (Viscount Dilhorne) (rejecting appellant's 'ingenious' submission which 'attempts to overcome the lack of consideration on which [their] contention founders').

80 *The Mahkutai* [1996] AC 650, 663–65 (Lord Goff of Chieveley).

81 (1809) 2 Camp 317, (1884) 9 App Cas 605. *cf Central London Property Trust v High Trees House Ltd* [1947] KB 130; *Williams v Roffey Bros & Nicholls* [1991] 1 QB 1.

82 See eg M Chen-Wishart, 'A Bird in the Hand: Consideration and One-sided Contract Modifications' in A Burrows and E Peel (eds), *Contract Formation and Parties* (Oxford, Oxford University Press, 2010); *Collier v P & M J Wright (Holdings) Ltd* [2008] 1 WLR 643 [42] (Arden LJ) (Denning J's 'brilliant obiter dictum' in *High Trees* had in substance implemented Law Revision Committee's 1937 Report).

83 [2018] UKSC 24; [2019] AC 119, [18].

84 Criticism of the latter is longstanding: see Jessel MR's Equitable sarcasm on hawks, horses, 'a canary or a tom-tit' constituting good consideration to vary a debt – but not '19 shillings and sixpence in the pound': *Couldery v Bartrum* (1881) 19 Ch D 394, 399. *cf* Swain (n 23) 218–19 (*Foakes v Beer* was 'perhaps a little surprising' given fate of 'other restrictions placed on consideration', noting contemporary criticisms of the case by Pollock and JB Ames).

85 Ibbetson (n 2) 294.

86 ibid 301.

87 [2023] UKSC 25; [2024] AC 346.

III. Constitution

I turn now to public law. 'Pragmatism' and 'gradualism' are no less important here. Differing from contract's continuity, English public law has undergone remarkable change.[88] But the transformation poses constitutional risks. To put it in stylised (no doubt oversimplified) terms: the British 'Political Constitution' tradition is moribund.[89] In its place, the 'Legal Constitution' reigns supreme, a partnership of judges and jurists. But it is a consensus from which I dissent. At least, courts should approach constitutional questions with prudent restraint.

There may be many reasons why legal scholars are inclined to praise *law's* role, while deploring *politics* as a forum to resolve fundamental constitutional questions. One powerful attraction, I suggest, is the apparent similarity of judicial and academic reasoning style, by contrast with the 'rough music' of politics.[90] I stress the word '*apparent*'. For I fear that Legal Constitutionalists hold a view of the law that is too rosy, and of politics too jaundiced.

To illustrate the argument, here is a summary defence of the political process. Parliament can, and does, reason using moral values and constitutional principles. Parliamentary debates could even be richer in character, lacking the constraints inherent in *legal* argument. Further, it is caricature to dismiss statutes as unreasoned impositions of sovereign will. Drafters take considerable care to fit legislation into the existing law, its concepts, and its reasoning. True, statutes can impose sharp distinctions, and embody political compromises. The common law cannot formulate such 'bright line' rules very successfully, and arguably it should not try.[91] But legislation is not simply horse-trading over arbitrary lines. Sometimes political compromise may be the best hope of social harmony on divisive questions. To insist on value-laden questions' *principled* resolution, while denigrating as 'impure' compromise solutions, may only entrench polarisation.

As I shall explain, public law judgments have become notably 'academic' in their reasoning style. In part it is a general stylistic trend, entailed by written judgments superseding extempore, oral opinions. Writing brings the apparatus of *academic* style: cross-referencing, subheadings and above all, footnotes.[92] The changes have been especially pronounced in *public* law, however. Courts now engage with theoretical questions about the very nature of the British Constitution, in a way that earlier generations of judges simply did not. Scholars will applaud the change. Quite apart from the 'flattery of imitation', deeper judgments, more ambitiously reasoned, give commentators more to get our teeth into – or perhaps (to quote Lord Neuberger) our 'claws'.[93] But I suggest caution. Judicial discussion of ultimate theoretical questions, such as the nature of

[88] Ibbetson (n 2) 299 ('In a system … dependent on case law, it is change that needs to be explained, not continuity').

[89] JAG Griffith, 'The Political Constitution' (1979) 42 *MLR* 1.

[90] Not beneath some scholars: FM Cornford, *Microcosmographia Academica: Being a Guide for the Young Academic Politician* (Cambridge, Bowes & Bowes 1908).

[91] *Fairchild v Glenhaven Funeral Services* [2002] UKHL 22; [2003] 1 AC 32; see J Morgan, 'Causation, politics and law: The English – and Scottish – asbestos saga' in R Goldberg (ed), *Perspectives on Causation* (Oxford, Hart Publishing, 2011).

[92] Rodger (n 3) 234–236.

[93] Neuberger (n 4).

parliamentary sovereignty, is undesirable unless strictly necessary to resolve a dispute. The comparative reticence of twentieth century courts should be seen as prudent self-restraint, not timidity or incuriosity.

Courts deciding constitutional cases were hailed by Ronald Dworkin as the 'Forum of Principle'.[94] But the rhetoric is tendentious. Dworkin overlooked how courts can and do *decline* to hear – or answer – questions of deep constitutional principle. I rely particularly on two other US scholars, Alexander Bickel[95] and Cass Sunstein.[96] They advocate restraint, lest every controversy about public values becomes a question of *law*. One aspect of 'restraint' is reasoning *style*. Modesty has its advantages. Bickel's 'passive virtues' have been tacit rather than explicit.[97] Increasingly, they are out of fashion in UK public law. Yet judicial statecraft requires a keen sense of when to intervene, and how far to go.[98] Let me expand these observations.

Jeremy Waldron questions legal reasoning's supposed superiority to the political process.[99] He argues that public-law orthodoxy both *under*-rates 'the Dignity of Legislation' and *over*-states the moral quality of judicial decisions. Take Waldron's analysis of abortion rights. He argues that the UK's 1967 Abortion Act liberalised far more successfully than *Roe v Wade* in 1973.[100] (Waldron was writing before *Dobbs v Jackson*).[101] Waldron's point is not simply that MPs are elected (although he does prefer democracy to Philosopher Kings' benevolent dictatorship).[102] Waldron praises the *style* of Parliament's reasoning. The Abortion Bill debates at Westminster considered a wide range of ethical and practical concerns. In Waldron's view, the House of Commons' deliberations were manifestly superior to Mr Justice Blackmun's oracular declaration in *Roe v Wade* that a Constitutional Right to abortion lay in the 'penumbra' of the US Bill of Rights.[103]

But isn't Waldron's example, a free vote of conscience on a Private Member's Bill atypical, even anomalous? Parliament is rarely as 'dignified' as this. Waldron's account might be thought romanticised, or even tendentious. Yet at least Parliament always scrutinises and *debates* Bills. (Admittedly, statutory instruments receive quite inadequate scrutiny).[104] The Government must justify and defend its proposed primary legislation. A *judgment* justifies the court's formal order. If we go behind the enacted text of a statute

[94] RM Dworkin, *A Matter of Principle* (Cambridge, MA, Harvard University Press, 1985) 69–71.

[95] AM Bickel, *The Least Dangerous Branch: The Supreme Court at the Bar of Politics* (New Haven, Connecticut, Yale University Press 1962).

[96] CR Sunstein, *Legal Reasoning and Political Conflict*, 2nd edn (Oxford, Oxford University Press, 2018).

[97] AM Bickel, 'Foreword: Supreme Court Term 1960: The Passive Virtues' (1961) 75 *Harv LR* 40.

[98] TRS Allan, 'Parliamentary Sovereignty: Lord Denning's Dexterous Revolution' (1983) 3 *OJLS* 22, 33 (at the 'high constitutional level … [judges] have to combine a cautious wisdom in estimating the readiness of the political climate for change and the courage and dexterity of Lord Denning in achieving it').

[99] J Waldron, *Law and Disagreement* (Oxford, Oxford University Press, 1999).

[100] 410 U.S. 113 (1973).

[101] *Dobbs v Jackson Women's Health Organization* 597 U.S. 215 (2022).

[102] *cf* Learned Hand, *The Bill of Rights* (Harvard University Press, 1958) 73–74 (Platonic Guardians' rule 'irksome' for one would 'miss the stimulus of living in a society where [one has], at least theoretically, some part in the direction of public affairs').

[103] *cf Griswold v Connecticut* 381 U.S. 479 (1965) (Douglas J) (privacy as unenumerated 'penumbral' Constitutional right).

[104] HJ Hooper, 'Delegated Legislation in an Unprincipled Constitution' in R Johnson and Y Yi Zhu (eds), *Sceptical Perspectives on the Changing Constitution of the United Kingdom* (Oxford, Hart Publishing, 2023).

(which lawyers tend *not* to do), Hansard similarly records *its* justification. Ignoring the deliberative legislative process misrepresents statutes as the unreasoned assertion of raw power.

Scholars may still prefer court judgments to legislative debates. Judges engage directly with legal and moral *principles*. This resembles scholarly writing on political morality – such theory is usually of little concern to Parliament. However, judgments too diverge from moral and political philosophy. Judicial reasoning obeys constraints that philosophers would think irrelevant. A court addresses the litigants' arguments – a judgment is essentially *reactive*.[105] Secondly, the court must naturally reason consistent with legal authority. I say 'naturally', but that is the *lawyer's* instinct speaking. A moral philosopher would find such constraints on their arguments very odd. Waldron, again, makes these points with great clarity.[106]

I am not suggesting some intellectual inferiority on the lawyer's part. Simply, the exercises are distinct – and also the styles of reasoning. Nor is it one-way traffic. Bernard Williams, no less, suggested that philosophers could learn from courts' approaches to moral dilemmas.[107] Williams emphasised that judges must actually decide real-life disputes, a corrective to philosophical 'frivolity' and 'irresponsibility'.[108] Those answers will be contested in future litigation (exposed to 'radiation at courtroom intensity') – a further source of pressure on the *judicial* problem-solver. Only robustly convincing answers will survive. Salutary though this is, Williams noted that judicial decisions are constrained also by the law's 'internal logic' – which is irrelevant to the moral philosopher.

Nonetheless, scholars have had unusual influence in *public* law. Constitutional law was always 'professors' law' – above all, Professor Dicey's. It was to be found primarily in his great treatise, rather than judicial decisions. Some even suggest that Dicey's work of 1885 became a de facto substitute for a written constitution.[109] In 1987, Atiyah noted the persistence of this anomalous academic pre-eminence.[110] Why in *public* law?

Jurists' influence correlated inversely with judges' reticence. Of such a central question as the sovereignty of Parliament, courts ventured little direct analysis. Students would consider dicta in cases like *British Coal v The King*, or *Madzimbamuto v Lardner-Burke*.[111] Decoding such judicial remarks required *academic* analysis. By considering Dicey of course, or Wade on 'The nature of legal sovereignty'.[112] In the Law Reports, however, such theory was not discussed. Scholars might derive oblique support, at best, from the laconic judicial reasoning.

[105] J Laws, 'Law and Democracy' [1995] *PL* 72, 93 ('[judges'] role is reactive; they cannot initiate; all they can do is to apply principle to what is brought before them by others').

[106] J Waldron, 'Judges as Moral Reasoners' (2009) 7 *Journal of Constitutional Law* 2.

[107] B Williams, 'Afterword: What has Philosophy to Learn from Tort Law?' in DG Owen (ed), *Philosophical Foundations of Tort Law* (Oxford, Oxford University Press, 1995).

[108] *cf* Burrows (n 9) 60 (noting, compared to legal scholars, the judge's 'particular pressure' to decide correctly, being 'very conscious of the possible detrimental consequences').

[109] JWF Allison, 'Editor's Introduction' in AV Dicey, *The Law of the Constitution* (Oxford, Oxford University Press, 2013) xiv (citing JF McEldowney, D Sugarman).

[110] PS Atiyah, *Pragmatism and Theory in English Law* (London, Stevens, 1987) 150–152 (citing Heuston's view that the Sovereignty of Parliament is an invention of Oxford academics).

[111] [1935] AC 500, [1969] AC 645.

[112] [1955] CLJ 172.

The House of Lords' *Factortame* decision was the most important on sovereignty in the twentieth century.[113] Yet Lord Bridge alone offered brief rationalisation of Parliament's subordination to the European Communities Act 1972. It was left to academic commentators, including (again) an exasperated Wade,[114] to explore the meaning.

Reading *Factortame* remains anti-climactic, perhaps frustrating. Professor Allan rejected Wade's explanation and criticised *Factortame* itself.[115] The decision was 'implausibly' presented as 'the ineluctable result of contemporary politics'. Such 'expediency', moreover, reflected no credit on the court. Merely 'an excuse for shirking the [necessary] *explicit* analysis of constitutional principle'. Allan dismissed Wade's suggestion that lawyers too might 'prudently … turn a blind eye to constitutional theory'. That was 'pusillanimous'. Against this, Professor Allison (at one time anyway) praised the 'economy' of *Factortame's* reasoning.[116] Judges understandably avoided the 'contentious abstractions' and 'unruly principles' of political morality.[117]

Of course, British courts' encounters with EU law are far from unique. Nor do the half-answers, even obscurities, of *Factortame* seem unusual. In Germany and elsewhere, constitutional courts have expressed reservations (at least!) about their national constitutions' compatibility with EU law's supremacy. Professor Barber analyses the 'pluralist' sovereignties that result.[118] Far from condemning this uncertainty, Barber praises compromise. Rather than *resolve* ultimate questions about sovereignty, courts on both sides (national, and European) have tacitly 'agreed to disagree'. The truce 'avoids unnecessary and potentially destructive conflict'. When both antagonists would suffer damage in a crisis, it being uncertain which would prevail, there is a strong, mutual interest in avoiding one.[119]

Such compromises may persist literally for centuries.[120] Barber cites the mutually inconsistent claims by the House of Commons, and the courts, definitively to decide the scope of parliamentary privilege – each side careful not to force the issue for almost 200 years. Barber elsewhere warns that drafting a written constitution would jeopardise such 'useful ambiguity'.[121] The *uncodified* constitution contains much vagueness which affords:

> a plausible constitutional argument against [other institutions] in a political struggle, *buying respect and moderation*.

[113] *R v Secretary of State for Transport, ex parte Factortame Ltd (No 2)* [1991] 1 AC 603.

[114] HWR Wade, 'Sovereignty – Evolution or Revolution?' (1996) 112 *LQR* 574.

[115] TRS Allan, 'Parliamentary Sovereignty: Law, Politics, and Revolution' (1997) 113 *LQR* 443.

[116] JWF Allison, 'Parliamentary Sovereignty, Europe and the Economy of the Common Law' in M Andenas and D Fairgrieve, *Judicial Review in International Perspective: Liber Amicorum in Honour of Lord Slynn of Hadley* (The Hague, Kluwer, 2000); *cf* JWF Allison, 'The Westminster Parliament's Formal Sovereignty in Britain and Europe from a Historical Perspective' (Munich, September 2016).

[117] JWF Allison, *The English Historical Constitution* (Cambridge, Cambridge University Press, 2007) 122, 125.

[118] NW Barber, 'Legal Pluralism and the European Union' (2006) 12 *ELJ* 306.

[119] ibid 327–29.

[120] *cf* Ibbetson (n 22) 136 (legal historians frequently find that formal rules' 'indeterminacy' permitted 'strongly held differences of opinion over what the law should be to remain unresolved').

[121] NW Barber, 'Against a Written Constitution' [2008] *PL* 11, 15–18.

Gladstone observed how much the British constitution 'boldly' presumes 'the good sense and the good faith of those who work it'. (Note that verb: to 'work').[122] This vital, practical 'good sense' is consistent with *Factortame's* glaringly *incomplete* theorisation. However unsatisfactory to a constitutional theorist, to avoid unnecessary conflict there is much to be said for the courts leaving ultimate constitutional questions until they actually arise – or perhaps not even then.

Thus we can defend *Factortame's* modest reasoning style. But all is now changed, changed utterly. Why, though, and to what effect? The turning point was *Thoburn*, in 2002.[123] Lord Justice Laws formulated not only a theoretical basis for *Factortame*, but invented 'Constitutional Statutes', immune from the rule of implied repeal. The Supreme Court has also analysed sovereignty's relation with EU law. I refer simply to engagement with Hart's theory of the 'Rule of Recognition' in *Miller I*.[124] Reversal of the *Factortame* generation's aversion to high theory was, by 2017, complete. Nor was this some European derangement. Compare *Anisminic* with *Privacy International*.[125] Both contain technical learning on the construction of ouster clauses. But only the 2019 decision explores the boundaries of parliamentary sovereignty. Professor Elliot notes how constitutional principles are today 'articulated and elaborated … [with] explicitness … uncharacteristic of … earlier generations [of judges]'.[126]

Given judicial freedom in judgment-writing, this sea-change in reasoning to some degree reflects personal choice. Sir John Laws was a pre-eminent constitutional theorist – later Goodhart Visiting Professor of Legal Science at Cambridge. (If time allowed, it would be amusing to deploy Sunstein's typology of judicial personae: 'Heroes, Soldiers, Minimalists, and Mutes').[127] I suggest another, *structural* explanation for the stylistic shift – ie *which* parties apply for judicial review, and why.

Milsom explained how *litigants* drove the common law's historical development. Each party had a direct material interest in winning, but cared not at all about developing the law, let alone its theoretical coherence. Counsel's arguments (framing the question the court must answer) aimed solely to advance their clients' material interests. Again, little room for flights of theory,[128] still less 'social engineering'. (For Milsom this explained how English law developed by 'unceasing abuse of its elementary ideas').[129]

Many parties challenging government decisions will have personal interests directly at stake. Historically, such applicants dominated. Take leading royal prerogative cases. De Keyer's Royal Hotel, the Burmah Oil Company, and the Council of Civil Service

[122] *cf* A Blick and P Hennessy, 'Good Chaps No More?' (London, Constitution Society, 2019).

[123] *Thoburn v Sunderland City Council* [2002] EWHC 195 (Admin); [2003] QB 151.

[124] *R (Miller) v Secretary of State for Exiting the European Union* [2017] UKSC 5, [2018] AC 61, [60] (Lord Neuberger et al), [223]–[228] (Lord Reed).

[125] *Anisminic Ltd v Foreign Compensation Commission* [1969] 2 AC 147; *R (Privacy International Ltd) v Investigatory Powers Tribunal* [2019] UKSC 22, [2020] AC 49.

[126] MC Elliott, 'Through the Looking-Glass? Ouster Clauses, Statutory Interpretation and the British Constitution' in M Hunt et al (eds), *Legislating Statutory Interpretation: Perspectives from the Common Law World* (Toronto, Carswell, 2018).

[127] CR Sunstein, *Constitutional Personae* (Oxford, Oxford University Press, 2013).

[128] Ibbetson (n 2) 297 (noting inertia in legal argument).

[129] Milsom (n 68) 6. *cf* Ibbetson (n 2) 296 ('Really significant shifts in law' the product of litigants' *procedural* manoeuvring '[without] the slightest suggestion that any [substantive] change … was contemplated; yet each brought about centrally important movements in the whole structure of the law of obligations').

Unions brought claims to protect their tangible interests.[130] Increasingly though, parties launch judicial reviews for more abstract reasons. Mr Blackburn, Lord Rees-Mogg, and Gina Miller, all sought judicial review to uphold parliamentary sovereignty, no less, in the EU context – albeit with different perspectives and records of success.[131] Here, counsel may well advance submissions of constitutional theory – for that *is* their client's interest. In *Privacy International* it was boldly submitted that Parliament's sovereignty does not extend to ousting judicial review. Lord Sumption complained that this posed the Supreme Court an 'examination question' (not a compliment).[132] Answering it would be neither 'appropriate [nor] wise'. Nevertheless, only Lord Lloyd-Jones resisted altogether the temptation of commenting on it.[133]

Whatever the reasons for this theoretical (or academic) turn in judicial style, is it not welcome? Of course full and transparent reasoning is vital.[134] Yet is judicial engagement with heavily-contested, abstract questions always wise? Adjudicating the British constitution must be controversial. (Recall Sidney Low: 'We live under a system of tacit understandings. But the understandings themselves are not always understood').[135] Far from authoritatively settling controversies, judicial intervention could upset a delicate constitutional balance.

There is a broader point. A court's decision is indeed authoritative. But decisive, litigious triumph on a morally-divisive question could inflame, not settle, the controversy. *Roe v Wade* and *Dobbs v Jackson* are prominent examples.[136] Lord Sumption identified litigation's polarising effect in his Reith lectures.[137] Political debate, in contrast, could broker *compromises* – legislation which gives some satisfaction to all protagonists.[138] As Bickel warned:

> no [large and heterogeneous] society ... can fail in time to explode if it is deprived of the arts of compromise, if it knows no ways to muddle through. No good society can be unprincipled; and no viable society can be principle-ridden.[139]

Many jurists have analysed the judicial process's abhorrence of compromise. Weir's wonderful late essay stressed the law's engrained preference for all-or-nothing outcomes.[140] Daube suggested that throughout history, the nature of adjudication has prevented *division* of its subject-matter.[141] But *statutory* innovations have

[130] *Attorney General v De Keyser's Royal Hotel Ltd* [1920] AC 508; *Burmah Oil Co Ltd v Lord Advocate* [1965] AC 75; *Council of Civil Service Unions v Minister for the Civil Service* [1985] AC 374.

[131] *Blackburn v Attorney General* [1971] 1 WLR 1037; *R v Secretary of State for Foreign and Commonwealth Affairs, Ex parte Rees-Mogg* [1994] QB 552; *Miller* (n 124).

[132] [2019] UKSC 22, [207].

[133] ibid [168].

[134] *cf* Allison (n 117) 126 ('general obfuscation' as one type of 'economical' reasoning).

[135] S Low, *The Governance of England* (London, T Fisher Unwin, 1904) 12.

[136] RB Ginsburg, 'Some Thoughts on Autonomy and Equality in Relation to *Roe v. Wade*' (1985) 63 *North Carolina LR* 375, 386 (*Roe* had 'provoked, not resolved, conflict [about abortion]').

[137] J Sumption, *Trials of the State: Law and the Decline of Politics* (London, Profile Books, 2019).

[138] Sunstein (n 96) 109, 113 (the 'moral foundations' of 'trimming': 'attempting to show respect to all sides – and to ensure no side feels offended, diminished, or aggrieved' – 'quintessentially political ... a pragmatic necessity').

[139] (1961) 75 *Harv LR* 40, 49.

[140] T Weir, 'All or Nothing' (2004) 78 *Tulane LR* 511.

[141] D Daube, 'The Scales of Justice' (1951) 63 *Juridical Rev* 109 (inaugural lecture at Aberdeen).

transformed English private law.[142] Under the 1945 Act, courts have enthusiastically made 'just and equitable' deductions for contributory negligence. (Weir thought it the *revival* of de facto apportionment, previously concealed beneath blank jury verdicts).

Those developments relate to damages. Being monetary, compensation is inherently divisible. But surely it remains impossible to apportion the subject-matter of public law adjudication. The government either has a given prerogative power, or not. There either is a Convention right to abortion, or asylum, or assisted suicide – or not. While this is true enough, the *scope* of a right or power may be stated more or less broadly. As may the underpinning rationale. Which leads back to Bickel's 'passive virtues'. Various devices afford leeway on answering divisive public-law questions – or the answers' scope.[143] There are procedural doctrines. Secondly, flexibility over remedies.[144] Thirdly and closest to our theme, the style and ambition of reasoning.

Procedural controls first. These include time limits; standing; leave to appeal; and 'mootness'. Standing in English administrative law has broadened to include the 'abstract' constitutional concerns noted earlier. But some courts have begun to question the propriety of politicians, or campaigning organisations, adding their names to challenges by *directly-affected* applicants.[145] Courts certainly disapprove of moot points. In *Rusbridger*, the House of Lords did not doubt that prosecution of newspapers advocating the monarchy's abolition, under the Treason Act 1848, would violate Article 10, ECHR.[146] But there was no prospect of the law being enforced. The 'threat' was unreal, the question 'hypothetical', and the litigation 'unnecessary'. The court would not 'spring-clean the statute book' by declaring obsolete legislation 'incompatible'.[147] It was not a 'debating society' or 'advisory bureau'.

Moreover, in judicial review *remedies* remain discretionary, within the boundaries analysed by Lord Bingham.[148] Flexibility has increased recently, or perhaps been reinstated, by the Judicial Review and Courts Act 2022.[149] The judicious use of postponed quashing is surely preferable to *HM Treasury v Ahmed*. The Supreme Court there exhibited conceptual purism, even puritanism, by declining to suspend the effect of its

[142] *cf* K Barker and J Steele, 'Drifting towards Proportionate Liability: Ethics and Pragmatics' [2015] *CLJ* 49 ('proportional' tendency influencing common law rules on causation and proof too). *cf* also Hale 'Private Law' (n 27), contrasting all-or-nothing effect of *ex turpi causa* defence with Estate Agents Act 1979, s 18.

[143] EF Delaney, 'Analyzing Avoidance: Judicial Strategy in Comparative Perspective' (2016) 66 *Duke LJ* 1.

[144] TRS Allan, 'Pragmatism and Theory in Public law' (1988) 104 *LQR* 422, 446 ('a flexible law of remedies offers a legitimate means of reconciling the applicant's grievance with the necessary demands of administration').

[145] See eg *R (Good Law Project Ltd) v Secretary of State for Health and Social Care* [2021] EWHC 346 (Admin) [106]–[107] (denying locus standi of second, third and fourth applicants (Members of Parliament)); *R (Good Law Project Ltd and Runnymede Trust) v The Prime Minister* [2022] EWHC 298 (Admin) (denying standing to first applicant) [57] ('No individual, even with a sincere interest in public law issues, would be regarded as having standing in all cases'); *R (Good Law Project Ltd) v Secretary of State for Health and Social* [2022] EWHC 2468 (TCC).

[146] *R (Rusbridger) v Attorney-General* [2003] UKHL 38; [2004] AC 357.

[147] ibid [36] Lord Hutton.

[148] T Bingham, 'Should public law remedies be discretionary?' [1991] *PL* 64.

[149] Section 1 (inserting section 29A Senior Courts Act 1981): applied in *R (Every Child Protected Against Trafficking) v Kent County Council* [2023] EWHC 2199 (Admin).

order.[150] This necessitated *emergency* legislation. Suspending quashing, to allow orderly, considered replacement of the lost '*vires*', would avoid unseemly legislative haste.[151]

The Human Rights Act declaration of incompatibility, as refused in *Rusbridger*, divided their Lordships in *Nicklinson*.[152] They considered human rights litigation's effect on parliamentary consideration of assisted dying. Notably, for Lord Neuberger, constitutional dialogue 'can be carried on with varying degrees of emphasis or firmness' – and he held 'an indication' from the court more appropriate in *Nicklinson* than a formal declaration's 'firm words'.[153] Thus through remedies too, courts consider the practicalities of government.[154]

I return to styles of reasoning. As we all know, the common law develops incrementally, by analogy – Lord Goff's 'gradualism'. In cricketing terms, courts score 'runs' in singles (like George Hirst and Wilfred Rhodes), with 'no boundaries, let alone sixes'.[155] Yet legal philosophers have attacked analogical reasoning. Dworkin, for example, states:

> analogy without theory is blind. An analogy is a way of stating a conclusion, not a way of reaching one, and *theory* must do the real work.[156]

Judges who are pre-determined to consider *only* facts and particulars may yet be forced to confront deep theoretical questions – the 'justificatory ascent'. (As Dworkin asks, is abortion 'similar' to appendectomy, or to infanticide?) Judges must not cloak their engagement with constitutional theory, nor ignore it like 'ostriches'.

To give the barest outline of Dworkinian jurisprudence,[157] while accepting that accounts of law must 'fit' the legal materials,[158] Dworkin emphasises how interpretations should 'justify' the law as a whole. Ambitious theory pervades this Dworkinian 'integrity'. It is not unfairly summed up by Richard Posner:

> The heart of Dworkin's conception … is the imposition of master themes, such as democratic legitimacy, or … equality, on the particulars of the law. The professors propose, and the judges impose.[159]

An exercise in high theory, in juristic style.

[150] [2010] UKSC 5; [2010] 2 AC 53. See Hale 'Public Law' (n 27): 'Not a hint of pragmatism there'. *cf* praising 'the logic of *Ahmed No. 2*' for restricting remedial discretion: CF Forsyth, 'The Rock and the Sand: Jurisdiction and Remedial Discretion' [2013] *JR* 360.

[151] J Morgan, '"O Lord Make Me Pure – But Not Yet": Granting Time for the Amendment of Unlawful Legislation' (2019) 135 *LQR* 585.

[152] *R (Nicklinson) v Ministry of Justice* [2015] 1 AC 657, [2014] UKSC 38.

[153] [117]. *cf* Lord Kerr at [343]. On Lord Neuberger's preference at [113] to give Parliament opportunity to consider the court's judgment, Lady Hale in 'Principle and Pragmatism in Public Law' (n 27) scented the Principle of Unripe Time (*cf* Cornford (n 90) above).

[154] *cf* CR Sunstein, *One Case at a Time: Judicial Minimalism on the Supreme Court* (Cambridge, MA, Harvard University Press, 1999) 38–39 (praising remedial 'minimalism' of the notorious 'all deliberate speed' order in *Brown v Board of Education II* 349 U.S. 294 (1955)). On *Brown* see further Bickel (n 95) ch 6.

[155] T Bingham, *The Business of Judging* (Oxford, Oxford University Press, 2000) 167.

[156] 'In Praise of Theory' (1997) 29 *Ariz St LJ* 353, 371 (emphasis added).

[157] RM Dworkin, *Law's Empire* (Cambridge, MA, Harvard University Press, 1986).

[158] See also RM Dworkin, 'Reply' (1997) 29 *Ariz St LJ* 431, 456. (*cf* Sunstein (n 96) 52 'lawyers could not try to reach full integrity without severely compromising the system of precedent').

[159] R Posner, 'Conceptions of Legal Theory: A Response to Ronald Dworkin' (1997) 29 *Ariz St LJ* 377, 380.

Other legal philosophers defend law's analogical tradition.[160] Professor Sunstein accepts that courts must *occasionally* 'ascend' to the theoretical heights.[161] But recommends avoidance, where possible, by 'incompletely theorised' decisions. Not simply because judges lack the time and perhaps expertise to elaborate 'master' theories (though they do).[162] Nor that the greater the court's ambition, the more damaging is a wrong decision. (Sunstein observes that in *Dred Scott v Sandford* (1857)[163] the US Supreme Court aimed to settle slavery's Constitutional status to defuse political disagreement – but disastrously triggered the Civil War).[164] Even entirely just decisions may provoke social backlash. Were human judges capable of single, unified, 'Herculean' moral theories of law, it would appear positively 'sectarian'.[165] Dworkin's 'Judge Hercules' is not heroic but 'a usurper'.[166]

Sunstein recommends the 'constructive use of silence' – deliberately leaving questions undecided, as space for democratic deliberation. At least, rulings should be relatively narrow.[167] And legal development, cautious and analogical. To decide too much, too quickly – he cites *Roe v Wade* and *Dred Scott* – can 'prevent social deliberation, give and take, learning, compromise and moral evolution'.[168] For Sunstein 'judges in a deliberative democracy [should] avoid the most contentious abstractions when they can'.[169]

In *Lochner v New York*, Oliver Wendell Holmes noted the Constitution was 'made for people of fundamentally differing views'.[170] Holmes thus dissented from the Supreme Court's infamous imposition of Freedom of Contract on the New York legislature. Judicial disagreements were then relatively courteous in the United States. Whereas in the 2015 same-sex marriage case, *Obergefell v Hodges*, Scalia J (dissenting) accused the majority of anti-democratic 'hubris'.[171] Pertinent for my theme was Scalia's extraordinary critique of Kennedy J's *style*. The majority opinion was 'silly … [and] pretentious', Kennedy's 'showy profundities' and 'would-be-memorable phrases' were merely 'the mystical aphorisms of the fortune cookie'.[172]

However regrettable, once courts are required (or if courts *choose*) to intervene in bitter political debates,[173] judges may pick up the saltier language of political combat.

[160] GJ Postema, '*A Similibus ad Similia*: Analogical Thinking in Law' in Douglas E Edlin (ed), *Common Law Theory* (Cambridge, Cambridge University Press, 2009). *cf* Burke, *Reflections on the Revolution in France* (1790) (precedents as 'collected reason of ages', 'the whole chain and continuity of the commonwealth'; in contrast with 'floating fancies or fashions', the 'dust and powder of individuality', and the 'arrogance' of 'usurping' precedent).

[161] CR Sunstein, 'On Analogical Reasoning' (1993) 106 *Harv LR* 741; Sunstein (n 96) 223 ('The impulse to theory should hardly be disparaged … and the conceptual ascent will require us to say broader and deeper things').

[162] CR Sunstein, 'From Theory to Practice' (1997) 29 *Ariz St LJ* 389, 391 ('judges have limited time and capacities, and … know that if they try to resolve large philosophical issues, they may blunder badly').

[163] 60 US 393.

[164] Sunstein (n 154) 37.

[165] Sunstein (1993) 106 *Harv L Rev* 741, 786.

[166] Sunstein (n 96) 49.

[167] See also CJ Peters, 'Assessing the New Judicial Minimalism' (2000) 100 *Colum LR* 1454.

[168] Sunstein (n 154) 59.

[169] (1997) 29 Ariz St LJ 389, 404.

[170] 198 US 45, 76 (1905).

[171] 576 US 644, 718 (2015).

[172] Ibid 719 (including fn 22).

[173] *cf* Sumption (n 137) 34 ('As politics loses its prestige, judges have been only too ready to fill the gap').

It is an irony if, to use Hart's terms, the 'noble dream' of soaring Dworkinian 'integrity' results in the 'nightmare' of a deeply politicised judiciary.[174] Better, then, to avoid grandiose dreams.

If this has seemed rather too *American* for a professor of English Law, I suggest we can learn much from the long US experience of constitutional adjudication, notwithstanding all the major differences. Do we see a beacon of liberty? Or a cautionary tale of vaulting ambition? Opinions will vary. But to revert to Bickel, 'prudential' courts must sometimes employ 'techniques of avoidance' – staying their hand not to 'sap the quality of the political process'.[175] Such prudence should not be despised as 'expediency' or 'whim'. To consider whether intervention would be 'wise and fruitful'[176] contributes to the 'great and stately jurisdiction' of a constitutional court.[177]

IV. Modesty

Milsom said that an inaugural lecture is a kind of sermon.[178] Lord Goff, I note, relied on ecclesiastical precedent: Pope Gregory and St Augustine's *pragmatic* evangelisation of England.[179] But I am reluctant to preach. Let me repeat: I do not proclaim one single valid style of legal scholarship. Doctrinal writing which takes judicial reasoning seriously remains valuable, indeed central. But law would be impoverished without historical, comparative, empirical and theoretical research.

Even if I *were* tempted to identify 'one right answer', such presumption would be self-contradictory.[180] My 'sermon', deep down, enjoins modesty in legal reasoning. Let us beware the sin of pride. Here endeth the lesson.

[174] HLA Hart, 'American Jurisprudence Through English Eyes: The Nightmare and the Noble Dream' (1977) 11 *Georgia LR* 969.

[175] Bickel, 'Passive virtues' (n 97) 74. *cf* Delaney (n 143) 40 on the European Court of Human Rights ('rather than a doctrine of principled institutional deference, the margin of appreciation is often an exercise in prudential restraint').

[176] Bickel (n 95) 205.

[177] Citing JB Thayer, 'The Origin and Scope of the American Doctrine of Constitutional Law' (1893) 7 *Harv LR* 129, 152.

[178] SFC Milsom, 'Reason in the Development of the Common Law' (1965) 81 *LQR* 496, 513 (inaugural lecture, LSE).

[179] Goff (n 10).

[180] *cf* Sunstein (n 96) xii ('A committed minimalist could not embrace minimalism all of the time; that would not exactly be minimalist. (Or would it?)'); *cf* ibid 56–57.

INDEX

www.ingramcontent.com/pod-product-compliance
Ingram Content Group UK Ltd.
Pitfield, Milton Keynes, MK11 3LW, UK
UKHW020231290926
15470UKWH00002B/471